# Puerto Ricans
# and Other Minority Groups
## in the
# Continental United States
### *An Annotated Bibliography*

### Edited by
# Diane Herrera

## With a New Foreword
## and Supplemental Bibliography by
# Francesco Cordasco

## BLAINE ETHRIDGE — BOOKS
### *13977 Penrod Street • Detroit, Michigan  48223*

*Originally Published by*
*Dissemination Center for Bilingual Bicultural Education, 1973*

PLEASE WRITE FOR OUR FREE ANNOTATED LIST OF LATIN

AMERICAN TITLES AND BILINGUAL BOOKS FOR CHILDREN.

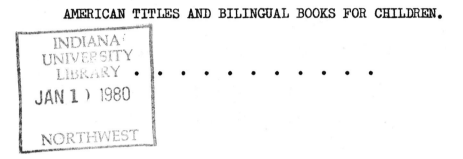

Copyright © 1979 Francesco Cordasco

Library of Congress Cataloging in Publication Data

Herrera, Diane.
    Puerto Ricans and other minority groups in the
continental United States: an annotated bibliography.

    Includes index.
    1.  Minorities—United States—Bibliography.
2.  Puerto Ricans in the United States—Bibliography.
I.  Cordasco, Francesco, 1920-      II.  Title.
Z1361.E4H47    [E104.A1]    016.30145'0973    78-27314
ISBN 0-87917-067-0

PH 1-8-80

Originally published as <u>Puerto Ricans in the</u>
<u>United States:  A Review of the Literature</u>

# TABLE OF CONTENTS

# NEW FOREWORD FOR THIS EDITION

The origins of this important volume are
noted by Diane Herrera in her note on acknowledg-
ments. For a number of reasons its distribution
was very limited, and, as a consequence, it re-
mains generally unknown, and its rich resources,
unfortunately, largely neglected. This new edition
is intended to make the work available: it is a
project with which I am proud to be associated.

Originally entitled <u>Puerto Ricans in the Uni-</u>
<u>ted States: A Review of the Literature</u>, the work
was a federally funded project under Title VII
(the Bilingual Education Act) of the Elementary and
Secondary Education Act of 1965: however, its scope
is much broader than its title suggests. Since its
focus is primarily educational (because of the funding auspices under which it was initiated), the editors wisely recognized that "many...areas...have
an impact on the educational experience of Puerto
Ricans in the United States;" and the volume incorporates "materials which have historical, economic,
sociological and anthropological relevance to the

Puerto Rican experience as a whole." Although it is
primarily concerned with Puerto Ricans on the mainland, it includes entries on other Hispanics in the
United States, and some notices of American blacks
and other minority groups. The new title is intended
to call attention to the broad and dimensional coverage of the work. There is, in my mind, no question about the volume's importance; its 2155 entries
(complete through December 1972) represent an extra-
ordinary corpus which affords educators and other
academicians a bibliographical register more comprehensive than any other presently available.

As noted, the focus of the work is primarily
educational; and beyond the federal funding auspices
(ESEA, Title VII) which mandated this orientation,
the emphasis on education (e.g., Part II, entries
59-1525) is singularly appropriate. No issue is more
important for the Puerto Rican community than education. Jobs and income (which are the ingredients of
the social mobility which characterizes a dynamic society) are irretrievably related to education: and
the evolving success or failure of the mainland Puerto Rican community is inextricably linked to meaningful educational opportunity. How important this is
has been dramatically shown in the recently published

iv

Puerto Ricans in the Continental United States:  An
Uncertain Future (1976), a report of the United States
Commission on Civil Rights:

"More than 30 percent of the 437,000
Puerto Rican students enrolled in mainland
schools are born in Puerto Rico.  Each year
thousands of children transfer from schools
in Puerto Rico to those on the mainland.
Spanish is the mother tongue of a major segment of the Puerto Rican school-age population
(and is the language used most often in the
home, even for those students born on the
mainland).

In New York City in 1970, of 362,000
Puerto Ricans under age 18, nearly one-fourth
(80,370) had been born in Puerto Rico.  About
one-fourth (nearly 80,000) of the Puerto Rican
and other Hispanic students in New York City's
public schools speak poor or hesitant English.
Birthplace is, obviously, a major determinent
of ability to speak English.

It is also clear that birthplace, language ability, and dropping out are closely
intertwined.  Great disparities exist in the
dropout rates of island-born and U.S.-born
Puerto Rican youngsters.  Those born on the mainland tend to enroll earlier in school and tend
to drop out less frequently.

About 47 percent of all mainland Puerto
Ricans age three to 34 are enrolled in school.
But this overall average is misleading:  67
percent of the mainland-born Puerto Ricans in
that age group are enrolled, compared with only
28 percent of those born in Puerto Rico.  The
disparity is very pronounced in the age 18 to
24 group.  Among males of this age group, for

example, 33 percent of the U.S.-born were still
in school, compared with only 13 percent of the
island-born. Among males age 16 to 21, about
12,000 of the U.S.-born are not enrolled in
school, compared with 32,000 island-born youngsters.

These figures indicate that the dropout
rate is more severe among Puerto Rican youngsters born on the island than among those youngsters of Puerto Rican parentage born on the mainland. Island-born youngsters are more likely to
have problems communicating in English, more
likely to be unemployed or underemployed, and
more likely to be doomed to a life of poverty.

While the education problems of mainland
Puerto Ricans are certainly not limited to the
island-born, this group is more adversely
affected by inadequate schooling. Language
is often the key factor that makes them different from other Puerto Rican students,
many of whom may sit in the same classroom,
or may even be siblings. The fact that
these language-handicapped students achieve
less and drop out more is compelling evidence that the schools' response to the problem has been inadequate.

One Puerto Rican parent expressed his
dismay at the lack of special instruction
for his children: '...They are practically
wasting their time because they are not learning anything. First of all, they don't understand the language. What good does it do to
sit there in front of the teacher and just
look at her face? It is wasting their time.
They don't learn anything because they don't
understand what she is saying.'" (pp. 96-99)

In a larger frame of reference, the continu-

vi

ing hardships faced by the mainland Puerto Rican community have provoked a revisionist socio-historiography which has challenged the prevailing intractability of a social system which continues to deny opportunity to Puerto Ricans.  It would be hazardous to ignore this new reaction, and its tenor is nowhere more clear than in the deliberations of a "Conference on Historiography" convened in April, 1974 by the Centro de Estudios Puertorriqueños of the City University of New York.  The issues are starkly enjoined in the foreword to the published Proceedings of the conference:

> "The publication of written materials
> such as the "Cuadernos," which the Centro de
> Estudios Puertorriqueños is producing, repre-
> sents much more than an attempt to fill a
> void in what is generally recognized as a
> need for literature on Puerto Ricans.  Our
> goal is a serious and critical statement
> about the Puerto Rican situation based on
> an analysis of the historical forces that
> have shaped our formation as a people and
> an understanding of the broader contexts
> with which we are inevitably interconnected.
> In that sense, we view Puerto Rican
> development not as a composite of isolated
> happenings determined by chance factors,
> but as a predictable unfolding of a process
> whose movement is basically tied to the
> growth patterns of a particular socio-eco-
> nomic system — in this case, Puerto Rico's
> colonial dependency on an advanced capital-

ist nation. The impact of that reality cannot be minimized, as is so often done, by compartmentalizing its relevance to only one or a few aspects of our national identity, e.g., our political status. This system has altered our cultural self-definition, occasioned the displacement of millions of Puerto Ricans from the Island, and forced economic impoverishment on a large majority of our population.

In these first "Cuadernos," we have addressed two vital areas of Puerto Rican life -- Puerto Rican culture and migration. The presentations dispute commonly-held assumptions about Puerto Ricans and about the causes or significance of historical events: they also challenge the interpretations and at times the basis on which current social theories were established. Our intent is to contradict unsubstantiated or erroneous conclusions that pass for facts, truth, or research findings, and to foster through scientific analysis an understanding of the dynamics that shape our lives. We hope to expose distortions of Puerto Rican reality that are so pervasive in the most common interpretations of social phenomena given by social scientists, and to uncover the reasons for those distortions. We do not attribute these distortions to conscious malice or the personal inadequacies of individual investigators, but rather to a generalized ideological perspective that necessarily flows from the socio-economic base of this society, including the institutional biases that impair objective analysis.

The importance of exposing those distortions relates to much more than an academic interest in objective facts or even
a sense of personal enlightenment. It relates to the need for knowledge as an essential base on which to realize any transformation of society and to individual or
group awareness as a pre-requisite for effective social action. The confusing and
fragmented pieces of information or false
analysis so often passed along as knowledge
in educational institutions, including universities, serve to incapacitate movements
for change by obfuscating goals and dissi-
pating energies into strategies of accommodation and reform. Our aim as a Centro de
Estudios Puertorriqueños is to develop mech-
anisms for producing new knowledge whose
form and content can provide a tool for
fundamental change and become an element
in our community's struggles toward self-
determination.

The production of these "Cuadernos,"
which in themselves reflect a process of
collective work and analysis, is a beginning step that must be added to, developed,
criticized and tested against reality.
Their effectiveness or validity can only be
judged by their use in different settings
throughout our community, particularly in
programs of Puerto Rican studies, where the
demand for substantive analysis and concrete
data is clearly sought as an organizing force
for action in the process of radical change.
(Taller de Migración, p. iv)

ix

Educational opportunities for Puerto Ricans
on the mainland largely depend on a correct understanding of bilingual education. Of all the new
developments in American schools, none has been
more challenging, and controversial, than bilingual education. What is bilingual education? And
how are the controversies which surround it to be
explained? The questions are very real: in 1977
the United States Department of Health Education,
and Welfare sponsored over 600 bilingual projects
in teacher training, curriculum development, and
classroom programs, in some 60 languages, at a
cost in excess of $200 million. These efforts have
been enthusiastically praised; and at the same
time bitterly condemned.

Some five million youngsters in the United
States come from homes in which the generally
spoken language is other than English; estimates
based on samplings in several states suggest that
between 1.8 and 2.5 million American children
need bilingual education. Bilingual education is
best defined as academic instruction in two languages: the child's native language and English.
The student also learns about the history and
culture associated with both languages; this is

x

what is meant by bicultural education.

There is no doubt that non-English speaking children encounter serious learning problems in American schools. A recent study conducted by the New York State Education Department concluded that "the most distressing incidence of academic failure occurs amoung a group of children who are handicapped by a language barrier in the classroom—those 160,000 children (in New York) whose native language is not English and whose difficulty comprehending English significantly impedes performance." A multitude of other studies from all regions of the United States confirm the New York findings.

Widespread efforts in the early 1960's to incorporate bilingual components into American school curricula resulted in the enactment by Congress in 1967 of the Bilingual Education Act as Title VII of the Elementary and Secondary Education Act, the far-reaching, massively funded federal educational statute for disadvantaged children enacted earlier in 1965. With limited resources of their own, states and school districts have relied principally upon the federal statutes to support programs to meet the needs of the bilingual child. The critical education challenges posed by growing numbers of non-English speaking children have resulted in a number of state legislatures (e.g., Colorado, Illinois, Massachusetts, New Jersey, and Texas) mandating bilingual education. A 1974 U.S. Supreme Court Ruling required San Francisco schools to provide bilingual education to non-English speaking pupils (largely Chinese) which will undoubtedly accelerate this trend.

Actually, bilingual education is not new in the United States: in a nation as diverse in its origins as ours, this should not be surprising. English has not always been the only language used in American schools. German immigrants (whose progeny make up the largest ethnic group in America) established German-English bilingual schools in Cincinnati, Indianapolis, Hoboken, N.J. Cleveland, and many other cities: these were public schools, and German was not only taught as a subject, it was used as a medium of instruction. Between 1880 and 1917, those schools flourished; they were eagerly supported by a powerful and socially-stratified German community. Only the political tensions of World War I ended their

history. In Louisiana, French was used as the
medium of instruction, and in New Mexico, Spanish
was used. These were limited efforts and largely
early and mid-19th century phenomena, but they
confirm a bilingual tradition in America. In New
York City, at different times and with differing
commitments, the public schools taught children
in Chinese, Italian, Greek, Yiddish, and French.
In a real sense, present-day efforts in bilingual
education are a rediscovery of a respected and
traditional American educational practice.

It is not altogether untrue, as a national weekly had critically affirmed, that "current
bilingual policy is a curious hybrid of pedagogy
and politics." Bilingual education is a product
of the social currents of equalitarianism which
engulfed our institutions in the 1960's. Bilingual education, in its <u>bicultural</u> orientations,
is a natural result of the new ethnic conscious-
ness which has gripped the American imagination.
It is a direct result of the Black civil rights
movement and new affirmations of identity and
proclamation of ethnic pride by Mexican Americans, Puerto Ricans, and earlier European
immigrants—Italians, Greeks, Jews, Poles, Slavs,

and others.

The preservation of languages is an important part of the ideology of the new ethnicity; and thus, bilingual education became embroiled in the controversy surrounding the new ethnicity, its ideologies and interventionist politics. And in these contexts, the resistance to bilingual/bicultural education is not unrelated to dominant themes in American society which have entertained and continue to entertain credence, e.g., interethnic rivalry, the Americanization movement, psychological testing and race typologies, eugenics and hereditarian persuasions, and the "melting pot" theory of assimilation. All of these issues are, and have been, highly controversial and emotionally disturbing episodes in our long history as a people. Many of these themes have served to obscure the very real pedagogic needs to which bilingual education adresses itself.

There is a clear consensus among American educators that the purpose of bilingual education is to help children who have little or no command of English to succeed in school. In the landmark decision in Lau v. Nichols, Associate Justice

William O. Douglas (who delivered the opinion of
the U.S. Supreme Court) said: "There is no equality of treatment merely by providing students with
the same facilities, textbooks, teachers, and
curriculum; for students who do not understand
English are effectively foreclosed from any meaningful education...basic English skills are at the
very core of what the schools teach. Imposition
of a requirement, that, before a child can effectively participate in the educational program, he
must already have acquired those basic skills is
to make a mockery of public education."

The ideologies of race, culture, and language (if not new phenomena in American history)
have a special importance now. For bilingual education, they have a crucial significance. How
successful bilingual education proves in the United States will depend in part on how congruent its
programs become with the aspiration of the ethnic
communities to which the programs are addressed;
on the awareness by American educators of the new
American ethnicity, and on the participation of
ethnic communities in program formulation and evaluation.

At this juncture in American history, the

new availability of a dimensionally comprehensive bibliographical register on Puerto Ricans and other Hispanics (with a primary focus on education) is singularly appropriate, and its publisher, Blaine Ethridge-Books, is to be commended. I have added as a supplemental register of titles my recently published "Bilingual and Bicultural Education in American Schools: A Bibliography of Selected References" (Bulletin of Bibliography, 35: 53-72, April-June, 1978), for which permission has been graciously extended by Sandra Conrad, editor of the Bulletin of Bibliography.

Francesco Cordasco
Montclair State College

# SUPPLEMENTARY BIBLIOGRAPHY

A basic bibliographical resource is William F. Mackey, *International Bibliography on Bilingualism* (Québec: Les Presses de l'Université Laval, 1972), which is a computer print-out of an alphabetized and indexed checklist of 11,006 titles. Reference also should be made to Einar Haugen, *Bilingualism in the Americas: A Bibliography and Reference Guide* (University of Alabama Press, 1965), and the valuable bibliographies in Theodore Andersson and Mildred Boyer, *Bilingual Schooling in the United States*, 2 vols. (Austin, Texas: Southwest Educational Development Laboratory, 1970).

Major sources of continuing information are the CAL/ERIC Clearinghouse on Languages and Linguistics which is operated by the Center for Applied Linguistics (1611 North Kent Street, Arlington, Va., 22209); and the Dissemination and Assessment Center for Bilingual Education (6504 Tracor Lane, Austin, Texas, 78721) whose *Cartel: Annotated Bibliography of Bilingual Bicultural Materials* is a monthly listing providing project personnel with information about relevant materials in bilingual/bicultural education for their programs. Reference should be made to the publications catalogue of the Georgetown University, School of Languages and Linguistics, (Washington, D.C., 20057), e.g., sociolinguistics, general linguistics, and the School's "Working Papers on Languages and Linguistics," and "Round Table on Languages and Linguistics."

A variety of publications is available from the TESOL (Teachers of English to Speakers of Other Languages) Central Office (455 Nevils Building, Georgetown University, Washington, D.C., 20057). A valuable retrospective resource is Virginia F. Allen and Sidney Forman, *English As a Second Language: A Comprehensive Bibliography* (Columbia University, Teachers College Press [1966]) which is a listing by subject categories of the special collection (English As a Foreign or Second Language) in the Teachers College Library. Newbury House Publishers (68 Middle Road, Rowley, Mass., 01969) is a specialized resource of materials in applied linguistics, sociolinguistics, and bilingual education texts.

A number of journals should be consulted; particularly useful are: *Florida FL Reporter; Human Organization; Journal of Verbal Learning and Verbal Behavior; Language Learning; Linguistic Reporter; The Modern Language Journal;* and *TESOL Quarterly.*

In the areas of poverty, socio-economic disadvantage, the equality of educational opportunity and related concerns, reference may be made to Francesco Cordasco, et al., *The Equality of Educational Opportunity: A Bibliography of Selected References* (Totowa, N.J.: Rowman and Littlefield, 1973); Francesco Cordasco, ed., *Toward Equal Educational Opportunity: The Report of the Select Committee on Equal Educational Opportunity, U.S. Senate* (New York: AMS Press, 1974), particularly Part V (Education of Language Minorities); and to Francesco Cordasco and David Alloway, eds., "Poverty in America: Economic Inequality, New Ideologies, and the Search for Educational Opportunity," *Journal of Human Relations* [Special Issue], vol. 20 (3rd Quarter, 1972), pp. 234-396, which includes articles on poverty contexts, minority responses to oppression, racial caste systems, the assimilation of Mexicans, and the educational neglect of Black, Puerto Rican, and Portuguese children.

Special note should be made of Harold B. Allen's *A Survey of the Teaching of English to Non-English Speakers in the United States* (Champaign, Illinois: National

Council of Teachers of English, 1966). Known generally as the TENES report, Dr. Allen's data are still very useful. In a class by themselves are the valuable explorations of Basil Bernstein of the effect of class relationships upon the institutionalizing of elaborated codes in the school, e.g., Basil Bernstein, *Class, Codes and Control* [Vol. I: *Theoretical Studies Towards a Sociology of Language;* Vol. II: *Applied Studies Towards a Sociology of Language;* Vol. III: *Towards a Theory of Educational Transmissions*] (London: Routledge & Kegan Paul, 1973-1975). Important bibliographical studies of the Center for Applied Linguistics should be noted: *A Bibliography of American Doctoral Dissertations in Linguistics, 1900-1964* (1968); *Reference List of Materials for English as a Second Language* (Three Parts, 1964, 1966, 1969); *Spanish and English of United States Hispanos: A Critical, Annotated, Linguistic Bibliography* (1975); and for native American Indian languages, the Center's *A Survey of the Current Teaching of North American Indian Languages in the United States and Canada* (1975). The Center has also published a *Vietnamese Refugee Education Series* (1975) which includes phrasebooks, cross-cultural materials, an annotated bibliography, a personnel resources directory, and a colloquium on the Vietnamese language.

In a class by themselves are the invaluable respository of documents which form the Congressional bilingual education *Hearings* out of which derived the enactment of the federal Bilingual Education Act as Title VII of the Elementary and Secondary Education Act:

*Hearings Before the Special Subcommittee on Bilingual Education of the Committee on Labor and Public Welfare* (U.S. Senate, 90th Congress, 1st. Session on S.428, Parts 1-2, 1967). 2 vols.
*Hearings Before the General Subcommittee on Education of the Committee on Education and Labor.* (House of Representatives, 90th Congress, 1st Session on H.R. 9840 and H.R. 10224, 1967).

A guide to much of the literature of social reform in American education which directly relates to the non-English speaking child and his social *milieu* is conveniently available in Francesco Cordasco, "Social Reform in American Education: A Bibliography of Selected References," *Bulletin of Bibliography & Magazine Notes,* 33 (April—June 1976), 105-10. This source should be supplemented by reference to Dorothy Christiansen, *Bilingualism: Teaching Spanish Speaking Students* (New York: Center for Urban Education, 1969), a valuable bibliographical handlist.

A miscellany of other titles are of value. A profile of doctoral dissertations on a large American minority community is available in Remigio U. Pane, "Doctoral Dissertations on the Italian American Experience Completed in the United States and Canadian Universities, 1908-1974," *International Migration Review,* 9 (Winter 1975), 545-56; many of the dissertations deal directly with bilingual/bicultural education, e.g., Walburga Von Raffler, *Studies in Italian-English Bilingualism* (Indiana University, 1953); and Herman C. Axelrod, *Bilingual Background and Its Relation to Certain Aspects of Character and Personality of Elementary School Children* (Yeshiva University, 1952), a study of more than 1200 children of Italian, Jewish, and Polish origin in metropolitan public schools in the New York City area. Two state documents of special value are Diego Castellanos, *Perspective: The Hispanic Experience in New Jersey Schools* (Trenton: New Jersey State Department of Education, 1972); and *Bilingual/Bicultural Education—A Privilege or a Right?* (Chicago: Illinois State Advisory Committee to the U.S. Commission on Civil Rights, 1974). Of the multitude of materials issued by the New York City Board of Education addressed to the needs of the non-English speaking child, *The Puerto Rican Study, 1953-1957 (see below* the 1972 reissue of the *Study* in the entry for J. Cayce Morrison) has continuing value. A million dollars was expended on the *Study* and its ancillary guides, but it has largely been neglected. Finally, a convenient general resource is Francesco Cordasco, *Bilingual Schooling in the United States: A Sourcebook for Educational Personnel* (New York: McGraw Hill, 1976) which includes materials on historical backgrounds; typology and definitions; linguistic perspectives; programs, practices, and staff development; an overview of court decisions and legislation affecting bilingual education; and selected program and project descriptions (e.g., California, Florida, New Jersey, New Mexico, New York, Texas, Illinois, Oklahoma, and Montana).

The selected references listed below are arranged alphabetically.

## BILINGUAL AND BICULTURAL EDUCATION: SELECTED REFERENCES

Aarons, Alfred C., Barbara Y. Gordon, and William A. Stewart, eds. "Linguistic-Cultural Differences and American Education." *Florida FL Reporter*, 7 (1969) (Special anthology issue).

Abrahams, Roger D., and Rudolph C. Troike, eds. *Language and Cultural Diversity in American Education*. Englewood Cliffs, New Jersey: Prentice-Hall, 1972.

Adkins, Dorothy C. *Cross-Cultural Comparisons of the Motivation of Young Children to Achieve in School*. 1971 [ERIC ED 60 053].

————, F. D. Payne, and B. L. Ballif. "Motivation Factor Scores and Response Set Scores for 10 Ethnic Cultural Groups of Preschool Children." *American Educational Research Journal*, 9 (1972), 557-72.

Agheyisi, Rebecca, and Joshua A. Fishman. "Language Attitude Studies: A Brief Survey of Methodological Approaches." *Anthropological Linguistics*, 12 (1970), 137-57.

Ainsworth, Len, and Gay Alford. *Responsive Environment Program for Spanish-American Children*. Evaluation Report, 1971-72. Lubbock, Texas: Adobe Educational Services, 1972. [ERIC ED 068 219].

Alatis, James E., ed. *Bilingualism and Language Contact: Anthropological, Linguistic, Psychological, and Sociological Aspects*. Monograph Series on Languages and Linguistics, 23. Washington: Georgetown University Press, 1970.

Alexander, David J., and Alfonso Nava. *A Public Policy Analysis of Bilingual Education in California*. San Francisco: R&E Research Associates, 1976.

Alfaro, Manuel R., Jr., and Homer C. Hawkins. *The Chicano Migrant Child*. 1972. [ERIC ED 072 900].

Allen, Harold B. *Teaching English as a Second Language*. New York: McGraw-Hill, 1972.

Alloway, David N., and Francesco Cordasco. *Minorities and the American City: A Sociological Primer for Educators*. New York: David McKay, 1970.

Altus, David M. *American Indian Education: A Selected Bibliography*. Supplement No. 2. Washington: Superintendent of Documents, U.S. Government Printing Office, 1971. [ERIC ED 58 980].

Anastasi, Anne, and Cruz de Jesus. "Language Development and Nonverbal IQ of Puerto Rican Children in New York City." *Journal of Abnormal and Social Psychology*, 48 (1953), 357-66.

Anderson, Nels, ed. *Studies in Multilingualism*. Leiden, The Netherlands: E. J. Brill, 1969.

Andersson, Theodore. "Bilingual Education: The American Experience." *The Modern Language Journal*, 55 (November 1971), 427-40.

————, and Mildred Boyer. *Bilingual Schooling in the United States*. 2 vols. Austin, Texas: Southwest Educational Development Laboratory, 1970. Rpt. Detroit: Blaine Ethridge, 1976.

Anisfeld, Moshe. *Language and Cognition in the Young Child*. 1965 [ERIC ED 019 636].

Aquino, Federico. "La Identidad Puertorriqueña y la Educación." *Quimbamba*, June 1972 (Bilingual Education Quarterly).

Arciniega, T.A. *The Urban Mexican-American: A Socio-Cultural Profile*. 1971. Austin: Southwest Ed. Dev. Lab., 1971.

Arndt, Richard. *La Fortalecita: A Study of Low-Income [Urban] Mexican-Americans and Implications for Education*. Unpub. diss., University of New Mexico, 1970.

Arnold, Richard D., and Thommasine H. Taylor. "Mexican-Americans and Language Learning." *Childhood Education*, 46 (1969), 149-54.

[Aspira]. *Hemos Trabajado Bien: A Report on the First National Conference of Puerto Ricans, Mexican-Americans and Educators on the Special Educational Needs of Puerto Rican Youth*. New York: Aspira, 1968.

Barclay, Lisa F.K. *The Comparative Efficacies of Spanish, English, and Bilingual Cognitive Verbal Instruction with Mexican-American Head Start Children*. Final Report. 1969 [ERIC ED 030 473].

Barik, H.C., and M. Swain. *Bilingual Education Project: Interim Report on the Spring 1972 Testing Programme*. Tor-

1974. (Originally, Duke University Press, 1954.)

———, ed. *Mexican-Americans in the United States.* Cambridge, Mass.: Schenkman, 1970.

Burt, Marina K., and Heidi C. Dulay, eds. *New Directions in Second Language Learning, Teaching and Bilingual Education.* Washington: Georgetown University Press, 1975. [TESOL]

Canedo, Oscar Octavio. *Performance of Mexican-American Students on a Test of Verbal Intelligence.* Unpublished dissertation, International University, 1972.

Cannon, Garland. "Bilingual Problems and Developments in the United States." *PMLA,* 86 (1971), 452-58.

Cárdenas, Blandina, and José A. Cárdenas. "Chicano—Bright-Eyes, Bilingual, Brown, and Beautiful." *Today's Education* [NEA Journal], (February 1973), 49-51.

Cárdenas, René. *Three Critical Factors that Inhibit Acculturation of Mexican-Americans.* Unpublished dissertation, University of California, Berkeley, 1970.

Carrow, Elizabeth. "Auditory Comprehension of English by Monolingual and Bilingual Preschool Children." *Journal of Speech and Hearing Research,* 15 (1972), 407-12.

———. "Comprehension of English and Spanish by Preschool Mexican-American Children. *Modern Language Journal,* 55 (1971), 299-306.

Carrow, Sister Mary Arthur. "The Development of Auditory Comprehension of Language Structure in Children." *Journal of Speech and Hearing Disorders,* 33 (1968), 105-08.

Castañeda, Alfredo, et al. *New Approaches to Bilingual, Bicultural Education.* Austin, Texas: Dissemination and Assessment Center for Bilingual Education, 1975.

Caudill, William, and Lois Frost. *A Comparison of Maternal Care and Infant Behavior in Japanese-American, American, and Japanese Families.* 1971 [ERIC ED 57 153]

Cazden, Courtney B. "The Hunt for the Independent Variables." In Renira Huxley and Elizabeth Ingram, eds., *Language Acquisition Models and Methods.* New York: Academic Press, 1971, pp. 41-49.

———. "The Situation: A Neglected Source of Social Class Differences in Language Use." *Journal of Social Issues,* 26 (1970), 35-59.

———. "Subcultural Differences in Child Language." *Merrill-Palmer Quarterly,* 12 (1966), 185-219.

———, ed. *Language in Early Childhood Education.* Washington: National Association for the Education of Young Children, 1972.

———, and Vera John. "Learning in American Indian Children." In *Styles of Learning Among American Indians: An Outline for Research.* Washington: Center for Applied Linguistics, 1968.

———, Vera John, and Dell Hymes, eds. *Functions of Language in the Classroom.* New York: Teachers College Press, 1972.

[Center for Applied Linguistics]. *Recommendations for Language Policy in Indian Education.* Arlington, Va.: Center for Applied Linguistics, 1973.

[Center for Applied Linguistics]. *Styles of Learning Among American Indians: An Outline for Research.* Washington: Center for Applied Linguistics, 1968.

[Certification]. "Proposed Guidelines for the Preparation and Certification of Teachers of Bilingual-Bicultural Education in the United States." *Linguistic Reporter* (October 1974).

Chafe, Wallace L. "Estimates Regarding the Present Speakers of North American Indian Languages." *International Journal of American Linguistics,* 28 (1962), 162-71.

Chilcott, John H., et al. *Handbook for Prima and Maricopa Indian Teacher Aides.* 1970 [ERIC ED 44 221].

Ching, D.C. "Reading, Language Development, and the Bilingual Child: An Annotated Bibliography." *Elementary English,* 46 (1969), 622-28.

Chomsky, Carol. *The Acquisition of Syntax in Children from Five to Ten.* Cambridge, Mass.: The M.I.T. Press, 1969.

Christian, Chester C., and John M. Sharp. "Bilingualism in a Pluralistic Society." In Dale Lange and Charles James, eds., *The ACTFL Review of Foreign Language Education,* vol. 4. Skokie, Illinois: National Textbook Co., 1972, pp. 341-75.

Christiansen, T., and G. Livermore. "A Comparison of Anglo-American and Spanish-American Children on the WISC." *Journal of Social Psychology,* 81 (1970), 1-14.

Christopherson, Paul. *Second-Language Learning: Myth and Reality.* London: Penguin Books, 1973.

Cintrón de Crespo, Patria. *Puerto Rican Women Teachers in New York, Self-Perception and Work Adjustment as Perceived in Themselves and by Others.* Ed. D. Report. New York: Columbia Uni-

———. "A Staff Institute for Teachers of Puerto Rican Students." *School & Society*, 99 (Summer 1972).

———, and Leonard Covello. *Studies of Puerto Rican Children in American Schools: A Preliminary Bibliography.* New York: Department of Labor, Migration Division, Commonwealth of Puerto Rico, 1967; also in *Education Libraries Bulletin,* Institute of Education, University of London, No. 31 (Spring 1968), 7-33; and in *Journal of Human Relations,* 16 (1968), 264-85.

———, Maurie Hillson, and Henry A. Bullock, eds. *The School in the Social Order: A Sociological Introduction to Educational Understanding.* Scranton, Pennsylvania: International Textbook, 1970.

Cornejo, Ricardo. "The Acquisition of Lexicon in the Speech of Bilingual Children." In Paul Turner, ed., *Bilingualism in the South West.* Tucson: University of Arizona Press, 1973, pp. 67-93.

———. *Bilingualism: Study of the Lexicon of the Five-Year-Old Spanish-Speaking Children of Texas.* Unpub. diss., University of Texas at Austin, 1969.

Cortés, Carlos E., advisory editor. *The Mexican American.* 21 vols. New York: Arno Press/New York Times, 1974.

Covello, Leonard. "Bilingualism: Our Untapped National Resource." *American Unity Magazine* (September-October 1960); also in *La Prensa* (Spanish text), 20 January 1960.

———, "A High School and Its Immigrant Community." *Journal of Educational Sociology,* 9 (February 1936), 333-46. [Benjamin Franklin High School, East Harlem, New York City.]

———. "Language as a Factor in Integration and Assimilation." *Modern Language Journal* (February 1939).

———. "Language Usage in Italian Families." *Atlantica,* (October-November 1934). (Part II, December 1934).

———. *The Social Background of the Italo-American School Child: A Study of the Southern Italian Family Mores and Their Effect on the School Situation in Italy and America.* Edited and with an Introduction by F. Cordasco. Leiden, The Netherlands: E. J. Brill, 1967; Totowa, N.J.: Rowman and Littlefield, 1972.

Crossland, F. *Minority Access to College.* Ford Foundation Report, New York: Schocken Books, 1971.

Darcy, N.T. "Bilingualism and the Measurement of Intelligence: Review of a Decade of Research." *Journal of Genetic Psychology,* 103 (1963), 259-82.

Davidson, M. Ruth. *A Comparative Pilot Study of Two First-Grade Programs for Culturally-Deprived Mexican-American Children.* Unpub. diss., University of Texas at Austin, 1967.

Del Campo, Philip E. *An Analysis of Selected Features in the Acculturation Process of the Mexican-American School Child.* Unpub. diss., International University, 1970.

Denzin, G. K. "Genesis of Self in Early Childhood." *Social Quarterly,* 13 (1972), 291-314.

Dickeman, Mildred. "The Integrity of the Cherokee Student." In Eleanor Leacock, ed., *The Culture of Poverty: A Critique.* New York: Simon and Schuster, 1971, pp. 140-79.

Diebold, A. Richard, Jr. *The Consequences of Early Bilingualism in Cognitive Development and Personality Formation.* 1966 [ERIC ED 020 491].

Dielman, T.E. "Childrearing Antecedents of Early School Child Personality Factors." *Journal of Marriage and the Family.* 34 (1972), 431-36.

Di Lorenzo, L.G., and R. Salter. "Evaluative Study of Prekindergarten Programs for Educationally Disadvantaged Children: Followup and Replication." *Exceptional Children,* 34 (1968), 111-19.

Donofrio, R.M. *Situations and Language: A Socio-Linguistic Investigation.* Final Report. Washington: National Center for Research and Development, 1972 [ERIC ED 168 236].

Doob, C.F. "Family Background and Peer-Group Development in a Puerto Rican District." *Sociological Quarterly,* 11 (1970), 523-32.

Drach, Kerry, Ben Kobashigawa, Carol Pfuderer, and Dan Slobin. *The Structure of Linguistic Input to Children.* Working Paper No. 14, Language Behavior Research Lab. Berkeley: University of California, 1969.

Drake, Diana. "Empowering Children Through Bilingual/Bicultural Education." *Educational Forum,* 40 (January 1976), 199-204.

Dulay, Heidi C. "Goofing: An Indicator of Children's Second Language Learning Strategies." *Language Learning,* 22 (1972), 235-52

Dumont, Robert V., Jr. "Learning English and How to be Silent: Studies in Sioux and Cherokee Classrooms." In *Functions of Language in the Classroom.* C. B. Cazden, et al., eds., New York: Teachers

University Press, 1970, 47-58.

———, "A Sociolinguistic Census of a Bilingual Neighborhood." *American Journal of Sociology*, 75 (1969), 323-39.

———. *Sociolinguistics: A Brief Introduction.* Rowley Mass.: Newbury House, 1971.

———, ed. *Readings in the Sociology of Language.* The Hague: Mouton, 1968.

———, et al. "Bilingualism in the Barrio." *Modern Language Journal*, 53 (March-April 1969).

———, and Heriberto Casiano. "Puerto Ricans In Our Press." *Modern Language Journal*, 53 (1969), 157-62.

———, Robert L. Cooper, and Roxana Ma, eds. *Bilingualism in the Barrio.* Language Science Monographs 7, Indiana University. The Hague: Mouton, 1971.

———, and John Lovas. "Bilingual Education in a Sociolinguistic Perspective." *TESOL Quarterly*, 4 (September 1970).

———, et al., eds. *Language Problems of Developing Nations.* New York: Wiley, 1968.

Fitzpatrick, Joseph. *Puerto Rican Americans: The Meaning of Migration to the Mainland.* Englewood Cliffs: Prentice-Hall, 1971.

Francescato, G. "Theoretical and Practical Aspects of Child Bilingualism." *Lingua Stile*, 4 (1969).

Freed, S.A., and R. S. "Technique for Studying Role Behavior." *Ethnology*, 10 (1971), 107-21.

Gaarder, A. Bruce. "Bilingual Education: Central Questions and Concerns." *New York University Quarterly*, 6 (Summer 1975), 2-6.

———. *Bilingual Schooling and the Survival of Spanish in the United States.* Rowley, Mass.: Newbury House, 1977.

[Gaarder, A. Bruce, Chairman]. "The Challenge of Bilingualism." *Reports*, Northeast Conference on the Teaching of Foreign Languages, 1965, pp. 57-101.

———. *Essays on Bilingual Schooling in the United States.* Rowley, Mass.: Newbury House, 1976.

———. "The First Seventy-Six Bilingual Education Projects." In James E. Alatis, ed., *Bilingualism and Language Contact.* Georgetown University Round Table on Languages and Linguistics, 1970. Washington: Georgetown University Press, 1970, pp. 163-78.

———. "Organization of the Bilingual School." *Journal of Social Issues*, 23 (1967) 110-20.

Gabet, Yvonne Helen Y. *Birth-Order and Achievement in Anglo, Mexican-American and Black Americans.* Unpub. diss.,

University of Texas at Austin, 1971.

Garbarino, M.S. "Seminole Girl: The Autobiography of a Young Woman Between Two Worlds." *Transaction*, 7 (1970), 40-46.

Garcia, A.B., and B. J. Zimmerna. "The Effect of Examiner Ethnicity and Language on the Performance of Bilingual Mexican-American First Graders." *Journal of Social Psychology*, 87 (1972), 3-11.

Gardner, R. C. "Attitudes and Motivation: Their Role in Second Language Acquisition." *TESOL Quarterly*, 2 (1968), 141-50. [ERIC ED 024 035].

Geffert, Hannah N., et al. *The Current Status of U.S. Bilingual Education Legislation.* Washington: Center for Applied Linguistics, 1975. (Bilingual Education Series, No. 4).

Gerber, Malcolm. *Ethnicity and Measures of Educability: Differences among Rural Navajo, Pueblo, and Rural-Spanish-American First Graders on Measures of Learning Style, Hearing Vocabulary, Entry Skills, Motivation, and Home Environment Processes.* Unpub. diss., University of Southern California, 1968.

Gievins, J. W., A. R. Neville, and R. E. Davidson. "Acquisition of Morphological Rules and Usage as a Function of Social Experience." *Psychology of the School*, 7 (1970), 217-21.

Gill, Joseph. *A Handbook for Teachers of Sioux Indian Students.* Unpub. diss., University of South Dakota, 1971.

Goldman, R., and J. W. Sanders. "Cultural Factors and Hearing." *Exceptional Children*, 35 (1969), 489-90.

Gonzáles, James Lee. *The Effects of Maternal Stimulation on Early Language Development of Mexican-American Children.* Unpub. diss., University of New Mexico, 1972.

González, Gustavo. "The Acquisition of Questions in Texas Spanish: Age 2 — Age 5." Arlington, Va.: Center for Applied Linguistics (mimeo), 1973.

———. *The Acquisition of Spanish Grammar by Native Spanish Speakers.* Unpub. diss., University of Texas at Austin, 1970.

———. *The English of Spanish-Speaking Migrant Children: Preliminary Report.* Austin, Texas: SEDL, 1969.

———. *A Linguistic Profile of the Spanish-Speaking First-Grader in Corpus Christi.* M.A. thesis, University of Texas at Austin, 1968.

Gordon, Susan B. *Ethnic and Socioeconomic Influences on the Home Language Expe-*

ment of Intelligence and Verbal Learning Abilities." *Exceptional Children,* 39 (1972), 24-28.

Hilger, Sister Inez. *Arapaho Child Life and Its Cultural Background.* Smithsonian Institution, Bureau of American Ethnology, Bulletin 148. Washington: Government Printing Office, 1952.

Hilton, Darla C. *Investigation of Internalization and Phonological Rules in Monolingual and Bilingual Children.* Master's thesis, University of Texas at Austin, 1969.

Hurt, M., Jr., and S.P. Mishra. "Reliability and Validity of the Metropolitan Achievement Tests for Mexican-American Children." *Educational and Psychological Measurement,* 30 (1970), 989-92.

Huxley, Renira. "Development of the Correct Use of Subject Personal Pronouns in Two Children." In Giovanni B. Flores d'Arcais and William J. M. Lavelt, eds., *Advances in Psycholinguistics.* Amsterdam: North Holland Publishing Co., 1970.

Hymes, Dell. "Bilingual Education: Linguistic vs. Sociolinguistic Bases." In James E. Alatis, ed., *Bilingualism and Language Contact* (Georgetown University Round Table on Language and Linguistics, 1970). Washington: Georgetown University Press, 1970, pp. 69-76.

_____. *Foundations in Sociolinguistics: An Ethnographic Approach.* Philadelphia: University of Pennsylvania Press, 1974.

_____, ed. *Language in Culture and Society: A Reader in Linguistics and Anthropology.* New York: Harper and Row, 1964.

_____, ed. *Studies in the History of Linguistics: Traditions and Paradigms.* Bloomington: Indiana University Press, 1974.

Ianni, Francis A.J., and Edward Storey, eds. *Cultural Relevance, Educational Issues: A Reader in Anthropology and Education.* Boston: Little, Brown, 1971.

Ingram, D. "Transitivity in Child Language." *Language,* 47 (1971), pp. 888-910.

Jakobovits, Leon A., and M. S. Miron. *Readings in the Psychology of Language.* Englewood Cliffs: Prentice-Hall, 1967.

Jampolsky, L. "Advancement in Indian Education." In *The Education of Indian Children in Canada.* Symposium by members of Indian Affairs Education. Toronto: Ryerson Press, 1965.

Jayagopal, R. *Problem Solving Abilities and Psychomotor Skills of Navajo Indians, Spanish Americans and Anglos in Junior High School.* Unpublished dissertation, University of New Mexico, 1970.

Jensen, Arthur R. "Learning Abilities in Mexican-American and Anglo-American Children." *California Journal of Educational Research,* 12 (1961), 147-59.

_____, and William D. Rohwer, Jr. *An Experimental Analysis of Learning Abilities in Culturally Disadvantaged Children.* 1970 [ERIC ED 43 690].

Jensen, J. Vernon. "Effects of Childhood Bilingualism, I." *Elementary English,* 39 (1962), 132-43; also, "Effects of Childhood Bilingualism, II." *Elementary English,* 39 (1962), 358-66.

John, Vera P., and Vivian M. Horner. *Early Childhood Bilingual Education.* New York: The Modern Language Association of America, 1971.

Johnson, Colleen L. *The Japanese-American Family and Community in Honolulu: Generational Continuities in Ethnic Affiliation.* Unpub. diss., Syracuse University, 1972.

Johnson, D. L., and C. A. "Comparison of Four Intelligence Tests Used with Culturally Disadvantaged Children." *Psychological Reports,* 28 (1971), 209-10.

Jorstad, D. "Psycholinguistic Learning Disabilities in Twenty Mexican-American Students." *Journal of Learning Disabilities,* 4 (1971), 143-49.

Justin, Neal. "Experiments in Bilingual Education." *School & Society,* (January 1970).

_____. "Mexican-American Achievement Hindered by Culture Conflict." *Sociology and Social Research,* 56 (1972), 271-79.

Kagan, Spencer, and Millard C. Madsen. "Co-operation and Competition of Mexican-American and Anglo-American Children of Two Ages under Four Instructional Sets." *Developmental Psychology,* 5 (1971), 32-39.

_____. "Rivalry in Anglo-American and Mexican Children of Two Ages." *Journal of Personality and Social Psychology,* 24 (1972), 214-20.

Karabinus, R.A., et al. "Van Alystyne Picture Vocabulary Test Used with Six-Year-Old Mexican-American Children." *Educational and Psychological Measurement,* 29 (1969), 935-39.

Karadenes, Mark. *A Comparison of Differences in Achievement and Learning Abilities between Anglo and Mexican-American Children when the Two Groups are Equated by Intelligence.* Unpub. diss., University of Virginia, 1971.

Karnes, M.B., J.A. Teska, and A.S. Hodgins. "The Effects of Four Programs of Classroom Intervention on the Intellectual and Language Development of Four-Year-Old Disadvantaged Children." *Ameri-*

Lamarche, Maurice M. *The Topic-Comment Pattern in the Development of English among Some Chinese Children Living in the United States.* Unpub. diss., Georgetown University, 1972.

Lambert, Wallace E. *Language, Psychology, and Culture.* Stanford: Stanford University Press, 1972.

_____, R.R. Gardner, R. Olton, and K. Tunstall. "A Study of the Role of Attitudes and Motivation in Second-Language Learning." In Joshua A. Fishman, ed., *Readings in the Sociology of Language.* The Hague: Mouton, 1968, pp. 473-91.

_____, J. Havelka, and C. Crosby. "The Influence of Language Acquisition Contexts on Bilingualism." *Journal of Abnormal and Social Psychology,* 56 (1958), 239-44.

_____, and Chris Rawlings. "Bilingual Processing of Mixed-Language Associative Networks." *Journal of Verbal Learning and Verbal Behavior,* 8 (1969), 604-09.

_____, and Y. Taguchi. "Ethnic Cleavage Among Young Children." *Journal of Abnormal and Social Psychology,* 53 (1956), 380-82.

_____, and Richard C. Tucker. *Bilingual Education of Children: The St. Lambert Experiment.* Rowley, Mass.: Newbury House, 1972.

Lampe, P.E. "The Acculturation of Mexican-Americans in Public and Parochial Schools." *Sociological Analysis,* 36 (Spring 1975).

Landy, David. *Tropical Childhood. Cultural Transmission and Learning in a Puerto Rican Village.* New York: Harper and Row, 1965.

Lassey, William R., and Gerald Navratil. *The Agricultural Workforce and Rural Development: The Plight of the Migrant Worker.* 1971 [ERIC ED 59 797].

Lastra, Yolanda. "El Hablar y la Educación de Niños de Origen Mexicano en Los Angeles." Paper read at Fifth Symposium of the Inter-American Program of Linguistics and Language Teaching, Sao Paulo, Brazil, January 5-14, 1965.

Lemus-Serrano, Francisco. *Mother-Tongue Acquisition and Its Implications for the Learning of a Second Language.* Unpub. diss., Claremont Graduate School, 1972.

Lenneberg, Eric H. *Biological Foundations of Language.* New York: John Wiley and Sons, 1967.

_____. "The Biological Foundations of Language." In Mark Lester, ed., *Readings in Applied Transformational Grammar.* New York: Holt, Rinehart and Winston, 1970a.

_____. "The Capacity for Language Acquisition." In Mark Lester, ed., *Readings in Applied Transformational Grammar.* New York: Holt, Rinehart and Winston, 1970b.

_____. "On Explaining Language." In Doris V. Gunderson, ed., *Language and Reading.* Washington: Center for Applied Linguistics, 1970.

_____, ed. *New Directions in the Study of Language.* Cambridge, Mass.: M.I.T. Press, 1964.

Lesser, G. S., G. Fifer, and D. H. Clark. *Mental Abilities of Children in Different Social and Cultural Groups.* Monograph of Society for Research in Child Development, Serial No. 102 (1965).

Levine, H. "Bilingualism, Its Effect on Emotional and Social Development." *Journal of Secondary Education,* 44 (1969), 69-73.

Le Vine, R.A. "Cross-Cultural Study in Child Psychology," In P. H. Mussen ed., *Carmichael's Manual of Child Psychology,* Vol. 2. New York: Wiley, 1970, pp. 559-614.

Lewis, Gordon K. *Puerto Rico: Freedom and Power in the Caribbean.* New York: Monthly Review Press, 1964.

Linton, Marigold. *Problems of Indian Children.* 1970 [ERIC ED 44 727].

Lombardi, Thomas D. "Psycholinguistic Abilities of Papago Indian School Children." *Exceptional Children,* 36 (1970), 485-93.

Long, Barbara H., and Edmund H. Henderson. "Self-Social Concepts of Disadvantaged School Beginners." *Journal of Genetic Psychology,* 113 (1968), 41-51.

Mace, Betty Jane. *A Linguistic Profile of Children Entering Seattle Public Schools Kindergartens in September, 1971, and Implications for Their Instruction.* Unpub. diss., University of Texas at Austin, 1972.

Mackey, William F. *Bilingual Education in a Binational School: A Study of Equal Language Maintenance Through Free Alternation.* Rowley, Mass.: Newbury House, 1972.

_____. *Bilingualism as a World Problem.* Montreal: Harvest House, 1967.

_____. *Theory and Method in the Study of Bilingualism.* Oxford: Oxford University Press, 1976.

_____, and Theodore Andersson. *Bilingualism in Early Childhood.* Rowley, Mass.: Newbury House, 1977.

_____, and Von N. Beebe, *Bilingual Schools for a Bicultural Community: Miami's Adaptation to the Cuban Refugees.* Row-

logical Linguistics, 12 (1970), 51-61.

Mishra, S. P., and M. Hurt, Jr. "Use of Metropolitan Readiness Tests with Mexican-American Children." California Journal of Educational Research, 21 (1970), 182-87.

Moore, Joan W. Mexican Americans. Englewood Cliffs, N. J.: Prentice-Hall, 1970.

[Morrison, J. Cayce, director]. The Puerto Rican Study, 1953-1957. New York: Board of Education, 1958. Reissued with an introductory essay by F. Cordasco New York: Oriole Editions, 1972.

Mycue, E. Testing in Spanish and the Subsequent Measurement of English Fluency. Texas: Texas Women's University, 1968. [ERIC ED 026 193].

Nagy, Lois B. Effectiveness of Speech and Language Therapy as an Integral Part of the Educational Program for Bilingual Children. Unpub. diss., International University, 1972.

Natalicio, Diana. Formation of the Plural in English: A Study of Native Speakers of English and Native Speakers of Spanish. Unpub. diss., University of Texas at Austin, 1969.

_____, and Frederick Williams. Repetition as an Oral Language Assessment Technique. Austin: Center for Communication Research, University of Texas at Austin, 1971.

Nava, Julian. "Cultural Barriers and Factors that Affect Learning by Spanish-Speaking Children." In John H. Burma, ed., Mexican-Americans in the United States. Cambridge, Mass.: Shenkman, 1970, pp. 125-34.

Naylor, Gordon Hardy. Learning Styles at Six Years in Two Ethnic Groups in a Disadvantaged Area. Unpub. diss., University of Southern California, 1971.

Ney, James W., and Donella K. Eberle, comps. [CAL/ERIC Clearinghouse on Languages. Selected Bibliographies 2] "Bilingual/Bicultural Education." Linguistic Reports, 17, No. 1 (January 1975).

Nichols, C. A. Moral Education among the North American Indians. New York: Bureau of Publications, Teachers College, Columbia University, 1930.

Nuñez, Louis. Puerto Ricans and Education. New York: Board of Education of the City of New York. Puerto Rican Heritage Lecture Series for Bilingual Professionals, May 17, 1971.

O'Donnell, R. C., William Griffin, and R. C. Norris. Syntax of Kindergarten and Elementary School Children: A Transformational Analysis. Champaign, Illinois: NCTE, 1967.

Ogletree, Earl J., and David Garcia. Education of the Spanish Speaking Urban Child: A Book of Readings. Springfield, Illinois: Charles C. Thomas, 1975.

Ohannessian, Sirarpi. The Study of the Problems of Teaching English to American Indians. Washington: Center for Applied Linguistics, 1967.

Oksaar, Els. "Bilingualism." In Thomas Sebeok, ed., Current Trends in Linguistics, vol. 9. The Hague: Mouton, 1972, pp. 476-511.

Olim, E. G. "Maternal Language Styles and Cognitive Behavior." Journal of Special Education, 4 (1970), 53-68.

Ortega, Luis, ed. Introduction to Bilingual Education. New York: Las Américas, 1975.

Osborn, L. R. "Rhetoric, Repetition, Silence: Traditional Requisites of Indian Communication." Journal of American Indian Education, 12 (1973), 15-21.

Ott, Elizabeth H. A Study of Levels of Fluency and Proficiency in Oral English of Spanish-Speaking School Beginners. Unpub. diss., University of Texas at Austin, 1967.

Owen, George M., et al. Nutrition Survey of White Mountain Apache Preschool Children. 1970. [ERIC ED 46 508].

Padilla, Elena. Up From Puerto Rico. New York: Columbia University Press, 1958.

Paquita, Vivó, ed. The Puerto Ricans: An Annotated Bibliography. New York: R. R. Bowker, 1973.

Parisi, Domenico. "Development of Syntactic Comprehension in Preschool Children as a Function of Socioeconomic Level." Developmental Psychology, 5 (1971), 186-89.

_____. "Differences of Socio-Cultural Origin in the Linguistic Production of Pre-School Subjects." Rassegna Italiana de Linguista Applicata, 2 (1970), 95-101.

_____, and Francesco Antinucci. "Lexical Competence." In d'Arcais and Levelt, eds., Advances in Psycholinguistics. Amsterdam: North-Holland Pub. Co., 1970, pp. 197-210.

Parker, Ronald K., et al. An Overview of Cognitive and Language Programs for 3, 4, and 5 Year Old Children. 1970. [ERIC ED 70 534].

Paulston, Christina B. Implications of Language Learning Theory for Language Planning: Concerns in Bilingual Education. Washington: Center for Applied Linguistics, 1974. (Bilingual Education Series, No. 1).

Peak, E., and Wallace Lambert. "The Relation

tion, April 14-15, 1972). Austin, Texas: Dissemination Center for Bilingual Bicultural Education, 1972, pp. 105-120.

Robbins, Lynn. "Economics, Household Composition and the Family Cycle: The Blackfeet Case." In June Helm, ed., *Spanish-Speaking People in the United States.* Proceedings of 1968 American Ethnological Society Meeting, 1968, pp. 196-215.

Rodriguez, Armando. "The Mexican-American Disadvantaged? Ya Basta!" In Alfred Aarons, et al., eds., "Linguistic-Cultural Differences and American Education." *Florida FL Reporter,* 7 (1969) (Special anthology issue).

Rohner, Ronald P. "Factors Influencing the Academic Performance of Kwakiutl Children in Canada." *Comparative Educational Review,* 9 (1965), 331-40.

Rosen, Carl L., and Phillip D. Ortego. "Resources: Teaching Spanish-Speaking Children." *The Reading Teacher,* 25 (1971), 11-13.

Rosenblatt, J. *Cognitive Impulsivity in Mexican-American and Anglo-American Children.* Unpub. diss., University of Arizona, 1968.

Rosenthal, Alan G. *Pre-School Experience and Adjustment of Puerto Rican Children.* Unpub. diss., New York University, 1955.

Samuels, S. Jay. "Psychological and Educational Considerations in Early Language Learning." In F. Andre Paquette, ed., *New Dimensions in the Teaching of FLES.* New York: American Council on the Teaching of Foreign Languages, 1969.

Sanches, Mary. *Features in the Acquisition of Japanese Grammar.* Unpub. diss., Stanford University, 1968.

_____, and Ben Blount, eds. *Sociocultural Dimensions of Language Use.* New York: Academic Press, 1975.

Sandler, L., et al. "Developmental Test Performance of Disadvantaged Children." *Exceptional Children,* 39 (1972), 201-08.

Sapir, Edward. "Language and Thinking." In Charlton Laird and Robert M. Gorrell, eds., *Reading about Language.* New York: Harcourt Brace Jovanovich, 1971.

_____, and Morris Swadesh. "American Indian Grammatical Categories." *Word,* 2 (1946), 103-12.

Sasser, C. *Motor Development of the Kindergarten Spanish-Speaking Disadvantaged Child.* M.A. thesis, Texas Women's University, 1970. [ERIC ED 167 186].

Saville, Muriel R. "Interference Phenomena in Language Teaching: Their Nature, Extent, and Significance in the Acquisition of Standard English." *Elementary English,* March 1971, pp. 396-405.

_____. "Linguistic and Attitudinal Correlates in Indian Education." Paper presented at the American Educational Research Association Convention, Chicago, 1972.

_____, and Rudolph C. Troike. *A Handbook of Bilingual Education.* Washington: Center for Applied Linguistics, 1971.

Saville-Troike, Muriel. "Basing Practice on What We Know About Children's Language." In *Classroom Practices in ESL and Bilingual Education,* Vol. 1. Washington: Teachers of English to Speakers of Other Languages, 1973.

_____. *Bilingual Children: A Resource Document.* Washington: Center for Applied Linguistics, 1973. (Bilingual Education Series, No. 2).

Say, Margaret Z., and William J. Meyer. *Effects of Early Day Care Experience on Subsequent Observed Program Behaviors.* 1970. [ERIC ED 68 149].

Schmidt, L., and J. Gallessich. "Adjustment of Anglo-American and Mexican-American Pupils in Self-Contained and Team-Teaching Classrooms." *Journal of Educational Psychology,* 62 (1971), 328-32.

*Selected Characteristics of Persons and Families of Mexican, Puerto Rican, and Other Spanish Origin.* 1972. [ERIC ED 70 546].

Serrano, Rodolfa G. "The Language of the Four Year Old Chicano." Paper presented at the Rocky Mountain Educational Research Association meeting, Boulder, Col., 1971. [ERIC ED 071 791].

Sharp, Derrick. *Language in Bilingual Communities.* London: Edward Arnold, 1973.

Shaw, Jean W., and Maxine Schoggen. *Children Learning: Samples of Everyday Life of Children at Home.* 1969. [ERIC ED 33 763].

Sherk, John K. *A Word-Count of Spoken English of Culturally Disadvantaged Preschool and Elementary Pupils.* Kansas City: University of Missouri, 1973.

Shriner, T. H., and L. Miner. "Morphological Structures in the Language of Disadvantaged and Advantaged Children." *Journal of Speech and Hearing Research,* 11 (1968), 605-10.

Shuy, Roger W., and Ralph W. Fasold, eds. *Language Attitudes: Current Trends and Prospects.* Washington: Georgetown University Press, 1973. [Georgetown University School of Languages and Linguistics.]

Siegel, Irving E., et al. *Psycho-Educational Intervention Beginning at Age Two: Reflections and Outcomes.* 1972. [ERIC ED 68 161].

Silberstein, R. *Risk-Taking Behavior in Pre-*

ism, and Code Acquisition." In *Conference on Child Language Preprints of Chicago Conference,* 1971. [ERIC ED 060 748].

Swanson, E., and R. DeBlassie. "Interpreter Effects on the WISC Performance of First Grade Mexican-American Children." *Measurement and Evaluation in Guidance,* 4 (1971), 172-75.

Swanson, Maria M. "Bilingual Education: The National Perspective." In Gilbert A. Jarvis, ed., *The ACTFL Review of Foreign Language Education,* vol. 5. Skokie, Illinois: National Textbook Co., 1974, pp. 75-127.

Swinney, J. S. *The Development of Education Among the Choctaw Indians.* M.A. thesis, Oklahoma A&M College, 1935.

Tagatz, C. E., et al. "Effects of Ethnic Background, Response Option, Task Complexity and Sex on Information Processing in Concept Attainment." *Journal of Experimental Education,* 39 (1971), 69-72.

Taylor, M. E. *Investigation of Parent Factors Affecting Achievement of Mexican-American Children.* Unpub. diss., University of Southern California, 1969.

[Teacher Training]. *Teacher Training Bibliography: An Annotated Listing of Materials for Bilingual-Bicultural Teacher Education.* Austin, Texas: Dissemination and Assessment Center for Bilingual Education, 1975.

Tharp, R., and A. Meadow. "Changes in Marriage Roles Accompanying the Acculturation of the Mexican-American Wife." *Journal of Marriage and the Family,* 30 (1968), 404-12.

Thomas, Elizabeth. *The Conceptualization Process in Advantaged and Disadvantaged Kindergarten Children.* Unpub. diss., University of Illinois.

Thomas, R. M. *Social Differences in the Classroom: Social-Class, Ethnic and Religious Problems.* New York: David McKay, 1965.

Thonis, Eleanor. *The Dual Language Process in Young Children.* 1971. [ERIC ED 061 812].

Topper, Martin D. *The Daily Life of a Traditional Navajo Household: An Ethnographic Study in Human Daily Activities.* Unpub. diss., Northwestern University, 1972.

Tremaine, Ruth V. *Syntax and Piagetian Operational Thought.* Washington: Georgetown University Press, 1975. [Georgetown University School of Language and Linguistics.]

Troike, Rudolph C., and Nancy Modiano, eds. *Proceedings.* First Inter-American Conference on Bilingual Education. Arlington,

Virginia: Center for Applied Linguistics, 1975.

Tucker, C.A. "The Chinese Immigrant's Language Handicap: Its Extent and Its Effects." *Florida FL Reporter,* 7 (1969).

Turner, Paul R., ed. *Bilingualism in the Southwest.* Tucson: University of Arizona Press, 1973.

Ulibarri, Horacio. *Interpretive Studies on Bilingual Education.* Washington: U.S. Office of Education, 1969.

[Ulibarri, Horacio, et al.] *Bilingual Research Project: Final Report.* Albuquerque: University of New Mexico, College of Education, 1959.

United States. Cabinet Committee on Opportunity for the Spanish Speaking. *The Spanish Speaking in the United States: A Guide to Materials.* With a Foreword by F. Cordasco. Detroit: Blaine Ethridge, 1975. (Originally, G.P.O., 1971)

United States Bureau of the Census. *American Indians: 1970 Census of Population.* Washington: U.S. Department of Commerce, 1973.

United States Bureau of the Census. *U.S. Census of Population and Housing: Puerto Rican Population Survey Areas, Employment Profiles of Selected Low Income Areas.* Final Report PHC (3). Washington: U.S. Government Printing Office, 1972.

United States Commission on Civil Rights. *Report 1: Ethnic Isolation of Mexican Americans in the Public Schools of the Southwest.* Washington: U.S. Government Printing Office, 1971.

United States Commission on Civil Rights. *Report 2: The Unfinished Education.* Washington: U.S. Government Printing Office, 1971.

United States Commission on Civil Rights. *Report 3: The Excluded Student: Educational Practices Affecting Mexican Americans in the Southwest.* Washington: U.S. Government Printing Office, 1972.

United States Commission on Civil Rights. *Report 4: Mexican American Education in Texas: A Function of Wealth.* Washington: U.S. Government Printing Office, 1972.

United States Commission on Civil Rights. *Report 5: Teachers and Students: Differences in Teacher Interaction with Mexican American and Anglo Students.* Washington: U.S. Government Printing Office, 1972.

Valencia, Atilano A. *The Effects of Bilingual/Bicultural Education among Spanish-Speaking, English-Speaking and Sioux-Speaking Kindergarten Children.* A report of statistical findings and recommenda-

## PREFACE TO FIRST EDITION

The Dissemination Center for Bilingual Bicultural Education is a federally funded project under Title VII of the Elementary and Secondary Act of 1965, as amended, responsible for disseminating materials relevant to bilingual-bicultural education.

PUERTO RICANS IN THE UNITED STATES - A REVIEW OF THE LITERATURE was developed by the New York Component, Nigda Nin, Manager, of the Multilingual Assessment Program, Joe Ulibarrí, Director. Intended for educators, it is an extensively annotated resource book, providing up-to-date information on current advances of bilingual education as well as information on the historical, economic, sociological and anthropological aspects of the Puerto Ricans, Mexican Americans, Blacks, Cubans, American Indians, Jews and other minority groups. Emphasis is on testing, cognitive style and teacher training.

PUERTO RICANS IN THE UNITED STATES - A REVIEW OF THE LITERATURE was edited by Sarah D. Frey, Assistant Editor, and Elsa Sánchez de la Vega-Lockler, Editor, of the DCBBE, Austin, Texas. The cover design was done by Consuelo Nin.

Requests for information concerning PUERTO RICANS IN THE UNITED STATES - A REVIEW OF THE LITERATURE or other bilingual materials should be addressed to the Dissemination Center for Bilingual Bicultural Education, 6504 Tracor Lane, Austin, Texas 78721.

Juan D. Solís
Director

Note:

Title IV funds categorically assigned to ensure the civil rights of non-English dominant minority group students have been used to reprint the review. It is understood that the contents of the publication do not necessarily reflect the views of the U.S. Office of Civil Rights.

Maria Ramirez
Coordinator Bilingual Education
New York State Education Department

ACKNOWLEDGEMENTS


Puerto Ricans in the United States:  A Review of the Literature
began in December 1971 under the supervision of James W. Hawkins, who is
now teaching English to Chicano children in Eagle Pass, Texas.  The majority of the entries assembled here were collected during the first
eight months of the project by Mr. Hawkins and Angel M. Pacheco.  Many
thanks go to both of them, of course.  I would especially like to thank
Mr. Pacheco, who was a great help to both Mr. Hawkins and myself whenever
we ran into difficulties, and was a constant source of moral support to
me.  Two previously published bibliographies were most useful:  Puerto
Ricans on the Mainland:  A Bibliography of Reports, Texts, Critical Studies
and Related Materials by Francesco Cordasco, Eugene Bucchioni and Diego
Castellanos; and Materials Relating to the Education of Spanish-Speaking
People in the United States:  An Annotated Bibliography by George I. Sánchez
and Howard Putnam.

I would also like to express my appreciation to the New York State
Department of Education and the Bilingual Education Unit for the use of
their facilities during the past fourteen months.  Special thanks are due
to Nancy Pollicino and Ellen Kurtzman, who helped me tremendously by
typing the final project.  Ms. Kurtzman proved to be a great help to me,
not only as a typist, but as a research assistant and editorial consultant.

Finally, I must thank everyone connected with the project for their
cooperation and goodwill.
                                                D.H.

# INTRODUCTION

The original purpose of this project was to review all the available literature on the educational experience of Puerto Rican children on the mainland, with an emphasis on educational testing, cognitive style and teacher training. Soon after the initial stages of research were completed, it became apparent that there are many other areas of interest which have an impact on the educational experience of Puerto Ricans in the United States. Consequently, it was decided to expand the scope of the study to include materials which have historical, economic, sociological and anthropological relevance to the Puerto Rican experience as a whole. The reader will also find information here on other non-English-speaking groups in the United States. This was done for several reasons: first, because of the scarcity of research on Puerto Ricans, it was often necessary to use studies in which "Spanish-speaking" subjects (Mexican-Americans) were used; second, to emphasize the need for further study of Puerto Ricans in areas where there is little data to date; and last, to give the reader an idea of how other minorities are faring in American institutions.

Among the sources used in preparation of this bibliography are Research in Education, Current Index to Journals in Education, Education Index, Exceptional Child Abstracts, Psychological Abstracts and Dissertation Abstracts International. Entries are complete through December 1972.

It is hoped that this review of the literature on Puerto Ricans on the mainland will be of great assistance to educators, counselors, social workers and all professionals interested in further research. We believe this is the most comprehensive collection of materials to date.

D.H.

PART I:  BIBLIOGRAPHIES

# BIBLIOGRAPHIES

1. Aarons, Alfred C. "ESL/EFL Materials." TESOL Newsletter. 2:3 and 4 (November 1968).

   A supplementary bibliography (to the author's "TESOL Bibliography" of a year and a half earlier) of ESL/EFL textbooks, language and linguistics, English language, special areas, and ESL/EFL related "supplementary materials that help to make one a better ESL:EFL teacher." (NYS Bibliography)

2. Aarons, Alfred C. "TESOL Bibliography." Florida FL Reporter. (Spring 1967). (Available as Florida FL Reprint).

   An extensive, partly annotated bibliography of TESOL textbooks, methodology, language anthologies, linguistics, English language, periodicals, resource centers, bibliographies, special issues, special areas and dictionaries. (NYS Bibliography)

3. Allen, Harold B., comp. Linguistics and English Linguistics. A Bibliography. New York: Appleton-Century-Crofts. 1966.

   An unannotated, selective listing of books and articles. Major divisions include bibliographies, dictionaries, linguistics, English language and English linguistics, language instruction and special topics.

4. Annotations on Selected Aspects of the Culture of Puerto Rico and Its People. Albany: New York State Education (ED 059 933)

   Intended for teachers who are currently working with Puerto Rican children, this manuscript provides an orientation to the cultural and historical background of Puerto Rico. The primary purpose of this is to depict significant contributions that occurred in Puerto Rico. Contents include information and materials obtained from national archives, official documents, and cultural institute reports, and offer a collection of selected notes relevant to Puerto Rico's history, music, everyday life and culture, horticulture, architecture and current trends. A series of descriptions about famous Puerto Ricans is also included, tracing the culture from 1580 to 1968. An alphabetical listing of information sources by author is presented from which educators may secure information about Puerto Rico. (RIE)

5. Barrios, Ernie, ed. Bibliografía de Aztlán; An Annotated Chicano Bibliography. San Diego, California: Centro de Estudios Chicanos Publications. 1971. 157pp. $3.95.

3

Selective, annotated bibliography arranged under the
following headings: 1, contemporary Chicano history; 2,
educational materials; 3, health research material; 4, high
school materials; 5, history of Mexico; 6, literature;
7, native Americans; 8, pre-Columbian history; 9, Southwest
history; 10, Chicano journals and publications; 11, reference
materials, and others. Particularly interesting for its
questioning of traditional ideas and definitions. (Proyecto
Leer Bulletin)

6. Benson, Susan Shattuck. Proyecto Leer Bulletin, Number 8.
     Washington, D.C.: Books for the People Fund, Inc.
     Washington, D.C.: National Endowment for the Humanities.
     1971. 10pp.
     (ED 063 821)

     This bulletin lists educational materials for the Spanish
speaking. Several hundred documents are listed in three main
sections: 1, organizations, programs, laws and news related
to the Spanish speaking; 2, a list of books selected; and 3,
a list of publishers and distributors with their addresses.
Several bibliographies are included. Entries are annotated
and include comments pertaining to grade level. (RIE)

7. Berger, Barbara. An Annotated Bibliography of Measurements for
     Young Children. New York: Center for Urban Education.
     1969. 50pp.

     A selective listing of assessment instruments for pre-
kindergarten children. Most of the entries describe research
instruments, but some standard commercially available measures
are also noted. Measurements are grouped under the following
headings: cognitive abilities, perceptual skills, reading
readiness, characteristics of cognitive style and personal
social development. References are included.

8. Bird, Agusto, ed. Bibliografía puertorriqueña de fuentes para
     investigaciones sociales: 1930-45. Rio Piedras:
     Centro de Investigaciones Sociales, Universidad de Puerto
     Rico. 1947. (Mimeographed).

9. Cabrera, Patricia, comp. An Introductory Bibliography for
     Teachers of English to Speakers of Other Languages.
     (ED 016 914)

10. Caskey, Owen L. and Jimmy Hodges, comps. <u>A Resource and Ref-</u>
    <u>erence Bibliography on Teaching and Counseling the</u>
    <u>Bilingual Student</u>. Texas Technological College, Lubbock.
    School of Education. March 1968.
    (ED 032 966)

    Citations for 733 selected references published between
    1914-1967 cover materials on the teaching and counseling of
    bilingual students. The purpose of the bibliography is to
    provide as many extensive helpful references as possible.
    Literature dealing with Indian and Mexican-American children
    is included. (RIE)

11. Coller, Alan R. and P.D. Guthrie. <u>Self-Concept Measures</u>:
    <u>An Annotated Bibliography</u>. Princeton, New Jersey:
    Educational Testing Service. 1971. 9pp.

    Includes self-concept measures appropriate for children
    from preschool through third grade. Annotation lists the
    purpose of each instrument, nature of the materials, groups for
    which it is intended, administration, scoring interpretation,
    and standardization. (Proyecto Leer Bulletin)

12. Cordasco, F. <u>The People of Puerto Rico: A Bibliography</u>.
    New York: Department of Labor, Migration Division,
    Commonwealth of Puerto Rico. (1968). Some 500 entries.

13. Cordasco, F., Eugene Bucchioni, and Diego Castellanos.
    <u>Puerto Ricans on the Mainland: A Bibliography of Reports</u>,
    <u>Texts, Critical Studies and Related Materials</u>. Totowa,
    New Jersey: Rowman and Littlefield. 1972.
    (ED 066 539)

    The contents of this annotated bibliography are divided
    into six parts, prefaced by a general description of the
    conditions and problems of the Puerto Ricans on the United
    States mainland. Part I comprises a list of general bibliographies.
    Part II concerns "The island experience," and first lists
    general works and then specific works. Part III concerns
    "The migration to the Mainland." Part IV concerns "The mainland
    experience," and first lists general studies and then studies
    specifically concerning conflict and acculturation. Part V
    focuses on "The mainland experience: education." In the
    first of three sections, it lists unpublished materials; then
    unpublished and published materials from the New York City
    Board of Education; and, finally, general studies. Part VI,
    "the mainland experience: the social context," first lists
    materials on "health, employment, and related social needs,"
    and then on miscellaneous topics. (RIE)

14. Cordasco, F. and Leonard Covello, comps. Studies of Puerto
    Rican Children in American Schools: A Preliminary
    Bibliography. New York: Puerto Rican Commonwealth,
    Department of Labor. 1967. 25pp.
    (ED 021 910)

    This unannotated bibliography lists works dealing with
    Puerto Rican children and their experience in the mainland
    American schools; however, it makes no attempt to cite compre-
    hensively studies which deal with migration or the overall
    experience of Puerto Ricans in the United States. Unpublished
    and published materials are listed separately; some are written
    in Spanish and a number of them were produced by the New York
    City Board of Education. (RIE)

15. A current Bibliography of ERIC-Processed TESOL Documents at
    the Secondary Level. Champaign, Illinois: NCTE/ERIC
    (Unpublished document). March 1970.

    Unannotated extensive listing of such materials in the
    areas of teaching techniques, cross-culture communications,
    methods and materials for special student populations, bilingual
    education and bilingual schools, multi-ethnic literature,
    audiovisual materials and resources, instructional materials,
    and miscellaneous references. (NYS Bibliography)

16. Dabbs, Jack A. "A Selected Bibliography on Bilingualism."
    Reports on Bilingualism. Third Annual Conference of the
    Southwest Council of Foreign Language Teachers. El Paso,
    Texas: the Council. 1966. pp. 27-30.

17. Dossick, Jesse J. Doctoral Research on Puerto Rico and Puerto
    Ricans. New York: New York University, School of Education.
    1967.

18. Eaton, Esther M. and others. Source Materials for Secondary
    School Teachers of Foreign Languages. Circular #788.
    Washington, D.C.: U.S. Department of Health, Education,
    and Welfare. 1966.

    A partially-annotated reference list of representative
    materials for secondary teachers. Includes information on:
    audiovisual aids, course outlines and guides, cultural aids
    from travel and information services, English as a foreign
    language, evaluation and testing, foreign language association
    journals, foreign language newspapers and periodicals,
    instructional aids, international understanding, language
    laboratories, linguistics, organizations offering professional
    services, professional references, programmed instruction,
    research, songs and dances, study, travel and exchange for
    students and teachers, textbooks, and vocational opportunities.
    (NYS Bibliography)

19. Hammer, John H. and Frank A. Rice, eds. A Bibliography of
    Contrastive Linguistics. Washington, D.C.:  Center
    for Applied Linguistics.  1965.

      An unannotated list, alphabetical by language, of con-
    trastive structure studies.  Includes books, theses and
    dissertations, articles, etc.  Majority of entires deal with
    English as one of languages treated.  (NYS Bibliography)

20. Harris, Arna S. and Allan C. Harris.  "A Selected Bibliography
    of American Literature for TESOL.  Part 1:  The Novel;
    Part 2:  The Short Story, Drama, Poetry."  TESOL Quarterly.
    1:3 (September 1967), 1:4 (December 1967).  Available
    as reprint from TESOL.

      Annotated.

21. Hess, Karen and John Maxwell.  What to Do About Non-Standard
    Dialects:  A Review of the Literature.  1969.  52pp.
    (ED 041 027)

      This paper, resulting from a comprehensive search of the
    literature on dialects and dialect learning from 1960-1969, sets
    forth some of the major ideas, points of view and recommendations
    in the following categories:  1, responsibility of the school to
    recognize and accept different varieties of the English language;
    2, early research on "correcting" usage "errors", 3, descrip-
    tive dialect studies (regional, ethnic, social); 4, effects of
    non-standard usage on learning to read, social status, etc.;
    5, descriptions of current programs; 6, what teachers should know
    to deal with non-standard usage; and 7, teacher preparation and
    classroom practices.  Extensive bibliography and glossary of
    terms included.  (RIE)

22. Jensen, J.V.  "Effects of Childhood Bilingualism."  Elementary
    English.  Vol. 39 (1962).  Part I, pp. 132-149.

      This is the first of two articles reviewing the effects of
    childhood bilingualism.  Some of the negative results discussed
    are 1, handicaps to speech development, such as sounds, stress
    and rhythm; 2, disadvantages in language development, such as
    vocabulary and confused structural patterns; 3, handicaps in
    intellectual development, especially for children with only
    superficial knowledge of one language or lacking superior
    intellectual ability; 4, retardation in educational progress, in
    reading and studying generally and in specific subjects; and
    5, emotional instability and social maladjustment because of his
    problems in communication.  The author also discusses some
    deleterious effects of bilingualism on society, from the family

to nations. The bibliography for both articles is included.
(ECK)

23. Klingstedt, Joe Lars. Teachers of Middle School Mexican
    American Children: Indicators of Effectiveness and
    Implications for Teacher Education. Washington, D.C.:
    Office of Education. [1972]. 47pp.

    A summary of research and related literature on the
    problem of identifying indicators of teacher effectiveness,
    this publication is divided into three sections: 1, traditional
    indicators of teacher effectiveness in terms of good teaching
    procedures and desirable personality characteristics; 2, new
    trends in identifying indicators of teacher effectiveness;
    and 3, implications for teacher education in the form of a
    teacher education model--with suggestions for further study.
    A bibliography of 83 citations is included. (RIE)

24. Materials Acquisition Project. Vol. 1, No. 1. San Diego Schools,
    California. Washington D.C.: Office of Education.
    February 1971. 15pp.
    (ED 060 716)

25. Materials Acquisition Project. Vol. 1, No. 2. San Diego Schools,
    California. Washington, D.C.: Office of Education.
    March 1971. 16pp.
    (ED 060 717)

26. Materials Acquisition Project. Vol. 1, No. 3. San Diego Schools,
    California. Washington, D.C.: Office of Education.
    April 1971. 11pp.
    (ED 060 718)

27. Materials Acquisition Project. Vol. 1, No. 4. San Diego Schools,
    California. Washington, D.C.: Office of Education.
    May 1971. 20pp.
    (ED 060 719)

28. Materials Acquisition Project. Vol. 1, No. 5. San Diego Schools,
    California. Washington, D.C.: Office of Education.
    June 1971. 19pp.
    (ED 060 720)

29. Materials Acquisition Project. Vol. 2, No. 1. San Diego Schools,
    California. Washington, D.C.: Office of Education.
    July 1971. 20pp.
    (ED 060 721)

30. Materials Acquisition Project. Vol. 2, No. 2. San Diego Schools,
     California. Washington, D.C.: Office of Education.
     September 1971. 16pp.
     (ED 060 722)

31. Materials Acquisition Project. Vol. 2, No. 3. San Diego Schools,
     California. Washington, D.C.: Office of Education.
     October 1971. 20pp.
     (ED 060 723)

32. Materials Acquisition Project. Vol. 2, No. 4. San Diego Schools,
     California. Washington, D.C.: Office of Education.
     November 1971. 20pp.
     (ED 060 724)

33. Materials Acquisition Project. Vol. 2, No. 5. San Diego Schools,
     California. Washington, D.C.: Office of Education.
     December 1971. 28pp.
     (ED 060 725)

34. Materials Acquisition Project. Vol. 2, No. 7. San Diego Schools,
     California. Washington, D.C.: Office of Education.
     February 1972. 35pp.
     (ED 064 967)

35. Materials Acquisition Project. Vol. 2, No. 8. San Diego Schools,
     California. Washington, D.C. Office of Education.
     April 1972. 38pp.
     (ED 065 004)

36. Materials Acquisition Project. Vol. 2, No. 8 [9]. San Diego
     Schools, California. Washington, D.C. Office of Education.
     May 1972. 59pp.
     (ED 066 095)

37. NCTE Committee on Teaching English to Speakers of Other
     Languages. "Some Materials for Teaching English as a
     Second Language in the Elementary School." Elementary
     English. 46:8 (December 1969).

     A basic, unannotated bibliography, which includes eleven
     methodology listings and fifteen sections on pre-school and
     primary school materials. (NYS Bibliography)

38. Ohannessian, Sirarpi and others. Reference List of Materials
     for English as a Second Language. Part I: Texts, Readers,
     Dictionaries, Tests. Washington, D.C.: Center for Applied
     Linguistics. 1964. 157pp.
     (ED 014 723)

     Annotated.

9

39. Ohannessian, Sirarpi, and others. Reference List of Materials
    for English as a Second Language. Part II: Background
    Materials, Methodology. Washington, D.C.: Center for
    Applied Linguistics. 1966. 115pp.
    (ED 014 724)

    Annotated.

40. Ohannessian, Sirarpi and Ruth E. Wineberg. Teaching English
    as a Second Language--Adult Education Programs.
    Washington, D.C.: Center for Applied Linguistics. 1966.
    (ED 018 788)

    An annotated bibliography of interest to teachers of English
    to adults. Includes background readings, teachers' guides and
    handbooks, adult education course materials, general course
    materials, and specialized English language texts and dictionaries.
    (NYS Bibliography)

41. O'Neill de Lopez, Maria Stella. Bibliografia puertorriqueña:
    1930-1959. Rio Piedras: Centro de Investigaciones
    Sociales. 1957. [Unpublished].

42. Pedtke, Dorothy A., and others. Reference List of Materials for
    English as a Second Language: Supplement (1964-1968).
    Washington, D.C.: Center for Applied Linguistics. 1969.
    207pp.
    (ED 025 773)

    Annotated.

43. "The Puerto Rican Experience on the United States Mainland."
    The International Migration Review. Vol. 2 (Spring 1968).
    Includes "An annotated bibliography on Puerto Rico and
    Puerto Rican migration", pp. 96-102.

44. Revelle, Keith. "A Collection for La Raza." Library Journal.
    96:20 (November 1971). pp. 3719-3726.
    (EJ 047 704)

    The 230 references include books, Spanish-language magazines
    and newspapers, the Chicano press and audiovisual materials
    which have proven successful with a Chicano public. (CIJE)

45. Rice, Frank A. and Allene Guss. Information Sources in Linguistics:
    A Bibliographical Handbook. Washington, D.C. Center for
    Applied Linguistics. 1965.

    A largely unannotated bibliography divided into sections on
    fields within linguistics, linguistics and related disciplines,

applied linguistics, abstracts, classification systems and manpower. (NYS Bibliography)

46. Rivers, Wilga M. Speaking in Many Tongues: Essays in Foreign Language Learning. Rowley, Massachusetts. 1972. $3.95.

     Considers problems such as student dissatisfaction with structural language courses, motivation difficulties, individual differences in means and goals of language learning, etc. and makes concrete proposals towards solving them. Guidelines are established for development and evaluation of language programs, new models of language teaching activities presented, and psychological insights discussed that will assist those involved in language teaching in assessing its meaning for today's students.

47. Rosen, Carl L. Assessment and Relative Effects of Reading Programs for Mexican Americans. A Position Papter. Albuquerque, New Mexico: Southwestern Cooperative Educational Laboratory. 1970. 39pp. (ED 061 000)

     The problems of teaching reading in English to Mexican American children with Spanish as their primary language is considered in this paper. Literature reviews are done on research dealing with 1, linguistics; 2, language-modification approaches; 3, linguistic approaches; 4, language experience approaches; 5, bilingual education; and 6, teacher-school factors. Conclusions on the basis of research in these six areas are given. Also given are implications and specific directions for 1, basic research in language and reading processes; 2, normative descriptive studies of processes involved in reading; 3, pre-school educational research and leadership; 4, language and bilingual education systems; and 5, basic and applied research into current school practices, conditions, and possible promising innovations. An 88-item bibliography is appended. (RIE)

48. Rosen, Carl L. and Phillip D. Ortego. "Resources: Teaching Spanish-Speaking Children." Reading Teacher. 25:1 (October 1971). pp. 11-13.

     Annotated bibliography.

49. Rosen, Pamela and Eleanor V. Horne. Tests for Spanish-Speaking Children: An Annotated Bibliography. Princeton, New Jersey: Educational Testing Service. 1971. 11pp. (ED 056 084)

Lists available instruments for measuring intelligence,
personality, ability and achievement. Excluded are culture-free
or -fair and non-language tests, tests in English with norms for
Spanish-speakers, and tests that have merely been translated
from English to Spanish. Annotation lists purpose of the test
and the groups for which it is intended, test subdivisions or
tested skills, behaviors, or competencies, administration,
scoring, interpretation, and standardization. (Proyecto Leer
Bulletin)

50. Sableski, J.A., ed. "A Selective Annotated Bibliography on
    Child Language." Linguistic Reporter. 7:2 (April 1965).

    A useful bibliography, almost alone in this area; some
    entries for bilingualism. (NYS Bibliography)

51. Sánchez, George I. and Howard Putnam. Materials Relating to
    Education of Spanish-Speaking People in the United States:
    An Annotated Bibliography. Latin American Studies XVII.
    Greenwood Press, Inc. 1959. 40pp.
    (ED 041 680)

    Concerned primarily with the education of Spanish-speaking
    people in the United States who are of Mexican descent, this
    annotated bibliography will also be of value to those working
    with other Spanish-speaking people such as Puerto Ricans. The
    list cites selected books, articles, monographs, bulletins,
    pamphlets, courses of study, bibliographies and unpublished
    theses and dissertations published between 1923 and 1954.
    (RIE)

52. Senior, Clarence. Bibliography of Puerto Ricans in the United
    States. New York: Department of Labor, Migration Division,
    Commonwealth of Puerto Rico. 1959.

53. The Spanish Speaking in the United States: A Guide to Materials.
    Washington, D.C.: the Cabinet Committee on Opportunity for
    the Spanish Speaking. 1971.

54. Status of Puerto Rico. Selected Background Studies Prepared for
    the United States-Puerto Rico Commission on the Status of
    Puerto Rico. Washington, D.C.: U.S. Government Printing
    Office. 1966. [Includes Clarence Senior and Donald O.
    Watkins, "Toward a Balance Sheet of Puerto Rican Migration:
    Bibliography."].

55. Ulibarrí, Horacio. <u>The Effects and Implications of Culturally Pluralistic Education on the Mexican-American</u>. Albuquerque, New Mexico: Southwestern Cooperative Educational Laboratory. 1970. 43pp.
(ED 058 971)

     Establishing that cultural diversity may be nothing more than ecological adjustment and then examining the literature and research related to culturally pluralistic education, the author deals with Mexican American children and children from other minority groups in terms of growth and development, language acquisition and learning, bilingual programs and methodology and tests and measurements. The author recommends three areas for basic research: 1, life-style studies; 2, sociopsychological studies; and 3, educational studies. In addition, it is suggested that a new start for the education of multicultural children utilize an organizational systems approach. One figure and a 74-item bibliography are included. (RIE)

56. Velázquez, Gonzalo, ed. <u>Annuario bibliografico puertorriqueño</u>. Rio Piedras: Editorial Universitaria. 1952. [Irregular].

57. Weinberg, Meyer, comp. <u>The Education of the Minority Child: A Comprehensive Bibliography of 10,000 Selected Entries</u>. Chicago: Integrated Education Associates. 1970.

     An unannotated bibliography.

58. Zirkel, Perry Alan. <u>A Bibliography of Materials in English and Spanish Relating to Puerto Rican Students</u>. Hartford, Connecticut: Connecticut State Department of Education. 1971. 51pp.
(ED 057 142)

     The contents of this listing of materials, intended as resources for teachers and other persons concerned with improving the educational opportunities of Puerto Rican pupils on the mainland as well as on the island, are organized in four sections: 1, books: Puerto Rican Culture in English, Puerto Rican Culture in Spanish, and Children's Fiction; 2, audio-visual materials: films, filmstrips, recordings, and others; 3, research studies; and 4, bibliographies. (RIE)

PART II:  THE PUERTO RICAN CHILD IN THE AMERICAN EDUCATIONAL SYSTEM

THE PUERTO RICAN CHILD IN THE AMERICAN EDUCATIONAL SYSTEM


A.  Anthologies or General Discussions

Puerto Ricans in Puerto Rico

59.  Cebollero, Pedro.  The School Language Policy of Puerto Rico.
         San Juan.  1945.  133pp.

60.  International Institute of Teachers College.  A Survey of the
         Public Educational System of Puerto Rico.  New York:
         Columbia University Bureau of Publications.  1926.

61.  Juncal, Hernan Poza.  "La escuela norteamericana y nuestros
         niños."  Plus Ultra.  (October 10, 1948).

62.  Landy, David.  Tropical Childhood:  Cultural Transmission and
         Learning in a Rural Puerto Rican Village.  New York:
         Harper and Row.  1965.

63.  Montilla, Aida Negrón de.  The Public School System and the
         Americanization Process in Puerto Rico from 1900 to 1930.
         Ph.D. Dissertation, New York University.  1970.
         (Dissertation Abstracts International.  Vol. 31 (1970).
         p. 2515-A.)

64.  Osuna, Juan J.  A History of Education in Puerto Rico.  Rio
         Piedras, Puerto Rico.  1949.

65.  Underwood, Ana R.  "La educacion pre-escolar en las escuelas
         publicas de Puerto Rico."  International Journal of Early
         Childhood.  2:1 (1970).  pp. 38-43.
         (EJ 029 662)

Puerto Ricans in Mainland Schools

66.  "Activaron la enseñanza del inglés básico en las communidades
         boricuas."  La Prensa.  (February 23, 1952).

67.  Bell, John.  "Puerto Rican Influx Jams Crowded Schools."
         New York World Telegram.  (May 3, 1947).

68.  Bucchioni, Eugene.  A Sociological Analysis of the Functioning
         of Elementary Education for Puerto Rican Children in the
         New York City Public Schools.  Unpublished Ph.D. Dissertation,
         New School for Social Research.  1965
         (Dissertation Abstracts.  Vol. 26 (1966).  pp. 6216-6217.)

The objectives of this paper were to examine and describe
the situation of Puerto Rican children in New York City
elementary schools. The author discusses the problem in sociological terms: the democratic idology of the schools, the role
of the school in assimilation, the conflict of values in the
educational program, and the "culturally loaded" curriculum,
methods and materials used in the school which generally lead
to severe educational retardation among Puerto Rican students.
Data were collected through participant observation and some
content analysis of relevant publications of the New York City
Board of Education.

As a result, the author states that "elementary education for
Puerto Rican children functions in the context of highly complex
arrangement of rhetoric, myth, and reality." Because the
"arrangement" makes it seem as if Puerto Rican children are
receiving a successful education, since they are receiving the
same program offered to other children, the special problems and
needs of these children are being ignored. According to Bucchioni,
the results further indicate that the school system is essentially
a "middle-class sorting device" whereby some children, primarily
those of North American middle-class background, are selected
in elementary school for sufficiently high academic achievement
throughout school and the successful attainment of middle-class
status. Access to these opportunities are severely limited for
Puerto Rican children, who are "sorted out" of the channels
for successful educational achievement early in the education
process. (DH)

69. "Children from Puerto Rico." Curriculum and Materials.
    (May-June, 1954). 16pp.

70. "Cívicas y culturales: Asociación de padres." El Diario de
    Nueva York. (June 13, 1952). p. 8

71. "Cívicas y culturales: Conferencia sobre educación escolar."
    El Diario de Nueva York. (May 21, 1952). p. 13.

72. "Cívicas y culturales: Escuela pública de la calle 109 (oeste)
    abre su matricula para kindergarten." El Diario de Nueva York.
    (May 17, 1952).

73. Collazo, Francisco. The Education of Puerto Rican Children in
    the Schools of New York City. San Juan: Department of
    Education Press. 1954. 14pp.

74. "Comprensión por conocimiento." (Editorial). El Diario de
    Nueva York. (May 27, 1952). p. 9.

75.  Cordasco, F.  "Educational Programs for Puerto Rican Pupils."
New York Times.  (May 30, 1967).

76.  Cordasco, F.  "The Puerto Rican Child in the American School."
Congressional Record.  111:195 (October 19, 1965).
pp. 26, 425-426.

_____  "The Puerto Rican Child in the American School."
American Sociological Association.  Abstracts of Papers
(61st Annual Meeting).  1966.  pp. 23-24.

_____  "The Puerto Rican Child in the American School."
Kansas Journal of Sociology.  Vol. 2 (Spring 1966).  pp. 59-65.

_____  "The Puerto Rican Child in the American School."
Journal of Negro Education.  Vol. 36 (Spring 1967).
pp. 181-186.

77.  Cordasco, F.  "Puerto Rican Pupils and American Education."
School and Society.  Vol. 95 (February 18, 1967).
pp. 116-119.

For the most part, the Puerto Rican child reflects a context
of bitter deprivation, poor housing, high unemployment, and a
record of disappointing educational achievement.  The child is
pressured both by a completely new environment and the negative
pressures of a ghetto mileu, ("the recurrent pattern of the
ghettoization of new arrivals").
Discussion of the two problems: 1, How to effectively teach
English as a second language and 2, How to promote a more rapid
and more effective adjustment of Puerto Rican parents and children
to the community and the community to them is included.
Acculturation is more important to the Puerto Rican child and
American society.  Just how can he retain his identity, culture
and language?
Cordasco suggests that a school that is not community-oriented
is a poor school, and that much more disturbing than the Puerto
Rican child's lack of English is the lack of economic security
and well-being that relate him to a noble family structure.  (DH)

78.  Cordasco, F. and E. Bucchioni.  Education Programs for Puerto
Rican Students.  [Jersey City Public Schools[.  Evaluation
and Recommendations.  Jersey City:  Board of Education.  1971.

79.  Cordasco, F. and E. Bucchioni.  Puerto Rican Children in Mainland
Schools.  Methuchen, New Jersey:  Scarecrow Press.  1968.

80.  Cordasco, F. and E. Bucchioni.  The Puerto Rican Community and Its
Children on the Mainland:  A Source Book for Teachers,
Social Workers and Other Professionals.  Metuchen, New Jersey:
The Scarecrow Press, Inc.  1972.

19

81. Covello, Leonard. *The Heart is the Teacher*. New York. 1958.

82. Covello Papers. Personal Files. [In the possession of F. Cordasco]

83. Covello, Leonard. "Recommendations Concerning Puerto Rican Pupils in Our Public Schools." May 1, 1953. [unpublished]

84. Cruz, Juan S. and George S. Richs. *Some Aspects of Puerto Rican Adaptation to Mainland U.S.A.* Chicago: Board of Education. 1967.

85. "Educadora boricua llevará a las cortes al City College de N.Y. Alega es víctima de descrimen." *El Diario de Nueva York*. (April 24, 1952).

86. *Education-in-the-News*. A monthly clip sheet for the use of U.S. editors and radio commentators. New York: Puerto Rican Public Relations Committee, Inc. (April 1, 1949). 3pp.

87. "Education of Puerto Rican Children in New York City." *Journal of Educational Sociology*. 28:4 (December 1954). pp. 145-192.

88. Emery, Helen T. "How the City's Schools Greet Puerto Ricans." *New York World Telegram and Sun*. (November 4, 1953).

89. Emery, Helen T. "Schools Here Aid Progress of Migrants." *New York World Telegram and Sun*. (February 11, 1953).

90. Emery, Helen T. "Schools Weigh Problems of Puerto Ricans." *New York World Telegram and Sun*. (February 11, 1953).

91. Emery, Helen T. Seward H.S. Makes Americans." *New York World Telegram and Sun*. (May 11, 1956). p. 34.

92. Entman, Frederick. "Our Puerto Rican Children: One School's Approach." *Strengthening Democracy*. (May 1955). pp. 3, 5.

93. Finocchiaro, Mary. *Education of Puerto Ricans on the Mainland: Overcoming the Communication Barrier*. Paper delivered at Conference on the Education of Puerto Rican Children on the Mainland in San Juan, Puerto Rico. 1970. 14pp. (ED 043 871)

The complexity of the problems concerning the teaching of English to Puerto Ricans in the U.S. has rarely been fully appreciated. Author discusses some factors involved: 1, learners may be admitted to school at any age and placed in advanced grades with their age peers; 2, some older learners may be functionally illiterate in their own language; 3, learners may or may not have had some previous instruction in English;

4, they may enter school at any time during the semester; 5, their schooling may be broken frequently; 6, many live in Spanish language enclaves; 7, language skills must be developed to allow students to participate in rest of curriculum, etc. (RIE)

94. Finocchiaro, Mary. "Our Schools Must Meet the Challenge of a New Migration." High Points. (March 1953). pp. 29-33.

95. Finocchiaro, Mary. "Puerto Rican Newcomers in Our Schools." Journal of Educational Sociology. Vol. 28 (December 1954). pp. 157-166.

_____ "Puerto Rican Newcomers in Our Schools." American Unity. 14:3 (January-February 1956). pp. 12-17.

This article describes the problems facing Puerto Ricans when they enter mainland schools and some of the modifications made in the regular school program to help the Puerto Rican students adjust. Illustrations for teacher techniques are also described and several problems which must be solved are also listed. (ECK)

96. Goodman, Samuel M., and others. Who Are the Puerto Rican Pupils in the New York City Public Schools? New York: Board of Education. 1956.

97. Greenstein, Marvin N. "Puerto Rican Children." Pathways in Child Guidance. 2:4 (June, 1960). pp. 1-3.

98. Guren, Louise. "A Special Class for Puerto Rican Students." High Points. (February 1948). pp. 77-80.

99. "Helping Puerto Rican Pupils to Achieve Status." Strengthening Democracy. 5:6 (May 1953). pp. 4-5.

100. Hochhauser, Aidalina. A Pilot Study of "Problem Children" of Puerto Rican Background. New York: The Puerto Rican Study of the New York City Board of Education. 1956.

101. "How to Teach Puerto Ricans." New York Herald Tribune. (February 13, 1951).

102. Ingraham, Leonard W. "Our Puerto Rican Students Must Become a Part of All the Children." High Points. (February 1951).

103. Lewis, C. "Some Puerto Rican Viewpoints." Childhood Education. Vol. 43 (October 1966). pp. 82-84.

104. Loretan, Joseph O. "Problems in Improving Educational Opportunities for Puerto Ricans in New York." High Points. (May 1963). pp. 23-31.

105. Margolis, Richard. The Losers: A Report on the Puerto Ricans and the Public Schools. New York: Aspira. 1968.

106. Materesi, Felicia. "No debe segregarse a los estudiantes de Puerto Rico." El Diario de Nueva York. (January 19, 1954).

107. Mayor's Advisory Committee on Puerto Rican Affairs in New York City, Sub-Committee on Education, Recreation and Parks. The Puerto Rican Pupils in the Public Schools of New York City: A Survey of Elementary and Junior High Schools. New York. 1951. 102pp.

108. Messer, Helaine R. The Puerto Rican Student in the New York City Public Schools: 1945-1965. Unpublished M.A. thesis, Columbia University. 1966.

109. Monserrat, Joseph. "Education of Puerto Rican Children in New York City." Journal of Educational Sociology. (December 1954).

110. Monserrat, Joseph. School Integration: A Puerto Rican View. San Juan: Commonwealth of Puerto Rico, Department of Labor, Migration Division. 1963. 16pp. Address, Teacher's College, Columbia University. May 1, 1963.

111. Montes, Marta. "La primera escuela puertorriqueña en la ciudad de Nueva York." La Prensa. (September 17, 1961).

112. Morrison, J. Cayce, Director. The Puerto Rican Study. New York City Board of Education. 1964.

113. McCuen, John J. "Puerto Rican Survey Seeks Best Methods." New York World Telegram and Sun. (April 7, 1954). p. 42.

114. "Need of the Puerto Rican Child." New York Teacher News. (November 8, 1952). p. 3.

115. The Needs of Children of Puerto Rico. Washington, D.C.: Federal Security Agency. 1950.

116. New York City Board of Education. Meeting the Needs of Puerto Rican Pupils in New York City Public Schools. New York: Board of Education. Supplement to Staff Bulletin. (March 23, 1964).

117. New York City Board of Education. Our Children from Puerto Rico. New York: Board of Education. 1957.

118. Oliveras, Candido. What Are the Educational Needs of Puerto Ricans Who Come to New York? Address, New York University. January 14, 1961.

119. Perlman, Ruth. "The American School: Cultural Crossroads."
     _The Elementary School Journal_. (November 1968). pp. 82-86.

120. Public Educational Association. _The Status of the Public School_
     _Education of Negro and Puerto Rican Children in New York_
     _City_. Presented to the Board of Education Commission on
     Integration. New York City Board of Education. October 1955.

     Following the Supreme Court decision to make school seg-
     regation illegal on May 17, 1954, Arthur Levitt, who was President
     of the New York City Board of Education at that time, requested
     this "full, impartial and objective inquiry" into the status of
     public school education for Black and Puerto Rican students in
     New York City. It is explained that New York City schools are
     community schools and therefore reflect the population make-up
     of the community. Since the Black and Puerto Rican communities
     are somewhat separated from the rest of the city's population,
     their schools are also separate. It is recognized here that the
     "separate but equal" facilities concept really amounts to de
     facto segregation; according to the data, the educational
     opportunities afforded the minority children are far from equal.
     President Levitt's stated goal was the "completely integrated
     school", so the study includes information about the present
     zoning situation and suggestions for its revision. (DH)

121. Public Education Association. "The Status of the Public School
     Education of Negro and Puerto Rican Children in New York
     City." Public Education Association. 1955.

122. "The Puerto Rican Child." _New York Teachers' News_. (November
     29, 1952). pp. 2, 7.

123. "Puerto Rican Children." _New York Teachers' News_. (April 3, 1954).
     p. 4.

124. _Puerto Rican Graduates of Morris High School, June 1961_.
     Migration Division, Commonwealth of Puerto Rico. 1963.

125. "Pupils from Puerto Rico." _The Elementary School Journal_.
     (November 1958). p. 74.

126. Rand, Christopher. "Puerto Ricans." _Saturday Review_. Vol. 41
     (September 13, 1958). p. 36.

127. Rand, Christopher. _The Puerto Ricans_. New York: Oxford. 1958.
     178pp.

128. Rand, Christopher. "A Reporter at Large: The Puerto Ricans." The New Yorker. (November 30, 1957). [Series of four articles].

129. "Reshaping Public Education: For Spanish-Speaking Children." United Teacher. (May 29, 1968).

   Discusses Puerto Rican children in New York City.

130. Sayers, Raymond S. "New York Teachers in Puerto Rican Schools." High Points. Vol. 39 (November 1957). pp. 5-16.

131. "Seek Better School Program for N.Y.C. Puerto Rican Youth." New York Teachers' News. (May 31, 1952). p. 4.

132. Senior, Clarence. "Schools, Newcomers and Community." Problems and Practices in New York City Schools. 1963 Yearbook of the Society for the Experimental Study of Education. Parts II and III, pp. 107-11. New York: Society for the Experimental Study of Education. 1963.

133. Strauss, Susan. "The Effect of School Integration on the Self-Concept of Negro and Puerto Rican Children." Graduate Research in Education. Vol. 3 (1967). pp. 63-76.

134. "Summary of Recommendations Made by the Puerto Rican Study for the Program in New York City Schools." Board of Education, City of New York. 1958. [Mimeographed].

135. "Teaching the Puerto Rican Child." New York Teachers' News. (February 24, 1953). p. 3

136. University of the State of New York. The State Education Department, Division of General Education, Bilingual Education Unit. Part III of Volume II, The Fleischmann Commission Report: Children with English-Language Difficulties. Albany, New York: 1972.

137. Vázquez, Hector I. "Puerto Rican Americans." National Elementary Principal. 50:2 (November 1970). pp. 65-71. (EJ 032 393)

   Summarizes briefly the low achievement rate of Puerto Ricans in New York Schools, including the background of the problem, the school situation, and the community involvement. (CIJE)

138. Weissman, Julius. An Exploratory Study of Communication Patterns of Lower Class Negro and Puerto Rican Mothers and Pre-School Children. Ph.D. Dissertation, Teachers College, Columbia

University. 1966.
(Dissertation Abstracts. Vol. 27 (1967). pp. 3960A-3961A).

The purpose of the investigation was to explore the assumption
that lower-class child-rearing patterns socialize passive behavior and lack of motivation for learning in children.  Ss were
mothers and pre-school age children from low-income Puerto Rican
and Black groups.  The nature and degree of the "assumed passivity"
were studied in terms of the forms and patterns of the verbal and
non-verbal communications between mother and child pairs in both
home and school settings.  The findings indicate that Puerto
Rican mother-child pairs are much more active at home than in the
school setting; the opposite was true for the Black group.
"The Puerto Rican group had higher activity rates in the 'teaching'
category, in the reinforcement of verbal praise, smiles, touch
contacts, and related areas.  The Black group was more active
in the use of verbal admonitions, 'don'ts' in critical comments,
in directing and coercing verbal and non-verbal communication."
The Puerto Rican mother-child pairs were more active and responsive in the interpersonal processes of communication than the
the Black mother-child pairs.  (DH)

139.  Zirkel, Perry Alan.  Puerto Rican Parents and Mainland Schools.
       Hartford Connecticut:  Hartford Model Cities.  November
       1971.  98pp.
       (ED 062 473)

       This study constitutes the promised product of an institute
on "Puerto Rican Pupils in Mainland Schools," sponsored by the
Educational Leadership Institute and the University of Hartford
during the summer of 1971.  The stated purposes of the institute
were: 1, to stimulate communications and understanding between
school and community representatives toward the improvement of the
educational opportunities of Puerto Rican pupils in mainland
schools; 2, to develop a data base concerning cultural and
linguistic factors in the home environment that may be significant
toward that end; and 3, to examine and interpret such data in
terms of present and potential school programs and practices.
The Institute focused on facilitating the relationship between the
home and school environment of Puerto Rican pupils in Hartford
as a possible model for other mainland school systems.  The formal
program of the Institute was concentrated in the week of June 28-
July 2.  The morning sessions provided the opportunity to interact
with several resource people in small group discussions.  The
afternoon sessions were devoted to conducting structured interviews
in the homes of a cross-section of Puerto Rican families who had
children in the Hartford schools.  The duration of the summer was
used for further research and the final writing of independent
individual reports, each culminating in recommendations for
improving the educational opportunities of these children in the
Hartford schools.  (RIE)

Spanish-Speaking Students in Mainland Schools

140. Anderson, James and Dwight Safar. Equality of Educational
     Opportunity for Spanish-American and Indian Students in
     Two Multi-Cultural Communities:  An Exploratory Assessment.
     1969.  34pp.
     (ED 029 746)

141. Austin, Mary.  "Rural Education in New Mexico." University of
     New Mexico Bulletin, Experimental School Series.  Vol. 2,
     no. 1.  Albuquerque:  University of New Mexico Press.  1931.

142. Biddick, Mildred L. and Esther A. Harrison.  "Spanish-American
     Children Receive Help in Achieving Status." School Management.
     (August 1947).

143. "The Community Speaks." National Elementary Principal.  50:2
     (November 1970).  pp. 29-33.

     Spanish-speaking parents reflect on the educational
     opportunities offered to their children.

144. Cooke, W. Henry.  "The Segregation of Mexican-American School
     Children in Southern California." School and Society.
     Vol. 67 (June 5, 1948).  pp. 417-421.

145. Cordasco, F. and Leonard Covello.  "Schools and the Spanish-
     Speaking Community." Congressional Record.  (June 12, 1962).
     pp. A4322-A4323.

146. "La educación y el emigrante." Temas.  Vol. 14 (November 1957).
     pp. 124-127.

147. The Excluded Student; Educational Practices Affecting Mexican
     Americans in the Southwest.  Mexican American Education Society.
     Washington, D.C.:  U.S. Government Printing Office.  May 1972.
     77pp.
     (ED 062 069)

148. Felder, D.  "The Education of Mexican-Americans:  Fallacies of
     the Monocultural Approach." Social Education.  Vol. 34 (1970).
     pp.  639-642.

149. Flicker, Jeanette.  "Classes for Spanish-Speaking Children."
     High Points.  (November 1947).  pp. 58-62.

150. "Helping the Migratory Mexican Child to Belong." California
     Elementary School Principals Association.  The Elementary
     School Faces the Problems of Migration, 15th Yearbook, 1943.
     by Jessica K. Pullis.  pp. 97-101.

26

151.  Holland, W.R.  "Language Barrier as an Educational Problem of
      Spanish-Speaking Children."  Exceptional Children.
      Vol. 27 (1960).  pp. 42-50.

152.  Howells, Simone.  "The Preschool Migrant Child."  Education News.
      Vol. 13, no. 4.  (August 1971).  pp. 9-14.
      (EJ 054-978)

153.  Link, Albert D., comp.  Mexican American Education, A Selected
      Bibliography (with ERIC Abstracts).  ERIC/CRESS Supplement
      No. 2.  New Mexico State University, University Park,
      ERIC Clearinghouse on Rural Education and Small Schools.
      Washington, D.C.:  National Center for Educational Research
      and Development.  May 1972.  345pp.
      (ED 065 217)

154.  Lozano, Diana.  "Historical Perspective."  (Education for the
      Spanish-Speaking).  National Elementary Principal.  50:2
      (November 1970).  pp. 20-23.

155.  Mangers, Dennis H.  "Education in the Grapes of Wrath."  National
      Elementary Principal.  50:2 (November 1970).  pp.  34-40.

      Comments on the educational situation in the San Joaquin
      Valley, California.

156.  Marland, S.P., Jr.  Completing the Revolution.  Speech presented
      at inauguration of Dr. Frank Angel as President of New Mexico
      Highlands'University, Las Vegas, New Mexico, June 5, 1972.  14pp.
      (ED 066 288)

      In this speech Mr. S.P. Marland, Jrs., U.S. Commissioner of
      Education, discusses both the shortcomings and accomplishments of
      the American education system when it comes to educating Mexican
      American Students.  (RIE)

157.  Martínez, Arnulfo S.  A Study of the Scholastic Census of the
      Spanish-Speaking Children of Texas.  Unpublished Master's
      thesis, University of Texas.  1944.

158.  Methodological Appendix of Research Methods Employed in the
      Mexican American Education Study.  Washington, D.C.:
      Commission on Civil Rights.  January 1972.  162pp.
      (ED 064 025)

159.  Nabokov, P.  Tijerina and the Courthouse Raid.  Albuquerque,
      New Mexico:  University of New Mexico Press.  1969.

160. "An Open Letter to Mexican-American Parents from an Anglo
     Elementary Teacher." La Raza. (May 11, 1968).

161. Ott, Elizabeth. Basic Education for Spanish-Speaking
     Disadvantaged Pupils. 1967. 23pp.
     (ED 020 497)

162. Raisner, Arnold. "New Horizons for the Student of Spanish-
     Speaking Background." High Points. (February 1966).
     pp. 19-23.

163. Rodríguez, A. "Education for the Spanish-Speaking: Mañana
     in Motion." National Elementary Principal. Vol. XLIX,
     no. 4 (February 1970). pp. 52-56.

     A history of Spanish-speaking people and their relationship
     with the schools; the author notes three main Spanish-speaking
     groups--Mexican Americans, Cuban refugees, and Puerto Ricans.
     There is a plea for a change in attitude from regarding the
     Spanish-speaking child as "disadvantaged" to helping him achieve
     bilingual and biculturalism, and for improvement of the
     relationship between the school and the community. (ECK)

164. Salazar, Rubén. Stranger in One's Land. Commission on Civil
     Rights, Washington, D.C. Washington, D.C.: U.S. Government
     Printing Office. May 1970. 52pp.
     (ED 054 908)

     An account of the hearing held by the U.S. Commission on
     Civil Rights on the Mexican American community's problems with
     civil rights, this report does not necessarily represent the
     views of the Commission but is published to stimulate public
     interest in the problems confronting Mexican Americans. Major
     areas explored were employment, education, the administration of
     justice, housing, and political representation. "The total
     picture of economic deprivation, of relegation to the meanest
     employment, of educational suppression, and of restricted
     opportunity in almost every phase of life unfolded." (RIE)

165. Salinas, Guadalupe, ed. Mexican-Americans and the Desegregation of
     Schools in the Southwest. California University, Riverside.
     Western Regional School Desegregation Projects. Washington,
     D.C.: Office of Education. Cooperative Research Program.
     December 1971. 41pp. Article originally appeared in
     "Houston Law Review." Vol. 8 (1971). p. 929.
     (ED 058 983)

166. Saunders, Lyle. "The Spanish-Speaking Population of Texas."
     <u>Inter-American Education, Occasional Papers, No. 5</u>.
     Austin: University of Texas Press. December 1949. 55pp.

167. Sepulveda, Betty. <u>Teaching the Educationally Disadvantaged
     Hispano Child at K-3 Level</u>. 1969. 4pp.
     (ED 036 807)

Educational Opportunity in the American Educational System

168. Blair, J.F. "When Nationalities Mix in the Classroom." <u>Instructor</u>.
     Vol. 63 (September 1953). p. 108.

169. Brameld, Theodore. <u>Minority Problems in the Public Schools</u>:
     <u>A Study of Administrative Policies and Practices in Seven
     School Systems</u>. New York: Harper and Brothers. 1946.

170. <u>The Children of Immigrants in Schools</u>. With an Introductory
     Essay by F. Cordasco. (Metuchen, New Jersey: Scarecrow
     Reprint Corporation, 1970; originally, 1911).
     5 vols. Originally Vols. 29-33 of <u>Report of the Immigration
     Commission</u>. [Washington, D.C.: U.S. Government Printing
     Office, 1911].

171. Cole, Stewart G. and Mildred W. Cole. <u>Minorities and the
     American Promise, the Conflict of Principle and Practice</u>.
     New York: Harper. 1954. 319pp. Bureau for Intercultural
     Education, Publication No. 10 in the series, "Problems of
     Race and Culture in American Education."

172. Coleman, J. and others. <u>Equality of Educational Opportunity</u>.
     Washington, D.C.: U.S. Government Printing Office. 1966.

173. Cordasco, Francesco. "The Challenge of the Non-English
     Speaking Child in the American School." <u>School and Society</u>.
     Vol. 96 (March 30, 1968). pp. 198-201.

174. Cordasco, Francesco. "Educational Pelagianism: The Schools and
     the Poor." <u>Teachers College Record</u>. Vol. 69 (April 1968).
     pp. 705-709.

175. Cordasco, Francesco. "Helping the Language Barrier Student."
     <u>Instructor</u>. Vol. 72 (May 1963). p. 20.

176. Cordasco, Francesco. "The Non-English Speaking Child in the
     American School: Continuing Challenge to Education in a
     Democratic Society." Statement and Testimony before the
     General Education Sub-Committee of the U.S. House of Re-
     resentatives. (June 29, 1967). Washington: 11pp.
     (H.R. Bill 9840).

29

_____ "The Non-English Speaking Child in the
American School: Continuing Challenge to Education in a
Democratic Society." Testimony before the Senate Sub-
Committee on Bilingual Education. (July 21, 1967).
Washington, D.C. 11pp. (Senate Bill 428).

177. Cordasco, Francesco and Maurie Hillson. "Poor Children and
Schools." in N.W. Brickman and S. Lehrer, eds. Education
and the Many Faces of the .Disadvantaged. New York:
John Wiley. 1972.

178. Díaz, Manuel and Roland Cintrón. School Integration and Quality
Education. New York: Puerto Rican Forum. 1964.

179. "Federal Judge Outlaws Segregation in Public Schools."
Common Ground. Vol. 8 (Winter 1947). pp. 102-103.

180. Green, Shirley E. The Education of Migrant Children. Washington,
D.C.: Department of Rural Education, N.E.A. 1954. 179pp.

181. Hillson, Maurie, and others. Education and the Urban Community:
Schools and the Crisis of the Cities. 1969. 506pp.
(ED 040 233)

Selection of 49 articles dealing with the crises and conflicts
of urban education. Articles discuss the impact of urbanization,
social stratification, the effects of urban poverty on Black and
Puerto Rican families, and the disadvantaged school dropout. (RIE)

182. Hnatek, Margaret. A Survey of Population Factors Relating to
the Education of Migrant Children in Victoria County, Texas.
Unpublished Master's thesis, University of Texas. 1952.

183. Law, William. "Problems for the Migratory Student." California
Journal of Secondary Education. Vol. 14 (March 1939).
pp. 170-173.

Problems confronting migratory students are: poor housing,
malnutrition, inferiority complex, inability to adjust socially,
mental retardation due to environment, the impossible task of
selecting subjects which can be followed through all of the
schools attended.

184. Light, Richard L. "The Schools and the Minority Child's
Language." Foreign Language Annals. 5:1 (October 1971).
pp. 90-91.
(ED 044 635)

185. McMurrin, Sterling M., ed. The Conditions for Educational
        Equality. CED Supplementary Paper, Number 34. Committee for
        Economic Development, New York. Research and Policy Committee.
        July 1971. 208pp.
        (ED 057 118)

186. Newcomb, W. Fred. "Caring for the Children of Seasonal Workers
        in Ventura County Schools." California Journal of Elementary
        Education. Vol. 6 (August 1937). pp. 54-59.

187. Newell, John, and others. Migrant Early Childhood Education
        Program in Hardee County, Florida: An Evaluation. Florida
        University, Gainesville College of Education; Florida
        University, Gainesville Institute for Development of
        Human Resources. Florida State Department of Education,
        Tallahassee Division of Elementary and Secondary Education.
        August 1971. 67pp.
        (ED 060 960)

188. Osborne, Marie A.S. The Educational Status of Intrastate Migrants
        in Texas, 1935-1940. Unpublished Master's thesis, University
        of Texas. 1954.

189. Rhine, W. Ray. Ethnic Minority Perspectives on the Evaluation
        of Early Childhood Education Programs. 3pp.
        (ED 062 010)

        Issues presented at a symposium on ethnic minority
perspectives and evaluation of early childhood education are
presented. Two presentations are summarized. The first,
"Evaluation Research and the Education of Oppressed Minority
Group Members," by Edward J. Barnes, emphasizes that the evaluation
of education programs must include a look at the person in a
social as well as academic context. It is stated that the
exclusion of ethnic minority values from the academic scene is
the cause for the school system's failure to educate ethnic
minority children. The second paper, "The Implications of
Cognitive Styles and Cultural Democracy for Evaluation Research,"
by Manuel Ramirez, states that cultures and values of minority
groups in the United States, especially those of Black and
Indians, have been viewed as pathological and inferior. It is also
stated that the results of ignoring these cultures is the alienation
of minority group children from the schools. (RIE)

190. Rice, J.P., Jr. "Education of Subcultural Groups." School and
    Society. Vol. 92 (1964). pp. 360-362.

    This article discusses intelligence testing, and includes
a very brief survey of the literature on "culturally loaded"
measures of intelligence. The author suggests compensatory
programs for the slower learners, TESOL programs for the non-
native speaker of English, and encourages the development of new
instruments for testing bilingual students. (DH)

191. Richey, Herman G. "Educational Status of Important Population
    Groups between the First and Second World War." School Review.
    Vol. 57 (January and February 1949). pp. 16-27, 89-100.

192. Rivera, Vidal A. "The Forgotten Ones: Children of Migrants."
    National Elementary Principal. 50:2 (November 1970).
    pp. 41-44.

    Discusses educational problems of migrant children.

193. Rodríguez, A. "The Challenge for Educators." National Elementary
    Principal. Vol. I, no. 2. (November 1970). pp. 18-19.

    Lists the problems faced by bilingual students in schools
that are exclusively Anglo-American and suggestions (such as
changes in teacher training and curriculum) that are necessary
to include the bilingual child in the school system. (ECK)

194. The Supreme Court of the State of California. "Serrano v. Priest:
    Implications for Educational Equality." Harvard Educational
    Review. 41:4 (November 1971). pp. 501-534.

    Reprint of the decision of the Supreme Court of the State of
California - Serrano v. Priest. Briefly, the Court found that the
school financing system in California is unconstitutional
because it does not provide children with equal protection as
guaranteed by the Fourteenth Amendment of the United States
Constitution. The decision was based on the fact that children
in wealthy communities receive greater educational offerings than
children growing up in poor communities. Commentary provided by
William N. Greenbaum.

195. The Unfinished Education; Outcomes for Minorities in the Five
    Southwestern States. Mexican American Educational Series.
    Washington, D.C.: Commission on Civil Rights. October 1971.
    94pp.
    (ED 056 831)

    "The basic finding of this report is that minority students
in the Southwest--Mexican Americans, blacks, American Indians--
do not obtain the benefits of public education at a rate equal to

that of their Anglo classmates. This is true regardless of the measure of school achievement used." The U.S. Commission on Civil Rights has sought to evaluate school achievement by reference to five standard measures: school holding power, reading achievement, grade repetitions, overageness for grade assignment, and participation in extracurricular activities. Without exception, minority students achieve at a lower rate than Anglos; their school holding power is lower; their reading achievement is poorer; their repetition of grades is more frequent; their overageness is more prevalent; and they participate in extracurricular activities to a lesser degree. (RIE)

196. The University of the State of New York. The State Education Department, Bureau of Pupil Testing and Advisory Services, Division of Educational Testing. Summary Report of State-wide Test Results. (October 1966-October 1970).

The Pupil Evaluation Program is an annual fall testing program required of all pupils in all public and non-public schools of New York State. It consists of reading and math achievement tests in grades 3 and 6 and reading and arithmetic minimum competence tests in grade 9. These tests have been developed by the State Education Department and are based on New York State courses of study. Includes: statewide analysis of educational disadvantage, analysis of educational disadvantage by type of school, schools with critical problems of educational disadvantage, statewide distribution of educationally disadvantaged pupils, and statistical information about the test itself.

No specific information on ethnic or non-English speaking linguistic groups.

B. Socioeconomic and Sociocultural Characteristics of the Puerto
   Rican Child in the United States and Their Relationship to the
   Educational Process

197. Anderson, James, and others. "Stability and Change among
     Three Generations of Mexican-Americans: Factors Affecting
     Achievement." American Educational Research Journal.
     8:2 (March 1971). pp. 285-309.
     (EJ 041 768)

198. Anderson, James and William H. Johnson. Sociocultural Deter-
     minants of Achievement Among Mexican-American Students.
     University Park, New Mexico: New Mexico State University.
     1968. 45pp.
     (ED 017 394)

199. Antonowsky, Aaron. "Aspiration, Class and Racial-Ethnic
     Membership," Journal of Negro Education. Vol. 36:4.
     pp. 385-393.

     Earlier studies of students from a small city show that
     Black youngsters have a higher level of aspiration than Whites.
     Three hundred seventy eight 10th-graders from five schools in a
     large city were tested to see if the same pattern could be
     found and to compare: 1, middle and low-class Blacks and Whites,
     and 2, Puerto Rican youths with Blacks and Whites. Senior
     guidance counselors asked eight questions dealing with "future
     socioeconomic-educational aspirations and expectations." It was
     found that middle-class Whites had the highest aspiration level,
     and Puerto Ricans were relatively low. Patterns of response were
     similar for lower-class Whites, middle-class Puerto Ricans, and
     middle and lower-class Blacks. The comparison between the
     small city and the metropolis showed "differences between lower-
     class Whites and similarities between lower-class Blacks. (PASAR)

200. Brameld, Theodore. "Explicit and Implicit Culture in Puerto
     Rico: A Case Study in Educational Anthropology." Harvard
     Educational Review. Vol. 28 (Summer 1958). pp. 197-213.

201. Caldwell, Floyd F. and Mary Mowry Davis. "Sex Differences in
     School Achievement Among Spanish-American and Anglo-American
     Children." Journal of Educational Sociology. Vol. 8
     (May 1935). pp. 168-173.

202. Casavantes, Edward J. Deviant Behavior in the Mexican-American
     Student and Its Relation to Education. A Position Paper.
     Albuquerque, New Mexico. Southwestern Cooperative Educational
     Laboratory. August 1970. 16pp.
     (ED 060 989)

34

Since the literature about the mental health of Mexican Americans has been consistent in reflecting that a low socio-economic level combined with extensive use of Spanish lowers IQ test scores of Mexican Americans, these factors should be studied in connection with the educational achievement of Mexican Americans and their mental health. This could be done because Mexican Americans are highly distinguishable from other ethnic groups. In such a study, eight hypotheses are proposed for testing on a random sample of large numbers of Mexican Americans from all socioeconomic levels and ages, from every state in the Southwest, from rural and urban settings, from the Chicano militant element, from colleges and from the Hispano component. The actual survey should be done by special questionnaire and a short adapted form of standard personality tests with some in Spanish. Examiners should be Mexican Americans highly trained in psychiatric interviewing procedures. In summary, this investigation should be a broad-based study on the mental health and educational achievement of Mexican Americans. (RIE)

203. Casavantes, Edward J. <u>Variables Which Tend to Affect (Impede or Retard) Learning of the Mexican American Student in American Education. A Position Paper</u>. Albuquerque, New Mexico. Southwestern Cooperative Educational Laboratory. August 1970. 15pp. (ED 060 990)

An interdisciplinary research study is suggested following a review of the more significant studies that have been attempted to explain the degree of educational retardation of the Mexican American as related to such factors as life stresses and learning styles. This study would be a combination of survey research and research for hypothesis testing wherein a random sample of the total Mexican American population would be used. It is noted that such a study would provide large quantities of data on sociologic, family education, cognitive, and personality functioning and would assess the co-variation and influence of each of these variables on each of the other variables. (RIE)

204. Cherkis, C. "School and the Puerto Rican Parent." <u>High Points</u>. Vol. 32 (March 1950). pp. 20-27.

This article stresses the need to bring parents of Puerto Rican school children in to the schools, to "educate" them about what goes on in the schools and show them that they are accepted as important members of the school community. Without the interest and cooperation of Puerto Rican parents during their children's experience in school, the children (who begin with a disadvantage) will have even more difficulty making adjustments to school life. The school is a very important agent in the socialization of children, and in the acculturation of children

from different ethnic backgrounds; without the cooperation of
Puerto Rican parents, the school cannot expect to succeed. (DH)

205. Christian, Chester C., Jr. "The Acculturation of the Bilingual
Child." Modern Language Journal. 49:5 (March 1965).
pp. 160-165.

Discusses the problem of confusion and frustration which
exists when a child learns one language and culture from his
parents and then must learn another language and culture when
he enters school. The author maintains the term "acculturation"
refers to the destruction of one culture to gain a second.
He suggests that education should attempt to involve the culture
of the child.

206. Clark, Madeline. A Preliminary Survey of the Employment
Possibilities of the Spanish-American Girls Receiving
Commercial Training in the San Antonio Secondary Schools.
Unpublished Master's thesis, University of Texas. 1936.

207. Cline, Marion, Jr. Achievement of Bilinguals in Seventh Grade
by Socioeconomic Levels. Ph.D. Dissertation, University
of Southern California. 1961.
(Dissertation Abstracts. Vol. 22 (1962). pp. 3113-3114.)

This study was designed to investigate the relative
achievement of Anglo-American and Spanish-American students within
socioeconomic levels in order to determine whether SES and
biculturalism have an effect on educational achievement. Ss were
354 seventh graders (156 Anglos, 197 Spanish-American); each
group was classified into three socioeconomic levels. Ss were
administered the Stanford Achievement test, the Otis Quick-Scoring
Mental Ability Test and a questionnaire. The groups and levels
were compared for all variables. Analysis of the data indicated
that: 1, socioeconomic status functions greatly in school
achievement; 2, biculturalism does not itself function in school
achievement, but in combination with SES it does become important;
and 3, Anglo-Americans at the upper and middle socioeconomic
levels did considerable better than Spanish-Americans at those
levels, but at the lower SES level, they did just as poorly.
Finally, there are recommendations for further research
concerning the materials and methods used in teaching all students
of the lower socioeconomic level. (DH)

208. Cobb, Albert F. Comparative Study of the Athletic Ability of
Latin American and Anglo American Boys on a Junior High
School Level. Unpublished Master's thesis, University of
Texas. 1952.

36

209. Cohen, S. Alan. "Some Learning Disabilities of Socially
     Disadvantaged Puerto Rican and Negro Children."
     Academic Therapy Quarterly. Vol. 2 (Fall 1966). pp. 37-41,
     52.

     This paper describes some of the learning disabilities and
patterns that are common in lower-class Puerto Rican and Black
children. The author's work with slum children has convinced him
that "cultural deprivation" includes many behaviors which can be
seen in dyslexia, SLD and perceptual dysfunction. He suggests
that schools stop labelling these children, begin to anticipate
their difficulties and teach to the behaviors in the disability
syndrome.
     Ss were 1721 third graders (489 Puerto Ricans, 626 Blacks, and
489 Whites, Others). Data were obtained from Marianne Frostig's
Developmental Test of Visual Perception, the Benton Visual
Retention Test, the WISC, and observations. Ss had a higher
incidence of perceptual dysfunction than test norms predict.
According to this study, poor visual discrimination of letters,
poor visual memory of unknown words, poor recognition of known
words, and letter reversals (p-b-d-q) were common among these
socially disadvantaged children. (DH)

210. Coole, Musgrave Ruth. A Comparison of Anglo-American and Latin-
     American Girls in Grades V-VI with Reference to Their
     Vocational, Academic, and Recreational Preferences and
     Aversions. Unpublished Master's thesis, University of Texas.
     1937.

211. Cruz, Juan S. and George S. Richs. Some Aspects of Puerto Rican
     Adaptation to Mainland U.S.A. Chicago: Board of Education.
     1967.

212. Delmet, D.T. "A Study of the Mental and Scholastic Abilities
     of Mexican Children in the Elementary School." Journal of
     Juvenile Research. Vol. 14 (January 1937). p. 31.

213. Deutsch, M. Minority Group and Class Status as Related to Social
     and Personal Factors in School Achievement. (Monograph #2).
     Ithaca, New York: The Society for Applied Anthropology.
     1960.

214. Elam, Sophie E. "Acculturation and Learning Problems of Puerto
     Rican Children." Teachers College Record. Vol. 61
     (February 1960). pp. 258-264.

     _____ "Acculturation and Learning Problems of Puerto
     Rican Children." in J.K. Robert, ed. School Children in the
     Urban Slums. New York: Free Press. 1965.

Suggests the problem for Puerto Rican children is changing
from rural peasant (tradition-oriented) culture to urban (other-
directed) complex. "Adjustment to one negates the other," and
rewards offered may not be as satisfying or easily adapted/inte-
grated into the patterns of the home and other culture: "culture
shock," inadequacy.

Discusses the language problem for the non-native; there is
some mention of nonverbal communication and confusion that can
result because certain expressive gestures may have different
meanings in the different cultures. Also discusses the weaknesses
of the American· education system, teacher preparation and classroom procedures, materials and orientation. "Our training
practices in education have dealt chiefly with the child who is
native to our land and has no outstanding language problems...
Most of our textbooks are written by middle-class professors for
middle-class teachers of middle-class children."

Proposes the concept of "fundamental education to cover the
whole of living; to teach not only new ways but the need and
incentive for new ways." In discussing the adjustment problems
of Puerto Rican children, Ms. Elan suggests that the family
condition may have something to do with the child's difficulty
in school: separation, instability, poverty, illness. She feels
that the school may be the most important institution in bringing
about the Puerto Ricans child's successful adjustment to the
new culture. (DH)

215. Fennessey, James. An Exploratory Study of Non-English Speaking
Homes and Academic Performance. Baltimore, Maryland:
Research and Development Center for the Study of Social
Organization of Schools and the Learning Process, Johns
Hopkins University. 1967.
(ED 011 613)

This paper is a re-analysis of data concerning Puerto Rican
schoolchildren in New York City collected as part of a larger
United States Office of Education survey. The answers to the
following questions were sought: 1, What relationships are
present between the language spoken in the home and other aspects
of ethnic background? and 2, What differences are present in
vocabulary test scores of Puerto Rican children with varying
home languages and at different grade levels? It was difficult
to analyze the data because of the apparent error in response to
several important interview questions. Two tentative conclusions
are 1, language is not very closely linked to other attributes of
Puerto Rican ethnicity and 2, "after taking into account some
confounding background variables, there is little difference
between Spanish-English homes and English-only homes on the
average vocabulary test scores of the children, except at grade
one." The author suggests further research to continue the
re-analysis of the USOE study. (ECK)

216. "From Puerto Rico to Pennsylvania:  Culture Shock in the
     Classroom."  _Pennsylvania Education_.  Vol. 2 (May-June 1971).
     pp. 22-29.

217. Garretson, O.K.  "A Study of the Causes of Retardation Among
     Mexican Children in a Small School System in Arizona."
     _Journal of Educational Psychology_.  Vol. 19 (January 1928).
     pp. 31-40.

218. Garth, Thomas R., and others.  "Mental Fatigue of Mexican School
     Children."  _The Journal of Applied Psychology_.  Vol. 16
     (December 1932).  pp. 675-680.

219. Gordon, C. Wayne, and others.  _Educational Achievement and
     Aspirations of Mexican-American Youth in a Metropolitan
     Context_.  Occasional Report 36, Center for the Study of
     Evaluation.  Los Angeles:  University of California.  1968.

220. Gross, Morris.  _Learning Readiness in Two Jewish Groups:  A
     Study in "Cultural Deprivation"_.  New York:  Center for
     Urban Education.  1967.  45pp.
     (ED 026 126)

         Study findings suggest that implicit cultural factors,
     aspirations, and more affect children's school readiness, even
     when poverty and other disadvantages are absent.
         Study involved 90 American born, middle class Jewish
     children, half of whom were Ashkenazic (of European descent)
     and half Sephardic (of Syrian descent).  Families of both groups
     had been in the United States at least 25 years. Results showed
     that the Ashkenazic children, whose cultural background possibly
     supported academic achievement, were more prepared than the
     Sephardic children, whose training seemed to stress financial
     success.  (RIE)

221. Guerra, Manuel H.  "Education Chicano Children and Youths."
     _Phi Delta Kappan_.  53:5 (January 1972).  pp. 313-314.

222. Halpern, Shelly.  _The Relationship between Ethnic Group Membership
     and Sex and Aspects of Vocational Choice of Pre-College
     Black and Puerto Rican High School Students_.  Ph.D. Dissertation,
     Fordham, University.  1972.
     (_Dissertation Abstracts International_.  Vol. 33 (1972).
     pp. 190A-191A.)

         The purpose of this study was to examine the relationship
     between sex and ethnic group membership and aspects of vocational
     choice.  The instruments used to measure the effects of these
     variables on the attitudes of the students were the Attitude
     Scale of the Vocational Development Inventory (VDI) and the

Vocational Aspiration Scale (VAS). The difference between
vocational expectation and aspiration was measured by VAS
discrepancy scores. Ss were 255 tenth graders from three high
schools in New York City (82 Black males, 116 Black females, 33
Puerto Rican males, and 24 Puerto Rican females). All were
enrolled in a pre-college program for minority youth, and were
required to meet these criteria in order to participate: low
socioeconomic status and academic underachievement with high
potential.

Analysis of the data indicated that both sex and ethnic
group membership are significant variables on vocational choice.
Black students tended to score higher than Puerto Rican students
and females tended to score higher than males. On the VAS,
however, males tended to score higher than females. The author
concludes with some suggestions for further research projects on
vocational expectation and aspiration. (DH)

223. Halstead, David W. _An Initial Survey of the Attitudinal Differences_
_Between the Mothers of Over-Achieving and Under-Achieving_
_Eleventh-Grade Puerto Rican Students._ Unpublished Ph.D.
Dissertation, Michigan State University. 1966.
(_Dissertation Abstracts._ 27:12 (1967). pp. 4127A-4128A.)

The purpose of the study was to examine the differences in
attitudes of mothers of over- and under-achieving students in
Puerto Rico. The sample was made up of mothers of 11th graders from
three geographical areas. These geographical areas were chosen
because of the hypothesized present-orientation (traditional
culture) found in the Rural areas, which changes over time to the
combination traditional/modern of Other Urban areas, and then to the
more modern, future-orientation of Urban San Juan residents.
The women were selected for the study on the basis of the
discrepancy between predicted and actual achievement of their
children. Interviewers used the Parental Interview Questionnaire
(PIQ) which was developed for this study. Results indicate that
the Urban San Juan and Rural mothers of over-achieving daughters
wanted their children to have a significantly greater amount of
education than did mothers of under-achievers. More mothers of
over-achievers than under-achievers of Rural and Other Urban areas
encouraged their children to ask questions and play with other
children. Most of the mothers believed that things would improve
in the future and all mothers thought their children's progress in
schools was above average. The author suggests that future researchers
use a different stratification procedure for sampling, as his
hypothesized shift in attitudinal patterns received little support in
vact. (DH)

224. Hernández, Norma G.  Variables Affecting Achievement of Middle
     School Mexican American Students. Texas University,
     El Paso. Washington, D.C.:  Office of Education.  August
     1971.  81pp.
     (ED 059 827)

     Literature pertaining to research done on academic achievement
of Mexican American students is reviewed in this paper.  The
literature deals with such variables as socioeconomic, physical,
psychological, and cultural aspects; language factors; attitudes;
language development; and environment.  A 15-page discussion of
recommendations for improving curriculum, instruction, and teacher
education for educating the Mexican American is included.  Also
included is a bibliography containing over 200 relevant citations.
(RIE)

225. Hobart, Charles W.  "Underachievement among Minority Group
     Students."  Phylon.  Vol. 24 (1963).  pp. 184-196.

     The author presents a sociological analysis of the situation
of minority group students in public schools.  There are four
conditions that seem to apply in all cases:  1, a damaged self-
concept; 2, inadequate motivation; 3, a lack of awareness of
employment opportunities and capabilities; and 4, resistance by
peers and community to self advancement.  Hobart notes that any
one of these circumstances would severely arrest the child's
development.  Combined, they function to guarantee that the
minority young person will finish school fitted only for unskilled
or semi-skilled work.  Hobart suggests that compensatory education
programs be instituted to counteract whatever deficiencies in
preparation which have accumulated during the student's previous
years of schooling, and provide the individualized attention so
badly needed to improve the student's self-evaluation.  (DH)

226. Henderson, Ronald.  Positive Effects of a Bicultural Pre-School
     Program on the Intellectual Performance of Mexican-American
     Children.  1969.  10pp.
     (ED 028 827)

227. Hermenet, Argelia María Buitrago.  Ethnic Identification of
     Puerto Rican Seventh Graders.  Unpublished Ph.D. Dissertation,
     University of Massachusetts.  1971.
     (Dissertation Abstracts International.  Vol. 32 (1971-1972).
     pp. 4350-4351A.)

     The project was designed to measure Puerto Rican ethnic
identity.  The sample consisted of seventh graders from Puerto
Rico and Soringfield, Massachusetts in the following breakdown:
93 Puerto Ricans from Puerto Rico who had had no experience in the

United States; 12 Puerto Ricans tested in Puerto Rico who had had
experience in the United States; 68 Puerto Ricans tested in
Springfield with varying experience in the United States and
Puerto Rico; 85 White, English-speaking Americans and 38
migrants from other countries (Italy and Portugal). The
instrument was a questionnaire which consisted of nine items
related to ethnic consistency. "The data showed that Puerto
Rican seventh graders in general are undergoing psychological
changes which are reflected in their view of themselves, their
parents, and their expressed wishes for political, cultural
and social alignments, whether with Puerto Rico and Puerto Ricans
and the Hispanic American culture, or with the United States,
the American and the English speaking culture." (ECK)

228. Jaramillo, Mari-Luci. Cultural Differences Revealed Through
      Language. NCRIEEO Tipsheet, Number 8. Columbia University,
      New York, New York, National Center for Research and Information
      on Equal Educational Opportunity. Washington, D.C.:
      Bureau of Elementary and Secondary Education (DHEW/OE).
      May 1972. 6pp.
      (ED 066 522)

      Biculturalism implies much more than bilingualism.
Bilingualism has been defined in a variety of ways, but perhaps
the most commonly accepted definition is varying degrees of
understanding of two languages. But biculturalism implies
knowing and being able to operate successfully in two cultures.
This means knowing two modes of behavior, and knowing the beliefs,
values, customs, and mores of two different groups of people.
The language used at a particular time and place would have the
referents in the culture the language represents. Teachers
must accept these differences in students and start working to
provide equal educational opportunity in the classrooms. One
could capitalize on the language children bring to school. The
students have already internalized the sound patterns of a language
and their written work could be based on these sounds. If these
sound patterns are Spanish, the instruction should be in Spanish.
Simultaneously, with this instruction, the second language should
be introduced systematically. (RIE)

229. Kandell, Alice S. Harlem Children's Stories: A Study of
      Expectations of Negro and Puerto Rican Boys in Two Reading-
      Level Groups. Unpublished Ph.D. Dissertation, Harvard
      University. 1967.
      (Dissertation Abstracts. 28:6 (1967). p. 2338A.)

      The purpose of the study was to investigate and compare the
educational and life expectations of lower socioeconomic-status
Black and Puerto Rican Harlem boys. Ss were 30 Puerto Rican boys
and 30 Black boys; half of each group had scored in the high

range on the Metropolitan Reading Test, and the other half had
scored in the low range. Ss were administered a projective test
combined with a direct questionnaire designed to elicit estimations
of their capabilities and chances to achieve their goals. Content
analysis of the Ss' stories and answers showed that the Black
boys had significantly lower estimates of their abilities and much
more negative life expectations than did the Puerto Rican boys.
The stories of the Black respondents were characterized by over-
tones of resignation and apathy, while the Puerto Rican Ss
expressed confidence in their eventual success, positive attitudes
about their families and school, and a much more optimistic
view of the environment. (DH)

230.  Katz, David.  The Effects of a Compensatory Educational Program
      on the Vocational Aspirations, Expectations, Self-Concept,
      and Achievement of Selected Groups of JHS Students.  Ph.D.
      Dissertation, Washington State University.  1968.
      (Dissertations Abstracts.  1969.  Vol. 29 (9-A0.  p. 2963.)

      This study was designed to investigate the effects of a
compensatory educational program on the vocational aspirations,
expectations, self-concepts and achievements of selected groups of
ninth grade junior high school students in New York City.  Ss
were male, average in grade, at least two years below grade level
in reading, and members of either Black or Puerto Rican minorities.
All students in the experimental group were in a Career Guidance
program.  Students in the control group were matched for characteristics equivalent to those of the experimental group, except that
they were either 1, in the same school as the Ss but not taking
part in the Career Guidance program, or 2, in schools which did
not have the compensatory program.  The instruments used by the
investigators were a personal adequacy scale based on the Whittaker
Scale, a modification of Hambruger's Life Planning Questionnaire,
and the Metropolitan Achievement Test.  All Ss were administered the
tests and questionnaire on two different occasions, at the
beginning and end of the school year.  Results of the statistical
analysis indicated that the Career Guidance program had no
significant positive effects on the variables under consideration.
In fact the effects that did occur were contrary to the goals of
the program.  In the experimental group congruency between
aspiration and expectation was reduced, rather than facilitated,
while the control groups showed a significant increase over the
same period of time.  Black students gained significantly more
than the Puerto Rican students in reading achievement, but the
control group gained more in reading than the experimental group
overall.  (DH)

231. Leach, John Nathaniel. Cultural Factors Affecting the
     Adjustment of Puerto Rican Children to Schooling in
     Hartford Connecticut. Unpublished Ph.D. Dissertation,
     The University of Connecticut. 1971.
     (Dissertation Abstracts International. Vol. 32 (1971-1972).
     p. 2308A.)

     This study was designed to identify differences between
migrant students originally from the coastal sugar plantations
of Puerto Rico and those originally from the tobacco-growing
hill areas of the island in the following school-related areas:
1, language usage; 2, social practices and conventions; 3,
attitudes toward legal authority; and 4, attitudes toward literary
pursuits. Ss were students from the above-mentioned areas of
Puerto Rico who attended Hartford Public High School. The inves-
tigator reached the following conclusions: 1. No significant
difference was found between students from the coastal areas and
students from the hill areas in English, mathematics, social
studies achievement, and quality point average; and 2. No
significant difference was found between the two groups in
attendance, school violations, and tardiness. (ECK)

232. Lopategui, Miguelina Nazario de. Needs and Problems of Puerto
     Rican High School Students Related to N Variables.
     Unpublished Ph.D. Dissertation, Purdue University. 1957.

233. Lowry, Sarah J. A Comparison of Certain Physical Abilities of
     Anglo and Latin American Fifth and Sixth Grade Girls.
     Unpublished Master's thesis, University of Texas. 1952.

234. Lucas, Isidro. Puerto Rican Dropouts in Chicago: Numbers and
     Motivations. Chicago: Council on Urban Education (sponsored
     by USOE). 1971. 101pp.
     (ED 053 235)

     Dropout rate was found to be 71.2% for pupils who had
received a substantial portion of their education on the
continent. Those remaining in school showed problems of self-
concept caused by discrimination, difficulty in relating to
parents, and a progressive strangement of pupil from school.
Schools did little to improve this image. Students' commitment to
study and future aspirations decreased the longer they stayed in
school. Knowledge of English was greater among dropouts than
among seniors staying in school; these seniors knew more Spanish
than dropouts. Study revealed that inclusion of Puerto Rican
studies courses and presence of Puerto Rican teachers helped
reduce the dropout rate substantially. (RIE)

235. Madeira, Eugene L. <u>The Puerto Rican Involvement in Educational</u>
     <u>Opportunity Fund Programs for the Disadvantaged</u>. New
     Jersey: Glassboro State College. (Social Science Seminar
     Thesis). 1970. 91pp.
     (ED 056 147)

     The purpose of this study was to analyze Puerto Rican re-
     sponse to the opportunities for higher education and to survey
     the prospects of recruiting more Puerto Ricans in "Educational
     Opportunity Fund Programs." Camden, New Jersey, was chosen as
     a representative medium-sized city with a Puerto Rican
     community. (RIE)

236. Mercer, Jane R. <u>Sociocultural Factors in the Education Evaluation</u>
     <u>of Black and Chicano Children</u>. Paper presented at the
     10th Annual Conference on Civil Rights Educators and Students,
     NEA, Washington, D.C. February 18-20, 1972. 16pp. Sacra-
     mento: California State Department of Mental Hygiene.
     Bureau of Research. Sacramento: California State Department
     of Education, Office of Compensatory Education. Bethesda,
     Maryland: National Institute of Mental Health.
     (ED 060 462)

     In a recent study the mothers of 268 children who were in
     classes for educable mentally retarded in two public school
     districts in Southern California were interviewed. The responses
     of some of these mothers dramatize three issues: 1, biases in
     the assessment procedures used to label children as mentally
     retarded; 2, the stigmatization associated with special class
     placement; and 3, inadequate programming. Disproportionally
     large numbers of black and Chicano children are labeled as mentally
     retarded by the public schools. Public schools rely more on IQ
     test scores than any other community agency. The schools label
     more persons as mentally retarded, share their labels with more
     other organizations, and label more persons with IQ's above 70 and
     with no physical disabilities than any other formal organizations
     in the community. Proportionately more low status persons and
     persons from minority ethnic groups were defined as comprehensively
     retarded as the cutoff level for sub-normality was raised.
     Stigmatization was a major concern of parents interviewed. Of a
     group of 108 children followed for several years and classified
     as retarded, only one in five ever returned to the regular class.
     Thus, many parents were justified in seeing the program as a
     "sentence of death." (RIE)

237. Miller, Henry. "New York City's Puerto Rican Pupils:  A
     Problem of Acculturation." <u>School and Society</u>. 76:1967
     (August 30, 1952). pp. 129-132.

238. Mingione, Ann D. "Need for Achievement in Negro, White, and Puerto Rican Children." Journal of Consulting and Clinical Psychology. 31:1 (1968). pp. 94-95.

Compared the need for achievement of Negro, White, and Puerto Rican fifth and seventh graders in low socioeconomic areas of a large New England city. The need-for-achievement test consisted of six topic sentences about which the subjects wrote stories. F tests of the need-for-achievement scores revealed no significant differences. These results contrast with the author's previous study in which White children had higher need-for-achievement scores than Negro children and seventh graders scored higher than fifth graders. There were more words per story, greater variety of story themes, and more stories concerning females written by both boys and girls than in the previous study, when the stories were written in response to drawings of people. School grades and group intelligence test scores did not correlate with the need-for-achievement scores in this study. (PASAR)

239. Nuttal, Ronald L. Do the Factors Affecting Academic Achievement Differ by the Socio-Economic Status or Sex of the Student? A Puerto Rican Secondary School Sample. Final Report. Boston College, Chestnut Hill, Massachusetts. Institute of Human Sciences. Washington, D.C.: National Center for Educational Research and Development (DHEW/OE). June 1972. 110pp.
(ED 064 465)

Variables expected to be associated with academic achievement were examined in a sample (generally exceeding 2500) from eight secondary schools in Baymon Norte, Puerto Rico. Concern was whether variables associated with academic achievement differed by sex or by socioeconomic status (SES). Multivariate analyses of variance with three factors of achievement, sex, and SES were made. High achievers tended to have accepting mothers, parents low on Hostile Psychological Control, and low on autonomy; and were more geographically mobile, had fewer siblings, were more intelligent, obedient, conscientious, artistic, group-minded, placid, self-disciplined, responsible, anxious (preocupado), mature, and less excitable. High achieving girls were less authoritarian, dogmatic, and test anxious, and gave fewer false but socially desirable responses. Students whose academic achievements were consistent with their SES were more assertive, less bragging, happier, and more esthetically sensitive than those whose achievement were discrepant with their SES. Self concepts were higher for achievers, especially for low SES students in junior high schools, and for all students in high schools. Low achievers, especially boys, disliked school. High achieving boys and low achieving girls were more self sufficient, while low achieving boys and high achieving girls were more group dependent. (RIE)

46

240. Nuttall, Ronald L., and others. <u>Family Background, Parent-Child Relationships and Academic Achievement Among Puerto Rican Junior and Senior High School Students</u>. <u>Report #4: Study of Factors Affecting Student Achievement</u>. Boston: Boston College. Massachusetts Institute of Human Sciences. 1969. 11pp.
(ED 043 698)

The reliability, validity, and relationships of a Spanish language adaptation of Schaefer's Child's Report of Parental Behavior Inventory (CRPBI) was examined. It was found the CRPBI had reliabilities averaging .78 and factor analysis indicated a 3 factor structure similar to Schaefer's previous work. Background variables, especially socioeconomic status (SES) were related to the CRPBI factors. Generally, higher SES went with higher acceptance and lower hostile psychological control. Children from large families were less accepted. The CRPBI factors predicted grades, especially among junior high school males. Background factors predicted college plans. (RIE)

241. Paschal, Franklin C. and Louis R. Sullivan. "Racial Influences in the Mental and Physical Development of Mexican Children." <u>Comparative Psychology Monographs</u>. Vol. 3. 76pp.

242. Pintner, R. and G. Arsenian. "The Relation of Bilingualism to Verbal Intelligence and to School Adjustment." <u>Journal of Educational Research</u>. Vol. 31 (1937). pp. 255-263.

243. Posner, Carmen Alberta. <u>Some Effects of Genetic and Cultural Variables on Self Evaluations of Children</u>. Unpublished Ph.D. Dissertation, Illinois Institute of Technology. 1969. (<u>Dissertation Abstracts</u>. 29:12 (1969). pp. 4833B-4834B)

The purpose of the investigation was to study the effects of socio-economic status (SES), ethnic affiliation, intelligence and sex on the self-perceptions of children. Ss were 300 first graders; ethnic groups included Black, White, and Puerto Rican children born on the mainland. The socio-economic groupings consisted of lower and upper-middle-class levels. Only the Puerto Rican sample was limited to children of lower SES (no Puerto Rican children of upper-middle-class status could be found). Within the ethnic affiliation and SES children were selected on three levels of intellectual ability: below average, average, and superior (based on their performance on the California Short Form Test of Mental Maturity, Level I). Two measures of self-perception were administered: The Illinois Index of Self-Derogation (IISD) and four different sets of a paper and pencil form of the Farnham-Diggory Children Self-Evaluation Scale (SE).
Results indicate that positive self-evaluations are directly related to healthy personality development: children who rate

47

themselves lower perceive their parents rating them low; children
of low SES and below average intelligence rate themselves consistently lower than their middle-class and intellectually superior
peers; Black children have significantly more negative self-
images than their White peers; the self-discrepancy of the Puerto
Rican children does not differ significantly from either White
or Black children. The need for preventive action to neutralize
the biological, psychological and social pathogenic factors which
so determind the developing child's self-perception is immense,
obviously. The author suggests that action be taken on the
community level, not limited to work with individual children. (DH)

244. Ramírez, Manuel, III. "Social Responsibilities and Failure in
     Psychology: The Case of the Mexican-American." Journal
     of Clinical Child Psychology. Vol. 1 (1972). pp. 5-8.

255. Sabatino, David A., and others. "Perceptual, Language and Academic
     Achievement of English, Spanish and Navajo Speaking Children
     Referred for Special Classes." Journal of School Psychology.
     Vol. 10 (March 1972). pp. 39-46.
     (EC 04 164)

        The purpose of this study was to determine the perceptual
     language and academic achievement functions of English, Spanish,
     and Navajo children experiencing learning difficulties and
     referred for placement into special education classes. Those
     test variables which discriminated among the native English-
     speaking children and the children who spoke Spanish or Navajo
     natively were, as predicted, those tasks which involved knowledge
     of the linguistic rules of English. It would seem that, taken
     as a group, the school learning problems experienced by the
     native Spanish- or Navajo-speaking children were the result of
     their limited linguistic competence in English, the language
     of instruction in their classrooms. (EC)

256. Sánchez, George I. "Group Differences and Spanish-Speaking
     Children. A Critical Review." Journal of Applied Psychology.
     Vol. 16 (October 1932). pp. 549-558.

257. Seda-Bonilla, Eduardo. "Cultural Pluralism and the Education
     of Puerto Rican Youths." Phi Delta Kappan. 53.5 (January
     1972). pp. 294-296.

258. Seda-Bonilla, Eduardo. "Ethnic Studies and Cultural Pluralism."
     The Rican. No. 1 (Fall 1971). pp. 56-65.

259. Sofietti, James P. "Bilingualism and Biculturalism." Journal
     of Educational Psychology. Vol. 46 (1955). pp. 222-227.

        This paper recognizes that biculturalism, both verbal

(language) and non-verbal (attitudes and everyday habits), is
part of bilingualism. It distinguishes four kinds of situations:
1, bilingual-bicultural i.e. the child of immigrant parents who
continue to speak their native language and retain traditional
customs and values; 2, bicultural-monolingual i.e. the child of
immigrant parents who give up their native language but continue
native customs; 3, mono-cultural-bilingual i.e. a child who
grows up in only one culture but who learns a second language
either at home or in school; and 4, monocultural-monolingual, the
most common situation in the United States. The author notes that
most studies which attribute learning difficulties to bilingualism
should look to the bicultural aspects of the situation to determine
the causes. It is not necessarily knowing two languages that
causes problems; it may be that living in two cultures causes
the conflict. (ECK)

260. Steubner, Josephine. "Racial Differences in Reading Achievement."
     Texas Outlook. Vol. 24 (January 1940). p. 32.

261. Tireman, L.S. "School Problems Created by the Homes of Foreign-
     Speaking Children." California Journal of Elementary
     Education. Vol. 8 (May 1940). pp. 234-238.

262. Walsh, P. "Dick and Jane on the Navajo Reservation." Journal of
     Continuing Education and Training. Vol. 1, no. 4 (May 1972).
     pp. 267-276.
     (EJ 058 636)

     Discusses the Bureau of Indian Affairs' failure to recognize
cultural differences in terms of the Bureau's unwillingness to
utilize a more acceptable philosophy of education with culturally
different children. (CIJE)

263. Zirkel, Perry Alan and John F. Grene. The Academic Achievement of
     Spanish-Speaking First Graders in Connecticut. Connecticut
     State Department of Education, Bureau of Compensatory and
     Community Educational Services. April 1971. 8pp.
     (ED 054 275)

     Study sought to demonstrate that deficiencies shown by
Puerto Rican children in verbal ability and academic achievement
might not exist if initial instruction and testing were in
Spanish. The Inter-American Test of General Ability was admin-
istered by the same examiner first in Spanish, then in English.
The Puerto Rican first graders scored significantly lower on the
English forms than all ethnic groups, including Puerto Ricans,
in Coleman's study on the subtest of verbal ability; however, on
the non-verbal ability subtest, the Puerto Ricans scored significantly higher than all groups in the Coleman study. The
Ss scored much higher on the Spanish form than on the English form.
(RIE)

264.  Zirkel, Perry Alan.  <u>Puerto Rican Perents and Mainland Schools</u>.
        Hartford, Connecticut:  Hartford Nodel Cities.  November
        1971.  98pp.
        (ED 062 473)

        This study constitutes the promised product of an institute on
"Puerto Rican Pupils in Mainland Schools," sponsored by the
Educational Leadership Institute and the University of Hartford
during the summer of 1971.  The stated purposes of the Institute were:
1, to stimulate communications and understanding between school
and community representatives toward the improvement of the
educational opportunities of Puerto Rican pupils in mainland
schools; 2, to develop a data base concerning cultural and
linguistic factors in the home environment that may be significant
toward that end; and 3, to examine and interpret such data in
terms of present and potential school programs and practices.
        The Institute focused on facilitating the relationship
between the home and school environment of Puerto Rican pupils
in Hartford as a possible model for other mainland school systems.
The formal program of the Institute was concentrated in the week
of June 28-July 2.  The morning sessions provided the opportunity
to interact with several resource people in small group
discussions.  The afternoon sessions were devoted to conducting
structured interviews in the homes of a cross-section of Puerto
Rican families who had children in the Hartford schools.  The
duration of the summer was used for further research and the
final writing of the independent individual reports, each
culminating in recommendations for improving the educational
opportunities of these children in the Hartford schools.  (RIE)

C. The Bilingual/Bicultural Child and the Question of Intelligence

265. Altus, G.T. "WISC Patterns of a Selective Sample of Bilingual School Children." Journal of Genetic Psychology. Vol. 83 (1953). pp. 241-248.

The purpose of the study was to compare intelligence patterns of "dull-minded" bilingual children of Mexican descent with "dull-minded" English-speaking unilinguals. Ss were matched for age, sex, and performance IQ, and the author suggests that future investigators control such factors as socioeconomic level and parental education as well. Ss in both groups were administered the Wechsler Intelligence Scale for Children. Results showed that the unilingual children averaged 17 points better on the Verbal Scale, a highly significant difference. A unique subtest pattern emerged for the bilinguals, and it was thought that this might be of value in the diagnosis of pshychometric retardation of bilingual of Mexican descent. The retardation is a linguistic one, but perhaps there is some evidence here of the handicapping influences of bilingualism for this group. On the Performance Scale, however, there was only one subtest which showed a significant difference between bilingual and unilingual children; this was the Picture Completion subtest, and it usually calls for a spoken answer. The author suggests that the retardation reflected in the verbal score could probably be alleviated if the children had been trained from birth in only one language, but notes that no generalizations could be made because this study involved only a small sample. It does seem reasonable to suppose that verbal-performance discrepancies might exist at any level of intelligence. (DH)

266. Anastasi, Anne. "Culture-Fair Testing." Educational Horizons. 43 (Fall 1964). pp. 26-30.

267. Anastasi, Anne and Fernando A. Córdova. "Some Effects of Bilingualism Upon the Intelligence Performance of Puerto Rican Children in New York City." Journal of Educational Psychology. 44:1 (January 1953). pp. 1-17.

The Cattell Culture Free Intelligence Test was administered to Puerto Rican children in grades 6-8 in Spanish Harlem. Half the group received test instructions in English during the first testing session (Form A) and in Spanish during the second session (Form B); the order was reversed for the second group. The most conspicuous finding was the marked improvement from first to second testing session, regardless of language. Over-all performance of group fell below test norms reported by Cattell. Reasons included low socio-economic level, bilingualism which makes them deficient in both languages, extreme lack of test sophistication and poor emotional adjustment to school situation. Maladjustment appears to have arisen from children's severe language handicap during initial school experiences. (author)

268. Anastasi, Anne and Cruz de Jesús. "Language Development and Non-Verbal IQ of Puerto Rican Preschool Children in New York City." Journal of Abnormal and Social Psychology. Vol. 48 (1953). pp. 357-366.

Three previous psychological studies of Puerto Rican children in New York City suggest that Puerto Rican children will do poorly on language tests whether the tests are administered in Spanish or English. Their performance on nonlanguage tests, however, generally seemed to equal or excell the American norms. The authors' hypotheses: 1, that the confusion of the two languages has made many Puerto Ricans "illiterate in two language", and has increased their educational difficulties; and 2, that the Puerto Rican child's attitude toward school is related to the first hypothesis, "that his initial school experience of being thrust into an exclusively English speaking environment at a time when he knows almost no English...produces a psychological insulation to whatever goes on in school," made it necessary to study the performance of Puerto Rican preschool children on both linguistic and nonlinguistic measures. In this way any evidence of the illiteracy in both languages or hostility or passive attitudes toward school could not be associated with negative reactions to the school environment.
Ss were 25 Puerto Rican boys and 25 Puerto Rican boys from day care centers in Spanish Harlem; all Ss were within six months of their fifth birthdays. The language test was recorded in the language spontaneously used by the child. Spanish was used almost completely, however, with only about 2% of the words and less than 1% of the sentences in English. When comparisons were made between the performance of the Puerto Ricans in this study and the Black and White subjects from an earlier study in which one of the authors participated, it was found that the Puerto Rican children did not differ significantly from any other group in Draw-a-Man IQ and that they excelled both Black and White groups in mean sentence length and in maturity of sentence structure. The authors suggest that the home environment of Puerto Rican children may be an important factor in their superior linguistic development. The findings of the present study indicate that the Puerto Rican pre-school children were not inferior to the White American norms, and seem to support the authors' hypotheses about the school environment. (DH)

269. Armstrong, C.P., and others. Reactions of Puerto Rican Children in New York City to Psychological Tests. Rep. Special Committee on Immigration and Naturalization, New York State Chamber of Commerce. 1935. 9pp.

270. Arnold, R.D. "Reliability of Test Scores for the Young 'Bilingual' Disadvantaged." Reading Teacher. Vol. 22 (1969). pp. 341-345.

This paper examines the results produced when tests whose norms were established on a middle class Anglo population were administered to minority students. Ss were over 200 Mexican-American third graders in various schools in San Antonio, Texas. The tests were the Metropolitan Achievement Tests, the Inter-American Reading Tests (parallel tests in Spanish and English) and the IPAT Culture Fair Test. Answers were sought for the following questions: 1, What will happen to the reliability of a test standardized on middle class Anglo-Americans if it is given to disadvantaged bilingual students? and 2, How does the reliability of a standardized test compare to that of a test designed specifically for a bilingual population? Results showed that the Inter-American English Test of Reading and the Metropolitan Achievement Tests were quite reliable for the group studied as long as tests of the proper difficulty were administered. (ECK)

271. Arsenian, Seth. Bilingualism and Mental Development. New York: Teachers College, Columbia University. 1937.

272. Atkinson, Rosa M. The Educational Retardation of the Spanish-Speaking Child and Recommendations for Remediation. Unpublished Master's thesis, University of Texas. 1953.

273. Bilingual Testing and Assessment, Proceedings of Bay Area Bilingual Education League (BABEL) Workshop and Preliminary Findings. Multilingual Assessment Program (Berkeley, California, January 27-28, 1969. B.A.B.E.L. Berkely, California. Multilingual Assessment Program, Stocton, California (ED 065 225)

The results and proceedings of the first annual Bilingual/Bicultural Testing and Assessment Workshop are presented. Approximately 150 bilingual psychologists and evaluators, educators working in bilingual-bicultural programs, and community representatives from California and Texas attended. Evaluations were made and the summaries are included of eight tests used extensively in bilingual programs: the Wechsler Intelligence Scale for Children, the Comprehensive Tests of Basic Skills, the Cooperative Primary, the Lorge-Thorndike, the Interamerican Series--General Ability, the Culture Fair Intelligence Test, the Michigan Oral Production Test and the Peabody Vocabulary Test. Also included in this publication are 1, and overview of the problem of assessment and evaluation in bilingual education, 2, a professional critique of the Inter-American series by Dr. Barbara Havassy; 3, a brief description of a Criterion Referenced System developed by Eduardo Apodaca; and 4, an article by Dr. Edward A. DeAvila discussing some of the complexities involved in testing and assessment of bilingual/bicultural children. (RIE)

274. Bordie, J.G. "Language Tests and Linguistically Different
Learners: the Sad State of the Art." Elementary English.
Vol. 47 (1970). pp. 814-828.
(ED 062 891)

Many schools use standardized language tests for both
placement and diagnostic devices, yet there is question as to
their validity. The paper discusses these questions: 1, To
what extent are current measures useful for identifying the
characteristics of linguistically different learners?; 2, Are
they helpful in planning instructional strategies?; 3, How can the
learning potentialities of linguistically different learners be
measured?; and 4, What are the high priority test needs? The
author notes that most programs he surveyed used tests designed
for specific research projects and that the confusion in the
goals of language, language learning, and curriculum design must
be clarified before test findings may be used with the same
meaning in each are. (ECK)

275. Bransford, L.A. A Comparative Investigation of Verbal and
Performance Intelligence Measures at Different Age Levels
with Bilingual Spanish-Speaking Children in Special Classes
for the Mentally Retarded. Unpublished Ph.D. Dissertation,
Colorado State College. 1966.
(Dissertation Abstracts. Vol. 27 (1967). p. 2267A.)

This study was designed to investigate the performance of
Spanish-speaking bilingual children in special classes for the
mentally retarded on the Wechsler Intelligence Scale for Children.
Ss were 60 Spanish-speaking bilinguals from Santa Fe, New Mexico;
they were compared with 34 non-bilingual English-speaking children
also attending special classes in Greeley, Colorado and from the
same socioeconomic background. Conclusions were as follows:
1, Spanish-speaking bilinguals scored significantly higher on
the WISC Performance Scale than on the Verbal Scale when compared
to English-speaking children from similar socioeconomic backgrounds;
2, the difference between Verbal and Performance scores of the
bilinguals tended to increase as age increased; this was not
found to be true for the control group; and 3, the disparity between
Verbal and Performance scores is greater for older than for
younger ages; this difference was not found for the control group.
(ECK)

276. Carlson, H.B. and N. Henderson. "Intelligence of American Children
of Mexican Parentage." Journal of Abnormal and Social
Psychology. Vol. 45 (July 1950). pp. 544-551.

54

277.  Cebollero, P.A.  Reactions of Puerto Rican Children in New York
      City to Psychological Tests.  An Analysis of the Study by
      Armstrong, Achilles, and Sacks of the Same Name.  San Juan,
      Puerto Rico:  The Puerto Rico School Review.  1936.  11pp.

278.  Christiansen, T. and G.A. Livermore.  "A Comparison of Anglo-
      American and Spanish-American Children and the WISC."
      Journal of Social Psychology.  Vol. 81 (1970).  pp. 9-14.

          This study compared the performance of lower and middle class
      Anglo-American with lower and middle class Spanish-American children
      on the Wechsler Intelligence Scale for Children.  The following
      were compared:  1, the Full Scale IQ score; 2, the Verbal IQ
      Scores; 3, the Performance Scale IQ Scores; 4, the intellective
      factors of Verbal Comprehension, Freedom from Distractability,
      Perceptual Organization and Relevance.  Ss were 92 Spanish and
      Anglo American children from 13-14 years old attending regular
      public school classes.  Social class was determined by father's
      occupation; ethnic group was determined by a child's having both
      or no parents with Spanish surnames.  Test conditions were as
      close as possible to those recommended in the WISC manual, and
      all testers were trained.  A 2 x 2 analysis of variance was computed
      for each of the measures examined in this study.   Results showed
      that general intelligence and the development of verbal abilities
      are related to ethnic origin and social class.  Nonverbal
      abilities, perceptual organization ability and the ability to
      concentrate on a task were found to relate only to social class.
      (ECK)

279.  Cook, J.M. and G. Arthur.  "Intelligence Ratings for 97 Mexican-
      American Children in St. Paul, Minnesota."  Exceptional
      Children.  Vol. 18 (1952).  pp. 14-15, 31.

280.  Cooper, J.G.  "Predicting School Achievement for Bilingual Pupils."
      Journal of Educational Psychology.  Vol. 49 (1958).
      pp. 31-36.

281.  Córdova, F.A.  A Comparison of the Performance of a Bilingual
      Group on a "Culture Free" Test Administered in English and
      in Spanish.  Unpublished M.A. thesis, Fordham University, 1951.

282.  Corwin, Betty.  "The Influence of Culture and Language on Performance
      of Individual Ability Tests."  Unpublished, duplicated paper.
      San Fernando Valley State College, California.  1961.

283.  Darcy, Natilie T.  "Bilingualism and the Measure of Intelligence:
      Review of a Decade of Research."  Journal of Genetic Psychology.
      Vol. 103 (1963).  pp. 259-282.

          This review of the research conducted in the field of
      bilingualism and the measurement of intelligence is divided into

several problems in dealing with bilingualism, such as differing
definitions of the term, the type of test used, the difficulty
in isolating linguistic from other environmental factors, etc.
Section three summarizes studies done on Spanish-English
bilinguals. The fourth deals with Welsh-English bilinguals in
Wales. Section five discusses studies made of other bilingual
groups. Section six is a general summary and the last section
lists some conclusions. (ECK)

284. Darcy, Natalie T. "The Effect of Bilingualism Upon the Measure-
      ment of the Intelligence of Children of Preschool Age."
      Journal of Educational Psychology. 37:1 (January 1946).
      pp. 21-44.

      Study designed to determine to what extent a non-verbal
test of intelligence, such as the Atkins Object-fitting Test,
can be employed as a substitute for a verbal test of intelligence,
such as the Stanford-Binet Scale. Results showed performance of
bilingual subjects to be significantly inferior to that of monolingual subjects on Stanford-Binet Scale, but significantly
superior to performance of monolingual subjects on the
Atkins Test. It was the general conclusion that the bilingual
subjects of this investigation (all Italian/English bilinguals)
suffered from a language handicap in their performance on the
Stanford-Binet Scale. (JH)

285. Darcy, Natalie T. "The Performance of Bilingual Puerto Rican
      Children on Verbal and Non-Language Tests of Intelligence."
      Journal of Educational Research. 45:7 (March 1952). pp.
      499-506.

      Study involved 235 bilingual children of Puerto Rican
parentage who were studying in grades five and six in New York
City public schools. Two group intelligence tests were administered: 1, the Pintner General Ability, Verbal Series, Intermediate Test, Form B; and 2, the Pintner General Ability Test,
Non-Language Series, Form K. As expected, results showed that the
bilingual subjects scored significantly higher on the non-language
test. The author suggests that the administration of both
verbal and non-verbal intelligence tests will yield a more valid
picture of the intelligence of a bilingual population than either
kind alone. (JH)

286. De Jesús, C. A Study of Language Development and Goodenough IQ of
      Puerto Rican Preschool Children in New York City. Unpublished
      M.A. thesis, Fordham University. 1952.

287. Deutsch, M. Minority Group and Class Status as Related to Social
      and Personal Factors in School Achievement. (Monograph #2).
      Ithaca, New York: The Society for Applied Anthropology.
      1960.

56

288. Droege, Robert G.  Alternatives to a Moratorium on Testing.  Paper
     presented at American Personnel and Guidance Convention,
     Atlantic City, New Jersey (April 1971).  14pp.
     (ED 053 199)

     The alternative suggested is comprised of three elements:
     1, working toward changes in attitudes of people and institutions
     to directly attack discriminatory applications of tests; 2,
     emphasizing test validation and development of new test
     instruments oriented to the needs of disadvantaged applicants;
     and 3, eliminating discriminatory selection procedures as stated
     in Title VII of the Civil Rights Act. (RIE)

289. Dunklin, L.D.  A Study of the Intelligence of Some Recent
     Puerto Rican Immigrant Children in a First Grade in a
     New York City School.  Unpublished M.A. thesis, Teachers
     College, Columbia University.  1935.

290. Dyer, Henry S.  Issues in Testing.  1969.  13pp.
     (ED 053 164)

     Certain concepts that are sometimes confused in discussions
     on testing socially disadvantaged children are clarified and a
     history of testing, beginning with Binet, is presented.  Finally,
     five programs for the disadvantaged are considered.  (RIE)

291. Finch, F.L.  Vamos.  To Develop a Bilingual Examination.  Paper
     presented to 5th Annual TESOL Convention, New Orleans,
     Louisiana, March 6, 1971.

292. Fishman, Joshua.  "Bilingualism, Intelligence and Language
     Learning."  Modern Language Journal.  Vol. 49 (1965).
     pp. 227-237.

     This paper examines the relationship between bilingualism,
     intelligence and learning.  Bilingualism is discussed from the
     viewpoints of several investigators, and as a social-psychological
     concept, subject to variance.  Variance in language use is
     explained in these terms:  media variance, role variance, and
     situational variance.  Language use relates to the situation and
     role relationship of the persons.  It is important to understand
     the concepts of switching, interference, and "domain" when
     speaking of the bilingual person.
     The author concludes that there is no substantial relationship
     between bilingualism and intelligence where everyone is of a
     similar class and similar bilinguality.  A person from a culturally
     deprived environment, whether mono or bilingual, will score lower
     on tests of verbal ability and on conceptual tests.  In an
     atmosphere in which bilingualism is accepted and considered
     prestigious, the bilingual person appears to be superior to the
     monolingual individual.  (DH)

293. Fishman, Joshua, and others. "Guidelines for Testing Minority
     Group Children." Journal of Social Issues. Vol. 20
     (1964). pp. 129-145.

        The author discusses the use of educational and psychological
     tests with respect to socially and culturally disadvantaged
     children. The three main problems created by standardized tests
     are 1, that they may not provide reliable differentiation in the
     range of scores; 2, their predictive validity for minority group
     children may be very different from their predictive validity
     for the standardization and validation groups; and 3, the validity
     of their interpretation depends, to a large extent, upon the
     interpreter's understanding of the social and cultural background
     of the minority group in question. Fishman notes that the
     reliability and predictive validity of standardized tests can
     not be arrived at by simple comparison of the norms and
     differentiation in the range of scores of the minority children
     and the standardization children. It is the examiner's responsibility
     to assess both the nature and composition of the samples and the
     test itself. In conclusion, the author appeals to the
     "conscientious educator" to reject the notion that test scores
     indicate fixed levels of performance or potential, and to plan
     compensatory programs in order to free the disadvantaged child
     from his handicap. (DH)

294. Fishman, J.A. and P.I. Clifford. "What Can Mass-Testing Programs
     Do For-and To- the Pursuit of Excellence in American Education?"
     Harvard Educational Review. Vol. 34 (1964). pp. 63-79.

295. Fishman, Joshua and Robert Cooper. "Alternative Measures of
     Bilingualism." Journal of Verbal Learning and Verbal
     Behavior. Vol. 8 (1969). pp. 276-282.

296. Fitch. M.J. Verbal and Performance Test Scores of Bilingual
     Children. Unpublished Ph.D. Dissertation, Ohio State Uni-
     versity. 1969.
     (Dissertation Abstracts. Vol. 27 (1966). pp. 1654A-1655A.)

        The purpose of the study was to investigate the effects of
     increased exposure to the English language on verbal and non-
     verbal of intelligence in bilingual children. Ss were 25 first
     and second grade bilinguals and 25 fifth and sixth grade bilinguals;
     the two age groups were matched according to sex, socioeconomic
     status and IQ. The Ss were administered the Ravens Colored
     Matrices test and the WISC. The younger children were expected to
     have some difficulty with the verbal exam, since they did not have
     a "clearly dominant language" to communicate concepts; the author
     also expected that the increased exposure to English would
     increase the bilinguals' facility with English, and that the
     verbal and non-verbal measures would correlate better at the older
     grade level. However, the verbal and non-verbal measures

correlated higher at the first and second grade level. Verbal
scores did approach non-verbal scores of intelligence as the
bilinguals became more proficient in English; and all five subtests
influenced by language showed improvement in the upper grade
Ss. (DH)

297.   Galvan, Robert Rogers. Bilingualism as it Relates to Intelligence
       Scores and School Achievement among Culturally Deprived
       Spanish-American Children. Ph.D. Dissertation, East Texas
       State University. 1967.
       (Dissertation Abstracts. Vol. 28 (1968). pp. 3021A-3022A.)

       This study was designed to investigate the relationship
between intelligence test scores and scholastic achievement as they
relate to bilingualism among "culturally deprived" children of
Spanish-American heritage. Ss were 100 Spanish-American children
from the third, fourth and fifth grades of a Dallas elementary
school. Ss were administered the Wechsler Intelligence Scale
for Children (WISC) in both English and Spanish. It was expected
that the Ss would score lower when the WISC was administered in
English than when it was administered in Spanish; this was found
to be true. The verbal section had a greater increase in points
than the non-verbal section. The author suggests that some other
measure of intelligence be developed for use with bilingual
children. The results here clearly point out the inadequacy of
using verbal tests of intelligence when testing bilinguals. (DH)

298.   García, Angela B. and Barry J. Zimmerman. "The Effect of Examiner
       Ethnicity and Language on the Performance of Bilingual
       Mexican American First Graders." Journal of Social Psychology.
       Vol. 87, no. 1 (June 1972). p. 3-11.
       (EJ 058 795)

299.   Green, Donald Ross. Biased Tests. CTB/McGraw Hill. 1971. 10pp.
       (ED 054 208)

       This paper is concerned with the accusations made by such
groups as the Association of Black Psychologists in their call for
a moratorium on testing because standardized tests are biased. A
biased test is one that measures one trait in one group but a
different trait in a second group. Evidence about the amount of
bias in tests is thin. Bias must be determined by research on
each instrument. A commitment to such research is in order. If
bias is found, reasonable courses of action include test revision,
alteration in interpretation, and discontinuance of testing. (RIE)

300.   Green, Donald Ross. Racial and Ethnic Bias in Test Construction.
       Final Report. Monterey, California: CTB/McGraw Hill.
       Washington, D.C.: Office of Education. September 1971. 104pp.
       (ED 056 090)

To determine if tryout samples typically used for item
selection contribute to test bias against minority groups, item
analyses were made of the California Achievement Tests using seven
sub-groups of the standardization sample. The best half of the
items in each test were selected for each group. Typically about
30% of the items in the upper half of the distribution of item-
test correlations for a group on a test did not meet this
criterion with another group.  By this criterion minority groups
were relatively similar as were the three suburban groups.  The
resulting unique item tests did not correlate well with each
other.  Scores of minority groups were relatively better on the
selected items.  Thus, standard item selection procedures produce
tests best suited to groups like the majority of the tryout
sample and are therefore biased against other groups to some
degree. This degree varies.  Ways to minimize this bias need to
be developed.  (RIE)

301.  Hernández, J.L.  <u>Testing, Guidance and Culture:  Their Theoretical
      and Practical Interaction.</u>  Unpublished paper prepared at
      Interamerican University, San German, Puerto Rico.  October
      1969.

302.  Hertzig, M.E. and H.G. Birch.  "Longitudinal Course of Measured
      Intelligence in Preschool Children of Different Social and
      Ethnic Backgrounds."  <u>American Journal of Ortho-psychiatry</u>.
      Vol. 41 (April 1971).  pp. 416-426.

      Examined the longitudinal course of measured intelligence
      (using the Stanford-Binet Intelligence Scale, Form L) in White
      middle-class and Puerto Rican working-class children at 3 and 6
      years of age.  Sixty Puerto Rican and 116 White Ss were examined
      at 3 years while 56 Puerto Rican and 110 of the White Ss were
      reexamined at 6 years of age.  Findings suggest that stability
      in IQ over this time was characteristic of both  groups, with
      greater stability manifested by Puerto Rican than by White Ss.
      No evidence for deterioration of IQ with age in the disadvantaged
      group was found.  Data are considered in relation to the problems
      of the stability of IQ and its utility in the assessment of the
      effects of compensatory education programs.  (DH)

303.  Hoffman, M.L. and C. Albizu-Mironda.  "Middle Class Bias in
      Personality Testing."  <u>Journal of Abnormal and Social Psychology</u>.
      1955.  pp. 150-152.

304.  Johnson, G.B.  "Bilingualism as Measured by a Reaction-time
      Technique and the Relationship Between a Language and a
      Non-language Intelligence Quotient."  <u>Journal of Genetic
      Psychology</u>.  Vol. 82 (1953).  pp. 3-9.

The purpose of the study was to determine the relation
between language and non-language intelligence tests and part
bilingualism, as measured by a reaction-time technique, plays
in the relationship. Ss were thirty boys ages 9-12 who used
English in school and had knowledge of Spanish. All were administered the Goodenough Draw-a-Man Test, the Otis Self-Administering
Test of Mental Ability, the Hoffman Test of Bilingualism; they
were also administered the Reaction-Time Test of Bilingualism, in
which they were asked to name as many words in English (or Spanish)
as they could in five minutes. Half the Ss were tested in English
first and Spanish two weeks later; for the other half the order
was reversed. The order was not found to be significant. Results
of the tests were correlated and the following conclusions were
reached: "An intelligence employing the English language is
probably not a valid measuring instrument when employed with subjects deficient in the assimilation of the culture of which
English is reflective...measuring the intelligence of bilingual
subjects presents complex problems which possibly render both
linguistic (Otis) and performance (Goodenough) tests invalid."
(ECK)

305. Karadenes, Mark. A Comparison of Differences in Achievement and
     Learning Abilities between Anglo and Mexican-American
     Children When the Two Groups are Equated by Intelligence.
     Unpublished Ph.D. Dissertation, University of Virginia. 1971.
     (Dissertation Abstracts International. Vol. 32 (1971-1972).
     pp. 4422A-4423A.)

     This study was designed to determine if differences in learning
     abilities exist between Anglo and Mexican American male
     kindergarten children, and how those differences relate to
     intelligence and academic achievement. Ss were 90 children
     (45 Anglo, 45 Mexican-American) who attended public elementary
     school in Santa Monica, California. School psychologists
     administered the Stanford-Binet Intelligence Test and the Wide
     Range Achievement Test (WRAT) to all Ss; the Meeker Profile was
     used to measure learning abilities. Findings indicate that
     achievement was affected by ethnicity and intelligence, and that
     learning abilities were not influenced by either ethnicity or
     intelligence. (DH)

306. Keston, M.J. and Carmina Jiménez. "A Study of the Performance on
     English and Spanish Editions of the Stanford-Binet Intelligence
     Test by Spanish-American Children." Journal of Genetic
     Psychology. Vol. 85 (1954). pp. 263-269.

     The purpose of the study was to determine whether Mexican-
     American children should be given the Stanford-Binet Intelligence
     Test in Spanish or in English. The study compares the children's
     scores on the two versions of the test rather than to any pre-
     established norms. Ss were 50 fourth graders from five different

schools. The children were administered form M of the Stanford-
Binet first and then Form L. The examiner was a bilingual person
and a native speaker of Spanish. Four weeks passed between the
two administrations. Results showed that the children performed
significantly better on the English version. The authors suggest
that the reason for the improved performance might be that
English becomes the child's dominant language after grade five;
before that time English tests are not valid. Since performance
on the Stanford-Binet depends, to a large extent, on education and
scholastic achievement, it seems likely that Spanish-American
children would perform better in the language of formal
instruction. The authors suggest that the Spanish version of the
test be given in a particular region and the results analyzed in a
similar fashion; this is necessary before effective research in
the area may proceed. (DH)

307. Killian, L.R. Cognitive Test Performance of Spanish-American
     Primary-School Children: A Longitudinal Study. Final Report.
     Kent State University, Ohio. Washington, D.C.: National
     Center for Educational Research and Development. November
     1971. 13pp.
     (ED 060 156)

     A twenty-six-month follow-up study was made of 75 Anglo- and
Spanish-American primary school children who were examined on the
Wechsler Intelligence Scale for Children, the Illinois Test of
Psycholinguistic Abilities, and the Bender Visual-Motor Gestalt
Test in order to determine the specific cognitive deficits which
might account for the poor school performance of Spanish-American
school children. After three years of schooling the children were
found to be deficient in verbal comprehension but have no deficits
in short-term memory, arithmetic, or perceptual organization.
Bilingualism does not appear to be as important as ethnic status.
There is some support for treating Spanish-American children as
a single group. If they are to be subdivided, it is probably
more important to consider the whole complex of variables making
up the ethnic class rather than just bilingualism. Remedial
efforts in the cognitive area with third and fourth grade
Spanish-American children should concentrate upon vocabulary,
general information, verbal analogies, experience with a wide
range of social situations and their corresponding rules, verbal
classifying procedures, and grammatical form. (RIE)

308. Killian, L.R. "WISC, Illinois Test of Psycholinguistic Abilities,
     and Bender Visual-Motor Gestalt Performance of Spanish-
     American Kindergarten and First Grade School Children."
     Journal of Consulting and Clinical Psychology. 37:1
     (August 1971). pp. 38-43.
     (EJ 043 081)

The specific cognitive deficits which might account for the poor school performance of Spanish-American children are examined. The results suggest that Spanish-American children are deficient on the input side of communicative skills, especially in understanding sentences and pictures. Bilingualism does not appear to be an important variable. (CIJE)

309. Kittell, J.E. "Bilingualism and Language: Nonlanguage Intelligence Scores of Third-Grade Children." *Journal of Educational Research*. Vol. 52 (1959). pp. 263-268.

Ss were 42 bilingual and 41 unilingual third graders at an elementary school in Berkeley, California. To reduce the cultural effects of only one ethnic background the bilingual group was drawn from all backgrounds (Chinese 19%, Japanese and Spanish 16.7% plus twelve other languages). The California Short-Form Test of Mental Maturity, Primary, 1953 S Form and the California Reading Test, Primary, Form AA had been given in the third grade and supplied data regarding the children's chronological and mental ages, IQ, language and non-language mental ages and reading age. The researchers also used the Warner's Revised Occupational Rating Scale to rate parents' occupations. Conclusions were 1, Bilingual children scored lower on the language section of the California Test of Mental Maturity; 2, Unilingual children scored higher on the language than on the non-language sections; 3, Unilingual children with parents in the middle occupational group were better in language mental ability than bilingual children with parents in the middle or lower occupational group; 4, Bilingual children did not differ significantly from unilingual children in mean reading differences in the language mental age scores on the mental maturity test; 5, Parents' place of birth, children's sex and children's chronological age did not account for differences in language mental maturity scores; and 6, Bilingual children did not differ significantly as a group from unilingual children in total mental age. "Although it was ascertained that language mental maturity scores were significantly lower for children with bilingual environments...this investigation failed to reveal what difference this might have in achievement in school. (ECK)

310. Kittell, J.E. "Intelligence Test Performances of Children from Bilingual Environments." Elementary School Journal. Vol. 64 (1959). pp. 263-368.

311. Koch, Helen L. and Rieta Simmons. "A Study of the Test Performance of American, Mexican and Negro Children." *Psychological Monographs*. Vol. 35, no. 5. 1926. 116pp. Also contained in *Texas Educational Survey Report 1925*.

312. Lerea, L. and S.M. Kohut. "A Comparative Study of Monolinguals and Bilinguals in Verbal Task Performance." *Journal of Clinical Psychology*. Vol. 17 (1961). pp. 49-52.

313.  Mahakian, C.  "Measuring Intelligence and Reading Capacity of
      Spanish-Speaking Children."  Elementary School Journal.
      Vol. 39 (1939).  pp. 760-768.

314.  Manuel, Herschel T.  Cooperative Inter-American Tests, 1050.
      Princeton, New Jersey:  Educational Testing Service.
      1950.  unpaged.

315.  Manuel, Herschel T.  Spanish and English Editions of the Stanford-
      Binet in Relation to the Abilities of Mexican Children.
      Austin, Texas:  University of Texas.  1935.  Cited by L.S.
      Tireman, "Bilingual Education."  Review of Educational Research.
      Vol. 21 (1970).  pp. 182-187.

316.  Mercer, Jane R.  Current Retardation Procedures and the Psychological
      and Social Implications on the Mexican-American.  A Position
      Paper.  Alburquerque, New Mexico:  Southwestern Cooperative
      Educational Laboratory.  1970.  40pp.
      (ED 052 848)

          Examining one California school system, it was determined that
      the pupil personnel department's clinical testing procedures
      rather than discriminatory referral processes produced a dis-
      proportionate representation of minority group children in
      special education classes.  Recommendations: 1, more refined
      scales need to be developed for assessing the child's adaptive
      behavior outside the school; 2, pluralistic norms need to be
      used in interpreting the meaning of both the IQ and the adaptive
      behavior score for children of Mexican-American heritage.  Five
      tables and 16 references included.  (RIE)

317.  Mishra, S.P. and J. Hurt, Jr.  "The Use of Metropolitan Readiness
      Tests with Mexican-American Children."  California Journal
      of Educational Research.  Vol. 21 (1970).  pp. 182-187.

318.  Mitchell, A.J.  "The Effect of Bilingualism in the Measurement
      of Intelligence.  Elementary School Journal.  Vol. 38 (1937).
      pp. 29-37.

          The purpose of the study was to determine whether an intelli-
      gence test administered in English is a fair estimate of the
      child's intelligence quotient when the child thinks in a language
      other than English.  Ss were 295 Spanish-speaking Mexican children
      from Arizona in grades 1-3.  They were administered the Otis
      Group Intelligence Scale (primary examination) on two different
      occasions, once in English and once in Spanish.  Comparison of the
      results indicates that Spanish-speaking children work under a
      serious handicap when taking an intelligence examination in
      English, especially in their early years.  The implications of
      the study can be applied to other children whose native language
      is not English.  The inferiority in the ability to respond

appropriately in an adopted language is not limited to Mexican
or Spanish-speaking people, but is common to all children who
are native speakers of foreign languages. (DH)

319. Morper, J. An Investigation of the Relationship of Certain
     Predictive Variables and the Academic Achievement of
     Spanish-American and Anglo Pupils in Junior High School.
     Unpublished Ph.D. Dissertation, Oklahoma State University.
     (1966)
     (Dissertation Abstracts. Vol. 27 (1967). p. 4051A.)

320. New York City Board of Education. Puerto Rican Study: Developing
     A Program for Testing Puerto Rican Pupils in New York City
     Public Schools. New York: Board of Education. 1959. 143pp.

321. New York City Board of Education, Bureau of Educational Research.
     The Effectiveness of the Cooperative Inter-American Tests of
     General Ability, Primary Level, Form A, as a Measure of the
     Intellectual Functioning of Spanish-Speaking Pupils
     Enrolled in the Elementary Schools. New York: Board of
     Education. 1954.

322. Oxman, Wendy G. The Effects of Ethnic Identity of Experimenter,
     Language of Experimental Task, and Bilingual vs. Non-
     Bilingual School Attendance on the Verbal Task Performance
     of Bilingual Children of Puerto Rican Background. Ph.D.
     Dissertation, Fordham University. 1972.
     (Dissertation Abstracts International. Vol. 33 (1972).
     p. 195A.)

     The purpose of this study was to determine whether bilingual
minority group children show evidence of alienation from a non-
bilingual school environment, and whether attendance at a bilingual
school would prevent that alienation. Ss were 256 fourth and fifth
bilinguals of Puerto Rican background; they attended either a
bilingual school or a non-bilingual school in the New York City
area. A paired associate verbal learning task was administered
individually to a random sample of 64 Ss in each school, equally
divided as to grade level and sex; Puerto Ricans and non-Puerto
Ricans administered the task. Results showed no significant
difference in the mean scores of students under any of the
experimental conditions in non-bilingual schools, and the performance of Ss in bilingual schools was not superior to the
performance of Ss in non-bilingual schools. Therefore, it was
inferred that bilingual Puerto Rican children were not alienated
from the non-bilingual school environment, and that attendance at
a fully bilingual school may be a factor in alienation. Finally,
the ethnic identity of the experimenter may reflect distraction
from a verbal task, but not alienation. (DH)

323. Pascale, Pietro J. and Shaena Jakuboric. The Impossible Dream:
    ·A Culture-Free Test. 1971. 25pp.
    (ED 054 217)

        This study reviewed the formats and psychometric rationale
    of several alleged culture-fair tests. Advantages and dis-
    advantages of each instrument were examined and implications for
    compensatory education were discussed. (RIE)

324. Peal, E. and W.E. Lambert. "The Relations of Bilingualism to
    Intelligence." Psychological Monographs. Vol. 76 (1962).
    pp. 1-23.

325. Personke, Carl R., Jr. and O.L. Davis. "Predictive Validity of
    English and Spanish Versions of a Readiness Test."
    Elementary School Journal. Vol. 70 (November 1969).
    pp. 79-85.

        The purpose of the study was to determine the predictive
    validity of the English and Spanish versions of the Metropolitan
    Readiness Tests in relation to current practice in reading
    instruction. Ss were 38 Spanish-speaking children in the first
    year of school in a South Texas city. Early in the school year,
    the Metropolitan Achievement Tests, Form A, were administered in
    both English and Spanish. In May of the same year, the Metropolitan
    Achievement Tests, Primary I Battery, Form B (1959) were administered
    in English. Coefficients of correlation between scores of the
    English and Spanish Metropolitan Reading Tests and selected scores
    on the Metropolitan Achievement Tests were determined. Findings
    indicate that the Metropolitan Readiness Tests are useful in
    predicting certain reading related achievements for Spanish-
    speaking children; administration in English does not seem to show
    test bias. The Spanish edition of the Metropolitan Readiness Test
    did result in one good preditor, Copying, but the subtest of
    the Metropolitan Readiness Test administered in English which best
    predicted school achievement was the Alphabet subtest. The authors
    note that it is not enough for a test to be a valid predictor if
    it predicts failure for a large number of children. (ECK)

326. Philippus, M.J. Test Prediction of School Success of Bilingual
    Hispano-American Children. Colorado: Denver Department of
    Health and Hospitals. 1967.
    (ED 036 577)

        Thirty bilingual Hispanoamerican students between the ages of
    eight and thirteen were given verbal and non-verbal intelligence
    tests which were then correlated with overall school grade point
    average. Non-verbal tests resulted in higher correlations; the
    Raven Coloured Progressive Matrices appeared to be the best
    predictor of school successes of these children. Following these

results, it was hypothesized that perceptual-motor skills were
used by these children in some way to accomplish verbal activities.
The author suggests that Spanish-speaking people should not be
evaluated primarily with tests depending on verbal skills. (ECK)

327.  Pintner, R.  "The Influence of Language Background on Intelligence
      Tests."  Journal of Social Psychology.  Vol. 3 (1932).
      pp. 235-240.

328.  Pintner, R. and G. Arsenian.  "The Relation of Bilingualism to
      Verbal Intelligence and to School Adjustment."  Journal
      of Educational Research.  Vol. 31 (1937).  pp. 255-263.

      This study was concerned with the relationship of bilingualism
to verbal intelligence and school adjustment of 469 American-born
Jewish children in sixth and seventh grades in Brooklyn, New York.
The Hoffman Bilingual Schedule was used to measure the extent of
bilingualism and the Pintner Intelligence Test was used to measure
intelligence; the Pupil Portraits Test, Form A, was used to measure
school adjustment.  The Pearson Product-Moment correlation
coefficients between the tests showed no significant statistical
difference.  It was concluded that for this population, bilingualism
bore no relation to verbal intelligence and school adjustment. (ECK)

329.  Rankin, C.J. and R.W. Henderson.  Standardized Tests and the
      Disadvantaged.  Research Report from the Arizona Center for
      Early Childhood Education.  November 1969.
      (ED 034 594)

      The purpose of the study was to evaluate the reliability of
the Wechsler Preschool and Primary Scale of Intelligence when the
Ss are from a disadvantaged group.  Ss were 25 male and 24 female
5 1/2 year old poor Mexican-Americans.  The test was shown to
be highly reliable for this sample but comparison with an
Anglo-American standardization group shows that the Mexican-Americans were below the norm in all subtests, especially the verbal,
information and similarities sections.  This evidence shows that
the Wechsler test was reliable even for children with a limited
ability in English; the authors suggest that a culture-free test
might not be required to predict skills, and that tests sampling
existing known factors be used to predict within groups.  Norms
should be established for the group that is being tested. (ECK)

330.  Rice, J.P., Jr.  "Education of Subcultural Groups."  School and
      Society.  Vol. 92 (1964).  pp. 360-362.

      This article discusses intelligence testing, and includes
a very brief survey of the literature on "culturally loaded"
measures of intelligence.  The author suggests compensatory
programs for the slower learners, TESOL programs for the non-
native speaker of English and encourages the development of new
instruments for testing bilingual students. (DH)

331. Roca, Pablo. <u>Construction of a General Group Test for Puerto Rican Students in the Elementary and Secondary Schools</u>. August 1962. (ED 002 770)

This study attempted to develop a group test of general ability which will accurately assess the intellectual capacities of elementary and secondary students in the Puerto Rican schools. The objectives were: 1, to determine what common intellectual tasks indicate mental ability in Spanish speaking Puerto Rican and other English speaking American children; and 2, to ascertain what cultural differences influence intelligence test scores to distort results in favor of or against Spanish speaking Puerto Rican children. The first step was a survey and analysis of published tests of intelligence and of the literature in the field to ascertain the common factors generally included in tests of intelligence. A pool of test items measuring different abilities at different grade levels was prepared. These items were tried out for validity and reliability, and some were selected for construction of a provisional scale. A second item sample included at least 500 children from primary, intermediate and advanced levels selected on the basis of normal age and average achievement for the grade. The schools were selected at random from the four geographical regions in Puerto Rico. A balanced selection of boys and girls from small, medium and large communities was used. In view of the results obtained by comparing the performance of Puerto Rican children in New York schools and the children in Puerto Rico, there were significant differences in favor of the latter at all three levels of the experimental edition of the test. It is considered advisable to make another comparison using the final edition of the test with a more representative sample from New York.
This document includes a complete copy of the <u>Test puerto-rriqueño de habilidad general</u>. (RIE)

332. Roca, P. "Problems of Adapting Intelligence Scales from One Culture to Another." <u>High School Journal</u>. Vol. 38 (1955). pp. 124-131.

Deals with the problem of the translation and adapting for use of schools in Puerto Rico of the following intelligence tests: Wechsler Intelligence Scale, Stanford-Binet and the Goodenough Intelligence Test. (RIE)

333. Roca, Pablo. <u>Research Report: Construction of a General Ability Group Test for Puerto Rican Students in the Elementary and Secondary Schools</u>. University of Puerto Rico: Rio Piedras, Puerto Rico. August 1960.

334. Rosen, Pamela and Eleanor V. Horne. <u>Tests for Spanish-Speaking Children: An Annotated Bibliography</u>. Princeton, New Jersey:

Educational Testing Service. 1971. 11pp.
(ED 056 084)

Lists available instruments for measuring intelligence,
personality, ability and achievement. Excluded are culture-free
or -fair and non-language tests, tests in English with norms for
Spanish-speakers, and tests that have merely been translated from
English to Spanish. Annotation lists purpose of the test and the
groups for which it is intended; test subdivisions or tested
skills, behaviors, or competencies; administration; scoring;
interpretation, and standardization. (Proyecto Leer Bulletin)

335. Saer, D.J. "An Inquiry into the Effect of Bilingualism upon
     the Intelligence of Young Children." Journal of Experimental
     Pedagogy. Vol. 6 (1922). pp. 232-240; 266-274.

336. Sánchez, George I. "Bilingualism and Mental Measures: A Word
     of Caution." Journal of Applied Psychology. Vol. 18
     (1934). pp. 765-772.

     This article is of historical importance in that the author's
purpose was to warn educators against the misuse and misinterpreta-
tion of standardized tests of intelligence. He points out that
any such test is valid only to the extent that the items are as
common to the child being tested as they were to the children
upon whom the norms were based. It should be obvious that the
"standardized" test cannot be valid for the bilingual child or
for the socially disadvantaged child. In 1934, Sanchez declared
that the instant application of the classification "moron" to
a native Spanish-speaking child who scored 70 on an IQ test is
much more than a misapplication of the test; it becomes an indict-
ment of these people. The author tested a group of bilingual
second-graders and found the median IQ to be 72. He assumed that
the low scores were due to insufficient work on language skills by
the school; he offered remedial instruction in language and
language arts over a two year period. After the instruction, the
median IQ was "raised" to 100, or normal. Sánchez concludes with
a discussion of the perhaps unintended prejudice and the school's
responsibility to be aware of the dangers (and to avoid them.)
The next step is a compensatory program to make up for the language,
disciplinary and informational deficiencies of the children, to
furnish those experiences which will make standardized measures
as valid for them as they were for the children in the original
sample. (DH)

337. Sánchez, George I. "Scores of Spanish-Speaking Children on
     Repeated Tests." Journal of Genetic Psychology. Vol. 40
     (March 1932). pp. 223-231.

     In this study, the Stanford Achievement Test (Primary and

Advanced) and the Haggerty Intelligence Test were administered to
the same group of 45 Spanish-speaking children in grades 3-8
four times over a period of 18 months from December 1928 to
April 1930 with the intent of measuring the differences in the
repeated tests. The author notes several points which must be
considered in evaluating scores of Spanish-speaking children so
the results will be valid. Significant gains occurred with
repeated testings, and the gains varied by age, grade and relative brightness of the children. The relation of language
ability (shown by reading tests) to both mental and educational
tests can also vary results. (ECK)

338. Seidl, J.C. The Effect of Bilingualism on the Measurement of
     Intelligence. Unpublished Ph.D. Dissertation, Fordham
     University. 1937.

339. Spanish Translations of Intelligence Tests. Bureau of Educational
     Research, Division of Tests and Measurements, Board of
     Education of the City of New York. 1951. (Manuscript).

     The purpose of this project was to translate these three
intelligence tests for use with Puerto Rican children attending
New York City schools: the Otis Quick Scoring Alpha Test, Form
A, the California Intelligence Test, Non Language Section,
Elementary Form; and the SRA, non Verbal Test. The members of the
research project concluded that the translation of the test "has
not completely eliminated the effect of cultural factors which
operate to depress the scores of Spanish-speaking pupils." (DH)

340. Spence, A.G., S.P. Mishra and S. Ghoseil. "Home Language and
     Performance on Standardized Tests." Elementary School
     Journal. Vol. 71 (1971). pp. 309-313.

341. Stablein, J.E., D.S. Willey, and C.W. Thomson. "An Evaluation
     of the Davis Eels (Culture Fair) Test Using Spanish and
     Anglo-American Children." Journal of Educational Sociology.
     Vol. 35 (1961). pp. 73-78.

     The purpose of this study was to determine if the Davis
Eels Test of General Intelligence or Problem Solving (DET)
is a culture-fair test, as its developers claim. The DET, the
Metropolitan Achievement Test Battery, the Primary Mental Abilities
Test and a 50 word vocabulary test were administered to 83 Anglo-
American and 127 Spanish-American children in grades 2-5 in a
southern New Mexico public school. The mean scores of the two
groups differed significantly on these four measures as well as
on the Sims Socko-economic Score Card. The comparison of test
results shows that the DET did not produce scores any less
divergent between the two cultural groups than other measures
which were supposedly less culture-fair. (ECK)

342. Stoval, Franklin L. *A Study of Scaled Scores with Special Reference to Inter-American Tests.* Unpublished Ph.D. Dissertation, University of Texas. 1945.

343. Swanson, Elinor and Richard R. DeBlassie. "Interpreter Effects on the WISC Performance of First Grade Mexican-American Children." *Measurement and Evaluation in Guidance.* 4:3 (October 1971). pp. 172-175. (EJ 046 379)

First grade rural Mexican-American children were tested to determine whether the use of a bilingual interpreter would significantly influence their Verbal, Performance and Total IQ scores. Results indicate no significant differences. (CIJE)

344. Talerico, Marguerite and Fred Brown. "Intelligence Test Patterns of Puerto Rican Children Seen in Child Psychiatry." *The Journal of Social Psychology.* Vol. 61 (October 1963). pp. 57-66.

345. "The 'test ban' in New York City Schools." *Phi Delta Kappan.* 46. 1964. pp. 105-110.

346. Thomas, A; M.E. Hertzig; I. Dryman and P. Fernández. "Examiner Effect in IQ Testing of Puerto Rican Working-Class Children." *American Journal of Orthopsychiatry.* Vol. 41 (October 1971). pp. 809-821. (EC 04 0824).

Examined were test reliability and examiner problems in which the Wechsler Intelligence Scale for Children scores of school-age Puerto Rican children were markedly affected by differences in examiner style between two examiners who were equivalent as to sex, ethnicity, fluency in Spanish and English and clinical experience. Higher performance level occurred with examiner behavior that encouraged active participation, verbalization and repeated effort on the child's part. (EC)

347. Tireman, L.S. "Results of Group Tests Given in the Original Survey of San Jose School." *University of New Mexico Bulletin, Training School Series.* Albuquerque. Vol. 1, no. 2. 1931.

348. Upshur, J.A. "Cross-Cultural Testing: What to Test." *Language Learning.* 16:3 and 4 (1966). pp. 183-196.

Given the need for cultural orientation programs, we must also have available test instruments and procedures which will supply reliable and valid measures of an individual's "cultural awareness." Upshur discusses Seelye's work in the field of cross-cultural testing, and goes further to suggest that the test

items should include not only observable behavior patterns but
also the intended meanings of behavior which are understood by
the members of the target culture.  The author then provides
a sample of the "universe of situations" such a test might
include, and points out the kinds of difficulties the examiner
might encounter.  (DH)

349.  Vincenty, Nestor I.  Racial Differences in Intelligence as
       Measured by Pictorial Group Tests with Special Reference to
       Puerto Rico and the United States. Unpublished Ph.D.
       Dissertation, Harvard University.  1929.

350.  Walsh, John F., and others.  "Performance of Negro and Puerto
       Rican Head Start Children on the Vane Kindergarten Test."
       Psychology in the Schools.  8:4 (October 1971).  pp. 375-385.
       (EJ 048 092)

       The data of the present study supplement those given by Vane
and also provide a context in which to assess the differential
abilities of Negro and Puerto Rican Head Start children on verbal
and performance tasks.  (Also tried to determine whether there
are different patterns as a consequence of age and sex).
       "Puerto Rican boys generally score higher than Negro boys on
the two performance subtests, as well as on the full scale, but
score lower on vocabulary."  Puerto Rican and Negro girls follow
a similar pattern of performance, but the magnitude of the
difference is considerably less.  (DH)

351.  Walsh, John F. and Rita D'Angelo.  "IQ's of Puerto Rican Head
       Start Children on the Vane Kindergarten Test."  Journal
       of School Psychology.  9:2 (1971).  pp. 173-176.
       (EJ 045 253)

       Comparison between Vane's standardization sample and the
Puerto Rican group yielded no significant differences in full
scale scores.  On the Vocabulary subtest, Puerto Rican subjects
earned lower mean scores; on the non-verbal subtests, they
scored higher than the normative group.  (CIJE)

352.  Zirkel, Perry Alan and John F. Greene.  The Academic Achievement of
       Spanish-Speaking First Graders in Connecticut.  Connecticut
       State Department of Education, Bureau of Compensatory and
       Community Educational Services.  April 1971.  8pp.
       (ED 054 275)

       Study sought to demonstrate that deficiencies shown by
Puerto Rican children in verbal ability and academic achievement
might not exist if initial instruction and testing were in Spanish.
The Inter-American Test of General Ability was administered by the
same examiner first in Spanish and then in English.  The Puerto

Ricans scored significantly higher than all groups in the Coleman
study.  The subjects scored much higher on the Spanish form than
on the English form.  (RIE)

353.  Zirkel, Perry Alan.  "Spanish-Speaking Students and Standardized
      Tests."  Urban Review.  Vol. 5 (June 1972).  pp. 32-40.
      (EJ 060 936)

          This is a review of the research done regarding linguistic,
      cultural and psychological difficulties encountered by Spanish-
      speaking children when they are administered standardized
      intelligence and achievement tests.  Conclusions of many studies
      are discussed and some general conclusions are given, i.e. there
      is a need to develop new measurements of IQ that utilize the
      language and cultural background of Spanish-speaking children;
      achievement tests that depend on English language skills generally
      result in poor performance; the ethnic background of the test
      administrator has some bearing on the results of both IQ and
      achievement tests.  (ECK)

D. Cognitive Development and the Bilingual Child

354. Barclay, Lisa and Frances Kurcz. Comparative Efficacies of
English, Spanish and Bilingual Cognitive Verbal Instruction.
1969. 309pp.
(ED 030 473)

Reports results of an experiment conducted with Mexican-
American Head Start children in California in 1967. Three
approaches were used: 1, structured English training program;
2, Spanish used as language of instruction; and 3, English used
as language of instruction; together with a control group
receiving usual preschool art and music activities. Results
showed no significant differences between the groups but
allowed that extraneous factors could have invalidated the
experiment. Though this experiment ended in failure,
much background material is presented in the introduction. (RIE)

355. Casavantes, Edward J. Variables Which Tend to Affect (Impede or
Retard) Learning of the Mexican American Student in American
Education. A Position Paper. Albuquerque, New Mexico:
Southwestern Cooperative Educational Laboratory. August 1970.
15pp.
(ED 060 990)

An interdisciplinary research study is suggested following a
review of the more significant studies that have been attempted
to explain the degree of educational retardation of the Mexican
American as related to such factors as life stresses and learning
styles. This study would be a combination of survey research and
research for hypothesis testing wherein a random sample of the
total Mexican American population would be used. It is noted
that such a study would provide large quantities of data on
sociologic, family education, cognitive, and personality functioning
and would assess the co-variation and influence of each of these
variables on each of the other variables. (RIE)

356. Chandler, J.T. and J. Plakos. Spanish-Speaking Pupils Classified
as Educable Mentally Retarded. Sacramento: California
State Department of Education. 1969.

357. Cohen, S. Alan. "Some Learning Disabilities of Socially Disadvantaged
Puerto Rican and Negro Children." Academic Therapy Quarterly.
Vol. 2 (Fall 1966). pp. 37-41, 52.

This paper describes some of the learning disabilities and
patterns that are common in lower-class Puerto Rican and Black
children. The author's work with slum children has convinced him

74

that "cultural deprivation" includes many behaviors which can be
seen in dyslexia, SLD and perceptual dysfunction. He suggests that
schools stop labelling these children, begin to anticipate their
difficulties and teach to the behaviors in the disability syndrome.
  Ss were 1721 third graders (489 Puerto Ricans, 626 Blacks,
and 489 Whites, Others). Data were obtained from Marianne
Frostig's Developmental Test of Visual Perception, the Benton
Visual Retention Test, the WISC, and observations. Ss had a
higher incidence of perceptual dysfunction than test norms
predict. According to this study, poor visual discrimination of
letters, poor visual memory of unknown words, poor recognition of
known words, and letter reversals (p-b-d-q) were common among
these socially disadvantaged children. (DH)

358. Diebold, A. Richard. The Consequences of Early Bilingualism on
       Cognitive Development and Personality Formation. 1966. 32pp.
       (ED 020 491)

     Compound bilingualism tends to result when the two languages
are acquired in a speech community offering the child equal and
simultaneous exposure to both and where the functions of both are
minimally differentiated. More typically one of the languages
is sociologically dominant and the social functions of each is
different. When bilinguals are studied in contexts where their
bilingual/bicultural backgrounds do not automatically assign them
to lower status within the monolingual community, it can be shown
that bilingualism is associated with and may facilitate
significantly superior performances on both verbal and non-verbal
tests of intelligence. Cases of bilingual psychopathology can
be traced to a crisis in social and personal identity engendered
by antagonistic acculturative pressures directed on a bicultural
community by a sociologically monolingual society. (RIE)

359. Dyer, Frederick N. "Color-Naming Interference in Monolinguals
       and Bilinguals." Journal of Verbal Learning and Verbal
       Behavior. 10:3 (June 1971). pp. 297-302.
       (EJ 042 845)

360. Feldman, Carol and Michael Shen. Some Language-Related Cognitive
       Advantages of Bilingual Five-Year-Olds. 1969. 27pp.
       (ED 031 307)

     Ss in this study were 15 bilingual students of Mexican
origin and 15 monolingual students; half the monolingual group
was Black and half was of Mexican origin. All lived in the same
neighborhood and attended the same Head Start program. Ss were
given three types of tasks. It was found that bilinguals, although
better at using names in relational statements, were not better
than monolinguals in the use of common names alone or nonsense
names alone. Bilingual Ss performed consistently better than
monolinguals where non-verbal pointing responses were required

but not where spoken responses were required. It was
suggested that having a notion of meaning as a function of use
facilitates acquisition of the ability of young children to use
labels in sentences. (RIE)

361. Hertzig, M.E., H.G. Birch and A. Thomas. "Class and Ethnic
     Differences in the Responsiveness of Preschool Children to
     Cognitive Demands." Monographs of the Society for Research
     in Child Development. Vol. 33 (1968). pp. 1-69.

     The findings demonstrate clearly that in the preschool years
native American middle-class and Puerto Rican working-class
children differ from each other in the behavioral styles with
which they respond to demands for cognitive functioning. These
differences include, the proportion of responses that are work
responses; 2, the tendency to make work responses after an
initial not-work response; 3, the proportion of verbally expressed
responses; 4, the style of making not-work responses; 5, the kinds
of verbalization that accompany not-work responses; 6, the
tendency to make spontaneous extensions; 7, the frequency with
which such spontaneous extensions are verbally expressed; and
8, the degree to which work responses are made verbal and nonverbal cognitive tasks, respectively. "Each of these differences
in style was sustained when IQ was at comparable levels in the
two groups as well as when the ordinal positions.of the children
were controlled for. They thus appear to be stylistic differences
characteristic of the different social groupings and not artifacts
of IQ differences or of differences in birth order." (PASAR)

362. Jacobs, John V. and M. Pierce. Bilingualism and Creativity.
     1966. 6pp.
     (ED 021 848)

     This study attempted to determine whether or not there is a
relationship between creativity, or divergent thinking and
bilingualism in fifth and sixth grade students. To assess the
degree of bilingualism the Adapted Hoffman Bilingual Schedule
was used. Two tests were administered. The bilingual students
scored higher on the non-verbal Uses test and slightly lower on the
**Word Meanings** test than did the monolingual students. Using
the combined score, the bilinguals were generally higher, or
more creative. (RIE)

363. Jensen. A.R. "Learning Abilities in Mexican-American and Anglo-
     American Children." California Journal of Educational Research.
     Vol. 12 (1961). pp. 147-159.

364. Karadenes, Mark. <u>A Comparison of Differences in Achievement</u>
<u>and Learning Abilities between Anglo and Mexican-American</u>
<u>Children When the Two Groups are Equated by Intelligence.</u>
Unpublished Ph.D. Dissertation, University of Virginia.
1971.
(<u>Dissertation Abstracts International.</u> Vol. 32 (1971-1972).
pp. 4422A-4423A.)

This study was designed to determine if differences in learning abilities exist between Anglo and Mexican American male
kindergarten children, and how those differences relate to
intelligence and academic achievement. Ss were 90 children
(45 Anglo, 45 Mexican-American) who attended public elementary
school in Santa Monica, California. School psychologists administered the Stanford-Binet Intelligence Test and the Wide Range
Achievement Test (WRAT) to all Ss; the Meeker Profile was used to
measure learning abilities. Findings indicate that achievement
was affected by ethnicity and intelligence, and that learning
abilities were not influenced by either ethnicity or intelligence.
(DH)

365. Kaufman, Maurice. <u>The Effect of Instruction in Reading Spanish</u>
<u>on Reading Ability in English of Spanish-Speaking</u>
<u>Retarded Readers.</u> Unpublished Ph.D. Dissertation, New York
University. 1966.
(<u>Dissertation Abstracts.</u> Vol. 28. p. 1299A.)

366. Killian, L.R. <u>Cognitive Test Performance of Spanish-American</u>
<u>Primary School Children: A Longitudinal Study. Final Report.</u>
Kent State University, Ohio. Washington, D.C.: National
Center for Educational Research and Development. November
(ED 060 156)

A twenty-six-month follow-up study was made of 75 Anglo-
and Spanish-American primary school children who were examined on
the Wechsler Intelligence Scale for Children, the Illinois Test
of Psycholinguistic Abilities, and the Bender Visual-Motor
Gestalt Test in order to determine the specific cognitive deficits
which might account for the poor school performance of Spanish-
American school children. After three years of schooling the
children were found to be deficient in verbal comprehension but
have no deficits in short-term memory, arithmetic, or perceptual
organization. Bilingualism does not appear to be as important
as ethnic status. There is some support for treating Spanish-
Americans children as a single group. If they are to be subdivided, it is probably more important to consider the whole
complex of variables making up the ethnic class rather than just
bilingualism. Remedial efforts in the cognitive area with
third and fourth grade Spanish-American children should concentrate
on vocabulary, general information, verbal analogies, experience

with a wide range of social situations and their corresponding
rules, verbal classifying procedures, and grammatical form. (RIE)

367. Killian, L.R. "WISC, Illinois Test of Psycholinguistic Abilities,
and Bender Visual-Motor Gestalt Test Performance of
Spanish-American Kindergarten and First Grade School
Children." Journal of Consulting and Clinical Psychology.
37: 1 (August 1971). pp. 38-43.
(EJ 043 081)

The specific cognitive deficits which might account for the
poor school performance of Spanish-American school children were
examined. The results suggest that Spanish-American children
are deficient on the input side of communicative skills, especially
in understanding sentences and pictures. Bilingualism does not
appear to be an important variable. (CIJE)

368. Kintsch, Walter. "Interlingual Interference and Memory
Processes." Journal of Verbal Learning and Verbal Behavior.
Vol. 8 (1969). pp. 16-19.

369. Knight, James. A Laboratory Study of the Reading Habits of
Spanish-Speaking Children. Ph.D. Dissertation, University
of Texas. 1931.

370. Lambert, W.E. and J. Macnamara. "Some Cognitive Consequences
of Following a First-Grade Curriculum in A Second Language."
Journal of Educational Psychology. 60:2 (April 1969).
pp. 86-96.

Presents results of a community-sponsored project to develop
skill in a second language (French) by using it as the sole
medium for instruction for pupils whose native language is
English. The experimental class is compared with both English
and French control classes and their relative standing in audio-
lingual and reading skills in both languages, in mathematics, in
sensitivity to novel phonemic sequences, and in measured
intelligence at the end of the year. Although the results, in
general, reveal a striking progress in French and considerable
transfer to English skills, the real value of the study will be
evident only after a replication with other first-grade experimental classes and a follow-up with the same students who are
currently continuing the experience into their second and third
years. (author)

371. Landry, Richard G. Bilingualism and Creative Abilities. 1968. 10pp.
(ED 039 602)

In this study, an attempt was made to examine the proposition
that experience with two languages during childhood is related
meaningfully to later verbal creative functioning. Findings

included: 1, no significant differences between bilingual and
monolingal groups on the second grade level in fluency or
flexibility on verbal and figural measures of creativity;
and 2, at the fourth grade level, significant differences between
the linguistic groups developed but not between the sexes.
The bilingual experience in childhood was felt to result in
subsequent greater development of potential creativity.  (RIE)

372.  Liedtke, W.W.  Linear Measurement Concepts of Bilingual and
        Monolingual Children.  Unpublished M.A. thesis, The University
        of Alberta, Edmonton.  1968.

373.  Liedtke, W.W. and L.D. Nelson.  Bilingualism and Conservation.
        1968.  8pp.
        (ED 030 110)

        Study attempts to use the Piagetian-type observations as an
assessment of intellectual capacities and to determine whether
learning a second language at an early age has beneficial or
detrimental effects on cognitive functioning.  A test dealing
with conservation (awareness of invariance) and measurement of
length was constructed dealing with the following topics:
reconstructing relations of distance, conservation of length,
conservation of length with change of positon, conservation of
length with distortion of shape, measurement of length and sub-
dividing a straight line.  The result of this study seems to be
in agreement with Peal and Lambert's finding that bilingualism has
favorable effects on intellectual function.  (RIE)

374.  Liedtke, W.W. and L.D. Nelson.  "Concept Formation and
        Bilingualism."  Alberta Journal of Educational Research.
        Vol. 14, no. 4 (December 1968).  pp. 225-232.

        The purpose of this study was to measure the effects of
bilingualism on mental development of young children.  The
instrument used was a Concepts of Linear Measurements Test, with
items similar to those devised by Jean Piaget.  Ss were grade one
students, 50 monolinguals and 50 bilinguals; each group had
an equal number of boys and girls.  Results of the test seemed to
show that the linguistic and cultural experience of the bilinguals
speeds up the normal process of some parts of mental development.
There were indications that bilingual students reach the state
of concrete operations before monolinguals do.  The authors note
that these findings have great implications for teachers and
administrators of these children.  (ECK)

375.  Mahakian, C.  "Measuring Intelligence and Reading Capacity of
        Spanish-Speaking Children."  Elementary School Journal.  Vol. 39
        (1939).  pp. 760-768.

376. Massad, C.E., K. Yamamoto, and O.L. Davis, Jr. "Stimulus Modes and Language Media." Psychology in the Schools. Vol. 7 (1970). pp. 38-42.

This experiment was devised to determine if verbal stimuli produce a greater proportion of sense-impressions than pictorial stimuli across two languages. Ss were 11 English-Spanish bilinguals, all of whom had finished the second year of college; this group was chosen because they were most likely to have equal proficiency in both languages. Ss were shown line drawings and English and Spanish printed words and were asked to respond an equal number of times in both languages. Conclusions are tentative because of the small size of the sample, but the data seem to indicate that words evoke more sensory reactions than pictures and Spanish evoked more sense impressions than English. The authors conclude with suggestions for further research. (ECK)

377. Peck, L. and A.M. Hodges. "A Study of Racial Differences in Eidetic Imagery of Preschool Children." Journal of Genetic Psychology. Vols. 50-51 (September 1937). pp. 141-161.

378. Rapier, J. "Effects of Verbal Mediation upon Learning of Mexican-American Children." California Journal of Educational Research. Vol. 18 (1967). pp. 40-48.

The study is an investigation into the role of verbal responses as behavioral controls in Mexican-American children. Two questions were proposed: 1, Is the Mexican-American child deficient in the use of verbal mediation processes to facilitate his learning?; and 2, Can Mexican-American children profit from training in the use of verbal mediating cues? To answer the first question, 20 Average and 20 Dull Mexican- and Anglo-Americans were selected from the third graders of four elementary school districts in California; to answer the second question, the numbers were the same but the children were fourth graders. The first experiment used followed the reversal and nonreversal shift design suggested by Kendler (1962) which involved discrimination between stimuli that differed in size and color. The second experiment studied the effects of supplying the necessary mediating links on paired-associates learning. The first experiment supported Kendler's finding that older children make more frequent use of mediating clues to facilitate their learning. The second experiment shows that Mexican-Americans will profit from the opportunity to use verbal mediators, which suggests that their learning disability may be due to a lack of verbal associations. (ECK)

379. Rodríguez, J.A. "Are Bilingual Children Able to Think in Either Language with Facility and Accuracy?" Bulletin of the Department of Elementary Principals. Vol. 10 (January 1931). pp. 98-101.

380. Smith, Frank. "Bilingualism and Mental Development." British
     Journal of Psychology. Vol. 13 (1921-1923). pp.271-282.

381. Stern, Carolyn and Diane Ruble. Teaching New Concepts to Non-
     English Speaking Preschool Children. California University,
     Los Angeles. Washington, D.C.: Office of Economic Opportunity;
     Office of Education, Cooperative Research Program. April
     1970. 36pp.
     (ED 054 903)

     Fifteen Mexican American children from four Head Start
classes participated in this study, which tested three
hypotheses: 1, that children whose first language is Spanish and
who are instructed in Spanish will require significantly fewer
trials to learn a new concept than children instructed either
in English or bilingually; 2, that children receiving the first
set of new concepts in English will learn a second instance of the
new concept taught in English more readily than children who
were taught the first use of the c oncept in Spanish; and 3, that
on a Spanish language criterion test, children taught concepts in
English will do as well as children taught those concepts in
Spanish or bilingually. The procedure included pretesting with
the Goodenough Draw-a-Man Test and the Expressive Vocabulary
Inventory in both English and Spanish; the instructional program;
a criterion test in the appropriate language using a series of
booklets developed to teach the conceptual task which was designed
to test the hypotheses; and a posttest. Study results rejected
hypotheses 1 and 2, while hypothesis 3 could not be rejected.
An appendix contains lessons used in the instructional program.
(RIE)

382. Thomas, Alexander. Retardation in Intellectual Development of
     Lower-Class Puerto Rican Children in New York City.
     New York: Department of Psychiatry, New York University.
     1967.
     (ED 017 591)

     The objectives of this study were 1, to identify any patterns
of behavioral and intellectual function which appear to be
detrimental to optimal learning and development; 2, to identify
inter- and extra-familial influences which produce the above
patterns; and 3, to identify favorable patterns which can be used
to prevent or remedy the situation. The Ss were two groups
of Puerto Rican children in New York City: 95 in one group which
was followed from infancy, and 155 in the other group which
consisted of their older siblings. For comparative purposes, two
groups of advantaged White children were also tested. All children
between the ages of 6 and 14 were administered the WISC; those
children between the ages of 15-17 were administered the WAIS.
Analysis of the data was not complete, as this was an interim

report. However, the following conclusions are presented:
1, the population of Puerto Rican children tested was retarded
in school achievement; 2, the findings do not show a decrement of
IQ level between pre-school and school ages, indicating that the
retardation in intellectual achievement is not a result of cultural
deprivation; 3, language development is not retarded by bilingualism;
and 4, other factors must be responsible, e.g. poor schooling,
inappropriate teaching methods. The author noted that some
factors in the home environment may also be at fault, but any
such conclusions must be withheld pending complete analysis of
the findings. (DH)

383. Tucker, G.R. and others. <u>Cognitive and Attitudinal Consequences</u>
<u>of Following the Curricula of the First Four Grades in a</u>
<u>Second Language</u>. McGill University, Montreal, Quebec.
February 1971. 78pp.
(ED 055 485)

384. Wolk, Elsie. "Reading Disabilities of Children Learning English
as a Second Language." <u>Elementary English</u>. Vol. 49,
no. 3 (March 1972). pp. 410-416.
(ED 056 673)

This article reports the results of a special study to
determine the specific problems of Puerto Rican children learning
to read. Over one hundred coordinators of ESL programs reported
on the reading habits of one child as observed through one year.
The article describes specific problems encountered by the children,
such as mispronunciation and problems in comprehension. It concludes with many procedures that should be useful in helping these
children learn to read. (ECK)

E. <u>Measures of Self-Concept and Socialization in Bilingual Children</u>

Puerto Ricans

385. Adams, John V. and Wallace K. Ewing. <u>A Study of Student Attitudes</u>
<u>Toward English as a Second Language in Puerto Rico</u>. (1971).
58pp.
(ED 057 695)

The results of a questionnaire designed to investigate
Puerto Rican students' attitudes toward learning English show
that there is a predominantly positive attitude toward English-
as-a-second-language in the Puerto Rican town studied in this
survey. The questionnaires solicit information from students in
grades five through eight concerning personal data, students'
contact with English, amount of English used, parental attitudes,
and student attitude toward learning English. The shortcomings
of Puerto Rico's standardized English curriculum may result from
inappropriate teaching methods rather than from a negative
attitude on the part of the students. The students may be
receiving too much language material in too little time without
reinforcing what is learned in class through use outside of
class. English might be better taught as a foreign language.
English and Spanish versions of the questionnaires are provided
along with graphs illustrating the results of this survey. (RIE)

386. Betances, Samuel. "Puerto Rican Youth: Race and the Search
for Identity." <u>The Rican</u>. No. 1 (Fall 1971). pp.4-13.

387. Blourock, Barbara. "Aspira in the Junior High School." <u>High</u>
<u>Points</u>. (February 1966). pp. 53-55.

388. Capone, Thomas A. <u>Interaction of Selected Needs and Perceived</u>
<u>Peer Orientation to Education as Related to Academic</u>
<u>Proficiency in Aspira Students</u>. Unpublished Ph.D. Dissertation,
Fordham University. 1969.
<u>(Dissertation Abstracts</u>. 30:12 (1970). p.5279A.)

The purpose of the study was to examine the need for
affiliation (n Aff), need for achievement (n Ach), and perceived
peer orientation toward education (P Peer O) of 120 Puerto Rican
male and female 12th grade acacemic students. Ss were all
members of the ASPIRA club in New York City, which is an agency
operated by people of Puerto Rican descent to encourage and support
Puerto Rican young people to enter and complete college. The
instruments used were the Edwards Personal Preference Schedule
(n Ach and n Aff) and the Peer Influence section of the Personal
Values Inventory (P Peer O). Also used in the investigation were

the SAT, to obtain a measure of general academic proficiency, and the comprehension section of the Nelson-Denny Reading Test, to obtain a rough index of language proficiency. Findings indicate that a positive relationship exists between a student's n Ach and his academic success as measured by the SAT. Also, students with a high n Aff more often perceive their peers as having academic orientations similar to their own than do students with a low n Aff. The author suggests that the n Aff may be countered somewhat by the student with a high n Ach who perceives that his peers do not value education as much as he does. (DH)

389. Epstein, Erwin H. Value Orientation and the English Language in Puerto Rican Attitudes Toward Second Language Learning Among Ninth Grade Pupils and Their Parents. Unpublished Ph.D. Dissertation, University of Chicago. 1966.

390. Greene, John F. and Perry Alan Zirkel. Academic Factors Relating to the Self-Concept of Puerto Rican Pupils. Paper presented at the American Psychological Association Convention, Washington, D.C. 1971. 10pp.
(ED 054 284)

Study investigated the relationship of the self-concept of Puerto Rican pupils with achievement, IQ, ethnic group mixture, and teacher ethnicity. The results of a correlational analysis indicated that self-concept was significantly related to achievement in English and Spanish, as well as to teacher ratings of aural ability in both languages, although self-concept was not significantly related to IQ. However, the relationship between self-concept and academic achievement is demonstrated to be complex and circular. (RIE)

391. John, Vera and Tomi Berney. Analysis of Story Retelling as a Measure of the Effects of Ethnic Content in a Story. New York: Yeshiva University. 1967. 92pp.
(ED 014 326)

The purpose of the study was to examine the psychological impact of stories and story books on Black, Puerto Rican, Mexican-American and American Indian preschool children and to discover patterns of language performance among the ethnic groups. The children were read various stories, some with specific ethnic content, others without, and were asked to retell the stories. It seemed that the inclusion of ethnic content is useful in a program aimed at non-white youngsters. (RIE)

392. Mangano, James F. and Richard C. Towne. Improving Migrant Students' Academic Achievement Through Self-Concept Enhancement. State University of New York College at Geneseo, Center for Migrant Studies. 1970. 55pp.
(ED 049 868)

Purpose of the research was to investigate whether an attempt to modify migrant parents' behavior in accordance with social psychological principles resulted in better academic achievement by their children. Ss were 21 Puerto Rican children; 12 in the experimental group (aged 6-16) and 9 in the control group (aged 7-14). Data were collected through use of reading and arithmentic subtests of the Metropolitan Achievement Test and the Spanish translation of the Michigan State General Self-Concept of Ability Scale. Results indicated that the self-concept of ability for the experimental group increased significantly and that academic achievement also increased, as measured by the above mentioned instruments. (RIE)

393. O'Brien, Sister Mary Gratia. Relationship of Self Perceptions of Puerto Rican and Non-Puerto Rican Parochial School Children to Selected School Related Variables. Ph.D. Dissertation, Fordham University. 1970.
(Dissertation Abstracts. Vol. 31 (1971). pp. 3347-3348A.)

The purpose of this study was to examine the self-perceptions of Puerto Rican children and to compare them with the self-perceptions of children from other ethnic backgrounds. Ss 2343 2796 fifth, sixth and seventh graders from twelve elementary parochial school in the Archdiocese of New York. Ss were divided into four groups (PR boys, PR girls, Other boys, Other girls); boys were compared with girls of the same ethnic group and Puerto Rican children were compared with Other children on each of the following variables: scholastic achievement, mental ability, socioeconomic status, teacher-ratings of behavior, and appraisal-perception. When mental ability and scholastic achievement, as measured by standardized tests, were comparable, the self perceptions of Puerto Rican children did not differ from those of Other children. When measures other than standardized tests were used, however, the Puerto Rican children did have significantly lower self-perceptions; this was true even when the comparisons were made between Ss of the same socioeconomic level. The relationships between the self-perception scores and the appraisal-perception scores were not significantly different for Puerto Rican Ss and Other Ss. (DH)

394. Puerto Rican Culture as it Affects Puerto Rican Children in Chicago Classrooms. Chicago: Chicago Board of Education. 1970. 20pp.
(ED 052 277)

Designed to develop better understanding and greater appreciation between the Puerto Rican child who enrolls in the Chicago public schools and his classroom teacher. Presents those aspects of the culture which would be likely to affect the child's classroom behavior. It is considered that an informed teacher may be able to assist the bicultural child to a considerable degree. (RIE)

395. Rosenthal, Alan Gerald. <u>Pre-School Experience and Adjustment of Puerto Rican Children</u>. Unpublished Ph.D. Dissertation, New York University. 1955.
(<u>Dissertation Abstracts.</u> Vol. 15 (1955). p. 1205.)

The purpose of this study was to determine the relationship between pre-school experiences of a non-academic nature and the absence of these experiences on the achievement of a group of bilingual children who made a successful school adjustment. Ss were five and six year old male and female children who were born in Puerto Rico; selection was partially based on socioeconomic, educational, and physical factors. Ss were divided into groups: the first had no pre-school orientation and the second was given cultural enrichment programs prior to entering school.
Data were based on the observations of the Ss' teachers. Results indicated a significant difference in the achievement of the two groups; the group that had the pre-school program received higher ratings overall. It was suggested that these programs be continued, and that further research in preschool orientation programs be undertaken. (DH)

396. Sobrino, James F. <u>Group Identification and Adjustment in Puerto Rican Adolescents</u>. Unpublished Ph.D. Dissertation, Yeshiva University. 1965.
(<u>Dissertation Abstracts.</u> Vol. 26 (1966). p. 4067.)

The author administered the Semantic Differential Scale, the EFOS and a questionnaire to 360 male and female Puerto Ricans between the ages of twelve and eighteen. Ss were selected from four parochial schools and from a child guidance clinic. Ss were divided into three groups: 1, the clinic group, clearly maladjusted; 2, school maladjusted but not in therapy; and 3, school well adjusted. It was found that 1, the clinic group identifies more with the majority group (in which it was unacceptable); 2, the adjusted group maintains a favorable self-concept while they do perceive differences between themselves and others; and 3, the maladjusted but non-clinic group seems to have a more positive self-image than the indicators would warrant. (DH)

397. Strauss, Susan. "The Effect of School Integration on the Self-Concept of Negro and Puerto Rican Children." <u>Graduate Research in Education and Related Disciplines</u>. Vol. 3 (1967). pp. 63-76.

Compared the self-concept of second and third grade Black and Puerto Rican children of low socioeconomic background in a paired school and in a non-paired school. "Pairing is the combining of two school populations," one predominantly white, the other predominantly black. It was hypothesized that for both grades the paired group would have a higher self-concept, and that the paired third grade would do better than the second.

A fifty question inventory was used. One hundred children were tested, 50 in each of the two schools, 25 in each of the two grades. The results showed that the paired groups' scores were significantly higher than the non-paired groups' scores. No significant difference was found between the scores of the paired second and third grade groups. It is concluded that pairing does increase the self-concept of Black and Puerto Rican children. The extent of its positive influence needs further study. (PASAR)

398.  Willis, Robert Manks. <u>An Analysis of the Adjustment and Scholastic Achievement of Forty Puerto Rican Boys Who Attend Transition Classes in New York City</u>. Unpublished Ph.D. Dissertation, New York University. 1961. (<u>Dissertation Abstracts</u>. Vol. 22 (1961). pp. 795-706.)

The objectives of this study were to identify the effects of transition classes on the adjustment, retention and scholastic achievement of forty Puerto Rican boys in a New York City school and to determine the implications their influence has for improvement of the curriculum. Ss were forty tenth grade boys from Morris High School; all were born in Puerto Rico and had attended transition classes. Data were collected from several sources. Students were classified as either in Group I, "Drop-Outs" or Group II, those students still attending school at the time of the survey. The findings indicate that there were no significant differences between the social and educational characteristics of the two groups. Recommendations include: 1, better transition classes; 2, improved TESL programs; 3, a more intensive guidance program; 4, more effective measures for the evaluation of these students; 5, more realistic placement of Puerto Rican students; 6, more effective programs in remedial reading; 7, an increased awareness and understanding of Puerto Rican students on the part of school personnel; and 8, increased participation of Puerto Rican students and adults in the educational process, including decision-making. (DH)

399.  Zirkel, Perry A. "Self-Concept and the 'Disadvantage' of Ethnic Group Membership and Mixture." <u>Review of Educational Research</u>. Vol. 14 (1971). pp. 211-225.

The author presents a brief review of the literature on the self-concept of minority group members, and discusses the relationship between low-self-evaluation and academic underachievement. He concludes that ethnic group membership may have some effect, positive or negative, on the self-concept of the disadvantaged child. The supposed "disadvantage" of minority students can be turned into an advantage by enhancing the self-concept, perhaps through such programs as bilingual-bicultural education and Black Studies. (DH)

400.  Zirkel, Perry Alan and E. Gnanaraj Moses. "Self-Concept and
      Ethnic Group Membership Among Public School Students."
      American Educational Research Journal. .8:2 (1971).
      pp. 253-265.

          Investigated the possible relationship of self-concept with
      ethnic group membership and mixture in the school setting.
      One hundred and twenty Negro, Puerto Rican and White students were
      selected from the fifth and sixth grades of three schools, each
      of which had a different one of these ethnic groups in the majority.
      Results on the Coopersmith Self-Esteem Inventory indicated that
      the self-concept of these children was significantly affected by
      their ethnic group membership but not by the majority-minority
      mixture of groups within the schools. The significant effect
      was ascribed to the lower self-concept of the Puerto Rican children
      in the study (significantly lower than both the White and Black
      children's self-concepts). (PASAR)

Other Non-English Speaking Groups

401.  Alvarado, M.B. "Lanier Students Revolt Against the System."
      Inferno. May 1968.

          Article about a predominantly Mexican-American school in
      San Antonio, Texas.

402.  Andersson, Theodore. "Foreign Language and Intercultural Under-
      standing." National Elementary Principal. Vol. 36 (February
      1967). p. 32.

          The bilingual needs to be proud of his heritage. The tech-
      niques studied in several school systems revealed that there are
      signs of better communication and improved attitudes toward non-
      English cultures. The bilingual children studied in these school
      programs seemed to become more literate in both the Spanish and
      English languages. (JH)

403.  Caskey, Owen L. and Doris J. Webb. [Keys to the Elementary School
      Environment (with Subgroup Reference Norms): How Children
      Perceive their School Environment.] Southwest Educational
      Development Laboratory. Austin, Texas. Texas Technological
      College. Lubbock. School of Education. Washington, D.C.:
      Office of Education. Cooperative Research Program. 1971.
      199 pp.
      (ED 059 822)

404.  Cervenka, Edward. Administrative Manual for Inventory of
      Socialization of Bilingual Children, Ages 3-10. 1968. 75 pp.
      (ED 027 062)

This battery of test instruments is one of a set of three developed for use in the study of bilingual instruction programs and other compensatory programs in Texas. The socialization inventory has been based on a sociological view of personality as a developing and changing entity. Four sub-measures are included: 1, a measure of self concept; 2, a behavior rating scale of a child's interpersonal behavior in an interview with the test administrator; 3, a behavior rating scale of a child's general social behavior in the classroom; and 4, a questionnaire given to parents of children in bilingual programs. Administration and rating directions are provided. Samples of socialization measures and their rating sheets form the bulk of this report. (REI)

405. Coller, Alan R. and P.D. Guthrie. Self Concept Measures: An Annotated Bibliography. Princeton, New Jersey: Educational Testing Service. 1971. 9 pp.

Includes self-concept measures appropriate for children from preschool through third grade. Annotation lists the purpose of each instrument, nature of the materials, groups for which it is intended, administration, scoring interpretation, and standardization. (PROYECTO LEER BULLETIN)

406. Coole, Musgrave Ruth. A Comparison of Anglo-American and Latin-American Girls in Grades V-VI with Reference to their Vocational, Academic, and Recreational Preferences and Aversions. Unpublished Master's thesis, University of Texas. 1937.

407. Dugas, Donald G. Facilitating the Self-Actualization of France-Americans. Paper presented at the Fifth Annual TESOL Meeting. New Orleans, Louisiana. March 6, 1971. 17 pp. (ED 055 482)

408. Durojaiye, S.M. "Social Context of Immigrant Pupils Learning English." Educational Research. Vol 13 (June 1971). pp. 179-184. (EJ 042 908)

409. Hernández, Norma G. Variables Affecting Achievement of Middle School Mexican American Students. Texas University, El Paso. Washington, D.C.: Office of Education. August 1971. 81 pp. (ED 059 827)

Literature pertaining to research done on academic achievement of Mexican American students is reviewed in this paper. The literature deals with such variables as socioeconomic, physical, psychological, and cultural aspects; language factors; attitudes; language development; and environment. A 15-page discussion of recommendations for improving curriculum, instruction, and teacher education for educating the Mexican American is included. Also included is a bibliography containing over 200 relevant citations. (RIE)

89

410. Leo, Paul F. The Effects of Two Types of Group Counseling Upon the Academic Achievement of Mexican-American Pupils in the Elementary School. Ph.D. dissertation, University of the Pacific, Stockton, California. Washington, D.C.: Office of Education, Cooperative Research Program. January 1972. 145p.
(ED 059 002)

411. Linton, Thomas H. A Study of the Relationship of Global Self-Concept, Academic Self-Concept, and Academic Achievement among Anglo and Mexican-American Sixth Grade Students. Paper presented at the annual meeting of the American Educational Research Association. Chicago: Illinois. April 3-7, 1972. 13 pp.
(ED 063 053)

A sample of 172 Anglo and 160 Mexican-American students from 16 elementary schools in a southern New Mexico city was stratified by three socioeconomic levels. The Piers-Harris Children's Self-Concept Scale and a Five-item factor analyzed scale developed from existing research were used to measure self-concept. Student a-chievement was measured by teacher-assigned grades in reading, arithmetic, and social studies and by the Iowa Test of Basic Skills. A three-way analysis of variance model (with students classified according to ethnicity, sex, and socioeconomic level) was used to test differences between students. Results indicated that no significant differences between ethnic groups in terms of global and academic self-concepts, and no sex differences were found. Significant differences were found in both self-concept measures between socioeconomic levels. High socioeconomic level was associated with high self-concept and low socioeconomic level was associated with low self-concept. However, middle socioeconomic level Mexican-American students' academic self-concept scores were almost the same as those of low socioeconomic level Anglo and Mexican American students. Results of actual achievement were consistent with findings of previous studies, and correlation analysis of the relationships between self-concept and achievement did not yield a consistent pattern across socioeconomic levels. (RIE)

412. Mans, Rolando. An Experimental Approach to the Teaching of Reading in Spanish at the Primary Level. Master's thesis, Sacramento State College. September 1971. 103 pp.
(ED 056 602)

An experiment in the teaching of reading in Spanish to second and third-grade students, conducted by the author at the Ethel Phillips elementary school, utilizes a modified version of Dr. Laubach's "Syllabic, analytic-synthetic method" of language instruction. Results indicate that success in school of children from Spanish-speaking homes may be directly related to the concept of self-identity. It is suggested that development of programs leading to curriculum-wide literacy in Spanish is considered by authorities in bilingualism to be one of the key factors in raising the Spanish-

90

speaking child's level of expectation in his academic achievement.
Major chapters in this study discuss: 1, the problem and definition
of terms; 2, review of related literature; 3, procedures of the
study; 4, analysis of data; and 5, summary, conclusions, and recommendations. A bibliography and an appendix containing sample
lessons and measurement tools are included. (RIE)

413. Mayans, Frank, Jr. Puerto Rican Migrant Pupils in New York City
Schools: A Comparison of the Effects of Two Methods of Instructional Grouping on English Mastery and Attitudes. Unpublished Ph.D. Dissertation, Columbia University. 1953.
(Dissertation Abstracts. Vol. 14 (1954). pp. 68-69.)

The purpose of this study was to compare the effects of two
types of instructional grouping on the English mastery and assimilation of Puerto Rican migrant students. Ss were recent immigrants
from Puerto Rico who were entering mainland schools for the first
time; the schools were two junior high schools in New York City's
Spanish Harlem. Ss were placed in two groups: 1) regular classes
with the other students in the school and 2) "vestibule" classes in
which all students were Puerto Ricans. At the start, Ss were pretested with the Cooperative Interamerican Test of General Ability
and a Test of Reading, both in Spanish; and Attitude Toward the
Surroundings Scale, also in Spanish, was administered. At the end
of one semester, all Ss were given the Cooperative Interamerican
Test of Reading, in English; Subtest I (oral vocabulary), Cooperative Interamerican Test of General Ability, in English; and the
Attitude Toward Surroundings Scales, in Spanish. The findings indicated that 1) the migrant will learn more English if (s) he has a
favorable attitude toward his surroundings; 2) the "regular" group
has more unfavorable attitudes toward school; 3) the "regular"
group has developed significantly more favorable attitudes toward
schoolmates; and 4) "regular" students score higher in all three
tests of English mastery. At the end of the semester, controls were
lifted and all students participated in "regular" classes. A follow-up study at the end of the year yielded these results: 1) the
original "regular" Ss retained their superiority in English oral
vocabulary, but not in reading; 2) all Ss have more favorable attitudes toward schoolmates with no differences between class groupings showing; 3) the original "regular" Ss have become more assimilated, "make more friends, speak English more often with their
friends;" and 4) Ss who preferred "regular" grouping felt they
learned more, while Ss who preferred the "vestibule" grouping felt
it helped them adjust better. The author suggests placing immigrant students in regular classes because of the rapid pace at
which assimilation can take place. (DH)

414. Muller, Douglas G. and Robert Leonetti. Primary Self-Concept
Scale: Boys. Dissemination Center for Bilingual Bicultural
Education. Austin, Texas. Washington, D.C.: Office of Education.
40 pp.
(ED 062 846)

415. Muller, Douglas G. and Robert Leonetti. Primary Self-Concept
     Scale: Girls. Dissemination Center for Bilingual Bicultural
     Education. Austin, Texas. Washington, D.C.: Office of Education.
     40 pp.
     (ED 062 845)

416. Muller, Douglas G. and Robert Leonetti. Primary Self-Concept
     Scale: Test Manual. Dissemination Center for Bilingual Bicultural
     Education. Austin, Texas. Washington, D.C.: Office of Education.
     39 pp.
     (ED 062 847)

     It is the purpose of the test described in this document to
     provide a procedure for economically evaluating several aspects of
     self-concept relevant to school success. The test was constructed
     specifically for use with the child of Spanish or Mexican descent
     in the southwest, but it is also appropriate for use with children
     from Anglo culture. The test consists of 24 items; in each item,
     the examinee is told a descriptive story about an illustration and
     is instructed to draw a circle around the person in the illustration
     that is most like himself. This document includes instructions
     for administering the test, the descriptive stories accompanying
     each test item, and details on scoring, interpretation, test con-
     struction, reliability, and validity. Statistical data and results
     are also included. (RIE)

417. Murray, Wayne Robert. Ethnic and Sex Differences as Related to
     Student Perceptions of a University Environment. Ph.D. Disser-
     tation, New Mexico State University. 1972.
     (ED 065 208)

418. Dissemination Center for Bilingual Bicultural Education. Austin, Texas.
     Washington, D.C: Office of Education.

     This series of instruments is designed to measure how very
     young students feel about Mexican-American and Anglo cultures. The
     test is based on pictures, some of which are culturally relevant
     only to Mexican-Americans. The manual provides a guide for the
     use of the inventory, including a rationale for the items used;
     a statement of the purpose of the test; instructions for adminis-
     tration; instructions for scoring results; and possible applications
     within the constraints of the test. (from document)

419. Ramirez, Manuel, III. Effects of Cultural Marginality on Education
     and Personality. Albuquerque, New Mexico: Southwestern Coope-
     rative Educational Laboratory. 1970. 15 pp.
     (ED 065 805)

     A review of the literature, this report concerns itself with the
     identification of the Mexican-American with his ethnic group as an
     asset or a liability. Examining the relationship of cultural mar-
     ginality to education, personality, and attitudes, the author points
     out a need for additional research in this area. (RIE)

92

420. Ramirez, Manuel, III. <u>Value Conflicts Experienced by Mexican-American Students</u>. 1968. 11pp.

The object of this study, conducted in a Northern California city school district, was to find evidence of cultural value conflicts experienced by Mexican-American secondary school students of low socioeconomic background. Those students experiencing the most difficulty in adjusting to the school setting and, thus, most likely to be dropouts, were interviewed, observed in class, and asked to tell stories about pictures depicting students, teachers and parents interacting in a school setting. Stories told about these pictures revealed Mexican-American value conflicts in terms of such factors as loyalty to family and ethnic group, female modesty, machismo, the role of education, and separation of sex roles. This paper contains discussions of eight Mexican-American values found to conflict most often with the value system of schools, along with an accompanying story for each as told by Mexican-American students; also contained are one-paragraph discussions of four measures that could be instituted to help alleviate value conflicts. (RIE)

421. Roca, Pablo. "The Construction of an Interest Inventory for Students of Different Linguistic and Cultural Backgrounds." <u>Journal of Educational Research</u>. Vol. 48 (November 1954). pp. 229-231.

422. Schwartz, Audrey James. "A Comparative Study of Values and Achievement: Mexican-American and Anglo Youth." <u>Sociology of Education</u>. Vol. 44 (Fall 1971). pp. 438-462.

Several value orientations and their relations with school achievement were examined with student samples from the Los Angeles City Schools. Findings show that Mexican-American pupils with value orientation most similar to those of Anglo pupils have the highest scholastic achievement. While it is recognized that pupils' values and achievements are substantially interdependent, the findings of this study suggest that affective factors in the cultural background of many Mexican-American pupils hinder their general academic achievement. (author)

423. "Student Strikes in East Los Angeles High Schools." <u>School and Society</u>. Vol. 100 (March 1972). pp. 182-185.

424. Tindall, Lloyd W. and others. <u>An Examination of the Receptivity of Mexican-American and Anglo Rural Disadvantaged to Education Programs</u>. Michigan State University. East Lansing, Michigan. Center for Rural Manpower and Public Affairs. March 1972. 34 pp. (ED 060 974)

425. Wilson, Alfred P. and others. <u>How Do You Feel About Things</u>? New Mexico State University. Las Cruces, New Mexico. Paper presented at the Annaul Meeting of the Rocky Mountain Educational Research Association. Boulder, Colorado. October 1971. 5 pp. (ED 058 281)

This 60-item questionnaire is designed to measure attitudes toward school among sixth grade Spanish American students. The respondents mark their answers on a 1 to 5, true to false continuum. Administration instructions are included.

F.  Linguistic Studies and the Measurement of Language Competence in Bilingual Children

General Discussions

426.  Alatis, James E., ed.  Report of the Nineteenth Annual Round Table: Contrastive Linguistics and Its Pedagogical Implications. Washington, D.C.: Georgetown University Press. 1968.

Discussions of contrastive analysis and lapsed time, the use of models in contrastive linguistics, contrastive analysis in discourse structure, and contrastive analysis and the notions of deep surface grammar. (NYS Bibliography)

427.  Allen, Harold B.  Linguistics and English Linguistics.  A Bibliography. New York: Appleton-Century-Crofts. 1966.

An unannotated, selective listing of books and articles.  Major divisions include bibliographies, dictionaries, linguistics, English language and English linguistics, language instruction and special topics.  (JH)

428.  Allen, Harold B., ed.  Readings in Applied English Linguistics, 2nd Edition. New York: Appleton-Century-Crofts. 1964. (paper)

A collection of 62 articles representative of current linguistic thought and applications, this anthology is a companion to Allen's Teaching English as a Second Language and includes coverage of transformational grammar and linguistic applications to reading, writing, speaking and listening. (NYS Bibliography)

429.  Andersson, Theodore.  "A New Focus on the Bilingual Child." Modern Language Journal.  Vol. 49 (1965).  pp. 156-160.

430.  Anisfeld, Moshe.  "Psycholinguistic Perspectives on Language Learning." in Albert Valdman, Trends in Language Teaching.  New York: McGraw-Hill. 1966

Discusses the nature of linguistic competence in terms of specific habits and general rules (non-introspective) and the psychological processes in language acquisition. (NYS Bibliography)

431.  Arapoff, Nancy. "Writing, a Thinking Process." TESOL Quarterly. Vol. 1 (June 1967).

Explains why teaching writing is different from teaching other language skills.  Presents a new method for teaching writing: an approach involving "transformations" in narration, paraphrase, summary, factual analysis, argumentative analysis, evaluation of arguments, and critical review.  (JH)

432. Barrows, Sarah T. "Speech Habits of the Foreign Child." Grade
     Teacher. Vol. 49 (February 1932), pp. 446-470; (April 1932),
     pp. 614-650.

433. Bever, Thomas and others. Linguistic Capacity of Very Young
     Children. 1968. 16 pp.
     (ED 018 796)

     Basic linguistic capacity is present extremely early in chil-
     dren. Two-year olds understand transitive active sentences and three
     year olds understand many passive sentences. The latter understand
     some sentences less well than the former. This brief decrease in
     comprehension ability is due to the temporary over-generalization
     of perceptual strategies which are drawn from the child's experience.
     This research indicates that the young child's capacity to under-
     stand and act out simple sentences goes through stages: 1, depen-
     dence on basic perceptual and conceptual mechanisms; 2, extension of
     these mechanisms by generalizations drawn from experience; and 3,
     development of a broad conceptual base which mediates between the
     basic mechanisms and the generalizations. (RIE)

434. Bracy, Maryruth. "Controlled Writing vs. Free Composition." TESOL
     Quarterly. Vol. 5 (September 1971). pp. 239-246.

     The purpose of this paper is to offer some suggestions for
     those who have tried to tackle the area of free (or advanced) com-
     position. The suggestions, based on a review of the literature and
     my experience in teaching composition courses at UCLA, center around
     the following three areas: 1, the revision of current classes in
     intermediate English so as to teach free composition instead of
     merely advanced controlled writing; 2, the unwanted and partially-
     opened Pandora's box of composition correction coupled with the
     question of what students do with the 'corrected' compositions to
     affect change and improvement in their writing techniques and use
     of language; and 3, the improvement of the over-all composition-
     teaching approach. (author)

435. Brooks, Nelson. Language and Language Learning: Theory and Practice.
     New York: Harcourt, Brace and World. 1964.

     Presenting the audiolingual method, this work is easy to read
     and covers many helpful topics: mother tongue and second language,
     language teaching, language and culture, language and literature,
     etc. (NYS Bibliography)

436. Brown, T. Grant. "In Defense of Pattern Practice." Language
     Learning. Vol. 19 (December 1969).

     Even though transformational grammar has shown the inadequacy
     of the pattern concept and behaviorist theories have been shown to
     be unable to account for first language acquisition, pattern prac-
     tice still seems to be of vital importance to students of foreign

96

languages. (NYS Bibliography)

437. Burt, Kim and Carol Kiparsky. <u>Gooficon - Common Errors in Spoken English.</u> Rowley, Massachusetts: Newbury House Publishers. 1972. $4.50.

Contains a broad sampling of speech errors made by speakers of other languages and arranged on the basis of errors that fall together structurally. The goal is to provide a practical guide to enable teachers to identify and treat errors made by non-native speakers of English. Each chapter provides the teacher with a summary of each type of error, an analysis of the error, and rules-of-thumb for correcting the faulty habits. (JH)

438. Calderon, C.I. "Seeing Sounds." <u>Texas Outlook</u>. Vol. 38 (October 1954). pp. 12-13.

439. Carroll, John B. "A Primer of Programmed Instruction of Foreign Language Teaching." <u>International Review of Applied Linguistics</u>. Vol. 1 (Special Issue, 1963). Reprints available from MLA.

A general introduction to methods of programmed instruction and its application to the teaching of foreign languages. (NYS Bibliography)

440. Carroll, John B. "Current Issues in Psycholinguistics and Second Language Teaching." <u>TESOL Quarterly</u>. Vol. 5 (June 1971). pp. 101-114.

It is urged that there is no real conflict between the audio-lingual habit and cognitive code learning theories as applied to language teaching. It is false to make an opposition between rule-governed behavior and language habits. The notion of habit is, however, more general than that of rule, and is not as conceptually inadequate as sometimes claimed. The learning of second languages requires both the acquisition of knowledge about rules and the formation of habits described by these rules. Language teaching procedures can be improved by application of psychological knowledge concerning the learning of language habits. It is stressed that situational meaning must be incorporated into language rules where it is applicable, and that the corresponding language habits must be made contingent upon these situational meanings. (author)

441. Carroll, John B. "The Contributions of Psychological Theory and Educational Research to the Teaching of Foreign Languages." in Albert Valdman, ed., <u>Trends in Language Teaching</u>. New York: McGraw-Hill. 1966.

Makes the proposal that specialists, analogous to agricultural county agents in their role, be employed to work with teachers by disseminating ideas, principles and materials from educational research. It points out the present problems that by and large prevent such contributions from finding use in the classroom. (NYS Bibliography)

442. Carrow, M.A. "Linguistic Functioning of Bilingual and Monolingual Children." _Journal of Speech and Hearing Disorders_. Vol. 22 (1957). pp. 371-380.

443. Catford, J.C. _A Linguistic Theory of Translation: An Essay in Applied Linguistics_. London: Oxford University Press. 1965.

    Sets up a theory of translation which may be drawn upon in any discussion of particular translation problems. Discusses phonological, graphological, grammatical and lexical translation as well as transliteration, translation shifts, language varieties in translation and the limits of translatability. (NYS Bibliography)

444. _Conference on Child Language. (Chicago, Illinois. November 22-24, 1971) Preprints_. Laval University, Quebec. International Center on Bilingualism. 1971. 530 pp. (ED 060 931)

445. Cooper, Robert and Lawrence Greenfield. "Word Frequency Estimation as a Measure of Degree of Bilingualism." _Modern Language Journal_. March 1969. pp. 163-166.

    The purpose of this study was to determine the utility of a word frequency estimation task as a measure of degree of bilingualism. Ss were 48 Puerto Ricans, age 13 or older, living in a Puerto Rican neighborhood in Jersey City, New Jersey. The procedure involved having a subject rate 75 commonly used English and Spanish words in terms of frequency that he had heard it or said it. Results showed that greater use of Spanish than English words was associated with greater facility in speaking Spanish than speaking English, use of Spanish more than English at home, greater word production in Spanish, a predominance of Spanish accent and use of fewer speech styles in speaking English. (ECK)

446. DiPietro, Robert J. _Bilingualism and Bidialectalism_. Paper presented at the 1970 Spring Institute on Teaching English as a Second Language and as a Second Dialect. Tallahassee, Florida. February 13-17, 1970. 15 pp. (ED 061 824)

447. Ervin, Susan. "Second Language Learning and Bilingualism." in C.E. Osgood, _Psycholinguistics: A Survey of Theory and Research Problems_. Baltimore, Maryland: Waverly Press, Inc. 1954. pp. 139-146.

448. Ervin, Susan M. "Semantic Shift in Bilingualism." _American Journal of Psychology_. Vol. 74 (June 1961). pp. 233-241.

449. Ferguson, Charles A. _Aspects of the Acquisition of English and Spanish Phonology_. Stanford University. California Commission

98

on Linguistics. 47 pp. (research proposal)
(ED 060 937)

450. Fishman, Joshua A. <u>Bilingual and Bidialectical Education: An Attempt</u>
<u>at a Joint Model for Policy Description</u>. In "Conference on Child
Language " preprints of papers presented at the Conference. Chi-
cago, Illinois. November 22-24, 1971. pp. 356-367.
(ED 060 751)

This paper questions whether the same theoretical model of educational policy decisions can be used for bilingual as well as bidialectical education. Three basic policies are discussed, first in
applications for second language learning and then in the field of
teaching a second dialect. Generally speaking, the same theoretical
models are applicable to both educational problems with variation in
administrative units between the two levels. (RIE)

451. Fishman, Joshua A. <u>Bilingual Education in Sociolinguistic Perspective</u>.
1970. 14 pp.
(ED 040 404)

Presents four broad categories of bilingual programs: 1, transitional bilingualism (until English skills develop); 2, monoliterate
bilingualism (oral-aural skills in both languages, literacy skills
only in English); 3, practical bilingualism (fluency and literacy in
both languages but use of mother tongue restricted to the ethnic
group and its heritage); and 4, full bilingualism (all skills in both
languages in all domains). Vitally needed are: 1, a survey establishing language and varieties employed by both parents and children,
by societal domain of function; 2, a rough estimate of the relative
performance level in each language, by societal domain; 3, an indication of community and school staff attitudes toward the existing
situation; and 4, an indication of community and school staff attitudes toward changing the existing situation. (RIE)

452. Fishman, Joshua A. <u>Language and Nationalism</u>. Rowley, Massachusetts:
Newbury House Publishers. 1972. $7.15.

Offers the results of a unique examination of nationalistic
influences in language planning. The guiding influences behind the
study are the social movements, attitudes, and ideologies which con-
strained and influenced nationalist planners and builders across
time and across nations. One result is a comprehensive study of
socio-historical, linguistic, and cross-national aspects relating to
language planning; another is an attempt to generate empirically
confirmable hypotheses from historical incidents spanning centuries
and continents. (catalogue)

453. Fishman, Joshua A., ed. <u>Language Loyalty in the United States</u>. The
Hague [Netherlands]: Mouton. 1966.

454. Fishman, Joshua A. "The Measurement and Description of Widespread
and Relatively Stable Bilingualism." <u>Modern Language Journal</u>.

March 1969. pp. 152-156.

The purpose of this article is to reiterate for the reader the
goals of the study Bilingualism in the Barrio and to promote better
understanding of them.  In the first section, Fishman explains what
the sociolinguist's goals are when studying a bilingual community.
The second section shows that the sociolinguists is interested in how
and when one language is used instead of another.  In the third section, the author describes the "usage of speech networks that utilize both standard and non-standard varieties of English."  In the
last section, he describes the samples used for the study and the
methods of collecting data.  (ECK)

455.  Fishman, Joshua A.  "Sociolinguistic Perspective on the Study of
          Bilingualism."  Linguistics.  Vol. 39 (1968).  pp. 21-49.

456.  Fishman, Joshua A.  Sociolinguistics:  A Brief Introduction.  Rowley,
          Massachusetts:  Newbury House Publishers. 1971.  $3.50.  (paper)

          An overview of the influences society has on language learning
and on maintaining a language.  Some kinds of linguistic behavior
are favorable to upward mobility; others are not.  Provides information about the varieties of language behavior in different communities.  (catalogue)

457.  Fishman, Joshua A.  The Sociology of Language.  Rowley, Massachusetts:
          Newbury House Publishers.  1971.  $6.95.

          Calling upon techniques and concepts of linguistics, sociology,
psychology, anthropology, and social psychology, the author presents
an interdisciplinary introduction to students of language and society
whose interests are primarily macrosociological and related to social
problems as well as to social theory.  (catalogue)

458.  Fishman, Joshua A.  "The Status and Prospects of Bilingualism in the
          United States."  Modern Language Journal.  Vol. 49 (1965).  pp.
          143-155.

          Cultural pluralism may determine the success of this country.
Discusses bilingualism and biculturalism.  Suggests that a commission
on bilingualism/biculturalism be established at the Federal, State
and local levels.

459.  Fishman, Joshua A.  "Who Speaks What Language to Whom and When?"
          Linguistique.  No. 2 (1965).  pp. 67-78.

460.  Fishman, Joshua A. and Robert Cooper.  "Alternative Measures of
          Bilingualism."  Journal of Verbal Learning and Verbal Behavior.
          Vol. 8 (1969).  pp. 276-282.

461.  Fishman, Joshua A. and John Lovas.  "Bilingual Education in Socio-
          linguistic Perspective."  TESOL Quarterly.  Vol. 4 (September

1970). pp. 215-222.

One of the avowed purposes of bilingual education is the maintenance and development of linguistic and cultural diversity.  The
authors believe that realistic societal information is needed for
realistic educational goals.  This information, which goes beyond
that normally available in school record and county census data, is
here described and presented as an aid in deciding what kind of
bilingual program to establish.  Four broad categories of bilingualism (transitional, monoliterate, partial, and full) are defined and
discussed in terms of their societal implications.  (author)

462.  Fishman, J.A. and Vladimir C. Nahirny.  "The Ethnic Group School and
      Mother Tongue Maintenance in the U.S."  Sociology of Education.
      Vol. 37 (1964).  pp. 306-317.

463.  Fraser, Bruce.  Non-Standard English.  1970.  22 pp.
      (ED 045 960)

      The present paper reviews recent research in the area of non-
standard English:  the major results to date, the significance of
this research for education, and suggestions for further research.
The notion of "standard" English resists definition; there is not
a simple set of linguistic features which can be said to define it.
A dialect may be classified from at least four points of view, according to 1, whether the speaker learned English as his first
language, or second or third; 2, the region of the U.S. where the
language was learned; 3, the cultural composition of the speech
community; and 4, the socioeconomic status (SES) of the speech
community.  A dialect may reflect all of these classifying labels.
The effect of SES on a speaker's dialect is not absolute presence
or absence of certain linguistic features but rather the relative
frequency of these features.  Speech style is distinguished from
social dialect.  (RIE)

464.  Friedlander, George H.  Report on the Articulatory and Intelligi-
      bility Status of Socially Disadvantaged Preschool Children.
      Institute for Retarded Children of Shield of David.  New York.
      December 1965.
      (ED 014 321)

465.  Fries, Charles C.  The Structure of English:  An Introduction to
      the Construction of English Sentences.  New York:  Harcourt,
      Brace, and Company.  1952.

      Does not deal with "grammar of usage" - language differences
according to social level - but with "grammar of structure" - the
systematic description of syntax patterns.  The analysis is based
on fifty hours of recorded conversations.  (JH)

466.  George, H.V.  Common Errors in Language Learning.  Rowley, Mass.:
      Newbury House Publishers.  1971.  $4.95.  (paper)

Provides basic guidelines for the causes and prevention of students' errors in foreign language learning. Incorporates a modern theory of language learning pedagogy based on the errors made by learners of a second language. Presupposes no previous linguistic training on the part of the reader. (catalogue)

467. Gudschinsky, Sarah C. <u>Literacy in the Mother Tongue and Second Language Learning</u>. In "Conference on Child Language." preprints of papers presented at the Conference. Chicago, Illinois. November 22-24, 1971. pp. 341-355. (ED 060 753)

Bilingual educations programs which foster literacy first in the mother tongue and then in the second language, before the second language is used as a medium of instruction, are proving to be successful in a number of locations around the world. Such programs encourage community understanding and support, minimize the culture shock for the child entering school, augment the child's sense of personal worth and identity, develop the child's habit of academic success, and utilize the child's fluency in his own language in learning the skills of reading and writing. Conscious control of one's own language facilitates the learning of a second language in the formal school setting. New ideas can be introduced in the mother tongue; reading ability facilitates the learning of a second language. In such bilingual programs, literacy in the mother tongue is followed immediately by learning to read and write in the second language. (RIE)

468. Gumperz, John J. "Linguistic and Social Interaction in Two Communities." <u>American Anthropologist</u>. Vol. 66 (December 1964). pp. 137-153.

469. Gumperz, John J. "On the Linguistic Markers of Bilingual Education." <u>Journal of Social Issues</u>. Vol. 23 (April 1967). pp. 48-58.

470. Hall, Robert A., Jr. <u>Linguistics and Your Language</u>. 2nd revised edition of <u>Leave Your Languae Alone</u>. Garden City, New York: Doubleday. 1960.

A brief, popular discussion relative to language and linguistics. Contains clear, non-technical statement of theories, principles, and methods. (JH)

471. Halliday, M.A.K.; Agnes McIntosh, and Peter Strevers. <u>The Linguistic Sciences and Language Teaching</u>. Bloomington: Indiana University Press. 1964.

A study of the application of modern linguistics to problems of language teaching. The linguistic theory embodied is mostly derived and developed from the works of Firth. The applications cited are largely directed towards ESL teaching. Provides valuable insights into the nature and structure of English. (NYS Bibliography)

472. Hammer, John H. and Frank A. Rice, eds. A Bibliography of Contrastive Linguistics. Washington, D.C.: Center for Applied
Linguistics. 1965. (paper)

An unannotated list, alphabetical by language, of contrastive
structure studies. Includes books, theses and dissertations, articles, etc. Majority of entries deal with English as one of
languages treated. (NYS Bibliography)

473. Hammers, Josiane F. and Wallace E. Lambert. "Bilingual Inter-
dependencies in Auditory Perceptions." Journal of Verbal
Learning and Verbal Behavior. Vol. 11 (June 1972). pp. 303-
310.
(EJ 059 241)

474. Harris, M.B. and W.G. Hassemer. "Some Factors Affecting the Complexity of Children's Sentences: The Effects of Modeling, Age,
Sex, and Bilingualism." Journal of Experimental Child Psychology. Vol. 13 (June 1972). pp. 447-455.
(EJ 060 780)

475. Haugen, Elinar. "Problems of Bilingualism." Lingua. Vol.2
(August 1950).

Social pressure becomes language pressure when one moves from
one linguistic community to another. Linguistic conformity takes
place when the learner has acclimated himself to the new environment.
This article points out that the bilingual, in the process of learning, goes from "erratic substitution" to "systematic substitution"
as he becomes more proficient in the new language. (JH)

476. Hess, Karen and John Maxwell. What to Do about Non-Standard
Dialects: A Review of the Literature. 1969. 52 pp.
(ED 041 027)

This paper, resulting from a comprehensive search of the literature on dialects and dialect learning from 1960-1969, sets forth
some of the major ideas, points of view and recommendations in the
following categories: 1, responsibility of the school to recognize
and accept different varieties of the English language; 2, early
research on "correcting" usage "errors;" 3, descriptive dialect
studies (regional, ethnic, social); 4, effects of non-standard
usage on learning to read, social status, etc.; 5, descriptions of
current programs; 6, what teachers should know to deal with non-
standard usage; and 7, teacher preparation and classroom practices.
Extensive bibliography and glossary of terms included. (RIE)

477. Hughes, M.M. and G.I. Sanchez. Learning a New Language. Washington,
D.C.: Association for Childhood Education International. 1958.

478. Hymes, Dell. "Models of Interaction of Language and Social Setting."
Journal of Social Issues. Vol. 23 (April 1967). pp. 8-28.

479. Jakobovits, Leon A. Foreign Language Learning: A Psycholinguistic ·
Analysis of the Issues. Rowley, Mass.: Newbury House. 1970.

A critical examination of psycholinguistic implications and
psychological and physiological aspects of foreign language
learning, compensatory foreign language instruction, problems
in the assessment of language learning, and foreign language
aptitude and attitude testing. Presents an approach that, the
author contends, is adaptable to any methods the teacher currently
uses to understand and take into account the strategies of the
learner. (NYS Bibliography)

480. Jakobovits, Leon A. "Implications of Recent Psycholinguistic
Developments for the Teaching of a Second Language,"
Language Learning, 18:1 and 2 (June, 1968).

Psycholinguistic theory emphasizes the developmental nature
of the language acquisition process; limitation, practice,
reinforcement, and generalization are no longer considered
theoretically productive concepts in acquisition. Points out
the implications of this principle for second language teaching:
"transformation exercises" at the phonological, syntactic and
semantic levels. (NYS Bibliography)

481. Jakobovits, Leon A. "The Psychological Bases of Second Language
Learning." Language Sciences. No. 14 (February, 1971).
pp. 22-28.
(EJ 042 819)

482. Jensen, J.V. "Effects of Childhood Bilingualism." Elementary
English Vol. 39 (1962). Part I, pp. 132-149

This is the first of two articles reviewing the effects of
childhood bilingualism. Some of the negative results discussed
are 1) handicaps to speech development, such as sounds, stress and
rhythm; 2) disadvantages in language development, such as
vocabulary and confused structural patterns; 3) handicaps in
intellectual development, especially for children with only
superficial knowledge of one language or lacking superior
intellectual ability; 4) retardation in educational progress, in
reading and studying generally and in specific subjects; and
5) emotional instability and social maladjustment because of his
problems in communication. The author also discusses some
deleterious effects of bilingualism on society, from the family
to nations. The bibliography for both articles is included. (ECK)

483. Jensen, J.V. "Effects of Childhood Bilingualism." Elementary
English Vol. 39 (1962). Part II, pp. 358-366.

The first part of this article offers evidence which is
contrary to that presented in the previous article. Some
researchers have found that bilingualism has no serious adverse

effects on speech and language development, that bilingualism does
not obstruct, and may actually help, educational achievement.
Research which contradicts findings that bilingualism can result
in emotional problems and conflicts in society is also discussed.
The second part of the article notes recommended attitudes for
parents, the elementary school and the public in order to understand and handle bilingualism better. The third section evaluates
the literature used for the article, with specific observations
about subjects, methodology and investigators. (ECK)

484. Johnson, Francis C. "The Failure of the Discipline of Linguistics
in Language Teaching," Language Learning, 19:3 and 4
(December, 1969).

According to the author, even though linguistics is one of the
prime variables in language pedagogy, recent concern with it has
overshadowed the learning and teaching discipline which,
accordingly, has fallen behind the times. (NYS Bibliography)

485. Johnson, L.W. "A Comparison of the Vocabularies of Anglo-
American and Spanish-American High School Pupils."
Journal of Educational Psychology. Vol. 29 (1938). pp. 135-144

486. Kintsch, Walter. "Interlingual Interference and Memory Processes."
Journal of Verbal Learning and Verbal Behavior. Vol. 8
(1969). pp. 16-19

487. Kinzel, Paul. Lexical and Grammatical Interference in the Speech
of a Bilingual Child, 1967, 116 pp.
(ED 029 273)

The spontaneous speech of a six-year-old bilingual child was
analyzed for this study. Grammatical and lexical interference
was shown to occur in both languages however the child does not
show any evidence of phonological interference in either language.
The author concludes that, in spite of considerable lexical and
grammatical interference, there is no evidence of a merger of
lexicons or grammatical structures. The author also feels that
these observations illustrate the validity and completeness of the
theoretical framework developed by Uriel Weinrich in Languages
in Contact. (RIE)

488. Koutsoudas, Andreas and Olympia Koutsoudas. "A Contrastive
Analysis of the Segmental Phonemes of Greek and English."
Language Learning, 12:3 (1962).

While specifically concerned with the problems that arise in
teaching English pronunciation to native speakers of Greek, this
paper provides an insight into the larger problem of language
learning and suggests some empirical solutions through the use of
contrastive analysis. (NYS Bibliography)

489. Krear, Serafina. <u>Development of Pre-Reading Skills in a Second Language or Dialect</u>. In "Conference on Child Language." preprints of papers presented at the Conference, Chicago, Illinois, November 22-24, 1971. p. 241-263. (ED 060 754)

   The bilingual education program in a given community should be based on a sociolinguistic assessment of that community, and community members should be involved in assessing the surrounding bilingual reality and in deciding whether they wish to mirror that reality in the biliteracy program. This paper presents alternatives for bilingual programs based on the nature and objectives of the community. The program models presented illustrate the relative use of the native language or dialect and the second language or dialect in areas of concept development, prereading skills, written and oral language development, and reading instruction. (RIE)

490. Lado, Robert. <u>Linguistics Across Cultures: Applied Linguistics for Language Teachers</u>. Ann Arbor, Mich.: University of Michigan Press. 1957. (paper)

   Uses non-technical vocabulary in demonstrating the role that descriptive linguistics can play in a language-teaching situation. Compares sound systems, grammatical structures, vocabulary systems and cultural patterns. (NYS Bibliography)

491. Lambert, Wallace E. "Measurement of the Linguistic Dominance of Bilinguals," <u>Journal of Abnormal and Social Psychology</u>. Vol. 50, no. 2 (March, 1955). pp. 197-200.

492. Lambert, Wallace. "Psychological Approaches to the Study of Language, Part I: On Learnings, Thinking and Human Abilities." <u>Modern Language Journal</u>. Vol. 47 (1963). pp. 51-62

493. Lambert, Wallace. "Psychological Approaches to the Study of Language, Part II: On Second Language Learning and Bilingualism." <u>Modern Language Journal</u>. Vol. 47 (1963).

494. Lambert, Wallace. "A Social Psychology of Bilingualism." <u>Journal of Social Issues</u>. 23:2 (1967). pp. 91-110

495. Lambert, Wallace and Chris Rawlings. "Bilingual Processing of Mixed-Language Association Networks." <u>Journal of Verbal Learning and Verbal Behavior</u>. Vol. 8 (1969). pp. 604-609.

496. Lambert, W.E. and G.R. Tucker. <u>Tu, Vous, Usted</u>. Rowley, Massachusetts: Newbury House Publishers. 1972. $5.50 (paper).

   When to be formal, when not? The way we choose to address another determines very clearly how we rank him socially. This book tells the story of how the authors examined the use of the familiar and the unfamiliar in spoken French and Spanish, and the revealing tests they made of the usages. (catalog)

497. Lefevre, Carl A. Linguistics and the Teaching of Reading. New York: McGraw-Hill 264 pp.

   Presents the fundamentals of structural linguistics, the study of language as it is spoken. The sound system of American English is described accurately from the smallest to the largest unit, since speech is considered basic to all language learning. A special chapter dealing with the musical qualities of spoken English is quite comprehensive. (NYS Bibliography)

498. Leopold, Werner F. "Speech Development of a Bilingual Child." Four Volumes. Evanston, Ill.: Northwestern University Press, 1939-1950.

499. Levinsky, Frieda L. Research on Bilingualism. March 1972. 74 pp. (ED 062 839)

   This discussion of bilingualism and second language learning concerns many linguistic considerations that figure in the problem of language instruction. The motor reports on current research and on the ideas of several noted linguists. Topics considered in this study are the goals of the bilingual education program, reasons for becoming bilingual, a definition of bilingualism, bilingual dominance and balance, types of bilingualism, bilingual barriers, second language study, two kinds of language learning theories, the effective teacher, and test validity. Included also are reports of observations in bilingual classroom observations. The summary from a national survey of linguistic methodology is provided along with a bibliography. (RIE)

500. Levinsky, Frieda L. Theory and Practice of Bilingualism. (1970). 39pp. (Ed 056 554)

501. Lieberson, Stanley. "Residence and Language Maintenance in a Multilingual City." South African Journal of Sociology. Vol. 1, No. 1 (November 1970). p. 13-22. (ED 055 465)

502. Lynn, K. "Bilingualism in the Southwest." Quarterly Journal of Speech. Vol. 31 (April 1945) pp. 175-180.

503. Mackey, William F. Free Language Alternation in Early Childhood Education. In "Conference on Child Language." preprints of papers presented at the conference, Chicago, Illinois, November 22-24, 1971. p. 396-432. (ED 060 755)

At the root of many early childhood bilingual education programs is the widespread belief that the two languages must be used and taught in different contexts, since the failure to do so would inevitably produce a single mixed language. From a study of the results achieved over a ten-year period, it would seem that, if at least one of the languages of the pre-school child is secure as a medium of communication, free language alternation in early childhood education can be used with mixed language populations as a means to promote bilingualism in the kindergarten and primary grades. The language program described in this report encourages free alternation between English and German on the part of teachers and students alike. The force dominating and determining the language alternation is the need to communicate and the desire to please. (RIE)

504. Macnamara, John. "The Bilingual's Linguistic Performance--a Psychological Overview." <u>Journal of Social Issues</u>. Vol. 23, No. 2 (April 1967). pp. 58-77.

505. Macnamara, John. "How Can One Measure the Extent of a Person's Bilingual Proficiency?" in <u>Preprints</u>, International Seminar on the Description and Measurement of Bilingualism, Ottawa: Canadian National Commission for UNESCO, 1967, pp. 68-90.

506. Macnamara, John, Marcel Krauthammer and Marianne Bolgar. "Language Switching in Bilinguals as a Function of Stimulus and Response Uncertainty." <u>Journal of Experimental Psychology</u>. Vol. 78 (1968). pp. 28-215.

The purpose of this study was to measure the speed of language switching. Ss were French-English bilingual college students who were either English-speaking with some knowledge of French, French-speaking with some knowledge of English or equally qualified in both languages. Ss were required to perform various tasks dealing with the naming of numbers. Findings showed that language switching takes an observable amount of time, that the time can be reduced if the bilingual is able to anticipate a switch. In comparison with an equivalent bilingual task, it is concluded that this type of language switching is not a psychological skill particular to bilingualism, but can be applied in a large number of operations in which it is necessary to switch modes of response rapidly. Some theoretical implications of these findings are also discussed. (ECK)

507. Marckwardt, Albert H. & Randolf Quirk. <u>A Common Language.</u> MLA-ACTFL Materials Center. 1964. 79pp. $2.50.

The script for 12 broadcasts over the Voice of American and the BBC. Lively discussion of the varieties of English spoken in different countries with the thesis that they are mutually understandable and equally good. (catalog)

508. Marckwardt, Albert H. The Relationship Between TESOL and the Center for Applied Linguistics. Paper presented at the Sixth Annual TESOL Convention. Washington, D.C., February 29, 1972. (ED 064 997)

509. Marquardt, William F. "The Tenth International Congress of Linguistics: Implications for Teaching English as a Second Language," TESOL Newsletter, 2:1 and 2 (January-March 1968).

 Notes that within the area of language study, syntactics, semantics and pragmatics have received much attention but that the "study of ways of bringing about competence in new language behavior" have received very little. Contends that the model the language learner should use ought not to be that of the linguist, but rather a fusion of it with that of the sociologist, the psychologist and the anthropoligist. Notes five major trends that may point up skills and techniques of possible use to teachers in the field. (NYS Bibliography)

510. Meyerson, Marion. "The Bilingual Child." Childhood Education. Vol. 45 (1969). pp. 525-527.

511. Morrison, J.R. "Bilingualism: Some Psychological Aspects." Advancement of Science. Vol. 14 (1958). pp. 287-290.

512. Moulton, William G. A Linguistic Guide to Language Learning. New York: Modern Language Association of America, 1966. (paper)

 A clear introduction to the principles of language learning and how language works, including sections on sounds, sentences, words, meaning and writing. Bibliography of useful books on linguistics, phonetics, contrastive structure and language learning. (NYS Bibliography)

513. Nedler, Shari. "Language, the Vehicle; Culture, the Content." Journal of Research and Development in Education. 4:4 (Summer, 1971). pp. 3-9. (EJ 044 589)

514. Ney, James W. "The Oral Approach: A Reappraisal," Language Learning, 18:1 and 2, (June, 1968).

 Discussed criticisms of audio-lingual approach by psychologists and transformational linguists, discriminating between those that are justified and those which are not. Suggests that many objectives have been anticipated by language teachers who have not been too doctrinaire. (NYS Bibliography)

515. Ney, James W. "Two Neglected Factors in Language Comparison." Modern Language Journal. 48:3 (1964).

 Suggests that pedagogically oriented contrastive studies

109

should take into account the forms that result from false analogy
as well as the frequency of occurrence of structures in the target
language. (NYS Bibliography)

516.  Nichols, Paul E.  A Study of the Cooperative Inter-American Tests of
      Language Usage at the Junior High School Level.  Unpublished
      Master's thesis, University of Texas.  1952.

517.  Nida, Eugene.  Learning a Foreign Language.  New York:  Free Press,
      Foreign Missions Conference of North America.  1957.  (revised
      edition)

      A guide for individual language study written from the point
of view of modern descriptive linguistics though with a minimum of
techinical vocabulary.  (JH)

518.  Paulston, Christina Bratt.  "The Sequencing of Structural Pattern
      Drills."  TESOL Quarterly.  Vol. 5 (September 1971).  pp. 197-
      208.

      This article is an attempt to re-examine the role and function
of structural pattern drills in language learning.  The first part
of the paper seeks to examine the relevant literature pertaining to
drills in order to 1) bring together some of the major references
for examining areas of concord and disagreement and 2) to consider
the implications for language teaching.  The second part of the
paper proposes a theoretical classification of structural pattern
·drills, incorporating the implications found relevant, in order to
allow a sequencing of drills which will provide a more efficient
working model for the classroom.  (author)

519.  Politzer, Robert L.  "Some Reflections on Pattern Practice."  Modern
      Language Journal.  Vol. 18 (1964).

      Discusses advantages and disadvantages of pattern practice while
cautioning that time devoted to thorough drilling necessarily limits
number of structures taught.  (NYS Bibliography)

520.  Politzer, Robert L.  "Toward Psycholinguistic Models of Language
      Instruction."  TESOL Quarterly.  Vol. 2 (September 1968).

      Discusses the congruence and clash of psychological and
pedagogical principles in language teaching and the use of
linguistic and psychological principles as tools in the analysis
of the teaching process.  Analyzes typical lessons.  (NYS Bibliography)

521.  Reeback, Robert T.  "Range of Effectiveness as a Comprehensive
      Measure of Communication Skill."  Language Learning.  Vol. 21
      (June 1971).  pp. 97-106.
      (EJ 042 831)

      Earlier version of this paper was presented at the annual TESOL
convention in New Orleans, Louisiana in March 1971.  (CIJE)

522. Rice, Frank A. and Allene Guss.  Information Sources in Linguistics:
     A Bibliographical Handbook.  Washington, D.C.:  Center for
     Applied Linguistics.  1965.  (paper)

     A largely unannotated bibliography divided into sections on
fields within linguistics, linguistics and related disciplines,
applied linguistics, abstracts, classification systems and manpower.
(NYS Bibliography)

523. Richards, I.A. and Christine Gibson.  Techniques of Language Control.
     Rowley, Massachusetts:  Newbury House Publishers.  1971.  $5.95.

     Control of vocabulary and structure is widely held to be a
prime influence on language learning.  In this book the authors
describe their tested approach to limiting vocabulary and syntax
in the teaching of English.  Their techniques of language control
are introduced through Every Man's English, a new list of high
utility words for learning English and for clarity of expression.
(catalogue)

524. Richards, Jack C.  "A Non-Contrastive Approach to Error Analysis."
     English Language Teaching.  Vol. 25 (June 1971).  pp.  204-219.
     (EJ 042 873)

     Based on a paper presented at the TESOL convention in San
Francisco, California in March 1970.  (CIJE)

525. Richards, Jack C.  Social Aspects of Language Learning.  Paper
     presented at the Sixth Annual TESOL Convention.  Washington,
     D.C.  February 28, 1972.  22 pp.
     (ED 061 829)

526. Rivers, Wilga M.  The Psychologist and the Foreign-Language Teacher.
     Chicago:  University of Chicago Press.  1964.

     A critical appraisal of foreign language teaching today (in
particular the audio-lingual method) in the light of current psychology and theories of learning.  The book is written for the
classroom teacher and concentrates on the high school level, with
most examples from French.  Includes recommendations for the
teacher and an appendix describing learning theories.  (NYS Bibliography)

527. Rivers, Wilga M.  Speaking in Many Tongues:  Essays in Foreign
     Language Learning.  Rowley, Massachusetts:  Newbury House.
     1972.  $3.95.

     Considers problems such as student dissatisfaction with
structual language courses, motivation difficulties, individual
differences in means and goals of language learning, etc. and
makes concrete proposals toward solving them.  Guidelines are
established for development and evaluation of language programs,
new models of language teaching activities presented, and psycho-

logical insights discussed that will assist those involved in language teaching in assessing its meaning for today's students.
(catalogue)

528.  Roeming, Robert F. "Foreword: Bilingualism and the Bilingual
      Child--A Symposium." Modern Language Journal. Vol. 49 (March
      1965). p. 143.

529.  Ronch, Judah; Robert L. Cooper, and Joshua A. Fishman. "Word
      Naming and Usage Scores for a Sample of Yiddish-English
      Bilinguals." Modern Language Journal. Vol. 53 (1969).
      pp. 232-235.

      Reviewed the findings of a study using 8 male and 7 female
      European-born Jewish adults who had used Yiddish as children and
      who continued active use in the United States. Ss were 55-80
      years old, and had resided in the United States for 40-60 years.
      The societal domains measured were home, ethnic behavior, work,
      neighborhood, and Jewish cultural activities. A Word Naming test
      in English and Yiddish was administered, and analysis of variance
      revealed that the "ratio of English to Yiddish words named varied
      as a function of domains." Ss rated themselves as using most
      Yiddish in the Jewish cultural domain. Results indicate that the
      Ss used the most English in the home domain. Compared with ana-
      logous Puerto Ricans, the Yiddish-English bilinguals use more
      English in the home domain than do the Puerto Ricans." Older
      Puerto Ricans are still Spanish dominant at work and in church,
      but appear to be moving toward greater use of English in their
      homes. (PASAR/DH)

530.  Sableski, J.A., Ed. "A Selective Annotated Bibliography on
      Child Language." Linguistic Reporter. Vol. 7 (April 1965).

      A useful bibliography, almost alone in this area; some entries
      for bilingualism. (NYS Bibliography)

531.  Samuels, Marilyn; Allan G. Reynolds, and W.E. Lambert. "Communication
      Efficiency of Children Schooled in a Foreign Language." Journal
      of Educational Psychology. Vol. 60 (October 1969). pp. 389-
      393.

      English-speaking children who had received their first two
      years of instruction exclusively in French, for them a foreign
      language, were tested for communication skills in both English and
      French. One experiment examined their ability as decoders of novel
      information; a second, their proficiency as encoders. In both in-
      stances they were found to be as capable as matched control groups
      of monolingual children. Apparently young children instructed ex-
      clusively in a foreign language can apply abilities developed
      mainly through teacher-pupil interaction, to nonacademic peer-to-
      peer communication settings, with no decrement in material language
      performance. (authors)

532. Sánchez, G.I. "The Crux of the Dual Language Handicap." New Mexico School Review. March 1954. pp. 13-15, 38.

533. Sánchez, G.I. "The Implications of a Basal Vocabulary to the Measurement of the Abilities of Bilingual Children." Journal of Social Psychology. Vol. 5 (August 1934). pp. 395-402.

534. Schmidt-Mackey, Ilonka. Language Strategies of the Bilingual Family. In "Conference on Child Language." preprints of papers presented at the conference in Chicago, Illinois, November 22-24, 1971. pp. 85-118. (ED 060 740)

The subject of language learning of children in bilingual families is considered in this paper. The author discusses practical problems and provides examples from his own family situation in which his children learned French, English and German. The possibility of language mixture is discussed and the author presents some tentative conclusions about the usage of a particular language in a particular situation. If the situation is a natural one, it is likely to motivate the child to use the language of the situation. If the parents do not interfere or force the child to speak a given language in a given situation, the overall linguistic development of the child is likely to be normal. If the parents inconspicuously lead the child into natural contexts in which the probability of language switch is high, the full language learning potential of the situation will have its effect upon the children. (RIE)

535. Spolsky, Bernard. "Language Testing: The Problem of Validation." TESOL Quarterly. Vol. 2 (June 1968).

Discusses the differences between tests for control of instruction, and tests for control of a person's career and the serious difficulty of validation in the second class. (JH)

536. Spolsky, Bernard. "The Limits of Language Education." Linguistic Reporter. Vol. 13 (Summer 1971). pp. 1-5. (EJ 046 147)

537. Spolsky, Bernard and Wayne Holm. Bilingualism in the Six-Year-Old Navajo Child. In "Conference on Child Language." preprints of papers presented at the Conference, Chicago, Illinois, November 22-24, 1971. pp. 225-239. (ED 060 747)

538. Stageberg, Norman C. "Structual Ambiguity and the Suprasegmentals." English Record. Vol. 21 (April 1971). pp. 64-68. (EJ 047 665)

After teaching the basic suprasegmental patterns, an ESL teacher can profitably continue with those other patterns which are useful in distinguishing meanings and whose absence on the printed page will sometimes result in double meaning. (CIJE)

539. Swain, Merrill. Bilingualism, Monolingualism and Code Acquisition. In "Conference on Child Language." preprints of papers presented at the conference. Chicago, Illinois. November 22-24, 1971. pp. 209-224. (ED 060 748)

540. Tarone, Elaine E. A Suggested Unit for Interlingual Identification in Pronunciation. Paper presented at the Sixth Annual TESOL Convention. Washington, D.C. February 28, 1972. 11 pp. (ED 060 726)

541. Thonis, Eleanor. The Dual Language Process in Young Children. In "Conference on Child Language." preprints of papers presented at the conference. Chicago, Illinois. November 22-24, 1971. 15 pp. (ED 061 812)

Problems attributed to dual language learning in early childhood have been exaggerated and may be the result of failure to control significant research variables. The relationship between a child's acquisition of a language and his ability to think must be better understood for closer investigation of the effects of dual language learning. Several conditions do appear to be conducive to promoting dual language acquisition. It seems that the two languages should be kept in separate contexts so that coordinated language systems might develop. The best language models must be available in both languages. A rich and varied background of environmental encounters is important as are acceptance of the child's uniqueness, respect for his native language, appreciation of his cultural heritage and attention to his specific language requirements. Curriculum design for early childhood bilingual education should take these conditions into account and encourage improved oral language ability and introductory literacy skills in the native language, intensive oral language development and readiness for literacy in the second language, and access to knowledge in the stronger language. (RIE)

542. Tireman, L.S. "The Bilingual Child and His Reading Vocabulary." Elementary English Review. Vol. 32 (January 1955). pp. 33-50.

543. Tireman, L.S. "Bilingual Children." Review of Educational Research. Vol. 14 (June 1944). pp. 273-278.

544. Troike, Rudolph and Roger Abrahams. Language and Cultural Diversity in American Education. New York: Prentice-Hall. 1972.

545. Upshur, John A. "Four Experiments on the Relation between Foreign Language Teaching and Learning." Language Learning. Vol. 18 (June 1968).

Experiments reported here indicated that 1, language learning is not related to the amount of formal language instruction for those students concurrently enrolled in academic classes, and that 2, sequential mastery of materials is not necessary for learning in an intensive foreign language program. (NYS Bibliography)

546. Upshur, John A. and Julia Fata, Eds. "Problems in Foreign Language Testing." <u>Language Learning</u>. Special Issue #3. August 1968.

Contains a wide selection of relevant articles from the proceedings of a conference at the University of Michigan in September 1967. (NYS Bibliography)

547. Valdman, Albert, Ed. <u>Trends in Language Teaching</u>. New York: McGraw-Hill. 1966. (.paper)

Includes articles, many hitherto unprinted, in the areas of linguistics, programmed instruction, language laboratory technology, literature, etc., related to current language teaching. (NYS Bibliography)

548. Van Syoc, Bryce, Ed. "Linguistics and the Teaching of English as a Foreign Language." <u>Language Learning</u>. Vol. 8 (June 1958).

A special issue devoted entirely to articles dealing with the topic from differing perspectives during the height of the "structuralist-approach" period. (NYS Bibliography)

549. Wolfram, Walt. <u>An Appraisal of ERIC Documents on the Manner and Extent of Non-Standard Dialect Divergence</u>. 1969. 23 pp. (ED 034 991)

This paper examines and evaluates 11 ERIC documents dealing with the manner and extent to which non-standard dialects differ from standard English. The author presents the deficit (non-standard dialect is a deficient form of standard English) and difference (different but equal status of all dialects) models of explicating language varieties. Also discusses the basic assumptions about the nature of language with which the deficit model is in conflict. (author/JH)

550. Yotsukura, Sayo. <u>A Structual Analysis of the Usage of the Articles in English.</u> Unpublished Ph.D. Dissertation, University of Michigan. 1963.

551. Young, Rodney W. <u>The Development of Semantic Categories in the Spanish-English and Navajo-English Bilingual Children</u>. In "Conference on Child Language." preprints of papers presented at the conference. Chicago, Illinois. November 22-24, 1971. pp. 193-208. (ED 060 749)

The experiment described in this report considers whether children who learn a second language will develop the same semantic system as monolingual children or whether their semantic system will be different because of linguistic or cultural interference, and also whether the bilingual child develops separate meaning systems for his two languages or whether he operates by means of a single system. The experiment compares the relative difficulty of certain semantic constructions in comprehension tests for two groups of young bilingual children: Spanish-English bilinguals and Navajo-English bilinguals. Details and results are provided. Findings indicate that bilingual children do not parallel monolingual children in patterns of difficulty of semantic categories. Categories not present in their first language are appreciably more difficult in relation to the other categories than for monolingual children. (RIE)

Linguistic Studies of Puerto Ricans on the Mainland

552. Berney, Tomi D., Robert L. Cooper, and Joshua A. Fishman. "Semantic Independence and Degree of Bilingualism in Two Puerto Rican Communities." Revista Interamericana de Psicologia. Vol. 2 (1968). pp. 289-294.

The Spanish and English word naming and word association responses of two groups of Puerto Rican respondents, one living on the island, the other on the Mainland, were analyzed in terms of words produced in the weaker language for each of five societal domains. Subjects on the Island gave significantly higher translation equivalent ratios than did the others. The domains of family and neighborhood exhibited the smallest translation equivalent ratios, and the domains of education and religion, the largest. Semantic independence and relative bilingual proficiency were found to be largely independent dimensions, with the former reflecting the coordinates of the bilingual's language system. (PASAR)

553. Cooper, Robert L., Barbara R. Fowles, and Abraham Givner. "Listening Comprehension in a Bilingual Community." Modern Language Journal. Vol. 53 (1969). pp. 235-244.

This article describes a technique which was designed to determine a more direct way of determining both bilingual proficiency and listening comprehension ability. It was also devised to reflect bilingual proficiency in different social contexts. Stimuli were five tape-recorded natural conversations between Spanish-English bilingual residents of New York; the "actors" agreed on a social situation and carried out a conversation, switching languages as they felt it appropriate. Ss were 48 Puerto Ricans over the age of 13, living within a four-block section of "dowtown" Jersey City. The conversations were played twice to the respondent and questions were asked which were designed to assess both comprehension and interpretation of social aspects, e.g. role relationships, degree of intimacy, etc. For each subtest, the percentage of correctly answered items assessing comprehension of the English portion was subtracted from the percentage of correctly answered items assessing comprehension of the Spanish portion. Thus, positive scores meant greater comprehension of English. Independent judges rated the respondents on the following five variables: accented speech, reading, writing, Spanish repertoire range and English repertoire range. The listening comprehension portions were also administered to 20 high

school students who had completed three or four years of Spanish and
19 Latin American students in an advanced course in English as a
Second Language at a New York City university. Results show mo-
derate correlations among the degree of bilingualism scales. The
authors note that bilingualism can vary along partially independent
dimensions; therefore, reliance upon performance in a single mode
can result in an inadequate estimate of bilingual ability. The
usefulness of a contextualized approach to measuring bilingual skills
is emphasized, and a discussion of the uses of this technique is
also included. (ECK)

554. Cooper, Robert and Lawrence Greenfield. "Word Frequency Estimation
as a Measure of Degree of Bilingualism." Modern Language
Journal. March 1969. pp. 163-166.

The purpose of the study was to determine the utility of a
word frequency estimation task as a measure of degree of bilingualism. Ss were 48 Puerto Ricans, age 13 or older, living in a
Puerto Rican neighborhood in Jersey City, New Jersey. The procedure
involved having a subject rate 75 commonly used English and Spanish
words in terms of frequency that he had heard it or said it. Results showed that greater use of Spanish than English words was
associated with greater facility in speaking Spanish than speaking
English, use of Spanish more than English at home, greater word
production in Spanish, a predominance of Spanish accent and use
of fewer speech styles in speaking English. (ECK)

555. DeJesús, C. A Study of Language Development and Goodenough IQ of
Puerto Rican Preschool Children in New York City. Unpublished
Master's thesis, Fordham University. 1952.

556. Fishman, Joshua. "A Sociolinguistic Census of a Bilingual Neighborhood." in Joshua A. Fishman, Robert L. Cooper and Roxana Ma,
et al., Bilingualism in the Barrio. Final Report. Washington,
D.C.: Office of Education. 1968. pp. 260-269.
(ED 026 546)

557. Fishman, Joshua A., et al. Bilingualism in the Barrio. Final Report.
(ED 026 546)

Presents excerpts from a report of bilingualism in a predominantly lower class urban Puerto Rican community in the United States, and
aspects of the larger network of communication media and communication
elites through which it is tied to the Puerto Rican community of a
larger metropolitan area. Those sections of the report judged relevant to language teachers are presented (in Modern Language Journal,
Vol. 53 (1969). pp. 151-185.), including papers by Joshua Fishman,
Cooper and Greenfield, Edelman, and Berney, dealing with: a) measurement and description of widespread and relatively stable bilingualism;
b) word frequency estimation as a degree of bilingualism; c) contextualized measures of degree of bilingualism; d) contextualization of
schoolchildren's bilingualism; and e) semantic independence and degree
of bilingualism in two communities. (PASAR)

558. Golaski, Clare T. <u>Language Interference and Visual Perception of</u>
     <u>Native and Puerto Rican Speakers of English in Second Grade</u>.
     Master's thesis, Rutgers University. 1971.
     (ED 051 981)

     Study sought to determine whether language interference would
     have a significant effect on visual perception. Puerto Rican par-
     ticipants had been instructed in aural-oral English skills for 2
     years. The Figure and Ground Test from the Holmes-Singer Language
     Perception Tests, Series E-J, was used. Study revealed no signi-
     ficant differences between the two groups. Test materials, tables,
     and a bibliography are included. (RIE)

559. Kriedler, Charles. <u>A Study of the Influence of English on the</u>
     <u>Spanish of Puerto Ricans in Jersey City, New Jersey</u>. Unpublished
     Ph.D. Dissertation, Michigan State University. 1958.
     (<u>Dissertation Abstracts</u>. Vol. 19 (1958). pp. 527-528.)

     The purpose of this study was to measure the amount and nature
     of change in the Puerto Rican dialect in Jersey City as a result of
     their exposure to English. Data for the study were obtained from
     30 Ss who responded to a prepared questionnaire. The 30 Ss were
     chosen to give representation to all groups according to age, length
     of residence, exposure to English, etc. The conclusions indicate
     that the Puerto Ricans in Jersey City adopted forms of English more
     readily than the English speakers adopted forms of Spanish. In
     borrowing linguistic forms, the occurrence of a native phoneme in
     a new position is more likely than the appearance of a new phoneme.
     When a new phoneme is "borrowed" into the language, it is usually
     because there is no Spanish phoneme that can be used in its place.
     (DH)

560. Labov, W., <u>et al</u>. <u>A Preliminary Study of the Structure of English</u>
     <u>Used by Negro and Puerto Rican Speakers in New York City</u>.
     Cooperative Research Project Report No. 3091. 1968.
     (ED 028 423) and (Ed 028 424)

     The purpose of this investigation was to ascertain the dif-
     ferences between non-standard Negro English of Northern ghetto
     areas (NNE) and the standard English required in the classroom (SE).
     Though the title of the project suggests that a study of Puerto Rican
     speech patterns is included, it should be noted that there is little
     material here for the student of bilingualism among Puerto Ricans
     in New York City. The field work for the study was done in Central
     Harlem; Ss were classified by the investigators as speakers of non-
     standard Negro English (NNE), standard English (SE), and White non-
     standard English (WNSE). An analysis of the structure of NNE presents
     the following differences: 1) frequent generalizations of rules
     found in other English dialects; 2) the systematic variation of
     past tense and stem clusters; 3) the irregularity of $\underline{s}$, $\underline{z}$ inflections;
     4) the negative syntax of NNE which distributes the negative particle
     more consistently and to a wider range of environments; and 5) some
     fluctuation in the use of tense inversion. Analysis of data collected

from repetition tests shows that many NNE speakers have an asymmetri-
cal system of perception and production; they understand SE forms but
produce NNE forms in response. Individual investigators vary greatly
in their perception of the differences between NNE and SE forms. As
a general conclusion, the authors state that the apparent categorical
rules of NNE prevent consistent repetition of SE forms. (DH)

561. Ma, Roxana and Eleanor Herasimchuk. "Linguistic Dimensions of a
Bilingual Neighborhood." In Joshua A. Fishman, Robert L. Cooper
and Roxana Ma, et al., Bilingualism in the Barrio. Final Report. Yeshiva University. Washington, D.C.: Office of
Education, Department of Health, Education and Welfare. 1968.

562. Mergal, Margaret Z. Structural Problems in the Written Use of
English by Puerto Ricans. Unpublished Ph.D. Dissertation,
Teachers College, Columbia University. 1959.

563. Reinstein, Steven and Judy Hoffman. "Dialect Interaction Between
Black and Puerto Rican Children in New York City: Implications
for the Language Arts." Elementary English. Vol. 49 (February
1972). pp. 190-196.

This article describes a project which was designed to measure
the effects of black peers upon the English dialect spoken by Puerto
Rican children in New York City. Two groups of 15 Puerto Rican
fourth graders were selected. The groups were alike in such things
as length of residence in the same area, lack of speech or auditory
defects or speech training, the fact that both parents were born in
Puerto Rico and that the children were Spanish-speaking; the distinguishing characteristic was the amount of opportunity to interact
verbally with black peers. Instruments used were Gross's Pronunciation
Test for Negro Dialect and Gross's Auditory Discrimination Test for
Dialect Sounds. Results showed that the dialect articulation of
Puerto Rican students who interacted with black children was significantly different from those Puerto Ricans with little interaction
and that dialect articulation and auditory discrimination on tests
validated for black children were highly correlated for Puerto Rican
children. The authors also discuss some implications for education
and indicate that they plan to do additional research. (ECK)

564. Sardy, Susan J. Dialect, Auditory Discrimination and Phonics Skills.
Unpublished Ph.D. Dissertation, Yeshiva University. 1969.
(Dissertation Abstracts. Vol. 30 (1970). pp. 2914-2915A)

The study was designed to investigate the relationship between
residential segregation in a large urban area and selected auditory
discrimination and phonics skills among 240 lower and middle class
Black, White and Puerto Rican fourth graders from segregated schools
in New York City. Ss responded to tapes prepared for this study
which included a 41-item Auditory Discrimination Test and an 81-item
decoding Phonics Test of regular sound. The ethnolinguistic group
distributions of auditory discrimination scores differed significantly, at .01 level, after correction for vocabulary score: the

Puerto Rican group had the greatest difficulty; the Black group had
the largest portion of highest scores; and the White group did significantly better than all the others.  On the Phonics Test, however,
the scores of the Puerto Rican and Black Ss did not differ significantly from the White group.  Socioeconomic class was found to be
a far more significant determinant, with middle class children far
outperforming their lower-class counterparts.  (DH)

565.  Shiels, Marie Eileen.  Dialects in Contact:  A Sociolinguistic
      Analysis of Four Phonological Variables of Puerto Rican English
      and Black English in Harlem.  Unpublished Ph.D. Dissertation,
      Georgetown University.  1972.
      (Dissertation Abstracts International.  Vol. 32 (1971-1972).
      p. 6959A.)

      This project studied the effects of Black English on Puerto
Rican English.  Information was gathered from tapes of informal
conversations with 43 adolescent boys.  The informants were from
three groups:  Puerto Ricans with little contact with blacks, Puerto
Ricans with extensive contact with blacks and blacks.  Four phonological variables were studied.  All three groups were similar for
one variable, showing almost complete assimilation of Puerto Ricans
to black patterns; for the other three variables, those Puerto Ricans
with more contact with blacks had speech patterns which approximated
black speech closer than those Puerto Ricans with less contact with
blacks.  (DH)

566.  Silverman, Stuart Harold.  The Effects of Peer Group Membership on
      Puerto Rican English.  Unpublished Ph.D. Dissertation, Yeshiva
      University.  1971.
      (Dissertation Abstracts International.  Vol. 32 (1971-1972).
      p. 5621A.)

      This study was designed to determine the effects of peer-group
influence on language development.  Ss were three groups of junior
high school students:  Group I, Puerto Rican students with black
friends; Group II, Puerto Ricans without black friends, and Group
III, blacks.  Each child was measured five ways to determine which
group used the greatest amount of Black Non-Standard English for
each of 11 phonological variables.  The hypothesis was that Group
III would have the greatest amount and Group II the least amount.
The results were discussed on the basis of their implications for
education, and seem to indicate that, unless the schools can dis-
place the peer group as the greatest influence on. language development, non-standard speakers of English will not speak standard
English.  The desirability of having society accept non-standard
English rather than teaching standard English was also discussed.  (ECK)

567.  Terry, Charles E. and Robert L. Cooper.  "A Note on the Perception
      and Production of Phonological Variation."  Modern Language
      Journal.  Vol. 53 (1969).  pp. 254-255.

      This article described a study on phonetic analysis of 36 bilingual Puerto Rican subjects in an urban setting. Sixteen taped English and Spanish items were presented to each subject in groups of three alternatives to test for perception of variation in "phonetic realizations." Linguists had devised three criteria scales: A) English repertoire range, B) accentedness, and C) reading. Results indicate that the bilingual subjects' perception of phonoligical variation in both English and Spanish was not significantly related to the frequency of their production of these variables. (PASAR)

568.  Thomas, Alexander. Retardation in Intellectual Development of Lower-
        Class Puerto Rican Children in New York City. New York:  De-
        partment of Psychiatry, New York University. 1967.
        (ED 017 591)

        The objectives of this study were 1) to identify any patterns of behavioral and intellectual function which appear to be detrimental to optimal learning and development; 2) to identify inter- and extra-familiar influences which produce the above patterns; and 3) to identify favorable patterns which can be used to prevent or remedy the situation. The population to be studied was lower-class Puerto Rican children in New York City. The Ss were two groups of Puerto Ricans: 95 in one group which was followed from infancy, and 155 in the other group which consisted of their older siblings. For comparative purposes, two groups of advantaged white children were also tested. All children between the ages of 6 and 14 were administered the WISC; those children between the ages of 15 and 17 were administered the WAIS. The areas of investigation were as follows:  the problem of IQ score decrement with increase in age; below normal academic achievement; differences in behavioral style; language development, as affected by bilingualism; and the effects of child care practices, home environment and family characteristics on the child's development. Analysis of data was not complete, as this was an interim report. However the following conclusions were presented by the author: 1) the population of Puerto Rican children tested were retarded in school achievement; 2) the findings do not show a decrement in IQ level between pre-school and school ages, indicating that the retardation in intellectual achievement is not a result of cultural deprivation, etc.; 3) language development is not retarded by bilingualism; and 4) other factors must be responsible, (e.g. poor schooling, inappropriate teaching methods). The author noted that some factors in the home environment may also be at fault, but any such conclusions must be withheld pending complete analysis of the findings. (DH)

569.  Weissman, Julius. An Exploratory Study of Communication Patterns of
        Lower-Class Negro and Puerto Rican Mothers and Pre-School
        Children. Unpublished Ph.D. Dissertation. 1966.
        (Dissertation Abstracts. Vol. 27 (1967). pp. 2960A-3961A.)

        The purpose of the investigation was to explore the assumption that lower-class child-rearing patterns socialize passive behavior and lack of motivation for learning in children. Ss were mothers and pre-school age children from low-income Puerto Rican and Black groups. The nature and degree of the "assumed passivity" were studied in terms of the forms and patterns of the verbal and non-verbal communications between mother and child pairs in both home and school settings. The findings indicate that Puerto Rican mother-child pairs are much more active at home than in the school setting; the opposite was true for the Black group. "The Puerto Rican group had higher activity rates in the 'teaching' category, in the reinforcement of verbal praise, smiles, touch contacts, and related areas. The Black group was more active in the use of verbal admonitions, 'don'ts' in critical comments, in directing and coercing verbal and non-verbal communications." The Puerto Rican mother-child pairs were more active and responsive in the interpersonal processes of communication than the Black mother-child pairs. (DH)

570. Williams, George M., Jr. Puerto Rican English: A Discussion of Eight Major Works Relevant to Its Linguistic Description. Cambridge, Masschusetts: Language Research Foundation Report #3. 1971. 49 pp.
(ED 051 709)

Discussion of eight major works relevant to a linguistic description of Puerto Rican English seeks to contribute a more unified theory of bilingualism and second language acquisition. The author's observations on phonological, lexical and morphological, and syntactic implications are presented in an attempt to coordinate the theory. (RIE)

571. Williams, George. Some Errors in English by Spanish-Speaking Puerto Rican Children. Cambridge, Massachusetts: Language Research Foundation Report #6. January 1972. pp. 85-102.
(ED 061 850)

The purpose of the investigation reported in this document is to determine the range of errors in the spontaneous speech of Puerto Rican children of intermediate English ability in order to provide specific information on phonetic and morphological deviations from standard English for use in curriculum development. The study first considers common pronunciation problems, many attributed to the influence of Spanish. Problems with vowels, diphthongs, consonants, consonant clusters, stops and aspirants are discussed. Syntactic problems with auxiliaries, tense and number, object complements, negation, structures difficult to understand and miscellaneous lexical items are also considered. Examples of errors are provided. (RIE)

572. Wolfram, Walt. Overlapping Influence and Linguistic Assimilation in Second Generation Puerto Rican English. Paper presented at the 1971 American Anthropological Association Conference. New York, New York. 1971. 48 pp.
(ED 057 665)

The English spoken by second generation Puerto Ricans in Harlem is influenced by black English heard in the surrounding community, standard English used in the school, and the Spanish-influenced English used by the first generation Puerto Rican community. The

study of these influences is conducted according to recently developed
sociolinguistic principles which state that various social dialects
in the United States are not differentiated from each other by dis-
crete sets of features but by variations in the frequency with which
certain features occur.  The author examines two phonological variables in Puerto Rican English and discusses the linguistic processes at work in the variations and the influences of contact with
the dialects mentioned above.  The author devises rules accounting
for various constraints in the variations.  The discussion of the
variables helps to isolate several sociolinguistic principles concerning such concepts as vestigal interference, convergent processes,
and assimilation variants.  A case of grammatical variation is also
considered in relation to the influencing dialects.  A bibliography
is included.  (RIE)

573.  Wolfram, Walt and others.  Overlapping Influence in the English of
      Second Generation Puerto Rican Teenagers in Harlem.  Final
      Report.  Washington, D.C.:  Center for Applied Linguistics.
      U.S. Office of Education, Cooperative Research Program.  1971.
      560 pp.
      (ED 060 159)

      This research is an attempt to determine the relative influence
of Black English and Puerto Rican Spanish in the speech of Puerto
Ricans raised contiguous to the black community in Harlem.  The first
chapter provides a general introduction to the study of this variety
of Puerto Rican English and a description of the sample on which this
study is based.  In Chapter Two, a general sociocultural picture of
various aspects of the Puerto Rican community is given, particularly
as it relates to the surrounding black community.  A number of
selected variables in Puerto Rican English are examined in Chapter
Three, building on the descriptive framework of variable rules in
generative-transformational grammar.  Chapter Four deals with the
assimilation of linguistic features from Black English in three
groups within the continuum of second generation Puerto Rican speakers in Harlem.  The final chapter consists of a nontechnical description of the differences between Puerto Rican English and Standard
English among second generation Puerto Ricans in Harlem, intended as
a practical guide for educators who want to know some of the main
characteristics of the dialect without the formalization or detail
that is involved in the third chapter.  (RIE)


Linguistic Studies of Other Non-English-Speakers on the Mainland

574.  Ajubita, Maria Luisa.  Language in Social Relation to the Mexican-
      American Problem.  Unpublished Master's thesis, Tulane University.
      1943.

575.  Arnold, Richard D.  Reading Skills of Afro-and Mexican-American
      Students.  Paper presented at the meeting of the International
      Reading Association.  Atlantic City, New Jersey.  April 19-23,
      1971.  12 pp.
      (ED 055 727)

576. Baugh, Lila. <u>A Study of Pre-School Vocabulary of Spanish-Speaking</u>
     <u>Children.</u> Unpublished Master's thesis, University of Texas,
     1933.

577. Broman, B.L. "Spanish-speaking Five-year old." <u>Childhood Education.</u>
     Vol. 48 (April 1972). pp. 362-364.
     (EJ 056 391)

578. Browning, Horace N. <u>A Comparison of the Spanish-Speaking and English</u>
     <u>Speaking Children in Nine Schools Over a Four-Year Period.</u>
     Unpublished Master's thesis, University of Texas. 1944.

579. Callicut, Laurie T. <u>Word Differences of Mexican and Non-Mexican</u>
     <u>Children.</u> Unpublished Master's thesis, University of Texas.
     1934.

580. Cervenka, Edward. <u>Final Report of Head Start Evaluation and Research</u>
     <u>1966-67 to the Institute for Educational Development, Section</u>
     <u>VI: ,The Measurement of Bilingualism and Bicultural Socializa-</u>
     <u>tion of the Child in the School Setting. The Development of the</u>
     <u>Instrument.</u> 1970. 236 pp.
     (ED 019 122)

     A study to develop instruments to measure child bilingualism
and bicultural socialization was conducted in Del Rio, Texas. Three
instruments were developed: 1) a series of six tests for measuring
linguistic competence in English; 2) a similar series for Spanish;
and 3) a series of three instruments for measuring socialization.
Test batteries focused on the oral-aural use of language in realistic
school situations. Analysis of results showed that children in the
bilingual program were as competent in English as those learning
only in English and they were also better adjusted socially. Test
instrument validity and reliability was determined and item analysis
carried out. Document mainly composed of test instruments and analysis of experimental data. (RIE)

581. Christian, Chester C., Jr. <u>Differential Response to Language Stimuli</u>
     <u>before Age 3: A Case Study.</u> In "Conference on Child Language."
     preprints of papers presented at the Conference. Chicago,
     Illinois. November 22-24, 1971. pp. 1-14.
     (ED 060 745)

     This case study describes the language development of a preschool
child exposed to Spanish in her home environment and to English outside the family. It is the parents' hope that the child will learn
to speak, read, and write Spanish first, while learning English before
entering school. Her progress is described in this report, as are
outside factors accounting for specific development. Prestige is
regarded as a key factor in the learning of a second language, with
the degree of success or failure of bilingual education in the home
or school proportionate to the degree to which prestige is associated
with each language being learned. (RIE)

582. Haught, B.F. "The Language Difficulty of Spanish-American Children." Journal of Applied Psychology. Vol. 15 (February 1931). pp. 92-95.

583. Levine, Helen Faith. "Linguistic and Paralinguistic Changes in Spanish-Speakers Learning English." English Language Teaching. Vol. 25 (June 1971). pp. 288-296. (EJ 042 877)

584. Linn, George B. "Linguistic Functions of Bilingual Mexican-American Children." Journal of Genetic Psychology. Vol. 111 (1967). pp. 183-193.

585. Linn, George B. A Study of Several Linguistic Functions of Mexican-American Children in a Two-Language Environment. San Francisco, California: R and E Research Associates. 1971. (originally published June 1965) (ED 065 263)

586. Moran, Mattie B. A Study of Oral and Reading Vocabulary of Beginning Spanish-Speaking Children. Master's thesis, University of Texas. 1940.

587. Manuel, Herschel T. "A Comparison of Spanish and English--Reading and Arithmetic." Journal of Applied Psychology. Vol. 19 (April 1935). pp. 189-202.

588. Natalicio, Diana S. and Frederick Williams. "What Characteristics Can 'Experts' Reliably Evaluate in the Speech of Black and Mexican-American Children." TESOL Quarterly. Vol. 6 (June 1972). pp. 121-127. (EJ 060 715)

589. New England Regional Spanish-Speaking Council. Overview of the Problems Encountered by New England's Spanish-Speaking Population. Hartford, Connecticut: New England Regional Spanish-Speaking Council. 1970.

590. Ornstein, Jacob. Language Varieties Along the U.S.-Mexican Border. 1969. 27 pp. (ED 032 520)

The U.S. Southwest, and particularly the region along the 1,000 mile U.S.-Mexican border, offers a ready laboratory for the observation of many phases of multilingualism and multiculturalism. The author feels, however, that the rich sociolinguistic material of the area has suffered from over-simplification and neglect. The author explains briefly the Sociolinguistic Study on Southwest Spanish (supported by the University of Texas at El Paso's Research Institute) and presents a survey of the historical evolution of the study of multilingualism. He also suggests a schema of the language situation in the Southwest. (RIE)

591. Palmer, M.B. "Effects of Categorization, Degree of Bilingualism,
     and Language upon Recall of Select Monolinguals and Bilinguals."
     Journal of Educational Psychology. Vol. 63 (April 1972). pp.
     160-164.

     This study was designed to measure the effects of categorization,
degree of bilingualism and language upon recall. Ss were schoolchildren in grades 5-8 who, on the basis of a self-report and a reaction
time technique, were determined to be monolingual English, strong
English, strong Spanish and balanced English-Spanish. The material
consisted of two word lists. The categorized list was made up of
40 words in four semantic categories; the non-categorized list was
composed of one word from each of 40 semantic categories. Results
showed that recall was better for all groups for the categorized
list and that students of lower socioeconomic class did better in
recall in English; it was also noted that recall in English was
superior for all groups. Because the results seem to show that
Spanish was not the "stronger" language for these students, the
author questions whether bilingual education programs are helping
the students or are creating more interference between the two
languages. (ECK)

592. Peña, Albar Antonio. A Comparative Study of Selected Syntactical
     Structures of the Oral Language Status in Spanish and English
     of Disadvantaged First-Grade Spanish-Speaking Children. Ph.D.
     Dissertation, University of Texas. 1967. 152 pp.
     (ED 045 961)

     This study presents an intensive comparative analysis of se-
lected basic sentence patterns and transformations in Spanish and
English manifested in the responses of Spanish-speaking disadvantaged
children selected to receive instruction in special programs. The
hypothese of this study, designed to test for similarities and
differences in the oral languages of the four groups selected were
that 1) there were no significant initial differences between the
groups, including sex, in pretest scores; 2) there were no significant
differences between group means and function of treatment. In general,
these hypotheses were "supported by the results." (RIE)

593. Peñalosa, Fernando. Chicano Multilingualism and Multiglossia. 12 pp.
     (ED 056 590)

     The linguistic situation of the Mexican-American community is
complex, involving multiglossia and multilingualism. Various language codes and different blendings of English and Spanish are in
use within the community. Educators should decide which code they
will use in their planning. Research is needed to consider the
various codes and their roles and relationships to improve the
educational system for the Mexican American. (RIE)

594. Rodríguez-Bou, Ismael. A Study of the Parallelism of English and
     Spanish Vocabulary. Rio Piedras: University of Puerto Rico,
     Superior Education Council of Puerto Rico. 1950.

595. Ryan, Louise T. <u>Common Errors in English Language Usage Made by Spanish-speaking Pupils</u>. Unpublished Ph.D. Dissertation, New York University. 1950.

596. Sabatino, David A. and others. "Perceptual, Language and Academic Achievement of English, Spanish and Navajo Speaking Children Referred for Special Classes." <u>Journal of School Psychology</u>. Vol. 10 (March 1972). pp. 39-46.
(EC 04 1641)

The purpose of this study was to determine the perceptual, language and academic achievement functions of English, Spanish and Navajo children experiencing learning problems and referred for placement into special education classes. Those test variables which discriminated among the native-English-speaking children and the children who spoke Spanish or Navajo natively were, as predicted, those tasks which involved knowledge of the linguistic rules of English. It would seem that, taken as a group, the school learning problems experienced by the native Spanish- or Navajo-speaking children were the result of their limited linguistic competence in English, the language of instruction, in their classrooms. (EC)

597. Skrabanek, R.L. "Language Maintenance among Mexican-Americans." <u>Civil Rights Digest</u>. Vol. 4 (Spring 1971). pp. 18-24
(EJ 044 625)

An examination of language retention among the Mexican-Americans and the factors involved in their language maintenance despite pressure from a dominant American society strongly supporting the use of the English language. (CIJE)

598. Spector, Sima. <u>Patterns of Difficulty in English in Bilingual Mexican-American Children</u>. Master's thesis. February 1972. 34 pp.
(ED 066 083)

The document first provides a review of relevant literature defining bilingualism, inherent characteristics of bilingualism, academic and psychological problems created by bilingualism, and essentials of language proficiency, and discusses specific patterns of difficulty to be expected in English-language performance. The author then describes an experiment conducted among 15 bilingual and 15 monolingual children to determine patterns of difficulty. The findings confirm the investigations and statements of linguists as to areas of difficulty for bilingual speakers; however, the similarity of performance by their monolingual, English-speaking peers indicates that other dynamics influence the language development of children in both groups. These factors must also be investigated. (RIE)

599. Stern, Carolyn and Diane Ruble. <u>Teaching New Concepts to Non-English Speaking Preschool Children</u>. California University, Los Angeles. Washington, D.C.: Office of Economic Opportunity, Office of

Education, Cooperative Research Program. August 1970. 36 pp.
(ED 054 903)

Fifteen Mexican-American children from four Head Start classes
were the Ss in this study, which tested three hypotheses: 1) that
children whose first language is Spanish and who are instructed in
Spanish will require significantly fewer trials to learn a new concept than children instructed either in English or bilingually; 2)
that children receiving the first set of new concepts in English will
learn a second instance of the new concept taught in English more
readily than children who were taught the first use of the concept
in Spanish; and 3) that, on a Spanish language criterion test, children taught concepts in English will do as well as children taught
those concepts in Spanish or bilingually. The procedure included
pretesting with the Goodenough Draw-A-Man Test and the Expressive
Vocabulary Inventory in both English and Spanish; the instructional
program; a criterion test in the appropriate language using a series
of booklets developed to teach the conceptual task which was designed
to test the hypotheses; and a posttest. Study results rejected hypotheses 1 and 2, while hypothesis 3 could not be rejected. An appendix contains lessons used in the instructional program. (RIE)

600. Stockwell, R.P. and J. Donald Bowen. The Sounds of English and
     Spanish. Chicago: University of Chicago Press. 1960.

     Contrastive linguistic analysis describing the similarities and
     differences between English and Spanish, and intended to offer a
     basis for the preparation of instructional materials, the planning
     of courses, and the development of classroom techniques. The style
     is moderately technical. (JH)

601. Stockwell, R.P.; J. Donald Bowen and J.W. Martin. The Grammatical
     Structures of English and Spanish. Chicago: University of
     Chicago Press. 1960.

     Contrastive linguistic analysis describing the similarities
     and differences between English and Spanish, and intended to offer
     a basis for the preparation of instructional materials, the planning
     of courses, and the development of classroom techniques. The style
     is moderately technical. (JH)

602. Tireman, L.S. "A Study of Fourth-Grade Reading Vocabulary of Native
     Spanish-Speaking Children." Elementary School Journal. Vol. 46
     (December 1945). pp. 223-227.

603. Tireman, L.S. and others. "Vocabulary Acquisition of Spanish-Speaking
     Children." Elementary English Review. Vol. 12 (May 1935). pp.
     118-119, 144.

604. Tireman, L.S. and V.E. Woods. "Aural and Visual Comprehension of
     English by Spanish-Speaking Children." Elementary English
     Review. Vol. 4 (November 1939). pp. 204-211.

605. Williams, Frederick and Geraldine Van Wart. On the Relationship of
     Language Dominance and the Effects of Viewing CARRASCOLENDAS.
     Texas University, Austin. Center for Communication Research.
     September 1972.  8 pp.
     (ED 066 058)

     A study was made of the relationship between the language domi-
nance of a child and the effects of viewing a bilingual television
program called Carrascolendas.  A previous study showed that the
program did have an effect on average knowledge gains among viewers.
In order to ascertain whether these gains were in some way related
to the language dominance of the child, and index was constructed to
determine the child's language dominance--Spanish, English, or bilingual.  When this index was correlated with gains made as a result
of viewing the program no significant evidence was found that the
effects of viewing Carrascolendas were related to, or dependent
upon, the child's language dominance.  (RIE)

G.  Studies of the Scholastic Achievement and Evaluation of Puerto
    Rican and other Non-English Speaking Children in Mainland Schools

606.  Anderson, James et al.  "Stability and Change among Three Genera-
        tions of Mexican-Americans:  Factors Affecting Achievement."
        American Educational Research Journal.  8:2  (March, 1971).
        pp.  285-309.
        (EJ 041 768)

607.  Anderson, James and William H. Johnson.  Sociocultural Determinants
        of Achievement Among Mexican-American Students.  University
        Park, New Mexico:  New Mexico State University.  1968.  45 pp.
        (ED 017 394)

608.  Arnold, R.D.  "Reliability of Test Scores for the Young 'Bilingual'
        Disadvantaged."  Reading Teacher.  Vol. 22 (1969).  pp. 341-345.

        This paper examines the results produced when tests whose norms
        were established on a middle class Anglo population were administered
        to minority students.  Ss were over 200 Mexican-American third
        graders in various schools in San Antonio, Texas.  The tests were
        the Metropolitan Achievement Tests, the Inter-American Reading Tests
        (parallel tests in Spanish and English) and the IPAT Culture Fair
        Test.  Answers were sought for two questions:  1) What will happen
        to the reliability of a test standardized on middle class Anglo-
        Americans if it is given to disadvantaged bilingual students? and
        2) How does the reliability of a standardized test compare to that
        of a test designed specifically for a bilingual population?  Results
        showed that the Inter-American English Test of Reading and the Metro-
        politan Achievement Tests were quite reliable for the group studied
        as long as tests of the proper difficulty were administered. (ECK)

609.  Caldwell, F.F. and M.D. Mowry.  "The Essay versus the Objective
        Examination as Measures of the Achievement of Bilingual
        Children."  Journal of Educational Psychology.  Vol. 25 (1933)
        pp. 696-702.

610.  Caldwell, Floyd F. and Mary Mowry Davis.  "Sex Differences in School
        Achievement Among Spanish-American and Anglo-American Children."
        Journal of Educational Sociology.  Vol. 8 (May 1935).  pp. 168-
        173.

611.  Caldwell, Floyd F. and Mary Mowry Davis.  "Teachers Grades as Criteria
        of Achievement of Bilingual Children."  Journal of Applied
        Psychology.  Vol. 18 (April 1934) pp. 288-292.

612.  Callicut, Laurie T.  The Construction and Evaluation of Parallel
        Tests of Reading in English and Spanish.  Unpublished Ph.D.
        Dissertation, University of Texas.  1942.

613.  Cantwell, George C.  Differential Prediction of College Grades for
        Spanish-American and Anglo-American Students.  Unpublished
        Master's thesis, University of Texas.  1946.

614.    Capone, Thomas A.  Interaction of Selected Needs and Perceived
        Peer Orientation to Education as Related to Academic Proficiency
        in Aspira Students.  Unpublished Ph.D. Dissertation, Fordham
        University.  1969.
        (Dissertation Abstracts. 30:12 (1970). p. 5279A.

        The purpose of the study was to examine the need for affilia-
tion (n Aff), need for achievement (n Ach), and perceived peer
orientation toward education (P Peer O) of 120 Puerto Rican male
and female 12th grade academic students.  The Ss were all members
of the ASPIRA club in NYC, which is an agency operated by people
of PR descent to encourage and support PR young people to enter
and complete college.  The instruments used to measure these 3
independent variables were the Edwards Personal Preference Schedule
(n Ach and n Aff) and the Peer Influence section of the Personal
Values Inventory (P Peer O).  Also used in the investigation were
the SAT, to obtain a measure of general academic proficiency, and
the comprehension section of the Nelson-Denny Reading Test, to
obtain a rough index of language proficiency.  Findings indicate
that a positive relationship exists between a student's n Ach and
his academic success as measured by the SAT.  Also, students with
a high n Aff more often perceive their peers as having academic
orientations similar to their own than do students with a low n Aff.
The authors suggest that the n Aff may be countered somewhat by the
student with a high  n Ach who perceives that his peers do not
value education as much as he does.  (DH)

615.    Cline, Marion, Jr.  Achievement of Bilinguals in Seventh Grade by
        Socioeconomic Levels.  Ph.D.  Dissertation, University of
        Southern California.  1961.
        (Dissertation Abstracts.  Vol. 22 (1962). pp. 3113-3114.

        This study was designed to investigate the relative achievement
of Anglo-American and Spanish-American students within socioeconomic
levels in order to determine whether SES and biculturalism have an
effect on educational achievement.  Ss were 354  seventh graders
(156 Anglos, 197 Spanish-Americans); each group was classified into
three socioeconomic levels.  Ss were administered the Stanford
Achievement test, the Otis Quick-Scoring Mental Ability Test and a
questionnaire.  The groups and levels were compared for all variables.
Analysis of the data indicated that 1) socioeconomic status functions
greatly in school achievement; 2) biculturalism does not itself
function in school achievement, but in combination with SES it does
become important; and 3) Anglo-Americans at the upper and middle
socioeconomic levels did considerably better than Spanish-Americans
at those levels, but at the lower SES level, they did just as poorly.
Finally, there are recommendations for further research concerning
the materials and methods used in teaching all students of the lower
socioeconomic level.  (DH)

616.    Coers, W.C.  "Comparative Achievement of White and Mexican Junior
        High School Pupils."  Peabody Journal of Education.  Vol. 12
        (January 1935).  pp. 157-162.

131

617. Cooper, J.G. "Predicting School Achievement for Bilingual Pupils." <u>Journal of Educational Psychology</u>. Vol. 49 (1958). pp. 31-36.

618. Davis, O.L., Jr. and C.P. Personke, Jr. "Effects of Administering the Metropolitan Readiness Test in English and Spanish to Spanish-Speaking School Entrants." <u>Journal of Educational Measurement</u>. Vol. 5 (1968). pp. 231-234.

This paper reports the results of administering the Metropolitan Readiness Tests (MRT) in English and Spanish to entering elementary school children with a view to determining if the customary English-only testing results in discriminatory practice against the children. Ss were 88 Spanish-speaking children from two elementary schools in a South Texas city. Fifty-three were enrolled in pre-first grade classes for those seen to be lacking in ability in English; thirty-five were in regular first-grade classes. All children took the test twice, once in Spanish and once in English, with about three weeks between the 2 administrations. Results are tentative, but seem to indicate that administering the MRT in English resulted in great testing bias toward and inadequate assessment of the Spanish-speaking children. The authors note that the mean scores fell in the test publisher's low average range, which does not augur well for success in school; it may be that the children tested have little ability in either Spanish or English and that perhaps a dificit in childhood experiences may be more important in determining low performance than the language in which the test was administered. (ECK)

619. Delmet, D.T. "A Study of the Mental and Scholastic Abilities of Mexican Children in the Elementary School." <u>Journal of Juvenile Research</u>. Vol. 14 (January 1937) p. 31.

620. Dreppa, J.J. <u>The Evaluation of English Skills of Puerto Rican High School Students</u>. Paper presented at the Conference on the Education of Puerto Rican Children on the Mainland. San Juan, Puerto Rico. October, 1970.

621. Deutsch, M. <u>Minroity Group and Class Status as Related to Social and Personal Factors in School Achievement</u>. (Monograph No. 2). Ithaca, New York: The Society for Applied Anthropology. 1960.

622. Fennessey, James. <u>An Exploratory Study of Non-English Speaking Homes and Academic Performance</u>. Baltimore, Maryland: Research and Development Center for the Study of Social Organization of Schools and the Learning Process, Johns Hopkins University. 1967. (ED 011 613)

This paper is a re-analysis of data concerning Puerto Rican schoolchildren in New York City collected as part of a larger United States Office of Education survey. The answers to the following two questions were sought: 1) What relationships are present between the language spoken in the home and other aspects of ethnic

background? and 2) What differences are present in vocabulary
test scores of Puerto Rican children with varying home languages
and at different grade levels? It was difficult to analyze the
data because of the apparent error in response to several important
interview questions. Two tentative conclusions are 1) language is
not very closely linked to other attributes of Puerto Rican ethnicity
and 2) "after taking into account some confounding background
variables, there is little difference between Spanish-English homes
and English-only homes on the average vocabulary test scores of
the children, except at grade one." The author suggests further
research to continue the re-analysis of the USOE study. (ECK)

623. Flaugher, Ronald L. Project Access Research Report No. 2: Patterns
of Test Performance by High School Students of Four Ethnic
Identies. Princeton, New Jersey: Educational Testing Service,
1971, 33pp.
(ED 055 102)

Participants included Blacks, Whites, Mexican-Americans and
Orientals. Findings: Overall level of performance varied with
social class, while the patterns remained rather constant within
ethnic group, regardless of social class. This new evidence adds
to the strength of the argument that our educational systems should
be attending to, and utilizing, the variety of talents and aptitudes
presented by the students, rather than attempting to treat everyone
as a member of the majority group. (RLE abridged)

624. Fussell, William D. Comparable Norms for Anglo-and Latin-American
Students on a Scholastic Aptitude Test. Unpublished Master's
thesis, University of Texas. 1940.

625. Galván, Robert Rogers. Bilingualism as it Relates to Intelligence
Test Scores and School Achievement among Culturally Deprived
Spanish-American Children. Ph.D. Dissertation, East Texas
State University. 1967.
(Dissertation Abstracts. Vol. 28 (1968). pp. 3021A-3022A .

This study was designed to investigate the relationship between
intelligence test scores and scholastic achievement as they relate
to bilingualism among "culturally deprived" children of Spanish-
American heritage. Ss were 100 Spanish-American children from the
third, fourth and fifth grades of aDallas, Texas elementary school.
Ss were administered the Wechsler Intelligence Scale for children
(WISC) in both English and Spanish. It was expected that the Ss
would score lower when the WISC was administered in English than when
administered in Spanish; this was found to be true. The verbal
section had a greater increase in points than the non-verbal section.
The author suggests that some other measures of intelligence be
developed for use with bilingual children. The results here clearly
point out the inadequacy of using verbal tests of intelligence when
testing bilinguals. (DH)

626. Gill, Lois J. and Bernard Spilka. "Some Intellectual Correlates of Academic Achievement Among Mexican-American Secondary School Students." *Journal of Educational Psychology*. Vol. 53 (June, 1962). pp. 144-156.

627. Gordon, C.Wayne et al. *Educational Achievement and Aspirations of Mexican-American Youth in a Metropolitan Context*. Occasional Report 36, Center for the Study of Evaluation. Los Angeles: University of California. 1968.

628. Greene, John F. and Perry Alan Zirkel. *Academic Factors Relating to the Self-Concept of Puerto Rican Pupils*, Paper for American Psychological Assn. Convention, Washington, D.C., 1971, 10 pp. (ED 054 284)

    Study investigated the relationship of the self-concept of Puerto Rican pupils with achievement, IQ, ethnic group mixture, and teacher ethnicity. The results of a correlational analysis indicated that self-concept was significantly related to achievement in English and Spanish, as well as to teacher ratings of aural ability in both languages, although self-concept was not significantly related to IQ. However, the relationship between self-concept and academic achievement is demonstrated to be complex and circular. (RIE)

629. Hernández, Carlos. *The Spanish Revision of the S.R.A. Junior Inventory, Form A*. Unpublished Ph.D. Dissertation. Purdue University, 1958.
    (*Dissertation Abstracts*. Vol. 19 (1958). pp. 354-355.)

    The S.R.A. Junior Inventory, Form A was revised for use among Puerto Rican students in grades four through seven. The purpose of the revision was to provide evidence about the needs and problems of Puerto Rican children as they themselves see them. The Spanish form would provide information comparable to that furnished by the English version, and would therefore facilitate transcultural studies of American and Puerto Rican schoolchildren. Most of the items included in the Revision came from the translation of the Junior Inventory. However, some items were eliminated from the English form by the author because they seemed obviously irrelevant to the experiences of Puerto Rican children. Some items were incorporated after talks with educational leaders, teachers, principals and students. After a pilot study, the final form of the S.R.A. Revision was administered to one thousand schoolchildren in specially selected places in Puerto Rico so that results would be representative of local school populations. (DH)

630. Hernández, Norma G. *Variables Affecting Achievement of Middle School Mexican American Students*. Texas University, El Paso. Washington, D.C.: Office of Education. August 1971. 81p. (ED 059 827)

Literature pertaining to research done on academic achievement of Mexican American students is reviewed in this paper. The literature deals with such variables as socioeconomic, physical, psychological, and cultural aspects; language factors; attitudes; language development; and environment. A 15-page discussion of recommendations for improving curriculum, instruction, and teacher education for educating the Mexican American is included. Also included is a bibliography containing over 200 relevent citations. (RIE)

631. Herr, S.E. "The Effect of Pre-First-Grade Training upon Reading Readiness and Reading Achievement among Spanish-American Children." Journal of Educational Psychology. Vol. 37 (1946). pp. 87-102.

632. Hobart, Charles W. "Underachievement among Minority Group Students: An Analysis and a Proposal." Phylon. Vol. 24 (1963). pp. 184-196.

The author presents a sociological analysis of the situation of minority group students in public schools. There are four conditions that seem to apply in all cases: 1) a damaged self-concept; 2) inadequate motivation; 3) a lack of awareness of employment opportunities and capabilities; and 4) resistance by peers and community to self advancement. Hobart notes that any one of these circumstances would severely arrest the child's development to his full potential. Combined, they function to guarantee that the minority young person will finish school fitted only for unskilled or semi-skilled work. Hobart suggests that compensatory educational programs be instituted to counteract whatever deficiences in preparation which have accumulated during the student's previous years of schooling, and provide the individualized attention so badly needed to improve the student's self-evaluation. (DH)

633. Johnson, B.E. Ability, Achievement and Bilingualism: A Comparative Study Involving Spanish-speaking and English-speaking Children at the Sixth Grade Level. Unpublished Ph.D. Dissertation, University of Maryland. 1962.

634. Johnson, G.F. "Metropolitan Tests: Inappropriate for ESEA Pupils." Integrated Education. Vol. 9, No. 6 (1971).

The article discusses the Metropolitan Achievement tests in terms of their middle-class cultural bias. The author's criticisms of the tests include "their fixation on verbal symbols, paragraph content, and problem solving that are most familiar to higher and middle socioeconomic groups." Furthermore, the Metropolitan tests do not measure some of the objectives of the ESEA programs. It is recommended that more work be done on this kind of standardized test, that some attempt be made to develop tests that "synthesize bicultural experiences." (DH)

635. Karadenes, Mark. A Comparison of Differences in Achievement and
     Learning Abilities between Anglo and Mexican-American
     Children When the Two Groups are Equated by Intelligence.
     Unpublished Ph.D. Dissertation, University of Virginia. 1971.
     (Dissertation Abstracts International. Vol. 32 (1971-72).
     pp. 4422A-4423A.)

        This study was designed to determine if differences in
     learning abilities exist between Anglo and Mexican American male
     kindergarten children, and how those differences relate to intelli-
     gence and academic achievement. Ss were 90 children (45 Anglo,
     45 Mexican-American) who attended public elementary school in
     Santa Monica, California. School psychologists administered the
     Stanford-Binet Intelligence Test and the Wide Range Achievement
     Test (WRAT) to all Ss; the Meeker Profile was used to measure
     learning abilities. Findings indicate that achievement was
     affected by ethnicity and intelligence, and that learning abilities
     were not influenced by either ethnicity or intelligence. (DH)

636. Katz, David. The Effects of a Compensatory Educational Program on
     the Vocational Aspirations, Expectations, Self-Concept, and
     Achievement of Selected Groups of JHS Students.
     (Dissertation Abstracts: 1969. Vol. 29 (9-A). p. 2963)

        This study was designed to investigate the effects of a com-
     pensatory educational program on the vocational aspirations, expec-
     tations, self-concepts and achievements of selected groups of ninth
     grade junior high school students in New York City. Ss were male,
     average in grade, at least two years below grade level in reading,
     and members of either Black or Puerto Rican minorities. All
     students in the experimental group were in a Career Guidance pro-
     gram. Students in the control groups were matched for character-
     istics equivalent to those of the experimental group, except that
     they were either 1) in the same school as the Ss but not taking part
     in the Career Guidance program, or 2) in schools which did not have
     the compensatory program. The instruments used by the investigators
     to measure the variables in question were a personal adequacy scale
     based on the Whittaker Scale, a modification of Hambruger's Life
     Planning Questionnaire, and the Metropolitan Achievement Test. All
     subjects were administered the tests and questionnaire on two
     different occasions, at the beginning and end of the same school
     year. Results of the statistical analysis indicated that the
     Career Guidance program had no significant positive effects on the
     variables under consideration. In fact, the effects that did
     occur were contrary to the goals of the program. In the experimen-
     tal group congruency between aspiration and expectation was reduced,
     rather than facilitated, while the control groups showed a signifi-
     cant increase over the same period of time. Black students gained
     significantly more than the Puerto Rican students in reading
     achievement, but the control group gained more in reading than the
     experimental group overall. (DH)

637. Leo, Paul F. <u>The Effects of Two Types of Group Counseling Upon the Academic Achievement of Mexican-American Pupils in the Elementary School</u>. Ph.D. dissertation, University of the Pacific, Stockton, California. Washington, D.C.: Office of Education, Cooperative Research Program. January 1972. 143p. (ED 059 002)

638. Linton, Thomas H. <u>A Study of the Relationship of Global Self-Concept, Academic Self-Concept, and Academic Achievement among Anglo and Mexican-American Sixth Grade Students</u>. Paper presented at the annual meeting of the American Educational Research Association. Chicago, Illinois. April 3-7, 1972. 13 p. (ED 063 053)

A sample of 172 Anglo and 160 Mexican American students from 16 elementary schools in a southern New Mexico city was stratified by 3 socioeconomic levels. The Piers-Harris Children's Self-Concept Scale and a 5-item factor analyzed scale developed from existing research were used to measure self-concept. Student achievement was measured by teacher-assigned grades in reading, arithmetic, and social studies and by the Iowa Test of Basic Skills. A 3-way analysis of variance model (with students classified according to ethnicity, sex, and socioeconomic level) was used to test differences between students. Results indicated that no significant differences between ethnic groups in terms of global and academic self-concepts, and no sex differences were found. Significant differences were found in both self-concept measures between socio-economic levels. High socioeconomic level was associated with high self-concept and low socioeconomic level was associated with low self-concept. However, middle socioeconomic-level Mexican American students' academic self-concept score were almost the same as those of low socioeconomic level Anglo and Mexican American students. Results of actual achievement were consistent with findings of previous studies, and correlation analysis of the relationships between self-concept and achievement did not yield a consistent pattern across socioeconomic levels. (RIE)

639. Littlefield, John H. <u>The Use of Norm-Referenced Survey Achievement Tests with Mexican-American Migrant Students; A Literature Review and Analysis of Implications for Evaluation of the Texas Migrant Education Program</u>. Austin, Texas: Texas Education Agency. (1972). 51p. (ED 063 983)

640. Mangano, James F. and Richard C. Towne. <u>Improving Migrant Students' Academic Achievement Through Self-Concept Enhancement</u>. State University of New York at Geneseo, Center for Migrant Studies. 1970. 55pp. (ED 049 868)

Purpose of research was to investigate whether an attempt to modify migrant parents' behavior in accordance with social psychological principles results in better academic achievement by their

137

children. Ss were 21 Puerto Rican children; 12 in the experimental
group (aged 6-16) and 9 in the control group (aged 7-14). Data was
collected through use of reading and arithmetic subtests of the
Metropolitan Achievement Test and the Spanish translation of the
Michigan State General Self-Concept of Ability Scale. Results
indicated that the self-concept of ability for the experimental
group increased significantly and that academic achievement also
increased, as measured by the above mentioned instruments. (ERIC)

641. Manuel, Herschel T. Cooperative Inter-American Tests, 1050.
Princeton, New Jersey: Educational Testing Service. 1950.

642. Mercer, Jane R. Sociocultural Factors in the Education Evaluation
of Black and Chicano Children. Paper presented at the 10th
Annual Conference on Civil Rights Educators and Students,
NEA, Washington, D.C. February 18-20, 1972. 16p. Sacramento:
California State Department of Education, Office of Com-
pensatory Education. Bethesda, Maryland: National Institute of
Mental Health.
(ED 060 462)

In a recent study the mothers of 268 children who were in
classes for educable mentally retarded in two public school districts
in Southern California were interviewed. The responses of some of
these mothers dramatize three issues: (1) biases in the assessment
procedures used to label children as mentally retarded; (2) the
stigmatization associated with special class placement; and (3)
inadequate programming. Disproportionately large numbers of black
and Chicano children are labeled as mentally retarded by the public
schools. Public schools rely more on IQ test scores than any other
community agency. The schools label more persons as mentally retarded
share their labels with more other organizations, and label more
persons with IQ's above 70 and with no physical disabilities than any
other formal organization in the community. Proportionately more
low status persons and persons from minority ethnic groups were
defined as comprehensively retarded as the cutoff level for sub-
normality was raised. Stigmatization was a major concern of parents
interviewed. Of a group of 108 children followed for several years
and classified as retarded, only one in five ever returned to the
regular class. Thus, many parents were justified in seeing the
program as a "sentence of death." (RIE)

643. Mingione, Ann D. "Need for Achievement in Negro, White, and Puerto
Rican Children." Journal of Consulting and Clinical Psychology.
31:1 (1968). pp. 94-95.

Compared the need for achievement of Negro, White, and Puerto
Rican fifth and seventh graders in low socioeconomic areas of a large
New England city. The need-for-achievement test consisted of 6 topic
sentences about which the subjects wrote stories. F tests of the
need-for-achievement scores revealed no significant differences.

These results contrast with the author's previous study in which
White children had higher need-for-achievement scores than Negro
children and seventh graders scored higher than fifth graders.  There
were more words per story, greater variety of story themes, and more
stories concerning females written by both boys and girls than in
the previous study, when the stories were written in response to
line drawings of people.  School grades and group intelligence test
scores. did not correlate with the need for achievement scores in
this study.  (PASAR)

644.  Mishra, S.P. and M. Hurt, Jr.  "The Use of Metropolitan Readiness
        Tests with Mexican-American Children." California Journal
        of Educational Research.  Vol. 21 (1970). pp. 182-187.

        The study was designed to test the assumption that reliability
and predictive validity for the Metropolitan Readiness Tests (MRT)
would be lower for Mexican-Americans who spoke Spanish at home than
for the standardization group.  Ss were 40 male and 33 female
Mexican-American elementary school students from a poor section of
Tucson, Arizona.  They were given the complete MRT battery of
tests at the beginning of first grade and the Metropolitan Achievement Tests in Word Knowledge and Reading at the end of their grade.
Results show that verbal tests in the MRT battery have a lower
reliability and predictive validity than the tests which do not
require skill in English to answer.  The authors note that these
findings have implications for educators working on programs for
the "culturally deprived."  (ECK)

645.  Morper, J.  An Investigation of the Relationship of Certain
        Predictive Variables and the Academic Achievement of
        Spanish-American and Anglo Pupils in Junior High School.
        Unpublished Ph.D.  Dissertation, Oklahoma State University. 1966.
        (Dissertation Abstracts. Vol. 27 (1967). p. 4051A.).

646.  New York City Board of Education, Bureau of Educational Research.
        The Effectiveness of the Cooperative Inter-American Tests
        of General Ability, Primary Level, Form A, as a Measure
        of the Intellectual Functioning of Spanish-Speaking Pupils
        Enrolled in the Elementary Schools.  New York:  Board of
        Education.  1954.

647.  Nichols, Paul E.  A Study of the Cooperative Inter-American Tests
        of Language Usage at the Junior High School Level.  Unpublished
        Master's theses, University of Texas.  1952.

648.  Nuttal, Ronald L.  Do the Factors Affecting Academic Achievement
        Differ by the Socio-Economic Status or Sex of the Student?  A
        Puerto Rican Secondary School Sample.  Final Report.  Boston
        College, Chestnut Hill, Massachusetts.  Institute of Human
        Sciences Washington, D.C.:  National Center for Educational
        Research and Development (DHEW/OE). June 1972.  110p.
        (ED 064 465)

Variables expected to be associated with academic achievement
were examined in a sample (generally exceeding 2500) from eight
secondary schools in Baymon Norte, Puerto Rico. Concern was whether
variables associated with academic achievement differed by sex or by
socioeconomic status (SES). Multivariate analysis of variance with
three factors of achievement, sex, and SES were made. High achievers
tended to have accepting mothers, parents low on Hostile Psychological
Control, and low on autonomy; and were more goegraphical mobile, had
fewer siblings, were more intelligent, obedient, conscientious,
artistic, group-mined, placid, self-disciplined, responsible,
anxious (preocupado), mature, and less excitable. High achieving
girls were less authoritarian, dogmatic, and test anxious, and
gave fewer false but socially desirable responses. Students whose
academic achievements were consistent with their SES. Self concepts
were higher for achievers, especially for low SES students in
junior high schools, and for all students in high schools. Low
achiever, especially boys, disliked school. High achieving boys
and low achieving girls were more self sufficient, while low achieving
boys and high achieving girls were more group dependent. (RIE)

649. Nuttall, Ronald L. et al. Family Background, Parent-Child Relation-
     ships and Academic Achievement Among Puerto Rican Junior and
     Senior High School Students. Report No. 4: Study of Factors
     Affecting Student Achievement. Boston: Boston College, Mass.
     Institute of Human Sciences. 1969. 11 pp.
     (ED 043 698)

     The reliability, validity, and relationships of a Spanish
language adaptation of Schaefer's Child's Report of Parental Behavior Inventory (CRPBI) was examined. It was found that CRPBI
had had reliabilities averaging .78 and factor analysis indicated a
3 factor structure similar to Schaefer's previous work. Background
variables, especially socioeconomic status (SES) were related to the
CRPBI factors. Generally, higher SES went with higher acceptance
and lower hostile psychological control. Children from large
families were less accepted. The CRPBI factors predicted grades,
especially among JHS males. Background factors predicted college
plans. (RIE abridged)

650. O'Brien, Sister Mary Gratia. Relationship of Self Perceptions of
     Puerto Rican and Non-Puerto Rican Parochial School Children to
     Selected School Related Variables. Ph.D. Dissertation, Fordham
     University. 1970.
     (Dissertation Abstracts. Vol. 31 (1971). pp. 3347A-3348A)

     The purpose of this study was to examine the self-perceptions
of Puerto Rican children and to compare them with the self-perceptions of children from other ethnic backgrounds. Ss were 2796
fifth, sixth and seventh graders from twelve elementary parochial
schools in the Archdiocese of New York. Ss were divided into four
groups (PR boys, PR girls, Other boys, Other girls); boys were

compared with girls of the same ethnic grouping and Puerto Rican
children were compared with Other children on each of the following
variables: scholastic achievement, mental ability, socioeconomic
status, teacher-ratings of behavior, and appraisal-perception. Ss
responded to a Checklist of Trait Names twice; first, in response
to "I think I am...," and second, "My teacher thinks I am...." (DH)

651. Palomares, Uvaldo H. and E.J. Cummins. Assessment of Rural
     Mexican-American Pupils Preschool and Grades One Through
     Six: San Isidro, California. Sacramento: California State
     Department of Education. 1968.

652. _____ Assessment of Rural
     Mexican-American Pupils Preschool and Grades One Through
     Twelve: Wasco, California. Sacramento: California State
     Department of Education. 1968.

653. Palomares, Uvaldo H. and L.C. Johnson. "Evaluation of Mexican-
     American Pupils for EMR Classes." California Education.
     Vol. 3 (1966). pp. 27-29.

654. Philippus, M.J. Test Prediction of School Success of Bilingual
     Hispano-American Children. Colorado: Denver Department of
     Health and Hospitals. 1967.
     (ED 036 577)

655. Pickett, G.D. "A Comparason of Translation and Blank-Filling as
     Testing Techniques," English Language Teaching, 23:1,
     (October, 1968).

     Points out the advantage of translating over slotfilling
     as a testing technique. (NYS Bibliography)

656. Rea, George H. A Study of Four Cooperative Inter-American Tests.
     Unpublished Master's thesis, University of Texas. 1954.

657. Readiness Checklist. Las Cruces School District, New Mexico;
     Dissemination Center for Bilingual Bicultural Education
     Austin, Texas. Washington, D.C: Office of Education. 12p.
     (ED 061 839)

     The Readiness Checklist is a 69-item instrument that provides a
measure of the psychomotor development of children. It covers seven
main areas: general health, movement patterns and muscular coordination, auditory skills, visual skills, speech and language, personal
independence, and social adjustment. The checklist is designed to
measure a child's level of physical maturity and can be used to
collect data as a diagnostic tool to isolate deficient children for
immediate remedial action. Collection of data through the checklist
can result in the establishment of norms. A score sheet is attached
to the checklist. (RIE)

658. Sabatino, David A. and Others. "Perceptual, Language and Academic Achievement of English, Spanish and Navajo Speaking Children Referred for Special Classes." _Journal of School Psychology_. Vol. 10 (March 1972). pp. 39-46. (EC 04 1641)

The purpose of this study was to determine the perceptual language and academic achievement functions of English, Spanish, and Navajo children experiencing learning problems and referred for placement into special education classes. Those test variables which discriminated among the native English-speaking children and the children who spoke Spanish or Navajo natively were, as predicted, those tasks which involved knowledge of the linguistic rules of English. It would seem that, taken as a group, the school learning problems experienced by the native Spanish-or Navajo-speaking children were the result of their limited linguistic competence in English, the language of instruction in their classrooms. (EC)

659. Schwartz, Audrey James. "A Comparative Study of Values and Achievement: Mexican-American and Anglo Youth." _Sociology of Education_. 44:4 (Fall, 1971). pp. 438-462.

Several value orientations and their relations with school achievement were examined with student samples from the Los Angeles City Schools. Findings show that Mexican-American pupils with value orientations most similar to those of Anglo pupils have the highest scholastic achievement. While it is recognized that pupils' values and achievements are substantially interdependent, the findings of this study suggest that affective factors in the cultural background of many Mexican-American pupils hinder their general academic achievement. (from article)

660. Spolsky, Bernard. "Language Testing: The Problem of Validation." _TESOL Quarterly_. 2:2 (June, 1968).

Discusses the differences between tests for control of instruction, and tests for control of a person's career and the serious difficulty of validation in the second class.

661. Stambler, Ada. _A Study of Eighth Grade Puerto Rican Students at Junior High School 65, Manhattan, with Implications for Their Placement, Grouping, and Orientation_. Unpublished Ph.D. Dissertation, Columbia University. 1958.

662. Steubner, Josephine. "Racial Differences in Reading Achievement." _Texas Outlook_. Vol. 24 (January 1940) p. 32.

663. The University of the State of NY, The State Education Department, Bureau of Continuing Education Curriculum Development. _Test of Readiness for Literacy (Pilot Edition)_, 1970.

This instrument is designed to assess the degree to which adults who are illiterate possess the requisites to learning to read. It will be administered by State Education Department, personnel at selected Adult Basic Education centers in New York State. Information gathered from this test, plus data from a standardized reading readiness test, will be used as guides for the development of comprehensive readiness for literacy programs.

N.B. This experimental test has been administered to non-native English speakers, among others, in New York City. (from the test booklet)

664. Vega Hernández, Elias. <u>Reading Retardation in Zavala School, Austin, Texas</u>. Master's thesis, University of Texas. 1954.

665. Willis, Robert Manks. <u>An Analysis of the Adjustment and Scholastic Achievement of Forty Puerto Rican Boys Who Attend Transition Classes in New York City</u>. Unpublished Ph.D. Dissertation, New York University. 1961.

The objectives of this study were to identify the effects of transition classes on the adjustment, retention and scholastic achievement of forty Puerto Rican boys in a New York City school and to determine the implications their influence has for improvement of the curriculum. Ss were forty tenth grade boys from Morris High School in New York City; all Ss were born in Puerto Rico and had attended transition classes. Data was collected from the following sources: class record forms, cumulative report cards; interviews with students, parents, teachers and guidance counselors. Students were put into two groups according to their status at the time of the study: Group I, "Drop-Outs," and Group II, those students still attending school. The findings indicate that there were no significant differences between the social and educational characteristics of the two groups. Recommendations were made for curriculum improvement in terms of each student, in terms of the community. The author suggests 1) better transition classes, 2) improved T.E.S.L. programs, 3) a more intensive guidance program, 4) more effective measures for the evaluation of these students, 5) more realistic placement of Puerto Rican students, 6) more effective programs in remedial reading, 7) an increased awareness and understanding of Puerto Rican students on the part of school personnel, and 8) increased participation of Puerto Rican students and adults in the educational process (including decision-making). (DH)

666. Zirkel, Perry A. "Self Concept and the 'Disadvantaged' of Ethnic Group Membership and Mixture." <u>Review of Educational Research</u>. Vol. 14 (1971). pp. 211-225

The author presents a brief review of the literature on the self-concept of minority group members, and discusses the relationship between low self-evaluation and academic under-achievement. He concludes that ethnic group membership may have some effect, positive or negative, on the self-concept of the disadvantaged

child. The supposed "disadvantage" of minority students can be
turned into an advantage by enhancing the self-concept, perhaps
through such programs as bilingual-bicultural education and Black
Studies. (DH)

667. Zirkel, Perry Alan and John F. Grene. The Academic Achievement of
      Spanish-Speaking First Graders in Connecticut, Conn. State
      Department of Education, Bureau of Compensatory and Community
      Educational Services, April, 1971, 8pp.
      (ED 054 275)

      Study sought to demonstrate that deficiencies shown by Puerto
Rican children in verbal ability and academic achievement might
not exist if initial instruction and testing were in Spanish. The
Inter-American Test of General Ability was administered by the same
examiner first in Spanish, then in English. The Puerto Rican first
graders scored significantly lower on the English forms than all
ethnic groups, including Puerto Ricans, in Coleman's study on the
subtest of verbal ability; however, on the non-verbal ability subtest, the Puerto Ricans scored significantly higher than all groups
in the Coleman study. The subjects scored much higher on the
Spanish form than on the English form. (from RIE rev. and abridged)

H.  Special Educational Programs and Efforts to Serve the Needs of
    Puerto Rican (and other Non-English-speaking) Children in Mainland
    Schools

General Programs

668.  ABE Phase III:  Progress and Problems.  September 1, 1969-April 1,
      1970.  Alburque, New Mexico:  Southwestern Cooperative Educa-
      tional Laboratory.  Washington, D.C.:  Office of Education.
      April 1, 1970.  166pp.  Interim Report.
      (ED 060 406)

      Interim information concerning the Adult Basic Education grants
is provided in the three parts of this report.  (RIE abridged)

669.  "Activaron La Enseñanza del Inglés Básico en las Communidades
      Boricuas."  La Prensa.  (February 23, 1952).

670.  Andersson, Theodore.  "A New Focus on the Bilingual Child."  Modern
      Language Journal.  Vol. 49 (1965).  pp. 156-160.

671.  Andrus, E.P.  "Social Living Classes for the Underprivileged."
      California Journal of Secondary Education.  Vol. 14 (November
      1939).  pp. 414-417.

672.  Andrus, E.P.  "Workshop Studies Education of Mexican Americans."
      California Journal of Secondary Education.  Vol. 18 (October
      1943)  pp. 328-330.

673.  Angel, Frank.  Program Content to Meet the Educational Needs of
      Mexican-Americans.  University Park, New Mexico:  New Mexico
      State University.  1968.  21 pp.
      (ED 017 392)

674.  Baldwin, Clare C.  "Education of the Non-English Speaking and
      Bilingual (Spanish) Pupils in the Junior High Schools of
      Districts 10 and 11, Manhattan."  June, 1952.  131 pp.
      (Unpublished material).

675.  Baldwin, Clare C.  "Program Outlined for Puerto Ricans."  The New
      York Times.  (December 5, 1947).

676.  Barclay, Lisa and Frances Kurcz.  Comparative Efficacies of English,
      Spanish and Bilingual Cognitive Verbal Instruction.  1969, 309p.
      (ED 030 473)

      Reports results of an experiment conducted with Mexican-American
Head Start children in California in 1967.  Three approaches were
used:  (1) structured English training program; (2) Spanish used as
language of instruction; and (3) English used as language of instruction; together with a control group receiving usual preschool art
and music activities.  Results showed no significant differences be-

145

tween the groups but allowed that extraneous factors could have
invalidated the experiment. Though this experiment ended in failure,
much background material is presented in the introduction. (from
document rev, substantially)

677. Benner, Ralph and Reyes, Ramiro. California Plan for Education of
     Migrant Children. 1967. 25 pp.
     (ED 020 831)

678. "Bilingual Problems in Puerto Rican Study." Curriculum and
     Materials. 11:2 (February, 1948). pp. 1-2.

679. Blancett, Bob L. Implementation of a Migrant Education Program in
     the Richgrove School District. July 1972. 189p.
     (ED 063 990)

680. Blourock, Barbara. "Aspira in the Junior High School." High Points.
     (February, 1966). pp. 53-55.

681. Bondarin, Arley. Assimilation Thru Cultural Understanding: Hoboken,
     New Jersey. New York: Center for Urban Education, 1969, 64p.
     (ED 034 804)

     This ESEA Title III project is aimed at assimilating foreign
     born and Puerto Rican children in the Hoboken, New Jersey public
     school system. Eight programs are described: two-week staff visits
     to Puerto Rican schools, teacher exchanges between Hoboken and Puerto
     Rican school systems, inservice course for teaching students with
     English handicaps, development of suitable instructional materials,
     human resource center, daily orientation programs, experimental
     bilingual classes, and a bilingual student aide program. (ERIC)

682. Booth, Jonathan L. "Meeting a Bilingual Problem: Elementary Spanish
     in the Tucson Public Schools." American School Board Journal.
     Vol. 117 (July 1948). pp. 15-17.

683. Broom, Perry Morris. An Interpretive Analysis of the Economic and
     Educational Status of the Latin American in Texas, with Emphasis
     on the Basic Factors Underlying an Approach to an Improved
     Program of Occupational Guidance, Training and Adjustment for
     Secondary Schools. Unpublished Ph.D. Dissertation, University
     of Texas. 1942.

684. Castañeda, Alfredo, ed. and Others. Mexican Americans and Educational
     Change. Symposium (University of California, Riverside, May 21-
     22, 1971). California University, Riverside. Mexican American
     Studies Program. Washington, D.C.: Office of Education. May,
     1971. 421p.
     (ED 063 988)

685. Childers, Jean. Some Secondary Level Curriculum Considerations for
     Teaching Spanish to the Mexican American in Austin, Texas.

The purpose of this study is to present curriculum considerations for the non-native who is interested in teaching Spanish to the Mexican-American at the secondary level of instruction. Approaches and directions are suggested to help bring about an effective type of cross-cultural teaching, particularly for certified Anglo teachers whose teaching experience has been exclusively with Anglo classes. The study includes: (1) introductory remarks, (2) review of related literature, (3) background, (4) classroom approaches and procedures, (5) textbooks and other materials, and (6) summary and conclusion. Appendixes contain sample questionnaires concerning sociological and educational information about Mexican-American students and sample communications to parents. (RIE)

686. "Classes for Mexican Workers in Michigan Aid Inter-American Understanding." _American Teacher_. Vol. 30 (January 1946) pp. 26-27.

687. Cordasco, F. "Educational Programs for Puerto Rican Pupils." _New York Times_. (May 30, 1967).

688. Cordasco, F. "Helping the Language Barrier Student." _Instructor_. Vol. 72 (May, 1963). p.20.

689. Cordasco, F. and E. Bucchioni. _Education Programs for Puerto Rican Students_. (Jersey City Public Schools). Evaluation and Recommendations. Jersey City: Board of Education. 1971.

690. Cordasco, Francesco and Eugene Bucchioni. _The Puerto Rican Community of Newark, N.J.: An Educational Program for Its Children_. Newark: Board of Education, Summer 1970.

691. _CVAE (Coordinated Vocational-Academic Education) Academic Curriculum Project. Evaluation Report, 1971-1972_. Education Service Center Regional, Edinburg, Texas. Austin: Texas Education Agency, Department of Occupational and Technical Education 1972. 78 pp.
    (ED 066 289)

692. DeWeaver, N.C. "NCTU Labor Schools for Spanish-speaking." _America_. Vol. 93 (August 6, 1955). pp. 451-453.

693. Dossick, Jesse J. "Workshop Field Study in Puerto Rican Education and Culture." _Journal of Educational Sociology_. Vol. 28 (December 1954). pp. 174-180.

This article discusses several workshops in Puerto Rican Education and Culture which were held in Puerto Rico to give teachers, administrators and community and social workers in New York City an understanding of the circumstances in which the Puerto Ricans they worked with grew up in order that they might be better able to deal with the problem of adjustment to life in the mainland United States. A description of the requirements of the workshops is included as are some of the comments by participants. Recommendations for improving the workshops are also included.(ECK)

147

694. Elementary Curriculum in Intergroup Relations:  Case Studies in
     Instruction.  Washington, D.C.:  American Council on Education:
     Work in Progress Series, 1950.

695. Espinosa, Renato.  Final Report on Head Start Evaluation and Re-
     search:  1967-68 to the Office of Economic Opportunity.  Section
     II:  Achievement Motivation and Patterns of Reinforcement in
     Head Start Children.  1968.  124 pp.
     (ED 023 458)

696. Evaluation of State Urban Education Programs, District 10, New York
     City, Board of Education, 1970-1971 School Year.  Fordham
     University, Bronx, New York.  Institute for Research and
     Evaluation.  June 1971.  199p.
     (ED 059 017)

697. Felder, D.  "The Education of Mexican-Americans:  Fallacies on the
     Monocultural Approach."  Social Education.  Vol. 34 (1970).
     pp. 639-642.

698. Fierro, Leonard.  Chicano Community Action Efforts at the Local
     Level and Their Effects on Promoting Educational Change for
     Mexican-Americans.  A Research Paper.  Alburquerque, New
     Mexico:  Southwestern Cooperative Educational Laboratory.  1970.
     16pp.
     (ED 057  972)

699. Filep, Robert T. and Others.  Voluntarias De Sesame Street: Manual
     Para Conducir Las Sesions "Sesame Street" Con Ninos De Edad
     Pre-Escolar.  Institute for Educational Development, El Segundo,
     California.  New York, New York:  John and Mary R. Markle
     Foundation.  July 28, 1971.  50 pp.
     (ED 057 897)

700. Fishman, J.A. and Vladimir C. Nahirny.  "The Ethnic Group School and
     Mother Tongue Maintenance in the U.S."  Sociology of Education.
     Vol. 37 (1964).  pp. 306-317.

701. Gaarder, Bruce.  "Teaching the Bilingual Child:  Research, Develop-
     ment and Policy."  Modern Language Journal.  Vol. 49 (1965).
     pp. 165-175.

702. González, Nancie L.  Positive and Negative Effects of Chicano Mili-
     tancy on the Education of the Mexican American.  Albuquerque,
     New Mexico:  Southwestern Cooperative Educational Laboratory.
     1970.  37p.
     (ED 061 004)

     Types of organizations involved in Chicano movements operating in
the five southwestern states and other areas with large numbers of
Mexican Americans are described in this paper.  They are examined
in terms of the possibilities of their philosophis or activism

affecting education either on a short-term or long-term basis. Additionally, the relationship between the kinds of demands made by the older Spanish-speaking activists and those of today's Chicanos is considered. It is recommended that further research be done on topics such as the various Chicano organizations, the interrelationship between Chicano militancy and other protest movements of the past and present, the implications of improved education along the lines demanded by today's Chicano activist, and how the Anglo power structure is likely to respond to the efforts of activist minority organizations. An appendix consisting of members of the Chicano Press Association, a list of 41 Chicano organizations, and a bibliography are included. (RIE)

703. Guerra, Emilio L. "Orientación de los estudiantes de Puerto Rico en la ciudad de Nueva York." El Diario de Nueva York. (March 28, 1949). p.6.

704. _____ "The Orientation of Puerto Rican Students in New York City." Modern Language Journal. (October, 1948). p415-420.

Adapting education the needs of immigrant Puerto Ricans in New York. Cultural and social adjustment stressed as most important part of the program. (from Sánchez, ED 041 680)

705. Guidelines for Educational Programs in the Commonwealth of Pennsylvania for Children Whose Dominant Language is Not English. Pennsylvania State Department of Education, Harrisburg. (May 1972. 27pp.
(ED 066 075)

706. Hacer Vida. First Year Evaluation Report, 1970-71. Riverside County Superintendent of Schools, California. Washington, D.C.: Office of Education. August 3, 1971. 194p.
(ED 064 018)

707. .Hall, Richard W. "Ann and Abby: The Agony Column on the Air." TESOL Quarterly, 5:3 (September, 1971), pp. 274-249.

This article suggests that the syndicated columns published under the by-lines "Dear Abby" and "Ann Landers" contain useful textual material for intermediate and advanced ESL students. The following characteristics seem valuable: 1) the columns offer sharp insights into implicit American cultural values; 2) they are modeled on the spoken, rather than written language; 3) they stimulate classroom discussion. (from the article)

708. Hefferman, H. "Reports of the Conference on the Education of Children of Seasonal Workers." California Journal of Elementary Education. Vol. 6-7 (February 1939) pp. 181-192.

709. "Hemos Trabajado Bien;" A Report on the First National Conference
of Puerto Ricans, Mexican-Americans, and Educators on "The
Special Educational Needs of Urban Puerto Rican Youth." New
York: Aspira, Inc. May, 1968. 78pp.
(ED 023-780)

710. Intergroup Education in Public Schools: Experimental Programs
Sponsored by the Project in Intergroup Education in in Cooperative
Schools: Theory, Practice, and In-Service Education. Washington,
D.C.: American Council on Education. 1952.

711. Kahnheimer, Leah W. "A Program in Social Living for Puerto Rican
Pupils." High Points. (June, 1954). pp. 58-68.

712. Katz, David. The Effects of a Compensatory Educational Program on
the Vocational Aspirations, Expectations, Self-Concept, and
Achievement of Selected Groups of JHS Students.
(Dissertation Abstracts: 1969. Vol. 29 (9-A). p. 2963)

This study was designed to investigate the effects of a compensatory educational program on the vocational aspirations, expectations, self-concepts and achievements of selected groups of ninth
grade junior high school students in New York City. Ss were male,
average in grade, at least two years below grade level in reading,
and members of either Black or Puerto Rican minorities. All
students in the experimental group were in a Career Guidance program. Students in the control groups were matched for characteristics equivalent to those of the experimental group, except that
they were either 1) in the same school as the Ss but not taking part
in the Career Guidance program, or 2) in schools which did not have
the compensatory program. The instruments used by the investigators
to measure the variables in question were a personal adequacy scale
based on the Whittaker Scale, a modification of Hambruger's Life
Planning Questionnaire, and the Metropolitan Achievement Test. All
subjects were administered the tests and questionnaire on two
different occasions, at the beginning and end of the same school
year. Results of the statistical analysis indicated that the
Career Guidance program had no significant positive effects on the
variables under consideration. In fact, the effects that did
occur were contrary to the goals of the program. In the experimental
group congruency between aspiration and expectation was reduced,
rather than facilitated, while the control groups showed a significant increase over the same period of time. Black students gained
significantly more than the Puerto Rican students in reading
achievement, but the control group gained more in reading than the
experimental group overall. (DH)

713. Kniefel, Tanya Suarez. Programs Available for Strengthening the
Education of Spanish-Speaking Students. Las Cruces, New
Mexico: ERIC Clearinghouse on Rural Education and Small
Schools. 1968.

714. **Lorge**, Irving and Frank Mayans, Jr. "Vestibules vs. Regular Classes for Puerto Rican Migrant Pupils." <u>Teachers College Record</u>. 15:5 (February, 1954). pp. 231-237.

715. Mans, Rolando. <u>An Experimental Approach to the Teaching of Reading in Spanish at the Primary Level.</u> Master's thesis, Sacramento State College. September 1971. 103pp. (ED 056 602)

   An experiment in the teaching of reading in Spanish to second- and third-grade students, conducted by the author at the Ethel Phillips elementary school, utilizes a modified version of Dr. Laubach's "Syllabic, analytic-synthetic method of language instruction. Results indicate that success in school of children from Spanish-speaking homes may be directly related to the concept of self-identity. It is suggested that development of programs leading to curriculum-wide literacy in Spanish is considered by authorities in bilingualism to be one of the key factors in raising the Spanish-speaking child's level of expectation in his academic achievement. Major chapters in this study discuss: (1) the problem and definition of terms, (2) review of related literature, (3) procedures of the study, (4) analysis of data, and (5) summary, conclusions, and recommendations. A bibliography and an appendix containing sample lessons and measurement tools are included. (RIE)

716. Mayans, Frank, Jr. <u>Puerto Rican Migrant Pupils in New York City Schools: A Comparison of the Effects of Two Methods of Instructional Grouping on English Mastery and Attitudes.</u> Unpublished Ph.D. Dissertation, Columbia University. 1953. (<u>Dissertation Abstracts</u>. Vol. 14 (1954). pp. 68-69.).

   The purpose of this study was to compare the effects of two types of instructional grouping on the English mastery and assimilation of Puerto Rican migrant students. Ss were recent immigrants from Puerto Rico who were entering mainland schools for the first time; the schools were two junior high schools in New York City's Spanish Harlem. Ss were placed in two groups: 1) "regular" classes with the other students in the school and 2) "vestibule" classes in which all students were Puerto Ricans. At the start, Ss were pretested with the Cooperative Interamerican Test of General Ability and a Test of Reading, both in Spanish; an Attitude Toward the Surroundings Scale, also in Spanish, was administered. At the end of one semester, all Ss were given the Cooperative Interamerican Test of Reading, in English; Subtest I (oral vocabulary), Cooperative Interamerican Test of General Ability, in English; and the Attitude Toward Surroundings Scales, in Spanish. The findings indicated 1) that the migrant will learn more English if (s)he has a favorable attitude toward his surroundings; 2) the "regular" group has more unfavorable attitudes toward school; 3) the "regular" group has developed significantly more favorable attitudes toward schoolmates; and 4) "regular" students score higher in all three tests of English mastery. At the end of the semester, controls were lifted and all

students participated in "regular" classes. A follow-up study at
the end of the year yielded these results: 1) the original "regular"
Ss retained their superiority in English oral vocabulary, but not in
reading; 2) all Ss have more favorable attitudes toward schoolmates
with no differences between class groupings showing; 3) the original
"regular" Ss have become more assimilated, "make more friends, speak
English more often with their friends"; 4) Ss who preferred "regular"
grouping felt they learned more, while Ss who preferred the "vestibule"
grouping felt it helped them adjust better.  The author suggests
placing immigrant students in regular classes because of the rapid
pace at which assimilation can take place.  (DH)

717.  Mercer, Jane R.  <u>Sociocultural Factors in the Education Evaluation of
      Black and Chicano Children</u>.  Paper presented at the 10th Annual
      Conference on Civil Rights Educators and Students, NEA,
      Washington, D.C.  February 18-20, 1972.  16p.  Sacramento,
      California State Department of Education, Office of Compensatory
      Educaton.  Bethesda, Maryland:  National Institute of Mental
      Health.
      (ED 060 462)

      In a recent study the mothers of 268 children who were in
classes for educable mentally retarded in two public school districts
in Southern California were interviewed.  The responses of some of
these mothers dramatize three issues:  (1) biases in the assessment
procedures used to label children as mentally retarded; (2) the
stigmatization associated with special class placement; and (3)
inadequate programming.  Disproportionately large numbers of black
and Chicano children are labeled as mentally retarded by the public
schools.  Public schools rely more on IQ test scores than any other
community agency.  The schools label more persons as mentally retarded
share their labels with more other organizations, and label more
persons with IQ's above 70 and with no physical disabilities than any
other formal organization in the community.  Proportionately more
low status persons and persons from minority ethnic groups were
defined as comprehensively retarded as the cutoff level for sub-
normality was raised.  Stigmatization was a major concern of parents
interviewed.  Of a group of 108 children followed for several years
and classified as retarded, only one in five ever returned to the
regular class.  Thus, many parents were justified in seeing the
program as a "sentence of death."  (RIE)

718.  Meriam, J.O.  "Learning English Incidentally.  A Study of Bilingual
      Children."  Bulletin No. 15, U.S. Office of Education. 1937 105p.

719.  Meyerson, Marion.  "The Bilingual Child."  <u>Childhood Education</u>.
      Vol. 45 (1969).  pp. 525-527.

720.  Montag, Jennie and Mary Finocchiaro.  "Guidance and Curriculum for
      Puerto Rican Children."  <u>High Points</u>.  (January, 1951).  pp. 32-42.

721.  Montes, Marta.  "La Primera Escuela Puertorriqueña en la Ciudad de
      Nueva York."  <u>La Prensa.</u>  September 17, 1961.

722. Morrison, J. Cayce. "The Puerto Rican Study---What It Is - Where It Is Going." <u>Journal of Educational Sociology</u>. Vol. 28 (December 1954). pp. 167-173.

The Puerto Rican Study, which was sponsored by the New York City Board of Education, was concerned with the education and adjustment of Puerto Ricans in New York City. During the first, exploratory year of the study, visits were made to twenty-seven schools which served Puerto Ricans; seven representative schools were studied intensively. Information was gathered to find out who the Puerto Rican students were, how they were adapting to the schools and how the schools were adapting to them. The second phase of the study was an experimental one in which fourteen schools cooperated in varying degrees. One major part of this phase was an experiment in teaching English as a second language; another was a study of means to promote the acculturation of Puerto Ricans. It was hoped that at the end of the study "a recommended program of action for adoption by all schools will emerge." (ECK)

723. Muckley, Robert L. "After Childhood, What Then? An Overview of Ethnic Language Retention (Elret) Programs in the United States." <u>Revista Interamericana</u>. Vol. 2 (Spring 1972). p. 1-15. (ED 061 808)

This paper describes some of the programs in bilingual education throughout the country. Some scholarly studies are mentioned and the author discusses "domain stability," the retention of the ethnic language in specific situations. Among Spanish-speaking groups, the author notes that Mexican-Americans conserve Spanish much better than Puerto Ricans, who tend to prefer English in all domains. Some suggestions for helping retention of the ethnic language are offered. The small amount of materials designed specifically for teaching ethnic-speakers their own language is discussed and some of those materials are evaluated. Almost all the bilingual programs and publications are aimed at Mexican-Americans, and the author suggests that there are other Spanish-speakers and speakers of Italian and other languages who could also benefit from such programs. (ECK)

724. McCuen, John J. "Puerto Rican Survey Seeks Best Methods." <u>New York World Telegram and Sun</u>. (April 7, 1954). p. 42.

725. Natalico, Diana S. and Frederick Williams. <u>Carrascolendas: Evaluation of a Bilingual Television Series. Final Report</u>. Texas University, Austin. Center for Communication Research. Washington, D.C.: Office of Education. June 1971. 204 pp. (ED 054 612)

726. National Education Association. <u>Las voces nuevas de Sudoeste: Symposium on the Spanish-speaking Child in the Schools of the Southwest</u>. Washington, D.C.: NEA Department of Rural Education. 1966.

727. Nedler, Shari. Early Education for Spanish-Speaking Mexican-American Children: A Comparison of Three Intervention Strategies. 1970. 8 pp.
(ED 037 778)

728. Nedler, Shari. A Preschool Program for Spanish-Speaking Children: Good Samaritan Center, San Antonio, Texas. 1966.
(ED 001 378)

729. Nedler, Shari. The Status and Educational Effect of Head Start Programs on Mexican American Children. Albuquerque, New Mexico: Southwestern Cooperative Educational Laboratory. 1970. 16 pp.
(ED 056 804)

Approximately five research studies relating to Project Head Start and reviewed in this document disclose a gap in the knowledge base regarding the effectiveness of various intervention strategies implemented with Mexican American children. Programs have varied from community to community and only general trends can be identified at the present time. Among the findings are (1) experiments in language programs suggest that children benefit more from a structured program than from an unstructured one; (2) as measured by tests not sensitized to subpopulation variations, children from low-income families perform below middle-class children in cognitive, intellectual l, and achievement behavior; and 3) children of parents have a high level of involvement in Head Start perform better on tests of achievement and development. Many questions remain unanswered regarding characteristics of learner, design and development or replicable instructional programs, training of teachers, and parental involvement and education. (RIE)

730. Nedler, Shari and Sebera, Peggy. "Intervention Strategies for Spanish-speaking Preschool Children." Child Development. Vol. 42 (1971). pp. 259-267.

This study compared 3 strategies of early intervention designed to increase the language and communication skills of disadvantaged 3-year-old Mexican-American children. Treatment group 1 (T1) included 16 children in a planned Bilingual Early Childhood Educational Program. Group T2 included 16 children who were indirectly involved in a Parental Involvement Program. Group T3 was composed of 14 children in a traditional day-care center. Before and after a 9-month intervention period, all Ss were tested with the Leiter International Performance Scale and the Peabody Picture Vocabulary Test in English and Spanish. On all measures, T1 made significantly greater gains than T2 or T3, indicating the greater effectiveness of the planned Bilingual Early Childhood Education Program. (from the article)

731. New York City Board of Education. <u>Puerto Rican Study: Developing</u> <u>a Program for Testing Puerto Rican Pupils in New York City</u> <u>Public Schools</u>. New York: Board of Education. 1959. 143 pp.

732. New York State Multiethnic Task Force. <u>Programs, services, materials</u> <u>of the New York State Education Department for Black and Puerto</u> <u>Rican Studies</u>. Albany: State Education Department. 1970.

733. <u>Nuevas Vistas. A Report of the Annual Conference of the California</u> <u>State Department of Education (3rd, Los Angeles, April 24-26,</u> <u>1969)</u>. California State Department of Education, Sacramento. 1970. 42 pp. (ED 055 700)

734. Núñez, Louis and Charles Bahn. <u>National Conference: Meeting the</u> <u>Special Educational Needs of Urban Puerto Rican Youth</u>. Final Report. New York: Aspira, Inc. September 30, 1968. 14pp. (ED 023 778)

"The available evidence, scant and incomplete though it may be, indicates that Urban Puerto Rican youth have distinctive educational problems of great severity." At a two-day conference of leaders of Spanish-speaking communities, sponsored by ASPIRA, an organization designed to develop Puerto Rican leadership, meetings were held to discuss the specific problems and needs of Puerto Ricans in the United States, to understand the reasons for the current situation and to plan programs to improve the educational situation of Puerto Ricans. After the conference, questionnaires were mailed to the participants, 3% of whom replied. Responses indicated that conference participants believed that positive action was necessary. Some of the steps that would be taken included exploration of bilingual education programs, parent education programs, and the creation of scholarship opportunities for Puerto Ricans. (ECK)

735. Osuna, J.J. "Report on Visits to New York City Schools." Government of Puerto Rico. Department of Labor and Employment and Migration Bureau. 1948.

736. Pallone, Nathaniel J. et al. <u>Evaluation Study: Augmented Services</u> <u>for Non-English Speaking Pupils in Selected Junior High Schools,</u> <u>Board of Education, City of New York</u>. New York: New York University. 1969.

737. <u>El plan de Santa Barbara: A Chicano Plan for Higher Education</u>. Santa Barbara, California: La Causa Publications. 1970.

738. <u>Puerto Rican Community Development Project</u>: A Proposal for a Self-Help Project to Develop the Community by Strengthening the Family, Opening Opportunities for Youth and Making Full Use of Education. New York: Puerto Rican Forum. 1964.

739. Raisner, Arnold; Philip Bolger; and Carmen Sanguinetti. <u>Science</u> <u>Instruction in Spanish for Pupils of Spanish-Speaking Background</u>. New York: New York City Board of Education. 1967.

740. Rapp, M.L. Case Studies in Educational Performance Contracting. Part 5. Gilroy, California. Rand Corporation. Santa Monica, California. Washington, D.C.: DHEW. December 1971. 61pp. (ED 056 291)

741. A Report of the University of New Mexico's College Enrichment Program. New Mexico University, Albuquerque Institute for Social Research and Development. Sante Fe: New Mexico State Board of Educational Finance. October 15, 1871 65p. (ED 058 997)

742. Report of Workshops of the Fourth Annual Conference on Puerto Rican Education Held at Hunter College of the City University, May 18, 1964. New York: National Conference of Christians and Jews.

743. "Reshaping Public Education: For Spanish-Speaking Children." United Teacher. (May 29, 1968).

Discusses Puerto Rican children in New York City.

744. Rice, J.P., Jr. "Education of Subcultural Groups." School and Society. Vol. 94 (1964). pp. 360-362.

This article discusses intelligence testing, and includes a very brief survey of the literature on "culturally loaded" measures of intelligence. The author suggests compensatory programs for the slower learners, TESOL programs for the non-native speaker of English, and encourages the development of new instruments for testing bilingual students. (DH)

745. Riggs, Virginia Fields. Action Research in Oral English for the Linguistically Different Secondary Student: Odessa, Texas. M.A. thesis, University of Texas of Austin. May 1971. 99p. (ED 058 763)

A program designed to decrease the number of linguistically differentiated, nonstandard speakers of English in Texas classrooms and to help potential dropouts attain proficiency in the use of English (thereby allowing them to achieve mobility in the dominant Anglo-American culture) is described in this report. The program provides linguistically different Negro and Mexican-American students the opportunity to acquire skills in standard spoken English. The problem is reviewed in general terms with emphasis placed on the sociocultural implications of dialectal variations. A review of the literature precedes a detailed description of the program implemented at Ector High School. A summary, limitations, conclusions, and recommendations concerning the project are included. Appendixes contain relevant project information and sample questions and exercises used. A bibliography is provided. (RIE)

746. Rubinstein, Annette T. (ed.). Schools Against Children; The Case for Community Control. Monthly Review Press. 1970. 299pp. (ED 040 221)

Collection of articles revolving around the struggle for full racial equality through community control of schools by Black and Puerto Rican people of New York City. (RIE abridged)

747. Salazar, Tony. A Summer Program for Hispano High School Students. A Report for the Second Year, June 15-July 10, 1970. Colorado University, Boulder, Department of Physics and Astrophysics. Denver County Public Schools, Colorado. 1970. 21p. (ED 058 978)

748. Sanguinetti, Carmen. Adapting Science Instruction in New York City Junior High Schools to the Needs of Puerto Rican Background Pupils. Unpublished Ph.D. Dissertation, Columbia University. 1956.

749. Seda Bonilla, Eduardo. "Ethnic Studies and Cultural Pluralism." The Rican. No. 1 (Fall 1971). pp. 56-65.

750. Smith, George W. and Owen L. Caskey, eds. Promising School Practices for Mexican Americans. Austin, Texas: Southwest Educational Development Laboratory; Texas Tech University, Lubbock. Washington, D.C.: Office of Education. 1972. 262p. (ED 064 003)

751. Strell, Joseph. "Elementary School Principals Visit Puerto Rico." High Points. Vol. 47 (February 1965). pp. 69-71.

752. Texas Education Agency. Preschool Instructional Program for Non-English Speaking Children. Austin: Texas: Texas Education Agency.

753. Thomas, Alexander, Retardation in Intellectual Development of Lower-Class Puerto Rican Children in New York City. New York: Department of Psychiatry, New York University. 1967. (ED 017 591)

The objectives of this study were 1) to identify any patterns of behavioral and intellectual function which appear to be detrimental to optimal learning and development; 2) to identify inter- and extra-familial influences which produce the above patterns; and 3) to identify favorable patterns which can be used to prevent or remedy the situation. The population to be studied was lower-class Puerto Rican children in New York City. The Ss were two groups of Puerto Ricans: 95 in one group which was followed from infancy, and 155 in the other group which consisted of their older siblings. For comparative purposes, 2 groups of advantaged White children were also tested. All children between the ages of 6 and 14 were administered the WISC; those children between the ages of 15 to 17 were administered the WAIS. The areas of investigation were as follows: the problem of IQ score decrement with increase in age; below normal academic achievement; differences in behavioral style; language development, as affected by bilingualism; and the effects of child care practices, home environment and family characteristics on the child's development. Analysis of data was not complete, as this was an interim report. However, the following conclusions are presented by the author: 1) the population of Puerto Rican children tested were retarded in school achievement; 2) the findings do not show a decrement of IQ level between pre-school and school ages, indicating that the retardation in intellectual achievement is not a result of cultural deprivation, etc.; 3) language development is not retarded by bilingualism; and 4) other factors must be responsible, (e.g. poor schooling, inappropriate teaching methods). The author noted that some factors in the home environment may also be at fault, but any such conclusions must be withheld pending complete analysis of the findings. (DH)

754. Thonis, Eleanor Wall. Evaluating the Effectiveness of Programs Designed to Improve the Education of Mexican-American Pupils. 2nd ed. Sacramento, California: California State Department of Education. Washington, D.C.: Office of Education. 1971 13p. (ED 062 047)

755. Threlkeld, Paul T. The Effectiveness of Michigan Migrant Primary Interdisciplinary Project (MPIP) Curricula in Helping Children with English Language Problems. (1970) 23p. (ED 063 979)

756. Tindall, Lloyd W. and Others. An Examination of the Receptivity of Mexican-American and Anglo Rural Disadvantaged to Education Programs. Michigan State University, E. Lansing. Center for Rural Manpower and Public Affairs. March, 1972. 34p. (ED 060 974)

In order to determine the willingness of rural disadvantaged to participate in educational programs, 125 rural male Anglo and Mexican-American household heads, both on and off welfare, were interviewed. The stratified sample was drawn from 4 Michigan counties. Based on findings from the 81 questions, these conclusion were made: Mexican-Americans were more willing to participate in educational classes than Anglos, and both groups desired to participate in such classes to get a job or a better job; there was no difference in willingness of these groups to participate in educational programs on the basis of welfare or nonwelfare status; decisions to participate would tend to be determined by the character of a prospective job; respondents were willing to participate in classes pertaining to their personal, educational, and social welfare (e.g. classes on buying food or obtaining credit); respondents tended to see themselves favorably in terms of ability to be hired for a job, run their own business, or be leaders, respondents indicated that classes should last no longer than 6 months; transportation to class was viewed as a problem; respondents would not spend their own money for tuition or supplies; age, residence, miles to high school, educational achievement, number of children, income, size of town shopped in, and time lived in Michigan did not affect willingness of the respondents to participate in classes; and proximity to a community college or university did

affect willingness to participate. Included in the document are the
study description, study implications, the questionnaire, and a guide
for identifying disadvantaged household heads. (RIE)

757. Tireman, L.S. "Discovery and Use of Community Resources in the
Education of Spanish-speaking Pupils." National Education
Association, Department of Rural Education. Yearbook 1939.
pp. 72-85.

758. Tireman, L.S. "New Mexico Tackles the Problem of the Spanish-
Speaking Child." Journal of Education. Vol. 114 (November
1931) pp. 300-301.

759. Tucker, G.R. and Others. Cognitive and Attitudinal Consequences of
Following the Curricula of the First Four Grades in a Second
Language. McGill University, Montreal, Quebec. February 1971.
78pp.
(ED 055 485)

760. University of the State of New York. The State Education Department,
Division of General Education, Bilingual Education Unit. Early
Childhood Programs for Non-English-Speaking Children. Albany,
New York: 1972 66pp.

761. Villaraonga, Mariano. "Program of Education for Puerto Rican
Migrants." Journal of Educational Sociology. Vol. 28 (December
1954). pp. 146-150.

This is a brief description of the educational programs in
Puerto Rico and how they affect prospective migrant, such as extension
of education to more people, improvement of textbooks and instruction
of English, adult education, social studies courses which include
the continental United States, expansion of vocational education and
establishment of exchange of personnel and educational materials with
mainland cities. (ECK)

762. Weikart, David P. Early Childhood Special Education for Intellectually
Subnormal and/or Culturally Different Children. Ypsilanti, Michigan:
High/Scope Educational Research Foundation. 1971. 28p.
(ED 061 684)

763. Willis, Robert Manks. An Analysis of the Adjustment and Scholastic
Achievement of Forty Puerto Rican Boys Who Attend Transition
Classes in New York City. Unpublished Ph.D. Dissertation, New
York University. 1961.
(Dissertation Abstracts. Vol. 22 (1961). pp. 795-796).

The objectives of this study were to identify the effects of
transition classes on the adjustment, retention and scholastic
achievement of forty Puerto Rican boys in a New York City school and
to determine the implications their influence has for improvement of

the curriculum. Ss were forty tenth grade boys from Morris High
School in New York City; all Ss were born in Puerto Rico and had
attended transition classes. Data was collected from the following
sources: class record forms, cumulative report cards; interviews
with students, parents, teachers and guidance counselors. Students
were put into two groups according to their status at the time of
the study: Group I, "Drop-Outs," and Group II, those students still
attending school. The findings indicate that there were no significant differences between the social and educational characteristics
of the two groups. Recommendations were made for curriculum
improvement in terms of each student, in terms of the community.
The author suggests 1) better transition classes, 2) improved TESL
programs, 3) a more intensive guidance program, 4) more effective
measures for the evaluation of these students, 5) more realistic
placement of Puerto Rican students, 6) more effective programs in
remedial reading, 7) an increased awareness and understanding of
Puerto Rican students on the part of school personnel, and
8) increased participation of Puerto Rican students and adults in
the educational process (including decision-making). (DH)

764. Zirkel, Perry Alan. Puerto Rican Parents and Mainland Schools.
      Hartford, Connecticut: Hartford Model Cities. November 1971. 98p.
      (ED 062 473)

      This study constitutes the promised product of an institute on
"Puerto Rican Pupils in Mainland Schools," sponsored by the Educational Leadership Institute and the University of Hartford during the
summer of 1971. The stated purposes of the Institute were: 1) to
stimulate communications and understanding between school and
community representatives toward the improvement of the educational
opportunities of Puerto Rican pupils in mainland schools; 2) to
develop a data base concerning cultural and linguistic factors in
the home environment that may be significant toward that end; and
3) to examine and interpret such data in terms of present and potential
school programs and practices. The Institute focused on facilitating
the relationship between the home and school environment of Puerto
Rican pupils in Hartford as a possible model for other mainland school
systems. The formal program of the Institute was concentrated in the
week of June 28-July 2. The morning sessions provided the opportunity
to interact with several resource people in small group discussions.
The afternoon sessions were devoted to conducting structured interviews in the homes of a cross-section of Puerto Rican families who had
children in the Hartford schools. The duration of the summer was used
for further research and the final writing of independent individual
reports, each culminating in recommendations for improving the educational opportunities of these children in the Hartford schools (RIE)

765. Zirkel, Perry A. "Self-Concept and the 'Disadvantage' of Ethnic
      Group Membership and Mixture." Review of Educational Research.
      Vol. 14 (1971). pp. 211-225.

The author presents a brief review of the literature on the
self-concept of minority group members, and discusses the relationship between low self-evaluation and academic under-achievement.  He
concludes that ethnic group membership may have some effect, positive
or negative, on the self-concept of the disadvantaged child.  The
supposed "disadvantage" of minority students can be turned into an
advantaged by enhancing the self-concept, perhaps through such
programs as bilingual-bicultural education and Black Studies. (DH)

Teaching English as a Second Language

766.   Abbey, Karin L.  Social Studies as Social Anthropology:  A Model
          for ESL Curricula.  Paper presented at the Sixth Annual TESOL
          Convention, Washington, E.D.C. February 28, 1972.  15p.
          (ED 060 735)

767.   Adair, J.B. and Robert L. Curry.  Talking It Over:  An Adult
          Reading Readiness Program for the Culturally Different. 2 vols.
          Chicago: Follet.  1966.

768.   Adams, John V. and Wallace K. Ewing.  A Study of Student Attitudes
          toward English as a Second Language in Puerto Rico.  (1971).  58p.
          (ED 057 695)

          The results of a questionnaire designed to investigate Puerto
       Rican students' attitudes toward learning English show that there is
       a predominantly positive attitude toward English-as-a-second lan-
       guage in the Puerto Rican town studied in this survey.  The question-
       naires solicit information from students in grades five through
       eight concerning personal data, students' contact with English, amount
       of English used, parental attitudes, and student attitude toward
       learning English.  The shortcomings of Puerto Rico's standardized
       English curriculum may result from inappropriate teaching methods
       rather than from a negative attitude on the part of the students.
       The students may be receiving too much language material in too
       little time without reinforcing what is learned in class through
       use outside of class.  English might be better taught as a foreign
       language.  English and Spanish versions of the questionnaires are
       provided along with graphs illustrating the results of this survey.
       (RIE)

769.   Anderson, Virginia.  "Teaching English to Puerto Rican Pupils."  High
          Points.  (March, 1964).  pp. 51-54.

770.   Andersson, Theodore.  "The Optimum Age for Beginning the Study of
          Modern Languages."  International Review of Education.  Vol. 6
          (1960).  pp. 298-306.

          This is a review of the way children learn language with
       suggestions as to when and how a second language should be taught.
       After describing the way infants learn language, the author describes
       situations where young children are able to use three or four languages

in appropriate situations without confusion; he notes that after a
certain age, approximately ten, children begin to lose the facility
to learn language. The author tentatively proposes age four as the
earliest recommended age to begin language study, and suggests that
the best method for language learning is in a natural situation with
an adult native speaker. He cites some opinions that bilingualism
may be harmful, but also mentions other opinions that knowing a
second language is worthwhile. (ECK)

771. Arthur, Bradford. "Reading Literature and Learning a Second
     Language." Language Learning, 18:3 and 4 (December, 1968).

     Demonstrates that literature in ESL programs must both teach
second language skills and retain its literary values for second
language learners. (NYS Bibliography)

772. Banathy, Bela et al. "The Use of Contrastive Data in Foreign
     Language Course Development: in Albert Valdman (ed.)
     Trends in Language Teaching, New York: McGraw-Hill, 1966.

     In the context of discussing the gap between the "how" and
"what" of ESL teaching, this article presents the use of contrastive
analysis and research data. It also presents an inventory of target
elements in an ESL course. (NYS Bibliography)

773. Bartlett, Alma J. From Spanish to English the Natural Way. El Paso
     Board of Education, Texas. 1949. 261pp. (mimeographed)

774. Basic Occupational Language Training (BOLT). Final Report. Puerto
     Rican Forum, Inc., New York, New York. Washington, D.C.:
     Manpower Administration (DOL), Office of Special Manpower
     Programs. 1969. 121pp.
     (ED 055 151)

     This 18-month phase of a continuing demonstration project was
designed to develop and test a program of English literacy training
for Puerto Rican workers. Participation in the Basic Occupational
Language Training (BOLT) program was based on the assumptions that
an intensive exposure basis will result in significant improvement
in job-related and non-job-related English language capability as
measured by designated tests and follow-up, and improvement in language
capability will contribute significantly to persistence, success in
and benefit from specific job upgrading programs, as derived from
analysis of skill training reports and follow-up in employment.
Other than the positive results that language improvement does, in
fact, occur, and that it contributes to job retention and upgrading,
other inferences can be made from the data from computer analysis and
a range of evaluation data compiled. The assumption that older men
resist training is unwarranted as shown by significant increases in
language competency in 40- and 50-year-old students. The report gives
an account of techniques and actions which resulted in a continuation
of the experimentation in a second phase now in progress. (RIE)

775. Behavioral Objectives for English as a Second Language (Developmental Copy). Four County Committee on Behavioral Objectives. California August 1969. 79pp.
(ED 035 874)

776. Bigelow, G.E. and D.P. Harris. The United States of America: Readings in ESL. New York: Holt, Rinehart and Winston. 1960. paper.

777. Blackburn, Ruth M. "English for Foreign Students Goes Out on the Streets," TESOL Quarterly, 5:3 (September, 1971), pp. 251-256.

There is much discussion these days about what to do in the FL classroom to develop skills in communication. For the foreign students in our universities the best laboratory is outside the classroom - in the community of native speakers of English. It is obvious that this setting is more natural and more challanging for the students and that, as they talk with Americans, their oral fluency will improve. What is not so obvious is that when students draw upon community experiences for their themes, their writing improves. Field experiences, featuring interviews with native speakers as a source of information and ideas, help to wean the foreign students away from over-reliance on the bilingual dictionary and on the authority of the textbook. Careful preparation for the field experiences will help the students to develop more self-confidence and to be more observant of details, more independent in their thinking, and more responsible in their statements. (author)

778. Blatchford, Charles H. A Theoretical Contribution to ESL Diagnostic Test Construction. Paper presented at the Fifth Annual TESOL Convention, New Orleans, Louisiana, March 7, 1971. 12pp.
(ED 055 484)

A diagnostic test in English as a second language should be a series of miniature tests on specific problems. Subscores in each area should be considered rather than a total score. The results should be used to probe mastery in an area rather than provide the means for comparing one student against another. The statistical reliability of the results does not necessarily depend on test length. The teacher should look at each item for each student rather than the score and should spend more time studying the analysis of each student's test. The criterion of the percent of correct decisions may be a more meaningful measure than ascertaining the traditional coefficients of reliability. Tables provide the statistical data under consideration. (RIE)

779. Bordie, John G. "When Should Instruction in a Second Language or Dialect Begin?" Elementary English. 48:5 (May, 1971) p. 551-558.
(EJ 042 896)

A preprint from a forthcoming pamphlet of the National Conference on Research in English. (RIE)

780. Bordwell, Constance. "The Film and the ESL Program: To View or Not to View," Journal of English as a Second Language, Vol. 4 (Spring, 1969).

   Presents considerations for and against the use of films in ESL teaching. (NYS Bibliography)

781. Bowen, J. Donald. "Characteristics of an Effective Program of Teaching English as a Second Language," California Education, Vol. 3, (February, 1966).

   Outlines the characteristics of a typical ESL program, centering on (1) how to produce an effective program and (2) how to appraise such a program. (NYS Bibliography)

782. Bracy, Maryruth (ed.) Workpapers in English as a Second Language, Volume III, Los Angeles: UCLA, 1969, 96pp. (ED 054 666)

   Several articles discuss teaching and learning a second language and practical considerations in second language learning such as reading and writing skills, the use of poetry, the concept of style among elementary school children, and procedures and objectives for analyzing classes. One article concerns attitudes toward the teaching of a particular pronunciation of English. Also contains abstracts of Masters Theses completed by students studying TESL. (RIE abridged)

783. Bracy, Maryruth (ed.). Workpapers in Teaching English as a Second Language, Volume IV, Los Angeles: UCLA, 1970, 130pp. (ED 054 664)

   Several articles concern topics on language instruction: the art of language teaching, bilingual education, literature study, composition writing, testing by dictation, problems of elementary school teachers, English curriculums for non-English speakers, computer applications and second language learning. Others concern language-teacher preparation: suggested areas of research by Masters-Degree students and programs for specializing in teaching English to the disadvantaged. Papers on linguistic theory include diacritics in modern English graphology and the pragmatics of communication. Abstracts of Masters theses approved during the year are also included. (RIE abridged)

784. Briere, Eugene J. "Quantity before Quality in Second Language Composition," Language Learning, 16:3 and 4 (1966).

   Citing the lack of empirical evidence about teaching composition in ESL classes, the author discusses a method of "free association" writing. Discussion includes subjects, procedure, and results.

785.  Bumpass, Faye. _Teaching Young Students English as a Foreign Language._
      New York: American Book Company, 1963. (paper) 198 pp.

      Discusses the advantages of introducing a foreign language early
      in school, the linguistic and psychological aspects of foreign language
      teaching in the elementary grades, teaching methods leading to aural-
      oral mastery of a language, the use of audio-visual materials, and the
      preparation of structured drills. (NYS Bibliography)

786.  Burt, Marina K. _Goof Analyses in English as a Second Language._
      Paper presented at Harvard University, Cambridge, Massachusetts.
      October 1971. 16p.
      (ED 061 838)

787.  Cabrera, Patricia (comp.) _An Introductory Bibliography for Teachers
      of English to Speakers of Other Languages._ 1965.
      (ED 016 914).

788.  Carr, Elizabeth B. "Teaching the 'TH' Sounds of English," _TESOL
      Quarterly_, 1:1 (March, 1967).

      A survey of reference materials on the oral production of the
      "th" sounds in English (/θ/,/ /) reveals certain confusion and disa-
      greement. Difficulties arise concerning not only the description of
      these two phonemes, but the manner in which they should be taught to
      non-native speakers. This article deals with the problems encountered
      in learning to produce the sounds and suggests techniques for
      creating materials in order to teach them. (RIE abridged and rev.)

789.  Carroll, John B. "Current Issues in Psucholinguistics and Second
      Language Teaching," _TESOL Quarterly_, 5:2 (June, 1971), p. 101-114.

      It is urged that there is no real conflict between the audiolingual
      habit and cognitive code learning theories as applied to language
      teaching. It is false to make an opposition between rule-governed
      behavior and language habits. The notion of habit is, however, more
      general than that of rule, and is not as conceptually inadequate as
      sometimes claimed. The learning of second languages requires both
      the acquisition of knowledge about rules and the formation of habits
      described by these rules. Language teaching procedures can be improved
      by application of psychological knowledge concerning the learning of
      language habits. It is stressed that situational meaning must be in-
      corporated into language rules where it is applicable, and that the
      corresponding language habits must be made contingent upon these sit-
      uational meanings. (author)

790.  Cervenka, Edward J. "TESOL-The State of the Art Today," _TESOL
      Newsletter_, 2:1 and 2 (January-March, 1968).

      Contends that, whereas previously most practice was based on
      faith in the linguists, controlled experimental study is possible
      now. Points out that most support is still given to "audio-lingual"

controlled and patterned intensive vocal practice, but that such is an oversimplification of ESL process. The greatest stimulus to research lies in federal government support of compensatory education programs for the socially disadvantaged at the elementary and secondary levels. Points out other promising areas: programmed learning, language laboratories, study of culture. (NYS Bibliography)

791. Chamot, Anna Uhl. English as a Third Language: Its Acquisition by a Child Bilingual in French and Spanish. Ph.D. Dissertation, University of Texas at Austin. May, 1972. 247p. (ED 060 770)

792. Ching, Doris C. "Reading Language Development and the Bilingual Child," Elementary English. 46:5 (May, 1969).

An annotated bibliography of articles, some from as early as 1930, concerned mainly with Negro and Spanish-speaking elementary and preschool youth. (NYS Bibliography)

793. Citizens' Committee for Children of New York. Do You Understand? N-E Program in the New York City Schools. New York: Citizens' Committee. 1961. 23pp.

794. Coindreau, J. "Teaching English to Spanish-speaking Children." National Elementary Principal. Vol. 25 (1946). p. 40-44.

795. Conway, William D. "The Undergraduate Major in TESOL." TESOL Quarterly. 3:1 (March, 1969).

Discusses in detail the B.A. program in TESL at the English Language Institute, Church College of Hawaii. (NYS Bibliography)

796. Cox, Adrienne F. Reading Is Whose Speech Written Down? Paper presented at the Sixth Annual TESOL Convention. Washington, D.C.: February 28, 1972. (ED 062 877)

Schools cannot change the language of children; the entire social structure is involved, particularly our patterns of social mobility and the values of lower class culture. At the early elementary level, children should be encouraged to use their own language to the fullest extent. Reading instruction for these youngsters should concern characters and experiences they can identify with. Having readers in the dialect may only further confuse the reading process. Standard English-as-a-second-dialect is a definite asset in our society but kindergarten or even earlier is not the place for drill to start. There has to be a desire and inward motivation on the part of the individual to switch his/her dialect. Until a youngster is old enough to reason and conceptualize the consequences involved in either acquiring or not acquiring the standard dialect, drill per se is a worthless endeavor on the part of the elementary school teacher. (RIE)

797. Darin, Steven. "Trends in EFL Teaching at American Universities." *TESOL Quarterly.* 1:3 (September, 1969).

The author surveys the development and implementation of programs during the past decade. (NYS Bibliography)

798. D'Arrigo, Peter. "Variables and Instructional Arrangements for the Non-English Speaking Child in the School Program." *Elementary English.* Vol. 49. No. 3 (March 1972). pp. 405-409.

799. Davis, Bertha M. and Others. *Teaching Reading to the Bilingual Child: Motivational Techniques. Sharing Ideas, Volume 7, Number 6.* Arizona State Department of Education, Phoenix. 1970. 69pp. (ED 055 698)

The motivational techniques presented in this document were prepared by participants in the Education 641 Workshop (Teaching Reading to Bilinguals) during a 1970 summer session at Northern Arizona University, Flagstaff. The 42 contributors (some are Navajo or speak Navajo) describe techniques that they have used in teaching reading of English to Navajo children in grades K-8. Activities and techniques are arranged by grade level. (RIE)

800. DiPietro, Robert J. *Bilingualism and Bidialectalism.* Paper presented at the 1970 Spring Institute on Teaching English as a Second Language and as a Second Dialect, Tallahassee, Florida, February 13-17, 1970. 15p. (ED 061 824)

801. Drennan, Orlena P. *The Progress of Reading of Second-Grade Spanish-Speaking Pupils.* Master's thesis, University of Texas. 1939.

802. Epstein, Erwin H. *Value Orientation and the English Language in Puerto Rican Attitudes Toward Second Language Learning among Ninth Grade Pupils and their Parents.* Unpublished Ph.D. Dissertation, University of Chicago. 1966.

803. Ervin, Susan. "Second Language Learning and Bilingualism." in C.E. Osgood, Psycholinguistics: *A Survey of Theory and Research Problems.* Baltimore, Maryland: Waverly Press, Inc. 1954. pp. 139-146.

804. *Evaluation Progress Report on Innovational Activities within the Applied Language Research Center under Title III of the Elementary and Secondary Education Act.* El Paso Public Schools, Texas. Washington, D.C.: Office of Education. April 1967. 76p. (ED 062 897)

This document discusses three educational experiments currently in progress within the Applied Language Research Center. Each of the programs concerns problems relating to teaching Spanish-speaking

pupils in a public school setting. The Grade One Experimental
Project is designed to determine if instruction in Spanish' at the
primary level (in an English-speaking school environment) would be
of value to the pupil who is principally Spanish oriented. The
second project concerns teacher training and involves an intensive
English and methods course as well as a beginning Spanish course for
non-Spanish-speaking school personnel. The third experiment involves
a course in English as a Second Language for the out-of-school neighborhood youth corps. The progress evaluation for each project is discussed and appendixes provide further details on each experiment. (RIE)

805. Feigenbaum, Lawrence. "Teaching English to Puerto Rican Youth."
     High Points. (January, 1952). pp. 45-48.

806. Finocchiaro, Mary. "A Suggested Procedure in the Teaching of
     English to Puerto Ricans." High Points. (May, 1949). p. 60-66.

807. Finocchiaro, Mary. "Teaching English to Speakers of Other Languages:
     Problems and Priorities." English Record. 21:4 (April, 1971).
     pp. 39-47.
     (EJ 047 662)

     Adapted from the address given by the current national president
of TESOL at the first meeting of the New York Affiliate (November,
1970). (CIJE)

808. Fishman, Joshua A. "Bilingual Sequences at the Societal Level." On
     Teaching English to Speakers of Other Languages, Series II.
     (Ed. by Carol J. Kreidler.) Champaign, Ill.: National Council
     of Teachers of English, 1966. pp. 139-144.

809. Fox, Melvin. "English as a Second Language: Development," Overseas,
     3:5, 1964.

     A survey of the increasing need for English in overseas
countries, how the need can be met, factors affecting the development
of English teaching resources overseas, and U.S. resources and activities in the field at home and abroad. (NYS Bibliography)

810. Gatbonton, Elizabeth C. and Richard G. Tucker. "Cultural Orientation
     and the Study of Foreign Literature" TESOL Quarterly, 5:2
     (June, 1971), pp. 137-143.

     In the Philippines, high school students study via English, a
second language. The results of the present research suggested that
Filipino high school students misunderstand American short stories
because they read into them inappropriate values, analysis was used
to isolate potential areas of difficulty. A group of students taught
using information provided by this technique, and then tested, performed
more like an American control group than Filipino students who had not
received this training. The implications of these findings for other
pupils studying via second languages are discussed. (author)

811.  Harris, David P. <u>Testing English as a Second Language</u>. New York:
      McGraw-Hill, 1969. 151pp.

      The objective of this book is to enable the ESL teacher to
      improve his own classroom measures and to make sound assessments of
      standardized tests which he may be asked to select, administer and
      interpret.  The opening chapters introduce the general purposes and
      methods of language testing.  Following chapters describe specific
      techniques for testing grammar, vocabulary, etc., and the processes
      involved in constructing and administering tests and interpreting
      the results.  The final chapter offers procedures for calculating
      a few basic test statistics.  Text does not assume previous
      training in tests and measurements or knolwedge of advanced
      mathematics. (NYS Bibliography)

812.  Harris, David P. and Leslie A. Palmer.  <u>CELT:  A Comprehensive
      English Language Test for Speakers of English as a Second
      Language</u>.  New York:  McGraw-Hill.  1970.

      Consists of test forms and examiner's books· for listening
      comprehension, structure, and vocabulary, accompanied by a <u>Technical
      Manual</u> with descriptions of the tests and information on test
      statistics and norms.  Suitable for high school students or older.
      Intended as a placement test but adaptable for use as a measurement
      of achievement as well. (CAL Bibliography)

813.  Harris, David P.  "The Intonation of English 'Yes-No' Questions:
      Two Studies Compared and Synthesized," <u>TESOL Quarterly</u>, 5:2
      (June, 1971), pp. 123-127.

      This paper summarizes two studies of the intonation patterns
      of English yes-no questions.  These studies were based on the
      analysis of informal, spontaneous speech occurring on radio and or
      television programs and followed similar analytical procedures, yet
      they produced different results.  The tentative conclusion proposed
      to explain these differences is based on dissimilarities in the
      corpuses upon which the analyses· were made:  when native speakers
      are asked a <u>succession</u> of yes-no questions to draw out specific
      information, falling intonation predominates; whereas when these
      questions occur only intermittently in extended discourse, rising
      intonation is definitely favored. (author)

814.  Hendrickson, R.H.  "ESL - Who Needs It?"  <u>English Record</u>.  21:4
      (April, 1971).  pp. 47-52.
      (EJ 047 663)

      Reviews the difficulties teachers face in evaluating the com-
      petence of their students in using English, and suggests recognition
      of the influences that may inhibit language performance in the class-
      room when the speaker comes from a minority sub-culture. (CIJE)

815. Hill, L.A. Selected Articles on the Teaching of English as a
     Foreign Language. London; Oxford University Press, 1967 (paper)

     Based on more than ten years' experience in Britain, the U.S.,
     Germany, India, Taiwan and Japan, these collected articles of the
     author touch on various aspects of EFL teaching: grammatical and
     usage questions, methodology, syllabi, examinations and audio-visual
     devices. (NYS Bibliography)

816. Hok, Ruth. "The Concept of 'General-Specific' and Its Application
     to The/A and Some/Any", TESOL Quarterly, 4:3 (September, 1970),
     pp. 231-239.

     The general-specific concept applied so widely in academic and
     philosophical concerns is defined as a matter of thinking in wholes,
     and in parts as they relate to wholes; or alternatively, taking a
     broad view versus a restricted view. This concept is examined as the
     key to the native English-speaker's use or non-use of the and a, as
     well as to his choice between some and any. Finding support in
     Miller's unitization theory of human knowlege with Mandler's
     hierarchical adjustment of it, the argument presented here suggests
     that in handling the various units a 'repositioning' process occurs
     resulting in a view which may be termed either macro- or microscopic,
     and that it is on this that the speaker's verbal choice depends. In
     other words, it is the adjustment of the view from general to spe-
     cific that explains the fact that 'non-count' nouns on occasion be-
     come 'count', that (regardless of the negative or affirmative con-
     struction of the sentence) some is used as distinct from any. (author)

817. Hok, Ruth. "Principles and Techniques Characteristic of the Oral
     Approach," Language Learning, 16:1 and 2 (June, 1966).

     Presents ESL teaching within the context of the goals of speaking
     and understanding the language as a system of patterns. Draws largely
     on the findings of structural linguistics, particularly in the area
     of contrastive analysis. (NYS Bibliography)

818. Jakobovits, Leon A. "Implications of Recent Psycholinguistic
     Developments for the Teaching of a Second Language," Language
     Learning, 18:1 and 2 (June, 1968).

     Psycholinguistic theory emphasizes the developmental nature of
     the language acquisition process; limitation, practice, reinforcement,
     and generalization are no longer considered theoretically productive
     concepts in acquisition. Points out the implications of this principle
     for second language teaching: "transformation exercises" at the
     phonological, syntactic and semantic levels. (NYS Bibliography)

819. Kaneda, Michikazu. Toward Constructing a Theory of Teaching English
     as a Foreign Language (1): Preliminary Consideration. Ehime
     University (Japan), School of Education. March 1972.
     (ED 064 999)

820. Kaufman, Maurice. The Effect of Instruction in Reading Spanish on
     Reading Ability in English of Spanish-Speaking Retarded Readers.
     Unpublished Ph.D. Dissertation. New York University. 1966.
     (Dissertation Abstracts. Vol. 28. p. 1299A)

     The problem was to determine the effect of instruction in reading
     Spanish on reading ability in English of Spanish-speaking children
     who were retarded in reading English. Ss were 139 Spanish-speaking
     seventh graders in two New York City junior high schools. The
     experimental procedure was instruction in standard Spanish with
     emphasis on reading skills: both the experimental and control groups
     received equivalent instruction in English. Initial tests used were
     the Cooperative Inter-American Pruebas de Lectura, Intermedio (CIA)
     the Durell-Sullivan Reading Capacity and Achievement Tests, Inter-
     mediate, the Hoffman Bilingual Schedule, and the California Test of
     Mental Maturity, Elementary. Some of the conclusions of this
     project are: 1) there is some evidence of positive transfer of
     learning and no evidence of interference from instruction in reading
     Spanish to reading ability in English; 2a) common abilities seem to
     play a part in determining the Spanish-English bilingual's reading
     ability in each language when instruction is given in both
     languages; 2b) there is no conclusive evidence that intelligence is
     more effectively utilized when reading instruction is based on the
     subject's total linguistic background; 3) there is no conclusive
     evidence that amount of transfer is directly related either to
     intelligence or to amount of Spanish used in the home; 4a) instruction
     in reading Spanish results in greater reading ability in Spanish;
     4b) IQ is unrelated to progress in reading Spanish in a given time
     interval; and 5) exposure to Spanish at home facilitates progress
     in reading Spanish when no school instruction in Spanish is given.
     (ECK)

821. Kaufman, Maurice. "Will Instruction in Reading Spanish Affect
     Ability in Reading English?" Journal of Reading. Vol. 11
     (April, 1968). pp. 521-527.

822. Klebaner, Ruth. "Providing for ESL Pupils During the Total School
     Day." TESOL Quarterly. 3:3 (June, 1969).

     Concerned with how English language learners interspersed
     among native English speakers in a regular classroom might
     participate in classroom activities at times when they are not
     receiving specific ESL instruction. (NYS Bibliography)

823. Knight, James. A Laboratory Study of the Reading Habits of Spanish-
     Speaking Children. Ph.D. Dissertation, University of Texas, 1931.

824. Kriedler, Carol J. and Pedtke, Dorothy A. (eds.). Teaching English
     to Speakers of Other Languages; United States: 1969. 1970.
     (ED 040 393)

The report summarizes a number of United States activities in or related to the teaching of English to speakers of other languages. Sources of information include reports from federal, state, and city government agencies; articles and notices in newsletters and professional journals; brochures; and personal contact. Sections cover (1) English language teaching and teacher training in the United States; (2) English language teaching and teacher training overseas; and (3) materials, testing and research. An index of organizations and addresses is appended. (from the document abridged)

825. Krohn, Robert. "The Role of Linguistics in TEFL Methodology," Language Learning, 20:1 (June, 1970).

Discusses three possible roles for linguistic theory in TEFL methodology and argues that its limited role of providing theoretical insights is by far the most defensible. (NYS Bibliography)

826. Lambert, Wallace. "Psychological Approaches to the Study of Language, Part II: On Second Language Learning and Bilingualism." Modern Language Journal. Vol. 47 (1963). pp. 114-119.

827. Lambert, W.E. and G.R. Tucker. The Home-School Language Switch Program: Grades K through 5. In "Conference on Child Language." preprints of papers presented at the Conference, Chicago, Illinois, November 22-24, 1971. p. 319-147. (ED 060 750)

828. Lambert, Wallace E. and others. A Study of the Roles of Attitudes and Motivation in Second-Language Learning. Montreal: McGill University, 1962. (Mimeo).

829. Lambert, W.E. and R.C. Gardner. Attitudes and Motivation in Second Language Learning. Rowley, Massachusetts: Newbury House Publishers. 1971. $5.95 (paper).

What is skill in language learning? How important is intelligence, motivation, attitude, and society to foreign language learners? Do negative ideas of a culture affect Americans' learning ability? Would knowledge of the social and psychological implications strengthen language teaching? These and other questions are answered.

830. Levenson, Stanely. "The Language Experience Approach for Teaching Beginning Reading in Bilingual Education Programs." Hispania. Vol. 55, No. 2 (May 1972). pp. 314-319. (EJ 056 358)

831. Levenson, Stanely. "Preparing for or Revitalizing ESL Programs: The Task Group Approach." TESOL Quarterly. 3:1 (March, 1969).

Presents phases for the work of such a task group, guidelines for establishing an ESL program, and suggestions for implementing the program. (NYS Bibliography)

832. Levinsky, Frieda L. Research on Bilingualism. March 1972. 74pp.
     (ED 062 839)

     This discussion of bilingualism and second language learning
concerns many linguistic considerations that figure in the problem
of language instruction. The author reports on current research
and on the ideas of several noted linguists. Topics considered in
this study are the goals of the bilingual education program, reasons
for becoming bilingual, a definition of bilingualism, bilingual
dominance and balance, types of bilingualism, bilingual barriers,
second language study, two kinds of language learning theories, the
effective teacher, and test validity. Included also are reports of
observations in bilingual classroom observations. The summary from a
national survey of linguistic methodology is provided along with a
bibliography. (RIE)

833. Lumpkin, James. "How Does an 'In-Betweener' Teach ESL?" School
     Management. Vol. 16, No. 4. (April 1972). pp. 32
     (EJ 054 961).

     This brief article describes how one school district that was
too poor to hire a regular ESL teacher and too rich for federal
aid (an "in-betweener") managed to institute a program for its
Spanish-speaking children. The solution was to use community
helpers who know both Spanish and English. The helpers visit
ESL classes at other schools and work closely with the principal
who gives them help with school equipment and ideas for teaching.
The children involved ususally have one hour of instruction, with
no more than four in a group. Some professional material is used,
but other material is adapted from regular classroom items. The
helpers are also involved in discussions with classroom teachers.(ECK)

834. MacCalla, Thomas A. "Organization and Administration of ESL
     Programs in the Public Schools," TESOL Quarterly. 2:2
     (December, 1968).

     Gives a six-step outline for reaching the objectives of such a
program. Serves as a model for organizing and administering ESL
programs in the public schools. (NYS Bibliography)

835. Marckwardt, Albert H. The Relationship between TESOL and the
     Center for Applied Linguistics. Paper presented at the Sixth
     Annual TESOL Convention. Washington, D.C., February 29, 1972.
     (ED 064 997)

836. Marckwardt, Albert H. "Teaching English as a Foreign Language: A
     Survey of the Past Decade," The Linguistic Reporter, Supplement
     No. 19 (October, 1967).

     A summary of American experience in teaching English to immigrants
and training teachers for teaching English abroad, this report highlights the developments and still-pressing problems of ESL/EFL
teaching. (NYS Bibliography)

837. Marquardt, William F. "Programmed Instruction; General Principles for the Teaching of English as a Second Language," _Language Learning_, 13;2 (1963).

Discusses the role of programmed instruction in teaching and the specific attention it gives to the special nature and circumstances of the learner in an ESL program. (NYS Bibliography)

838. Marquardt, William F. "The Tenth International Congress of Linguistics: Implications for Teaching English as a Second Language," _TESOL Newsletter_, 2:1 and 2 (January-March, 1968).

Notes that within the area of language study, syntactics, semantics and pragmatics have received much attention but that the "study of ways of bringing about competence in new language behavior" have received very little. Contends that the model the language learner should use ought not to be that of the linguist, but rather a fusion of it with that of the five major trends that may point up skills and techniques of possible use to teachers in the field. (NYS Bibliography)

839. Matthies, Barbara P. "TESOL at the '5 and 10'." _TESOL Quarterly_. 2:4 (December, 1968).

Presents models for teacher-made TESOL Materials such as: Woolworth's and the Vocabulary Class, Simon and Garfunkel in the Language Lab, Comprehensive News Coverage, Mail-Order Americana, and Beware the Innocent "Educational" Film. (NYS Bibliography)

840. Maynes, J.O., Jr. House Bill No. 1: _Special English Classes. Evaluation._ Arizona State Department of Education, Phoenix. October 1971. 31 pp. (ED 055 703)

Defining the overall objective of bilingual education to be the integration of the child into the mainstream of American life while maintaining audiolingual skills in both English and the native language, without losing certain aspects of the subculture, this report summarizes information from 19 school districts involved in special English classes funded under the Arizona State House Bill No. 1. Utilizing results derived from the Monroe Oral Language Scale for 16 of the 19 school districts involving approximately 6,000 predominately Spanish-speaking or American Indian children (grades 1 through 3), significant progress in oral language development during the interim between pre- and post-tests was found. Although no controls were used to account for maturation effects, it was deemed probable that the gains were due to the special English classes. Among the recommendations, it is noted that a uniform testing methodology be implemented and that the comparison of results between different school districts be avoided. (RIE)

841. Menton, Seymour. "Teaching English to Puerto Rican Students." _High Points_. (November, 1952). pp. 67-70.

842. Mercer, O.R.  "The Non-English-Speaking Learn Our Language."
     _Instructor_.  Vol. 53  (November 1943).  p. 14.

843. Morrisroe, Michael and Sue Morrisroe.  "TESL: A Critical Evaluation
     of Publications, 1961-1968."  _Elementary English_.  Vol. 49
     (January 1972).  pp. 50-61.

     The authors surveyed 20 periodicals for articles relating to the
     field of Teaching English as a Second Language.  They classified
     the articles into two main divisions, scientific and non-scientific;
     of the 230 articles read  there were only 17 that could be classified
     as scientific descriptions of research.  Much of the research dealt
     with reading and oral English; the second largest group was second
     language testing.  Other, one-of-a-kind articles were described by
     the term miscellaneous.  The authors note that in general the articles
     are limited in application and show the great need for more research
     and more control and care in conducting and reporting the projects.
     (ECK)

844. Mullen, Dana.  _LEREC:  Learning English as a Second Language through
     Recreation_.  Saskatchewan New Start, Inc. Canadian Dept. of
     Regional Economic Expansion, Ottawa.  1972.  263 pp.
     (ED 064 993)

845. Murra, Elizabeth.  "Learning English as a Second Language."  _Journal
     of Educational Sociology_.  Vol. 28 (December, 1954), pp. 181-192.

     This is a report of observations made of children aged 3-8
     learning English; they were either born in New York of Puerto Rican
     parents or reached New York by the time they were pre-school age.
     The observations were made over a period of two years at a Harlem
     day-care center where the Spanish-speaking children were a minority.
     The children learned English through interaction with the English-
     speaking children, but there were differences in the way the language
     was learned.  The 3-4 1/2 year olds learn English on their own intia-
     tive in order to interact; they feel no shame at speaking Spanish and
     continue to use it in appropriate situations (with parents, for example).
     On the other hand, older children feel pressure to learn English and
     seem ashamed of and reluctant to speak Spanish.  Also noted was the
     conflict with parents when their children stop speaking Spanish, with
     a suggestion that it would be worthwhile to look for ways to lessen
     the inter-generational conflict.  (ECK)

846. Nash, Rose.  "The Place of the English Language in the U.S.S.R. (as
     compared to Puerto Rico),"  _Revista Interamericana Review_, 1:1
     (Spring, 1971), 13pp.
     (ED  053 583)

     The author notes that English language instruction in the Soviet
     Union is characterized by well-trained teachers, good facilities, and

an emphasis on practical phonetics, although writing skills are not
up to contemporary standards. The program there suffers some from
lack of contact with an English-speaking country. In Puerto Rico
there is that contact but a lack of well-trained teachers and good
facilities. Also, the Soviet student studies English to enrich his
life and is not afraid he will lose his Russian culture. In Puerto
Rico many students regard the study if English as a necessary evil
that will soon be done away with, making it a waste of time. (RIE)

847. Natalico, Diana S. and Frederick Williams. "What Characteristics
     Can 'Experts' Reliably Evaluate in the Speech of Black and
     Mexican-American Children?" TESOL Quarterly. Vol. 6, No. 2
     (June 1972). pp. 121-127.
     (EJ 060 715)

848. National Council on the Testing of English as a Foreign Language.
     Test of English as a Foreign Language (TOEFL). Princeton,
     New Jersey: Educational Testing Service (1964) (revised
     annualy).

     A battery of five diagnostic subtests: Listening Comprehension,
     Structure, Vocabulary, Reading Comprehension and Writing. (NYS
     bibliography)

849. Ohannessian, Sirapi. "TESOL Today - A View from the Center." TESOL
     Quarterly. 3:2 (June, 1969).

     Surveys ESL teaching from the founding of the Center for Applied
     Linguistics through the beginning of International Conferences on
     Second Language Problems and other activities, conferences and
     publications that have come into being over the past decade. (NYS
     bibliography)

850. Ohannessian, Sirarpi and Ruth E. Wineberg. Teaching English as a
     Second Language-Adult Education Programs. Washington, D.C.:
     Center for Applied Linguistics, 1966. (paper)
     (ED 018 788)

     An annotated bibliography of interest to teachers of English to
     adults. Includes background readings, teachers' guides and handbooks,
     adult education course materials, general course materials, and
     specialized English language texts and dictionaries. (NYS bibliography)

851. Oller, John W., Jr. Assessing Competence in ESL: Reading. Revised
     version of a speech presented at the Sixth Annual TESOL Convention
     Washington, D.C. March 1, 1972. 25p.
     (ED 060 757)

     Results from research with eye movement photography (EMP) are
     discussed with a view to defining differences between native-speaker
     and non-native reading processes. The greatest contrast is in terms
     of the duration of eye fixations; non-native speakers at the college

level require about as much time for a fixation as an average native-
speaker at the third grade level.  Various tests of reading skill
are discussed and correlations with other tests are given.  The
hypothesis is advanced that high correlations between tests of listening, speaking, reading, and writing are an indication of test validity.
Support for tests which can easily be constructed by classroom teachers
is provided.

852.  Pascual, Henry W. ed.  <u>Reading Strategies for New Mexico in the 70's</u>
      Resource Guide No. 2.  January 1972.  29p.
      (ED 061 022)

      The three papers in this resource guide are oriented to the needs
of Spanish-surnamed and Indian children.  The first paper points out
three concerns to be examined before selecting reading materials:
(1) the population for whom selection is planned, (2) criteria emphasizing children's needs, and (3) apparent trends in reading instruction.  The second paper stresses teacher-student interaction, diagnostic teaching, and classroom management in the elementary school.
The author feels that standardized tests, especially their norms
should not be used with minority groups, but that the informal reading
inventory is best for these children.  The third paper observes that
schools are serving the interests of the dominant social forces, and
that while unable to reform schools, teachers can humanize their
classrooms by examining and revising certain beliefs which lead to anti-
humanistic school practices.  References are included.  (RIE)

853.  Payne, R.  "Learning to Say Good Morning as Well as 'Buenos Dias.'"
      <u>N.E.A. Journal</u>.  Vol. 41  (March 1952)  p. 165.

854.  Pinson, Rose Barajas and Others.  <u>I Do and I Understand (Glen Helen</u>
      <u>Workshop:  April 29-May 1, 1971)</u>.  Columbus:  Ohio State
      Department of Education.  Presentations adapted from Glen Helen
      Workshop, Yellow Springs, Ohio, April 29-May 1, 1971.  27 p.
      (ED 058 976)

855.  Preston, Dennis R.  "English as a Second Language in Adult Basic
      Education Programs," <u>TESOL Quarterly</u>.  5:3, (September 1971).
      pp. 181-196.

      There seems to be a reluctance on the part of ABE professionals
to adopt modern FL teaching methods.  Many see a conflict between the
strict methods of the audio-lingual approach and the psychology of
the learner being served by ABE centers.  TESOL specialists must make
sure that they understand the purposes of ABE and that ABE teachers
understand the depth and variety of ESL methodology.  This paper suggests several specific organizational and methodological solutions to
problems posed by ESL-ABE classes:  It is recommended that the ESL-ABE
classes be geared to time-learned (student attendance) rather than
time-taught (teacher attendance) figures and that polystructural,
small-unit sequences be cycled to allow for both open enrollment and
irregular attendance.  The inclusion of the content material of ABE

in the ESL segment of the program is especially recommended as a
practical corollary to the immediacy of ABE students' needs for
survival information. (from the article)

856. Quirk, Randolph. "English Today: A World View." TESOL Quarterly.
3:1 (March, 1969).

Discusses the necessary collaboration of psychologists, socio-
logists, linguists, teachers, etc., in the world view that ESL
teaching is taking. (NYS Bibliography)

857. Ramírez, Jean A. Hearing and Speaking Skills in Teaching English
as a Second Language. Speech presented at the Fifth Annual
TESOL Conference, New Orleans, Louisiana, March 3, 1971. 19p.
(ED 056 581)

858. Rand, Earl (ed.). Workpapers in English as a Second Language,
Volume II. Los Angeles: UCLA, 1968, 92 pp.
(ED 054 665)

Includes discussions of several practicalities in the field
of teaching ESL such as choosing literature for non-native speakers,
criteria for selecting textbooks, educational problems involved
in TESL, English language teaching at home and abroad, TESL in a
planned multilingual situation and free recall of orally predented
sentences as a test of English competence. Several articles discuss
applied linguistic theory on such topics as the role of rules in
second language learning, teaching pronunciation, and a rationale
for teaching a second language. (RIE abridged)

859. Rogde, Margaret. "Learning to Speak English in the First Grade."
Texas Outlook. Vol. 22 (September 1938) pp. 40-41.

860. Rogers, Melvin L. "For Puerto Rican Pupils: Crash Program in
Reading." The Elementary School Journal. (November, 1958).
pp. 87-89.

The article discusses the many problems that Puerto Rican
children experience in learning to read. The author traces some
of these difficulties to the following sources: parents who speak
little or no English; parents who fail to supervise their children's
activities because economic necessity demands that both parents must
work; parents who fail to recognize the need for academics; etc. The
other problems that confront these children are compounded by the
school system itself. First, in order to attend remedial reading
classes, the child must score 85 on various IQ examinations. The
eligibility requirement is necessary because of the shortage of
remedial reading teachers in public schools. In effect, this compels
the schools to limit the remedial reading programs to those students
who can already read.
The author suggest the temporary revision of school schedules so
that all textbooks would be used as readers. The teacher would launch

a new subject and develop it with the use of the textbook, rather than a question and answer period. Monotony must be avoided and techniques in which the student himself is actively involved, such as silent reading, oral reading, and workbook exercises, must become more prevalent. Rogers advocates special training for teachers in remedial reading, preferably two years extra plus some supervised practice-teaching. He suggests that remedial reading programs become a regular, full-time operation in schools with students who are native speakers of a language other than English. (DH)

861. Rosen, Carl L. Assessment and Relative Effects of Reading Programs for Mexican Americans. A Position Paper. Albuquerque, New Mexico: Southwestern Cooperative Educational Laboratory. 1970. 39p.
(ED 061 000)

The problem of teaching reading in English to Mexican American children with Spanish as their primary language is considered in this paper. Literature reviews are done on research dealing with (1) linguistics, (2) language-modification approaches, (3) linguistic approaches, (4) language experience approaches, (5) bilingual education and (6) teacher-school factors. Conclusions on the basis of research in these six areas are given. Also given are implications and specific directions for (1) basic research in language and reading processes, (2) normative descriptive studies of processes involved in reading, (3) pre-school educational research and leadership, (4) language and bilingual education systems, and (5) basic and applied research into current school practices, conditions, and possible promising innovations. An 88-item bibliography is appended. (RIE)

862. Russell, Lois. "Second Languages in New Brunswick: 1972 Edition." Canadian Modern Language Review. Vol. 28 No. 3 (March 1972). pp. 14-19.
(EJ 056 336)

863. Selected Articles from Language Learning: Series I, English as a Foreign Language. Ann Arbor, Michigan: Research Club in Language Learning, (1953). (paper)

Has sections on language learning, language teaching, grammar, pronunciation, vocabulary and testing. The articles represent practical applications of the principles of structural linguistics. (NYS Bibliography)

864. Selected Articles from Language Learning: Series 2, Theory and Practice in English as a Foreign Language. Ann Arbor, Michigan: Research Club in Language Learning, (1963) (paper)

Has sections on teacher education, techniques, pronunciation, vocabulary, grammar, reading and composition. The articles reflect contemporary linguistic theories. (NYS Bibliography)

865. Sepúlveda, Betty. <u>Teaching the Educationally Disadvantaged Hispano Child at K-3 Level</u>. 1969. 4pp.
(ED 036 807)

This teacher's contention is that primary grade Hispano children are not non-verbal, but have learned a nonstandard "poverty dialect" of English in their community, Therefore, before these children can learn to read, the schools must provide time for them to learn standard English. The author's premises are as follows: "(1) the present curriculum does not provide for a transitional-type program to help bridge the formal language gap that exists initially; and (2) that attempts to teach reading without first teaching formal language usage nourishes a language barrier to the degree that it blocks out progress in all areas of learning." As a result, she has developed a Formal Language Learning Program to help the child acquire formal spoken usage. (ECK)

866. Smith, Larry E. <u>An Individualized Seminar in American Culture and English as a Second Language at the Culture Learning Institute, East-West Center</u>. Honolulu: Hawaii University, East-West Center. Paper presented at the Sixth Annual TESOL Convention, Washington, D.C. March 11, 1972 and published as Working Paper No. 11 of the East-West Culture Learning Institute. January 1972. 18 p.
(ED 060 731)

This report presents a description of a seminar in American culture and English-as-a-second-language which allows the students to learn what they want, at their own rate. The teacher serves as a guide and helps the student plan and evaluate his studies. Students may also assume the function of communicating knowledge or ability to each other. Instructional materials depend on the interests of the participants. Basic and constant in the course is a textbook designed to promote language fluency which provides resource material for group discussions usually lasting 20 to 30 minutes. A variety of 15-minute tapes, ranging from simple dialogues to complex lectures and directions, are also used; each tape includes comprehension questions and answers. Each student maintains a folder to record his classroom activity. Students spend at least half their seminar time cultural "adventures" outside the classroom. In the classroom, they record their impressions and ask any questions. The teacher listens to the tapes and makes suggestions for language development. A list of suggested cultural activities is provided. (RIE)

867. Smoker, David. <u>Working Conference on Research Activity in the Language Arts for Pre-Primary/Primary Culturally Diverse Non-English Speaking Child</u>. 1967.
(ED 013 163)

868. Spolsky, Bernard. "Attitudinal Aspects of Second Language Learning." <u>Language Learning</u>. 19:3 and 4 (December, 1969).

Discusses the importance of the attitude held by the learner
of a language to its speakers and an instrument measuring the nature
and influence of this attitude. The social role of language cannot
be overlooked in the development of a second language acquisition
theory. (NYS Bibliography)

869. Spolsky, Bernard. "Language Testing: The Problem of Validation."
TESOL Quarterly. 2:2 (June, 1968).

Discusses the differences between tests for control of instruction, and tests for control of a person's career and the serious
difficulty of validation in the second class.

870. Stageberg, Norman C. "Structural Ambiguity and the Suprasegmentals"
English Record. 21:4 (April, 1971). pp. 64-68.
(EJ 047 665)

After teaching the basic suprasegmental patterns, an ESL
teacher can profitably continue with those other patterns which are
useful in distinguishing meanings and whose absence on the printed
page will sometimes result· in double meanings. (CIJE)

871. Strain, Jeris E. "Teaching a Pronunciation Problem," Language
Learning. 12:3 (1962).

A presentation of the approach and methodology employed for
over two decades by the English Language Institute of the University
of Michigan: a concise, concrete presentation of pronunciation
techniques and problems. (NYS Bibliography)

872. Streiff, Virginia. Question Generation by First Graders: A Heuristic
Model. In "Conference on Child Language." preprints of papers
presented at the Conference, Chicago, Illinois, November 22-24,
1971. p. 119-138.
(ED 061 807)

This paper describes the design and practical application of a
program called "Listening" which has been developed to help young
learners of English as a second language gain some strategies for
comprehension in their new language. The long-range goal of the
program is to develop the learner's active involvement in thinking
about the facts he listens to, in applying language thinking
processes which help him comprehend and retain the salient features
of a message which often exceed the explicit facts, and then in
thinking more about them. Inquiry is the principal device of the
program. The children learn to ask relevant, appropriate, and substantial questions, and to value such inquiry by actually engaging
in the activity. Question-asking acts as the pivot from second
language learning to learning in the second language. A description
of the program is provided, on the objectives and language
learning to learning in the second language. A description of
the program is provided, with remarks on the objectives and char-

acteristics of the various states of the program. (RIE)

873. Thonis, Eleanor Wall. <u>Teaching Reading to Non-English Speakers</u>.
New York: Collier-Macmillan. 1970. 270pp.

A broad analysis of the reading process and of the problems
involved in the teaching of reading, beginning from the viewpoint
of reading in the vernacular, then turning to reading in a second
language. (CAL Bibliography)

874. Tireman, L.S. "Reading in the Elementary Schools of Mexico."
<u>Elementary School Journal</u>. Vol. 30 (April 30) pp. 621-626.

875. Tireman, L.S. and M. Houghes. "A Reading Program for Spanish-
Speaking Pupils." <u>Elementary English Review</u>. Vol. 14
(April 1937) pp. 138-140, 152.

876. Titone, Renzo. "Guidelines for Teaching a Second Language in Its
Own Environment." <u>Modern Language Journal</u>. Vol. 52 (1969)
pp. 306-309.

877. <u>A Total System Approach Attacking the Educational Problems of the
Illiterate Spanish-Surnamed Adults</u>. Albuquerque, New Mexico:
Southwestern Cooperative Educational Laboratory. Washington,
D.C.: Office of Education. August 1969. 49p.
(ED 060 405)

A program for the development and production of basic oral
English lessons for the non-English-speaking, Spanish-speaking
adults is discussed. This program is conceptualized incorporated
animation, choreography, and other entertaining elements coupled
with the instructional features of the lessons. Steps were
taken to develop a total educational TV package. (RIE)

878. Ulibarrí, Mari-Luci. <u>Pensamientos Sobre (Thoughts On) Teaching
English as a Second Language</u>. New Mexico University, Albuquer-
que. College of Education. Washington, D.C.: Office of
Education. 1969. 26p.
(ED 060 703)

879. Valdés, Joyce. "Starting English Late," <u>TESOL Quarterly</u>, 4:3
(September, 1971), pp. 277-282.

When the League of Mexican-American Students of Houston re-
quested that the administration of the University provide English
instruction for the Spanish-speaking custodians and groundskeepers
on campus, every effort was made to comply with the request. Complications developed at once, but results indicate that strong
motivation can overcome almost insurmountable difficulties in an
adult course. The first complications were of a psychological and
sociological nature. The men varied in ages and ability to speak
English and were embarrassed to reveal their inadequacies to one

another. The second type of complication was pedagogical. Theory again did not work out in practice, but the enthusiasm of the men and the dedication of one of the teachers worked together to produce gratifying results. Ultimate progress was achieved in the program; but since testing is tabu, the estimate of that progress must be informal. (from the article)

880. Van Syoc, Bryce. (ed.). "Linguistics and the Teaching of English as a Foreign Language," Language Learning, 8:1 and 2 (June, 1958).

A special issue devoted entirely to articles dealing with the topic from differing perspectives during the height of the "structuralist-approach" period. (NYS Bibliography)

881. Wardhaugh, Ronald. "Some Current Problems in Second-Language Teaching." Language Learning 17:1 and 2 (July, 1967).

Discusses problems related to the inadequacies of current views of language as being systematic and second language learning as a habit-forming activity. Suggests areas that need further exploration. (NYS Bibliography)

882. Wardhaugh, Ronald. "Teaching English to Speakers of Other Languages: The State of the Art," TESOL Newsletter, 4:1 (February, 1970) (Available from CAL/ERIC).

A document commissioned by the ERIC Clearinghouse for Linguistics, this summary presents a thorough overview of the field, giving sources for further information. (NYS Bibliography)

883. Wasserman, Paul and Susan Wasserman. "No Hablo Inglés." Elementary English. Vol. 49 (October 1972). pp. 832-835, 852.

The first part of this article briefly describes three different types of English as a Second Language programs, where all non-English speaking children in a school have English together but return to regular classes for the rest of the day, where non-English-speaking children are in classrooms only with others with similar needs and where a bilingual-bicultural approach is used for all children. The authors list some basic information for the teacher of English to Spanish-speaking children. A sample ESL lesson is given, with examples of different types of drills and other language activities.(ECK)

884. Wissot, Jay. "HESL and MESL: The Teaching of History and Math as Components of an ESL Program," English Record, 21:4 (April, 1971), pp. 68-73. (ED 053 609)

Within a school curriculum featuring ESL, classes such as History for ESL and Math for ESL can play an important role. In these classes, the teacher can present content-subject matter, keeping in mind the linguistic capabilities of the students. Principles are not watered down; rather, they are presented in terms of

linguistic achievement of the students. Such classes are best
taught by the ESL teacher, because he knows and understands the
linguistic problems of the students and he has more experience
with adapting materials for the foreign-born student. When the
student's linguistic ability makes competing in English feasible,
such classes should be discontinued. (RIE)

885. Wolk, Elsie. "Reading Disabilities of Children Learning English
        as a Second Language." Elementary English. Vol. 49. No. 3.
        (March 1972). pp. 410-416.
        (EJ 056 673)

        This article reports the results of a special study to deter-
mine the specific problems of Puerto Rican children learning to
read. Over one hundred coordinators of ESL programs reported on the
reading habits of one child as observed through one year. The
article describes specific problems encountered by the children, such
as mispronunciation and problems in comprehension. It concludes
with many procedures that should be useful in helping these
children learn to read. (ECK)

886. Wolk, E. "The Teaching of English as a Second Language in the
        Elementary Schools of New York City." Hispania. Vol. 49
        (May, 1966). pp. 293-296.

887. Workpapers: Teaching English as a Second Language. Vol. V.
        California University, Los Angeles. June 1971. 161 pp.
        (ED 056 556)

888. Wright, Carrie E. An Experiment with a Spanish Reading Test. Un-
        published Master's thesis, University of Texas. 1927.

* 889. Young, Robert B. Contributions of the Latin American TESOL Ex-
        perience. Speech presented at the Fifth Annual TESOL Convention
        New Orleans, Louisiana, March 6, 1971. 10pp.
        (054-671)

890. Zintz, Miles V. Corrective Reading. 2nd Edition. Dubuque, Iowa:
        William C. Brown Co., 1972. 449 pp.
        (EC 04 1234)

        The text is intended for classroom teachers who need assistance
with students who have reading difficulties. After an introduction
to reading problems, discussed immediately are several informal tests
the teacher can use to evaluate oral and silent reading and thereby
identify children in need of corrective reading. Teaching and testing
techniques and devices are emphasized. In addition to evaluation and
diagnosis, major topics covered are: planning remedial work with the
student, scheduling, teaching bilingual and non-standard dialect-
speaking children, emotional factors in reading, working cooperatively
with parents, attitudes of teachers toward students who fail, use of

standardized tests and progress records, and specific learning disability. (EC, abridged by DH)

Bilingual Education

891.  Adkins, Dorothy C. and Others. Interative Research in Curriculum Development: A Preschool Language Module. A Section of the Final Report for 1969-70. Hawaii University, Honolulu. Education Research and Development Center. Washington, D.C. Office of Economic Opportunity. December 1970. 12pp. (ED 055 483)

The child in a bilingual or bidialectal situation must increase his skills so that he may function successfully in a wider variety of situations and know how and when to use both language codes. The curriculum described here, used in Head Start ckasses, is a carefully programmed, very detailed presentation of syntactic patterns that appear with high frequency in the standard dialects of American English. Details of the classroom techniques are provided as are the results observed from tests administered to young children under the new curriculum and to those under other nursery school programs. The various tests and their particular results are discussed. A list of references is given. (RIE)

892.  Ainsworth, C.L. and Chester C. Christian, Jr. Lubbock Bilingual Elementary Education Program, Title VII, Elementary and Secondary Education Act of 1965. Evaluation Report, 1970. Lubbock Independent School District, Texas. Washington, D.C.: Office of Education. 1970. 32 pp. (ED 065 213)

893.  Anderson, Merlin. Bilingual Education in Nevada. 1967. 2 pp. (ED 017 387)

894.  Andersson, Theodore. "Bilingual Education: The American Experience." Modern Language Journal. 55:7 (November, 1971). pp. 425-438. (EJ 044 608)

Revision of a paper presented at the Conference on Bilingual Education in Toronto, Canada (March 13, 1971) at the Ontario Institute for Studies in Education. (CIJE)

895.  Andersson, Theodore. Bilingual Schooling: A Cross-Disciplinary Approach. 1970. 9 pp. (ED 038 628)

896.  Andersson, Theodore and Mildred Boyer. Bilingual Schooling in the United States. 1970. 2 vols. 589pp. (ED 039 527)

Presents a history of bilingual schooling both in the U.S. and in other parts of the world; alternative concepts of bilingual schooling; sample curriculum models; implications for education and society; an outline of needs as related to action and research; an annotated bibliography; data on the Bilingual Education Act; demographic data; a typology of bilingual education; sociohistorical notes on bilingualism in the U.S.; descriptions of non-English-speaking ethnic groups in the U.S.; a directory of persons, organizations and sources of teaching materials; and many other subjects of interest.

Available from the Supt. of Documents, U.S. Govt. Printing Office, Washington, D.C. for $6.00. (from document abridged)

897. Andersson, Theodore. "A New Focus on the Bilingual Child." Modern Language Journal. Vol. 49 (March 1965). pp. 156-160.

The author reviews some of the failures of foreign-language education and outlines principles and goals for setting up a bilingual-bicultural education program. He calls the failure "seven 'deadly' sins" and their solutions are: 1) two years of language instruction in high school--a six-year sequence with four years of Latin and/or Greek; 2) the late start in learning modern languages--beginning language study at age 10-12; 3) waiting till first grade to begin education--opening public kindergartens and nursery schools to make use of the ability of young children to learn; 4) concentrating on grammar, reading and literature--learning of speech patterns first, and study of culture; 5) hiring Americans to teach foreign languages--hiring more native-born people to teach their language; 6) inflexible teacher education--using examinations- not credits, to measure proficiency; and 7) the policies of destroying non-English languages and cultures - the establishment of bilingual-bicultural programs to help bilinguals adjust to American schools while retaining pride in their own culture. The author notes that changes such as bilingual education might also result in a revolution in teaching all foreign languages. (ECK)

898. Andersson, Theordore and Others. An Experimental Study of Bilingual-Affective Education for Mexican-American Children in Grades k-1 Southwest Educational Development Laboratory, Austin, Texas. April 27, 1970. 77pp. (ED 056 536)

This paper proposed an educational study to determine the best way to educate Mexican-American children. It suggests an experiment comparing the traditional approach, the English as a second language approach, and a bilingual affective approach as described by the authors. The details of the proposed program are presented, and the three language teaching methods are discussed. Teacher preparation and selection are described as are the criteria for school and student selection. The program is designed to operate through a scientific/democratic decision-making process where the teachers decide as a group

on objectives, strategies, and assessment. The teacher's tasks
through out the year are listed along with details on the support
they will receive. Criterion measures for testing program effectiveness
are presented. Attachments to the main proposal chart the differences
in instructional activities that characterize the three methods,
provide time and scheduling rules and a typical daily schedule,
list assumptions held in each method, describe an experimental
research design for evaluative innovative learning activities, and
present a theory of parent effectiveness. (RIE)

899. Andrade, Ernest. "Bilingual-Bicultural Education--An Answer."
     Colorado Journal of Education Research. Vol. 2. No. 1.
     (February 1971). pp. 27-30.
     (EJ 054 792).

900. Baker, Jean M. Bicultural Socialization Project: A Group Process
     Approach to Bilingual Instruction - Title VII. Final Report.
     1970-71. Arizona University, Tucson. Arizona Center for Early
     Childhood Education. Washington, D.C.: Office of Education
     August 1971. 107pp.
     (ED 057 973)

        This final report relates to student socialization through a
     bilingual (Spanish/English), bicultural program involving six
     second grades in three schools of Phoenix, Arizona, for the 1970-71
     school year. As reported, the major objective of the program was to
     develop and implement a group process approach to bilingual education;
     in addition, classroom instructional personnel were trained by site
     coordinators. Program success was regarded as outstanding in class-
     rooms having strong administrative support for the program; partial
     success was achieved in overall efforts to create classroom environ-
     ments and appropriate activities to facilitate small group inter-
     action. The relatively unsuccessful aspects of the program were
     attributed to lack of (1) bilingual teachers, (2) a true hetero-
     genious student population, and (3) supporting administration. The
     document contains discussions of program rationale, the group process
     approach and procedures for implementing it, training and research
     procedures, and bilingual and bicultural activities; results,
     evaluation, a summary, and recommendations are also provided; and
     appendixes include tabular summaries of the training evaluations, a
     checklist for program classrooms, noted reactions to various prog-
     gram components, results of analysis of variance for the Peabody
     Vocabulary Test and the Artoa-Stewart Spanish-English Vocabulary Test,
     selected language samples, a composite of the parent questionnaire;
     a description of the teacher's manual, and the Natural Method of
     Language Acquisition Checklist. (RIE)

901. Baker, Jean M. and James Martin. Bicultural Socialization: A Group
     Process Approach to Bilingual Instruction; Behavior Observation
     Schedules. Arizona University, Tucson. Arizona Center for Early
     Childhood Education. Washington, D.C.: Office of Educ. 1971. 41p.
     (ED 062 383)

902. Ballesteros, David. "Toward an Advantaged Society; Bilingual
     Education in the 70's." <u>National Elementary Principal</u>.
     50;2 (November, 1970). pp. 25-28.

903. Bauer, Evelyn. "Bilingual Education in BIA Schools," <u>TESOL
     Quarterly</u>, 4:3 (September, 1970), pp. 223-229.

     Because of a persistent lack of success in enabling Indian
     students to equal the academic achievement of the general school
     population, the Bureau of Indian Affairs is taking a close look at
     bilingual programs and related research as a possible answer to
     retardation among their non-English-speaking students. In this
     paper a brief survey of the history of bilingualism in the Bureau
     is presented which includes the program to promote native-tongue
     literacy, begun in the late 30's, and the Navajo Five-Year Program.
     Present day programs, such as those at the Rough Rock and Rock
     Point Schools, bilingual materials development, and projected
     projects, including a Navajo bilingual kindergarten program and a
     reading study similar to that carried out in Mexico by Nancy
     Modiano, are described. (from the article)

904. Benítez, Mario. "Bilingual Education: The What, the How, and the
     How Far." <u>Hispania</u>. 54:3 (September, 1971). p. 499-503.
     (EJ 042 856

905. Benjamín, Richard. "A Bilingual Oral Language and Conceptual
     Development Program for Spanish-Speaking Preschool Children."
     <u>TESOL Quarterly</u>. 3:4 (December 1969). pp. 315-319.
     (ED 030 087)

906. Bernal, E.M., Jr., (ed.). <u>Bilingual-Bicultural Education: Where
     Do We Go From Here?</u> San Antonio, Texas; Sponsored by the
     Bureau of Educational Personnel Development, U.S. Office of
     Education, and St. Mary's University. 28, 29 (March 1969).

907. Bernabaum, Marcia. <u>Early Childhood Programs for Non-English
     Speaking Children. OCD Topical Paper</u>. ERIC Clearinghouse
     on Early Childhood Education, Urbana, Illinois. Washington, D.C.
     National Center for Educational Communication (DHEW/OE), Division
     of Information Resource. Washington, D.C. Office of Child
     Development (DHEW). May 1971. 70pp.
     (ED 054 872)

     Guidelines based on research and reports from bilingual pre-
     school programs are offered to assist teachers and administrators
     interested in the general problems of bilingualism and bilingual
     education. In addition to summarizing research and describing
     existing models for bilingual preschool programs, this document lists
     recommended teacher-administrator handbooks and useful materials for
     teachers. Model bilingual programs are classified both as to compo-
     sition of the classes as to approach. Several programs are described.
     (RIE)

908. Bernbaum, Marcia. Early Childhood Programs for Non-English Speaking Children, PREP-31. Urbana, Illinois: ERIC Clearinghouse on Early Childhood Education. National Center for Educational Communication (DHEW/OE) Washington, D.C. Washington, D.C.: U.S. Government Printing Office. 1972. 34p. (ED 060 397)

Research findings on bilingual preschool children (2-1/2 to 6 years of age) and programs are presented. Working definitions are given for some of the terms used in the report. Research findings are divided into four categories: (1) "The Community" focuses on the findings from the fields of social psychology and sociolinguistics; (2) "The Bilingual Child" considers those findings from linguistics and psycholinguistics; (3) "Of Special Interest to Educators" answers some specific questions; and (4) "Testing the Bilingual Preschooler" summarizes several issues associated with assessing to what extent a child is bilingual, and draws attention to possible approaches that may be used to assess the intelligence of a bilingual child. Practical Guidelines for the Teacher and Administrator are given, followed by specific guidelines that relate to the community, the parents, the children, the teacher and her aide, and goals. Examples of existing bilingual preschool programs that fit into one of the four following categories are given: (1) one way; dominant language; (2) one way: bilingual; (3) mixed: dominant language; and (4) mixed: bilingual. Additional sources of information on bilingual programs and teaching aids are presented in two categories: Handbooks and Teaching Aids, which are for use in Spanish-speaking or Indian-speaking classes. A bibliography concludes the report. (RIE)

909. Bilingual Education. 5pp.
(ED 057 916)

This document reports on the Bilingual Education Program established under Title VII of the Elementary and Secondary Education Act of 1965, as amended in 1967. The Bilingual Education Act is specifically designed for those children who come from environments where the dominant language is not English. A significant requirement of the Bilingual Office of the Office of Education is the inclusion of a section for accountability for results in every bilingual project. It was decided to select discretionary programs such as Title VII and implement and develop evaluative procedure. Major requirements for accountability included the following: (1) Objectives must be stated in terms of desired student performance; (2) A school system must recognize its own capabilities and deficiencies and must seek to utilize appropriate technical assistance in an effort to develop and operate an effective program; and (3) All projects must provide for an independent educational accomplishment audit of the project. Program evaluation is done on a project basis. Individual project data emerging from first and second year projects show that concrete results are already being achieved. Of great significance is the fact that programs have reduced the number of student absences. (RIE)

910. Bilingual Education; Hearings before the Special Subcommittee on
     Bilingual Education of the Committee on Labor and Public
     Welfare, United States Senate, Ninetieth Congress, First
     Session on S. 428. A Bill to Amend the Elementary and Secon-
     dary Education Act of 1965 in order to provide assistance to
     Local Educational Agencies in Establishing Bilingual American
     Education Programs, and to Promote such programs. Washington:
     U.S. Government Printing Office. 1967. (2 Volumes)

911. Bilingual Program Applications for Continuation Proposal: Compton
     Unified School District. Compton City Schools, California.
     Washington, D.C.: Office of Education. 1972 258p.
     (ED 061 835)

912. Bilingual Testing and Assessment, Proceedings of Bay Area Bilingual
     Education League (BABEL) Workshop and Preliminary Findings.
     Multilingual Assessment Program (Berkeley, California,
     January 27-38, 1969.) Washington, D.C.: January 28, 1972. 122p.
     (ED 065 225)

     The results and proceedings of the first annual Bilingual/Bi-
     cultural Testing and Assessment Workshop, held in Berkeley, Cali-
     fornia, January 27-28, 1972, are presented in this publication.
     Approximately 150 bilingual psychologists and evaluators, edu-
     cators working in bilingual/bicultural programs, and community
     representatives from California and Texas attended. Evaluations
     were made and the summaries are included of 8 tests used exten-
     sively in bilingual programs: the Wechsler Intelligence Scale
     for Children, the Comprehensive Tests of Basic Skills, the Coop-
     erative Primary, the Lorge-Thorndike, the Interamerican Series--
     General Ability, the Culture-Fair Intelligence Test, the Michigan
     Oral Production Test, and the Peabody Picture Vocabulary Test. Also
     included in this publication are (1) an overview of the problem of
     assessment and evaluation in bilingual education, (2) a professional
     critique of the Inter-American series by Dr. Barbara Havassy,
     (3) a brief description of a Criterion Referenced System developed
     by Eduardo Apodaca, and (4) an article by Dr. Edward A. DeAvila
     discussing some of the complexities involved in testing and
     assessment of bilingual/bicultural children. (RIE)

913. "Bilingualism." The Center Forum. Vol. 4 (September 1969).

914. "Bilingualism and the Bilingual Child: A Symposium" Modern
     Language Journal, 49:3 (1965).

     A series of seven articles commenting on the language resources
     represented in bilinguals. Discusses topics such as acculturation,
     bilingual schools, first and second language learning, and instruc-
     tional materials. (NYS Bibliography)

915. Black, Eric D. "Bilingual Education for Nation's Spanish-Speaking."
     Inter-American Scene. 3;1-2 (1971). pp. 20-28.
     (EJ 047 577)

     Article presented in Spanish and English versions.

916. Blanco, George. Texas Report on Bilingual Education for Students.
     1967. 5pp.
     (ED 017 388).

917. Borrego, E.R. "American Child with a Two-Language Heritage."
     National Elementary Principal. Vol. 25 (June 1940). pp. 32-35.

918. Bortin, Barbara H. Milwaukee Bilingual Education Program 1970-1971.
     Evaluation Report. Milwaukee Public Schools, Wisconsin. June
     1971. 105p.
     (ED 058 299)

919. Bryson, Juanita. Comparison of Bilingual Vs. Single Language
     Instruction in Concept Learning in Mexican-American 4 Year Olds.
     Washington, D.C.: Office of Education. March, 1970. 67p.
     (ED 062 043)

     Bilingual vs. unilingual instruction was studied in the
     teaching of 5 positional-prepositional concepts (e.g. under) to
     Mexican-American Headstart 4-year olds. Treatments consisted of
     instruction in Spanish only, English only, or bilingually to the 48
     subjects exposed to the prepositional concepts via tape-recorded
     programmed instruction given daily for 10 minutes. Assignment to
     control and treatment groups was randomly stratified by sex, and
     subjects were pretested the first day of instruction and posttested
     on the final (3rd) day. Analysis of test results indicated that
     posttest scores of the treatment group, were higher than those of the
     control group, reflecting the effect of instruction vs. no instruc-
     tion. Significant differences were found as a function of language
     exposure in the home, but no significant differences were found
     between treatment groups. The study is limited by sampling prac-
     tices and restricted treatment time. An appendix contains the
     instructional treatments used. (RIE)

920. Burbeck, Edith. "Problems Presented to Teachers of Bilingual Pupils."
     California Journal of Elementary Education. Vol. 8 (August 1939)
     pp. 49-54.

921. Cervenka, Edward. Final Report of Head Start Evaluation and Research
     1966-67 to the Institute for Educational Development, Section
     VI: The Measurement of Bilingualism and Bicultural Socialization
     of the Child in the School Setting - the Development of the
     Instrument, 1970, 236pp.
     (ED 019 122)

191

A study to develop instruments to measure child bilingualism and bicultural socialization was conducted in Del Rio, Texas. Three instruments were developed; (1) a series of 6 tests for measuring linguistic competence in English; (2) a similar series for Spanish; and (3) a series of 3 instruments for measuring socialization. Test batteries focused on the oral-aural use of language in realistic school situations. Analysis of results showed that children in the bilingual program were as competent in English as those learning only in English and also better adjusted socially. Test instrument validity and reliability was determined and item analysis carried out. Document mainly composed of test instruments and analysis of experimental data. (from document abridged)

922. Cline, Marvin G. and John F. Joyce. <u>An Evaluation of the EDC Role in the Bilingual Transitional Clusters of the Boston Public Schools</u>. Newton Massachusetts: Education Development Center, Inc. 1971, 88pp.
(ED 050 652)

This report documents the early stages and reflections of some of the staff of the Boston Bilingual Transitional Clusters. These separate schools were located in the Puerto Rican neighborhoods so students would not have to be bussed and so parents could become involved; the curriculum was to be taught in Spanish so children would find it easier to adjust. When the teachers considered them ready they would be transferred to regular classrooms. Thus, these Clusters were a transitional educational experience.
Interviews were conducted with the head teacher, teachers and teacher aides as part of the effort to evaluate the program. Several problems became obvious: the purpose of the program needs clarification, and, once that was done, specific criteria for student behavior should be established. Other problems included matching the teaching style with the cultural values of the community, the importance of understanding linguistic development and methods of instruction, coordination with the Boston School Department, and communication about style of teaching among teachers and teacher aides.
Appendixes include assessment instruments, interview questions used in evaluations by the staff, and reports on the teacher-aide workshops. (ECK)

923. Cohen, Bernard and Others. <u>Final Evaluation Report of the 1970-71 New Haven Bilingual Education Program</u>. New Haven Board of Education, Connecticut. Darien Connecticut: Dunlap and Associates Inc. September 1971. 50p.
(ED 064 459)

This final evaluation report of the 1970-71 New Haven Bilingual Education Program's effectiveness in the various areas of instruction is a presentation of analyses of data gathered on student performance in oral language proficiency (English only), reading comprehension (English only), mathematics, and student self concept (administered

in the dominant language only)--the students having been pre-and
post-tested in these areas. Among the findings were; (1) teachers
felt that the learning of a second language for Anglos was enough of
an advantage to the students to include them as participants of the
ESEA Title VII program--and the evaluators felt that the program
must enhance its efforts in this area; (2) analyses of sociometric
data did not yield clearly discernable results--it being not possible
to argue that the program had generally improved mixing between
Puerto Rican and Anglo children; (3) in word knowledge, reading,
and mathematics, it was found that the program classes showed a
positive and, in many cases, significant growth; and (4) in general,
there was no significant difference between the program and control
children on T-tests done on scores for self-concept. (RIE.

924.   Cohen, Bernard and David M. Promisel. Final Evaluation Report
       (1969-70), New Haven Bilingual Education Program, New Haven,
       Connecituct. Darien, Connecticut: Dunlap and Associates,
       Inc.; New Haven Board of Education, Connecticut, Washington, D.C.:
       Office of Education. August 27, 1970. 104p.
       (ED 064 461)

       The New Haven Bilingual Education Program had two primary
       components: grade K-1 and grade 2-6. Puerto Rican and Anglo students
       in the younger age groups had a daily Spanish lesson; Puerto Rican
       children were also given English as a second language (ESL) lessons.
       The older children attended their regular classes in the morning
       and were given subject matter lessons in Spanish as well as ESL and
       Spanish language lessons. The evaluation design for the program was
       modified several times due to time and money constraints; the evalua-
       tion as performed concentrated on the more traditional product evalua-
       tion as well as a description of procedures carried out to assess
       student change in the areas of language development and self concept
       and/or attitude twoard education. Among the findings were the
       following: (1) there was management which seemed to be aware of the
       problems in the program and which would take steps to make adjustments
       in the program; (2) overall teacher performance was rated as quite
       satisfactory; (3) course outlines were considered more than adequate
       when supplemented by Spanish language materials; (4) the dissemination
       program aimed at the Anglo teachers had failed; and (5) no significant
       difference could be made on the student self concept scales. (RIE)

925.   "The Compelling Case for Bilingual Education." Saturday Review.
       Vol. 55, no. 18 (April 29, 1972). pp. 54-58.
       (EJ 056 252)

926.   Cordasco, F. "The Bilingual Education Act." Phi Delta Kappan.
       Vol. 51 (October 1969).

927.   Cordasco, F. and E. Bucchioni. Newark Bilingual Program, 1970-71.
       Newark: Board of Education. 1971.

928. Dugas, Don. Research Relevant to the Development of Bilingual
     Curricula. 1967, 6pp.
     (ED 018 298)

     Discusses contributions to be made by psycholinguistics to
     bilingual education planning. Psycholinguistics established two
     types of bilinguals: compound and coordinate. The new field of
     developmental psycholinguistics has made some recent findings
     which seem relevant to methodology. This field is interested in
     plotting all stages of concept and language development in
     children, and some of its observations seem to contradict
     hypotheses language teachers have held regarding the acquisition
     process.
     Paper read at the Annual Conference of Foreign Language
     Teachers, El Paso, Texas, 1967. (from document)

929. Edgewood Independent School District, Title VII Bilingual Education
     Program. Final Evaluation Report, 1970-71. Edgewood Indepen-
     dent School District, San Antonio, Texas. Washington, D.C.:
     Office of Education. August 1971. 67p.
     (ED 064 024)

930. "La Enseñanza bilingüe en las escuelas públicas de Nueva York."
     Yelmo. No. 5 (April-May 1972). pp. 11-12.
     (ED 056 309)

931. Final Report of the Evaluation of the Bilingual Mini-School (P.S.
     Number 45), 1970-71, ESEA Title VII. Teaching and Learning
     Research Corp. New York, New York. Brooklyn, New York: New
     York City Board of Education. 1971. 30pp.
     (ED 066 521)

     The program of the Bilingual Mini-School, funded under
     Title VII of the 1965 Elementary Secondary Education Act, and
     located in a junior high school in that area of Manhattan commonly
     characterized as East Harlem, was designed to reach the junior high
     school student who had had all his previous schooling in Spanish, as
     well as those students who, having been taught in English, have
     achieved poorly as a result of inadequate English facility. The
     program at this school represents the first attempt in New York
     City at a bilingual program for junior high school children. Approx-
     imately 72 seventh graders and 44 eithth graders were selected to
     participate in the program. Eighty-five are Spanish speaking, while
     31 are English speaking. The key personnel are bilingual. The
     general objective of the bilingual program is to prepare children
     more adequately for the higher academic instruction of high school
     than has been accomplished in the past. By providing instruction via
     a language they now know best, by fostering pride in the culture of
     their parents, and by encouraging active participation of their
     parents in school affairs, it is hoped this goal will be accomplished.
     (RIE)

932. Finocchiaro, Mary. Bilingual Readiness in Earliest School Years; A
     Curriculum Demonstration Project. 1966. 124 pp.
     (ED 012 903)

933. Finocchiaro, Mary. <u>Bilingual Readiness in Primary Grades: An Early Childhood Demonstration Project</u>. (Final Report, 1970). 1970. 272pp.
(ED 033 248)

934. Fisher, John C. "Bilingualism in Puerto Rico: A History of Frustration," <u>English Record</u>, 21:4 (April, 1971). pp. 19-24.
(ED 053 608)

The implementation of English language instruction presents problems for Puerto Ricans both in Puerto Rico and in the U.S. In Puerto Rico, the role of English in the schools has always been a political issue with widespread implications. Both there and in the States, the greatest problem in English instruction is the lack of trained, well qualified teachers. To alleviate the problem, the Puerto Rican Department of Public Instruction is granting aid to 425 men and women to improve the teaching of English. Several universities in the States are instituting graduate and undergraduate programs designed to prepare teachers of English as a second language. (RIE)

935. Fishman, Joshua A. <u>Bilingual and Bidialectal Education: An Attempt at a Joint Model for Policy Description</u>. In "Conference on Child Language." preprints of papers presented at the Conference, Chicago, Illinois, November 22-24, 1971. p. 356-367.
(ED 060 751)

This paper questions whether the same theoretical model of educational policy decisions can be used for bilingual as well as bidialectal education. Three basic policies are discussed, first in applications for second language learning and then in the field of teaching a second dialect. Generally speaking, the same theoretical models are applicable to both educational problems with variation in administrative units between the two levels. (RIE)

936. Fishman, Joshua. <u>Bilingual Education in Socio-Linguistic Perspective</u>. 1970, 14pp.
(ED 040 404)

Presents four broad categories of bilingual programs: (1) transitional bilingualism (until English skills develop); (2) monoliterate bilingualism (oral-aural skills in both languages, literacy skills only in English); (3) practical bilingualism (fluency and literacy in both languages but use of mother tongue restricted to the ethnic group and its heritage); and (4) full bilingualism (all skills in both languages in all domains).
Vitally needed are: (1) a survey establishing language and varieties employed by both parents and children, by societal domain of function; (2) a rough estimate of the relative performance level in each language, by societal domain; (3) an indication of community and school staff attitudes toward the existing situation; and (4) an indication of community and school staff attitudes toward changing the existing situation. (from document abridged)

937. Fishman, Joshua A. and John Loyas. "Bilingual Education in Socio-
        linguistic Perspective," TESOL Quarterly, 4:3 (September, 1970),
        pp. 215-222.

        One of the avowed purposes of bilingual education is the main-
    tenance and development of linguistic and cultural diversity.  The
    authors believe that realistic societal information is needed for
    realistic educational goals.  This information, which goes beyond
    that normally available in school records and county census data,
    is here described and presented as an aid in deciding what kind of
    bilingual program to establish.  Four broad categories of bilingual-
    ism (transitional, monoliterate, partial, and full) are defined and
    discussed in terms of their societal implications.  (from article)

938. Flores, S.H.  The Nature and Effectiveness of Bilingual Education
        Programs for the Spanish-speaking Child in the United States.
        Unpublished Ph.D. Dissertation, Ohio State University. 1969.

939. Gaarder, A.B.  "Statement Before the Special Subcommittee on
        Bilingual Education of the Committee on Labor and Public
        Welfare, U.S. Senate, May 18, 1967." Florida Foreign Language
        Reporter. Vol. 7 (1969). pp. 33-34, 171.

940. Gaarder, Bruce.  "Organization of the Bilingual School." Journal
        of Social Issues. 23:2 (1967). pp. 110-121.

941. Gaarder, Bruce.  "Teaching the Bilingual Child:  Research, Develop-
        ment and Policy." Modern Language Journal. Vol. 49 (1965).
        pp. 165-175.

942. Gaarder, Bruce et al.  Bilingualism From the Viewpoint of the
        Administrator and Counselor.  paper for Southwest Council of
        FL Teachers, El Paso, Texas. 1966. 18pp.
        (ED 018 286)

        The most difficult problem in bilingualism is that of gaining
    favorable administrative attitude and policy.  Bilingual schooling
    is profitable because it makes for superior educational achievement
    and students can learn best through their mother tongue.  Through this
    approach, biculturalism can be achieved, rather than the cutting of
    ties from the original culture.  Included are a supporting bibliography
    and an appendix which describes a number of bilingual projects in
    various schools.  (RIE)

943. Gates, J.R.  "The Bilingually Advantaged." Today's Education. Vol.
        59 (1970). pp. 38-40, 56.

944. Giles, W.H.  Cultural Contrasts in English-French Bilingual Instruc-
        tion in the Early Grades.  In "Conference on Child Language."
        preprints of papers presented at the Conference, Chicago, Illinois,
        November 22-24, 1971.  p. 368-395a.  Laval University, Quebec.
        International Center on Bilingualism.
        (ED 061 810)

196

945. Goodman, Frank M. <u>Bilingual Bicultural Education in the Compton Unified School District and Its Relevance to a Multi-Ethnic Community</u>. Compton City Schools, California. 5p. (060 705)

The Compton Bilingual Plan is a multi-cultural program designed to foster language preservation as a national resource to promote a well-educated, well-adjusted citizenry able to function effectively in two languages and in two or more cultures. The children are taught in two languages, Spanish and English, and are openly participating in trans-racial communication in a multi-cultural classroom and community. All the children, within an integrated classroom environment, are offered the opportunity to become functional bilinguals and participate in one another's culture. (RIE)

946. Goodman, Frank M. and Carolyn Stern. <u>Bilingual Program Evaluation Report, ESEA Title VII, 1970-1971</u>. Compton City Schools, California. Washington, D.C.: 1971. 121pp. (ED 054 672)

This report presents an evaluation of a bilingual education plan in its second year of operation. The major emphasis is on establishing a comprehensive, experimental, educational program utilizing the native language abilities of Spanish-speaking children as the primary medium of instruction until such time as the student is bilingual and capable in both English and Spanish. The program's hypothesis and design are discussed as are the personnel involved. The program and its scope are described, as are the bilingual-bicultural curriculum; acquisition, adaptation, and development of materials; and procedures for kindergarten and first and second grades. Community involvement and bilingual education as a tool for positive social change are considered. Finally, there is a discussion of staff development, budget requirements, and results. (RIE)

947. Gudschinsky, Sarah C. <u>Literacy in the Mother Tongue and Second Language Learning</u>. In "Conference on Child Language." preprints of papers presented at the Conference, Chicago, Illinois, November 22-24, 1971. p. 341-355. (ED 060 753)

Bilingual education programs which foster literacy first in the mother tongue and then in the second language, before the second language is used as a medium of instruction, are proving to be successful in a number of locations around the world. Such programs encourage community understanding and support, minimize the culture shock for the child entering school, augment the child's sense of personal worth and identity, develop the child's habit of academic success, and utilize the child's fluency in his own language in learning the skills of reading and writing. Conscious control of one's own language facilitates the learning of a second language in the formal school setting. New ideas can be introduced in the mother tongue; reading ability facilitates the learning of a second language. In such bilingual programs, literacy in the mother tongue is followed immediately by learning to read and write in the second language. (RIE)

948. Guerra, Emilio L. "The Role of the Teacher of Spanish in the Orientation of Non-English Speaking Pupils." Hispania. 32:1 (February, 1949). pp. 59-63.

Teaching the Anglo culture to Puerto Rican children in New York. Program procedure is outlined.

949. Gumperz, John. "On the Linguistic Markers of Bilingual Education." Journal of Social Issues. 23:2 (April, 1967). pp. 48-58.

950. Hall, Richard. Learning to Read in Two Languages: Statements from the Research Literature on Reading in Bilingual Programs. Philadelphia School District, Pennsylvania. October 1970. 9pp. (ED 057 653)

This collection of statements describes the rationale and research behind the bilingual reading education program in the Philadelphia public schools where students are learning to read in two languages. The native Spanish speakers learn to read in Spanish and are taught to read in English only after having mastered the aural-oral skills of understanding and speaking. Statements included cover learning to read in Spanish, transfer of skills, the problem of interference, affective factors in learning readiness and results of the Philadelphia program. A bibliography listing 22 relevant books and articles provides the sources for the statements. (RIE)

951. Haynes, J. Bilingual Education in Arizona. 1966. 5pp. (ED 017 385)

952. Helping Advance Bilingual Learning in Abernathy (HABLA). Evaluation Report. 1970-71. Abernathy Independent School District, Texas. Washington, D.C.: Office of Education. 1971. 102pp. (ED 065 209

953. Henderson, Ronald. Positive Effects of a Bicultural Preschool Program on the Intellectual Performance of Mexican-American Children. 1969. 10pp. (ED 028 827)

954. Herbert, Charles H., Jr. The Bilingual Child's Right to Read. Paper presented at the Claremont (California) Reading Conference. February 4-5, 1972. 12pp. (ED 062 841)

This document presents some ideas about initial reading instruction in bilingual education. The bilingual programs created in 1969 seek the creation of equal educational opportunities through the use

of instruction in a native language to children who speak a language
other than English. Such programs attempt to teach two languages
concurrently and to deal with subject matter instruction in both
languages. The problem of teaching reading skills to accompany the
oral language skills is a current topic of research. One reading
theory states that the ability to understand what is read depends
upon the child's experience with the subject matter as well as his
comprehension of the language in which it is written. The "Initial
Reading in Spanish" project produced a detailed descriptive analysis
of procedures used to teach Spanish-speaking children in Mexico to
read in their native language. Evaluation of student achievement in
the experimental use of the Mexican reading instruction methods in
the United States indicates success in learning to read in both
Spanish and English. (RIE)

955. Herbert, C.H., Jr. "The Bilingual Child's Right to Read."
     Claremont Reading Conference Yearbook. Vol. 36 (1972). p. 50-58.

956. Herbert, Charles H., Jr. Initial Reading in Spanish for Bilinguals.
     In "Conference on Child Language." preprints of papers presented
     at the Conference, Chicago, Illinois, November 22-24, 1971.
     pp. 501-519. Laval University, Quebec. International Center
     on Bilingualism.
     (ED 061 813)

     "Initial Reading in Spanish" is a project designed to produce a
     detailed, descriptive analysis of procedures used to teach Spanish-
     speaking children in the United States to read in their native
     language. This document describes the procedures in developing and
     evaluating such a reading program. The initial step in the program
     was to observe Spanish reading instruction in several Mexican schools.
     Observations of procedures and methods used in Mexico were used to
     devise a program tested in four locations in the United States.
     Several forms were developed to standardize the procedures for evalua-
     ting the program. Extensive videotaping was done in the four experi-
     mental classrooms. The final report on the project shows the results
     of the observations and evaluations made during the project and
     describes the teaching methodologies that were used. This report
     summarizes the teaching methodologies and the general results of the
     project. (RIE)

957. Hernández, Norma G. Mathematics for the Bicultural Student. Paper
     presented at the Mathematics Colloquium, New Mexico State
     University, Las Cruces. April 5, 1972. 17p.
     (ED 060 987)

958. Holland, R. Fount. "School in Cherokee and English." Elementary
     School Journal Vol. 72, no. 8 (May 1972). pp. 412-418.
     (ED 061 184)

     Describes the activities of the Cherokee Bilingual Education
     Center, created in 1969 by the Northeastern State College at
     Tahlequah, Oklahoma. (CIJE)

959. Howe, Elliot. Program for Bilingual Students of Utah. 1967. 4pp.
(ED 017 389)

960. Hughes, B.E. and Helene W. Harrison. Evaluation Report of the
Bilingual Education Program: Harlandale Independent School
District; San Marcos Independent School District; Southwest
Texas State University, 1970-1971. Harlandale Independent
School District, San Antonio Texas. San Marcos Independent
School District, Texas. Southwest Texas State College, San
Marcos.Washington, D.C.: Office of Education. 1971. 72pp.
(ED 055 686)

961. John, Vera P. and Vivian M. Horner. Early Childhood Bilingual
Education. MLA/ERIC Clearinghouse, 1971. 207pp.

Provides information helpful to communities attempting to
present their demands for better bilingual education more cogently
and helps educators meet such demands with appropriate programs.
Three major groups - the Puerto Rican, the Mexican American, and
the American Indian - are discussed. Includes a history of
bilingual education in the U.S., demographic information, program
descriptions, teacher training, curriculum materials, testing,
research, and models for bilingual education.
Price: $4.00 - order No. A290.

962. Kindergarten Bilingual Resource Handbook. Lubbock Independent
School District, Texas. Dissemination Center for Bilingual
Bicultural Education, Austin, Texas. Washington, D.C.:
Office of Education. October 1971. 194p.
(ED 059 636)

This curriculum bulletin has been developed to assist
kindergarten teachers who work with bilingual five year-olds. It
contains activities which are appropriate for this age which relate
to his cultural background and which deal with concepts within his
immediate range of experiences. The handbook includes details on
such topics as early childhood education and the bilingual approach,
curriculum design, characteristics of the five-year-old, activities
of teacher aides, suggestions for bulletin boards and room arrangements, suggested daily schedules and plans, strategies and suggestions, resource and activity units, resource material in Spanish,
and the construction of various teaching aids. A bibliography is
included. (RIE)

963. Kloss, Heinz. The American Bilingual Tradition. Rowley. Massachu-
settes: Newbury House Publishers. 1971. $8.95 (paper).

An up-to-date account of the political, social, educational,
and federal treatment of language minority groups in America -
from earliest colonial times to the present. This exhaustive search
reveals the causes of friction and harmony between ethnic groups
and provides each reader with an historical conscience which is
thoroughly relevant today. (catalog)

964. Krear, Serafina. Development of Pre-Reading Skills in a Second Language or Dialect. In "Conference on Child Language." pre-prints of papers presented at the Conference, Chicago, Illinois, November 22-24, 1971. p. 241-263. (ED 060 754)

The bilingual education program in a given community should be based on a sociolinguistic assessment of that community, and community members should be involved in assessing the surrounding bilingual reality and in deciding whether they wish to mirror that reality in the biliteracy program. This paper presents alternatives for bilingual programs based on the nature and objectives of the community. The program models presented illustrate the relative use of the native language or dialect and the second language or dialect in areas of concept development, prereading skills, written and oral language development, and reading instruction. (RIE)

965. Lambert, W.E. and G.R. Tucker. The Bilingual Education of Children. Rowley, Massachusetts: Newbury House Publishers. 1972. $5.95 (paper).

Do children taught in a foreign tongue for the first two years suffer in linguistic development of their native tongue? Does bilingual education affect childrens' intelligence? What are some ways to establish bilingual programs? What are some materials and methods used to teach in a bilingual school? The results of a five year study of the bilingual education program at St. Lambert School clearly answers the above questions. (catalog)

966. Larson, Donald N. and William A. Smalley. Becoming Bilingual: A Guide to Language Learning. New Canaan, Connecticut: Practical Anthropology. Pre-publication edition. 1972. 426pp. (ED 066 076)

Becoming bilingual as defined in this book is a process by which an adult acquires an additional language in the environment in which it is spoken, surrounded by the culture in which it is used. The book seeks to present the learner with an integrated and systematic treatment of his task--linguistic, cultural, and practical--in learning a new language abroad. The authors believe that habit formation and practice have important roles in the language learning process, cultural alienation is seen as the primary problem in living abroad, and learning the local language is a major factor in adjustment to new surroundings. The book covers such topics as motivation, language learning, programs, opportunities, techniques for learning a language, and widening one's range of communication.(RIE)

967. Lesley, Tay. Bilingual Education in California. Master's thesis, University of California, Los Angeles. 1971. 132pp. (ED 057 661)

This study investigates the development of bilingual education in
California along with the impact of federal legislation and seeks to
evolve a descriptive definition of the term "bilingual education" in
terms of programs for Mexican Americans in the state. Bilingual
programs in the United States and typologies for bilingual programs
are discussed for background information. The author considers 23
of the 26 bilingual programs in California on the basis of objectives,
participants, curriculum, methods and materials, teachers and teacher
training, and community involvement. In light of his findings, the
author presents a classification of current programs and discusses
implications for further investigations. A list of references is
included along with the questionnaire used in the survey of current
programs and the questions used in interviews with program directors.
A list of state programs, their directors and locations is provided.
(RIE)

968.  Levenson, S. "Language Experience Approach for Teaching Beginning
         Reading in Bilingual Education Programs." Hispania. Vol. 55
         (May 1972). pp. 314-319.
         (EJ 056 358)

This article discusses the LEA approach to teaching reading to
Spanish-speaking children. The author feels that reading should be
taught in the native language as well as in English, and that
beginning with the native language enables the child to experience
success at the start of the program. Following a brief description
of the development of reading programs and the approaches currently
used by most bilingual projects, the author explains the benefits
of the LEA approach and offers some illustrations of the techniques
employed by his program. (DH)

969.  Levenson, Stanley. Planning Curriculum for Bilingual Education
         Programs: K-12. Paper for TESOL Convention, New Orleans,
         March, 1971, 13pp.
         (ED 053 587)

This speech provides an outline of the planning procedure and
framework for the curriculum used in the bilingual education program,
Project Frontier, at Chula Vista, California. It explains the goals
of the project which is gradually being expanded to all grade levels,
and it describes how the goals are interwoven into a framework made
up of units of learning at any one level. A diagram showing the
framework is included along with a chart showing the steps followed
in the curriculum development. Bibliography included. (RIE)

970.  Lubbock Bilingual (Elementary) Education Program. Evaluation Report.
         Lubbock Independent School District, Texas. Washington, D.C.:
         Office of Education. 1971.
         (ED 065 216)

971. Mackey, William F.  The Bilingual Community School.  Rowley,
        Massachusetts:  Newbury House Publishers. 1971,  $6.95.

        To get away from unproductive generalizations about bilingual
    education, the author developed a topology of bilingual education.
    Using it as a reference, he examined the bilingual program at the
    John F. Kennedy School in Berlin.  The objective was to determine
    which goals in bilingual education are obtainable and by whom
    and under what kind of conditions.  The results provide a frame-
    work and point of reference for teachers, administrators, and
    students of bilingual education.  ( Catalog)

972. Mackey, W.F.  Bilingual Education in a Binational School.  Rowley,
        Massachusetts:  Newbury House Publishers.  1972. $7.95.

        A study of bilingual-education-at-work for persons who wish to
    profit from the experience of others.  Devoted to the description of
    a type of school serving a community composed of families using
    two different languages - German and English.  Describes the
    objectives and curriculum of the bilingual school, the manner of
    teacher selection and training, and the selection and preparation
    of materials.  Includes Mackey's typology of bilingual education
    which was developed as a reference to get away from unproductive
    generalizations about bilingual education and to provide a frame-
    work of reference for teachers, administrators, and students. (catalog)

973. Mackey, William F.  "A Typology of Bilingual Education."  Quebec:
        International Center for Research on Bilingualism, 1969. (Mimeo).

974. Mackey, William F.  Free Language Alternation in Early Childhood
        Education.  In "Conference on Child Language."  preprints of
        papers presented at the Conference, Chicago, Illinois, November
        22-24, 1971.  p. 396-432.
        (ED 060 755)

        At the root of many early childhood bilingual education programs
    is the widespread belief that the two languages must be used and
    taught in different contexts, since the failure to do so would
    inevitably produce a single mixed language.  From a study of the
    results achieved over a ten-year period, it would seem that, if at
    least one of the languages of the pre-school child is secure as a
    medium of communication, free language alternation in early childhood
    education can be used with mixed language populations as a means
    to promote bilingualism in the kindergarten and primary grades.  The
    language program described in this report encourages free alternation
    between English and German on the part of teachers and students alike.
    The force dominating and determining the language alternation is the
    need to communicate and the desire to please.  (RIE)

975. Magaña, Conception L.  "Some Thoughts for Improving the Effectiveness
        of Bilingual Programs."  Hispania.  Vol. 55 (March 1972).
        pp. 109-110.

976. Malkoç, Anna Maria. "NCTE-ERIC Report: Bilingual Education; A Special Report from CAL/ERIC." *Elementary English* 47;9 (May, 1970). pp. 713-725.

977. Medinnus, Gene R. and Others. *Parent Attitudes Toward Education Scale*. Las Cruces School District, New Mexico. Dissemination Center for Bilingual Bicultural Education , Austin, Texas. Washington, D.C.: Office of Education. 14p. (ED 058 804)

   This document provides a questionnaire to be used to determine the attitudes and influence of parents who have children in bilingual education programs. Fifty-three statements to be classified by varying degrees of agreement and disagreement are listed concerning parental attitudes toward schools and teachers, the value of education, the value of the parent's own education, and language education in general. Techniques for administering the questionnaire are suggested along with possible uses of the resulting information. (RIE)

978. *The Memramcook Conference of North American Indian Young People (Memramcook, New Brunswick, July 1969)*. Teaching and Research in Bicultural Education, Inc. Princeton, Maine. Washington, D.C.: National Endowment for the Humanities. July 1969. 163p. (ED 063 054)

   A meeting of over 100 American Indian and non-Indian young people and adults from the eastern United States and Canada is described in this publication. Significant events of the 6-day conference are reported in order to show the evolution of ideas, changes in attitude and behavior, thoughts, feelings, and creative energy and determination of today's young Indian men and women. Discussion of the concept of an all-Indian school directed by Indians is emphasized, and plans for continuing study of such a project are reported as the major accomplishment of the conference. (RIE)

979. Modiano, Nancy. *Reading in Bilingual Education*. Paper presented at the Sixth Annual TESOL Convention. Washington, D.C., February 28, 1972. 8pp. (ED 065 000)

   In a bilingual education program, reading should be introduced in the child's stronger language. Reading in the second language should be delayed until the child has become fully literate in the first language. Ideally, that point should be determined for each child individually. The relative emphasis given to reading in each language is based on different factors, basically depending on language role. In the case of newly transcribed languages, the creation of a written literature should be encouraged. (RIE)

980. Muller, Douglas G. and Robert Leonetti. A Cumulative Summary of the
     3 Years of the Sustained Primary Program for Bilingual Students,
     1967-1970. Division of Plans and Supplementary Centers BESE.
     1970. 24p.
     (ED 060 981)

        In this report of the final evaluation of the Las Cruces (New
Mexico) Sustained Primary Program for Bilingual Students (funded
under Title III of the Elementary and Secondary Education Act), the
major findings for the academic years of 1967-68, 68-69, and 69-70 are
cited following a program description in terms of schools, students,
teachers, class size, classrooms and treatments, and objectives for
each year. As reported, K-3 bilingual children in 4 public elementary
schools that tended to be homogeneous with regard to the children's
cultural and socioeconomic backgrounds were placed in one of three
instructional settings; (1) an experimental English program where
only English was used as an instructional language; (2) an experimental Spanish/English program where both languages were used, and
(3) a control program. The report discusses the program's effectiveness in terms of such factors as Spanish vs. English instruction,
children's intellectual development and self-concept, parental involvement, and the children's bicultural interaction. Although "results
of the K-3 experiment still are...inconclusive," it is indicated
that the program is providing "...a very valuable set of learning
experiences in both the cognitive and affective domains." (RIE)

981. National Conference on Bilingual Education. Washington, D.C.:
     Educational Systems Corporation. 1969.
     (ED 033 256)

        This final report of the Bilingual Education Conference presents
an overview of the state of the art in America and position papers on
various theoretical aspects of bilingual education. The work of
over 40 leading specialists in the field includes discussion of a
typology of bilingual education, problems of research in a "pluri-
lingual universe", and children's second language learning in a
natural environment is incorporated. Other significant topics are a
government report on the Bilingual Education Program (Elementary
and Secondary Education Act: Title VII, 1967 Ammendments), a keynote
address on the realities of bilingual education and the components
and objectives of a bilingual program. Charts and an appendix with a
conference guide, list of participants, and a typology questionnaire
are furnished. (ERIC)

982. Nedler, Shari and Judith Lindfors. Bilingual Learning for the Spanish
     Speaking Preschool Child. In "Conference on Child Language".
     preprints of papers presented at the Conference, Chicago,
     Illinois, November 22-24, 1971. p. 149-169.
     (ED 060 746)

        It is easier for non-English-speaking preschool children to learn
new concepts if they are introduced in their own language. Once the

child has mastered the concept, it can be introduced in the second language. The program described in this report is designed for Mexican-American preschool children. Content of the program is selected to relate meaningfully to the child's experience, background, knowledge, and skill building. The English component of the program views language as an internalized, self-contained system of rules according to which sentences are created, spoken, or understood. The child is not explicitly told a rule; he is shown how a rule works through carefully selected and sequenced representative examples of English sentences. The English program is characterized by realistic situations, meaningful responses, individual response, acceptance of all appropriate responses, emphasis on questioning, use of complete forms, and initial emphasis on syntax, not vocabulary. (RIE)

983. Offenberg, Robert M. Let's Be Amigos:  Title VII Bilingual Project Report. Evaluation of the First Year, 1969-1970, Philadelphia, Pa.:  School District of Phila., 1970, 134pp.
(ED 046 295)

This study assesses the implementation of the "Let's Be Amigos" program for Spanish and English-speaking students during its first year. The program, operating in Philadelphia at the elementary and secondary school levels, is described in terms of instructional objectives, evaluation criteria and procedures, student performance, teacher perceptions of student behavior, reading and writing skills of first-grade students, and the continuing-education-in-Spanish program. Commentary on a summer institute (1969) for training teachers in bilingual education programs concludes the report. Statistical data, linguistic examples, and graphs are used extensively. (ERIC)

984. Olstad, Charles. Bilingual Education in Three Cultures. 1968. 32pp.
(ED 027 515)

985. Owens, Thomas R. Analysis of a Spanish Bilingual Preschool Program. Paper presented at AERA (Chicago, Illinois, April 1972). April 1972. 22p.
(ED 064 397)

A report is given of student learning outcomes investigated over a one and one half year period on the Spanish Dame School Project. This project provided instruction in Spanish and English for approximately 100 children between the ages of three and six. A pretest-posttest control group design was used involving eight groups. Four tests were used on a pre-post basis in the evaluation of the project and control group children. Language acquisition was measured by three instruments:  The Comprehension of Directions, Tests of Basic Competence in English and Spanish, and The Test of English Grammar and Vocabulary. School readiness was measured through five categories of the Inventory of Developmental Tasks (IDT). An analysis of the correlations among the project developed instruments revealed low intercorrelations among the tests, thus indicating that they are measuring separate skills. Children's family and background data were collected from a parent interview. Findings include: (1) In the area of oral development in Spanish, both the three and four year old bilingual project preschool students demonstrated greater growth than three control groups; (2) On a performance task for four and five-year olds involving the correct use of the past tense in Spanish, ten out of 26 second year bilingual preschool children were able to perform successfully as were five out of 14 bilingual kindergarten class children. In contrast to this, no children in any of the control groups were able to successfully perform this task. In the area of oral English development, the preschool groups showed greater gains than the comparison groups. (RIE)

986. Owens, Thomas R. and Others. Final Evaluation Report for ABRAZO-
      Title VII Bilingual Project. 1970-1971. San Jose Unified
      School District, California. Washington, D.C.: Office of
      Education. September 1971. 70pp.
      (ED 065 212)

987. Oxman, Wendy G. The Effects of Ethnic Identity of Experimenter,
      Language of Experimental Task, and Bilingual vs. Non-Bilingual
      School Attendance on the Verbal Task Performance of Bilingual
      Children of Puerto Rican Background. Ph.D. Dissertation, Fordham
      University. 1972.
      (Dissertation Abstracts International. Vol. 33 (1972). p. 195A.).

      The purpose of this study was to determine whether bilingual minority group children show evidence of alienation from a non-bilingual school environment, and whether attendance at a bilingual school would prevent that alienation. Ss were 256 fourth and fifth grade bilinguals of Puerto Rican background; Ss attended either a bilingual school or a non-bilingual school in the New York City area. A paired associate verbal learning task was administered individually to a random sample of 64 Ss in each school, equally divided as to grade level and sex; Puerto Ricans and non-Puerto Ricans administered the task. The author hypothesized that the Ss performance on the task would be inferior if he or she were alienated from school in the non-bilingual environment, his performance would also be inferior if the examiner were not of the same ethnic background. Finally, it was expected that the performance of Ss in bilingual schools or programs would be superior to the performance of Ss in the supposed alien (non-bilingual) environment.
      There was no significant difference in the mean scores of students under any of the experimental conditions in non-Bilingual schools, and the performance of Ss in bilingual schools was not superior to the performance of Ss in non-bilingual schools. Therefore, it was inferred that bilingual Puerto Rican children were not alienated from the non-bilingual school environment, and that attendance at a fully bilingual school may be a factor in alienation. Finally, the ethnic identity of the experimenter may reflect distraction from a verbal task, but not alienation. (DH)

988. Parent Questionnaire. Las Cruces School District, New Mexico.
     Dissemination Center for Bilingual Bicultural Education,
     Austin, Texas. Washington, D.C.: Office of Education.
     September 1971. 11pp. (ED 061 811)

     This instrument provides questions for determining parental
     attitudes toward aspects of the bilingual education programs in
     which their children participate. The questions appear in both
     English and Spanish. Techniques for administering the questionnaire
     are suggested along with possible uses of the information. (RIE)

989. Parent Questionnaire on Bilingual Education. Jersey City State
     College, New Jersey. Dissemination Center for Bilingual
     Bicultural Education, Austin, Texas. Washington, D.C.:
     Office of Education. 16p.
     (ED 058 803)

     This document provides a questionnaire to be used to determine
     the attitudes and influence of parents who have children in bilingual
     education programs. Thirty seven questions are listed, covering
     such factors as family background, language usage at home, and
     aspirations for the education of the children. Techniques for
     administering the questionnaire are suggested along with possible
     uses of the resulting information. (RIE)

990. Peso Bilingual Language Development Project. Project Evaluation,
     June 30, 1970. Peso Education Service Center Region 16, Amarillo,
     Texas. Division of Plans and Supplementary Centers, BESE.
     June 1970. 102p.
     (ED 064 010)

     The "PESO" Bilingual Language Development Project was a 1-year
     pilot study in 4 West Texas county school districts involving 451
     Anglo and Mexican American 1st and 2nd grade students. The project
     contained three components: (1) the development of bilingual oral
     and written language skills--instruction in the Spanish language,
     and the concomitant development of concept formation ability, self-
     image, and cultural awareness; and instruction in English, within the
     regular school program; (2) the development of a well-trained staff
     of bilingual teachers, and (3) through parent involvement, the
     development of a positive relationship between the school and community
     concerning the bilingual program. The objectives of the instructional
     component were achieved to a significant level; however, the attempt
     to develop Spanish written language skills failed. Testing indicated
     the need for an entire year to develop Spanish oral language skills.
     Staff development and parent involvement objectives were met. Pro-
     cedures for the attainment of these objectives were deemed practical,
     but the evaluation design was thought to need further development
     owing to the lack of adequate measurement devices in Spanish language
     development. Eight exhibits, including a parent attitude survey and
     evaluation reports, and 12 tables of tests results are appended. (RIE)

991. Questionnaire: Parent Attitude Toward Bilingual Education. Las
     Curces School District, New Mexico. Dissemination Center for
     Bilingual Bicultural Education, Austin, Texas. Washington, D.C.:
     Office of Education. 14pp. (ED 066 066)

992. Rebert, Robert J. ed. and Others. Bilingual Education for American
     Indians. Washington, D.C.: Bureau of Indian Affairs (Depart-
     ment of Interior). 1971 102p.
     (ED 061 789)

993. Region XIII Bilingual Education Program. Evaluation Report.
     Washington, D.C.: Office of Education. August 1971. 194pp.
     (ED 065 221)

994. Robinett, Ralph. Developing Curriculum for Bilingual Education. In
     "Conference on Child Language." preprints of papers presented
     at the Conference, Chicago, Illinois, November 22-24, 1971. 30pp.
     Laval University, Quebec. International Center on Bilingualism.
     Miami, Florida: Spanish Curricula Development Center.
     (ED 061 811)

     This document describes the work of the Spanish Curricula
     Development Center, a project funded by the Bilingual Education
     Program Branch of the United States Office of Education. It is the
     function of the Center to develop multidisciplinary resource kits
     to help support the major areas of instruction in Spanish at the
     primary level. Forth-eight kits are planned; kits 1-8 have been
     completed and kits 9-24 are in progress, covering first grade and
     the first half of second grade. Each kit provides two weeks of
     work and covers five areas of instruction: Language Arts--Vernacular,
     Social Science, Science/Mathematics, Fine Arts and Spanish--Second
     Language. The means for evaluation of pupils' progress are provided
     in each kit along with supplementary audiovisual and manipulative
     materials. A product design or overview is included. Further details
     on the design and use of the kits and on the educational strands
     and assessment activities are provided here. (RIE)

995. Rowan, B. and Others. "Teaching of Bilingual Children." Education.
     Vol. 70 (March 1950) pp. 423-426.

996. Rowland Bilingual/Bicultural Education Project. Evaluation Report.
     Rowland School District, Rowland Heights, California. Washington,
     D.C.: Office of Education. July 1971. 149p.
     (ED 064 015)

997. Russo, John V. The Administrative Aspects of the Development of a
     Bilingual Secretarial/Clerical Program at Santa Ana College.
     Seminar paper. 21pp. June 1972.
     (ED 062 986)

998.  Sancho, Anthony R.  Spanish:  <u>A New Approach to Bilingual Programs</u>.
      Paper presented at the Sixth Annual TESOL Convention. Washington,
      D.C.  February 29, 1972. 9pp.
      (ED 062 842)

      The child in the bilingual education situation must be aware of
      the two languages involved as two separate systems corresponding to
      the two distinct cultural entities that are part of his environment.
      The child must learn to separate, yet identify with, each system as
      a useful and necessary means of communication.  The teacher-directed
      method is being used currently to teach Spanish as part of a bilin-
      gual curriculum.  According to this method, children receive teacher-
      directed instruction in Spanish as a native language and Spanish as
      a foreign language, in bilingual switching, and in rhetoric to teach
      effective speech in both languages and an awareness of human emotions
      in both cultures.  Another method currently being used is the small
      groups process which groups together children with varied language
      abilities, backgrounds, and academic skills.  It is based on the
      theory that children from different language backgrounds, if exposed
      to one another's language in a bilingual setting which encourages
      and reinforces both languages equally, will develop the second lan-
      guage naturally and easily, while improving the first language. (RIE)

999.  Saville, Muriel P. and Rudolph C. Troike.  <u>A Handbook of Bilingual</u>
      <u>Education</u>.  Center for Applied Linguistics, Washington, D.C.
      ERIC Clearinghouse for Linguistics. January 1970. 69pp.
      (ED 035 877)

      This is a handbook for teachers and administrators of bilingual
      education programs.  The first chapter is a historical view of
      bilingualism, with a discussion of questions raised by educators
      and a glossary of linguistic terms.  Chapter II gives the linguistic,
      psychological, social and cultural factors involved in bilingualism.
      Chapter III gives suggestions for setting up bilingual programs,
      stressing that the need must first be recognized by the community.
      The fourth chapter describes English phonology and grammar and
      contrasts them with Spanish and Navajo to illustrate common teaching
      problems.  Chapter V bases practical teaching suggestions "on
      traditional axioms adapted to bilingual education."  Chapter VI
      notes the importance of evaluation and discusses language and
      intelligence tests.  (RIE; ECK)

1,000.  Simmons, Raymond S.  <u>Final Evaluation Report for Colorado (City)</u>
        <u>Bilingual Education Program, Colorado (City) Independent School</u>
        <u>District, Colorado City, Texas</u>.  Colorado City Independent
        School District, Texas. Washington, D.C.: Office of Education.
        1971. 12p.
        (ED 064 022)

1,001.  Singer, H.  "Bilingualism and Elementary Education."  <u>Modern Lan-</u>
        <u>guage Journal</u>.  Vol. 40 (1956). pp. 444-458.

1,002.  Smith, Merle. <u>Pontiac Title VII Bilingual Education Program, 1970-</u>
        <u>71 Final Evaluation Report</u>. Pontiac City School District,
        Michigan. Washington, D.C.:  Office of Education. 1970. 72p.
        (ED 061 840)

1,003.  Spolsky, Bernard (ed.). <u>The Language Education of Minority Children</u>.
        Rowley, Massachusetts:  Newbury House Publishers. 1972
        (expected). $4.95.

            Brings together writings on the problems of minority groups
        in the United States grouped into three topical sections:  (1)
        Multilingualism in the United States, (2) Bilingualism and Bilingual
        Education, and (3) Language Education in Practice.  Articles
        provide a basis for a course in the language education of minority
        children, and the background to applied courses, such as bilingual
        education, language arts methodology, applied linguistics, TESOL,
        English education, and foreign language education.  (catalog)

1,004.  Stern, Carolyn and Diane Ruble.  <u>Teaching New Concepts to Non-</u>
        <u>English Speaking Preschool Children</u>.  California University,
        Los Angeles.  Washington, D.C.:  Office of Economic Opportunity;
        Office of Education, Cooperative Research Program.  August
        1970.  36pp.
        (ED 054 903)

            Fifteen Mexican American Children from four Head Start
        classes participated in this study, which tested three hypotheses:
        (1) that children whose first language is Spanish and who are instruc-
        ted in Spanish will require significantly fewer trials to learn a
        new concept than children instructed either in English or bilingually;
        (2) that children receive in the first set of new concepts in English
        will learn a second instance of the new concept taught in English
        more readily than children who were taught the first use of the
        concept in Spanish; and (3) that, a Spanish language criterion test,
        children taught concepts in English will do as well as children
        taught those concepts in Spanish or bilingually.  The procedure in-
        cluded pretesting with the Goodenough Draw-A-Man Test and the Ex-
        pressive Vocabulary Inventory in both English and Spanish; the
        instructional program; a criterion test in the appropriate language
        using a series of booklets developed to teach the conceptual task
        which was designed to test the hypotheses; and a posttest.  Study
        results rejected hypotheses 1 and 2, while hypothis 3 could not be re-
        jected.  An appendix contains lessons used in the instructional program.
        (RIE)

1,005.  Stubing, C.H. and Others.  <u>Reports:  "Bilingual Education:  The</u>
        <u>Status of the Art, 1970" (7th Annual Conference of the South-</u>
        <u>west Council for Bilingual Education, El Paso, Texas, November</u>
        <u>20-21, 1970)</u>. Las Cruces, New Mexico:  Southwest Council for
        Bilingual Education. 1970. 82p.
        (ED 059 818)

A report on the status of bilingual education during 1970, this document is composed of presentations from the 7th Annual Conference of the Southwest Council for Bilingual Education. Five papers are included as is a section describing a proposed program to increase the proficiency of bilingual teachers. Also included are six paradigms relating to the proposed program. (RIE)

1,006. Swain, Merrill, ed. Bilingual Schooling: Some Experiences in Canada and the United States. Toronto, Ontario, Canada: The Ontario Institute for Studies in Education. 1972. 102p. (ED 061 849)

1,007. Thonis, Eleanor Wall. Bilingual Education for Mexican-American Children: A Report of an Experiment Conducted at the Marysville Unified School District. Sacramento: California State Department of Education. 1967.

1,008. Thonis, Eleanor Wall. Bilingual Education for Mexican-American Children....an Experiment. A Report of the Second Year, September 1967 - June 1968. Marysville, California: Marysville Unified School District. 1969.

1,009. Thonis, Eleanor. The Dual Language Process in Young Children. In "Conference on Child Language." preprints of papers presented at the Conference, Chicago, Illinois, November 22-24, 1971. 15p. Laval University, Quebec. International Center on Bilingualism. (ED 061 812)

Problems attributed to dual language learning in early childhood have been exaggerated and may be the result of a failure to control significant research variables. The relationship between a child's acquisition of a language and his ability to think must be better understood for closer investigation of the effects of dual language learning. Several conditions do appear to be conducive to promoting dual language acquisition. It seems that the two languages should be kept in separate contents so that coordinated language systems might develop. The best language models must be available in both languages. A rich and varied background of environmental encounters is important as are acceptance of the child's uniqueness, respect for his native language, appreciation of his cultural heritage and attention to his specific language requirements. Curriculum design for early childhood bilingual education should take these conditions into account and encourage improved oral language ability and introductory literacy skills in the native language, intensive oral language development and readiness for literacy in the second language, and access to knowledge in the stronger language. (RIE)

1,010. Treviño, Bertha. "Bilingual Instruction in Primary Grades." Modern Language Journal. (April, 1970). pp. 255-256.

1,011. Tucker, G.R. and Alison D'Anglejan. "Some Thoughts Concerning
         Bilingual Education Programs." Modern Language Journal. 55:8
         (December, 1971). pp. 491-493.
         (EJ 047 576)

         Discusses advancements made in bilingual programs in the
United States and Canada. (CIJE)

1,012. Ulibarrí, Horacio. Bilingual Education: A Handbook for Educators.
         Interpretive Studies on Bilingual Education. New Mexico
         University, Albuquerque. College of Education. Office of
         Education (DHEW), Washington, D.C. Bureau of Research, March,
         1970. 151pp.
         (ED 038 078)

         This comprehensive handbook on bilingual education, designed
to aid administrators primarily, presents program guidelines, procedures for program initiation, and an annotated bibliography. Based
on analyses of some 2,000 reports on bilingual and bicultural
education, the work stresses social, cultural and psychological
concepts in sections treating: (1) objectives of bilingual education
programs, (2) program description, (3) teacher role, (4) materials,
(5) evaluation, (6) counseling, and (7) program initiation and
implementation. (RIE)

1,013. Ulibarrí, Horacio. The Effects and Implications of Culturally
         Pluralistic Education on the Mexican-American. Albuquerque,
         New Mexico: Southwestern Cooperative Educational Laboratory.
         1970. 43p.
         (ED 058 971)

         Establishing that cultural diversity may be nothing more than
ecological adjustment and then examining the literature and research
related to culturally pluralistic education, the author deals with
Mexican American children and children from other minority groups
in terms of growth and development, language acquisition and learning,
bilingual programs and methodology and tests and measurements. The
author recommends three areas for basic research: (1) life-style
studies, (2) sociopsychological studies, and (3) educational studies.
In addition, it is suggested that a new start for the education of
multicultural children utilize an organizational systems approach.
One figure and a 74-item bibliography are included. (RIE)

1,014. Ulibarrí, Horacio. Interpretive Studies on Bilingual Education.
         Final Report. New Mexico University, Albuquerque. College of
         Education. Office of Education (DHEW), Washington, D.C.
         Bureau of Research. March, 1970. 99pp.
         (ED 038 079)

         This final report contains speeches on bilingualsim given at
conferences in San Antonio, Los Angeles, and Albuquerque. "Bilingualism and Socioculture", "Community Involvement Through Effective Use

213

of Mass Media Communication", "In-Service Training", "Folklore",
"Dilectic Education", and "What's the Score on Bilingual Education?"
are reprinted in this work. A series of on-going, public school
projects in bilingual education are examined individually. The
history of the entire project is reviewed and abstracts provided
for four mongraphs concerning project-funding and function, a
compendium on bilingual education administrator guidelines, and a
collection of ideas and materials on bilingual education drawn
from various sources. Pre- and post-questionnaires, evaluation of
conferences, and a concluding statement are included. (RIE)

1,015.  University of the State of New York.  The State Education Department,
        Division of General Education, Bilingual Education Unit.
        Administrative Procedures for the Bilingual Education Act.
        Albany, New York:  1971. 26pp.

1,016.  University of the State of New York.  The State Education Department,
        Division of General Education, Bilingual Education Unit.
        Bilingual Education, A Position Paper. Albany, New York
        August 1972.

1,017.  University of the State of New York.  The State Education Department,
        Division of General Education, Bilingual Education Unit.
        Bilingual Educational Services.

1,018.  University of the State of New York.  The State Education Department,
        Division of General Education, Bilingual Education Unit.
        Programs under the Bilingual Education Act--Title VII ESEA:
        Manual for Project Applicants and Grantees. Albany, New York:
        1971. 202pp.

1,019.  Valencia, Atilano A.  Bilingual/Bicultural Education:  A Perspective
        Model in Multicultural America.  Southwestern Cooperative
        Educational Laboratory.  Alberquerque, New Mexico. April 1969.
        (ED 028 017)

        Bilingual/bicultural education, with its focus on the linguistic
and cultural needs of America's multicultural population, is emerging
as a potential type of educational curriculum.  Difficulties encountered by the non-English-speaking child, with instruction
presented in a language essentially foreign to him, point to the
value of bilingual and cross-cultural education in the instructional
program.  However, demographic data and careful examination of the
educational needs of the children are necessary in ascertaining the
type of bilingual program for a geographical area.  In this volume,
19 models (some operative, some theoretical) and 9 bilingual programs
for Spanish-speaking children are presented to illustrate differences,
similarities, and potentialities of the models for implementation
elsewhere.  (RIE)

1,020.  Valencia, Atilano A.  Bilingual/Bicultural Education--An Effective
        Learning Scheme for First Grade and Second Grade Spanish Speak-
        ing, English Speaking, and American Indian Children in New
        Mexico.  Southwestern Cooperative Educational Laboratory.
        August 1971.  134pp.
        (ED 054 883)

1,021.  Verner, Zenobia and Josue Gonzalez.  "English Language Teaching in
        a Texas Bilingual Program."  English Language Teaching. 25:3
        (June, 1971).  pp. 296-302.
        (EJ 042 878)

1,022.  Walsh, Donald D. and Others.  "Teaching Spanish in School and
        College to Native Speakers of Spanish."  Hispania.  Vol. 55
        (October 1972).  pp. 619-631.

              This is a report of recommendations of the American Association
        of Teachers of Spanish and Portuguese about the education of the
        Spanish-speaking in the United States.  The basic recommendations
        is that each school, elementary through college, that has Spanish-
        speaking students should establish special sections to develop
        literacy in Spanish and reinforce or complement other areas of the
        curriculum.  The program on which all the premises were based
        is the Spanish-S program (Spanish for Spanish speakers) in Dade
        County, Miami, Florida, which was begun in 1969 for Cuban immigrants.
        The report discusses the relationship of Spanish-S to other Spanish
        teaching, the curriculum and teaching methods, a seven-step strategy
        to develop literacy, teacher training and includes a bibliography
        of teaching materials.  (ECK)

1,023.  White, Ronald V.  "Activating Advanced ESL Students:  A Problem
        and a Solution,"  TESOL Quarterly, 5:3 (September, 1971),
        pp. 231-238.

              This paper concerns itself with problems in teaching advanced
        ESL students.  The first of these is contextualization, the problem
        of making the connection between the linguistic features of an
        utterance and the non-linguistic features of the situation operating
        when the utterance is made.  The second is the difficulty of the
        learner in identifying himself with the language he is being required
        to learn.  The author describes a simulation study-role playing
        project carried on with advanced students which resulted in an
        enlivened English program.  (from the article)

1,024.  Williams, Frederick and Others.  Carrascolendas:  Effects of a
        Spanish/English Television Series for Primary School Children.
        Final Report. Evaluation Component. Texas University, Austin.
        Center for Communication Research.
        (ED 066 048)

1,025.  Williams, Frederick and Diana S. Natalicio.  Evaluating Carrascol-
        endas:  A Television Series for Mexican-American Children.

Texas University, Austin. Center for Communication Research.
Washington, D.C.: Office of Education. Paper presented at the
annual meeting of the American Educational Research Association,
(Chicago, Illinois) April, 1972. 19p.
(ED 062 367)

1,026. Williams, Frederick and Geraldine Van Wart. On the Relationship of
Language Dominance and the Effects of Viewing CARRASCOLENDAS.
Texas University, Austin. Center for Communication Research.
September 1972. 8pp.
(ED 066 058)

A study was made of the relationship between the language
dominance of a child and the effects of viewing a bilingual television program called Carrascolendas. A previous study showed that
the program did have an effect on average knowledge gains among
viewers. In order to ascertain whether these gains were in some
way related to the language dominance of the child, an index was
constructed to determine the child's language dominance--Spanish,
English, or bilingual. When this index was correlated with gains
made as a result of viewing the program no significant evidence
was found that the effects of viewing Carrascolendas were related
to, or dependent upon, the child's language dominance. (RIE)

1,027. Wilson, Robert D. Assumptions for Bilingual Instruction in the
Primary Grades of Navajo Schools. Paper presented at
Conference on Child Language (Chicago, November 22-24, 1971).
38p.
(ED 059 766)

1,028. Zirkel, Perry Alan. Aural-Oral Skills and Different Models of
Bilingual Education. Paper presented at the Sixth Annual TESOL
Convention, Washington, D.C. February 29, 1972.
(ED 061 792)

This paper seeks to define the program title "Basic Skills in
Bilingual Education: Grammar and Pronunciation." The author
considers the terms separately. Grammar and pronunciation should
perhaps be defined as aural-oral skills to better specify what is
involved. Various definitions of bilingual education are discussed,
as are the linguistic and sociolinguistic factors that should be
considered in a typology of bilingual education. The idea of basic
skills in bilingual education programs cannot be limited to language.
The output as well as the input of such programs must be seen in
terms of concept as well as of language development. Linguistic,
sociolinguistic, and educational factors must all be taken into
consideration when defining bilingual education. (RIE)

1,029. Zirkel, P.A. "Two Languages Spoken Here." Grade Teacher. 1971. 88.
36-40,59

This article describes the first two years of the elementary
bilingual education program for Puerto Rican children in New Haven,
Connecticut. It explains the organization of lessons and staff and
describes some of the teacher-made and commercial materials used. (ECK)

I. Educational Materials for Teachers of Non-English-Speaking Students

1,030    Aarons, Alfred C. "ESL/EFL Materials," TESOL Newsletter, 2:3 and 4 (November, 1968).

        A supplementary bibliography (to the author's "TESOL Bibliography" of a year and a half earlier) of ESL/EFL textbooks, language and linguistics, English language, special areas, and ESL/EFL related "supplementary materials that help to make one a better ESL/EFL teacher." (NYS Bibliography)

1,031    Aarons, Alfred C. "TESOL Bibliography." Florida FL Reporter, (Spring 1967). (Available as Florida FL Reprint) (paper)

        An extensive, partly annotated bibliography of TESOL textbooks, methodology, language anthologies, linguistics, English language, periodicals, resource centers, bibliographies, special issues, special areas and dictionaries. (NYS Bibliography)

1,032    Alesi, Gladys and Dora Pantell. Family Life in the U.S.A. New York: Regents Publishing Company.

        An adult reader for beginning students. Relates the daily lives of an average immigrant family in the U.S. Vocabulary and sentence structures are simple and carefully graded, but the content reflects adult interests. Each lesson includes two readings - the second more difficult than the first - plus exercises in comprehension, grammar, pronunciation, and conversation. Price (1972): $1.25 (catalog)

1,033    Alesi, Gladys E. and Dora F. Pantell. First Book in American English. New York: Oxford Book. 1962. 241 pp.

        Designed for adult basic education courses. Second Book in American English published in 1964.

1,034    Agard, F.B. et al. El inglés hablado: Para los quen hablan español. New York: Holt, Rinehart and Winston. 1953.

        One of a series for eleven languages, prepared by the American Council of Learned Societies. Most of the others are out of print. What are available are sold by the Columbia University Press (Spoken English Series). Includes records. High school and above. (CAL Bibliography)

1,035    Allen, Harold B. (comp.). Linguistics and English Linguistics. A Bibliography. New York: Appleton-Century-Crofts. 1966.

        An unannotated, selective listing of books and articles. Major divisions include bibliographies, dictionaries, linguistics, English language and English linguistics, language instruction and special topics. (Hefferman-Cabrera)

1,036    Allen, Harold B.  (ed.)  <u>Readings in Applied English Linguistics</u>,
         2nd Edition.  New York:  Appleton-Century-Crofts, 1964.
         (paper)

         A collection of 62 articles representative of current
         linguistic thought and applications, this anthology is a compan-
         ion to Allen's <u>Teaching English as a Second Language</u> and includes
         coverage of transformational grammar and linguistic applications
         to reading, writing, speaking and listening.  (NYS Bibliography)

1,037    Allen, Harold B.  (ed.).  <u>Teaching English as a Second Language</u>:
         <u>A Book of Readings</u>.  New York:  McGraw-Hill, 2nd ed. 1972.
         $9.50.

         Contains the work of 45 authors in the areas of linguistics,
         psychology and education, from Australia, England, the U.S.,
         Canada and the Philippines; some theoretical and some practical.
         Nine subject areas, each with an overview:  Theories and Approaches,
         Teaching English Speech, Teaching English Structure, Teaching
         English Vocabulary, Teaching English Usage and Composition,
         Teaching the Printed Word, Reading and Literature, Methods and
         Techniques, Teaching with Audio-Visual Aids and Testing.  (NYS
         Bibliography)

1,038    Allen, Robert L.; Allen, Virginia French; and Margaret Shute.
         <u>English Sounds and Their Spellings:  A Handbook for Teachers</u>
         <u>and Students</u>.  New York:  Thomas Y. Crowell Co., 1966.
         (paper)  $2.75.

         This book can be used in different ways for different
         purposes in different kinds of classes for students of any age.
         Its distinctive features:  a systematic sequence for coordinating
         teaching sounds with patterns of spelling; a procedure from
         regular to irregular spellings; calling "short" vowels the <u>basic</u>
         sounds, and "long" vowels the <u>name</u> sounds of vowels; avoidance of
         conventional phonetic symbols by representing vowel sounds by
         numbers; 40 lessons include explanations, instructions and
         practice.  Films available.  (NYS Bibliography)

1,039    Allen, V.F.  <u>People in Fact and Fiction:  Selections Adapted for</u>
         <u>Students of English as a Foreign Language</u>.  New York:
         Thomas Y. Crowell Co.  1957.  paper.

1,040    Allen, V.F.  People in Livingston:  <u>A Reader for Adults Learning</u>
         <u>English</u>.  New York:  Thomas Y. Crowell Co.  1953.  paper.

1,041    Allen, Virginia French and Robert Allen.  <u>Listen and Guess!</u>  New
         York:  McGraw-Hill.  144 pp.

         A program for auditory comprehension practice, designed for
         pupils who have studied English by the audio-lingual approach
         for at least one year.  Listening to the conversations, the

student is familiarized with idioms, a basic vocabulary of 800-1000 words, and the native speech patterns and rhythms of the English language. A Laboratory Book accompanies each of the tapes or recordings; it includes notes, typical grammatical and sentence structures, a worksheet of questions on each conversation, and a vocabulary list of new words used in the conversations. (NYS Bibliography)

1,042    Allen, V.F. and R.L. Allen. Review Exercises for English as a Foreign Language. New York: Thomas Y. Crowell Co. 1961. paper. 149 pp.

For oral and written practice at the intermediate level. Contains suggestions to the teacher on method of presentation. (Hefferman-Cabrera)

1,043    Allen, Walter Powell. Easy Crossword Puzzles. Rockville, Maryland: English Language Services, Inc. Two volumes @ $0.85 ea.

Each book (Easy Crossword Puzzles for Learners of English and More Easy Crossword Puzzles for ... etc.) contains 20 puzzles. The first puzzle in each book is made from the list of the first 500 most frequently used words in English, and the remaining puzzles gradually add less frequently used words. The words in the clues to each puzzle are parallel in frequency with those in the puzzle. (catalog)

1,044    Allen, Walter Powell. More Easy Crossword Puzzles for People Learning English. Washington, D.C.: English Language Services, Inc., 1970.

1,045    Allen, Walter Powell. Selecting Reading Materials for Foreign Students. Rockville, Maryland: English Language Services, Inc. $1.70.

Designed as a guide for teachers of ESL in helping them select materials containing reading selections which will provide people from other lands with background for understanding the language. (catalog)

1,046    Alter, Jason B. et al. Utterance-Response Drills for Students of English as a Second Language. Englewood Cliffs, New Jersey: Prentice-Hall. 1966.

Conversational practice for upper high school or college age students.

1,047    Alvarado, Patricio R. and Luis Montalvo. Mi Primer Libro de Máquinas Simples: Trabajo y Fuerza. Escuela Intermedia Grados 7, 8 y 9 (My First Book of Simple Machines: Work and Force. Intermediate School Grades 7, 8 and 9). Dissemination Center for

Bilingual Bicultural Education, Austin, Texas. Washington, D.C.: Office of Education. October 1971. 18 p.
(ED 059 638)

1,048   Alvarado, Patricio and Luis Montalvo. Mi Segundo Libro de Máquinas Simples: Las Palancas. Escuela Intermedia Grades 7, 8 y 9 (My Second Book of Simple Machines: Levers. Intermediate School Grades 7, 8 and 9). Dissemination Center for Bilingual Bicultural Education, Austin, Texas. Washington, D.C.: Office of Education. October 1971. 25p.
(ED 059 640)

1,049   Alvarado, Patricio R. and Luis Montalvo. Mi Tercer Libro de Máquinas Simples: La Rueda y la Polea. Escuela Intermedia Grados 7, 8 y 9 (My Third Book of Simple Machines: The Wheel and the Pulley. Intermediate School Grades 7, 8 and 9). Dissemination Center for Bilingual Bicultural Education, Austin, Texas. Washington, D.C.: Office of Education. October 1971. 25 p.
(ED 059 637)

1,050   Alvarado, Patricio R. and Luis Montalvo. Mi Cuarto Libro de Máquinas Simples: Otras Modificaciones de la Rueda. Escuela Intermedia Grados 7, 8 y 9 (My Fourth Book of Simple Machines: Other Modifications of the Wheel. Intermediate School Grades 7, 8 and 9). Dissemination Center for Bilingual Bicultural Education, Austin, Texas. Washington, D.C.: Office of Education. October 1971. 22p.
(ED 059 639)

1,051   Alvarado, Patricio and Luis Montalvo. Mi Quinto Libro de Máquinas Simples: El Plano Inclinado. Escuela Intermedia Grados 7, 8 y 9 (My Fifth Book of Simple Machines: The Inclined Plane. Intermediate School Grades 7, 8 and 9). National Consortia for Bilingual Education, Fort Worth, Texas. Philadelphia District, Pennsylvania. Washington, D.C.: Office of Education. October 1971. 19p.
(ED 059 641)

1,052   American English Charts with Teacher's Manual. New York: American Book Company. 14 charts and manual.

Charts (17" x 23") are of everyday life: the home, office, city, country, etc. Teacher's Manual gives suggested uses. Sold in binder which converts to easel for the charts. (CAL Bibliography)

1,053   The American Language Institute (New York City). American English: An Integrated Series for International Students. Philadelphia, The Center for Curriculum Development, Inc. 1970

A complete course in modern American English which includes

four basic texts, books on pronunciation and dictation and guided composition, tapes for laboratory exercises (coordinated with the basic texts), a laboratory workbook and three readers (also coordinated with the basic texts). This series is primarily designed for older students studying here or abroad. The cultural orientation is largely New York City centered. Evaluation kit available for $15.00 from:

> The Center for Curriculum Development, Inc.
> 401 Walnut Street
> Philadelphia, Pennsylvania 19106

1,054    American University Language Center Tests. Washington, D.C.: Educational Services. 1961.

A series of diagnostic tests: 1. English Usage, 2. Aural/Oral rating, 3. Vocabulary and Reading Tests, and 4. Listening Test. Used for United States State Department Grantees and for college-oriented students. (Hefferman-Cabrera)

1,055    Amsden, Constance et al. A Reading Program for Mexican-American Children. Revision 1. Los Angeles: Youth Opportunities Foundation. 1965. 69 pp.
(ED 016 757)

1,056    Annotations on Selected Aspects of the Culture of Puerto Rico and Its People. Albany: New York State Education Department. (1969). 85p.
(ED 059 933)

Intended for teachers who are currently working with Puerto Rican children, this manuscript provides an orientation to the cultural and historical background of Puerto Rico. The primary purpose of this survey is to depict significant contributions that occurred in Puerto Rico. Contents include information and materials obtained from national archives, official documents, and cultural institute reports, and offer a collection of selected notes relevant to Puerto Rico's history, music, everyday life and culture, horticulture, architecture and current trends. A series of descriptions about famous Puerto Ricans is also included, tracing the culture from 1580 to 1968. An alphabetical listing of information sources by author is presented from which educators may secure information about Puerto Rico. (RIE)

1,057    Arapoff, Nancy. Writing Through Understanding. New York: Holt, Rinehart and Winston. 1970.

Composition practice for upper high school or college age students.

1,058       Aurbach, Joseph et al. <u>Transformational Grammar:  A Guide for</u>
<u>Teachers.</u> Rockville, Maryland:  English Language Services,
Inc.  $3.50.

An instructional course designed to provide the English
teacher with an introduction to transformational grammar theory
and application.  Includes sections on syntax, morphology, and
phonology oriented to classroom texts using the new grammar.
(catalog)

1,059       Baird, Cynthia, Comp. La Raza in Films:  <u>A List of Films and</u>
<u>Filmstrips.</u> 1972.  77pp.
(ED 065 245)

A listing of over 200 films and filmstrips concerning the
Spanish-speaking people in the United States is given in this
publication.  (RIE)

1,060       Bauder, Robert G. <u>American English Rhetoric:  Writing from</u>
<u>Spoken Models for Bilingual Students.</u> New York:  Holt,
Rinehart and Winston.  1971.

Composition practice for upper high school or college age
students.

1,061       Baumwoll, Dennis and Robert L. Saitz. <u>Advanced Reading and</u>
<u>Writing:  Exercises in English as a Second Language.</u> New
York:  Holt, Rinehart and Winston.  1965.

Reading and composition practice for upper high school and
college age students.

1,062       Benson, Susan Shattuck. <u>Proyecto Leer Bulletin, Number 8</u>.
Washington, D.C.:  Books for the People Fund, Inc.
Washington, D.C.:  National Endowment for the Humanities.
1971.  10p.
(ED 063 821)

This bulletin lists educational materials for the Spanish
speaking.  Several hundred documents are listed in three main
sections:  (1) organizations, programs, laws and news related
to the Spanish speaking;  (2) a list of books selected; and (3)
a list of publishers and distributors with their addresses.
Several bibliographies are included.  Entries are annotated and
include comments pertaining to grade level.  (RIE)

1,063       Benson, Susan Shattuck. <u>Proyecto Leer Bulletin, Number 9</u>.
Washington, D.C.:  Books for the People Fund, Inc.
Washington, D.C.:  National Endowment for the Humanities.
1971.  10p.
(ED 063 822)

This bulletin lists addresses of publishers and distributors of audiovisual instructional materials in Spanish in the United States and Latin America. Sources are listed in four categories: (1) federal sources of materials, information on materials, names of resource people, programs, and proposal guidelines concerning the Spanish speaking; (2) consumer education materials in Spanish or for the Spanish speaking; (3) folk music of the Americas; and (4) books, bibliographies, and periodicals. Two sections listing children's and adults' books in Spanish are included with annotations. (RIE)

1,064      Bernardo, Leo U. and Dora F. Pantell. <u>English: Your New Language</u>. Morristown, New Jersey: Silver Burdett. 2 vols. 1966-67.

Designed for adult basic education courses. Records and tapes available.

1,065      Binner, Vinal O. <u>American Folktales: A Structural Reader</u>. New York: Thomas Y. Crowell Company. 1966.

Graded supplementary reader. Contains 15 simplified reading passages for students with knowledge of basic English structures and a 1,000-word basic vocabulary. Selected vocabulary, idioms, related words and opposite word lists, which follow readings, provide for vocabulary building. Specific sentence structures taken from context provide controlled exercises for practice. Conversation questions, write-or-tell exercises, and pronunciation drills with modified Trager-Smith transcriptions follow. Appendixes include table of punctuation marks, guide to pronunciation, glossary of grammatical terms, vocabulary and index. (Hefferman-Cabrera)

1,066      Black, John W. <u>American Speech for Foreign Students</u>. Springfield, Illinois: Charles C. Thomas, Publisher. 1963.

A fairly complete edition for foreign students which describes American speech and gives exercises in speech and listening. (Hefferman-Cabrera) (rev. and abridged)

1,067      Boggs and Dixson, Robert J. <u>English Step by Step With Pictures</u>, New York: Regents Publishing Company, (revised edition).

The pictures which form an integral part of this text are used to introduce and reinforce new vocabulary, aid retention through association, assist comprehension, and help maintain a high level of student interest and motivation. Designed for beginning students. Covers vocabulary of approx. 800 words (16 new words/lesson). Presents basic grammar and structure in conversational context.
     Price (1972): Book/$1.75 ea.; Posters (20" x 24", color)/ $4.00. (catalog)

1,068     Boggs, and Dixson, Robert J.  <u>Sound Teaching:  A Laboratory</u>
          <u>Manual of American English</u>.  New York:  Regents Publishing
          Company.

              An audio-lingual course for conversational practice in
          American English consisting of a manual and tapes.  May be used
          as a complete course or as a course supplement.  Lessons are
          divided into three steps:  grammar practice; question and
          answer exercises; and phrasing, intonation, and pronunciation.
          Each lesson averages approx. 13 minutes of playing time.  Manual
          may also be used as a basic text.
              Prices (1972):  text @ $1.75 tapes and manual @ $75.00
          (catalog)

1,069     Brooks, Nelson.  <u>Language and Language Learning:  Theory and</u>
          <u>Practice</u>.  New  York:  Harcourt, Brace and World, 1964.

              Presenting the audiolingual method, this work is easy to
          read and covers many helpful topics:  mother tongue and second
          language, language teaching, language and culture language and
          literature, etc.  (NYS Bibliography)

1,070     Bumpass, Faye L.  <u>Let's Read Stories</u>.  Five volumes.  New York:
          McGraw-Hill, 1965.  (paper).

              A series of readers, including adaptations from Irving
          through Twain.  Each lesson contains a part of a story and a
          section of oral practice on words and patterns with intonation
          indicated.  Review practice is provided after every two parts,
          and a general test on comprehension at the end of each story.
          Notes on the author's life, a word list, and suggestions to the
          teacher are also included in each book.  (NYS Bibliography)

1,071     Bumpass, Faye L.  <u>The New We Learn English</u>.  New York:  American
          Book Company.  5 vols. 1968.

              Series for early grades.  Revised international edition of
          the English version, <u>We Learn English</u> (1959), of an earlier
          Spanish language series, <u>Vamos a aprender el inglés</u> (1955).
          Illustrations, songs and games accompany a pattern practice
          approach modelled for children.  Emphasis on oral skills but
          reading and writing practice included.  First volume, <u>Language</u>
          <u>Readiness Book</u>, consists entirely of pictures.  Reading introduced
          in second volume.  Series brings students to low intermediate level,
          leading up to sequel series, <u>We Speak English</u>.  From second
          volume on, two-page notes to the teacher suggest steps for develop-
          ing aural-oral skills and for teaching reading and writing.
          (CAL Bibliography)

1,072     Bumpass, Faye L.  <u>We Speak English.</u>  New York:  American Book
          Company.  2 vols.  1967.

Beginning course designed for 10-13 year olds of no
specific language background. Aural-oral "functional" approach.
Book I based on 630-word vocabulary. Each of 8 units contains a
short conversational dialog and extensive sequenced drills.
Songs and games also included. Book II has 7 units and is based
on a 829-word vocabulary. Teacher's editions discuss teaching
methods and techniques, and provide guides to exercises and drills.
(CAL Bibliography)

1,073    Burnett, Richard W. Basic Reading Inventory. Rensenville,
            Illinois: Scholastic Testing Service. 1966.

         A basic reading test for illiterates and up to fourth or
fifth-grade literacy level. Identifies basic skill strengths.
Part I, Vocabulary; Part 2, Ability to hear beginning sounds;
Part 3, Synonymous reading; Part 4, Synonymous listening;
Part 5, Reading context and listening. (Hefferman-Cabrera)

1,074    Burt, Kim and Carol Kiparsky. Gooficon - Common Errors in
            Spoken English. Rowley, Massachusetts: Newbury House
            Publishers. 1972. $4.50.

         Contains a broad sampling of speech errors made by speakers
of other languages and arranged on the basis of errors that fall
together structurally. The goal is to provide a practical guide
to enable teachers to identify and treat errors made by non-native
speakers of English. Each chapter provides the teacher with a
summary of each type of error, an analysis of the error, and
rules-of-thumb for correcting the faulty habits. (catalog)

1,075    California Achievement Test. 11th edition. California Test
            Bureau. 1957.

         Scores are given in the areas of reading, arithmetic, and
language; grades one through fourteen. Performance is given by
grade placement and in profile form. Percentile and age norms
are provided. These tests are useful with advanced ESL students
to determine their readiness for high school subjects.
(Hefferman-Cabrera)

1,076    Caskey, Owen L. (comp.) and Jimmy Hodges, (comp.). A Resource
            and Reference Bibliography on Teaching and Counseling the
            Bilingual Student. Texas Technological College, Lubbock.
            School of Education. March 1968.
            (ED 032 966)

         Citations for 733 selected references published between
1914-1967 cover materials on the teaching and counseling of
bilingual students. The purpose of the bibliography is to
provide as many extensive helpful references as possible.
Literature dealing with Indian and Mexican-American children is
included. (RIE)

1,077 Center for Applied Linguistics. <u>Aural Aids in English for</u>
<u>Foreigners</u>, 2nd Ed., Washington, D.C.: Center for Applied
Linguistics, (1964).

An annotated list of sources for tapes and records.
(NYS Bibliography)

1,078 Center for Applied Linguistics. <u>English as a Second Language in</u>
<u>Elementary Schools: Background and Text Materials</u>.
Washington, D.C.: Center for Applied Linguistics, (1967).
(paper)

Gives information on programs and materials. (NYS Bibliography)

1,079 Center for Applied Linguistics. <u>Visual Aids for English as a</u>
<u>Second Language</u>. Washington, D.C.: Center for Applied
Linguistics, (1965).

This annotated list gives sources of charts, pictures,
films, filmstrips, slides and games useful to the teacher.
Included are background readings and articles on making and
using the aids. (NYS Bibliography)

1,080 Cervenka, Edward. <u>Administrative Manual for Inventory of</u>
<u>Socialization of Bilingual Children Ages 3-10, 1968</u>, 75pp.
(ED 027 062)

This battery of test instruments is one of a set of three
developed for use in the study of bilingual instruction programs
and other compensatory programs in Texas. The socialization inventory has been based on a sociological view of personality as
a developing and changing entity. Four sub-measures are included: (1) a measure of self concept; (2) a behavior rating
scale of a child's interpersonal behavior in an interview with
the test administrator; (3) a behavior rating scale of a child's
general social behavior in the classroom; and (4) a questionnaire
given to parents of children in bilingual programs. Administration and rating directions are provided. Samples of socialization measures and their rating sheets form the bulk of this report.
(RIE)

1,081 Cervenka, Edward. <u>Administrative Manual for Tests of Basic Lan-</u>
<u>guage Competence in English and Spanish: Level I (Preschool):</u>
<u>Children Ages 3-6</u>, 1968, 146pp.
(ED 027 063)

This battery of test instruments is one of three developed for
use in the study of bilingual instruction programs and other
compensatory programs in Texas. The tests are to be individually
administered and are designed to measure the child's basic
language competence via the perceptual and motor sides of
linguistic and communicative phenomena. In this manual, guidelines for the selection and training of test administrators

suggest desireable professional and personal qualifications. The importance of a trial testing period is stressed. Forms A and B of the test in both language versions are included. Samples in the appendix include pictures for the oral vocabulary tests, the scoring sheet for subtests, and the rating sheet of the child's interpersonal behavior in an interview with the test administrator. (RIE)

1,082    Clarey, Elizabeth and Robert J. Dixson. <u>Curso práctico de pronunciación del inglés</u>. New York: Regents Publishing Company. $1.25.

This Spanish edition of Pronunciation Exercises in English was adapted by Julio I. Andújar to give particular emphasis to the problems most frequently encountered by Spanish-speakers in the pronunciation of English. See entry under English title for additional information.
    Price (1972): text @ $1.25, records and text @ $8.95, tapes and text @ $21.00 (catalog)

1,083    Clarey, Elizabeth and Robert J. Dixson. <u>Pronunciation Exercises in English.</u> New York: Regents Publishing Company. 1963, $1.25 (paper).

Each lesson deals with a single sound. After a concise explanation of its production, each sound is practiced in single words, minimal pairs, sentences, intonation exercises, and short review paragraphs. This book may be used with beginners to establish good pronunciation, or with advanced students to correct faulty pronunciation.
    Also available in Spanish edition under the title: <u>Curso práctico de Pronunciación del inglés.</u> (catalog)

1,084    Close, R.A. <u>English as a Foreign Language: Grammar and Syntax for Teachers and Advanced Students.</u> Cambridge, Mass.: Harvard University Press, 1962.

Source book for teachers containing many discussions and examples of grammatical and usage distinctions. From his background of experience in his native England and abroad the author discusses problems and makes suggestions regarding the study of grammar and usage.

1,085    Coleman, Algernon and Clara B. King. <u>English Teaching in the Southwest: Organization and Materials for Instructing Spanish-Speaking Children.</u> Washington, D.C.: American Council on Education. 1940. 307 pp.

1,086    Coller, Alan R. and P.D. Guthrie. <u>Self-Concept Measures: An Annotated Bibliography.</u> Princeton, New Jersey: Educational Testing Service. 1971. 9 pp.

Includes self-concept measures appropriate for children
from preschool through third grade. Annotation lists the
purpose of each instrument, nature of the materials, groups
for which it is intended, administration, scoring interpretation,
and standardization. (Proyecto Leer Bulletin)

1,087    Committee on the Language Program. Structural Notes and
Corpus: A Basis for the Preparation of Materials to Teach
English as a Foreign Language. Washington, D.C.:
American Council of Learned Societies. 1952. (Hefferman-
Cabrera)

1,088    Cordasco, Francesco and Eugene Bucchioni. Course Outline:
Puerto Rican Children in Mainland Schools. (Lehman
College, City University of New York, 1971).

1,089    Cordasco, Francesco and Eugene Bucchioni. The Puerto Rican
Community and Its Children on the Mainland: A Source Book
for Teachers, Social Workers and Other Professionals.
Metuchen, New Jersey: The Scarecrow Press, Inc. 1972.

1,090    Cornelius, Edwin T. First Lessons in English. Rockville,
Maryland: English Language Services, Inc. $1.50.

A 20-lesson course useful as a beginning text for slow-
paced adult courses where is a need to restrict to a minimum
the rate of introduction of new vocabulary and sentence
patterns. Each lesson contains sentences for repetition drill,
word study, and simple notes on grammar. (catalog)

1,091    Cornelius, Edwin T. Jr. Teaching English. Rockville, Maryland:
English Language Services, Inc. $2.00.

An orientation manual for teachers and teacher trainees
who have had no previous training in linguistics and linguistic
concepts of language teaching. Emphasis is given to basic
attitudes and assumptions in language teaching, rather than to
the efficacy of a particular method. Chapters include: (1)
objectives, (2) techniques, (3) and (4) problems, (5) exercises
used in language teaching and the use of pictures, illustrations
and objects, and (6) the preparation of the teacher. (catalog)

1,092    Croft, Kenneth. A Practice Book on English Stress and Intonation.
Rockville, Maryland: English Language Services, Inc.

Designed to provide systematic study and drill on the
patterns of English stress and intonation. Uses dot-and-line
notation devised by Croft and Davis. Four major and five minor
English intonation patterns are given in the text, with appropriate drills for classroom and language laboratory work.
Price (1972): text @ $1.50, tapes @ $51.00 (catalog)

1,093   Croft, Kenneth (ed.). Reader's Digest Readings: ESL. Books
        Five and Six. Pleasantville, New York: Reader's Digest
        Services. 1963-64.

1,094   Croft, Kenneth. Reading and Word Study for Students of English
        as a Second Language. New York: Prentice-Hall, (1960).
        (paper)

        Part I has ten stories carefully adapted from American
        Literature and presented in 24 selections, within an assumed
        vocabulary of approximately 2,000 words (gradually increased
        to 4,000), explanatory footnotes and objective comprehensive
        questions. Part II contains 24 chapters, each corresponding
        with one of the previous selections and intended to be used with
        it. Stress here is on word study, but some attention is given
        to separating major word classes. Emphasis given to the
        derivation of words, suffixes, prefixes and inflectional endings.
        A variety of exercises accompany explanations in each chapter.
        High intermediate level.

1,095   Croft, Kenneth (ed.). Readings on English as a Second Language:
        For Teachers and Teacher Trainees. Cambridge Mass.:
        Winthrop Publishers, Inc., 1972, 496pp. (paper).

        A collection of 34 articles by 30 contributors designed to
        help the practicing teacher or the teacher trainee gain a broad
        view of ESL through a close look at some of the specific areas of
        the subject. The selections are divided into nine sections, each
        dealing with a specific area of second language teaching and learn-
        ing: (1) Trends and practices; (2) Speaking and understanding;
        (3) Grammar; (4) Reading; (5) Writing; (6) Vocabulary; (7) Testing;
        (8) Teaching aids; and (9) Other selected topics. (catalog)

1,096   Croft, Kenneth and Bylle Walker Brown. Science Readings for
        Students of English as a Second Language With Exercises for
        Vocabulary Development. New York: McGraw-Hill 184 pp.

        In this text, .general science readings were selected and
        adapted for individual and classroom use by the intermediate‾
        student. Topics include science education, biology, chemistry,
        earth sciences, engineering, mathematics, oceanography, physics,
        and space exploration. To an assumed vocabulary of 3,500 words,
        700 new terms are added; each term is footnoted and in some cases
        illustrations are used. Exercises at the end of each chapter test
        the understanding of the text material as well as reinforce the
        learning and retention of vocabulary. (NYS Bibliography)

1,097   Croft, Kenneth and E.P. Croft.(eds.). Graded Readers for ESL.
        Englewood Cliffs, New Jersey: Prentice-Hall. 1962.

1,098    Crowell, Thomas Lee, Jr.  Index to Modern English.  New York:
           McGraw-Hill  1964.

           Grammatical explanations for upper high school and college
      age students.

1,099    Crowell, Thomas Lee, Jr.  Modern English Workbook.  New York:
           McGraw-Hill.  1961.

           Designed for upper high school or college age students.

1,100    Crowell, Thomas Lee, Jr.  Modern Spoken English.  New York:
           McGraw-Hill.  1961.

           Designed for upper high school or college age students.

1,101    Da Cruz, Daniel.  Men Who Made America.  New York:  Thomas Y.
           Crowell Company.  1962.

           A collection of brief biographies of famous men in the
      history of the United States.  Vocabulary and syntax are
      controlled, and there are accompanying exercises. (Hefferman-
      Cabrera)

1,102    Davis, A.L.  Diagnostic Test for Students of English as a Second
           Language.  New York: McGraw-Hill.

           This examination, consisting of 150 multiple choice
      questions, tests the student's understanding of English structure
      and idiomatic vocabulary.  The test is easy to administer and
      score.  A one page answer sheet with carbon tissue and underlay
      is used by the student; the instructor scores on the second
      sheet which compares the correct answer to the student's answer.
      (NYS Bibliography)

1,103    Díaz, Luisa V.  It Takes All Kinds of People.  Dade County Public
           Schools.  Miami, Florida.  1971.  13 pp.

           This is a course in English as a second language designed to
      make students further understand cultural differences and to
      accept and adjust to environmental changes in conflict with their
      own culture without damage to their self-image or that of their
      culturally different parents in a pluralistic society.  Students
      are to discuss, according to specified performance objectives,
      read, and write about cultural differences and different culture
      groups in the community using controlled language patterns.
      Linguistic difficulties caused by "going to" "will," "be," and
      "do" are treated in several exercises.  A list of resource
      materials is provided.

1,104  Dixson, Robert J. <u>American Classics</u>. New York: Regents Pub-
     lishing Company. 5 volumes at $1.00 each.

     Ten classics of American literature graded according to
vocabulary level and divided into sections suitable for a single
class period. Comprehension and vocabulary exercises accompany
each reading section, and drills are provided for idioms,
spelling, and grammar. Titles: (1) The House of Seven Gables,
(2) Moby Dick, (3) Murders in the Rue Morgue and The Gold Bug,
(4) The Pathfinder, (5) The Outcasts of Poker Flat, The Luck of
the Roaring Camp, (6) The Hoosier Schoolmaster, (7) The Portrait
of a Lady, (8) The Rise of Silas Lapham, (9) Huckleberry Finn,
and (10) The Red Badge of Courage. (catalog)

1,105  Dixson, Robert J. <u>Complete Course in English</u>. New York: Regents
     Publishing Company (revised edition).

     Comprehensive course designed for high school or college.
Books 1 and 2 offer an intensive course in basic English,
emphasizing the forms of American spoken English and practicing
these forms in dialogues, grammar drills, and reading and
conversation exercises. Also includes work on pronunciation and
anecdotes. Books 3 and 4 cover additional grammatical points,
but place greater emphasis on reading and conversation. Cultural
setting: New York City.
     Price (1972): Books 1-4 @ $1.25 ea.; Tapes (7" reels)
@ $70.00/book.
     (Books 1 and 2 also available in Spanish/English edition
under the title <u>Curso completo de inglés</u>. (catalog)

1,106  Dixson, Robert J. <u>Curso completo de inglés: libros 1 and 2</u>.
     New York: Regents Publishing Company. $1.25 ea.

     Contains the same material as Complete Course in English,
Books 1 and 2 except that all grammar rules and explanations are
presented in Spanish. It is recommended that those using these
books continue their studies with books 3 and 4 of the all English
series. See entry under English title for additional information.
(catalog)

1,107  Dixson, Robert J. <u>Easy Reading Selections in English</u>. New York:
     Regents Publishing Co. (rev. ed.).

     Contains short stories by authors such as O. Henry, Poe,
and Hawthorne, simplified and adapted for intermediate and
advanced students. Each story is divided into sections suitable
for a single class period and is followed by questions and exercises for conversational practice. This book may serve as a
sequel to <u>Elementary Reader in English</u>, by the same author.
     Price (1972): $1.50 (catalog)

1,108     Dixson, Robert J. Elementary Reader in English. New York:
              Regents Publishing Company. (rev. ed.).

              An easy reader containing interesting short stories,
          articles, and anecdotes, adapted and simplified for the beginning
          student. Limited to a vocabulary of approx. 1,000 words, it may
          be used as early as the end of the first six months of English
          study. Each reading selection is followed by exercises in
          comprehension, conversation, and vocabulary. This is the first
          in a series of three readers. The second and third in the series
          are Easy Reading Selections in English and Modern Short Stories
          in English.
              Price (1972): $1.50 (catalog)

1,109     Dixson, Robert J. El inglés én acción. New York: Regents
              Publishing Company. $0.50.

              Basic course in English for students whose native language
          is Spanish. All instructions, explanations, and notes are in
          Spanish. Places main emphasis on the oral aspect of learning
          English without sacrificing practice in basic grammar principles.
          (catalog)

1,110     Dixson, Robert J. English in Action, New York: Regents
              Publishing Company.

              Offers a basic course with emphasis on spoken English.
          Pictures used for vocabulary development and comprehension.
          Simple explanations, easy reading selections, exercises and
          opportunities for constant review.
              Price (1972): Book/$1.25 ea. (catalog)

1,111     Dixson, Robert J. Essential Idioms in English. New York:
              Regents Publishing Company.

              Contains approximately 600 high-frequency idioms and gives
          definitions, illustrations, example sentences, and practice
          exercises in each lesson. The book is divided into elementary,
          intermediate, and advanced levels, each with a review lesson.
          An appendix gives the Spanish, French, and German equivalents
          for every idiom.
              Price (1972): $1.50 (catalog)

1,112     Dixson, Robert J. Everyday Dialogues in English. New York:
              Regents Publishing Company, (rev. ed.)

              A book in advanced conversation, with drills and exercises,
          designed to acquaint the student with the vocabulary and idiomatic
          forms used in a wide variety of circumstances. Each dialogue is
          accompanied by questions for conversation practice, vocabulary
          drills, and sentence construction exercises.
              Price (1972): $1.50 (catalog)

1,113       Dixson, Robert J. <u>Exercises in English Conversation</u>. New
             York: Regents Publishing Company, (rev. ed.)

             Two-book series in conversational English using the direct
        method and introducing grammar through conversation practice.
        Each lesson is divided into three parts: a dialogue, or short
        reading, oral exercises, and a review. Lessons are graded
        according to vocabulary and grammar. This series is coordinated
        with the author's <u>Tests and Drills in English Grammar</u>.
             Price (1972): Book 1 (beginning/intermediate) and Book 2
        (intermediate/advanced) @ $1.25 ea. (catalog)

1,114       Dixson, Robert J. <u>Graded Exercises in English</u>. New York:
             Regents Publishing Company.

             Defines each grammatical principle and presents each part
        of speech in its different forms. Also deals with special
        difficulties of structure, usage and punctuation. Abundant
        exercises arranged in topical form.
             Price (1972): Book @ $1.50 ea. (catalog)

1,115       Dixson, Robert J. <u>Modern American English Series</u>, New York:
             Regents Publishing Co. (revised edition).

             Six-level series for secondary ESL program. Each book is a
        controlled and integrated step toward conversational fluency,
        writing proficiency, and reading comprehension. Emphasis on
        oral competency and careful control of sentence patterns and
        vocabulary. Extensive pattern practice on all structures.
        Book (1) introduces basic vocabulary and grammatical structures;
        readings in form of dialogues and anecdotes; (2) reviews
        patterns from first level and introduces more complex forms;
        (3), (4) and (5) continue building more complex forms and pro-
        gressively advanced reading selections. (6) short articles,
        stories, conversation exercises, and grammar review.
             Price (1972): Books 1-6/$1.75 ea.: Workshops 1-6/$1.00 ea.;
        Tapes (reels or casettes)/$75.00 per book. Posters (20" x 24",
        color): in preparation. (catalog)

1,116       Dixson, Robert J. <u>Modern Short Stories in English</u>. New York:
             Regents Publishing Company, (rev. ed.).

             Contains seventeen short stories written by well-known
        authors and only slightly adapted for use by advanced students.
        Each story is only four or five pages long and can easily be
        studied within one or two class periods. Comprehension questions,
        sentence construction exercises, and vocabulary practice follow
        each story. This book is the third in a series which includes
        <u>Elementary Reader in English</u> and <u>Easy Reading Selections in</u>
        <u>English</u>, both by the same author.
             Price (1972): $1.50

1,117    Dixson, Robert J. <u>Oral Pattern Drills in Fundamental English</u>.
         New York: Regents Publishing Company.

         Source of pattern drills on every major aspect of English
         grammar.  The table of contents is arranged alphabetically
         according to grammatical categories.  May be used as a class-
         room text or as a language laboratory supplement for any basic
         course.
         Price (1972): text at $1.00, tapes and text at $60.00 (catalog)

1,118    Dixson, Robert J. <u>Practical Guide to the Teaching of English</u>
         <u>as a Foreign Language</u>. New York:  Regents Publishing
         Company.  1960.  $1.00.

         Suggestions on classroom procedures based on author's
         experience as a teacher and textbook writer.  Chapters on
         general principles and the teaching of grammar, conversation,
         reading, vocabulary and pronunciation.  Bibliography of author's
         materials.  (NYS Bibliography)

1,119    Dixson, Robert J. <u>Practice Exercises in Everyday English</u>.
         New York: Regents Publishing Company.

         Designed for advanced students in third or fourth year of
         study.  Provides a review of fundamental grammar while introduc-
         ing and drilling more advanced material.  Explanations precede
         each exercise and an index to all grammatical rules.
         Price (1972):  Book at $1.75 ea.  (catalog)

1,120    Dixson, Robert J. <u>Regents English Workbooks</u>. New York:
         Regents Publishing Company.

         Contain exercises in grammatical structure, idiomatic usage,
         vocabulary building, pronunciation, spelling and punctuation.
         Each page of this series is a lesson a single feature of English,
         and intensive exercises follow each concise explanation.
         Adaptable to most any basic course.  Book 1:  elementary/inter-
         mediate; Book 2:  intermediate/advanced; Book 3:  advanced.
         Price (1972):  Workbooks 1-3 at $1.25 ea. Teacher's key
         free with class order.  (catalog)

1,121.   Dixson, Robert J. <u>Second Book in English</u>, New York: Regents
         Publishing Company, (revised edition).

         Continues work of Boggs and Dixson's Beginning Lessons in
         English.  Designed for intermediate students.  In combination
         with first book, covers all essential grammar, vocabulary, and
         sounds of English language.  Introduces new vocabulary; extended
         reading, conversational and pronunciation exercises; and
         additional grammar practice.
         Price (1972):  Book/$1.50 ea.  (catalog)

1,122.  Dixson, Robert J. _Tests and Drills in English Grammar_, New York:
        Regents Publishing Company (revised edition).

        Companion volumes to Exercises in English Conversation, but
        may be adapted to other programs. Emphasizes the acquisition of
        correct usage through drill and repetition. Each lesson contains
        a brief explanation. Each lesson contains a brief explanation of
        grammatical structure followed by a variety of practice exercises.
        Price (1972): Books 1 and 2 at $1.25 ea. (catalog)

1,123.  Dixson, Robert J. _The U.S.A._ Two volumes. New York:  Regents
        Publishing Company. 1959-60.

        Designed to give simple, readable information about geography,
        history, people, events, customs, and ideals of the United States.
        Each book is independent in content and contains exercises for
        conversation and discussion, comprehension and vocabulary review.

1,124.  Dixson, Robert J. and Julio I. Andújar. _Resumen práctico de la
        gramática inglesa._ New York:  Regents Publishing Company.
        $0.85.

        A comprehensive compendium of English grammar and syntax
        designed for speakers of Spanish. Explains all elements of English
        construction with special emphasis given to difficulties most
        commonly encountered by Spanish-speaking students. All model
        English sentences appear with their Spanish equivalents. Includes
        sections on orthography, syllabification, and capitalization, a
        guide to the use of prepositions and conjunctions, and a list of
        irregular verbs. (catalog)

1,125.  Dixson, Robert J. and Fox. _Mi primer diccionario ilustrado de
        inglés._ New York:  Regents Publishing Company. $0.75.

        A beginning word book for the very young Spanish-speaking
        student who is learning English. Each of 650 words included in this
        book is defined in three ways: (1) by means of the Spanish equiva-
        lent of the word; (2) by means of an illustration; (3) by means of a
        sentence in both Spanish and English that defines the word through
        use. (catalog)

1,126.  Dorry, Gertrude Nye. _Games for Second Language Learning._ New York:
        McGraw-Hill. 64pp.

        A collection of 72 games. Relieving the tedium of constant drill
        and practice, most of the games require a great deal of oral partici-
        pation by the entire class. Each game is classified according to the
        aspect of the language that it emphasizes, the size and level of the
        group to which it is suited, and its type. Appropriate for students
        at various levels of maturity and language skill, they may be repeat-
        ed from time to time with more advanced material. (NYS bibliography)

1,127. Dykstra, Gerald et al. A Course in Controlled Composition: Ananse
Tales. New York: Columbia University Teachers College Press.
1966.

Composition practice for upper high school and college age
students.

1,128. Eaton, Esther M. et al. Source Materials for Secondary School
Teachers of Foreign Languages. Circular No. 788. Washington,
D.C.: U.S. Department of Health, Education and Welfare, 1966.
(paper)

A partially-annotated reference list of representative
materials for secondary teachers. Includes information on:
aduiovisual aids, course outlines and guides, cultural aids from
travel and information services, English as a foreign language,
evaluation and testing, foreign language association journals,
foreign language newspapers and periodicals, instructional aids,
international understanding, language laboratories, linguistics,
organizations offering professional services, professional
references, programmed instruction, research, songs and dances,
study, travel and exchange for students and teachers, textbooks,
and vocational opportunities. (NYS bibliography)

1,129. Educational Attitude Survey. Healdsburg Union School District,
California. Dissemination Center for Bilingual Bicultural
Education, Austin, Texas. Washington, D.C.: Office of Education.
September 1971. 11pp.
(ED 062 844)

This instrument was developed for use with parents of children
participating in bilingual education programs. It seeks to determine
parental attitudes toward education in general and toward using
both Spanish and English to teach courses in public schools. Statements requiring parental agreement or disagreement appear in both
Spanish and English. Techniques for administering the questionnaire
are suggested along with possible uses of the information. (RIE)

1,130. Educational Services of Washington, D.C. Commercial Correspondence
for Students of English as a Second Language. New York:
McGraw-Hill 148pp.

A simple treatment of American business English for the intermediate student, this text is suitable for self-study, classroom,
or office use. Lessons contain four sections: a presentation of
types and parts of business letters and forms, a discussion of this
material, grammar review, and exercises. A brief appendix provides
abbreviations, irregular verbs, and a reference list of frequently
used business terms. (NYS bibliography)

1,131. Educational Services of Washington, D.C. Reading Selections for
Students of English as a Second Language. New York: McGraw-
Hill, 158pp.

236

Stories and articles from American magazines have been selected
to provide an introduction to the American people and their customs.
Rewritten for the intermediate student, complicated vocabulary
and sentence construction have been eliminated, but common idiomatic
expressions have been retained and footnoted.  "Questions for
Conversation" follow each selection.  (NYS bibliography)

1,132.  Educreative Systems, Inc.  A Listening-Reading Program for Grades
        1-6.  Lexington, Massachusetts:  D.C.  Heath and Company.

A supplementary series designed to strengthen listening,
reading and comprehension skills.  One of the major aims of·the
program is to introduce children to new people and life-styles.
Therefore, many of the stories deal with different ethnic groups
and customs, placing emphasis on the positive contributions of
these people.  Other stroies deal with ideas and experiences more
familiar to most children.  Each grade level unit contains 6
records, 12 stories, response sheets, and a teacher's manual.(catalog)

1,133.  Elkins, Robert J. and Christian Bruggemann.  Comic Strips in the
        Teaching of English as a Foreign Language.  Paper presented to a
        conference on the teaching of English, Kassel, West Germany,
        February 5-6, 1971.  20pp.
        (ED 056 591)

1,134.  English Around the World.  Glenview, Illinois:  Scott, Foresman
        and Company.  1970-71.

A three-level program in ESL for elementary school children,
including a full level of aural-oral work before reading is introduced.  The program includes Pupils' Skills Books, Teacher's
Guidebooks, display cards, posters  (level 1), word cards (levels
2 and 3), practice pads and test booklets, records, and tapes.
See catalog for detailed description and prices of individual
components.  (catalog)

1,135.  English Examination for Foreign Students:  Including a Test of Non-
        Verbal Reasoning.  Princeton, New Jersey:  Educational Testing
        Services, 1947.

1,136.  English Language Institute.  ELI Achievement Series: Sentence
        Structure Examinations, A, B, and C.  Ann Arbor, Michigan:
        Follett's Michigan Bookstore.  Summer, 1972. $12.00/20 students.

An adjunct to Robert Krohn's grammar textbook, English Sentence
Structure.  The three 50-item, multiple-choice forms correspond to
three progressive levels of achievement, and are designed to aid
the teacher who wishes to evaluate his students' mastery of the
material in the text.  Punched scoring stencils, answer sheets and
reusable test booklets for each test.  (catalog)

1,137.  English Language Institute.  English Conversation Practices.  Ann
        Arbor, Michigan:  The University of Michigan Press.  130pp. $2.25

Part of An Intensive Course in English. Designed for use by intermediate and advanced students of ESL, primarily on the university level. The practices in it will help develop conversational ease. Modals, two-word verbs, time expressions, relative clauses, and many other sentence parts are emphasized. (catalog)

1,138.   English Language Institute. English Pattern Practices. Ann Arbor, Michigan: The University of Michigan Press. 3rd rev. ed. 362pp. $2.95.

Part of An Intensive Course in English. Designed primarily for foreign students on the university level. This text develops the automatic use of English patterns. Includes a picture sequence exercise that can be used by teachers for class drill or by students for home study. (catalog)

1,139.   English Language Institute. English Pronunciation. Ann Arbor, Michigan: The University of Michigan Press. 2nd rev. ed. 212pp. $2.95.

Part of An Intensive Course in English. Designed primarily for foreign students on the university level. Stresses not only the pronunciation of English sounds but also their recognition, utilizing the following three methods: imitation, articulatory description, and comparison with the nearest sound in Spanish. (catalog)

1,140.   English Language Institute. English Sentence Structure. Ann Arbor, Michigan: The University of Michigan Press. 320pp. $3.25.

Part of An Intensive Course in English. The successor to the well-known English Sentence Patterns of Lado/Fries. Tapes available. Designed for foreign students on the university level. (catalog)

1,141.   English Language Institute. An Intensive Course in English. Ann Arbor, Michigan: The University of Michigan Press. 5 volumes.

A well-known course developed under the direction of Charles C. Fries and Robert Lado which applies the advances of structural linguistics and language-learning psychology to all areas of language teaching. Titles: (1) English Sentence Structure, (2) English Conversation Practices, (3) English Pattern Practices, (4) English Pronunciation, and (5) Vocabulary in Context. See individual titles for details. Primarily designed for foreign students on the university level.   (catalog)

1,142.   English Language Institute. Michigan Test of Aural Comprehension: Forms 1, 2, and 3. Ann Arbor, Michigan: Follett's Michigan Bookstore. Spring, 1972. $60.00/100 students.

Designed to measure a subject's understanding of spoken English. Three 90-item forms, equivalent in level of difficulty and content, use the same test booklet and answer sheet. The student hears either a statement or question and responds by

indicating the appropriate written choice. Magnetic tapes, punched
scoring stencils, answer sheets and reusable test booklets. (catalog)

1,143. English Language Institute. Placement Test. Ann Arbor, Michigan:
Follett's Michigan Bookstore. Summer, 1973. $70.00/100 student-.

This is a non-diagnostic, objectively scored test designed
for quick placement of students into homogeneous ability levels.
It contains problems of listening comprehension, grammar in context,
vocabulary recognition, and reading comprehension of sentences.
Punched scoring stencil, magnetic tape, answer sheets and reusable
test booklets. (catalog)

1,144. English Language Institute. Vocabulary in Context. Ann Arbor,
Michigan: The University of Michigan Press. 206pp. $3.25.

Part of An Intensive Course in English. Designed primarily
for foreign students on the university level. Develops skill in
using vocabulary in everyday situations. The student progresses
from simple conversation to dialogue involving specialized words
and usage. (catalog)

1,145. English Language Services, Inc. Collier-Macmillan English Readers.
21 volumes. New York: Collier-Macmillan. 1965-68.

A series of 21 graded readers progressing in vocabulary
level from 500 to 4,000 words. (Hefferman-Cabrera)

1,146. English Language Services. Drills and Exercises in English Pronunciation: Consonants and Vowels. New York: Collier-Macmillan
International. 1966-67.

Provides basic drill material on all the individual sounds
and the more important combinations of sounds in the English sound
system. A table of symbols is provided, and any unusual spellings
are given in phonemic symbols. There is a spelling and pronunciation
aid section in the back of the book. Tapes available. Designed for
upper high school and college age students. (catalog)

1,147. English Language Services. Drills and Exercises in English Pronunciation: Stress and Intonation: Part I. New York: Collier-
Macmillan International. 1966-67.

Introduces word and word combination stress, and the study
of intonation in ordinary speech patterns. A system of stress
marking and intonation patterns is introduced, and completely marked
practice dialogs are included. Tapes available. Designed for upper
high school or college age students. (catalog)

1,148. English Language Services. Drills and Exercises in English Pronunciation: Stress and Intonation: Part II. New York: Collier-
Macmillan International. 1966-67.

Provides practice drills concerned mainly with non-emphatic
phrase stress, and phrase stress and intonation for contrast and
emphasis. Practice material is given through marked dialogs,
readings, anecdotes, speeches, and poetry. The speeches and poems
are read on the accompanying tapes by their authors. Designed for
upper high school or college age students. (catalog)

1,149.  English Language Services. English Grammar Exercises. New York:
        Collier-Macmillan International. Three volumes.

        Provides intensive practice with the basic structure patterns
of English for secondary school or adult learners. Since these
books are intended primarily to supplement a basic text, grammar
explanations are limited to the inclusion of instructions and an
example or two at the beginning of each exercise. Exercises are
useful for homework assignments as well as oral drill. A progression in difficulty from the beginning of Book 1 through the
end of Book 2 is suitable for use with basic elementary-to-inter-
mediate language courses. Book 3 is designed for advanced students
and is based on a progression in difficulty with respect to the
treatment of individual grammatical points. (catalog)

1,150.  English Language Services. English 900. New York: Collier-
        Macmillan, 1964-65. (paper) (Thirteen volumes)

        A basic instructional series for adults, consisting of six
textbooks, six workbooks, a teacher's manual, and 180 tapes. The
course is based on 900 English utterances, ranging from greetings
to quite complex sentences. Each lesson includes a number of basic
utterances, intonation practice, questions and answers, verb study,
substitution drills, conversation and exercises. Keys to the
exercises are provided. The workbooks are programmed for self-
study. The Teacher's Manual contains each unit's grammar and a
general word index indicating in which textbook each word occurred
first. Readers supplement to texts: Collier-Macmillan English
Readers. Tapes. (NYS bibliography)

1,151.  English Language Services. English Teaching Kit. Rockville,
        Maryland: English Language Services, Inc. $25.00.

        Developed as an aid to the non-professional who becomes in-
volved in teaching ESL, and who needs immediate and practical guidance. Includes 4 booklets, a color filmstrip, 2 tapes and a sample
proficiency test. Covers general approaches and techniques of
second language teaching and stresses a number of the problems
inherent in teaching English to non-native speakers. The sound
system of English and the English structure are also covered, as
well as methods of teaching using oral-aural approaches. (catalog)

1,152.  English Language Services. English This Way. New York: Macmillan
        16 vols. 1963-65.

A 6-year course in ESL for secondary schools (uses 2 books for each year). Books 1-6 emphasize spoken language, with more extensive comments on grammar appearing in Books 7-8 and exercises on vocabulary and composition predominating in Books 9-12. New structures and vocabulary are introduced in dialog and pattern sentences, with practice provided by substitution, completion, conversion, and question-answer exercises. Teacher's manuals and keys to exercises in separate volumes. (CAL bibliography)

1,153. English Language Services. Intensive Course in English. Rockville, Maryland: English Language Services, Inc.

A four level course designed for secondary schools or adult programs on the intermediate or advances levels using an aural-oral approach with dialogs, basic sentences, repetition drills, and reading and comprehension materials. The intermediate level includes 30 lessons. Advanced levels 1 and 2 contain 50 lessons each. The fourth level - Specialized Studies - prepares foreign students for undertaking university studies. It includes reading passages, dialogues, and introductory training in note taking, outlining, and preparing research papers.
Prices (1972): text (first 3 levels) @ $1.65 ea. (level 4) @ $1.35 ea. tapes (level 1) $67.50 Levels 2 and 3 $112.50 (level 4) $45.00. (catalog)

1,154. English Language Services. The Key to English. New York: Collier-Macmillan International.

Designed for students at the intermediate and advanced level, these 10 paperbound books focus on major aspects of grammar and usage, bringing mastery of the most difficult areas of the language within easier reach. Each book is concerned with one specific subject and contains expositions, examples, drills, and exercises with answers. The series can be used for independent study or as supplementary and reference material in the classroom. It is also suitable for use in courses developed for students who have completed their work with a basic text. Although not restricted, the vocabulary is generally on the intermediate level. See Separate entries for each of the 10 books. (catalog)

1,155. English Language Services. The Key to English Adjectives 1. New York: Collier-Macmillan International. 1965, 94pp.

Rejects as inadequate and confusing the traditional concept of a "word that modifies a noun." Follows modern structuralist methodology instead, placing emphasis on syntax. Treats the basic use of the adjective and its most closely associated structures such as intensifiers, constructions with for and to, adjectival clauses, and word order. Also discusses the definite article, the possessive pronoun and other noun determiners. (catalog)

1,156. English Language Services. The Key to English Adjectives II. New York: Collier-Macmillan International. 1965.

Includes sections on the comparison of adjectives, the study of derivational affixes, problems in distinguishing true adjectives from related adjective-like structures, and idiomatic uses of adjectives. (catalog)

1,157.  English Language Services.  The Key to English Figurative Expressions. New York:  Collier-Macmillan International.

Includes more than a thousand expressions chosen because of their frequency of occurrence in both literary and colloquial usage. Arranged alphabetically, each is accompanied by a definition and an example.  Especially useful because these expressions are not ordinarilly found in dictionaries or classroom texts. (catalog)

1,158.  English Language Services.  The Key to English Letter Writing.  New York:  Collier-Macmillan International. 1966. 76pp.

Ten lessons discuss the different types of letters, describe the different parts of a letter, set forth some general rules on composition and mechanics, and give samples and practical exercises. Particular attention is given to business correspondence but guidance is also offered on other types of letters such as applications, invitations and cables. (catalog)

1,159.  English Language Services.  The Key to English Nouns.  New York: Collier-Macmillan International. 1965 106pp.

Thirteen lessons discuss noun forms and their use in sentences, treating such aspects as nouns with irregular plurals, mass and count nouns, and agreement of subject and verb.  Also discusses pronouns and the rules governing their replacement of nouns. Includes drills and exercises. (catalog)

1,160.  English Language Services.  The Key to English Prepositions I. New York:  Collier-Macmillan International.

Fourteen lessons present in context the most important and frequently encountered meanings of the common prepositions.  Sometimes the context consists of a single sentence, but there are also consecutive reading selections and short conversations.  Exercises of various kinds and several tests for check-up use have been provided.  Includes discussion of one-, two-, and three-word prepositions (e.g. in, out of, in front of). (catalog)

1,161.  English Language Services.  The Key to English Prepositions II. New York: Collier-Macmillan International. 88pp.

The choice of the right preposition often seems quite unpredictable and the student must familiarize himself with a great many phrases.  Several hundred idiomatic usages of prepositions are presented in this book.  Lessons include short expository statements, exercises and tests.  A detailed index is provided, arranged according to the noun if it is the noun that determines the choice of preposition. (catalog)

1,162.  English Language Services.  The Key to English Two-Word Verbs.  New
York:  Collier-Macmillan International. 132pp.

The two-word verb consists of a verb and adverb (or preposition),
with or without a following noun object.  In this book, two-word
verbs are classified as "separable" and "inseparable" and they are
distinguished from ordinary combinations of verbs and prepositions.
The 14 lessons in this book contain exercises and drill material
including practice with intonation patterns.  A glossary about 400
two-word verbs is included. (catalog)

1,163.  English Language Services.  The Key to English Verbs.  New York:
Collier, Macmillan International.

This ten lesson book covers the verb and the verb phrase; the
meanings of the various verb structures (often called "tenses");
and a number of verbal idioms.  Special verb problems, such as be,
do and have are treated separately because their grammar is so
different from that of ordinary verbs.  One appendix lists forms of
irregular verbs and another gives examples of archaic verb forms.
Lessons provide dialogues, practice sentences and exercises. (catalog)

1,164.  English Language Services.  The Key to English Vocabulary.  New
York:  Collier-Macmillan International. 1965, 125pp.

Designed to bridge the gap between elementary and more advanced word levels.  All lessons include practice and text exercises.
Also included is a 2,000 word list prepared for ESL students, and
lists of suffixes and prefixes. (catalog)

1,165.  English Language Services.  Reading and Conversation for Intermediate and Advanced Students of English.  Rockville, Maryland:
English Language Services, Inc.  Two volumes.

Provides practice in both literary and coloquial styles of
English.  The 20 lessons in each volume also include vocabulary
drills, writing exercises and punctuation practice.  Volume 1:
geography, history, holidays, government, education, American speech,
transportation and communications.  Volume 2:  architecture and
housing, food and drink, entertainment, sports, vacation, American
cities, country living, art and music, and American literature.
Price (1972): text at $2.75 ea. tape at $45.00/volume. (catalog)

1,166.  English Language Services, Inc.  Special English.  New York:
Collier-Macmillan International. 15 volumes.

A series of 15 books for intermediate level students to aid
them in acquiring the specialized vocabulary and understanding of
terms commonly used in professions such as medicine, aviation, en-
gineering, banking, international trade, agriculture, and journal-
ism.  Each book is divided into a number of lessons containing
dialogues, readings, word studies, and exercises.  Accompanying tapes
provide practice in comprehension, pronunciation and intonation.  All
books were prepared in cooperation with experienced specialists in the
relevant fields. (catalog)

1,167.  English Language Services. <u>Technical English Tape Library</u>. Rock-
        ville, Maryland: English Language Services, Inc.

        Designed to furnish study materials for students of English
        who need to learn terminology peculiar to specialized areas of
        study such as: (1) agriculture and natural resources, (2) industry
        and mining, (3) transportation, (4) labor, (5) health and sanitation,
        (6) education, (7) public safety and administration, (8) community
        development and social welfare, and (9) general and misc. topics.
        Each lesson module is identified by the approx. Pedagogical level,
        specific learning activity, and a lesson title. Useful as a
        language laboratory resource.
              Price (1972): Tapes at $4.90 ea. Complete set at $515.00. (catalog)

1,168.  Erazmus, Edward and Harry Cargas. <u>English as a Second Language</u>:
        <u>A Reader</u>. Dubuque, Iowa: William C. Brown. 1970.

        Reader for upper high school or college age students.

1,169.  <u>Ethnic Studies Elective Resource Bulletin</u>. Junior High School.
        Intermediate School; High School. July 1970. Includes "The
        Puerto Ricans." pp. 109-126.

1,170.  Feeney, Joan V., Comp. <u>Chicano Special Reading Selections 1972</u>. 72p.
        (ED 065 255)

1,171.  Feigenbaum, Irwin. <u>English Now</u>. New York: New Century. 1971.

        An oral language program developed through ESL research and
        methodology for Black students who speak non-standard informal
        English. Based on the premise that social situations determine
        "appropriate" language usage. Its main objective is to teach
        students an alternative way of speaking by concentrating on
        certain features of grammar and pronunciation that distinguish
        formal English from Black informal English.
              Price (1972): Write and See Student Workbooks 5/$9.90
        teacher's manual $1.98, tapes (reels) $117.00 (cassettes) $63.00 (catalog)

1,172.  Filep, Robert T. and Others. <u>Voluntarias De Sesame Street: Manual</u>
        <u>Para Conducir Las Sesions "Sesame Street" Con Niños De Edad</u>
        <u>Pre-Escolar</u>. Institute for Educational Development, El Segundo,
        California. New York, New York: John and Mary R. Markle
        Foundation. July 28, 1971. 50pp.
        (ED 057 897)

1,173.  Finkel, Lawrence S. and Ruth Krawitz. <u>Learning English as a Second</u>
        <u>Language</u>. (from the Phillipine Center for Language Study),
        Dobbs Ferry, New York: Oceana Publications, Inc. 1970-1971.

        A series of workbooks for ESL on six levels. These workbooks are
        for classroom use and cover six levels of instruction, beginning with
        an essentially auditory approach, then moving on to writing and
        reading. The lessons are sequential and presented in a manner to

establish a foundation on which to build and expand necessary skills
in reading, writing and speaking. Pupil interest is stimulated
through involvement in classroom dialogues and activities.
> Cultural content drawn mostly from the Phillipines.
> Primary Use: Elementary Levels. (Oceana catalog)

1,174. Finocchiaro, Mary. English as a Second Language: From Theory to
Practice. New York: Regents Publishing Company. 1964.
$1.95. (paper). 143pp.

> Designed for beginning and advanced teachers. Presents back-
ground reading for language learning and teaching, based largely
on author's experience. Includes suggestions for preparing curriculum, developing language skills, materials, techniques and testing.
(PREP on B.E. rev.)

1,175. Finnochiaro, Mary. Learning to Use English. New York: Regents
Publishing Company.

> Levels: upper elementary, secondary or college. Audio-lingual
course stressing balanced achievement in the full range of language
skills. Wide variety of graded exercises based on common spoken
English. Each lesson emphasizes the interrelatedness of language
skills and progresses through a four-phrase sequence of listening,
speaking, reading and writing. Very comprehensive teacher's manual.
> Price (1972): Books 1 and 2 at $1.75 ea.; Teacher's manual
at $2.50; Tapes (7" reels) at $55.00/set. (catalog)

1,176. Finocchiaro, Mary. Let's Talk, New York: Regents Publishing
Company.

> Book of dialogues designed for maximum textbook flexibility.
Dialogues present patterns of everyday spoken English designed to
reinforce grammatical structures, practice pronunciation and
intonation, and increase conversational fluency. Progresses from
simple to complex speech patterns. Includes pattern practice
exercises within the dialogues.
> Price (1972): Book at $1.75 ea. (catalog)

1,177. Finocchiaro, Mary. Teaching Children Foriegn Languages. McGraw-Hill.
1964.

> Non-technical guide with specific examples of tested classroom
procedures. Includes chapters on techniques, teacher attitude,
development of language skills, making teaching effective, and the
preparation and adaptation of materials. Bibliography and glossary
of useful terms. (NYS bibliography)

1,178. Finocchiaro, Mary and Michael Bonomo. The Foreign Language Learner:
A Guide for Teachers. New York: Regents Publishing Company. $3.95.

A comprehensive professional guide in the field of foreign or second language learning. Includes topics such as determining beginning proficiency levels, planning the curriculum, classroom utilization of teaching materials, and ways of evaluating student achievement and teaching efficiency. Useful as a reference book or for teacher training. (catalog)

1.179. Finocchiaro, Mary and Lavenda. Selections for Developing English Language Skills. New York: Regents Publishing Company, (rev.ed.)

A workbook type publication suitable for intermediate and advanced students and designed to improve listening, reading, and writing skills. The book is divided into two major parts: listening comprehension and reading comprehension. The reading selections, followed by comprehension questions, may also be used in a variety of related activities described in the instructions to teachers and students.
Price (1972): $1.50. (catalog)

1,180. Fisher, and Dixson, Robert J. Beginning Lessons in English. New York: Regents Publishing Company (revised edition).

A text for beginners. Emphasizes conversation and pronunciation; covers grammar through pattern practice rather than rule memorization. Frequent re-entry and review exercises. Each lesson consists of three parts: pronunciation, grammar exercises, and conversation practice.
Price (1972): Book/$1.50 ea. (catalog)

1,181. Francis, W. Nelson. The Structure of American English. New York: The Ronald Press. 1958.

Intended for a one-semester course in the English language for prospective teachers. Attempts to synthetize "current linguistic knowledge, especially as applied to present-day American English." (Hefferman-Cabrera)

1,182. Friend, Jewell A. Writing English as a Second Language. Glenview, Illinois: Scott, Foresman. 1971.

Composition practice for upper high school or college age students.

1,183. Fuller, H.R. and F.F. Wasell. Advanced English Exercises. Saxon Series in ESL. New York: McGraw-Hill.

Offers the opportunity for drill in and mastery of the English language for students who have thoroughly grasped the fundamentals. 253 grammar, vocabulary, and pronunciation exercises comprise the text. The material is interrelated in the belief that learning a language is the acquisition of habits, not merely the learning of rules. (NYS bibliography)

1,184.  Gibson, Christine and I.A. Richards.  First Steps in Reading English.
        4 vols. New York:  Washington Square Press. 1959.

        Introduction to reading for beginners.  Graded for letter-
        intake and vocabulary of about 316 words.  Stick drawings illustrate
        meanings.  (Hefferman-Caberea)

1,185.  Grindell, Robert et al.  American Readings.  Saxon Series in ESL.
        New York:  McGraw-Hill.

        A text for the upper-intermediate ESL student, designed
        primarily to develop English language skills adequate for study of
        college subjects in English.  Features 15 short selections by such
        distinguished American writers as Mark Twain, Jack London, Washington
        Irving, and O. Henry.  Many of the themes are humorous, and they
        range from the philosophical to the factual.  Intensive study of
        this book should increase the student's ability to reproduce the
        most complicated vocabulary and structure accurately.  (NYS
        bibliography)

1,186.  Guerra, Manuel H. and Others.  Listing of Resource Material Con-
        cerned with the Spanish-Speaking.  Olympia:  Washington State
        Office of Public Instruction. Washington, D.C.:  Office of
        Education. June 1971. 37p.
        (ED 059 830)

        An enumeration of teaching-learning resources pertaining to
        Spanish-speaking groups in America, this publication contains a 40-
        item selected bibliography on Mexican Americans, a list of 150
        sources of general information, over 60 citations of selected materials,
        and a 28-item list of migrant education materials.  The resources
        cited encompass children's and adults' books, meetings, periodicals,
        audiovisual aids, educational opportunities, organizations, and
        Federal programs concerned with the Spanish-speaking, bibliographies
        articles, speeches, and textbooks.  Some of the bibliographic
        citations are annotated.  Also included is an article on the
        language-instruction programs for Spanish-speaking learners in
        California, as related to intergroup relations.  (RIE)

1,187.  Hall, Eugene J.  Basic Literacy Series:  Reading Improvement for
        Adults.  New York:  Regents Publishing Company. 6 volumes $1.25 ea.

        Series designed to teach literacy, reading improvement, and
        other communication skills to adults.  The graded selections describe
        everyday situations and activities, and include such special areas
        as application forms and letter writing.  Titles:  (1) Sounds and
        Syllables, (2) The Signs of Life, (3) A Handful of Letters,
        (4) The Food We Eat, (5) How Government Works, and (6) Making
        Government Work for You.  (catalog)

1,188.  Hall, Eugene J.  Building English Sentences, New York:  Regents
        Publishing Company.

Series of workbooks designed to help student synthesize basic
sentence patterns into unified speech. Can be used individually or
collectively as a supplement to almost any English course. Deals
with the formation of sentence patterns, providing graded oral and
written exercises proceeding from basic patterns to more complex
syntactic structures. Topics include: (1) Sentences with be
(2) One-word verbs, (3) Two-word verbs, (4) Verbals, (5) Adverbs,
(6) Alternatives in Building English Sentences, (7) Building Complex
English Sentences, and (8) Adjectives in separate books.
Price (1972): Books 1-7 at $1.00 ea.; Book 8: in preparation.
(catalog)

1,189.  Hall, Eugene J.  Estudios del inglés: intermedio-avanzado.  New
York:  Regents Publishing Company. $1.50.

Identical to Practical Conversation in English for Intermediate Students with a corresponding translation in Spanish on
facing pages of all dialogues, sentences for practice, and idiomatic expressions. See entry under English title for additional
information.
Price (1972): text at $1.50 records and text at $9.95 tapes
and text at $28.00 casettes and text at $22.50. (catalog)

1,190.  Hall, Eugene J.  Practical Conversation in English for Beginning,
Intermediate and Advanced Students. New York: Regents
Publishing Company.

These three conversation books present English as it is
actually spoken in homes, offices, and a variety of other situations.
Each dialogue is built around one or more grammatical structures
and is accompanied by exercises in comprehension, structure, stress,
and intonation.
Price (1972): Books 1-3 at $1.50 ea.   (catalog)

1,191.  Hall, Eugene et al.  Orientation in American English. Washington,
D.C.:  American Express Language Centers. 1970.

A series of 6 texts, 4 workbooks, 4 tapebooks, 3 readers,
and 50 tapes or 24 cassettes designed for upper high school or
college age students.  (CAL bibliography)

1,192.  Hall, Robert A., Jr.  Linguistics and Your Language. 2nd Rev. ed.
of Leave Your Language Alone. Garden City, New York:
Doubleday. 1960.

A brief popular discussion relative to language and linguistics.
Contains clear, non-technical statement of theories, principles,
and methods.  (Hefferman-Cabrera)

1,193.  A Handbook for Teachers of English (Americanization - Literacy).
rev. ed. Sacramento: California State Department of Education.
1967.
(ED 016 191)

1,194. Harding, Deborah A. and Others. A Microwave Course in English as a
Second Language (For Spanish Speakers). La Jolla, California:
Lingoco Corp. 1969. 257p.
(ED 035 876)

1,195. Harris, Arna S. and Allan C. Harris. "A Selected Bibliography of
American Literature for TESOL. Part 1: The Novel; Part 2:
The Short Story, Drama, Poetry." TESOL Quarterly. 1:3
(September, 1967), 1:4 (December, 1967). (Available as
reprint from TESOL)

Annotated bibliography. (NYS bibliography)

1,196. Harris, David P. Reading Improvement Exercises for Students of
English as a Second Language. Englewood Cliffs, New Jersey:
Prentice-Hall, 1966. (paper)

For high-intermediate and advanced students. Part I
consists of a diagnostic vocabulary test and a reading comprehension test (which covers both speed and comprehension) and
gives suggestions for increasing vocabulary. Parts II-VII
consist of exercises to increase speed in recognition and comprehension, first of words, then of sentences, paragraphs and whole
compositions. Part VIII deals with scanning techniques. Part IX
contains exercises to develop speed and accuracy in using a dictionary. Includes key to exercises and reading-time conversion
table. (NYS bibliography)

1,197. Harris, David P. and Leslie A. Palmer. CELT: A Comprehensive
English Language Test for Speakers of English as a Second
Language. New York: McGraw-Hill. 1970.

Consists of test forms and examiner's books for listening
comprehension, structure, and vocabulary, accompanied by a
Technical Manual with descriptions of the tests and information
on test statistics and norms. Suitable for high school students
or older. Intended as a placement test but adaptable for use as
a measurement of achievement as well. (CAL bibliography)

1,198. Hayden, R.E. et al. Mastering American English. Englewood Cliffs,
New Jersey: Prentice-Hall. 1956. paper.

1,199. The Heath Reading Program (for grades 7-9). Lexington, Massachusetts
D.C. Heath and Company. 1971.

A three-level reading program with tabloid-style format and
contemporary themes designed to motivate reluctant readers.
Though the stories deal with such specific topics as racial and
ethnic prejudice, environmental problems, political assassinations,
illegitimate births, and urban riots, the underlying themes express
universal human interests and values. After-reading activities are
am important feature of this program. Each grade-level kit contains
20 stories, 3 filmstrips, 4 records, a teacher's guide and duplicating
masters for student activities. (catalog)

1,200. Hefferman-Cabrera, Patricia. <u>Audio-Visual English</u>. Collier-
Macmillan International. 191.

Objective is to provide visual and oral support in the
teaching of ESL. The materials carefully control structures
and use vocabulary in context. Each set in the series consists
of 10 color filmstrips, records or tapes, and a teacher's guide/
script. The tapes contain the recorded script and sound effects
while the teacher's guide/script includes each filmstrip script,
explanatory notes to the teacher, and suggestions for using the
materials. Each filmstrip treats a separate language topic. (catalog

1,201. Hill, L.A. and R.D.S. Fielden. <u>Vocabulary Tests and Exercises</u>
<u>for Overseas Students</u>. London: Oxford University Press. 1962.

1,202. Hines, Mary Elizabeth. <u>Skits in English as a Second Language</u>.
New York: Regents Publishing Company. 1972 (in preparation).

Combines pattern practice with role-playing. Consists of 36
carefully graded skits designed to reinforce basic structures.
Vocabulary is rigidly controlled: in each skit, material beyond
the structure being reinforced is kept to the absolute minimum.
Each skit is followed by a variety of exercises. Enables the
student to overcome his inhibitions and achieve free use of the
target language by assuming various roles. (catalog)

1,203. Hirschhorn, Howard H. <u>Spanish-English/English-Spanish Medical</u>
<u>Guide (Guía médica español-inglés/inglés-español)</u>. New
York: Regents Publishing Company. $1.00.

Presents words, phrases, and sentences, with their equivalents,
bilingually to help communication between medical personnel and
patients when one is Spanish-speaking and the other English-
speaking. (catalog)

1,204. Hirschhorn, Howard H. <u>Technical and Scientific Reader in English</u>
<u>(Temas técnicos y científicos en inglés)</u>. New York: Regents
Publishing Company. $1.75.

Non-graded reading selections drawn from a wide variety of
technical and semitechnical writings (e.g. architecture, electronics,
auto mechanics, agriculture, data processing, navigation, chemistry,
television, etc.) designed especially for students who plan to take
technical or scientific courses in American schools. Lexical items
of a technical nature or with specialized contextual meanings are
defined in Spanish in the margins. Exercises following each reading
selection are based on comprehension, vocabulary, and conversation.
(catalog)

1,205. Hocking, Elton. <u>Language Laboratory and Language Learning</u>. Monograph
2. Washington, D.C.: Department of Audio-Visual Instruction,
National Education Association of the United States, (1964). (paper)

Discusses the language laboratory and developments that should aid language learning and teaching; a basic document in this area. (NYS bibliography)

1,206.  Holland, B.F. and G. McDaniel. "Teaching Latin-Americans to Read by Means of Visual Aids." Texas Outlook. Vol. 26 (July 1942) pp. 20-22.

1,207.  Hollander, Sophie. Impressions of the United States. New York: Holt, Rinehart and Winston. 1964.

A reading textbook for students at the intermediate-advanced level. The text is a series of letters written by newcomers with various backgrounds describing the individual's reaction to some aspect of the American scene. (Hefferman-Cabrera)

1,208.  Imamura, Shigeo and James W. Ney. Audio-Lingual Literary Series. Boston: Blaisdell. 3 vols. 1969.

Structured readers for upper high school and college age ESL students.

1,209.  Institute of Modern Languages. Contemporary Review Exercises. New York: Thomas Y. Crowell. 1967.

Grammar review exercises for upper high school or college age students.

1,210.  Institute of Modern Languages. Contemporary Spoken English. New York: Thomas Y. Crowell. 5 vols. 1967-68.

Basic course for adult or secondary school beginners. Linguistically graded and controlled. Lessons are based on short dialogs, followed by pattern practice of various types. New Patterns are introduced in frames to emphasize structure. Occasional notes to students point out facts about the patterns, and how and where to use them. Later lessons include reading passages. Reaches high intermediate level. (CAL bibliography)

1,211.  Institute of Modern Languages. Situational Reinforcement. Washington, D.C.: Institute of Modern Languages. 1967.

Course for beginners intended for college age or older students but usable in high school as well. Use-oriented rather than structure-oriented. Oral approach, controlled within each situation by question-response type of practice. Reading and writing introduced at beginning level. Course consists of 8 texts (5 general and one each on schools and universities, American politics and government, and style and usage); workbooks accompany first 4 texts; readers accompany levels 2-5; tapes and tapebooks for levels 1-5. (CAL bibliography)

1,212. Intergroup Relations in Teaching Materials:  A Survey and Appraisal.
Washington, D.C.:  The Council. 1949.  231pp. Report of the
Committee on the Study of Teaching Materials in Intergroup
Relations of the American Council on Education.

1,213. Kane, John and Mary Kirkland.  Contemporary Spoken English.  New
York: Thomas Y. Crowell Co. 1967. Six volumes.

1,214. Karp, T.B. et al.  Principles and Methods of Teaching a Second
Language:  A Motion Picture Series for Teacher Training.  A
five-film series. New York: Teaching Film Custodians. 1962.

A series of films entitled: "The Nature of Language," "The
Sounds of Language," "The Organization of Language," "Words and
their Meanings," "Modern Techniques for Teaching Foreign Languages."
A helpful base from which to loft preservice and inservice teacher
training programs. (Hefferman-Cabrera)

1,215. Kennedy, Dora F.  Mexican Americans:  A Teaching and Resource Unit
for Upper Level Spanish Students, to be Executed in Spanish
or in English for Social Studies Classes, or Classes in
Hispanic Cultures.  Prince George's County Board of Education.
Upper Marlboro, Maryland. 1971. 91pp.
(ED 056 577)

1,216. Kenyon, J.S. and T.A. Knott.  A Pronouncing Dictionary of American
English.  Springfield, Mass.:  G. and C. Merriam Co. 1953.

Gives standard colloquial pronunciation of American English
transcribed in the IPA.  Records variant pronunciations when
there are differences among educated speakers.  Regional differences
are also given.  A handy reference book.  (NYS bibliography)

1,217. King, Harold V.  Irregular Verbs.  Rockville, Maryland:  English
Language Services, Inc.  $1.25.

A series of lessons with oral drills designed to give non-
native English speakers an active oral command of all the important
irregular verbs.  Auxiliaries and a few of the commonest irregular
verbs are reviewed first, then other verbs are covered in separate
lists grouped together according to the way their principal parts
are formed.  (catalog)

1,218. King, Harold V. and Russell Campbell.  An English Reading Test.
Rockville, Maryland:  English Language Services, Inc. $0.15.

A 30-minute test of reading ability accompanied by a detailed
interpretation of scores.  Designed as a scale for measuring reading
skill over a wide range of ability.  Especially useful as an aid in
determining readiness to enter an American college or university.
(catalog)

1,219. Kitchin, A.T. and V.P. Allen (eds.). Reader's Digest Readings: ESL. Books One through Four. Pleasantville, New York: Reader's Digest Services. 1963-64. paper.

1,220. Kreidler, Carol J. and Beatrice M. Sutherland. Flash Pictures - A Set of 252 Cards Used as an Aid to Teachers of English as a Foreign Language. Ann Arbor, Michigan: Follett's Michigan Bookstore. 1963.

Simple figures and drawings on 7" x 10" cards. Word families are catalogued by color for quick organization of drills. A four-page brochure gives examples of drills that may be constructed with the cards.

1,221. Kurilecz, Margaret. Man and His World: A Structured Reader. New York: Thomas Y. Crowell. 1969.

Structured reader for upper high school or college age ESL students.

1,222. Lado, Robert. Lado English Series: A Complete Course in English as a Second Language. New York: Regents Publishing Company.

Comprehensive course in ESL designed for use in high school or college on the beginning, intermediate and advanced levels. Each lesson presents patterns, first established by audio-lingual drills and simple explanations, then reinforced by speaking and reading exercises. Includes Practice in intonation, pronunciation, and writing. Graded presentations, continuous review and numerous illustrations.
Price (1972): Books 1-4/$1.75 ea.; Books 5-6/ in preparation; Workbooks 1-4/$1.00 ea.; Workbooks 5-6/ in preparation; Teachers Manual 1-3/$2.50; Posters (20" x 24", color) for books 1-3/$10.00; Tapes (reels or cassettes)/$75.00 per book. (catalog)

1,223. Lado, Robert. Language Teaching: A Scientific Approach. New York: McGraw-Hill, 1964. (paper) 239pp.

Presents a scientific approach to language teaching, including linguistic background, language learning, teaching techniques, testing, use of language laboratories and other aids, reading, writing, cultural content, literature, teaching machines and programmed learning. Contains many practical suggestions for language teaching. (NYS bibliography)

1,224. Lancaster, Louise. Introducing English, An Oral PreReading Program for Spanish-Speaking Primary Pupils (Ages 4-6). Boston: Houghton Mifflin Company, 1966. 294pp.

A 28-Unit oral program organized to give the child some under-standing and command·of spoken English before being introduced to reading. A basic speaking vocabulary of 500-600 words, used in meaningful sentence patterns, is presented in graded and controlled sequences. In addition to the text, which provides detailed, step-by-step directions to the teacher for each lesson, a file box of 316 picture cards and a set of 35 duplicating masters was also prepared for the course. (RIE abridged)

1,225. Landrum, Roger and Others. A Day Dream I Had at Night and Other Stories: Teaching Children How to Make Their Own Readers. Teachers and Writers Collaborative, New York, New York. New York State Council on the Arts, New York. (Contributions by children from PS 1 and PS 42 in New York City) 1971 131p. (ED 064 208)

1,226. Lawrence, Mary S. Writing as a Thinking Process. Ann Arbor, Michigan: The University of Michigan Press. 1972. $3.95.

Employs a cognitive approach to teaching composition, capitalizing on the student's ability to think inductively. The student is given data, and the relevant vocabulary, on a variety of interesting topics. He manipulates the data according to a sequence of logical relationships, making extrapolations and syntheses, and engaging in problem-solving. The writing process which he learns is generative and widely applicable. (catalog)

1,227. Lee, Mary Elizabeth. Learning to Learn English. Van Nuys, California: DFA Publishiers. 1971. Two volumes.

The vocabulary of each 256-page volume in this ESL program for adults includes topics relevant to the problems encountered by new immigrants - colors, numbers, money, addition, prices, traffic signs, time, daily routine, days of the week and months of the year, food, materials, styles, clothing, housing, furniture, credit and charge accounts, checking and savings accounts, telephone and postal services.
Price (1972): texts/$8.50 ea.; 6 tape cassettes at $36.50 per volume; Multi-media learning kit/$97.50 per volume. (catalog)

1,228. Lismore, Thomas. Welcome to English. New York: Regents Publishing Company.

Designed to teach ESL to young children: teaching basic skills, providing a solid foundation for future study, and inspiring confidence and interest. Emphasizes spoken English. Each lesson has a four-phase design: listening, speaking, reading, and writing. Illustrated in color.
Price (1972): Books 1-5 at $1.25 ea.; Tapes No. 1 at $12.00; No. 2-5 at $24.00 ea. (catalog)

1,229. Lorenz, Marian Brown. Patterns of American English: A Guide for Speakers of Other Languages. Dobbs Ferry, New York: Oceana Publications, Inc. 1971, 224pp.

This textbook is intended for students who have some knowledge of English but who need guidance and intensive structured practice in the speaking of the language. The emphasis is on the spoken form

of standard American English. Lessons varied in content and format
(e.g. questions about the students' lives, interests and hobbies;
stories, dialogues, quiz programs, debates, exercises, etc.).
Cultural items are United States centered. The book contains ten
units and provides grammar lessons for at least a one semester
course.

Primarily designed for senior high schools, universities and
adult education programs. (catalog)

1,230.  Mackey, Ilonka Schmidt. <u>English 1:  A Basic Course for Adults</u>.
Rowley, Massachusetts:  Newbury House Publishers. 1972. $1.25.

A course for adults designed to: (1) give newcomers the
English they require immediately on arrival in the U.S. (2) provide
the basis for a more thorough study of English, and (3) be a
remedial program for students whose knowledge of English fundamentals needs firmer footing.  It includes a Teaching Manual de-
tailing the oral work, which constitutes the core of the program,
and a Learner's Book reinforcing the oral work through exercises,
dialogues, and reading passages.

Price (1972):  Learner's Book $1.25, Teaching Manual $3.95.
(catalog)

1,231.  Madrigal, Margarita and Ursula Meyer.  <u>Invitación al inglés</u>.  New
York:  Regents Publishing Company.

A complete course in beginning English with all instruction
and explanations in Spanish.  All basic English structures are
introduced easily and gradually through examples and exercises.
Vocabulary is introduced in context and reinforced by pictures.
Prices (1972):  text at $1.50; records and text/$9.95;
tapes and text $28.00; cassettes and text/$22.50.  (catalog)

1,232.  Maldonado et al.  <u>Tito</u> (Beginning Reading in Spanish).  Indianapolis,
Indians:  The Economy Company. 1972.  $1.41.

This audio-readiness text for Spanish-speaking children is a
dual purpose  tool:  (1) used prior to English language reading
instruction, it teaches the concept of decoding; (2) used prior
to basic Spanish language primers, it teaches the basic skills
necessary for reading Spanish.  The special significance of <u>Tito</u>
is that it teaches vital transferable decoding essentials in the
language in which the Spanish-speaking child is most comfortable.
(catalog)

1,233.  Marckwardt, Albert H. and Randolf Quirk.  <u>A Common Language</u>.
MLA-ACTFL Materials Center. 1964. 79pp. $2.50.

The script for 12 broadcasts over the Voice of America and
the BBC.  Lively discussion of the varieties of English spoken in
different countries with the thesis that they are mutually understandable and equally good.  (catalog)

1,234. Marquardt, William F. et al. <u>English Around the World</u>. Gleview,
Illinois: Scott Foresman and Co., 1970. 4 volumes. 575pp.

Aural-oral program for teaching ESL/EFL in the primary grades.
Provides an international context in which pupils are introduced to
customs and styles from around the world. Course includes: (1)
teachers' guidebooks with detailed instructions for lesson preparation and presentation; (2) pupils' skills books which present the
lesson content; (3) posters, vocabulary developing display cards
and word cards; (4) practice pad/test books containing exercise
materials for pattern practice; and (5) record albums presenting
conversations, songs, and patterns in a range of voices and
regional variations. (RIE abridged)

1,235. Martin, Joseph F. <u>Let's Speak English</u> (adults). Los Angeles:
The Last California Company. 1971.

A series of three text-workbooks that takes the adult
learner from the introductory level to a functional fluency in
English. These books are designed to be used as a basic textbook
for level 1-6. Each lesson of each book contains practice in all
four basic language skills, meaningful dialogues, substitution
drills, a reading and comprehension exercise, sound drills, a
writing exercise and a simple explanation of the grammar of each
lesson.
Price (1972): text-workbook $3.00 ea.; cassettes (Book 1)
$59.50, manual for Book 1 (Spanish) $1.50. (catalog)

1,236. Martin, Joseph F. <u>Let's Speak English</u> (children). Los Angeles:
The Last California Company. 1971.

A text-workbook for children learning ESL with accompanying
tapes. Each lesson contains practice in all four language skills,
a simple and meaningful dialogue, substitution drills, a reading
exercise, sound drills, and a simple writing exercise. The book
contains a step by step, easy to follow lesson plan, some simple
poems and games, as well as lessons designed to develop comprehension and listening skills.
Price (1972): text $1.50, tapes $11.95 (with text) (catalog)

1,237. Martin, Joseph F. <u>Let's Speak Spanish</u>. Los Angeles; The Last
California Company. 1971.

A textbook-workbook for children from 3rd-6th grade who are
studying Spanish for the first time or for those Spanish-speaking
children who need to be taught to read and write in Spanish. Each
lessson contains practice in all four language skills, one grammatical principle within the context of a dialogue, substitution drills,
a reading exercise with a vocabulary list, and a simple writing
exercise. The book contains a step by step, easy to follow lesson

plan, some simple poems, songs and plays put in an easy to
dramatize form.
      Price (1972): text at $1.50; tapes and text at $11.95. (catalog)

1,238.  Materials Acquisition Project. Vol. 1, No. 1.  San Diego Schools
        California. Washington D.C.: Office of Education. February 1971
        15p.
        (ED 060 716)

1,239.  Materials Acquisition Project.  Vol. 1, No. 2.  San Diego Schools,
        California. Washington D.C.: Office of Education. March 1971 16p.
        (ED 060 717)

1,240.  Materials Acquisition Project.  Vol. 1, No. 3.  San Diego Schools,
        California. Washington D.C.: Office of Education. April 1971 11p.
        (ED 060 718)

1,241.  Materials Acquisition Project.  Vol. 1, No. 4.  San Diego  Schools
        California. Washington D.C.: Office of Education. May 1971 20p.
        (ED 060 719)

1,242.  Materials Acquisition Project.  Vol. 1, No. 5.  San Diego Schools
        California. Washington D.C.: Office of Education. June 1971. 19p.
        (ED 060 720)

1,243.  Materials Acquisition Project.  Vol. 2, No. 1.  San Diego Schools
        California. Washington D.C.: Office of Education. July 1971 20p.
        (ED 060 721)

1,244.  Materials Acquisition Project.  Vol. 2, No. 2.  San Diego Schools
        California. Washington D.C.: Office of Education. September 1971
        16p.
        (ED 060 722)

1,245.  Materials Acquisition Project.  Vol. 2, No. 3.  San Diego Schools
        California. Washington, D.C.: Office of Education. October 1971.
        20p.
        (ED 060 723)

1,246.  Materials Acquisition Project.  Vol. 2, No. 4.  San Diego Schools,
        California. Washington D.C.: Office of Education. November 1971
        20p.
        (ED 060 724)

1,247.  Materials Acquisition Project.  Vol. 2, No. 5.  San Diego Schools,
        California. Washington D.C.: Office of Education. December 1971.
        28p.
        (ED 060 725)

1,248.  Materials Acquisition Project.  Vol. 2, No. 7. San Diego Schools,
        California, Washington D.C.: Office of Education. February 1972.
        35pp.
        (ED 064 967)

1,249.  Materials Acquisition Project. Vol. 2, No. 8.  San Diego City Schools,
        California. Washington D.C.: Office of Education. April 1972. 3
        38pp.
        (ED 065 004)

1,250.  Materials Acquisition Project. Vol. 2, No. 8.  San Diego Schools,
        California. Washington D.C.: Office of Education. 1972 59pp.
        (ED 066 095)

1,251.  Matus, Sue.  Count and Mass Nouns.  Santa Monica, California:
        Pyramid Films. 14 captioned filmstrips at $100.00/set.

        Filmstrip titles: (1) Introduction to Count Nouns (2) Use
        of "a" and "an" (3) Use of "a" and "an" with singular and plural
        nouns (4) Singular and plural of count nouns (5) plural endings
        (exceptions) (6) Introduction to mass nouns (7) Plural comparison:
        count and mass nouns (8) Article comparison: count and mass nouns
        (9) Mass noun indicators (10) Much and many (11) A little and a
        few (12) Some, any, a lot of (lots of) (13) Mass nouns used as
        count nouns (14) Review test.  (catalog)

1,252.  Miami Linguistic Readers, 53 volumes. Experimental Edition. Boston:
        D.C. Heath, 1964-66. (paper)

        An introductory reading course for non-English-speaking or
        cultural disadvantaged elementary school children, prepared under
        the aegis of the Ford Foundation and the Dade County (Florida)
        Public Schools.  Linguistically structured and controlled, the
        material is designed to provide aural comprehension, speaking and
        writing practice as well as reading instruction, in a four fold
        language arts program in standard English.  Consists of Pupil's
        Books (21 pre-primers, primers and readers); Seatwork Booklets
        (16 workbooks providing for writing practice); Teacher's Manuals
        (16 volumes providing specific guides for each step in each lesson);
        and "Big Books"; charts for language practice and special work on
        reading problems.  Reading content and illustrations designed to
        appeal to young children. (NYS bibliography)

1,253.  Michigan Oral Language Series: ACTFL Edition. MLA-ACTFL Materials
        Center. 1970. $50.00.

        Structured oral language lessons for 4, 5, or 6 year old
        Spanish-background children, accompanied by evaluation and teacher-
        training materials.  All items in the series are loose-leaf, held
        secure with paper bands.  Descriptive catalog free.  (catalog)

1,254.  Michigan Oral Language Series: ACTFL Edition - Bilingual Conceptual
        Development Guide - Preschool. MLA-ACTFL Materials Center.
        1970. 396pp. $7.50.

Designed for the 4 year old, provides activities to introduce basic English language patterns and sounds. Activities focus on basic intellectual skills introduced in Spanish and then reinforced in English. Provides an 8-week period of instruction with 3 separate 15-minute activities for each day. (catalog)

1,255. Michigan Oral Language Series: ACTFL Edition - Developing Language Curricula: Programmed Exercises for Teachers. MLA-ACTFL Materials Center. 1970. 78pp. $2.50.

A manual to introduce teachers to basic principles of language analysis which can be applied in classrooms with non-English-speaking or language-handicapped children. (catalog)

1,256. Michigan Oral Language Series: ACTFL Edition - English Guide - Kindergarten. MLA-ACTFL Materials Center. 1970. 146pp. $3.50.

For teaching English to Speakers of Other Languages and Standard English as a Second Dialect. Conceptually, these materials provide a bridge from the development of basic intellectual skills to their application in subject matter. The activities are planned for 30 minutes per day for one academic year. (catalog)

1,257. Michigan Oral Language Series: ACTFL Edition - Interdisciplinary Oral Language Guide - Primary One. MLA-ACTFL Materials Center. 1970.

A program to teach first grade children who speak Spanish, or who are limited in their command of standard English, the oral language necessary for success in the usual school environment. The content is drawn principally from social science, science, and mathematics. Each lesson lasts about 30 minutes.
Part 1: 214pp. $6.00; Part 2: 470pp. $9.00; Part 3: 342pp. $7.75; Part 4: 360pp. $7.75. (catalog)

1,258. Michigan Oral Language Series: ACTFL Edition - Michigan Oral Language Productive Tests. MLA-ACTFL Materials Center. 1970. $5.00.

A set of two individually-administered tests, "Structured Response Test" and "Conceptual Oral Language Test," with administration and evaluation materials, the first tests for grammatical and phonological features of English; the second for conceptual understanding relatively free from the effects of dialect or language differences of the examiner. (catalog)

1,259. Michigan Oral Language Series: ACTFL Edition - Spanish Guide - Kindergarten. MLA-ACTFL Materials Center. 1970. 282pp. $5.50.

For teaching Spanish as a Second Language or Standard Spanish as a Second Dialect. The activities are planned for 30 minutes per day for one academic year. (catalog)

259

1,260. Mi diccionario ilustrado. Glenview. Illinois: Scott, Foresman and
       Company. 1971 $1.38.

       Reference book of 525 words, all pictured, for use in kinder-
       garten. Two editions available:
       (1) Edición Bilingüe - Spanish-English bilingual pictionary,
       primarily designed for use in the United States with children of
       Spanish backgrounds.
       (2) Edición Hispanoamericana - Standard Spanish edition,
       primarily for use in Spanish-speaking Latin American countries. (catalog)

1,261. Mitchell, Elizabeth Gillian. Beginning American English. Englewood
       Cliffs, New Jersey: Prentice-Hall. 1957.

       Twenty-five units of simple conversational English. Each unit
       contains dialogue, exercises on vocabulary, sentence structure,
       pronunciation and review. (Hefferman-Cabrera)

1,262. Molina, Hubert. "Language Games and the Mexican-American Child
       Learning English", TESOL Quarterly, 5:2 (June, 1971).
       pp. 145-148.

       This paper describes a set of criteria and their use in the
       development of games that are a part of a tutorial component of the
       Language and Concept Skills for Spanish Speakers Program developed
       at Southwest Regional Laboratory for Educational Research and
       Development. Included are the 1969-1970 results of field tryouts
       of the program. (from article)

1,263. Morley, Joan. Improving Aural Comprehension. Ann Arbor, Michigan;
       The University of Michigan Press. 1972.

       Presents a graded series of 132 lessons in concentrated
       listening. It is designed for classroom and laboratory use by
       secondary/adult ESL students. Lesson flexibility permits use at
       low-intermediate through advanced levels. Lessons provide ample
       opportunity for vocabulary-building, pronunciation practice and
       class discussion.
       Price (1972): student's workbook $4.95; teacher's book of
       readings $3.95; tapes - will be available. (catalog)

1,264. Moulton, William G. A Linguistic Guide to Language Learning. New
       York: Modern Language Association of America, 1966 (paper)

       A clear introduction to the principles of language learning
       and how language works, including sections on sounds, sentences,
       words, meaning and writing. Bibliography of useful books on
       linguistics, phonetics, contrastrive structure and language
       learning. (NYS bibliography)

1,265. Muller, Douglas G. and Robert Leonetti. Primary Self-Concept Scale:
       Boys. Dissemination Center for Bilingual Bicultural Education,
       Austin, Texas. Washington, D.C.: Office of Education. 40pp.
       (ED 062 846)

1,266.  Muller, Douglas G. and Robert Leonetti. <u>Primary Self-Concept Scale:</u>
        <u>Girls</u>. Dissemination Center for Bilingual Bicultural Education.
        Austin, Texas. Washington, D.C.: Office of Education. 40pp.
        (ED 062 845)

1,267.  Muller, Douglas G. and Robert Leonetti. <u>Primary Self-Concept Scale:</u>
        <u>Test Manual</u>. Dissemination Center for Bilingual Bicultural Educa-
        tion. Austin, Texas. Washington, D. C.: Office of Education.
        39pp. (ED 062 845)

        It is the purpose of the test described in this document to
        provide a procedure for economically evaluating several aspects of
        self concept relevant to school success. The test was constructed
        specifically for use with the child of Spanish or Mexican descent
        in the Southwest, but it is also appropriate for use with children
        from Anglo culture. The test consists of 24 items; in each item,
        the examinee is told a descriptive story about an illustration and
        is instructed to draw a circle around the person in the illustration
        that is most like himself. This document includes directions for
        administering the test, the descriptive stories accompanying each
        test item, and details on scoring, interpretation, test construction,
        reliability, and validity. Statistical data and results are also
        included. (RIE)

1,268.  McCallum, George P. (adaptor). <u>Seven Plays from American</u>
        <u>Literature</u>. Rockville, Maryland: English Language Services, Inc.

        Combinations of one text and 7 tapes designed for use with
        intermediate to advanced level adult students. The 10-15 minute
        plays are adapted from short stories by American authors, chosen
        for their portrayal of American life and values and for their
        dramatic interest, as well as for their usefullness in the class-
        room situation.
                Price (1972): text at $3.10, tapes at $15.75. (catalog)

1,269.  McGillivray, James H. <u>People at Work: Readings with Drills and</u>
        <u>Exercises for Beginners in English</u>. New York: American Book
        Company. 1961.

        Reading selections simplified for beginning students at high
        school adult levels. Readings followed by drills, exercises and
        dramatization for dialogue practice. Limited to 600-word vocabulary.
        (Hefferman-Cabrera)

1,270.  McIntosh, Lois. <u>How to Teach English Grammar</u>, 1967. 19pp.
        (ED 012 438)

        Presents a discussion of the basic tenets of teaching English
        grammar to non-native speakers, as followed in the ESL program at
        UCLA. The introduction of grammar points to be practiced and the
        generalization process which follows are described in non-technical
        language. Various types of drills illustrate implementation of the
        grammar lesson. Particular importance is given to the age levels of
        the students as affecting the type of grammar presentation. (RIE)

1,271. McIntosh, Lois et al. <u>Advancing in English</u>. New York: American
       Book Company. 1970.

       Designed for upper high school or college age students.

1,272. McWilliams, Carey, ed. <u>The Mexicans in America; A Students' Guide</u>
       <u>to Localized History. Localized History Series</u>. New York,
       New York: Teachers College Press, Columbia University. 1968 32p.
       (ED 058 979)

       The four main sections of this publication are (1) Special
       Minority, which deals with the settlement in the Southwest and
       historical background of the Hispanos; (2) The Great Invasion,
       which discusses Mexican immigration and Hispanos and industrial
       employment; (3) The Mexican Problem, which treats the Hispano
       "language problem" and social discrimination; and (4) New
       Stirrings in the Borderlands, which deals with Hispano action
       against discrimination, political role, and influence of the
       Spanish Mexican. A 12-item bibliography is appended. (RIE)

1,273. Nance, Mrs. Afton D. <u>Spanish for Spanish-Speaking Pupils</u>.
       Sacramento:  State of California Department of Education,
       1963 (Mimeo).

1,274. Dissemination Center for Bilingual Bicultural Education. Austin, Texas.
       <u>Cross Cultural Attitude Inventory</u>

       This series of instruments is designed to measure how very
       young students feel about Mexican-American and Anglo cultures.
       The test is based on pictures, some of which are culturally
       relevant only to Mexican-Americans. The manual provides a guide
       for the use of the inventory, including a rationale for the items
       used; a statement of the purpose of the test; instructions for
       administration; instructions for scoring results; and possible
       applications within the constraint of the test. (from introduction
       somewhat revised)

1,275. National Council of Teachers of English. <u>English for Today</u>. Eight
       Volumes. William R. Slager and Luella B. Cook, eds. New York:
       McGraw-Hill, 1964-66. (paper)

       Six books from beginning to lower advanced, include reading
       passages, comprehensive questions and exercises and sections on
       grammar and composition. Book Six contains unabridged but
       stylistically simple fiction, non-fiction, plays, and poetry from
       English-speaking countries. Teachers' editions for each volume
       include special section with general comments on teaching
       procedures, sample lesson plans, and specific notes on each lesson.
       Two workbooks and picture cue cards available for <u>Book One</u>. Tapes
       and records also available. (NYS bibliography)

1,276.  NCTE Committee on Teaching English to Speakers of Other Languages.
        "Some Materials for Teaching English as a Second Language in
        the Elementary School," _Elementary English_, 46:8 (December, 1969).

        A basic, unannotated bibliography, which includes eleven
        methodolody listings and fifteen sections on pre-school and primary
        school materials.  (NYS bilbiography)

1,277.  Newmark, Leonard et al. _Using American English_.  New York: Harper
        and Row.  1964.

        Conversational practice for upper high school or college
        age students.

1,278.  New York City Board of Education. _Puerto Rican Study: Resource
        Units for Classes with Puerto Rican Pupils:  Grades 1-6
        and Secondary School, 1-3_.  New York:  Board of Education. 1955.

1,279.  New York City, Board of Education. _Scope and Sequence in the
        Teaching of English as a New Language to Adults, Beginning
        Level_. Curriculum Bulletin: 1967-68, Series No. 22. 1968.

1,280.  New York City,  Board of Education. _Teaching English as a New
        Language to Adults_.  Curriculum Bulletin: 1963-64, Series
        No. 5.  New York: New York Superintendent of Schools. 1964.
        180pp.

        A presentation of guiding principles and methods for teaching
        beginners through advanced students with references for teachers.

1,281.  New York City Board of Education. _Teaching of English to Puerto
        Rican Children_. Four volumes. New York: Board of Education. 1957.

1,282.  Nichols, Ann Eljenholm.  _English Syntax: Advanced Composition for
        Non-Native Speakers_.  New York:  Holt, Rinehart and Winston.
        1965.

        Composition practice for upper high school or college age
        students.

1,283.  Nida, Eugene.  _Learning a Foreign Language_.  New York: Free Press.
        Foreign Missions Conference of North America. 1957. (rev. ed.)

        A guide for individual language study written from the point
        of view of modern descriptive linguistics though with a minimum of
        technical vocabulary.  (Hefferman-Cabrera)

1,284.  Nilsen, Don L.F. and Alleen Pace Nilsen.  _Pronunciation Contrasts in
        English_. New York: Regents Publishing Company. $4.25 (cloth)
        $2.25 (paper)

                                    263

Deals with sounds that are difficult for the non-native
student of English to distinguish and produce. Each lesson compares
and contrasts pairs of sounds in lists of minimal pairs, minimal
contrast sentences, and sentences with contextual clues. Sound
production charts and profile diagrams illustrate the position of
the lips, teeth, and tongue during the articulation of the sounds.
In addition, each lesson contains unique lists of problem-area
language backgrounds. (catalog)

1,285.  Ohannessian, Sirarpi et al.  Reference List of Materials for English
as a Second Language. Part I: Texts, Readers, Dictionaries,
Tests, 1964, 157pp.
(ED 014 723).

Annotated bibliography prepared by the Center for Applied
Linguistics, Washington, D.C.

1,286.  Ohannessian, Sirarpi et al.  Reference List of Materials for English
as a Second Language.  Part II: Background materials, Methodology
1966. 115pp.
(ED 014 724)

Annotated bibliography prepared by the Center for Applied
Linguistics, Washington, D.C.

1,287.  Ohannessian, Sirarpi (ed.).  30 Books for Teachers of English as a
Foreign Language. Washington, D.C.: Center for Applied Linguistics.
1963. paper.

1,288.  Olsher, Larua and Robert D. Wilson.  Beginning Fluency in English as
a New Language. North Hollywood, California: Bowman Records.
6 vols. 1967.

Audio visual course for children, consisting of 5 sets of
coordinated records and filmstrips, a script for each set and a
teacher's manual for the whole series.  Practices phrasing, transformation, substitution and expansion types of language activity.
No isolated pronunciation or vocabulary practice.  Students repeat,
recite and eventually act out the parts of the characters, first
following the given script, then elaborating in free expressions.
Teahcer's manual outlines rationale for the course, suggest additional
activities, and presents the syllabus for the whole series. (CAL
bibliography)

1,289.  Orientation in American English.  Washington, D.C.: Institute of
Modern Languages, Inc.  1971.

A six-level course employing the Situational Reinforcement
methodology designed to produce orderly progression through three
levels of proficiency - basically S. 1-2-3 as established by the
Foreign Service Institute.  Each level is designed for 80-100 hours
of classroom instruction. Materials include texts, workbooks, tapes,

tapebooks and readers. Program designed for adult learners. For
more detailed information, contact company.
Prices (1972): texts/$1.65 ea.; tapebooks and workbooks/$1.00
ea.; readers/$1.20 ea.; tapes vary according to level. (catalog)

1,290. Owen, George H. <u>Effective Pronunciation: A Textbook for Teaching</u>
<u>English Sounds</u>. Experimental ed. Detroit, Michigan: Detroit
Public Schools, Department of Adult Education and Summer
Schools. 1957. 215pp.

Designed for Adult basic education courses.

1,291. Pantell, Dora F. and Angelica W. Cass. <u>We Americans</u>. New York:
Oxford Book. 1957. 279pp.

Designed for adult basic education courses.

1,292. Paratore, Angela. <u>Conversational English:</u> ESL. Englewood Cliffs,
New Jersey: Prentice-Hall. 1961.

Designed to give supplementary aural-oral practice to adult
non-beginning students. Emphasis on selected points of grammar,
especially constructions and usages employing auxiliary verbs.
Group recitation, memorization, and repetitive drills. Each of
30 lessons begins with dialogue drill, dialogue notes and variety
of exercises. Accent marks and arrows indicate stress and intonation.
(Hefferman-Cabrera)

1,293. Parker, Sandra. <u>Social Studies: School, Home, and Neighborhood.</u>
<u>Getting to Know More People and Places. English as a Second</u>
<u>Language</u>. Miami, Florida: Dade County Public Schools. 1971. 36p.
(ED 062 233)

1,294. Paulston, Christina Bratt and Gerald Dykstra. <u>Controlled Composition</u>
<u>in English as a Second Language</u>. New York: Regents Publishing
Company, $1.75.

This advanced composition text consists of 65 literary passages
and 122 instructional steps covering the specific language patterns
and grammar rules of English. Following each passage, the student
is presented with a number of situations and correlated assignments
requiring him, for example, to change the voice, tense, person, or
word order of the selection, or to rewrite the passage imaginatively.
The emphasis in this book is on the mechanics of English: grammar,
sentence structure, idiomatic usage, spelling, and punctuation.
Though not intended to replace the grammar textbook, it can be used
effectively in conjunction with it. (catalog)

1,295. <u>Peanut Butter and Yogurt: Case Studies and Activities in Cultural</u>
<u>Understanding</u>. Glenview, Illinois: Scott, Foresman and Company
1971. 96pp. $1.50.

Although primarily directed toward American students in other
lands, this book can be used effectively with any group of students

experiencing the problems and conflicts that arise when different
cultures come together. (catalog)

1,296. Pedke, Dorothy A. et al. Reference List of Materials for English
as a Second Language Supplement (1964-1968). 1969. 207pp.
(ED 025 773)

Annotated bibliography prepared by the Center for Applied
Linguistics, Washington, D.C.

1,297. Plaister, Ted. English Monosyllables: A Minimal Pair Locator
List for English as a Second Language. Honolulu: East-West
Center Press, 1965 (paper)

Intended as a tool for teaching and testing pronunciation, in
building drill materials, etc. A handy reference work. (NYS bibliography)

1,298. Politzer, Robert L. "Pattern Practice for Reading," Language
Learning. 14:3 and 4 (1964).

Presents rationale behind pattern practice approach to
developing reading skills, and suggests methods for teaching instant
recognition of visual cues expressing grammatical meaning. (NYS
bibliography)

1,299. Praninskas, J. Rapid Review of English Grammar. Englewood Cliffs,
New Jersey: Prentice-Hall. 1959.

A review text for use by foreign students and others with some
background in grammar, English or otherwise. (Hefferman-Cabrera)

1,300. Prator, C.H., Jr. Manual of American English Pronunciation. rev. ed.
New York: Holt, Rinehart and Winston. 1957. paper.

1,301. Preston, Dennis R. and Michael B. Kozoll. English Language and
Literacy: Book One. (Wisconsin Series in Adult Basic Education
for Spanish-Speaking Agricultural Workers.) Madison: University
Extension, University of Wisconsin. 1967. 232pp.

Designed for adult basic education courses.

1,302. Prevocational English. Washington, D.C.: Institute of Modern
Languages, Inc. 1971.

A two-level prevocational English course designed to prepare
non-English speakers for employment requiring technical skills. On
each level the course includes both a textbook and a workbook divided
into twenty-lesson segments. Each level should require 120-150 hours
of classroom instruction. The lessons are divided into four parts:
(1) covers language used in social situations: greetings, discussing
the weather, etc. (2) introduces new structures and vocabulary through
situation sequences. (3) presents technical material through situations.
(4) presents an illustrated reading followed by comprehensive questions.
Price (1972): textbooks/$3.00 ea. and workbooks/$1.75 ea. (catalog)

1,303. Puerto Rican Department of Education. _American English as a Second Language._ Three volumes. Boston, Massachusetts: D.C. Heath. 1965-67.

1,304. Rahtz, Robert (ed.). _American English for All the World._ St. Louis, Missouri: Webster. 4 vols. 1957-60.

Beginners texts for primary school children. Two editions: one general and the other specifically designed for Catholic schools. Pictures and classroom activities used to drill children in vocabulary, formulas of politness, and a few structural patterns. Separate manuals for each edition provide lesson by lesson guide to the use of materials in the text. (CAL bibliography)

1,305. _Readiness Checklist._ Las Cruces School District, New Mexico; Dissemination Center for Bilingual Bicultural Education, Austin, Texas. Washington, D.C.: Office of Education. 12pp. (ED 061 839)

The Readiness Checklist is a 69-item instrument that provides a measure of the psychomotor development of children. It covers seven main areas: general health, movement patterns and muscular coordination, auditory skills, visual skills, speech and language, personal independence, and social adjustment. The checklist is designed to measure a child's level of physical maturity and can be used to collect data as a diagnostic tool to isolate deficient children for immediate remedial action. Collection of data through the checklist can result in the establishment of norms. A score sheet is attached to the checklist. (RIE)

1,306. _Reading Skill Builders._ Pleasantville, New York: Reader's Digest Services, Inc., Educational Division.

A series of 50 books on reading levels 1-10 which contain a variety of high-interest stories of mystery, adventure, history, animals, science, sports, etc. Exercises and quizzes following most selections help pupils measure their achievement in terms of specific educational objectives, such as summarizing, making comparisons, learning word parts and new words and applying ideas creatively. Separate teacher's editions offer specific suggestions for reading instruction, exercises and quizzes, as well as skills and subject matter charts. Twelve audio lessons are available on each level 1-6 on tape cassette or LP record. Practice pads also available.
Prices vary according to plan of purchase. See catalog for details. (catalog)

1,307. _A Regional Educational Television Project for Non-English Speaking Spanish-Surname Adults. Final Report._ Albuquerque, New Mexico: Southwestern Cooperative Educational Laboratory. Washington, D.C. Office of Education. 1967. 112p.
(ED 061 477)

1,308.  Resource Material for Bilingual Education. Dissemination Center for
        Bilingual Bicultural Education, Austin, Texas. Washington, D.C.:
        Office of Education. September 1972
        217p.
        (ED 063 808)

        This handbook consists of materials written in Spanish and
    English and serves as a reference book to aid the bilingual class-
    room teacher and instructional aide at the primary level by pro-
    viding material for language enrichment and supplementary learning
    activities. There is material to supplement each area of the curricu-
    lum. Poems, finger plays, stories, and songs are provided for use in
    aural-oral activities to supplement the areas of language, and
    music. No grade-level limitations are placed on the use of the
    material; it is suggested that teachers adapt the different ideas
    and activities which are suitable for their grade level. (RIE)

1,309.  Revelle, Keith. "A Collection for La Raza." Library Journal.
        96:20 (November, 1971). pp. 3719-26.
        (EJ 047 704)

        The 230 references include books, Spanish-language magazines
    and newspapers, the Chicano press and audiovisual materials which
    have proven successful with a Chicano public. (CIJE)

1,310.  Richards, I.A. and Christine Gibson. English Through Pictures. New
        York: Washington Square Press. 1952-60.

        A series of 2 texts, 1 workbook, films, filmstrips and records
    for upper high school or college age students.

1,311.  Richards, Jack and Michael Poliquin. English Through Songs. Rowley,
        Massachusetts: Newbury House Publishers. 1971.

        A collection of 65 songs and rhymes written with a graded vocab-
    ulary. Selections have been chosen for their teaching ability with
    children and adults in their first years of learning ESL. Each
    song is graded according to difficulty and a vocabulary index is
    provided. Songs are classed both by content and general interest.
    A teacher's guide shows how to integrate the songs into the normal
    classwork, and how to use the songs to improve pronunciation and
    control of a growing vocabulary in appropriate contexts.
        Price (1972): pupil's book $2.25, teacher's guide $5.95, tape
    $6.50. (catalog)

1,312.  Robinson, Lois. Guided Writing and Free Writing: A Text in Compo-
        sition for English as a Second Language. New York: Harper and
        Row. 1967.

        Composition practice for upper high school or college age
    students.

1,313.  Rojas, P.M. "Reading Materials for Bilingual Children." Elementary School Journal. Vol. 47 (December 1946) pp. 204-211.

1,314.  Roscoe, Carole. "Developing Instructional Materials for a Bilingual Program." TESOL Quarterly. Vol. 6, No. 2 (June 1973). p. 163-166. (EJ 060 718)

1,315.  Rosen, Carl L. and Phillip D. Ortego. "Resources: Teaching Spanish-Speaking Children." Reading Teacher. 25:1 (October, 1971). pp. 11-13.

        Annotated Bibliography.

1,316.  Ross, Janet. "Controlled Writing: A Transformational Approach." TESOL Quarterly. 2:4 (December, 1968).

        Presents exercises in combining sentence patterns as well as slot substitution, question and answer, and paraphrasing. (NYS bibliography)

1,317.  Ross, Janet and Gladys Doty. Writing English: A Composition Text in English as a Foreign Language. New York: Harper and Row. 1965.

        Composition practice for upper high school or college age students.

1,318.  Rutherford, William E. Modern English: A Textbook for Foreign Students. New York: Harcourt, Brace and World. 1968.

        Designed for upper high school or college age students.

1,319.  Saitz, Robert L. and Donna Carr (eds.). Selected Readings in English: For Students of English as a Second Language. Cambridge, Mass.: Winthrop Publishers, Inc., 1972.

        A collection of twelve short stories and essays designed to aid the foreign student in mastering English vocabulary and idiomatic expressions. Selections were chosen to represent a wide range of writing styles, rhetorical techniques, and patterns of narration, description, and argumentation. Each reading is accompanied by exercises which require the student to understand the content and the structure of the selection. (catalog)

1,320.  San Bernardino County Schools. Mi Libro: A Pre-Reading Workbook. San Bernardino, California: Regional Project Office, San Bernardino County Schools. 1972. $.35.

        A 12-page illustrated workbook giving children practice in basic cursive writing strokes. The booklet also develops such concepts as colors, numbers and visual perception. A teacher's edition accompanies individual child's copies. (catalog)

1,321. San Bernardino County Schools. The Open Classroom - Part I. (Videotape). San Bernardino, California: Regional Project Office, San Bernardino County Schools. 15:00. B/W. $24.95 ($10.00 if tape is provided).

   Scenes of open classrooms include examples of small group learning centers, individualized learning, team teaching and the use of student contracts at the elementary level. An interview with a team teaching leader explains the organization, planning and operation of classes in these North Dakota schools.
   Designed for teacher in-service, grades K-12. (catalog)

1,322. San Bernardino County Schools. The Open Classroom - Part II. (Videotape). San Bernardino, California: Regional Project Office, San Bernardino County Schools. 15:00. B/W. $24.95 ($10.00 if tape is provided).

   Actual lessons within the free structure of the open classroom setting include language arts, science and mathematics. An interview with a principal indicates the necessity of community support and good parent relations. Classes shown are in the Grand Forks, North Dakota, area.
   Designed for teacher in-service, grades K-12. (catalog)

1,323. San Bernardino County Schools. Each One Learning: A Small Group Process Manual. San Bernardino, California: Regional Project Office, San Bernardino County Schools. $1.75.

   A 70-page illustrated manual describing rationale, room environment, grouping procedures, activities and materials, and the teacher's role. (catalog)

1,324. San Bernardino County Schools. Language Arts and Motor Activities in a TMR Classroom. (Videotape). San Bernardino, California: Regional Project Office, San Bernardino County Schools. 20:00 B/W. $36.95 ($15.00 if tape is provided).

   Two intermediate level TMR classrooms are shown. A structured language communication skills lesson is followed by scenes of independent motor skill practice. Mrs. Jeanne Davis, special education consultant, narrates describing the methods and teaching techniques demonstrated.
   Designed for teacher in-service, grades K-12. (catalog)

1,325. San Bernardino County Schools. Language Experience and Reading Practices. (Videotape). San Bernardino, California: Regional Project Office, San Bernardino County Schools. B/W. $24.95 ($10.00 if tape is provided).

Mrs. Emily Sumahara, a fourth grade teacher, demonstrates through her class' activities the application of many language experience techniques. The class is shown making tortillas, dictating stories, using a tape recorder, playing language games, and building illustrated storybooks. An interesting feature of the tape is the extensive use of volunteer teacher and student aides in the classroom.
Designed for teacher in-service. (catalog)

1,326. San Bernardino County Schools. Literary Study in Secondary Schools. (Videotape). San Bernardino, California: Regional Project Office, San Bernardino County Schools. B/W. $24.95 ($10.00 if tape is provided).

Dr. G. Robert Carlsen, well-known consultant and author, delivers an informal lecture to a class of teachers. He deals with the teaching of literature at the secondary level.
Designed for teacher in-service. (catalog)

1,327. San Bernardino County Schools. Overview (Tape No. 1 from Initial Reading in Spanish for Bilinguals Series). (Videotape). San Bernardino, California: Regional Project Office, San Bernardino County Schools, 30:00 B/W. $36.95 ($15.00 if tape is provided).

Offers a sampling from the various teaching techniques which appear more in depth in each of the seven films of the series: Readiness, Developmental Language, Phonics, Syllabication, Story Sequence, Cursive Writing and Supplemental Techniques. The methods are shown just as they were filmed in the first grade classrooms in Mexico and in Texas.
Designed for teacher in-service. (catalog)

1,328. San Bernardino County Schools. Puedo Leer - I Can Read: Initial Reading in Spanish for Bilinguals. San Bernardino, California: Regional Project Office, San Bernardino County Schools. 1972.

An initial reading in Spanish manual describing methods used by Mexican teachers in a special project in Texas first grade class-roims. The method combines phonic and language experience approaches in a reading program, integrating the four major components of language learning - reading, listening, speaking and writing. (catalog)

1,329. San Bernardino County Schools. Readiness (Tape No. 2 from Initial Reading in Spanish for Bilinguals Series). (Videotape). San Bernardino, California: Regional Project Office, San Bernardino County Schools. 15:00 B/W. $24.95 ($10.00 if tape is provided).

This tape demonstrates the application of various techniques to the readiness phase of initial reading in Spanish for bilinguals. Methods of three first grade teachers are shown as they were filmed in their bilingual classrooms in Texas.
Designed for teacher in-service. (catalog)

1,330. San Bernardino County Schools. Small Group Activity Charts. San
       Bernardino, California:  Regional Project Office, San Bernardino
       County Schools.  $4.95.

       A set of 12  16 x 20 inch instruction charts providing lessons
       which develop skills in writing, vocabulary, general language develop-
       ment and numbers.  The charts, in color, are in Spanish (five) and
       English (seven).                                      (catalog)

1,331. San Bernardino County Schools. Small Group Process. (Videotape).
       San Bernardino, California: Regional Project Office, San
       Bernardino County Schools. 15:00. B/W. $24.95 ($10.00 if tape
       is provided).

       Bilingual-bicultural second grade children have been grouped
       heterogeneously, each group having five or six members and a child
       leader.  The group members remain together and move through several
       independent learning centers each day.  The room environment, teacher
       aides, lessons, independent groups, teacher oriented groups and the
       end of the day's evaluation with all of the class are viewed in
       progress.
               Designed for teacher in-service, grades K-6.  (catalog)

1,332. San Bernardino County Schools. Spanish Reading Charts. San
       Bernardino, California:  Regional Project Office, San Bernardino
       County Schools.  1972.  $10.00.

       A set of 25 four-color charts (17 x 23 inch) which reinforces
       the phonic approach used in initial reading in Spanish.  Illustrative
       charts apply the phonic method to letters, syllables, phrases and
       complete sentences.  Completely in Spanish.  (catalog)

1,333. San Bernardino County Schools. They Help Each Other Learn:  A
       Group Participation and Leadership Training Manual. San
       Bernardino, California: Regional Project Office, San Bernardino
       County Schools. $1.75.

       A 48-page illustrated manual describing five basic lessons to
       help children learn skills necessary to function in small groups.
       Skills include reading and understanding group instructions, distri-
       buting materials, helping each other and evaluating group progress.
       (catalog)

1,334. San Bernardino County Schools.  Fullerton Elementary School District.
       Using H-200 ESL Materials. (Videotape). San Bernardino,
       California:  Regional Project Office, San Bernardino County
       Schools.  B/W.

       Mrs. Betty Fulton Poggi demonstrates the use of H-200 materials
       to teach English vocabulary and structures to elementary school
       students.  The students are beginners in an ESL class.  The lesson
       deals with sentence structures used in H-200 materials to present
       dialog sentences relating to the family.  A variety of techniques

are shown.
Designed for teacher in-service. (catalog)

1,335. Sandberg, Karl C. and Thomas H. Brown. Conversational English. Waltham, Massachusetts: Blaisdell. 1969.

Designed for upper high school or college age students.

1,336. Sarantos, R.L. Advanced Composition: English as a Second Language
Dade County Public Schools, Miami, Florida. 1971. 32p.
(ED 063 825)

1,337. Sarantos, Robin L. How Much English Do You Know? Dade County
Public Schools. Miami, Florida. 1971
(ED 064 966)

1,338. Schneider, Velia. Bilingual Lesson for Spanish Speaking Preschool
Children. 1969. 121pp.
(ED 031 465)

1,339. Schotta, Sairta G. Teaching English as a Second Language. Davis,
California: Davis Publications in English, 1966. (paper)

An introduction to the materials and methods that recent
linguistic studies have provided teachers of English as a second
language or dialect. (NYS bibliography)

1,340. Sé quién soy. Glenview, Illinois: Scott, Foresman and Company.
1972 (in preparation). 32pp. $0.66.

Consumable Spanish-English pupil book for grades K-3 supplementary to English Around the World. Contains bilingual picture
essays designed to develop cultural awareness and improve both
Spanish and English abilities in Mexican-American children. Vocabulary coordinated with Mi diccionario ilustrado. (catalog)

1,341. Sheeler, Willard D. Elementary Course in English. Rockville,
Maryland: English Language Services, Inc. 1971.

A two-level course designed for secondary schools or adult
programs, using an oral-aural approach with dialogs, basic sentences,
repetition drills, and reading and comprehension materials. Each
level consists of 50 lessons and accompanying tapes. Presumes no
previous oral-aural training in English. The two levels introduce a
vocabulary    approx. 1350 items and provide material for 25-300 hours
of combined classroom and language laboratory work.
Price (1972): text/$2.75/level, tapes /$112.50/level   (catalog)

1,342. Slager, William R. et al. Core English: Levels One and Two. Lexington, Massachusetts: Ginn and Company. 1971.

A two-level program specifically designed to meet the particular needs of the non-English-speaking child in the primary grades.
Using highly motivational materials, an oral approach, and step-by-
step teaching guides, the program provides a core of oral English
skills that enables the child to participate fully in the regular
classroom. The program includes teacher's manuals, wall charts,
picture cards, puppets, a flannel kit, language games and songs,
workbooks and records. Sample lesson and price list available from
publisher on request. (catalog)

1,343. Southwestern Cooperative Educational Laboratory. Oral Language
Program. Albuquerque: SWCEL.

OLP is designed to be used daily by one teacher with groups of
up to 10 children from ages 5 to 7. Each lesson is approx. 25
minutes long, although the teacher encourages the children to use
sentence patterns learned in the lessons during the rest of the day.
The lessons deal entirely with oral and auditory aspects of English;
there is no instruction in either reading or writing contained in
the program. This is based on the premise that fluency in a language is prerequisite to facility in reading and writing that language.
(catalog)

1,344. The Spanish Speaking in the United States: A Guide to Materials.
Washington: the Cabinet Committee on Opportunity for the
Spanish Speaking. 1971.

1,345. Stack, Edward M. The Language Laboratory and Modern Language
Teaching. New York: Oxford University Press, (1966).

Treats techniques for the classroom and the laboratory. Also
contains materials about testing. Problems and exercises are
given throughout. (NYS bibliography)

1,346. Steel de Meza. Business Letter Handbook: Spanish-English (Manual
de correspindencia comercial español-inglés). New York: Regents
Publishing Company. $3.95.

This complete guide to bilingual letter-writing includes comprehension sections on letter styles, word separation, punctuation, and
many other aspects of personal and commercial correspondence in
Spanish and English. Model letters in both languages are presented
by categories (requests, offers, orders, claims, etc.). (catalog)

1,347. Steeves, Roy W. et al. Handbook for Teachers of English as a
Second Language: Americanization-Literacy. 2nd rev. ed. Sacramento, California: California State Department of Education.
1969. 85pp.
(ED 036 784)

1,348. Stevick, Earl W. Helping People Learn English. New York:
Abingdon Press. 1957.

Slanted to the non-professional teacher. Attempts to touch
on all related techniques, backgrounds and problems. (Hefferman-
Cabrera)

1,349. Stevick, Earl. "UHF and Microwaves in Trasmitting Language Skills."
TESOL Newsletter, 2:1 and 2 (January-March, 1968).

Presents "a way of individualizing instruction so that a single
set of materials may be used by students of many different temper-
ments and diverse interests, under widely varying circumstances with
instructors who are unskilled and/or inexperienced in language
teaching." Teaching cycles have two phases: an M-phase of mimicy,
memorization and meaning and a C-phase of real communication, in the
sense that it refers to real persons, objects and events, in short
conversations. The author presents several sequences of each cycle,
pointing out how through "small vocabulary, but structures to be
mastered remaining constant, choice is localization and personal-
ization of vocabulary or delexicalized language," thus like UHF
localized trasmission. (NYS bibliography)

1,350. Stevick, Earl. A Workbook in Language Teaching: With Special
Reference to English as a Foreign Language. Nashville,
Tennessee: Abingdon Press, 1963. (paper) 127pp.

For initial training of new language teachers and for inservice
use by experienced teachers. Treats three selected topics: English
phonology, basic types of drills, and fundamentals of grammar.
Frequent exercises and discussion questions assist user in acquiring
skills and in keeping check on his own progress. (NYS bibliography)

1,351. Stieglitz, Francine. P.A.L. Progressive Audio-Lingual Drills in
English. New York: Regents Publishing Company.

A grammar practice supplement suitable for any basic course
in English as a second language. It consists of sixty units
recorded on tape and a manual. Each unit focuses on a single
grammatical structure and drills it in a series of audio-lingual
exercises. These exercises are graded according to difficulty,
from simple to more complex forms. Available in sets of 12 units
or as a complete program of 60 units.
Price (1972): manual/$2.50, set of 12 units and manual/$18.00
complete set of 60 units and manual/$90.00. (catalog)

1,352. Stockwell, R.P. and Donald J. Bowen. The Sounds of English and
Spanish. Chicago: University of Chicago Press. 1960.

Contrastive linguistic analysis describing the similarities
and differences between English and Spanish, and intended to offer
a basis for the preparation of instructional materials, the planning
of courses, and the development of classroom techniques. The style
is moderately technical. (Hefferman-Cabrera)

1,353. Stockwell, R.P.; Donald J. Bowen, and J.W. Martin. The Grammatical
       Structures of English and Spanish. Chicago: University of
       Chicago Press. 1960.

       Contrastive linguistic analysis describing the similarities
       and differences between English and Spanish, and intended to offer
       a basis for the preparation of instructional materials, the planning
       of courses, and the development of classroom techniques. The style
       is moderatelt technical. (Hefferman-Cabrera)

1,354. Taylor, Grant. American English Reader. Saxon Series in ESL. New
       York: McGraw-Hill.

       Presents 12 stories on American themes for the intermediate
       student learning American English. Questions, summary sentences,
       and exercises emphasize the conversion of "passive" language
       ability (reading and listening) into the "active" counterpart
       (writing and speaking).

1,355. Taylor, Grant. English Conversation Practice. Saxon Series in
       ESL. New York: McGraw-Hill 260pp.

       Primarily for oral practice in English with adult students who
       have completed at least a beginning course. Contains conversa-
       tional drills, plus substitution and expansion exercises. In all,
       500 structure-oriented conversations are provided ("short answers,"
       "active vs. passive," etc.) as well as a programmed section of a
       structure and work study drills. All cues or cue sentences are
       presented at the left of the page and all answers or expected
       responses at the right. This enables the student to use the book
       for home study by covering the right hand column with a strip of
       paper. (NYS bibliography)

1,356. Taylor, Grant. Learning American English. Saxon Series in ESL.
       New York: McGraw-Hill 372pp.

       A textbook for beginning and intermediate students. Describes
       the informal spoken English used by the majority of native American
       speakers. Emphasis is on building a core vocabulary of 1500 words
       and idioms. Focuses on developing control of the basic elements of
       English through constant drill and a comprehensive grammar and
       structure program. (NYS bibliography)

1,357. Taylor, Grant. Mastering American English. Saxon Series in ESL.
       New York: McGraw-Hill.

       An exercise book containing review and exercise material for
       students at the intermediate and advanced levels. Emphasizes
       teaching English grammar and structure through examples rather
       than through grammatical explanations. The very large number of
       short exercises is arranged to allow the teacher complete flex-
       ibility. (NYS bibliography)

1,358.  Taylor, Grant.  Practicing American English.  Saxon Series in ESL.
New York:  McGraw-Hill   325 pp.

Specifically designed for systematic audio-oral and written
practice.  Composed of 516 pattern drills, word lists furnishing
material for additional drill, and over 300 picture groups which
help the student to attain his most important goal - automatic
control over sentence patterns.  For advanced as well as elementary
students.  (NYS bibliography)

1,359.  Texas Education Agency.  Teaching English as a Second Language:
Adult Basic Education Teacher's Guide.  Austin, Texas:
Texas Education Agency. 1969. 130pp.
(ED 034 147)

1,360.  Thomas.and Allen.  Oral English, Learning a Second Language.
Indianapolis, Indiana:  The Economy Company.

Designed to aid the very young child who may have trouble
succeeding in school due to little or no command of the English
language.  Objectives:  (1) to help the pupil communicate in
English in school; (2) to help the pupil hear and pronounce
the sounds of  the English language; (3) to help the pupil become
familiar with language patterns and vocabulary; and (4) to help
the pupil learn about the English-speaking culture while maintaining
appreciation of his own culture.
Price (1972): text $1.47, language development cards $75,00,
pocket chard and wall charts $21.75. (catalog)

1,361.  Trager, Edith Crowell and Sara Cook Henderson.  Pronunciation Drills
(The PD's) for Learners of English.  Rockville, Maryland:  English
Language Services, Inc.

Each vowel, consonant and stress phoneme is drilled alone, then
in contrast with similar phonemes, and finally, in short sentences.
Words used in the drills are of ultra-high frequency.  Although
problems are introduced in order of importance (determined by frequency of item and effect on intelligibility), teachers may often
find it more satisfactory to use the lessons in a different order,
in accordance with specific needs of their classes.
Price (1972): text/$2.75 ea., tapes/$31.75.  (catalog)

1,362.  U.S. Defense Language Institute.  American Language Course.  Twelve
volumes.  Lackland Air Force Base, Texas: Lackland Military
Training Center, 1963-64.  (paper)

Elementary Phase consists of four study guides which contain
detailed grammatical explanations and build up to a more advanced
level.  Instructor's Guide explains a general approach to pronunciation, intonation, structure, etc.  Accompanying workbook for Elementary Phase is programmed.  In the first volume of the Fundamental
Phase, each unit begins with a reading passage based on some immediate
aspect of American culture.  Three more advanced volumes follow the
Fundamental Phase.  Two Student Workbooks accompany the Fundamental
Phase.  Tapes available.  (NYS bibliography)

1,363. The U.S.A. Readers. New York: Regents Publishing Company. Four
Volumes at $1.25 ea.

Each book in this series contains short stories or articles
at carefully graded vocabulary levels. Each article or story is
followed by comprehension, vocabulary, and conversation exercises.
Book 1: The Land and the People - deals with the different
regions of the U.S. and describes the men and events that helped
shape these regions. (1,200 words).
Book 2: Men and History - A historical profile of twenty-
three famous Americans. (1,600 word range).
Book 3: Men and Machines - Challenges, triumphs, and achievements of men in science (2,400 word range).
Book 4: Customs and Institutions - An overall survey of the
traditions, customs, and social institutions of the U.S. (vocabulary
range: 3,000 words). (catalog)

1,364. The University of the State of New York, The State Education
Department, Bureau of Continuing Education Curriculum
Development. Test of Readiness for Literacy (Pilot Edition),
1970.

This instrument is designed to assess the degree to which
adults who are illiterate possess the requisites to learning to
read. It will be administered by State Education Department personnel
at selected Adult Basic Education centers in New York State. Information gathered from this test, plus data from a standardized
reading readiness test, will be used as guides for the development
of comprehensive readiness for literacy programs.
N.B. This experimental test has been administered to non-
native English speakers, among others, in New York City. (from the
test booklet)

1,365. University of the State of New York, The State Education Department,
Division of General Education, Bilingual Education Unit. Books
and Materials in English on Puerto Rico and the Puerto Ricans.
Albany, New York: 1972. 11pp. Originally appeared in the
Newsletter of Philadelphia Bilingual Programs. 1971.

1,366. University of the State of New York, The State Education Department,
Division of General Education, Bilingual Education Unit. Books
in Spanish for Children: An Annotated Bibliography (K-8).
Albany, New York: 1972. 25pp. Originally published in the
Newsletter of the Philadelphia Bilingual Programs. 1971.

1,367. University of the State of New York, The State Education Department,
Division of General Education, Bilingual Education Unit. Con-
ceptual and Oral Language Development, Bilingual Series. Guide I
(Pre-K): A Guidebook for Bilingual Teachers. First Series.
Albany, New York: 1970. 66pp.

1,368.  University of the State of New York.  The State Education Department,
        Division of General Education, Bilingual Education Unit. Concep-
        tual and Oral Language Development, Bilingual Series, Guide II
        (Pre-K):  A Guidebook for Bilingual Teachers.  Albany, New York:
        1970.  65pp.

1,369.  University of the State of New York.  The State Education Department,
        Division of General Education, Bilingual Education Unit. English
        as a Second Language:  Audiolingual Series (K).  First Series.
        Albany, New York:  1970.  67pp.

1,370.  University of the State of New York.  The State Education Department,
        Division of General Education, Bilingual Education Unit. English
        as a Second Language:  Audiolingual Series (K).  Second Series
        Albany, New York:  1970.  67pp.

1,371.  University of the State of New York.  The State Education Department,
        Division of General Education, Bilingual Education Unit.  Facts
        About Puerto Rico.  Albany, New York:  1972.  8pp.

1,372.  University of the State of New York.  The State Education Department,
        Division of General Education, Bilingual Education Unit.  A
        Handbook for Teachers of English as a Second Language Instruction.
        Albany, New York:  1970. 136pp.

1,373.  University of the State of New York.  The State Education Department,
        Division of General Education, Bilingual Education Unit.
        Listings of Textbooks Used by the Department of Education in
        Puerto Rico, and Available Materials for Puerto Rican Studies
        Programs.  Albany, New York:  1971.

1,374.  University of the State of New York.  The State Education Department,
        Division of General Education, Bilingual Education Unit.
        Materials Acquisition Project.  (Vol. 1, Nos. 1, 2, 4  and
        Vol. 2, Nos. 3, 4, 5, 8).  Albany, New York:  1972.

1,375.  University of the State of New York.  The State Education Department,
        Division of General Education, Bilingual Education Unit.  Resource
        Material for Puerto Rican History and Culture.  Albany, New York.

1,376.  University of the State of New York.  The State Education Department,
        Division of General Education, Bilingual Education Unit.
        Suggested Activities for the Celebration in the Public Schools
        of New York City of the Discovery of Puerto Rico by Christopher
        Columbus on November 19, 1493.  Albany, New York: 1972.  16pp.
        Originally developed by the Board of Education of the City of
        New York.

1,377.  The University of the State of New York.  The State Education Department,
        Bureau of Continuing Education Curriculum Development.  Consumer
        Education:  Educación del Consumidor, 1969, 98pp.

279

This manual has been designed to provide teachers with suggested lesson plans in the area of consumer education. Each lesson plan contains background material for the teacher, specific information on the subject, aims of the lesson, and the development of essential understandings. The manuals to accompany the filmstrip Getting Credit and the flipchart Shopping for Money are also included. Discussion questions are suggested throughout the materials to encourage the greatest possible student involvement. In this Spanish edition, material which is to be presented orally to the students or read by the students appears in Spanish. All other material appears in English. This publication covers 10 topics in the area of consumer education. (from introduction)

1,378. The University of the State of New York. The State Education Department, Bureau of Continuing Education Curriculum Development. Health and Nutrition: Salud y Nutrición, 1969, 101pp.

This manual has been designed to provide teachers with suggested lesson plans in the area of health and nutrition. Each lesson plan contains background material for the teacher, specific information on the subject, aims of the lesson, and the development of essential understandings. The manuals to accompany the filmstrip Shots for Your Health and the flipchart Keep Well With Vaccine are also included. Discussion questions are suggested to encourage the greatest possible student involvement. In this Spanish edition, material which is to be presented orally to the students, or read by the students, appears in Spanish. All other material appears in English. Ten topics are included. (from introduction)

1,379. The University of the State of New York. The State Education Department, Bureau of Continuing Education Curriculum Development. Practical Government: Gobierno Práctico, 1969, 97pp.

This manual has been designed to provide the teacher with suggested lesson plans in the area of practical government. Each lesson plan contains background material for the teacher, specific information on the subject, aims of the lesson, and the development of essential understandings. The manuals to accompany the filmstrip The Silent Voice and the flipchart Using the Voting Machine are also included. Discussion questions are suggested throughout the material to encourage the greatest possible student involvement. In this Spanish edition, material which is to be presented orally to the students or read by the students appears in Spanish. All other material appears in English. This publication covers 10 topics in the area of practical government. (from introduction)

1,380. Wall, Muriel (comp.). Audiovisual Aids to Enrich the Curriculum for the Puerto Rican Child in the Elementary Grades, Part 1 and 2. City University of New York, Hunter College. 1971. 33pp. (ED 049 659)

In part one, a short article on listening skills and information
on the classroom use of tape recordings precedes an annotated list
of more than 60 records and tapes for use in enriching the curriculum.
A list of "Read-With-Me-Recordings" and addresses of distributors
of sheet music, records, and tapes are included. Part two contains
additional lists of appropriate films and filmstrips, film evaluation
forms, and sources of other types of bilingual instructional materials.
(RIE abridged)

1,381. Wallace, Betty. The Pronunciation of American English for Teachers
of English as a Second Language. Ann Arbor, Michigan: George
Wahr, 1957. (paper)

Although written primarily for Spanish speakers learning
English, it is also useful in other linguistic contexts or as a
reference book for the teacher. (NYS bibliography)

1,382. Wheeler, Gonzalez. Let's Speak English. Six volumes. New York:
McGraw-Hill, 1967. (paper)

A graded and controlled course for elementary schools. Designed to teach spoken usage only, although the text page may be
used for reading and writing if the teacher desires. Books 1-3
follow inductive method, providing large amounts of generally
structured practice material rather than isolated patterns. Books
4-6 have materials divided into three part units: a dialog,
exercises, and the "Program Steps." "Language Hints" and "Word Study"
isolate patterns in a colored block. General exercises are well-
structured, with numerous examples and answers in the margin for
home study. Color is used extensively in illustrations and to
coordinate parts of the lessons and identify types of drills.
Instructions to the teacher are provided in each book. (NYS
bibliography)

1,383. Whitehouse and Robert J. Dixson. Inglés práctico sin maestro. New
York: Regents Publishing Company.

A self-instructional program in English for Spanish-speaking
people consisting of 20 graded lessons, with instructions and explanations in Spanish. Phonetic transcriptions and Spanish equivalents accompany all new vocabulary. Text provides intensive
practice for all grammatical and structural forms.
Prices (1972): text/$1.50, records and text/$9.95, tapes and
text/$28.00. (catalog)

1,384. Whitford, Harold C. A Dictionary of American Homophones and Homographs. New York: Teachers College, Columbia University,
1966. (paper)

Part I lists over 1,000 homophones (pairs of words identically
pronounced but different in spelling and meaning). Part II deals
with 160 homographs (pairs of words identical in spelling but
differently in pronunciation and meaning). Part III has an additional
list of 800 less frequent homophones; Part IV has a series of oral
and written exercises. Useful as a textbook or as a reference work.
(NYS bibliography)

1,385. Whitford, Harold C. and Robert J. Dixson. Handbook of American
Idioms and Idiomatic Usage. New York: Regents Publishing Co.

A reference book containing over 5,000 of the most common
idiomatic words and phrases. Each idiom is defined and its use
illustrated in a sentence. Price (1972): $2.95. (catalog)

1,386. Wiener, Soloman. Manual de modismos americanos más comunes. New
York: Regents Publishing Company.

This book contains about 1,200 basic American idioms, listed
and defined for Spanish-speaking people who are learning English.
Using both Spanish and English, it defines each idiom and shows its
use in a sentence. This book is also available in an all-English
version under the title: A Handy Book of Commonly-Used American
Idioms.
Price (1972): Spanish/English version: $0.75, English version:
$0.60. (catalog)

1,387. Wilson, Alfred P. and Others. How Do You Feel About Things? New
Mexico State University, Las Cruces. Paper presented at the
Annual Meeting of the Rocky Mountain Educational Research
Association, Boulder, Colorado, October 1971. 5pp.
(ED 058 281)

The 60-item questionnaire is designed to measure attitudes
toward school among sixth grade Spanish American students. The
respondents mark their answers on a 1 to 5, true to false
continuum. Administration instructions are included. (RIE)

1,388. Wishon, George E. and Julia M. Burks. Let's Write English. Two
volumes. New York: American Book, (1968). (paper)

Provides methodical practice in the written forms of English.
Book I deals with sentence patterns, leading up to paragraph and
short composition writing. Book 2 deals with various prose forms
from letters to description, narration, argumentation, and explanation. Includes lessons on outlining, note-taking, the use of the
library, summarizing and preparation of research papers, intending
to bring the student to a level of competence enabling him to handle
college work. Lessons begin with explanation and comment on several
patterns, illustrating each with several examples. Examples
follow. (NYS bibliography)

1,389. Withers, Sara. The United Nations in Action: A Structured Reader.
New York: Thomas Y. Crowell. 1969.

Structured reader for upper high school or college age ESL
students.

1,390. Workpapers: Teaching English as a Second Language. Vol. V. California University, Los Angeles. June 1971. 161pp.
(ED 056 556)

1,391.  Wright, Audrey L. and McGillivroy. Let's Learn English. 3rd ed.
        New York: American Book Company. 1966.

        Emphasis is on oral English. Good beginning lessons in pro-
nunciation. Vocabulary and patterns of structure taught in context.
Every fourth lesson is a review. Latter part of book can be used
with intermediate students. (Hefferman-Cabrera)

1,392.  Yo Puertorriqueño. Glenview, Illinois: Scott, Foresman and
        Company. 1972 (in preparation). 32pp. $.66

        Consumable Spanish-English pupil book for grades K-3 sup-
plementary to English Around the World. Contains bilingual picture
essays designed to develop cultural awareness and improve both
Spanish and English abilities in Puerto Rican children living in
Puerto Rico or the United States. Vocabulary coordinated with
Mi diccionario ilustrado.      (catalog)

1,393.  Yorkey, Richard C. Study Skills for Students of English as a
        Second Language. New York: McGraw-Hill. 1970.

        Reading improvement and study skill book for foreign students
on the upper high school or college age level.

1,394.  Zintz, Miles V. Corrective Reading. 2nd Edition. Dubuque, Iowa:
        William C. Brown Co., 1972. 449pp.

        The text is intended for classroom teachers who need assis-
tance with students who have reading difficulties. After an
introduction to reading problems, discussed immediately are
several informal tests the teacher can use to evaluate oral and
silent reading and thereby identify children in need of corrective
reading. Teaching and testing techniques and devices are emphasized. In addition to evaluation and diagnosis, major topics
covered are: planning remedial work with the student, scheduling,
teaching bilingual and non-standard dialect-speaking children,
emotional factors in reading, working cooperatively with parents,
attitudes of teachers toward students who fail, use of standardized
tests and progress records, and specific learning disability.
(EC, abridged by DH)

1,395.  Zirkel, Perry Alan. A Bibliography of Materials in English and
        Spanish Relating to Puerto Rican Students. Hartford, Connec-
        ticut: Connecticut State Department of Education. 1971. 51pp.
        (ED 057 142)

        The contents of this listing of materials, intended as resources
for teachers and other persons concerned with improving the educational
opportunities of Puerto Rican pupils on the mainland as well as on
the island, are organized in four sections: (1) books: Puerto Rican
Culture in English, Puerto Rican Culture in Spanish, and Children's
Fiction; (2) audio-visual materials: films, filmstrips, recordings,
and others; (3) research studies; and (4) bibliographies. (RIE

J.  Teacher and Counselor Attitudes, Recruitment and Training for Working
    with Puerto Rican or Other Non-English-Speaking Children

1,396.  Ainsworth, C.L. (ed.)  Teachers and Counselors for Mexican-American
        Children.  Southwest Educational Develop-Laboratory, Austin,
        Texas:  Texas Technological College, Lubbock, Texas. 1969. 137pp.
        (ED 029 728)

1,397.  Allen, Harold B. (ed.).  Teaching English as a Second Language:  A
        Book of Readings.  New York:  McGraw-Hill, 2nd ed. 1972. $9.50.

        Contains the work of 45 authors in the areas of linguistics,
        psychology and education, from Australia, England, the U.S., Canada
        and the Philippines; some theoretical and some practical.  Nine
        subject areas, each with an overview:  Theories and Approaches,
        Teaching English Speech, Teaching English Structure, Teaching
        English Vocabulary, Teaching English Usage and Composition, Teaching
        the Printed Word, Reading and Literature, Methods and Techniques,
        Teaching with Audio-Visual Aids and Testing.  (NYS bibliography)

1,398.  Allen, Harold B.  TENES:  A Survey of the Teaching of English to
        Non-English Speakers in the United States.  Champaign, Illinois:
        National Council of Teachers of English, 1966.  (paper)

        A survey to date of publications based on 500 replies to de-
        tailed questionnaire sent to schools, colleges and institutions
        throughout the country.  Analyzes and discusses findings under
        TENES programs:  the teacher, the teaching situation, aids and
        materials, problems and needs.  Includes conference report and
        recommendations on representative TENES programs.  (NYS bibliography)

1,399.  Allen, Robert L.; Virginia French Allen; and Margaret Shute.
        English Sounds and Their Spellings:  A Handbook for Teachers
        and Students.  New York: Thomas Y. Crowell Co., 1966. (paper)
        $2.75.

        This book can be used in different ways for different purposes
        in different kinds of classes for students of any age. Its dis-
        tinctive features: a systematic sequence for coordinating teaching
        sounds with patterns of spelling; a procedure from regular to
        irregular spellings; calling "short" vowels the basic sounds, and
        "long" vowels the name sounds of vowels; avoidance of conventional
        phonetic symbols by representing vowel sounds by numbers; 40
        lessons include explanations, instructions and practice.  Films
        available.  (NYS bibliography)

1,400.  Allen, V.F.; C.J. Kreidler, and B.W. Robinett.  On Teaching English
        to Speakers of Other Languages:  Series I-III.  Washington,
        D.C.:  TESOL. 1965-67.

        Proceedings of the first three annual conferences of the
        Association of Teachers of English to Speakers of Other Languages.
        Papers cover a variety of theoretical and practical topics in the
        field for teachers of all age groups and levels of instruction.
        (CAL bibliography)

1,401.  Alloway, David and F. Cordasco.  <u>Minorities and the American City:
        A Sociological Primer for Educators</u>.  New York: David McKay. 1970.

1,402.  Anastasiow, Nicholas J. and Espinosa, Iraida. "The Guadalajara
        Project:  An In-Service Approach in Training Teachers in
        Spanish." <u>California Journal for Instructional Improvement</u>.
        (October, 1968).

        Discusses a project conducted in Palo Alto, California.

1,403.  Anderson, James F.  <u>Teachers of Minority Groups:  The Origins of
        Their Attitudes and Instructional Practices</u>.  Las Cruces,
        New Mexico:  New Mexico State University. 196.  72pp.
        (ED 026 192)

            This study was designed to gain some understanding of the origin
        of teacher attitudes and instructional methods when dealing with
        Mexican-American students.
            A questionnaire was developed to question teachers about their
        academic background, experience, career aspirations, instructional
        practices, and attitudes toward students, parents and special
        programs for disadvantaged minority students; it was administered
        to 72 mathematics teachers in three districts in South El Paso.
        Factor analysis was used to clarify the complex variables among
        teachers.  Results suggest that the kind of professional training
        they receive may have some effect on teacher' attitude toward
        minority groups.  Teachers' approaches to teaching Mexican-
        Americans, views regarding compensatory and bilingual programs,
        evaluation of student ability and progress, and the kind of student
        they enjoyed teaching were all related to their professional
        training and career aspirations.  There are many charts and
        figures illustrating the narrative, and the teacher questionnaire
        is included.  (ECK)

1,404.  Arapoff, Nancy. "Writing, a Thinking Process." <u>TESOL Quarterly</u>.
        1:2  (June, 1967).

            Explains why teaching writing is different from teaching other
        language skills.  Presents a new method for teaching writing:  an
        approach involving "transformations" in narration, paraphrase,
        summary, factual analysis, argumentative analysis, evaluation of
        arguments, and critical review.

1,405.  Armas, José.  <u>Cultural Communications</u>.  Paper presented at the
        Sixth Annual TESOL Convention.  Washington, D.C., March 1, 1972.
        29pp.
        (ED 064 998)

            It is too often taken for granted that the communication process
        with culturally different children takes place as readily as it might
        with children from Anglo cultures.  Most teachers receive training
        in verbal and formal communication skills; children come to school
        with nonverbal and informal communication skills.  This initially

can create problems of communication breakdown. To complicate the situation, nonverbal messages that do not support verbal communication messages assure communication breakdown. This paper proposes cultural differences as the number one consideration for the school when it deals with children from different cultures and provides recommendations for teachers, curriculum, and community on affecting the change required to meet the educational needs of the culturally different child. (RIE)

1,406. Baca, Joseph Donald. A Comparative Study of Differences in Perception of Mexican American Students Between Anglo and Mexican American Secondary School Teachers in Dona Ana County (New Mexico). Specialist in Education thesis submitted to New Mexico State University, Las Cruces, New Mexico. July 1972. 131p. (ED 065 218)

1,407. Barbour, Elizabeth et al. Teaching Foreigners. San Antonio. 1916. 19pp.

1,408. Bathurst, Effie G. "Inter-American Understanding and the Preparation of Teachers." U.S. Office of Education Bulletin No. 15. 1946. 100pp.

1,409. Baty, Roger M. Reeducating Teachers for Cultural Awareness: Preparation for Educating Mexican-American Children in Northern California. Praeger Special Studies in U.S. Economic and Social Development Series. New York, New York: Praeger Publishers. 1972. 147pp. (ED 066 545)

1,410. Blatchford, Charles H. A Theoretical Contribution to ESL Diagnostic Test Construction. Paper presented at the Fifth Annual TESOL Convention, New Orleans, Louisiana, March 7, 1971 12pp. (ED 055 484)

A diagnostic test in English as a second language should be a series of miniature tests on specific problems. Subscores in each area should be considered rather than a total score. The results should be used to probe mastery in an area rather than provide the means for comparing one student against another. The statistical reliability of the results does not necessarily depend on test length. The teacher should look at each item for each student rather than the score and should spend more time studying the analysis of each student's test. The criterion of the percent of correct decisions may be a more meaningful measure than ascertaining the traditional coefficients of reliability. Tables provide the statistical data under consideration. (RIE)

1,411. Bowen, J. Donald. "Maximum Results from Minimum Training." TESOL Quarterly. 3:1 (March, 1967).

Contrasts the goals of long-term and short-term training programs. Presents the potential weaknesses of NDEA Institutes and Peace Corps-type programs and suggestions for strengthening these programs, including an analysis of the training cycle. (NYS bibliography)

286

1,412.  Bracy, Maryruth. "Controlled Writing vs. Free Composition."
        TESOL Quarterly. 5:3 (September, 1971), pp. 239-246.

        The purpose of this paper is to offer some suggestions for
        those who have tried to tackle the area of free (or advanced) com-
        position. The suggestions, based on a review of the literature and
        on my experience in teaching composition courses at UCLA, center
        around the following three areas: 1) the revision of current
        classes in intermediate English so as to teach free composition
        instead of merely advanced controlled writing; 2) the unwanted and
        partially-opened Pandora's box of composition correction coupled
        with the question of what students do with the 'corrected' compo-
        sitions to affect change and improvement in their writing techniques
        and use of language; and 3) the improvement of the over-all compo-
        sition-teaching approach. (from the article)

1,413.  Bracy, Maryruth (ed.). Workpapers in English as a Second Language,
        Volume III. Los Angeles: UCLA, 1969, 96pp.
        (ED 054 666)

        Several articles discuss teaching and learning a second lan-
        guage and practical considerations in second language learning such
        as reading and writing skills, the use of poetry, the concept of
        style among elementary school children, and procedures and objectives
        for analyzing classes. One article concerns attitudes toward the
        teaching of a particular pronunciation of English. Also contains
        abstracts of Masters Theses completed by students studying TESL. (RIE)

1,414.  Bracy, Maryruth (ed.). Workpapers in Teaching English as a Second
        Language, Volume IV. Los Angeles: UCLA, 1970, 130pp.
        (ED 054 664)

        Several articles concern topics on language instruction:  the
        art of language teaching, bilingual education, literature study,
        composition writing, testing by dictation, problems of elementary
        school teachers, English curriculums for non-English speakers,
        computer applications and second language learning. Others concern
        language-teacher preparation: suggested areas of research by Masters-
        Degree students and programs for specializing in teaching English to
        the disadvantaged. Papers on linguistic theory include diacritics in
        modern English graphology and the pragmatics of communication. Ab-
        stracts of Masters theses approved during the year are also included.
        (RIE)

1,415.  Brice, Edward Warner et al. Teaching Adults the Literacy Skills.
        Washington, D.C.: General Federation of Women's Clubs. n.d. 112p.

1,416.  Briggs, Frances M. "As Five Teachers See Themselves." Educational
        Forum. 28:4 (May, 1964). pp. 389-397. (reprinted by Migration
        Division, Commonwealth of Puerto Rico, 1965).

1,417.  Brown, T. Grant.  "In Defense of Pattern Practice,"  Language Learning,
        19:3 and 4 (December, 1969).

        Even though transformational grammar has shown the inadequacy
        of the pattern concept and behaviorist theories have been shown to
        be unable to account for first language acquisition, pattern practice
        still seems to be of vital importance to students of foreign
        languages.  (NYS bibliography)

1,418.  Cabrera, Patricia (comp.).  An Introductory Bibliography for Teachers
        of English to Speakers of Other Languages. 1965.
        (ED 016 914).

1,419.  Carter, T.  Preparing Teachers for Mexican-American Children.  Las
        Cruces, New Mexico:  ERIC Clearinghouse on Rural Education. 1969.

1,420.  Carroll, John B.  "A Primer of Programmed Instruction of Foreign
        Language Teaching," International Review of Applied Linguistics,
        1:2 (Special Issue, 1963) (Reprints available from MLA).

        A general introduction to methods of programmed instruction
        and its application to the teaching of foreign languages. (NYS
        bibliography)

1,421.  Cintron de Crespo, Patria.  Puerto Rican Women Teachers in New
        York:  Self Perception and Work Adjustment as Perceived by
        Themselves and Others.  Unpublished Ph.D. Dissertation
        Columbia University. 1965.

1,422.  "City College da satisfacción a maestra boricua."  El Diaro de
        Nueva York. (July 30, 1952). pp. 1, 17.

1,423.  Concepción, Abigail Díaz de.  Resources in Which the Lives and
        Culture of Puerto Rican Students Will Aid in the Understanding
        and Use of Basic Concepts in Social Psychology. Unpublished
        Ph.D. Dissertation, Columbia University. 1960.

1,424.  Cook, Katherine M.  "Opportunities for the Preparation of Teachers
        of Native and Minority Groups." Bulletin No. 77, U.S. Office
        of Education. 1937. 11pp.

1,425.  Cordasco, F. and Bucchioni  "Institute for Preparing Teachers of
        Puerto Rican Students."  School and Society. Vol. 100 (Summer
        1972). pp. 308-309.
        (EJ 059 480).

        The authors note that there is a lack of specially trained
        teachers to deal specifically with Puerto Rican students and
        propose a Staff Development Institute for Elementary and Secondary
        School Teachers of Puerto Rican Students.  A team of four teachers
        and other personnel is suggested to insure a variety of professional
        skills.  Some of the topics to be studied in the institute would be
        the Puerto Rican culture and experience in the United States;

remedial reading, English as a Second Language and guidance for
Puerto Rican students; conversational Spanish; and bilingual
education. Criteria for participants, especially commitment to
the education of Puerto Ricans, are listed. The authors suggest
that funds from the Elementary and Secondary Education Act may be
used to help defray the costs of the program. (ECK)

1,426. Crespo, Patricia Cintrón de. Puerto Rican Women Teachers in New
York: Self Perceptions and Work Adjustment as Perceived by
Themselves and Others. Unpublished Ph.D. Dissertation,
Columbia University. 1965.

1,427. Cross, William C. and Bonnie Maldonado. "The Counselor, the
Mexican-American and the Stereotype." Elementary School
Guidance and Counseling. 6:1 (October, 1971). pp. 27-31.
(EJ 044 910)

To understand the cultural differences of Mexican-Americans
the authors recommend an internship within the barrio or the inclusion of Mexican-American history or culture courses in the
Anglo counselor's program of study. (CIJE)

1,428. Decaney, Fe R. Techniques and Procedures in Second Language
Teaching. Phillipine Center for Language Study, Monograph
Series No. 3. Dobbs Ferry, New York: Oceana Publications,
Inc., 1967, 538pp.

The reader should keep in mind that this book was primarily
created to help Filipino teachers of English. It was written for
the classroom teacher who needs a wide variety of aids in presenting, drilling and testing the material she is teaching. The
author did not intend it to be a sophisticated treatise on
linguistics. Thus, linguists might object, and with some justi-
fication, to the cursory treatment of terms like phonemes, allo-
phones and phonetics. The book includes ways in which the
structures of English can be effectively presented by means of
dialogues, visuals, stories, newspaper articles and comic strips.
(from MLJ review LIV:4 rev.)

1,429. De Todo un Poco (A Little of Everything). Chicago Public Schools,
Illinois. Washington, D.C. Office of Education. March 1972. 137p.
(ED 066 082)

This document seeks to underline the importance of cultural
awareness by providing examples of the folkways, customs, art, traditions, and life styles of different ethnic groups. Included here
are teaching techniques designed to motivate understanding of the uni-
versality of man and to show how cultural differences enrich everyone's life. Suggestions are offered to teachers, and examples of
activities for and by students are provided. The document concerns
such diverse topics as free pamphlets available on bilingual and bicultural education, statistics on foreign speakers in Chicago, communication problems, international geographical facts, and cultural

insights into many different countries, especially through the eyes
of children from those countries. (RIE)

1,430. Dinsmore, Cyrena B. Teacher Guide for English Speaking. Albuquerque,
New Mexico: Home Education Livelihood Program. 1967. 139pp.
(ED 017 347)

1,431. Dulay, Heidi and Jeffrey Shultz. Crosscultural Miscommunication in
the Classroom. Cambridge, Massachusetts: Languag Research
Foundation. New York, New York: Ford Foundation, paper
presented at the joint annual meeting of the Society for
Applied Anthropology and the American Ethnological Society,
Montreal, Quebec, April 8, 1972. 36p.
(ED 064 439)

Communication between students and teachers is a basic requirement for learning to take place in a classroom. Like words
and phrases, behaviors carry specific meanings which may vary across
cultures. When teachers are not aware of cultural differences, when
they assume that a behavior has a particular meaning while students
assume it has another, then there is a misunderstanding--a breakdown in communication. One basic reason for the failure of Puerto
Rican students in mainland classrooms is the lack of communication
between them and their Anglo teachers--due to a lack of cross-
cultural sensitivity. The purpose of this research project was
to find evidence of culture conflicts, resulting in miscommunication
between Puerto Rican students and Anglo students. Four classes
in a Boston public school were observed and tape recorded, and information compiled on Puerto Rican culture and the Anglo teacher
subculture. The findings encompassed instances of miscommunications
manifested by the behavior of the students and teachers which could
be explained by their respective cultural norms. (RIE)

1,432. Ekmekci, Oxden. Teaching Composition through Comprehension:  A
Survey of Teaching English Composition to Foreign Students and
Its Application to the English Program at the Middle East
Technical University in Turkey. Master's thesis, University of
Texas at Austin. August 1971. 97p.
(ED 060 739)

1,433. English Language Services, Inc. ELS Teacher Education Program.
Washington, D.C., 1967.

An experimental multi media self-instructional course in the
techniques of TESOL. Designed for an estimated 200 hours of self-
paced independent study in order to provide well-trained new teachers
without a professional training staff. Course includes: (1) 26
programmed workbooks covering English phonology and grammar, principles of language learning, classroom techniques, and general
teaching methodolody; (2) 163 8mm sound films; (3) 140 audio tapes;
(4) 20 packages of worksheets, participation forms, and other
training aids; and (5) 28 volumes of professional reference books

in linguistics, methodology, phonology and grammar. The trainee
reads lessons, listens to tapes, observes demonstration films and
practice teaches in simulated classroom situations. (RIE)

1,434. Epstein, Erwin H. and Joseph J. Pizzillo, eds. A Human Relations
Guide for Teachers: Linguistic Minorities in the Classroom.
Wisconsin State Department of Public Instruction, Madison.
1972. 101pp.
(ED 066 417)

This resource book is a collection of articles and reports of
classroom observations, discussion questions, learning strategies,
and suggested classroom activities appropriate to various curricular
areas such as language arts and social studies on topics that often
arise in the schooling of children from minority groups, especially
from linguistic minorities. Its purpose is to enlighten teachers
and school personnel about the implications of educating children
of diverse cultural backgrounds, especially Mexican Americans,
Puerto Ricans, and American Indians to accept an "American" ethnic
and ideal. (RIE)

1,435. Espinoza, Marta. Cultural Conflict in the Classroom. Speech to
TESOL Convention, New Orleans, 1971, 7pp.
(ED 054 669)

A cultural conflict exists between the Mexican-American child
and the Anglo teacher within the classroom situation. Punishment
for adherence to his own culture results in loss of identity for the
child and increases his tendency toward what may be termed deviant
behavior. The more weighted the school curriculum is toward the
middle-class Anglo expectations, the more difficult it will be for
the child to participate. A positive attitude must be established
and the cultural gap must be bridged; total acceptance of the
validity of another culture is what should and must be the end
goal.(RIE abridged)

1,436. "'Ethno-lematics': Evoking 'Shy' Spanish American Pupils by Cross-
Cultural Mediation." Adolenscence. Vol. 6, no. 25 (Spring 1972).
pp. 61-76.
(EJ 055 587)

1,437. Finocchiaro, Mary. English as a Second Language: From Theory to
Practice. New York: Regents Publishing Company. 1964. $1.95.
(paper). 143pp.

Designed for beginning and advanced teachers. Presents background reading for language learning and teaching, based largely on
author's experience. Includes suggestions for preparing curriculum,
developing language skills, materials, techniques and testing.
(PREP on B.E. rev.)

1,438. Finocchiaro, Mary. "A Suggested Procedure in the Teaching of English
to Puerto Ricans." High Points. (May, 1949). pp. 60-66.

1,439.  Finocchiaro, Mary.  <u>Teaching Children Foreign Languages</u>.  McGraw-Hill 1964.

        Non-technical guide with specific examples of tested classroom procedures.  Includes chapters on techniques, teacher attitude, development of language skills, making teaching effective, and the preparation and adaptation of materials.  Bibliography and glossary of useful terms.  (NYS bibliography)

1,440.  Finocchiaro, Mary.  <u>Teaching English as a Second Language:  In Elementary and Secondary Schools;</u> rev. ed. Harper and Row. 1968 478pp.

        Updated version brings together theories in general education, second language teaching and applied linguistics.  Emphasis remains on the activities approach, stressing cultural orientation as an important aim in language learning.  Practical suggestions for teachers and supervisors.  (NYS bibliography)

1,441.  Finocchiaro, Mary and Michael Bonomo.  <u>The Foreign Language Learner: A Guide for Teachers</u>. New York: Regents Publishing Company. $3.95.

        A comprehensive professional guide in the field of foreign or second language learning.  Includes topics such as determining beginning proficiency levels, planning the curriculum, classroom utilization of teaching materials, and ways of evaluating student achievement and teaching efficiency.  Useful as a reference book or for teacher training.  (catalog)

1,442.  Fowler, Mary Elizabeth.  <u>Teaching Language, Composition, and Literature</u>.  New York: McGraw-Hill. 435pp.

        Provides a thorough study of areas of major concern to the teacher of secondary English:  language, composition, and literature.  Specific teaching suggestions; assignments in linguistics, usage, and composition; and thematic teaching units in biography, drama, the novel, and nonfiction are among the special features of this text.  (NYS bibliography)

1,443.  Francis, W. Nelson.  <u>The Structure of American English</u>.  New York: The Ronald Press. 1958.

        Intended for a one-semester course in the English language for prospective teachers.  Attempts to synthetize "current linguistic knowledge, especially as applied to present-day American English." (Hefferman-Cabrera)

1,444.  Fries, Charles C.  <u>Linguistics and Reading.</u>  New York: Holt, Rinehart and Winston, 1963.

        A survey of developments in modern linguistics relative to the teaching of reading in English.  Includes historical surveys of

methods of teaching reading and the development of modern linguistics. Discusses the nature of the reading process, the place of
phonics, and the development of English spelling; also suggests
essentials for a linguistic approach in the development of
materials and methods to teach reading. (NYS bibliography)

1,445. Fries, Charles C. <u>Teaching and Learning English as a Foreign
Language</u>. Ann Arbor, Mich.: University of Michigan Press,
1945. (paper)

Still useful more than 25 years after its publication, this
work contains information in support of the theory behind the linguistic approach to teaching and learning English as a foreign
language. There is much emphasis on the use of the oral approach
based on a contrastive analysis of the learner's language. (NYS
bibliography)

1,446. Gaarder, Bruce et al. <u>Bilingualism From the Viewpoint of the
Administrator and Counselor</u>. paper for Southwest Council of
FL Teachers, El Paso, Texas, 1966, 18pp.
(ED 018 286)

The most difficult problem in bilingualism is that of gaining
favorable administrative attitude and policy. Bilingual schooling
is profitable because it makes for superior educational achievement
and students can learn best through their mother tongue. Through
this approach, biculturalism can be achieved, rather than the
cutting of ties from the original culture. Included are a
supporting bibliography and an appendix which describes a number
of bilingual projects in various schools. (RIE)

1,447. García, Ernesto F. <u>Modification of Teacher Behavior in Teaching the
Mexican-American</u>. Albuquerque, New Mexico: Southwestern Coop-
erative Educational Laboratory. 1970. 1pp.
(ED 047 971)

1,448. Greenstein, Raymond and Moises Tirado. Operation <u>P.R.I.M.A. - RECLAIM</u>.
(Recruitment of Teachers of Puerto Rican Extraction). 1966.
(ED 010 775)

1,449. George, H.V. <u>Common Errors in Language Learning</u>. Rowley, Mass.: Newbury House Publishers. 1971. $4.95 (paper).

Provides basic guidelines to the causes and prevention of
students' errors in foreign language learning. Incorporates a modern
theory of language learning pedagogy based on the errors made by
learners of a second language. Presupposes no previous linguistic
training on the part of the reader. (catalog)

1,450. Greenstein, Marvin N. "Puerto Rican Children." <u>Pathways in Child
Guidance</u>. 2:4 (June, 1960). pp. 1-3.

1,451. Halliday, M.A.K.; Agnes McIntosh; and Peter Strevers. *The Linguistic Sciences and Language Teaching.* Bloomington: Indiana University Press, 1964.

A study of the application of modern linguistics to problems of language teaching. The linguistic theory embodied is mostly derived and developed from the works of Firth. The applications cited are largely directed towards ESL teaching. Provides valuable insights into the nature and structure of English. (NYS bibliography)

1,452. *A Handbook for Teachers of English* (Americanization - Literacy). rev. ed. Sacramento: California State Department of Education. 1967. (ED 016 191)

1,453. Harris, David P. *Testing English as a Second Language.* New York: McGraw-Hill, 1969. 151pp.

The objective of this book is to enable the ESL teacher to improve his own classroom measures and to make sound assessments of standardized tests which he may be asked to select, administer and interpret. The opening chapters introduce the general purposes and methods of language testing. Following chapters describe specific techniques for testing grammar, vocabulary, etc., and the processes involved in constructing and administering tests and interpreting the results. The final chapter offers procedures for calculating a few basic test statistics. Text does not assume previous training in tests and measurements or knowledge of advanced mathematics. (NYS bibliography)

1,454. Hausler, Jeanette. *Selling a Book.* Dade County Public Schools, Miami, Florida. 1971. 24pp. (ED 062 876)

Intended primarily for use with Spanish-speaking students from South and Central America and the Caribbean who have migrated to the United States, this text outlines ways to develop interest in reading good literature. The main literary theme reflected through the literary selections concerns the worldwide problem of maintaining an ecological balance between nature and mankind. Performance objectives are prescribed which help develop skills related to literary analysis, vocabulary development, and oral expression. The guide is written principally in Spanish. (RIE)

1,455. Heffernan-Cabrera, Patricia. *A Handbook for Teachers of English to Non-English Speaking Adults.* Washington, D.C.: Center for Applied Linguistics, 1969. (paper)

An introduction to and summary of the field, including sections on the why and who of TESOL teaching, some how's of TESOL teaching, some what's to teach, some kinds of evaluation and a bibliography. (NYS bibliography)

1,456.  Hendricks, Herbert W.  "The Mexican-American Student and Emigrated
Values."  College Student Journal.  5:2 (September-October, 1971).
pp. 52-54.

The author believes that the teacher should serve as a model
of conduct for his students in the eyes of Mexican students.  With
a solid foundation of tradition brought into the schools by these
children, teachers would receive the kind of support needed to
conduct a program adaptable to their needs.  (CIJE)

1,457.  Jakobovits, Leon A.  The Encounter-Communication Workshop.  June
1970.  47pp.
(ED 062 883)

This paper outlines a program of inservice training for teachers
and administrative school personnel designed to foster a better
understanding of the problems involved in the education of children
from minority groups within an educational system that is defined
and administered by the cultural interests of the dominant social
or national community.  The Encounter-Communication Workshop, a
program of study conducted in the bilingual school setting, is designed to give the individual a better understanding of himself
within the context of interpersonal communication.  The study
program involves two types of activities:  an objective analysis
of role dyadic interactions in the school in terms of a linguistic-
communication model, and an analysis of the subjective aspects of
interpersonal relations, including social contracts, trust, risk-
taking, self-image and its management, and personal metaphysics. (RIE)

1,458.  Jakobovits, Leon A.  Foreign Language Learning:  A Psycholinguistic
Analysis of the Issues.  Rowley, Mass.:  Newbury House. 1970.

A critical examination of psycholinguistic implications and
psychological and physiological aspects of foreign language
learning, compensatory foreign language instruction, problems in
the assessment of language learning, and foreign language aptitude
and attitude testing.  Presents an approach that, the author contends,
is adaptable to any method the teacher currently uses to understand
and take into account the strategies of the learner.  (NYS bibliography)

1,459.  Klingstedt, Joe Lars.  Teachers of Middle School Mexican American
Children:  Indicators of Effectiveness and Implications for
Teacher Education.  Washington, D.C.:  Office of Education. (1972).
46p.
(ED 059 828)

A summary of research and related literature on the problem of
identifying indicators of teacher effectiveness, this publication is
divided into three sections: (1) traditional indicators of teacher
effectiveness in terms of good teaching procedures and desirable
personality characteristics; (2) new trends in identifying indicators
of teacher effectiveness; and (3) implications for teacher education
in the form of a teacher education model--with suggestions for further
study.  A bibliography of 83 citations is included.  (RIE)

1,460. Krear, Serafina and Frank Voci. The Role of the Teacher Aide in
       Second Language Programs. California Association TESOL News-
       letter. Vol. 3, no. 3. Spring 1972.
       (ED 061 798)

       To investigate the role of the teacher aide in second language
       programs, the California Association of Teachers of English to
       Speakers of Other Languages (CATESOL) has issued a questionnaire to
       teacher aides in the Title VII bilingual projects in California. The
       questionnaire and conclusions drawn from replies are presented here.
       Information is provided on the attitudes, background, and activities
       of teacher aides. An increasing number of paraprofessionals can be
       found in second language programs, but the oversupply of certified
       teachers is likely to curb the need for and the growing number of
       teacher aides. (RIE)

1,461. Kreidler, Carol J. and Dorothy A. Pedtke (eds.). Teaching English
       to Speakers of Other Languages; United States: 1969. 1970.
       (ED 040 393)

       The report summarizes a number of United States activities in
       or related to the teaching of English to speakers of other languages.
       Sources of information include reports from federal, state, and city
       government agencies; articles and notices in newsletters and pro-
       fessional journals; brochures; and personal contact. Sections
       cover (1) English language teaching and teacher training in the
       United States; (2) English language teaching and teacher training
       overseas; and (3) materials, testing and research. An index of
       organizations and addresses is appended. (from the document)

1,462. Lado, Robert. Language Teaching: A Scientific Approach. New York:
       McGraw-Hill, 1964. (paper) 239pp.

       Presents a scientific approach to language teaching, including
       linguistic background, language learning, teaching techniques,
       testing, use of language laboratories and other aids, reading,
       writing, cultural content, literature, teaching machines and pro-
       grammed learning. Contains many practical suggestions for language
       teaching. (NYS bibliography)

1,463. Lado, Robert. Language Testing: The Construction and Use of
       Foreign Language Tests. New York: McGraw-Hill, (1961).

       Contains discussions of construction and use of language tests.
       Suggests types of tests and describes the theory and practice of
       refining and standardizing tests. (NYS bibliography)

1,464. Lado, Robert. Linguistics Across Cultures: Applied Linguistics for
       Language Teachers. Ann Arbor, Mich.: University of Michigan
       Press. 1957. (paper)

Uses non-technical vocabulary in demonstrating the role that
descriptive linguistics can play in a language-teaching situation.
Compares sound systems, grammatical structures, vocabulary systems
and cultural patterns. (NYS bibliography)

1,465. Lefevre, Carl A. Linguistics and the Teaching of Reading. New York:
McGraw-Hill 264pp.

Presents the fundamentals of structural linguistics, the study
of language as it is spoken. The sound system of American English
is described accurately from the smallest to the largest unit, since
speech is considered basic to all language learning. A special
chapter dealing with the musical qualities of spoken English is
quite comprehensive. (NYS bibliography)

1,466. Leo, Paul F. The Effects of Two Types of Group Counseling Upon The
Academic Achievement of Mexican-American Pupils in the Elementary
School. Ph.D. dissertation, University of the Pacific, Stock-
ton, California. Washington, D.C.: Office of Education,
Cooperative Research Program. January 1973. 143p.
(ED 059 002)

1,467. Libbish, B. (ed.) Advances in the Teaching of Modern Languages.
New York: Macmillan, 1964.

A collection of articles from British and other authors concerning advances in language teaching due primarily to the influence of the oral approach. Articles discuss methods, trends
and techniques in many nations. (NYS bibliography)

1,468. Littlejohn, Joseph E. A Handbook for Teachers and Aides of the
Choctaw Bilingual Education Program. Southeastern State
College, Durant, Oklahoma. August 1971. 26pp.
(ED 054 902)

1,469. Magee, Bettie and Others. A Description of Simulation Technique
to Develop Teacher and Counselor Empathy with the Spanish-
Speaking Student. 1972. 4pp.
(ED 065 254)

1,470. A Manual for the Teaching of American English to Spanish-Speaking
Children in Puerto Rico. Puerto Rico: Department of Education.
1949. 674pp.

1,471. Marquardt, William F. "The Training of Teachers of English as a
Second Language in the Peace Corps," Language Learning, 12:2,
(1962).

Presents concepts and skills desirable for and of importance
to elementary and secondary ESL teachers, supervisors and teacher-
trainers. (NYS bibliography)

1,472. Medina T., René. "Planeamiento de la unidád didactica en la ensenanza del inglés como idioma extranjera (Planning the Teaching Unit in the Instruction of English as a Foreign Language)." Lenguaje y Ciencias. Vol. 11, no. 2 (June 1971). pp. 44-54.
(ED 057 655)

This paper discusses the use of the teaching unit as a means for organization in English-as-a-foreign-language classes. It lists the essentials in the construction of such a unit: cultural topics, linguistic elements, time period, main objectives, instructional materials, focus, specific activities, intended results, evaluation techniques and bibliographies for students and teachers. An example of a teaching-unit plan is provided, including content material, main objectives and introductory activities. Activities for six classes are described along with optional and concluding activities for three other classes. Means for evaluation are presented; bibliographies for students and teachers are included. (RIE)

1,473. Michel, Joseph. The Preparation of the Teacher for Bilingual Education. Speech presented at Edinboro State College, Edinboro, Pennsylvania, February 4, 1972. 21p.
(ED 063 830)

This document contains a proposed curriculum for a Bachelor of Sciences program in elementary education with an academic concentration in bilingual education for Spanish-English bilinguals. A questionnaire sent to selected individuals provided ideas on some of the issues and problems discussed. The questionnaire, included with results, covers general considerations, training in linguistics, training in English and Spanish, competence in Spanish, training in culture, training in methodology, practice teaching, training in educational foundations, and training in testing. Suggestions for the teacher education curriculum are presented along with explanations. The program developed here is weighted toward the language arts. Several basic ideas for the preparation of the teacher for bilingual education are listed. (RIE)

1,474. Migrant Education Tutorial Aide Training Manual. Butte County Superintendent of Schools, Oroville, California: California State Department of Education, Sacramento. Bureau of Community Services and Migrant Education. Washington, D.C.: Office of Education. Office of Programs for the Disadvantaged. (1971). 263pp.
(ED 060 976)

Designed by California's Region II Office of Migrant Education to aid in training teacher aides working with migrant children, this manual outlines activities used in teaching by the aides. Each activity is described in terms of the concept to be taught, the tutorial skill required, standard instructional media, rationale for the media, expected learner response, and the criterion test (what the aide will actually do). Activities are provided for 33 arithmetic concepts, 68 reading concepts, and 20 English as a second language concepts for grades K-3. Also included is a list of 50 English survival words considered essential to non-English-speaking children in order that their immediate needs are met. (RIE)

1,475. Mir, Sister Margarita María. Training of Paraprofessionals in a Teacher Education Program for Puerto Rico, Ph.D. Dissertation, Columbia University. 1972.
(Dissertation Abstracts International. Vol. 33 (1972). p. 214-A).

The objectives of the study were to assess the needs of Puerto Rican schools and to investigate the idea of the paraprofessional could be used to alleviate the overcrowding and understaffing now at the critical stage in Puerto Rican schools. Paraprofessionals in four New York City schools were interviewed and observed in practice to provide data on the responsibilities and working relationships of the paraprofessional within the school system. Nineteen recommendations for the implementation of a paraprofessional program are included. (DH)

1,476. Mulvaney, Iris. "Teaching Students from Bilingual or Non-English-Speaking Homes." Audiovisual Instruction. Vol. 10 (January 1965). pp. 34-35.

1,477. McCullough, Constance M. Preparation of Textbooks in the Mother Tongue: A Guide for Those Who Evaluate Textbooks in Any Language. New Delhi, India: Department of Curriculum, Methods and Textbooks, 1965. (paper)

Although designed primarily for those who are to develop or evaluate textbooks in language, this study can serve as a guide for the use of texts already in print. Particularly relevant chapters include: "The Study of Children's Spoken Vocabulary," "Approaches to Teaching the Reading of a Language," "Controlled Vocabulary," "The Meaning Dimensions of a Word," and "Bases for Evaluation of a Language Text and Related Materials." (NYS bibliography)

1,478. McGrail, Richard F. The Relationships Between the Organizational Climate of Schools and the Personality Characteristics of Teachers: A Puerto Rican Sample. Unpublished Ph.D. Dissertation, Boston College. 1970.
(Dissertation Abstracts. 31:10 (1971). pp. 5085A-5806A).

The purpose of the study was to relate the organizational climate of schools with teacher personality characteristics. The study was conducted in the Bayamón Norte School District in Puerto Rico; the results were returned by 309 teachers from 8 secondary schools and 15 elementary schools. McGrail used the Organizational Climate Index (OCI) developed by Stern and Steinhoff to establish the climate measures and the Sixteen Personality Factor Questionnaire (16 PF) developed by Cattell to assess the teachers' personality

characteristics. Analysis of the data indicated 10 relationships
which were significantly correlated at all 3 levels of analysis:
1. Individual teachers compared on OCI and 16 PF
2. Correlation of school measures for OCI and individual
   teacher scores on 16 PF
3. Comparison of various schools in terms of mean scores for
   each school of all teachers in given school on OCI and 16 PF.

Only 3 of the 6 OCI factors were involved: Fantasy Climate,
Orderliness, and Fearful Climate; Four 16 PF factors were found to
be significantly correlated with Fantasy Climate: Assertive,
Happy-go-lucky, Venturesome, and Extraversion. The 16 PF factors
called Humble, Tenderminded, and Tenderminded Emotionality were
significantly related with both Orderliness and Fearful Climate
of all 3 levels. Further analysis showed that the elementary
school teachers in the sample saw their schools as being more
Supportive, Orderly, Affective, and Fearful than did Secondary
school teachers. Female teachers, more than male teachers, perceived their schools as Orderly and Fearful; and private school
teachers rated their schools higher than did the public school
teachers on all 6 factors, with 4 showing a significant difference:
Supportive, Orderliness, Affective and Fearful. (DH)

1,479.  McIntosh, Lois. _How to Teach English Grammar_, 1967. 19pp.
        (ED 012 438)

        Presents a discussion of the basic tenets of teaching English
grammar to non-native speakers, as followed in the ESL program at
UCLA. The introduction of grammar points to be practiced and the
generalization process which follows are described in non-technical
language. Various types of drills illustrate implementation of the
grammar lesson. Particular importance is given to the age levels
of the students as affecting the type of grammar presentation. (RIE)

1,480.  McRae, Susan. _Relations Between Teacher Bilingualism in Spanish and_
        _English and Attitudes Toward a Bilingual Television Program_.
        Washington, D.C. Office of Education. August 1972.
        (ED 066 033)

1,481.  Naun, Robert J. _Comparison of Group Counseling Approaches with_
        _Puerto Rican Boys in an Inner City High School_. Ph.D. Disserta-
        tion, Fordham University. 1971.
        (_Dissertation Abstracts International_: (August 1971) Vol. 32
        (2-A). p 742-743).

        The purpose of this study was to ascertain if different approaches
to group counseling would have different effects on 31 ninth and tenth
grade Puerto Rican boys from an inner city high school. Ss were
randomly assigned to three groups: 1) a group receiving interventionist
counseling based upon the theory of Glasser's Reality Therapy, 2) a
group receiving non-interventionist counseling based upon Rogers'

theory, and 3) a group receiving no counseling at all.  In order to
compare the effects of the different approaches, all Ss were administered the Occupational Aspiration Scale (O.A.S.) at the beginning and at the end of the group counseling sessions.  For
additional data, each of the S's teachers was asked to rate the
subject as he was at the beginning of the term and at the end;
grade averages, attendance, lateness percentages and number of disciplinary referrals were computed for each Ss.  Results of the
analysis of the data indicate that the different approaches to
group counseling employed in this study did not produce any significant changes in occupational aspiration level as measured by the
O.A.S. or in school or teacher ratings.  When each of the experimental groups was compared to the control group no significant
difference was found in occupational aspiration level or school
behavior.  (DH)

1,482.   New York City, Board of Education.  Teaching English as a New
            Language to Adults.  Curriculum Bulletin: 1963-64.  Series
            No. 5.  New York: New York Superintendent of Schools. 1964.
            180pp.

         A presentation of guiding principles and methods for teaching
beginners through advanced students with references for teachers.

1,483.   Ney, James W.  "The Oral Approach:  A Reappraisal," Language
            Learning, 18:1 and 2, (June, 1968).

         Discusses criticisms of audio-lingual approach by psychologists
and transformational linguists, discriminating between those that
are justified and those which are not.  Suggests that many objectives
have been anticipated by language teachers who have not been too
doctrinaire.  (NYS bibliography)

1,484.   Ney, James W.  "Predator or Pedagogue?:  The Teacher of the Bilingual
            Child."  English Record, 21:4 (April, 1971). pp. 12-18.
            (ED 053 602)

         Cultural factors should be taken into consideration in a bilingual
education program.  The cultural background of students learning
English as a second language should not be regarded inferior.  A
realistic analysis of a student's language capability must be made so
that his language-learning problems can be recognized and solved as
much as possible.  The student must be able to cope with the English
used  in the classroom, and teaching materials must be developed to
handle those problems.  Instruments of measurement must be used to
determine the linguistic capability of the student.  (RIE)

1,485.   Pascual, Henry W. ed.  Reading Strategies for New Mexico in the 70's
            Resource Guide No. 2.  January 1972. 29p.
            (ED 061 022)

The three papers in this resource guide are oriented to the needs of Spanish-surnamed and Indian children. The first paper points out three concerns to be examined before selecting reading materials: (1) the population for whom selection is planned, (2) criteria emphasizing children's needs, and (3) apparent trends in reading instruction. The second paper stresses teacher-student interaction, diagnostic teaching, and classroom management in the elementary school. The author feels that standardized tests, especially their norms should not be used with minority groups, but that the informal reading inventory is best for these children. The third paper observes that schools are serving the interests of the dominant social forces, and that while unable to reform schools, teachers can humanize their classrooms by examining and revising certain beliefs which can lead to anti-humanistic school practices. References are included. (RIE

1,486. Past, Ray et al. Bilingualism - From the Viewpoint of Recruitment and Preparation of Bilingual Teachers. 1966. 19pp. (ED 018 297)

1,487. Paulston, Christina Bratt. "The Sequencing of Structural Pattern Drills", TESOL Quarterly. 5:3 (September, 1971). pp. 197-208.

This article is an attempt to re-examine the role and function of structural pattern drills in language learning. The first part of the paper seeks to examine the relevant literature pertaining to drills in order to (1) bring together some of the major references for examining areas of concord and disagreement and (2) to consider the implications for language teaching. The second part of the paper proposes a theoretical classification of structural pattern drills, incorporating the implications found relevant, in order to allow a sequencing of drills which will provide a more efficient working model for the classroom. (from article)

1,488. Pickett, G.D. "A Comparison of Translation and Blank-Filling as Testing Techniques," English Language Teaching, 23:1 (October, 1968).

Points out the advantage of translating over slotfilling as a testing technique. (NYS bibliography)

1,489. Politzer, Robert L. "Toward Psycholinguistic Models of Language Instruction." TESOL Quarterly. 2:3 (September, 1968).

Discusses the congruence and clash of psychological and pedagogical principles in language teaching and the use of linguistic and psychological principles as tools in the analysis of the teaching process. Analyzes typical lessons. (NYS bibliography)

1,490. Potts, Alfred M. "Teaching the 'Big City' to the Migrant Child." Audiovisual Instruction. Vol. 10 (January 1965). pp. 37-38.

302

Stresses the importance of audio-visual/non-verbal materials
for the teacher of migrant "bilingual" children. Since verbal
competence is limited at the outset, "seeing things" will contribute
considerably to the meaningfulness of things, ideas and words, and
therefore aid in language association and acquisition. (DH)

1,491. Puerto Rican Culture as it Affects Puerto Rican Children in Chicago
Classrooms. Chicago: Chicago Board of Education. 1970. 20pp.
(ED 052 277)

Designed to develop better understanding and greater appreciation between the Puerto Rican child who enrolls in the Chicago public
schools and his classroom teacher. Presents those aspects of the
culture which would be likely to affect the child's classroom behavior. It is considered that an informed teacher may be able to
assist the bicultural child to a considerable degree. (RIE revised)

1,492. Puerto Rican Forum, Inc. Instructor's Curriculum Guide; Building
Services Personnel. New York: Puerto Rican Forum, Inc. 1970.
83pp.
(ED 038 645)

This B.O.L.T. curriculum guide based on an audiolingual method
of language training, consists of 20 lessons representing 50-100
hours of classroom instruction including structured "Shop Talk",
visits by the supervisors, tours of the job sites, actual on-the-
job sessions emphasizing the vocabulary and/or structures related
to a particular job skill, and post course testing. Directed to
hospital-building services personnel, the materials in this guide
may be adapted to suit other job areas by changing pertinent vocabulary and reading materials. (RIE abridged)

1,493. "The Puerto Ricans in New York City: Background Information for
Teachers." Curriculum and Materials. 18:3 (Spring, 1956).
pp. 6-7.

1,494. Richards, I.A. and Christine Gibson. Techniques of Language Control.
Rowley, Massachusetts: Newbury House Publishers. 1971. $5.95.

Control of vocabulary and structure is widely held to be a
prime influence on language learning. In this book the authors
describe their tested approach to limiting vocabulary and syntax
in the teaching of English. Their techniques of language control
are introduced through Every Man's English, a new list of high
utility words for learning English and for clarity of expression.
(catalog)

1,495. Richards, Jack C. and John W. Oller (eds.). Language Learning and
Language Teaching: Psycholinguistic Perspectives for the
Teacher of ESL. Rowley, Massachusetts: Newbury House Publishers.
July, 1972. $4.95.

303

An anthology which surveys the psychology of second language
learning. Its purpose is to provide practicing and student teachers
with a balanced introduction which can be applied to classroom
teaching, which can be used to assess new trends as they develop,
and which can help develop more individualized ways of dealing with
learners at all levels. (catalog)

1,496.  Rivers, Wilga M.  The Psychologist and the Foreign-Language Teachers.
Chicago: University of Chicago Press, 1964.

A critical appraisal of foreign language teaching today (in
particular the audio-lingual method) in the light of current psychology and theories of learning. The book is written for the
classroom teacher and concentrates on the high school level, with
most examples from French. Includes recommendations for the
teacher and an appendix describing learning theories. (NYS
bibliography)

1,497.  Rivers, Wilga M.  Speaking in Many Tongues: Essays in Foreign
Language Learning. Rowley, Massachusetts. 1972. $3.95.

Considers problems such as student dissatisfaction with
structural language courses, motivation difficulties, individual
differences in means and goals of language learning, etc. and
makes concrete proposals towards solving them. Guidelines are
established for development and evaluation of language programs,
new models of language teaching activities presented, and psychological insights discussed that will assist those involved in language
teaching in assessing its meaning for today's students. (catalog)

1,498.  Rivers, Wilga M.  Teaching Foreign Language Skills.  Chicago:
University of Chicago Press, 1968. 403pp.

Includes Chapters on objectives and methods, the audio-lingual
method, the place of grammar, construction of grammatical drills
and exercises, teaching sounds, listening comprehension, speaking
and reading skills, cultural understanding, testing, and language
laboratories. "Areas of Controversy" section ends each chapter.
(NYS bibliography revised)

1,499.  Rodríguez-Bou, Ismael, et al.  "Problemas de lectura y lengua en
Puerto Rico."  Publicaciones Pedagógicas.  Series 2, No. 6.
Río Piedras: Universidad de Puerto Rico.

Spanish-language handbook on the problems of reading and
language in Puerto Rico. The appendices contain reports by United
States officials in English which could be very informative to the
teacher of ESL. (from Sánchez)

1,500.  Roscoe, Carole.  "Developing Instructional Materials for a Bilingual
Program."  TESOL Quarterly. Vol. 6, No. 2 (June 1972). 163-166 pp.
(EJ 060 718)

1,501. Rosen, Carl L. and Phillip D. Ortego. Problems and Strategies in Teaching the Language Arts to Spanish-Speaking Mexican-American Children. ERIC Rural Education Clearinghouse, New Mexico State University, Box 3-AP, University Park Branch, Las Cruces, New Mexico, 88001.

1,502. Rosen, Carl L. and Phillip D. Ortega. "Resources: Teaching Spanish-Speaking Children." Reading Teacher. 25:1 (October 1971). pp. 11-13.

Annotated Bibliography.

1,503. Saunders, Jack. Blueprint Potential for Cooperative Teacher Education Preparation: Utilizing the Talented Mexican-American. Las Cruces, New Mexico: ERIC Clearinghouse on Rural Education. 1969.

1,504. Selected Articles from Language Learning: Series I, English as a Foreign Language. Ann Arbor, Michigan: Research Club in Language Learning, (1953). (paper)

Has sections on language learning, language teaching, grammar, pronunciation, vocabulary and testing. The articles represent practical applications of the principles of structural linguistics. (NYS bibliography)

1,505. Selected Articles from Language Learning: Series 2, Theory and Practice in English as a Foreign Language. Ann Arbor, Michigan: Research Club in Language Learning, (1963) (paper)

Has sections on teacher education, techniques, pronunciation, vocabulary, grammar, reading and composition. The articles reflect contemporary linguistic theories. (NYS bibliography)

1,506. Sharpe, Sarah Ellen. A Comparative Analysis Between the Teaching of a Native Language and a Foreign Language Literature. M.A. thesis, University of Texas at Austin. August 1971. 94p. (ED 060 769)

1,507. Slager, William. "The Foreign Student and the Immigrant - Their Different Problems as Students of English." Language Learning. 6:3 and 4 (1956).

Shows implications for differing language pedagogy and makes specific recommendations based on these differences. (NYS bibliography)

1,508. Smith, Larry E. "Don't Teach - Let Them Learn," TESOL Quarterly, 5:2 (June, 1971), pp. 149-151.

People have different learning styles, ability levels, threshold of boredom, interests, and motivation. These are some of the variables the language teacher must keep in mind as he faces his class. The idea of trying to meet each person's learning style has been considered an impossible goal, and homogeneous grouping has become the substitute. Individualization is not a new learning concept, yet it is rarely found in the language classroom. This paper describes an attempt to set up an environment for learning so flexible that any person at any level of proficiency with an interest in any of the language skills may be successful in learning. It has been tried at the East-West Center on the University of Hawaii campus and in Bahgkok, Thailand with encouraging results. (From the article)

1,509. "Some Aspects of Teaching Languages in the Grades in the Southwest." Hispania. Vol. 38 (May 1940) pp. 171-174.

1,510. Southwestern Cooperative Educational Laboratory. Cross Cultural Communication Program. Albuquerque: SWCEL.

Aids the teacher in communicating with adults with children from minority backgrounds. It helps the teacher understand and accept standards, values, and behaviors differing from his own so culturally relevant materials will have more meaning in the classroom. The training is directed toward developing verbal and non-verbal communication skills. Instructional techniques include lecture, simulation, and role playing. Media is an integral ingredient and is used to build the teacher's awareness of cultural differences as well as the importance of verbal and non-verbal communication. (catalog)

1,511. Southwestern Cooperative Educational Laboratory. Systems Approach to Lesson Planning. Albuquerque: SWCEL.

Package provides teachers with training on techniques for converting written objectives to lesson plans through utilization of the teaching systems matrix. The matrix is a record-keeping tool by which the teacher can record planned entry conditions, teaching procedures, and learner outcomes as well as what actually happens. In this way, the teacher can decide what to do if the actual outcomes do not meet those that are planned.
Package price: $195.00 (catalog)

1,512. Stack, Edward M. The Language Laboratory and Modern Language Teaching. New York: Oxford University Press, (1966).

Treats techniques for the classroom and the laboratory. Also contains material about testing. Problems and exercises are given throughout. (NYS bibliography)

1,513. Steeves, Roy W. et al. Handbook for Teachers of English as a Second Language: Americanization-literacy. 2nd rev. ed. Sacramento, California: California State Department of Education. 1969. 85pp.

1,514.  Stevick, Earl W. <u>Helping People Learn English</u>. New York: Abington
        Press. 1957.

        Slanted to the non-professional teacher. Attempts to touch on
        all related techniques, backgrounds and problems. (Hefferman-Cabrera)

1,515.  Stevick, Earl. <u>A Workbook in Language Teaching: With Special</u>
        <u>Reference to English as a Foreign Language</u>. Nashville, Tennessee:
        Abington Press, 1963 (paper) 127pp.

        For initial training of new language teachers and for inservice
        use by experienced teachers. Treats three selected topics: English
        phonology, basic types of drills, and fundamentals of grammar.
        Frequent exercises and discussion questions assist user in acquiring
        skills and in keeping check on his own progress. (NYS bibliography)

1,516.  Thonis, Eleanor Wall. <u>Teaching Reading to Non-English Speakers</u>. New
        York: Collier-Macmillan. 1970. 270pp.

        A broad analysis of the reading process and of the problems
        involved in the teaching of reading, beginning from the viewpont of
        reading in the vernacular, then turning to reading in a second
        language. (CAL bibliography)

1,517.  Tireman, L.S. <u>Teaching Spanish-Speaking Children</u>. Albuquerque:
        University of New Mexico Press, revised. 1951. 252pp.

1,518.  Titone, Renzo. "Guidelines for Teaching a Second Language in Its
        Own Environment." <u>Modern Language Journal</u>. Vol. 52 (1969).
        pp. 306-309.

1,519.  Turner, H.C. <u>Team Teaching, Employing a Variety of Methods for</u>
        <u>Spanish/Anglo-American Integration. Title IV, 1969-70. Final</u>
        <u>Report</u>. Las Vegas City Schools, New Mexico. Washington, D.C.:
        Office of Education. 1970. 52pp.
        (ED 056 130)

1,520.  Ulibarrí, Mari-Luci. <u>Pensamientos Sobre (Thoughts On) Teaching</u>
        <u>English as a Second Language</u>. New Mexico University, Albuquerque.
        College of Education. Washington, D.C.: Office of Education.
        1969. 26p.
        (ED 060 703)

1,521.  Ulibarrí, Horacio. <u>Teacher Awareness of Sociocultural Differences in</u>
        <u>Multicultural Classrooms</u>. The University of New Mexico Graduate
        School, Albuquerque. 1959.

        Teachers and administrators need to be aware of sociocultural
        differences as they affect the bilingual. Ulibarri's study showed a
        general lack of teacher sensitivity toward sociocultural differences.

1,522. Valdman, Albert. (ed.). <u>Trends in Language Teaching</u>. New York: McGraw-Hill, (paper).

Includes articles, many hitherto unprinted, in the areas of linguistics, programmed instruction, language laboratory technology, psychology, literature, etc., related to current language teaching. (NYS bibliography)

1,523. Varena-Cartada, Laudalina Fernández. <u>Some Procedures for Using Pictures in Teaching English as a Second Language</u>. Unpublished Ph.D. Dissertation, Teacher's College, Columbia University. 1956.

1,524. Witherspoon, Paul. "A Comparison of the Problems of Certain Anglo and Latin-American Junior High School Students." <u>Journal of Educational Research</u>. 53:8 (April, 1960). pp. 295-299.

Witherspoon found a general lack of teacher sensitivity toward sociocultural differences of the bilingual. There are really more likenesses than differences between Anglos and bilinguals; but teachers, counselors and administrators need to be aware of the main problems involved in the differences. (NYS bibliography)

1,525. Woolsey, A.W. "What Are We Doing for the Spanish-Speaking Students?" <u>Hispania</u>. vol. 44 (March 1961). pp. 119-123.

The author addresses himself to the problem of teaching a Spanish class which has Spanish-speaking students. His first general point is that Spanish-speaking students should have the benefits of bilingualism emphasized, as well as pride in their native language. He also gives many suggestions for teaching Spanish-speaking students to write Spanish, and explains how these will also benefit English-speaking students in the Spanish class. (ECK)

III.  THE PUERTO RICAN EXPERIENCE ON THE MAINLAND

A. General Discussions of the Topic

1,526. Abrams, Charles. "How to Remedy Our 'Puerto Rican Problem'."
       Commentary. 19:2 (February, 1955). pp. 120-127.

1,527. Abrams, Charles. "New York's New Slums." New Leader. (January
       1956). pp. 20-23.

1,528. Adamic, Louis. From Many Lands. New York: Harper and Brothers.
       1940. 350pp.

1,529. Adamic, Louis. A Nation of Nations. New York: Harper and Brothers.
       1944.

1,530. Alcalá, Roberto de. "Nueva York - Ciudad Hispana." Temos.
       (February, 1953). pp. 7-8.

1,531. Alvarado. M.B. "Juan Gallo." Inferno. (August, 1968).

       Article about David Sánchez, 19 year old leader of the Los
       Angeles Brown Berets.

1,532. Arnold, Elliott. Time of the Gringo. New York: Knopf. 1953. 612pp.

1,533. Aumann, Jon and Others. The Chicano Addict: An Analysis of Factors
       Influencing Rehabilitation in a Treatment and Prevention Program.
       Phoenix, Arizona: Valle Del Sol, Inc. Bethesda, Maryland:
       National Institute of Mental Health. (1972). 53p.
       (ED 064 007)

1,534. Bates, Barbara. "New York and Puerto Ricans." Survey. Vol. 85
       (September 1949). p. 487.

1,535. Berlant, Rose. "¿Cómo has pasado el domingo?" New York City Education.
       (Winter, 1969).

1,536. Beshoar, Barron B. "Report from the Mountain States." Common Ground.
       Vol. 4 (Spring, 1944). pp. 23-30.

1,537. Bienvenidos A Paterson, Amigos! Paterson, New Jersey: Paterson
       Inter-group Council. 1958.

1,538. Blair, W.C. "Spanish-Speaking Minorities in a Utah Mining Town."
       Journal of Social Issues. No. 1 (1952). p. 409.

1,539. Bogardus, Emory S. The Mexicans in the United States. Los Angeles:
       University of California Press. 1934.

1,540. Bone, Bob. (Series of eight articles on Puerto Ricans in Middletown,
       New York). Middletown Daily Record. March 9-13. 16-18. 1959.

1,541. Boroff, David. "Jews and Puerto Ricans." Congress Weekly. (American Jewish Congress). Vol. 24 (April 15, 1957). 10-13pp.

1,542. Bourne, Dorothy D. and James R. Bourne. Thirty Years of Change in Puerto Rico. New York: Prager, 1966.

1,543. Bowman, Leroy. "The Puerto Ricans in America." Humanist. Vol. 22 (January/February 1962). pp. 27-29.

1,544. Braestrup, Peter. "New York's Puerto Ricans." New York Herald Tribune. October 16-18, 20, 21, 1957. (series of five articles).

1,545. Brooks, Tom. "The Puerto Rican Story." Industrial Bulletin. Vol. 39 (June 1960). pp. 6-12.

1,546. Brown, Francis J. and Joseph S. Roucek. One America: The History and Contributions and Present Problems of Our Racial and National Minorities. New York: Prentice-Hall. 1946.

1,547. Browning, Frank. "From Rumble to Revolution: The Young Lords." Ramparts. October 1970.

1,548. Burma, John H. Puerto Ricans in the United States. Chicago: Quadrangle. 1961.

1,549. Burma, John. Spanish Speaking Groups in the United States. Durham, North Carolina: Duke University Press. 1954.

1,550. Burnham, David and Sophy Burnham. "El Barrio's Worst Block is Not All Bad." New York Times Magazines. (January, 1969).

Discusses one block in Spanish Harlem.

1,551. Calitri, Charles J. "A Puerto Rican Story." American Unity. 15:1 (September-October, 1956). pp. 19-24.

1,552. Cannon, Antoinette. "The Puerto Ricans." Interpreter Releases. 24:37 (August 28, 1947). pp. 296-304.

1,553. Caplovitz, David, et al. The Poor Pay More. Free Press, 1963.

1,554. Celso Barbosa, José. Problema de Razas. San Juan: Biblioteca de Autores Puertorriqueños, 1942.

1,555. Chenault, Lawrence R. The Puerto Rican Migrant in New York City. New York: Columbia University. 1938. 190pp.

This book was one of the first to be published on the massive Puerto Rican migration to New York City. The author discusses the conditions on the island first, in order to give the reader an understanding of the early migrants' motivations for coming to New York. The bulk of the book deals with the problems the migrants faced upon

their arrival on the mainland: language barrier, substandard
housing, un-and underemployment, ill health, and social disorgan-
ization. The book was reissued in 1970 with a foreword by Francesco
Cordasco (Russell and Russell, 1970). (DH)

1,556. "Chicago's Puerto Ricans." New Republic. Vol. 130 (February 22, 1954).
pp. 3-4.

1,557. "Cívicas y Culturales: Reunión Cívica." El Diario de Nueva York.
June 2, 1952. p. 5.

1,558. Clark, Rosemarie. "New York and the Puerto Rican 'Problem'."
UNESCO Features. January 12, 1959. pp. 4-6.

1,559. Clark, Victor S. Puerto Rico and Its Problems. Washington, D.C.:
The Brookings Institution, 1930.

1,560. Clarke, Blake. "The Puerto Rican Problem in New York." Readers
Digest. Vol. 62 (February 1953). pp. 61-65.

1,561. Cole, Stewart G. and Mildred W. Cole. Minorities and the American
Promise, the Conflict of Principle and Practice. New York:
Harper. 1954. 319pp. Bureau for Intercultural Education,
Publication No. 10 in the series, "Problems of Race and
Culture in American Education."

1,562. Colman, Hilda. Girl from Puerto Rico. New York: William Myra. 1961.

1,563. Colón, Jesús. A Puerto Rican in New York and Other Sketches. New
York: Mainstream. 1961.

1,564. Coon, Barlette E. A Comparative Study of the American and Mexican
Children in the 'Big Bend' Area for 1935-1936. Unpublished
Master's thesis, University of Texas. 1936.

1,565. Cordasco, F. "Studies in the Disenfranchised: The Puerto Rican
Child." Psychiatric Spectator. Vol. 3 (November, 1966). 3-4pp.

1,566. Cotto-Thorner, Guillermo. Trópico en Manhattan. San Juan:
Editorial Occidente. 1951.

1,567. Crawford, W. Rex. "The Latin-American in Wartime United States."
pp. 123-131 in Minority People in a Nation at War. American
Academy of Political and Social Science, the Annals. September
1942. 276pp.

1,568. "Cree Jansen que el gobierno federal y el estatal deben ayudar a
boricuas." La Prensa. (February 1, 1954).

1,569. ¿Cuales son sus Derechos Civiles en Connecticut? Bridgeport,
Connecticut: Bridgeport Inter-group Council. (n.d.)

1,570. Denny, M.C. "Chicago Meets San Juan." Instructor. Vol. 76.
(February, 1967). pp. 38-39.

1,571. "De Puerto Rico al Universo." Life. (Spanish Ed.). Vol. 22
(December 9, 1963). pp. 66-67.

1,572. DeRowan, Josefina. "New York's Latin Quarter; The Story of Our
Little-Known Fellow Americans from Puerto Rico Who Live in
Manhattan." InterAmerican. Vol. 5 (January 1946). pp. 10-13.

1,573. Díaz, Eileen. "A Puerto Rican in New York." Dissent. 8:3
(Summer, 1961). pp. 383-385.

1,574. Directorio de Chicago para Nuevos Vecinos. Chicago: Comision de
Relaciones Humanas y Comite del Alcalde pro Nuevos Residentes.
1959.

1,575. "Division Lesson: Problems of Chicago's Puerto Rican Community."
Time. Vol. 87 (June 24, 1966). pp. 30-31.

1,576. Dodson, Dan W. Between Hell's Kitchen and San Juan Hill. New York:
Center for Human Relations, New York University. 1952.

1,577. Dossick, Jesse J. Doctoral Research on Puerto Rico and Puerto
Ricans. New York: New York University, School of Education.
1967.

1,578. Doviak, Joan. Fourteen Beautiful People. Washington, D.C.:
Educational Systems Corp. 1970. 69pp.
(ED 065 220)

    Brief biographies are given of 14 Mexican Americans who are
representative of the accomplishments of the Mexican American
community in the United States in such areas as sports, politics,
labor, and entertainment. (RIE abridged)

1,579. Elman, R.M. "Puerto Ricans." Commonwealth. Vol. 83 (January 7,
1966). pp. 405-408.

1,580. El Ojo, Chicano Newsletter. Washington, D.C.: Montal Systems,
Incorporated, monthly, $1.50/year.

    Proposes to "...direct itself to informing Chicanos throughout
Aztlán of activities affecting Chicano programs." Includes areas
such as: (1) curriculum development, (2) program actions, (3)
fellowships and financial assistance, (4) legislation, (5) publications, (6) employment, and (7) items of general interest that will
aid Chicano education. (Proyecto Leer Bulletin)

1,581. The Emerging Puerto Rican Community of New York. New York: New
York Chapter of the Public Relations Society of America.
October 22, 1963.

1,582. Fishman, Joshua and Heriberto Casiano. "Puerto Ricans in Our Press."
The Modern Language Journal, March 1969. pp. 157-162.

The purpose of the study was to investigate the treatment of
Puerto Ricans in four New York City daily newspapers, two published
in English and two in Spanish. Content analyses during a six-month
period showed that the English newspapers had little interest in
Puerto Ricans either before or after the major flare-up in Spanish
Harlem. In comparison with the Spanish dailies, the English dailies
were more concerned with Puerto Rican/Anglo relations, referred more
often to the Spanish Language (generally for identification purposes)
attributed negative traits to the Puerto Ricans more often than
positive traits, frequently mentioned Blacks and Puerto Ricans together as problem populations, discussed their needs or problems
rather than solutions or remedial measures that could be taken to
counter the problems. In the Spanish press there was some indication
of Puerto Rican/Black tension, primarily in terms of competition for
anti-poverty funds and Puerto Rican reluctance to being classified
with Blacks in most Anglo-American references. (DH)

1,583. Fitzpatrick, J.P. "Helping the Mainland." _Time._ Vol. 74 (October
26, 1956). p. 34.

1,584. Fitzpatrick, J.P. "Puerto Rican Story." _America._ (September 3, 1960).

1,585. Fox, Rosa Rudami. "Puerto Ricans in Your Town." _American Unity._
11:5 (May-June, 1953). pp. 3-8.

1,586. Furts, Philip W. _Puerto Ricans in New York City._ Puerto Rican
Social Services, Inc. New York City. (March 1963).

1,587. Galarza, E.; H. Gallegos, and J. Samora. _Mexican-Americans in the
Southwest._ Goleta, California: Kimberley Press. 1969.

1,588. Galíndes-Suárez, Jesús. _Puerto Rico en Nueva York: Aspectos de la
vida en el Harlem Hispano._ New York: Cuadernos Americanos. 1956.

1,589. Glazer, Nathan. "New York's Puerto Ricans." _Commentary._ Vol. 26
(December 1958). pp. 469-478.

1,590. Gonzáles, R. _Yo soy Joaquín._ Denver, Colorado: Crusade for
Justice. 1967.

1,591. Gosnell, Patria Arán. _The Puerto Ricans in New York City._ Unpublished Ph.D. Dissertation, New York University. 1945.

1,592. Grebler, Leo; Joan Moore, and Ralph Guzman. _The Mexican-American
People._ New York: The Free Press. 1970.

1,593. Grebler, Leo and Others. _The Mexican-American People: The Nation's
Second Largest Minority._ Santa Barbara, California: La Causa
Publications. 1970. 777pp.
(ED 054 901)

1,594. Gruber, Ruth. "E. 110th Street Isn't the Universe: The Puerto Rican
in New York." _New York Herald Tribune._ December 6, 1958.

315

1,595. "Guidance is Asked for Puerto Ricans." The New York Times.
(October 28, 1947).

1,596. Haddox, John. Los Chicanos: An Awakening People. Southwestern
Studies, Monograph No. 28. El Paso, Texas: Texas Western
Press. 1970. 44pp.
(ED 062 054)

1,597. Hammer, Richard. "Report from a Spanish Harlem'Fortress'." New
York Times Magazine. January 5, 1964. pp. 22, 32.

1,598. Hamil, P. "Coming of Age in Nueva York." New York. Vol. 2
(November 24, 1969). pp. 37-47.

1,599. Handlin, Oscar. The American People in the Twentieth Century.
Cambridge: Harvard University Press. 1954. 244pp.

1,600. Handlin, Oscar. The Newcomers, Negroes and Puerto Ricans in a
Changing Metropolis. New York: Doubleday, 1962. 177pp.

1,601. Harrington, Janette T. "Puerto Rico: Bridge Between the Americas."
Presbyterian Life. Vol. 17 (February 1964). pp. 14-21.

1,602. Hartford Y Usted: Un Guía. Hartford, Connecticut: Greater Hartford
Council of Churches. (n.d.)

1,603. Hasting, W.F. "Our Puerto Rican Friends." Christian Century.
Vol. 67 (December 20, 1950). p. 1525.

1,604. Haus, W.H. Puerto Ricans in New York City. Cambridge, Massachusetts:
Harvard University. 1959.

1,605. Helm, June, ed. Spanish Speaking People in the United States.
Seattle: University of Washington Press. 1969.

1,606. Hernández, J. "El Centro en Jersey City." America. Vol. 102
(November 14, 1959). pp. 199.

1,607. Horgan, P. Conquistadores in North America. New York: Macmillan.
1963.

1,608. Howard, John R. and Others. Awakening Minorities: American Indians,
Mexican Americans, Puerto Ricans. Chicago, Illinois: Aldine
Publishing Company. 1970. 189pp.
(ED 054 909)

As one in a series of books published by "Trans-action" magazine
which deals with social changes such as organizational life-styles,
concepts of human ability and intelligence, changing patterns of
norms and morals, and the relationship of social conditions to physical
and biological environments, this book contains five essays on the
American Indians, two on Mexican Americans, and four on Puerto Ricans.
(RIE)

1,609. Imse, Thomas P. _Puerto Ricans in Buffalo_. City of Buffalo. Board of Community Relations, 1961.

1,610. Jahn, A.V. "Spanish Harlem." _Today's Health_. Vol. 31 (February 1953). pp. 30-34.

1,611. Jones, Robert C. _Mexicans in the United States: A Bibliography_. Washington, D.C.: Pan American Union, Division of Labor and Social Information. Bibliography Series No. 27. 1942. supplement to Bogardus, 1929.

1,612. Klein, Woody. _Let in the Sun._ New York. 1963. an account of the "barrio" communities.

1,613. _Know Your Fellow American Citizens from Puerto Rico_. Washington, D.C. Office of the Government of Puerto Rico (n.d.)

1,614. Koch, J.E. "Puerto Ricans Come to Youngstown." _Commonweal_. Vol. 59 (October 8, 1953). pp. 9-11.

1,615. Lelyveld, J. "Se Habla Espanol?" _New York Times Magazine_. (June 14, 1964). pp. 65-68.

1,616. Lewis, Oscar. "In New York You Get Swallowed by a Horse." _Commentary_. Vol. 38 (November 1964). pp. 69-73.

1,617. Lockett, Edward B. _The Puerto Rican Problem._ New York: Exposition Press, 1964.

1,618. Loeffler, H.W. "San Antonio's Mexican Child." _Texas Outlook_. Vol. 29 (March 1945) p. 28.

1,619. Machiran Sague, Consuelo. _El Folklore de Cuba: Primera Parte (The Folklore of Cuba: Part I)_. Pennsylvania State Modern Language Association. Speech presented at the Pennsylvania State Modern Language Association Conference, Gannon College, Erie, Pennsylvania. October 1970. 1971. 5p. (ED 058 812)

1,620. Manuel, Herschel T. "The Mexican Population of Texas." _Southwest Review_. Vol. 17 (1932) pp. 290-302.

1,621. Marden, Charles F. _Minorities in American Society_. New York: American Book Company. 1952. 493pp.

1,622. Massimine, E. Virginia. "The Puerto Rican Citizen of New York." _The Journal of Pi-Lamda Theta_ (New York University). (April, 1950). p.2.

1,623. Mayerson, C. _Two Blocks Apart_. New York: Holt, Rinehart and Winston. 1965.

1,624. Mayor's Advisory Committee on Puerto Rican Affairs in New York City, Sub-Committee on Education, Recreation and Parks. The Puerto Rican Pupils in the Public Schools of New York City: A Survey of Elementary and Junior High Schools. New York. 1951. 102pp.

1,625. Meier, Matt S. and Feliciano Rivera. The Chicanos: A History of Mexican Americans. American Century Series. New York: Hill and Wang. 1972. 302pp.
(ED 065 231)

1,626. Mexican-American and Public Aid Recipients Project (MAPAR). Final Report. Washington, D.C.: Office of Education (DHEW). November 1969. 65p.
(ED 061 476)

1,627. Meyerson, Michael. "Puerto Rico: Out Backyard Colony." Ramparts (June 1970).

1,628. Midcentury Pioneers and Protestants. A Survey Report. Protestant Council of the City of New York, (1954).

   Discusses the religious affiliations of the Puerto Ricans in New York City. (DH)

1,629. Mills, C. Wright. Puerto Ricans in New York. New York: Harper and Row. 1950.

1,630. Mills, C. Wright et al. The Puerto Rican Journey. New York: Harper and Row. 1950. 238pp.

1,631. Mirkin, Sydney. "The Puerto Rican Problem." Daily News. January 5, 1955. pp. 3, 29.

1,632. Mirkin, Sydney. "The Puerto Rican Problem: Island Fights for Better Living." Daily News. January 5, 1955. pp. 2, 32.

1,633. Mirkin, Sydney. "The Puerto Rican Problem: They Change Her, Island Feels." Daily News. January 4, 1955. pp. 3, 24.

1,634. Monserrat, Joseph. "Industry and Community--A Profitable Partnership." Journal of Educational Sociology. Vol. 27 (December 1953). pp. 171-181.

1,635. Monserrat, Joseph. "Literacy Tests: Puerto Rican Perspective." New York Herald Tribune Magazine. October 13, 1963. pp. 9-10.

1,636. Monserrat, Joseph. Puerto Ricans in New York City. New York: Migration Division, Commonwealth of Puerto Rico. 1967.

1,637. Montez, Phillip. "Will the Real Mexican-American Please Stand Up?" Integrated Education. 8:3 (May-June, 1970). pp. 43-49.

1,638. Moore, Joan W. and Alfredo Cuellar. Mexican Americans. Ethnic Groups in American Life Series. Englewood Cliffs, New Jersey: Prentice-Hall, Inc. 1970. 174p.
(ED 063 994)

1,639. Moquin, Wayne, and Charles Van Doren, eds. A Documentary History of the Mexican Americans. New York, New York: Praeger Publishers. 1971. 399pp.
(ED 059 821)

A documentary history of the Mexican Americans from 1536 to 1970 is presented in this book consisting of 65 documents arranged chronologically and divided into five main chapters that deal with the periods of (1) the Spanish rule, (2) Mexico's rule over the Southwest, (3) the Anglo American take-over of the Southwest and its integration into the society and economy of the United States, (4) the Mexican immigration to the United States during 1911-1939 and (5) the reawakening of La Raza from 1940 to 1970. (RIE)

1,640. Moreno; Joseph A. Clark. "A Bibliography of Bibliographies Relating to Studies of Mexican Americans." El Grito: A Journal of Contemporary Mexican American Thought. Vol. 5, No. 2, (Winter 1971-72). pp. 47-79.
(EJ 059 448)

1,641. Morgan, T.B. "Real West Side Story--Life of José Rivera." Look. Vol. 24 (February 16, 1960). pp. 22-27.

1,642. Moskin, J. Robert. "Puerto Rico: Island at Crossroads." Look. Vol. 28 (March 24, 1964). pp. 26, 42.

1,643. Mozer, R.J. "Victims of Exploitation: New York's Puerto Ricans." Catholic World. Vol. 189 (September 1959). pp. 441-446.

1,644. New England Regional Spanish-Speaking Council. Overview of the Problems Encountered by New England's Spanish-Speaking Population. Hartford, Connecticut: New England Regional Spanish-Speaking Council. 1970.

1,645. "New York's Puerto Ricans." America. Vol. 97 (May 11, 1957). p. 185.

1,646. "No Hablo Inglés: Police Blamed for Puerto Rican Riots." New Republic. Vol. 154 (June 25, 1966). p. 7.

1,647. O'Gara, J. "Strangers in the City." Commonweal. Vol. 57 (October 10, 1952). pp. 7-9.

1,648. One in Twenty: The Facts about the Puerto Ricans among Us and What the Boys Athletic League is Doing About It. New York: Boys Athletic League, 1956.

1,649. O'Neill, George C. and Nena O'Neill. <u>Vocational Rehabilitation Needs of Disabled Puerto Ricans in New York City</u>. Puerto Rican Social Services, Inc. 1964.

1,650. "Our Minority Groups: Spanish-Speaking People." <u>Building America</u>. Vol. 8, No. 5 (1940). Society for Curriculum Study. Americana Corporation, New York.

1,651. <u>Our Puerto Rican Fellow Citizens</u>. New York: National Conference Sponsored by AFL-CIO Community Service Activities. January 15, 1960.

1,652. Owens, James M. "These Are Puerto Ricans." <u>Hartford Courant</u>. March 15-22, 1959. (series of eight articles)

1,653. Parker, E.C. "Spanish Speaking Churches." <u>Christian Century</u>. Vol. 78 (August 12, 1962). pp. 466-468.

1,654. Perloff, Harvey. <u>Puerto Rico's Economic Future</u>. Chicago: University of Chicago Press. 1950.

1,655. "Power of Words: Exploitation of Puerto Rican Workers in New York City." <u>Nation</u>. Vol. 185 (August 17, 1957). p. 62.

1,656. Poyatos, Fernando. <u>Hacia una visión total del hablante español</u> (Toward a Total View of the Spanish Speaker.) Paper presented at the annual meeting of the American Association of Teachers of Spanish and Portuguese. San Francisco, California, December 1970.
(ED 061 778)

1,657. Price, G.W. <u>Origins of the War with Mexico: The Polk-Stockton Intrigue</u>. Austin: University of Texas Press. 1967.

1,658. Probst, Nathan and Sophia A. Olmsted. "The Rising Puerto Rican Problem." <u>Bar Bulletin</u> (New York County Lawyers Association) Vol. 9 (March 1952). pp. 5-12.

1,659. "The Puerto Rican Experience on the United States Mainland." <u>The International Migration Review</u>. Vol. 2 (Spring 1968). Includes "An annotated bibliography on Puerto Rico and Puerto Rican migration," pp. 96-102.

1,660. Puerto Rican Forum, Inc. <u>Puerto Rican Community Development Project</u>. New York: Puerto Rican Forum, 1964.

1,661. <u>Puerto Rican Neighbors</u>. New York: National Council of the Episcopal Church. 1958.

1,662. "Puerto Rican Number." <u>The Bible in New York</u>. (New York Bible Society). Vol. 49 (February 1958). pp. 1-8.

1,663. "The Puerto Ricans." Civil Rights Digest. Vol. 4, No. 4. (December 1971). pp. 17-21. (EJ 052 318),

1,664. "Puerto Ricans and the ILGWU." New Politics. Vol. 1 (1962). pp. 6-17; Vol. 2 (1963). pp. 7-27.

1,665. "Puerto Ricans and Inter-American Understanding." The Journal of Educational Sociology. 35:9 (May, 1962); pp. 385-440.

1,666. "Puerto Ricans Find Church Homes." Christian Century. Vol. 75 (March 26, 1958). p. 365.

1,667. Puerto Ricans in New York City. New York: Commonwealth of Puerto Rico, Department of Labor, Migration Division, 1965.

1,668. Puerto Ricans in New York City. New York: Welfare and Health Council of New York City. April 1953.

1,669. Puerto Ricans in Philadelphia. Philadelphia Commission on Human Relations. April 1959. (Prepared by Raymond Metauten and Burton Gordon).

1,670. "Puerto Ricans Not Guilty." Economist. Vol. 193 (October 3, 1959). pp. 44.

1,671. The Puerto Ricans of New York City. Washington: Office of the Government of Puerto Rico. 1948.

1,672. Palomares, Uvlado H. "Viva La Raza!" Personnel and Guidance Journal. 50:2 (October, 1971). pp. 119-129. (EJ 044 929)

Viva La Raza is the rallying cry of the Chicano movement. Viva La Raza illustrates the historical forces that spark its present eruption and the current pressures for social change from new and dynamic leadership. (CIJE)

1,673. Rand, Christopher. "Puerto Ricans." Saturday Review. Vol. 41 (September 13, 1958). p. 36.

1,674. Rand, Christopher. The Puerto Ricans. New York: Oxford. 1958. 178p.

1,675. Rand, Christopher. "A Reporter at Large: The Puerto Ricans." The New Yorker. November 30-December 21, 1957. (Series of four articles.)

1,676. Raushenbush, Winifred. "New York and the Puerto Ricans." Harper's Vol. 206 (May 1953). pp. 13-15.

1,677. "Really Fantastic Bronx Puerto Rican Theater." Time. Vol. 53 (March 28, 1949). p. 83.

1,678. "Really Fantastic Bronx Puerto Rican Theater." <u>Time</u>. Vol. 53 (March 28, 1949). p. 83.

1,679.. Rendón, Armando. "El Puertorriqueño: No More, No Less." <u>Civil Rights Digest</u>. (Fall, 1968).

1,680. Ribes Tovar, Federico. <u>Handbook of the Puerto Rican Community</u>. New York: Colección Grandes Emigraciones. 1968. (New York: Plus Ultra. 1970).

1,681. Ribes Tovar, Federico. <u>El libro puertorriqueño de Nueva York</u>. New York: Colección Grandes Emigraciones. 1968. (New York: Plus Ultra. 1970).

1,682. Rice, John L. <u>Health Problems Among Puerto Ricans in New York City</u>. New York: Health Department, 1934. (Unpublished).

1,683. Rigau, Angel. "Un Estudio Puertorriqueño." <u>La Prensa de Nueva York</u>. April .3-10, 1956.

1,684. Rogler, L. <u>Migrant in the City: The Life of a Puerto Rican Action Group</u>. New York: Basic Books, 1972.

1,685. Roman, Josefina de. "New York's Latin Quarter." <u>The Inter-American</u>. Vol. 1 (January 1946) pp. 9-13, 36-37.

1,686. Rosten, Norman. "Puerto Ricans in New York." <u>Holiday</u>. Vol. 29 (February 1961). pp. 48-49.

1,687. Ruíz, R.E. (ed.). <u>The Mexican-American War: Was it Manifest Destiny?</u> New York: Holt, Rinehart and Winston. 1963.

1,688. Ruíz, Ruperto. <u>Understanding Civil Liberties and Human Relations as they Affect Puerto Ricans and Negroes</u>. New York, 1960.

1,689. Ruíz, Ruperto. <u>What can a Puerto Rican Person of Hispanic Descent Do to Become an Effective American Citizen?</u> New York, 1966. (pamphlet)

1,690. Ruíz, Ruperto and H.L. Present. <u>Puerto Ricans in the United States</u>. New York: Spanish American Youth Bureau. June 1966.

1,691. Ruoss, M. "What About New York's Puerto Ricans?" <u>National Council Outlook</u>. Vol. 4 (May 1954). p. 12.

1,692. Rusk, Howard A. "The Facts Don't Rhyme: An Analysis of Irony in Lyrics Linking Puerto Rico's Breezes to Tropic Diseases." <u>New York Times</u>. September 19, 1957.

1,693. Salazar, Ruben. <u>Stranger in One's Land</u>. Commission on Civil Rights, Washington, D.C. Washington, D.C.: U.S. Government Printing Office. May 1970. 52pp. (ED 054 908)

An account of the hearing held by the U.S. Commission on Civil
Rights on the Mexican American community's problems with civil rights
this report does not necessarily represent the views of the Commission but is published to stimulate public interest in the problems
confronting Mexican Americans. Major areas explored were employment,
education, the administration of justice, housing, and political
representation. "The total picture of economic deprivation, of
relegation to the meanest employment, of education suppression, and
of restricted opportunity in almost every phase of life unfolded." (RIE)

1,694. Samora, J. (Ed.). La Raza: Forgotten Americans. Notre Dame, Indiana: University of Notre Dame Press. 1966.

1,695. Samuels, Gertrude. "I Don't Think the Cop is My Friend." New York
Times Magazine. March 29, 1964. p. 28.

1,696. Samuels, Gertrude. "Two Case Histories out of Puerto Rico." New
York Times Magazine. January 22, 1956. pp. 26-27.

1,697. Samuels, Gertrude. "Walk Along the Worst Block: East 100th
Street." New York Times Magazine. September 30, 1962. 18-19pp.

1,698. "San Juan Day: Mainland Puerto Ricans Honor their Patron Saint."
Jubilee. September 1946. pp. 48-51.

1,699. Sánchez, D.J., Jr. "Equal Opportunity for the Spanish Speaking
American." Educational Forum. Vol. 36 (March 1972). p. 383-387.

1,700. Sauna, Victor D., et al. The Vocational Rehabilitation Problems of
Disabled Puerto Ricans in New York City. The Institute of
Physical Medicine and Rehabilitation, New York University--
Bellevue Medical Center. Rehabilitation Monograph 12. 1957.

1,701. Schnitzler, W.F. "Puerto Rican Workers get Labor's Help to the
Better Life." American Federationist. Vol. 67 (February 1960).
pp. 6-7.

1,702. "Senate Hearings." Center Forum. 1969. 4. 5-23.

1,703. Senior, Clarence. Bibliography of Puerto Ricans in the United
States. New York: Department of Labor, Migration Division,
Commonwealth of Puerto Rico. 1959.

1,704. Senior, Clarence. Our Citizens from the Caribbean. New York:
McGraw-Hill. 1965.

1,705. Senior, Clarence. "The Puerto Ricans in the United States." In
Joseph Gittler, ed. Understanding Minority Groups. New York:
John Wiley, 1956. pp. 109-125.

1,706. Senior, Clarence. The Puerto Ricans of New York City. Washington,
D.C. Office of the Government of Puerto Rico. 1948.

1,707. Senior, Clarence. "Puerto Ricans on the Mainland." Americas. Vol. 13 (August 1961). pp. 36-47.

1,708. Senior, Clarence. The Puerto Ricans: Strangers-Then Neighbors. Chicago: Quadrangle. 1965. 128pp.

1,709. Seplowin, Virginia M. Training and Employment Patterns of Puerto Ricans in Philadelphia. Unpublished Ph.D. Dissertation, University of Pennsylvania. 1969.

1,710. Shotwell, Louisa. "Puerto Rican Neighbors." The Presbyterian Tribune. Vol. 68 (September 1953). pp. 1-3.

1,711. Silen, Juan A. We, The Puerto Rican People: A Story of Oppression and Resistance. New York: Monthly Review Press. 1971.

1,712. Simmons, W.R., et al. "The Spanish-Speaking Scene: Silhoutte on New York City Today." El Diario-La Prensa. February 1963.

1,713. Soto, P.J. Spiks. San Juan: Departamento de Instrucción Pública. 1967.

1,714. Status of Puerto Rico. Selected Background Studies Prepared for the United States-Puerto Rico Commission on the Status of Puerto Rico. Washington, D.C. U.S. Government Printing Office, 1966. (Includes Clarence Senior and Donald O. Watkins, "Toward a Balance Sheet of Puerto Rican Migration: Bibliography.

1,715. Steiner, S. La Raza: The Mexican-Americans. New York: Harper and Row. 1968.

1,716. String, Alvin. "Puerto Ricans in New Jersey." Public Health News. August 1962.

1,717. "Sugar-Bowl Migrants, New York's Spanish Harlem." Time. Vol. 50 (August 11, 1947). p. 20.

1,718. Su Guía a New Haven. New Haven, Connecticut: New Haven Human Relations Council. 1959.

1,719. Tebbel, John and Ramon Eduardo Ruiz. South by Southwest: The Mexican-American and His Heritage. New York: Doubleday and Company. 1969. 122pp. (ED 063 065)

1,720. "Thank Heaven for Puerto Rico." (An Editorial). Life. March 15, 1954.

1,721. "Tropics in New York." Americas. Vol. 4 (June 1952). pp. 32-33.

1,722. "Un Esfuerzo Encomiable." (Editorial). El Diario de Nueva York. February 18, 1954. p. 13.

1,723. Vandow, Jules E. "Venereal Disease among Puerto Ricans in New York City." Public Health Reports. Vol. 70 (December 1955). pp. 1242-1246.

1,724. Vivas, Julio. The Puerto Ricans of Cleveland: A Challenge to Community Organization. Cleveland: Western Reserve University, 1951.

1,725. Wagner, Geoffrey. "Puerto Rico in Harlem." New Republic. Vol. 131 (August 23, 1954). pp. 16-18.

1,726. Wakefield, Dan. "The Gang that Went Good." Harper's. Vol. 216 (June 1958). pp. 36-43.

1,727. Wakefield, Dan. Island in the City. Boston: Houghton Mifflin. 1959. 278pp.

1,728. Wakefield, Dan. "The Other Puerto Ricans." New York Times Magazine. October 11, 1959. pp. 24-25.

1,729. Wakefield, Dan. "Politics and the Puerto Ricans." Commentary. Vol. 25 (March 1958). pp. 226-236.

1,730. Wakefield, Dan. "200,000 New Yorkers Can't Vote." Nation. Vol. 188 (February 28, 1959). pp. 183-185.

1,731. Weales, Gerald. "New Yorker's Puerto Rican Dilemma." The New Leader. (March 7, 1955). pp. 8-10.

1,732. Weitzman, Judy. "Reheating the Melting Pot." The New Leader. (June 28, 1954). pp. 11-12.

1,733. Welfare and Health Council of New York City: Brooklyn Council for Social Planning. Report on Survey of Brooklyn Agencies Rendering Services to Puerto Ricans. June 1953.

1,734. Welfare Council of New York City, Committee on Puerto Ricans in New York City. Puerto Ricans in New York City. New York. 1948. 60pp.

1,735. Werner, M.R. "The Puerto Ricans in New York." The Reporter. Vol. 3 (September 26, 1950). pp. 20-23.

1,736. Willoughby, W. "Puerto Rican Story." Globe-Times (Bethlehem, Pa.). July 7-12, 1958. (series of six articles)

1,737. Woodbury, Clarence. "Our Worst Slum, New York's Spanish Harlem." American Magazine. Vol. 148 (September 1949). pp. 30-31.

1,738. Yezierska, Anzia. "Lower Depths of Upper Broadway." Reporter Vol. 10 (January 19, 1954). pp. 26-29.

1,739. Young Lords Party. Palante. New York: McGraw-Hill. 1971.

B. Demographic Studies and Patterns of Migration

1,740. Bogardus, Emory S. Immigration and Race Attitudes. Boston: Heath. 1928.

1,741. Bogardus, Emory S. The Mexican Immigrant: An Annotated Bibliography. Los Angeles: Council on International Relations. 1929. 21pp.

1,742. Breisler, B. "Looking for the Promised Land." Saturday Evening Post. April 11, 1959.

1,743. Bureau of Applied Social Research of Columbia University. "Letter to Governor Jesus T. Pinero Summarizing the Principal Findings of the Study of Puerto Rican Migrants which the Bureau has been Conducting since November, 1947." June 15, 1948. 15pp. In the Covello Papers - Personal Files.

1,744. Carleton, R.O. "New Aspects of Puerto Rican Migration." Monthly Labor Review. Vol. 83 (February 1960). pp. 133-135.

1,745. Carter, Hugh and Bernice Doster. "Residence and Occupation of Naturalized Americans from Mexico." Monthly Review, Immigration and Naturalization Service. U.S. Department of Justice. Vol.8 (October 1950) pp. 47-53.

1,746. Castaño, Carlos. "The First 10 Years...The Puerto Rican Migratory Program." Employment Security Review. Vol. 25 (March 1958). pp. 31-33.

1,747. "Channel Puerto Rican Migration." Commweal. Vol. 47 (February 27, 1948). p. 484.

1,748. Colón, Petroamerica Pagán de. Migration Trends. New York: Migration Division, Department of Labor, Commonwealth of Puerto Rico. 1959.

1,749. "Columbia Plans Study of Puerto Rican Migration to New York City." PM. October 14, 1947.

1,750. Community Council of Greater New York. Manhattan Communities: Summary Statements of Population Characteristics. Community Council of Greater New York, Research Department, 1955.

1,751. Community Council of Greater New York. Our Changing Community. Community Council of Greater New York. 1957.

1,752. Community Council of Greater New York. Research Department. Bureau of Community Statistical Services. "Population of Puerto Rican Birth or Parentage for New York City, by borough: 1960." April 15, 1962.

1,753. Cordasco, F. and David Alloway. "Spanish Speaking People in the
United States: Some Research Constructs and Postulates."
_International Migration Review_. Vol. 4 (Spring 1970). 76-79pp.

This is a review of the volume of _Proceedings_ of the Spring
1968 meeting of the American Ethnological Society. Two of the
papers are theoretical, cautioning against generalizing from too-
scanty data about the 5.1 million Spanish-speaking people in the
United States, and another which comments on two opposing views
of ethnicity and the social class system. Other papers study the
Mexican-American experience in Racine, Wisconsin; the child's view
of life in the city; the Spanish-speaking community in Florida; and
the role of the non-Spanish-speaking in acculturation and cultural
assimilation. The authors suggest other publications which deal
with the Puerto Rican experience. (ECK)

1,754. Cordasco, F. and R. Galatioto. "Ethnic Displacement in the Inter-
stitial Community: The East Harlem (New York) Experience."
Phylon: _The Atlanta Review of Race and Culture_. Vol. 31
(Fall, 1970). pp. 302-312.

1,755. Costa, Richard H. "Latest Migration: Puerto Rico Moves Upstate."
_Utica_ (New York) _Observer Dispatch_. May 27-29, 1957. (series
of three articles)

1,756. Cunningham, John T. "Migrants Pose Problems for N.J. Farmers Who
Need Them." Reprinted from _Newark News Magazine_. September 1,
1957. Commonwealth of Puerto Rico, Department of Labor,
Migration Division. (n.d.).

1,757. Davis, H.D. "Golden Door." _New Statesman_. Vol. 50 (September 24,
1955). pp. 355-356.

1,758. Davis K. and C. Senior. "Immigration from the Western Hemisphere.
_Annals of the American Academy of Political and Social Science_.
Vol. 262 (Marcy 1949) pp. 76-77.

1,759. "Demographic Tables." (for East Harlem) Appendix. September 1964.
Unpaged. Unpublished.

1,760. _La División de Migración...Sirviendo a los Puertorriqueños en los
Estados Unidos_. Nueva York: Estado Libre Asociado de Puerto
Rico, Departamento del Trabajo, Division de Migración. 1957.

1,761. Donahue, Frances M. _A Study of the Original Puerto Rican Colony in
Brooklyn, 1938-1943_. Master's Thesis, Fordham University School
of Social Work. 1945.

1,762. Donchain, Daniel. _A Survey of New Haven's Newcomers: The Puerto
Ricans_. New Haven, Connecticut: Human Relations Council of
Greater New Haven. 1959.

1,763.  Dooey, Merrill H.  The Migrant Puerto Rican in Bridgeport, Hartford
        and New Haven.  New Haven, Connecticut: Yale University. 1956.

1,764.  Dworkis, Martin B.  Impact of Puerto Rican Migration on Governmental
        Services in New York City.  New York: New York University. 1957.

1,765.  Eagle, Morris.  "The Puerto Ricans in New York City."  In N. Glazer
        and D. McEntire, Housing and Minority Groups.  University of
        California Press, 1960.  pp. 144-177.

1,766.  "Effects of Labor Costs and Migration on Puerto Rican Workers."
        Monthly Labor Review.  Vol. 76 (June 1953).  pp. 625-627.

1,767.  Elinson, Jack; Paul W. Haberman; Cyrille Gell.  Ethnic and Educa-
        tional Data on Adults in New York City, 1963-1964.  New York:
        School of Public Health and Administrative Medicine, Columbia
        University.  1967.

1,768.  "Emigrating Puerto Ricans."  Commonweal.  Vol. 46 (August 15, 1947)
        p. 420.

1,769.  Ethnic Survey.  A Report on the Number and Distribution of Negroes,
        Puerto Ricans and Others Employed by the City of New York.
        New York City Commission on Human Rights.  1964.

1,770.  Fitzpatrick, J.P.  "Intermarriage of Puerto Ricans in New York City."
        The American Journal of Sociology.  71:4 (1966).  pp. 395-406.

        This paper discusses the rate of assimilation of Puerto Ricans
        in New York City as indicated by the rate of intermarriage with
        members of another ethnic group.  A study of out-group marriages
        in 1949 and 1959 showed that increases in such marriages among
        second-as compared with first-generation.  Puerto Ricans were as
        large as those found by Drachsler for all immigrants in New York,
        1908-1912.  This indicates that the cultural assimilation of Puerto
        Ricans is taking place quite rapidly.  For women, intermarriage was
        highly correlated with higher occupational status ("This suggests
        that they may be marrying out in order to marry up.")  There was no
        such visible trend for men.  Both men and women married younger in
        the second generation.  Catholic ceremonies increased in 1959 over
        1949 and in the second generation over first.  However, as compared
        with Puerto Rico, civil and Catholic ceremonies decreased in New
        York; Protestant ceremonies increased.  (DH)

1,771.  Fitzpatrick, J.P.  "Puerto Ricans in Perspective:  The Meaning of
        Migration to the Mainland."  International Migration Review.
        Vol. 2 (1968).  pp. 7-20.

1,772.  Fleischer, Belton M.  "Some Economic Aspects of Puerto Rican Migration
        to the U.S."  Review of Economics and Statistics.  Vol. 45
        (August 1963).  pp. 221-230.

1,773.  Fleisher.  Belton M.  <u>Some Economic Aspects of Puerto Rican Migration</u>
        <u>to the United States</u>.  Unpublished Ph.D.  Dissertation, Stan-
        ford University. 1961.
        (<u>Dissertation Abstracts</u>. Vol. 22 (1962). p. 3434.).

        This study attempts to explain Puerto Rican migration to the
        mainland in terms of economic variables, particularly during the
        period immediately following World War II.  It is hypothesized that
        migration is a response to labor market disequilibrium.  According
        to the author's sources, mainly published and unpublished government
        documents, the hypothesis is valid in the case of Puerto Rican
        migration to the United States.  There is also some discussion of
        the impact of the migration upon the source and receiving regions
        involved.  (DH)

1,774.  Galarza, E.  <u>Merchants of Labor:  The Mexican Bracero Story</u>. Santa
        Barbara, California: MacNally and Leften.  1964.

1,775.  García, Carmen Sylvia.  <u>Study of the Initial Involvement in the</u>
        <u>Social Services by the Puerto Rican Migrants in Philadelphia</u>.
        Ph.D. Dissertation, University of Pennsylvania. 1968.
        (<u>Dissertation Abstracts</u>. Vol. 29 (1968). p. 1294A.)

1,776.  Gernes, Arthur C.  "Implicaciones de la Emigración Puertorriqueña
        al Continente Fuera de la Ciudad de Nueva York."  <u>La Torres</u>
        (Enero-Marzo, 1956).  pp. 97-111.

1,777.  Glazer, Nathan.  "Puerto Rican Migration--Right Place, Wrong Time."
        <u>America</u>.  Vol. 125.  No. 13.  (October 30, 1971).  pp. 339-341.
        (EJ 054 979).

1,778.  Goldsen, Rose K.  <u>Puerto Rican Migration to New York City</u>.  Unpub-
        lished Ph.D.  Dissertation, Yale University.  (1953).

1,779.  Goldwin, Irwin J; Roslyn G. McDonald; and Joyce Epstein.  "Charac-
        teristics of Jobs Held by Economically Disadvantaged Youth."
        <u>American Journal of Orthopsychiatry</u> 40:1 (1970). pp. 97-105.

        "Studied job histories of 112 16-18 year-olds from low-income
        neighborhoods.  An interview schedule and the Hamburger Occupational
        Scale with respect to characteristics of jobs held, extent of
        employment, nature of first jobs, and ethnic differences were
        utilized.  The median number of full-time jobs held by Ss (from
        first job to time of interview) was 4.  Findings indicate the
        possibility of vertical mobility among available jobs, but limited
        primarily to the 3 lowest occupational levels.  Median pay of
        35-45 Hr./Wk. jobs was $53.  The jobs of Ss tend not to be in their
        own neighborhood.  Source of job was predictive of pay (P: .001),
        duration (P: .001), and non-significantly, of evaluation (P: .20).
        A major difference in jobs held by Blacks and jobs of Puerto Rican
        Ss was found in the source of employment.  Almost twice as many jobs

of Puerto Ricans were referred by friends, neighbors, and relatives than jobs of Blacks." Although personal source of job and higher pay are often associated with each other, this is not the case for the Puerto Ricans in this study. In fact, for jobs over 45 hours/ week the Puerto Ricans were paid significantly less than Blacks. The greatest difference was in the lowest pay category (under $50/week) which accounted for 22% of jobs held by Puerto Ricans and only 14% of jobs held by Blacks. (PASAR and DH)

1,780. Goodman, Mary Ellen and Others. The Mexican-American Population of Houston: A Survey in the Field, 1965-1970. Monograph in Cultural Anthropology, Houston, Texas: Rice University Studies Vol. 57. No. 3 Summer 1971. 130p. (ED 060 997)

1,781. Gray, Lois Spier. Economic Incentives to Labor Mobility: The Puerto Rican Case. Ph.D. Dissertation, Columbia University. 1966. (Dissertation Abstracts. Vol. 27 (1967). p. 2263A.)

Explains migration behavior based on economic incentives, using the recent migration of Puerto Ricans to the U.S. mainland as a case in point. (DH)

1,782. Grieser, Normal. "Airborne from San Juan." New Republic. Vol. 117 (November 3, 1947). pp. 21-24.

1,783. Hernández Alvarez, José. Return Migration to Puerto Rico. (Population Monograph Series No. 1). Berkley, California: University of California, Institute of International Studies. 1967.

Though the main focus of the monograph is the migrant Puerto Rican's return to the island, there is quite a lot of material about the migrant's situation during his stay on the mainland. In his introduction, Hernández presents a general description of Puerto Rican migration to the United States since the early 1900's and discusses the disappointments and great difficulties the migrants face here. Puerto Rican migrants in the United States and Puerto Rican return migrants are compared for these demographic variables: economic characteristics, social characteristics, age distribution and sex ratios, fertility and marital status of Puerto Rican women, school attendance, areas of residence, and industrial distribution of the Puerto Rican migrant labor force. (DH)

1,784. Hnatek, Margaret. A Survey of Population Factors Relating to the Education of Migrant Children in Victoria County, Texas. Unpublished Master's thesis. University of Texas. 1952.

1,785. How to Hire Agricultural Workers from Puerto Rico. New York: Commonwealth of Puerto Rico. Department of Labor, Migration Division. (In: Employment Security. U.S. Employment Service. Farm Placement Service. 1953, 1954, 1955, 1957, 1958.) (irregular)

1,786.  Interim Report. New York: Labor Advisory Committee on Puerto Rican
        Affairs. AFL-CIO, New York, 1955.

1,787.  Jaffe, Abraham J. (ed.). Puerto Rican Population in New York City.
        New York: Columbia University, Bureau of Applied Research. 1954.

1,788.  Jones, Isham B. The Puerto Rican in New Jersey: His Present Status.
        New Jersey State Department of Education. Division Against
        Discrimination, July 1955.

1,789.  Kantrowitz, Nathan and Donnell M. Pappenfort. 1960 Fact Book for the
        New York-Northeastern New Jersey Standard Consolidated Area;
        the Non-White, Puerto Rican, and White Non-Puerto Rican Popu-
        lations: Selected Characteristics for Counties and Cities of
        50,000 or More. New York: Columbia University, 1966. (Social
        Statistics for Metropolitan New York. Monograph No. 2.)

1,790.  Kihss, Peter. "Gains Made by Puerto Ricans Here." and "City Relief
        Roll Held Down Despite Job Hunter Influx." both in: New York
        Times. May 31, 1957 and June 2, 1957. Reprinted by Commonwealth
        of Puerto Rico, Migration Division, Department of Labor.

1,791.  King, Joh. "From Caguas to New York." San Juan Review. Vol. 2
        (June 1965). pp. 62-64.

1,792.  Koss, Joan D. Puerto Ricans in Philadelphia: Migration and Accomo-
        dative Processes. Unpublished Ph.D. Dissertation, Unversity
        of Pennsylvania. 1965.
        (Dissertation Abstracts. Vol. 26 (1966). pp. 4958-5959.).

        The purpose of this study was to determine the effects of
    migration upon Puerto Ricans in Philadelphia and how they reorganize
    or adjust their lives to the new sociocultural environment. Data
    was collected by the author in both Puerto Rico and Philadelphia,
    using the field techniques of ethnography. Focal aspects of Puerto
    Rican life styles are considered and described: structure of the
    family, kinship organization, patterns of friendship, and the develop-
    ment and function of voluntary associations. The norms and patterns
    of behavior related to social class and race, including the
    quality of interpersonal behavior and the function of religious
    beliefs, are also discussed.
        Analysis of the data revealed a pattern of accomodation to
    Philadelphia life which included a change in basic attitudes. Given
    those conditions that favor it, the presence of accomodation within
    the process of acculturation functions to offset the descriptive
    effects of certain cultural changes, and acts as a deterrent to
    personal and social disorientation. (DH)

1,793.  Kurtis, Arlene Harris. Puerto Ricans from Island to Mainland. New
        York: Messner. 1969.

1,794.  Law, William. "Problems for the Migratory Student." California
        Journal of Secondary Education. Vol. 14 (March 1939) p. 170-173.

Problems confronting migratory students are: poor housing, malnutrition, inferiority complex, inability to adjust socially, mental
retardation due to environment, the impossible task of selecting
subjects which can be followed through all of the schools attended.
(Sanchez and Putman)

1,795. Leviton, Bertha. "Census of Puerto Rican and Foreign-Born Pupils,
Provisional Report." Board of Education of the City of New York.
February 1956.

1,796. Leviton, Bertha. "Special Census of School Population: Classification
of non-Englisn-Speaking Pupils." October 31, 1960. No. 171. New
York City Board of Education. 1961.

1,797. Maciso, John J. "Assimilation of Puerto Ricans on the Mainland: A
Socio-Demographic Approach." _International Migration Review_.
Vol. 2 (1968). pp. 21-39.

The purpose of this paper is to describe the social and demographic characteristics of Puerto Ricans on the U.S. mainland, and
the direction of change between the first and second generation of
Puerto Ricans. Most of the data come from the 1960 census. First
and second generation Puerto Ricans are compared in regard to
(1) education, (2) age, (3) labor force status, (4) income,
(5) occupation, (6) age at first marriage, (7) per cent of out-
group marriages, and (8) fertility. The total U.S. population was
arbitrarily selected as the standard. It was discovered that second
generation Puerto Ricans are younger, have more schooling, are less
likely to be unemployed, have higher incomes, are employed in
higher status occupations, marry earlier, tend to marry non-Puerto
Ricans in greater proportions and have fewer children than first
generation Puerto Ricans. An exception is that second generation
females have higher incomes and lower fertility than total U.S.
females, which may indicate that the traditionally dominant role is
being weakened by the woman's role as wage earner and that they are
adjusting more effectively to mainland patterns. In short, except
for the one point noted above, from first to second generation, the
Puerto Ricans have moved in the direction of the total U.S. population.
(ECK)

1,798. Main, Willett S. Memorandum on _In-Migration of Puerto Rican Workers_.
Wisconsin State Employment Service. September 3, 1952.

1,799. Maldonado, A.W. "The Migration Reverses." _The Nation_. Vol. 198
(March 16, 1964). pp. 255-257.

1,800. Maldonado, A.W. "The Puerto Rican Tide Begins to Turn." _New York
Times Magazine_. September 20, 1964.

1,801. Meyers, George C. "The Elusive Male: Some Methodological Notes on
Survey Research." _Public Opinion Quarterly_. 33:2 (1969). p. 255-259.

"The initial decisions made in a study can result in situations
that materially after a research design. A field study in Puerto
Rico supplies an illustration:" In order to study the effects of
housing conditions on household members differentially, it was decided to interview the head of the household and the spouse. Rather
than interview family members simultaneously, they decided on
"repeat interviewing," returning unannounced to talk to another
member of the household. As they had anticipated, it was much more
likely to find a woman at home, than a man. They had not anticipated
such high percentages of woman heads of households, however, nor did
they expect such difficulty rescheduling a return interview. Finally,
even the males who were "theoretically 'at home'," were difficult, if
not impossible, to locate. Meyers suggests that what evolved here
was a "pattern of evasion," which served as an alternative to an out-
right refusal. Thus, the decisions made early in the study placed
obstacles in the way of completing the investigation. (DH)

1,802.  Mintz, Shirley. "Puerto Rican Emigration: A Threefold Comparison."
        Social and Economic Studies. Jamaica: University College of the
        West Indies. Vol. 4 (December 1955). pp. 311-325.

1,803.  Monserrat, Joseph. Background and General Information on Puerto Rico
        and the Puerto Rican Migrant. New York: Commonwealth of Puerto
        Rico, Department of Labor, Migration Division. (1963)

1,804.  Monserrat, Joseph. "La emigración, realidad y problema en la ciudad
        de Nueva York." La Torre (Universidad de Puerto Rico). (March
        1956).

1,805.  Monserrat, Joseph. "Some Data on Population Trends in New York:
        'Must' Information for Its Citizens." Journal of Educational
        Sociology. Vol. 28 (November, 1952). pp. 108-114.

1,806.  Montross, Harold K. "Meeting the Needs of the Puerto Rican Migrant."
        Employment Security Review. Vol. 26 (January 1959). pp. 31-33.

1,807.  Moskin, J.R. "Million on the Mainland." Look. Vol. 25 (January 17,
        1961). p. 44.

1,808.  Muñoz Marín, Luis. Un Mensaje a Los Comunidades Puertorriqueñas del
        Continente. Nueva York: Estado Libre Asociado de Puerto Rico,
        Departamento del Trabajo, División de Migración. 25 de julio de
        1953.

1,809.  Myers, George C. and George Masnick. "The Migration Experience of
        New York Puerto Ricans: A Perspective on Return." International
        Migration Review. Vol. 2 (1968). pp. 80-90.

        In this article, Puerto Ricans who indicated that they would like
to return to the island and Puerto Ricans who indicated that they intend to remain on the mainland are compared as to factors that relate
to that choice, such as residence and return visits to Puerto Rico.

Those that wish to return are more demanding in their assessments
of aspects of life on the mainland that would compose a satisfactory
residence in New York City, and they are more likely to maintain ties
with the island through visits. The authors suggest that prospective
return migrants be trained as carriers of social change to the areas
to which they return. (ECK)

1,810. McWilliams, C. North from Mexico: The Spanish-Speaking People of
the United States. New York: Greenwood Press. 1968.

1,811. New York State Commission Against Discrimination. Employment in the
Hotel Industry. Published by the Commission, March 1958.

1,812. New York State Commission for Human Rights. Division of Research. The
Puerto Rican Populations of the New York City Area: Populations
of New York State: 1960 Report No. 2. 1962. 22pp.

1,813. New York State Department of Labor. Occupations of Puerto Ricans in
New York City. Special Labor News Memo No. 50. New York State
Department of Labor. June 17, 1954.

1,814. "900,000 Puerto Ricans in the United States: Their Problems and
Progress." U.S. News and World Report. Vol. 47 (December 7,
1959). pp. 91-95.

1,815. Novak, Robert T. "Distribution of Puerto Ricans on Manhattan Island."
Geographical Review. Vol. 46 (April 1956). pp. 182-186.

1,816. Nueva York y Usted. Nueva York: Estado Libre Asociado de Puerto
Rico, Departamento del Trabajo, División de Migración. 1951.

1,817. O'Brien, Robert W. Cleveland Puerto Rican Survey Tabulations.
Cleveland: Nationalities Services Center of Cleveland and Ohio
Wesleyan University (Sociology Department) 1954.

1,818. O'Brien, Robert W. A Survey of the Puerto Ricans in Lorain, Ohio.
Neighborhood House Association of Lorain, 1954.

1,819. Padilla, Elena. Up from Puerto Rico. New York: Columbia University.
1958. 317pp.

1,820. Pagán de Colón, Petroamérica. Northeastern Ohio and the Puerto Rican
Migration. New York: Commonwealth of Puerto Rico, Department of
Labor, Migration Division. 1955.

1,821. Pagán de Colón, Petroamérica. Programa de Colocaciones de Trabajadores
Agrícolas Puertorriqueños en Estados Unidos. San Juan: Estado
Libre Asociado de Puerto Rico, Departamento del Trabajo. (n.d.)

1,822. Pagán de Colón, Petroamérica. "The Status of the Migrant: People with
the Same Aspirations." Vital Speeches. Vol. 28 (May 1, 1962).
pp. 445-448.

1,823.  Peña, Joan Finkle de.  Standards of Growth and Development for
        Puerto Rican Children.  Ph.D. Dissertation, Indiana University.
        1958.
        (Dissertation Abstracts.  Vol. 19 (1959).  pp. 3081-3082.).

1,824.  "Persons of Spanish Origin in the United States: November, 1969,
        Bureau of Census."  Journal of Mexican American Studies.  1:2
        (Winter, 1971).  pp. 106-119.

1,825.  Philadelphia's Puerto Rican Population with 1960 Census Data.  City
        of Philadelphia, Commission on Human Relations.  March, 1964.

1,826.  Puerto Rican Farm Workers in Florida.  Washington: U.S. Department of
        Labor.  Bureau of Employment Security.  February 1955.

1,827.  Puerto Rican Farm Workers in the Middle Atlantic States.  Bureau
        of Employment Security.  1954.

1,828.  Puerto Rican Forum, Inc.  The 1964 Study of Poverty Conditions In
        the New York City Puerto Rican Community.  New York:  Puerto
        Rican Forum.  1964.

1,829.  "Puerto Rican Migrants Jam New York" Life.  August 25, 1947. p. 25-29.

1,830.  "Puerto Rican Migrants on the Mainland of the United States."  In
        formation Retrieval Center on the Disadvantaged.  Bulletin.
        Vol. 4, No. 1 (1968).  Includes Gertrude S. Goldberg,  "A
        Review of the Literature."

1,831.  "Puerto Rican Migration."  Real Estate News.  March, 1949.

1,832.  "Puerto Rican Migration Dwindles in a Recession."  New York Times.
        September 7, 1971.

1,833.  Puerto Rican Migration to New York City.  New York: New York City De-
        partment of City Planning.  February 1957.

1,834.  Puerto Rican Population of New York City.  New York: Bureau of Applied
        Social Research, Columbia University.  1954.  61pp.

1,835.  Puerto Ricans Filling Manpower Gap.  Washington: Office of the
        Government of Puerto Rico.  1951.

1,836.  "Puerto Ricans in New York City."  Geographical Review.  Vol. 44
        (January 1954).  pp. 143-144.

1,837.  Puerto Ricans in the United States.  U.S. Department of Commerce.
        Bureau of the Census.  Final Report PC (2)--ID. U.S. Census of
        Population: 1960, July 1963.  III-XIV and 140pp.

1,838.  "Puerto Ricans Key Source of Labor."  Highlights.  (New York City
        Department of Commerce and Public Events).  Vol. 1 (October 1956).
        pp. 1-3.

1,839.  "Puerto Ricans Start Up Labor Ladder." Business Week. May 2, 1953.
        pp. 150-152.

1,840.  Report on the Protestant Spanish Community in New York City. Protes-
        tant Council of the City of New York, (1960).

1,841.  Sandis, Eva E. "Characteristics of Puerto Rican Migrants to, and
        from, the United States." The International Migration Review.
        Vol. 4 (1970). pp. 22-43.

        This article reviews the data and attempts to draw some conclu-
        sions from a comparison of Puerto Rican migrants to the United States,
        migrants who have returned to the island, and Puerto Ricans who have
        never left the island. The data used in this study were obtained
        from the U.S. Census and two surveys made by the Commonwealth of
        Puerto Rico (all of which had certain shortcomings). From the
        available data, it seemed that educational and occupational selec-
        tivity characterized the migrants, who had more schooling than the
        average Puerto Rican non-migrant and came from the skilled and semi-
        skilled occupations. When they come to the mainland, however, it
        appears that there is a downward mobility in terms of occupation but
        an increase in income. Return migrants living in Puerto Rico have
        more education, more white-collar workers and lower incomes than
        Puerto Rican migrants remaining in the United States, but more data
        are needed to determine whether this difference existed before
        migration or resulted from differing experiences on the mainland.
        More data are also needed to improve knowledge of motivational
        characteristics of Puerto Rican migrants and return migrants, internal
        migrants and those who do not migrate at all. (ECK)

1,842.  Senior, Clarence. "Migration and Economic Development in Puerto Rico."
        Journal of Educational Sociology. Vol. 28 (December 1954). pp. 151-15

        This article describes the improvements in the economy of
        Puerto Rico. For example, the lowering of the death rate, improve-
        ment of education, public health and per capita income, cuts in unem-
        ployment and construction of public housing are mentioned. The author
        notes that "all this adds up to an economy full of vitality, to a
        culture which, after four and a half centuries of colonialism, has
        worked out new solutions for old problems." (ECK)

1,843.  Senior, Clarence. "Migration and Puerto Rico's Population Problem."
        The Annals. Vol. 285 (January 1953). pp. 130-136.

1,844.  Senior, Clarence. "Migration to the Mainland." Monthly Labor Review.
        Vol. 78 (December 1955). pp. 1354-1358.

1,845.  Senior, Clarence. "Puerto Rican Dispersion in the United States."
        Social Problems. Vol. 2 (October 1954). pp. 93-99.

1,846.  Senior, Clarence. Puerto Rican Migration. Rio Piedras: University of
        Puerto Rico. Social Science Research Center. 1947.

1,847.   Senior, Clarence.  <u>Puerto Rican Migration: Spontaneous and Organized</u>.
         Commonwealth of Puerto Rico, Department of Labor, Migration
         Division. 1957.

1,848.·  Senior, Clarence and Donald O. Watkins.  "Toward a Balance Sheet of
         Puerto Rican Migration."  <u>In Status of Puerto Rico: Selected
         Background Studies for the United States-Puerto Rico Commission
         on the Status of Puerto Rico</u>. Washington, D.C.: U.S. Government
         Printing Office, 1966. pp.  689-795.

1,849.   Siegel, Arthur; Harold Orland; and Loyal Greer.  <u>Puerto Ricans in
         Philadelphia:  A Study of Their Demographic Characteristics,
         Problems, and Attitudes</u>. Philadelphia: Philadelphia Institute for
         Research in Human Relations.  1954.

1,850.   Slaiman, Donald.  "Discrimination and Low Incomes." <u>Federationist</u>.
         Vol. 88 (January 1961).  pp. 17-19.

1,851.   Smart, Pearl.  "Experiment in Boston: Services to Puerto Rican New-
         comers." <u>Wilson Library Bulletin</u>. Vol. 34 (February 1960). p. 415.

1,852.   Suter, Larry E.  <u>Selected Characteristics of Persons and Families
         of Mexican, Puerto Rican, and Other Spanish Origin: March 1971</u>.
         <u>Population Characteristics: Current Population Reports</u>. Bureau
         of the Census, Suitland, Maryland. Washington, D.C.: Government
         Printing Office. October 1971. 23pp.
         (ED 065 224)

            Data on a variety of social and economic characteristics for
         persons and families of Mexican American, Puerto Rican and other
         Spanish origins and comparative data for the total white and black
         population are presented in this report...The median family income
         in 1970 for all families of Spanish origin was lower than the
         median income for all white families but higher than that for
         black families.  Unemployment rates were higher for persons of
         Spanish origin than the national average and about the same as the
         rate for men of Negro and other races.  Among persons 25 to 29
         years old, 48% of persons of Spanish origin had graduated from high
         school compared to 58% of blacks and 80% of all whites.  One-third
         of the black and Puerto Rican families had a female head.  (RIE)

1,853.   Talbert, Robert H.  <u>Spanish-Name People in the West and Southwest</u>.
         Fort Worth: Leo Potishman Foundation, Texas Christian
         University. 1955.  90pp.

1,854.   Tannenbaum, Dora, et al.  <u>The Puerto Rican Migration: A Report</u>.  New
         York: Hudson Guild Neighborhood House, Colony House, and Grand
         Street Settlement. 1955.

1,855.   Taylor, Travis H.  "Migratory Farm Labor in the United States."
         <u>Monthly Labor Review</u>. U.S. Department of Labor, Bureau of Labor
         Statistics. Vol. 44 (March 1937) pp. 539-549.

1,856. Tough, Rosalind and Gordon D. Mac Donald. "Manhattan's Real Property Values and the Migrant Puerto Ricans." Land Economics: A Quarterly Journal of Planning, Housing and Public Utilities. (University of Wisconsin).

1,857. Trade Unions and Puerto Rican Workers: Report on Conference Held May 17, 1962. New York: Commonwealth of Puerto Rico, Department of Labor, Migration Division. 1962.

1,858. Transient Youth in California; a National, State and Local Problem Report and Recommendations. California Commission for the Study of Transient Youth. 1948. 48pp.

1,859. Tubbs, Lowell L. A Survey of the Problems of Migratory Mexicans. Unpublished Master's thesis, University of Texas. 1952.

1,860. Walker, Helen W. "Mexican Immigrants and American Citizenhsip." Sociology and Social Research. Vol. 13 (1923-1929) pp. 465-471.

1,861. Welfare and Health Council of New York City. Population of Puerto Rican Birth or Parentage: New York City, 1950. Published by the Council. September 1952.

1,862. Wells, Robert W. "Our Latin Newcomers." The Milwaukee Journal. April 6-9, 1958. (series of four articles).

1,863. Wenk, M.G. "Adjustment and Assimilation: The Cuban Refugee Experience." International Migration Review. Vol. 3. pp. 38-49.

1,864. Werner, M.R. "The Puerto Ricans: Slum to Slum." Reporter. September 12, 1950. pp. 20-22 and September 26, 1950. pp. 20-23.

C. Psychological Adjustment of Puerto Rican Migrants on the Mainland

1,865. Abelardo. *Chicano: 25 Pieces of a Chicano Mind*. Denver, Colorado: Barrio Publications. 1971.

1,866. Araoz, Daniel Leon. *Male Puerto Rican Parental Self-Image*. Unpublished Ph.D. Dissertation, Columbia University. 1969. (*Dissertation Abstracts*: Vol. 30 (1969). pp. 1629A-1630A.).

1,867. Betances, Samuel. "Puerto Rican Youth: Race and the Search for Identity." *The Rican*. No. 1 (Fall 1971). pp. 4-13.

1,868. Budner, Stanley; Lawrence Goodman; and Rosa Aponte. "The Minority Retardate: A Paradox and a Problem in Definition." *Social Service Review*. Vol. 43, No. 2 (June, 1969). pp. 174-183.

The authors divide the article into two sections, each dealing with a specific problem concerning the minority retardate. First, why is the institutionalization rate of retardates among minority groups so great when these groups are generally believed to be more tolerant of retardates? Previous studies have shown that lower-income groups do tend to accept such abnormalities more readily than do upper-income groups. Ss in the aforementioned studies were White, however. In order to ascertain if the hypothesis is equally valid for non-White minority groups, the sample in the present study consisted of the following groups: native Whites maintaining a retardate at home; Puerto Ricans maintaining a retardate at home; and Puerto Ricans voluntarily institutionalizing a retardate. Analysis of the data was based on these four variables: severity of retardation; life-stress; use for community resources; and reactions to retardation, which dealt with the possibility that Puerto Ricans react differently to a retardate than do Whites- The authors conclude that class position is related to familial response to retardation on two levels: the lower the class position, the higher the tolerance for retardation; the lower the socioeconomic position, the less able the family is to cope with the reality problems involved. The authors note that the higher rate of institutionalization of minority retardates may result from a higher incidence of retardation among lower-class groups or selective or discriminatory operations on the part of public agencies toward these groups. They recommend changing current treatment programs so that they become more appropriate for the Puerto Rican family.

The remainder of the article dealt with the lack of knowledge about the minority retardate, and the lack of clarity in the concept itself. The authors attempt to clarify the phenomenon, noting that there are several approaches to the problem. It may be that the difficulty is not retardation, but minority status; hence, proverty. There is a difference in extent of retardation, a higher incidence among minorities, and a difference, too, in the quality of the retardation. (DH)

1,869. "Campaña de Saneamiento en Harlem." *El Diario de Nueva York*. June 20, 1949. p. 3.

339

1,870.  Casavantes, Edward J.  Deviant Behavior in the Mexican-American Stu-
        dent and Its Relation to Education.  A Position Paper. Albuquerque
        New Mexico. Southwestern Cooperative Educational Laboratory
        August, 1970.  16p.
        (ED 060 989)

        Since the literature about the mental health of Mexican Americans
        has been consistent in reflecting that a low socioeconomic level com-
        bined with extensive use of Spanish lowers IQ tests scores of Mexican
        Americans, these factors should be studied in connection with the
        educational achievement of Mexican Americans and their mental health.
        This could be done because Mexican Americans are highly distinguishable
        from other ethnic groups.  In such a study, 8 hypothesis are proposed
        for testing on a random sample of large numbers of Mexican Americans
        from all socioeconomic levels and ages, from every state in the South-
        west, from rural and urban settings, from the Chicano militant element,
        from colleges and from the Hispano component.  The actual survey should
        be done by special questionnaire and a short adapted form of standard per-
        sonality tests with some in Spanish.  Examiners should be Mexican
        Americans highly trained in psychiatric interviewing procedures.  In
        summary, this investigation should be a broad-based study on the
        mental health and educational achievement of Mexican Americans. (RIE)

1,871.  Cole, M. and J. Bruner.  "Cultural Differences and Inferences about
        Psychological Processes."  American Psychologist. Vol. 26
        (1971). pp. 867-876.

1,872.  Covian, Sherrill.  "The Effect of Unemployment and Under-employment
        on the Puerto Rican Male in New York City." October 27, 1965.
        (unpublished)

1,873.  Dohrenwend, Bruce P.  "Social Status, Stress and Psychological Symp-
        tons."  Milbank Memorial Fund Quarterly. 47:1 (1969) - Part 2.
        pp. 137-150.

        "Examined the incidence of psychiatric disorder among Black and
        Puerto Rican groups relative to their social class counterparts in
        more advantaged ethnic groups in the Washington Heights area of New
        York City.  Subjects consisted of a sample from the general popu-
        lation of approximately 1,000 21-59 year old adults, of whom 150
        were seen for follow-up.  In addition, about 100 psychiatric outpatients
        served as subjects.  Results generally confirm earlier reports of an
        inverse relationship between social class and psychological disorder.
        However, Puerto Rican subjects showed larger proportions of symptons
        than their counterparts in other groups.  Black subjects did not show
        higher rates than Jewish or Irish ethnic groups.  Findings suggest
        that there are strong ethnic and class differences in modes of ex-
        pressing distress."  It was found that both Puerto Ricans and Blacks
        tend to score higher than subjects in the other groups on sets of
        items that indicate sociopathic ("most people are honest for fear of
        being caught") and possible paranoid ("it's safer to trust nobody")
        tendencies.  Members of different ethnic groups differ greatly in
        their ratings of the social desirability of many of the symptons.
        (PASAR + DH)

1,874.  Fernández-Marina, R.  "The Puerto Rican Syndrome: Its Dynamics and
        Cultural Determinants".  _Psychiatry_. Vol. 24 (1961). pp. 79-82.

1,875.  Garretson, O.K.  "A Study of the Causes of Retardation Among Mexican
        Children in a Small School System in Arizona." _Journal of Educa-
        tional Psychology_. Vol. 19 (January 1928) pp. 21-40.

1,876.  Goodenough, F.L. and D.B. Morris.  "Studies in the Psychology of
        Children's Drawings." _Psychology Bulletin_. Vol. 47 (1969).
        pp. 369-433.

1,877.  Lubchansky, Isaac; Gladys Ergi; and Janet Stokes.  "Puerto Rican
        Spirtualists View Mental Illness: the Faith Healer as a
        Paraprofessional."  _American Journal of Psychiatry_. 127:3
        (September, 1970). pp. 312-321.

        "Examines the attitudes and beliefs about mental illness of
        twenty faith healers in the Puerto Rican Community of New York
        City: these were compared with data collected earlier from samples
        of Spanish-speaking community leaders and a cross-section of Puerto
        Rican household heads.  Spiritualists appear to be an idiosyncratic
        group differentiated within their culture for the purpose of healing.
        The lack of professional acknowledgement of the role native healers
        play in this and other minorities is emphasized, and two case studies
        that may help to explain this lack of acknowledgement are presented."
        (PASAR)

1,878.  Malzberg, B.  "Mental Disease among Puerto Ricans in New York City."
        _Journal of Nervous and Mental Disease_. Vol. 123 (1956). pp. 262-269.

        This study examines the prevalence of mental disease among
        migrants and native-born citizens who have at least one parent born
        in Puerto Rico.  The author notes that Puerto Rican migration has
        concerned itself mainly in New York City, with the population at
        355,000 in 1953 (est.).  Migration is influenced by economic factors,
        notably, the search for employment.  Puerto Ricans are faced with
        the severe handicap of the language barrier upon their arrival in
        this country, and this leads them to the segregated areas of the city
        where Spanish is readily understood, and where housing and health
        conditions are noticeably substandard.  Hospital admissions for
        Puerto Ricans between October 1, 1948, and September 30, 1951,
        numbered 1,163 first admissions, or 157.7 per 100,000 people.  For
        the population of New York City as a whole, the number was 144.5
        per 100,000 people.  When the rates are compared on the basis of age
        and sex, they become 229.3 for Puerto Ricans and 185.5 for others.
        Because the Puerto Rican admissions tend to be younger, as does the
        whole Puerto Rican population in the city, there was a high propor-
        tion suffering from dementia praecox and an extremely low proportion
        suffering from psychoses of old age.  Mental illness among Puerto
        Ricans is attributable, to a large extent, to the difficult life
        circumstances they face in this country, low wages, substandard
        housing, poor standard of living, etcetera.  The author also feels

that migration is an important factor, that a person of Puerto Rican origin is much more likely to develop a mental disease than an average person in the city's population. (DH)

1,879. Malzberg, Benjamin. "Mental Disease Among Puerto Ricans in New York State." Psychiatric Quarterly. Vol. 22 (1948). pp. 300-308.

1,880. Mercer, Jane R. The Origins and Development of the Pluralistic Assessment Project. Sacramento: California State Department of Mental Hygiene, Bureau of Research. Sacramento: California State Department of Education, Office of Compensatory Education. Bethesda, Maryland: National Institute of Mental Health. January 1972. 26p.
(ED 062 461)

The Pluralistic Assessment Project, which has been funded for three years by the National Institute of Mental Health, was developed in response to the results of earlier studies on the epidemiology of mental retardation in the City of Riverside, California. It was found that the criteria for classification of persons as mentally retarded varied as a function of sociocultural group in a study conducted in 1963-64. The present project will produce an Adaptive Behavior Inventory for Children standardized on representative samples of Anglo, Mexican-American, and black public school children, five through 11 years of age, which can be used to assess a child's performance in non-academic rules using socioculturally relevant norms. The project will produce socioculturally relevant norms on the 1973 edition of the Wechsler Intelligence Scale for Children for use with Anglo, Mexican-American, and black children. The project will also produce a Health History and Impairment Inventory standardized on a representative sample of Anglo, Mexican-American and black children. (RIE)

1,881. Opler, Marvin . "The Social and Cultural Nature of Mental Illness and Its Treatment." in S. Lesse, ed. An Evaluation of the Results of the Psychotherapies. pp. 280-291.

1,882. Pagán de Colón, P. Emotional Adjustment Problems of the Puerto Rican Migrant. New York: Commonwealth of Puerto Rico, Department of Labor, Migrant Division. (c. 1960).

1,883. Palomares, Geraldine Dunne. The Effects of Stereotyping on the Self-Concept of Mexican Americans. Albuquerque, New Mexico: Southwestern Cooperative Educational Laboratory. 1970. 35pp.
(ED 056 806)

Purposes of this literature review on the Mexican American child were to explore the self concept; cultural marginality; the occurrence and effects of stereotyping; and the results of studies undertaken to measure self-concept. Findings included that (1) the manner in which a person is dealt with by "significant others," especially in the early years, is considered to have a great deal to do with that

person establishing a satisfactory identity and a positive self-view;
(2) Mexican American children have been found to experience ever-
present conflicting demands and pressures to do and be at school something other than what they do and are in the subculture; (3) many
educators are seen to hold stereotypic views of Mexican American
children due to over-generalization of the literature regarding
specific Mexican American populations--this affects the children's
performance, as is maintained in the "self-fulfilling prophecy"
theory; and (4) due to inconclusiveness of research on the Mexican
American child's self-concept, the broadly accepted idea that Mexican American children, as a group, have a negative self-concept is
a stereotypic view.  Discussion of the review concludes that
educators, "by seeing all or most Mexicans as 'fatalistic,' 'unable
to delay gratification,' 'lazy', 'dependent,' 'having negative self-
concepts,' etc., and then reflecting these beliefs to the children
with whom they deal," are forcing the Mexican American child either
to reject the majority culture or to deny what he is.  The only
recommendation is to research why the Anglo insists on cultural
homogeneity.  (RIE)

1,884.  Paschal, Franklin C. and Louis R. Sullivan.  "Racial Influences in
the Mental and Physical Development of Mexican Children."
Comparative Psychology Monographs. Vol. 3. 76pp.

1,885.  Posner, Carmen Alberta.  Some Effects of Genetic and Cultural
Variables on Self Evaluations of Children. Unpublished Ph.D.
Dissertation, Illinois Institute of Technology. 1969.
(Dissertation Abstracts. 29:12 (1969). pp. 4833B-4834B).

The purpose of the investigation was to study the effects of
socio-economic status (SES), ethnic affiliation, intelligence and
sex on the self-perceptions of children.  Subjects were 300 first
graders; ethnic groupings included Black, White and PR children
born on the U.S. mainland.
The socio-economic groupings consisted of lower and upper-
middle-class levels.  Only the PR sample was limited to children of
lower SES (no PR children of upper-middle-class status could be
found).  Within the ethnic affiliation and SES children were
selected on 3 levels of intellectual ability; below-average,
average and superior (based on their performance on the California
Short Form Test of Mental Maturity, Level I).  Two measures of self-
perception were administered: The Illinois Index of Self-Derogation
(IISD) and 4 different sets of a paper and pencil form of the
Farnham-Diggory Children Self-Evaluation Scale (SE).
Results indicate that positive self-evaluations are directly
related to healthy personality development; children who rate themselves lower perceive their parents rating them low; children of low
SES and below average intelligence rate themselves consistently
lower than their middle-class and intellectually superior peers;
Black children have significantly more negative self-images than
their White peers; the self-discrepancy of the PR children does not
differ significantly from either White or Black children.  The need

343

for preventive action to neutralize the biological, psychological and social pathogenic factors which so determine the developing child's self-perception is immense, obviously. The author suggests that action be taken on the community level, not limited to work with individual children. (DH)

1,886. Ramírez, Manuel, III. Effects of Cultural Marginality on Education and Personality. Albuquerque, New Mexico: Southwestern Cooperative Educational Laboratory. 1970. 15pp.
(ED 065 805)

A review of the literature, this report concerns itself with the identification of the Mexican American with his ethnic group as an asset or a liability. Examining the relationship of cultural marginality to education, personality, and attitudes, the author points out a need for additional research in this area. (RIE)

1,887. Ramírez, Manuel III. "Social Responsibilities and Failure in Psychology: The Case of the Mexican-American." Journal of Clinical Child Psychology. Vol. 1 (1972). pp. 5-8.

1,888. Ramírez, Manuel, III. Value Conflicts Experienced by Mexican-American Students. (1968). 11p.
(ED 059 829)

The object of this study, conducted in a Northern California city school district, was to find evidence of cultural value conflicts experienced by Mexican American secondary school students of low socioeconomic background. Those students experiencing the most difficulty in adjusting to the school setting and thus most likely to be dropouts were interviewed, observed in class, and asked to tell stories about pictures depicting students, teachers and parents interacting in a school setting. Stories told about these pictures revealed Mexican American value conflicts in terms of such factors as loyalty to family and ethnic group, female modesty, machismo, the role of education, and separation of sex roles. This paper contains discussions of eight Mexican American values found to conflict most often with the value system of schools, along with an accompanying story for each as told by Mexican American students; also contained are 1-paragraph discussions of four measures that could be instituted to help alleviate value conflicts. (RIE)

1,889. Reville, J.N. and A. Rivera. The Psychological Adjustment of Puerto Rican Boys. Project 4623. New York School of Social Work. 1956.

1,890. Rosenthal, Alan Gerald. Pre-School Experience and Adjustment of Puerto Rican Children. Unpublished Ph.D. Dissertation, New York University. 1955.
(Dissertation Abstracts. Vol. 15 (1955). p. 1205.).

The purpose of this study was to determine the relationship between pre-school experiences of a non-academic nature and the absence of these experiences on the achievement of a group of bilingual

children who made a successful school adjustment.  Ss were five
and six year old male and female children who were born in Puerto
Rico; selection was partially based on socioeconomic, educational
and physical factors.  Ss were divided into two groups:  the first
group had no pre-school orientation; the second group was given
cultural enrichment programs prior to entering school.
    Data was based on the observations of the S's teachers.
Results indicate a significant difference in the achievement of
the  two groups; the group that had the pre-school program received
higher ratings overall.  It was suggested, therefore, that these
programs be continued, and that further research in pre-school
orientation programs be undertaken.  (DH)

1,891.  Rosner, Milton S.  A Study of Contemporary Patterns of Aspirations
        and Achievements of the Puerto Ricans of Hell's Kitchen.  Un-
        published Ph.D.  Dissertation, New York University. 1957.

1,892.  Soares, Louise M. and Anthony T. Soares.  Age Differences in the
        Personality Profiles of Disadvantaged Females.  Paper presented
        at the American Psychological Association Annual Convention,
        Washington, D.C.  September 1971.  8pp.
        (ED 056 135)

        This study systematically investigated age differences in per-
        sonality characteristics of advantaged and disadvantaged high school
        and college females.  Two hundred and thirty three Ss were randomly
        selected from an urban environment.  The test norms for the study
        instrument, Cattell's 16 Personality Factor Questionnaires, were
        based on a group of 86 advantaged college women.  The disadvantaged
        group was 50% black and Puerto Rican, while the advantaged group was
        75% White.  Both disadvantaged and advantaged high school girls
        showed a pattern of group dependence, self-assurance, expediency,
        and relatively little frustration, with the disadvantaged girls
        indicating greater emotional instability, less intelligence, lower
        ego strength, and tough-mindness.  Disadvantaged and advantaged
        college women seemed more sociable, assertive, conscientious,
        venturesome, sensitive, guilt-prone, self-sufficient, tense and
        controlled.  The advantaged women demonstrated an even greater
        tendency toward intelligence and enthusiasm.  (RIE)

1,893.  Sobrino, James F.  Group Identification and Adjustment in Puerto
        Rican Adolescents.  Unpublished Ph.D. Dissertation, Yeshiva
        University. 1965.
        (Dissertation Abstracts. Vol. 26 (1966). p. 4067).

        The author hypothesized that the social adjustment of a Puerto
Rican adolescent depends, to a great extent, on his or her identification within the ethnic group itself.  The person's idealized image
(what group he or she identifies with) must then be compared with his
or her self-image; adjustment would seem to depend upon the relative
similarity of these two images.
        To test his hypothesis, Sobrino administered the Semantic
Differential Scale, the EFOS and a questionnaire to 360 male and

female Puerto Ricans between the ages of twelve and eighteen. Ss were
selected from four parochial schools and from a child guidance clinic.
Ss were divided into 3 groups on the basis of these tests: 1) the
clinic group, clearly maladjusted; 2) school maladjusted but not in
therapy; and 3) school well adjusted. Correlations were made between
the author's hypothesis and the groups of Ss, and it was found that:
1) the clinic group identifies more with the majority group (in
which they are unacceptable); 2) the adjusted group maintains a
favorable self-image while they do perceive differences between
themselves and others; and 3) the maladjusted but non-clinic group
seems to have a more positive self-image than the indicators would
warrant. (DH)

1,894.  Stanton, Howard R. "Social Research into Mental Retardation and
        Employment: A Puerto Rican Study." in A. Field (ed.). Urban-
        ization and Work in Modernizing Societies. pp. 9-13.

        "A sample of the total population of Puerto Rico was screened
with intelligence tests 'to determine who had what level of intelligence, and what they were doing.' If mental retardation is defined by
by IQ test scores, 'then societies like Puerto Rico have as high as
30 or 35% retardation. The person suffers less in many such societies
not because he has been rehabilitated in some way, but because the
society takes the low levels of ability into account.' The two main
criteria were: '(1) The extent to which a disabling condition is
compounded by structural position, by ethnic group membership, age
category, social class, or place of residence and (2) The difference
in effect of a disabling condition depending on the way economic and
social factors are structured.'"     (PASAR)

1,895.  Strauss, Susan. "The Effect of School Integration on the Self-Concept
        of Negro and Puerto Rican Children. Graduate Research in Educa-
        tion and Related Disciplines. Vol. 3 (1967). pp. 63-76.

        Compared the self-concept of second and third grade Black and
Puerto Rican children of low socioeconomic background in a paired
school and in a non-paired school. "Pairing is the combining of two
school populations," one predominantly white, the other predominantly
black. It was hypothesized that for both grades the paired group
would have a higher self-concept, and that the paired third grade
would do better than the second. A 50 question inventory was used
in which there were three possible answers to each question. The
possible score range was 100-150. One hundred children were tested,
50 in each of the two schools, 25 in each of the two grades. The
results showed that the paired groups' scores were significantly higher
than the non-paired groups' scores. No significant difference was
found between the scores of the paired second and third grade groups.
It is concluded that pairing does increase the self-concept of Black
and Puerto Rican children. The extent of its positive influence needs
further study. (PASAR Vol. 14 (1967) DC 237501 Abst. No. 12495)

1,896. Sunshine, Nancy J. <u>Cultural Differences in Schizophrenia</u>. Unpublished
Ph.D. Dissertation, The City University of New York. 1971.
(<u>Dissertation Abstracts</u>. 32:2 (1971). pp. 1197B-1198B).

Researchers have concluded that schizophrenias are manifesta-
tions of culturally conditioned responses to stress. Culture
provides the values, life styles and interpersonal attitudes fundamental to the different symptons. A study by Singer and Opler
found such symptomatic differences between Irish and Italian
schizophrenics, and related them to the cultural factors of
family and energy distribution. The present study worked with
the hypothesis that differences in psychopathology, again due to
cultural distinctions, would be found between 40 Black and 40
Puerto Rican male schizophrenics being hospitalized at Manhattan
State Hospital. Class, ethnicity and educational level were controlled for and the Ss were divided into two age groups: over
thirty, and under thirty. The first part of the study involved a
census of hospital records, checking for incidence of alcoholism, etc.
the second part involved the administration of the Wittenborn
Psychiatric Rating Scale, the MACC II Behavioral Adjustment Scale
and a hostility scale. The results reaffirm the Singer and Opler
fundings, Blacks being similar to the Irish and Puerto Ricans
resembling the Italians, and provide further evidence of the role
of culture in transmitting sympton styles.
     The Puerto Rican Ss were considered less of a management
problem than the Black Ss, whose symptons were characterized by
withdrawal. The Puerto Rican Ss were prone to acting out and
assaultive behavior; they had more visitors than the Black Ss and
exhibit much more sociable behavior. (DH)

1,897. Suraci, Anthony B. <u>Reactions of Puerto Rican and Non-Puerto Rican
Parents to Their Mentally Retarded Boys</u>. Ph.D. Dissertation,
New York University. 1966.
(<u>Dissertation Abstracts</u>. Vol. 27 (11-A) pp. 3739-3740.).

The study dealt with the differences between Puerto Rican and
non-Puerto Rican parents' reactions to their mentally retarded boys.
It was hypothesized that there were differences in parents' reaction
to etiology of retardation, child-rearing practices, reactions toward institutionalization and reactions to special education classes.
Ss were 120 parents of mentally retarded boys; 60 Puerto Rican and
60 non-Puerto Rican, all from the Mental Retardation Clinic of New
York Medical College. It was found that differences do exist in
Puerto Rican and non-Puerto Rican parental attitudes toward retardation: Puerto Rican parents tend to be more superstitious and
religious. Puerto Rican parents tend to be more authoritarian in
their child-rearing practices than do non-Puerto Rican parents, and
have more favorable attitudes concerning institutionalization than
non-Puerto Rican parents. The non-Puerto Rican Ss had more favorable
attitudes toward special education classes in publc schools, however.
No significant differences could be found concerning: a) chronological
ages of retarded boys and their families; b) education of the parents;
c) family size; d) employment, or parental income. Differences noted

were the levels of intelligence of the retarded boys and the parents' religious preference.  (DH DC 28309 1)

1,898.  Troutman, E.C.  "Suicide Attempts of Puerto Rican Immigrants." Psychiatric Quarterly. Vol. 35 (1961). pp. 544-554.

D. Sociological and Anthropological Studies of Puerto Rican Communities on the Mainland

1,899. Aiello, John R. and Stanely E. Jones. "Field Study of the Proxemic Behavior of Young School Children in Three Subcultural Groups." Journal of Personality and Social Psychology. 19:3 (September, 1971). pp. 351-356.

Observed the proxemic relationships of 210 interacting pairs of Black, Puerto Rican, and White first and second graders in school playgrounds. Interaction distance and directness of shoulder orientation (axis) were recorded. Middle-class White subjects stood farther apart than lower-class Black and Puerto Ricans. Sex differences among White subjects in distance scores and culture and sex differences in axis scores were also found. Results suggest that proxemic patterns are acquired early in life and support the contention that differences between the dominant culture and other groups in the use of space are basic, with the qualification that sex roles may also influence proxemic behavior. (PASAR)

1,900. Abramson, Harold J. Ethnic Pluralism in the Connecticut Central City. Storrs, Connecticut: Institute of Urban Research, University of Connecticut. 1970.

1,901. Alers-Montalvo, M. The Puerto Rican Migrants of New York City: A Study of Anomie. Unpublished M.A. Dissertation, Columbia University. 1971.

1,902. Allen, Ruth A. "Mexican Peon Women in Texas."Sociology and Social Research. Vol. 15 (November-December 1930). pp. 131-142.

1,903. The American Catholic Family. Englewood Cliffs, New Jersey: Prentice Hall, Inc. 1956. Chapter VI.

1,904. Anderson, James and William H. Johnson. Social and Cultural Characteristics of Mexican-American Families in South El Paso, Texas. Interim Reports of the Mathematics Education Program. Las Cruces, New Mexico: New Mexico State University. 1968. 47pp. (ED 026 175)

1,905. Antonowsky, Aaron. "Aspiration, Class and Racial-Ethnic Membership." Journal of Negro Education. Vol. 36:4 pp. 385-393.

Earlier studies of students from a small city show that Black youngsters have a higher level of aspiration than Whites. Three hundred seventy eight 10th-graders from 5 schools in a large city were tested to see if the same pattern could be found, and to compare: (1) middle and low-class Blacks and Whites, and (2) Puerto Rican youths with Blacks and Whites. Senior guidance counselors asked 8 questions dealing with "future socioeconomic-educational aspirations and expectations". It was found that middle-class Whites had the highest aspiration level, and Puerto Ricans were relatively low. Patterns of response were similar for lower-class Whites, middle-class Puerto Ricans, and middle and lower-class Blacks. The comparison between the small city and the metropolis showed "differences between lower-class Whites and similarities between lower-class Blacks." (PASAR)

1,906.  Arter, Rhetta M. Between Two Bridges: A Study of Human Relations in the Lower East Side of Manhattan, the Area Served by the Educational Alliance. Human Relations Monograph No. 5. Interpretation by Dan W. Dodson. New York University Center for Human Relations. 1956.

1,907.  Arter, Rhetta M. Mid-City. Human Relations Monograph No. 3. New York University Center for Human Relations Studies. 1953.

1,908.  Atkins, James A. "A Cultural Minority Improves Itself." Human Relations in Colorado. Denver: Colorado State Department of Education, 1961.

1,909.  Baglin, Roger F. The Mainland Experience in Selected Puerto Rican Literary Works. Unpublished Ph.D. Dissertation, State University of New York at Buffalo. 1971.
        (Dissertation Abstracts International. Vol. 32 (1971-72). p. 3290A.)

        This study examines the mainland experience in the Puerto Rican short story, novel, and theater. Themes such as liberty and identity appear constantly in works on this subject. The study includes an introduction to Puerto Rican literature dealing with these themes before 1940, a discussion of the radical demographic and osciological changes since 1940 and a detailed examination of six works on the mainland experience by recognized authors. (ECK)

1,910.  Barry, David W. "Opportunity for Protestant Churches among Puerto Ricans." National Council Outlook. Vol. 9 (May 1959). pp. 9-10.

1,911.  Barry, David W. "The Puerto Rican Adapts Remarkably." Washington Post and Times Herald. March 8, 1959.

1,912.  Beecher, Robert Houston. A Study of Social Distance Among Adolescents of Ethnic Minorities. Ph.D. Dissertation, New York University. 1968.
        (Dissertation Abstracts International. Vol. 29 (2-A), 1968. pp. 398-399.)

        The purpose of the study was to determine the nature of social distance between Puerto Rican and Black adolescents in New York City. Three hypotheses were tested: 1) length of residence; 2) color is related to the sociometric choices made by the youngsters; and 3) whenever either Puerto Ricans or Blacks are in the minority, the acceptance scores will be higher than when both are in the majority or in the minority. Results of testing on both the Ohio Acceptance Scale and the Bogardus Scale only partially substantiated the first hypothesis. In order to test the second hypothesis, the investigator used photographs; the Ss were asked to classify the

students "light," "dark," or "medium." The correlation was at the
.05 level, which was not significant. The third hypothesis was rejected after the t-test was calculated. Scores on the social
acceptance scale were not necessarily higher when either group
was in the minority. The author suggests that the social climate
of the school environment was probably more responsible for the
positive relationship between Puerto Rican and Black adolescents
than was the minority/majority representation. (DH)

1,913. Bender, L. and S. Nichtern. "Two Puerto Rican Boys in New York."
in G. Seward (ed.). Clinical Studies in Cultural Conflict.
New York: Ronald. 1958.

1,914. Benitez, Jaime. "El Problema Humano de la Emigración." La Torre.
(Enero-Marzo, 1956). pp. 13-21.

1,915. Berger, S. "Puerto Rican Migrants Create Housing Problems." Real
Estate News. Vol. 33 (August 1942). pp. 265-267.

1,916. Berkowitz, Elaine. "Family Attitudes and Practices of Puerto Rican
and Non-Puerto Rican Pupils." High Points. (March, 1961).
pp. 25-34.

In the past 8 years the number of Puerto Rican children in
New York City's public schools has increased 150% and many difficulties in teaching these children have come up. A great deal has
been written about the language handicaps and cultural differences
of the Puerto Rican children, but this home economics teacher set out
to see if those supposed family backgrounds were really different.
The results of a survey of 247 students (120 PR and 127 non-PR)
at J.H.S. 263 in Brooklyn, New York, indicated that the differences
in family patterns were really not that siginificant. "It would
appear that both groups of pupils, Puerto Rican as well as non-
Puerto Rican pupils, need help in the typical concerns of youth at
the adolescent level. If there are any differences they would
appear in the following: Puerto Rican pupils more than non-Puerto
Rican pupils need help in the area of family relationships; Puerto
Rican pupils need help in improving facilities for living within the
home and for carrying on normal family life. Since they are living
under more crowded conditions, emphasis needs to be on providing
some kind of privacy for the members, and help sharing in limited
facilities. Since there is more unemployment among the Puerto
Rican group, help must be furnished in the better use of the money....
The non-Puerto Rican pupils more than the Puerto Rican pupils need
help in the appreciation of the companionship of the family group;
The non-Puerto Rican pupils have to assume more responsibility for
household management because there are more working parents in the
group..." (DH)

1,917. Berle, Beatrice B. Eighty Puerto Rican Families in New York City.
New York: Columbia University Press. 1958.

1,918.  Berle, Beatrice B.  "Sterilization and Birth Control Practices in a
        Selected Sample of Puerto Rican Living in a Manhattan Slum."
        Fertility and Sterility. Vol. 8 (May/June 1957). pp. 267-281.

1,919.  Beytagh, L.A.  Family Dynamics in Thirty-two Puerto Rican Families.
        Unpublished Ph.D. Dissertation, Columbia University. 1967.

1,920.  Bienstock, Herbert.  Labor Force Experience of the Puerto Rican
        Worker.  New York:  United States Bureau of Labor Statistics.
        (May 20, 1968).

1,921.  Bodarsky, C.J.  "Chaparonage and the Puerto Rican Middle Class."
        Journal of Marriage and Family.  26:347-348, August 1964.

1,922.  Bogardus, Emory S.  "Second Generation Mexicans."  Sociology and
        Social Research.  Vol. 13 (1928-1929) pp. 276-283.

1,923.  Bouquet, Susana.  Acculturation of Puerto Rican Children in New
        York and Their Attitudes toward Negroes and Whites.  Unpublished
        Ph.D. Dissertation, Columbia University. 1961.
        (Dissertation Abstracts. Vol. 22 (1962). p. 4105-4106.)

The purpose of this study was to investigate the relationship
between the acculturation of Puerto Ricans in New York and their
physical type.  Ss were 140 Puerto Ricans, 31 Blacks, and 32 Whites,
all males, between the ages of 10.5 and 12.5.  The schedule for
interviewing consisted of a questionnaire and photographs protraying
different physical types and different occupations, and some showing
hostile and friendly situations.  The boys were asked to match
physical types with occupations and the various situations pictured
in the photographs.  Each of the Ss' verbal responses were recorded
and classified according to the length of time he had lived in New
York and his physical type.  The findings indicate that 1) individual
behavior within a family changes less during acculturation than behavior within a community; 2) the degree of acculturation of Puerto
Ricans does not vary according to the physical types (i.e. light or
dark Puerto Ricans); 3) the Puerto Rican Ss made use of physical
discrimination to the same extent as the Black and White Ss. (DH)

1,924.  Boxhill, C.J.; T.V. Kalarickal; M. Curcio.  "Certain Expressed Moral
        Beliefs of Three Groups of Early Adolescent Boys."  National
        Catholic Guidance Conference Journal. Vol. 14 (1969). pp. 21-24.

So were 63 Black, 68 Puerto Rican, and 51 White eighth grade
boys from Catholic schools of East and Central Harlem whose families
were in upper-low and lower-low socioeconomic levels.  The instrument
used was Isler's revision of the Havighurst and Taba Student Belief
Inventory.  Whites scored higher on honesty and responsibility than
did the other two groups.  No significant difference was found in
regard to friendliness, loyalty, and moral courage among any of the
groups. (PASAR)

1,925.  Braestrup, Peter.  "Life among the Garment Workers."  New York Herald
        Tribune.  September 29-October 10, 1958. (series of ten articles.)

1,926.  Bram, Joseph.  The Lower Status Puerto Rican Family. Revised.  New
        York: Mobilization for Youth, Inc.  (March, 1963). 14pp.
        (ED 016 690)

1,927.  Brameld, Theodore.  "Explicit and Implicit Culture in Puerto Rico:
        A Case Study in Educational Anthropology."  Harvard Educational
        Review.  Vol. 28 (Summer, 1958). pp. 197-213.

1,928.  Brameld, Theodore.  The Remaking of a Culture.  New York: 1959. 478pp.

1,929.  Brody, E.  "Cultural Exclusion, Character and Illness."  American
        Journal of Psychiatry.  Vol. 122 (1966). pp. 852-858.

1,930.  Brown, Myrtle Irene.  Changing Maternity Care Patterns in a Migrant
        Puerto Ricans:  A Study of Acculturation in a Group of Puerto
        Rican-Born Women in New York City, Relevant to the Extent of their
        Utilization of Professional Health Care during the Maternity
        Cycle.  Ph.D. Dissertation, New York University. 1961.
        (Dissertation Abstracts.  Vol. 22 (1962). p. 4330.)

1,931.  Brown, Stuart.  "Philadelphia's Puerto Ricans: Language Barrier is
        Chief Source of Problems Faced by Migrants."  Philadelphia
        Sunday Bulletin. March 16, 1958.

1,932.  Bryce, Herrington J.  Social Origin as an Obstacle or as an Aid to
        Mobility:  A Comparative Analysis of Long-Run Occupational
        Mobility.  Ph.D. Dissertation, Syracuse University. 1966.
        (Dissertation Abstracts.  Vol. 28 (2-A) 1967. pp. 333-334).

        The purpose of this study was to determine to what extent a
father's social origin and occupation affect the son's opportunities
for social mobility, either upward or downward.  It is a cross-
national study in that the investigation was carried out in the
United States, Puerto Rico, Japan, and seven countries of Western
Europe.  The study revolves around these variables: 1) the efficient
utilization of human talent; 2) the occupational wage structure;
3) the level and distribution of employment; and 4) economic equity.
Three broad occupational categories were used: middle-class, working-
class, and elite; the nebulous quality of the classification system
may have some bearing on the validity of the study, the author notes.
For the purposes of this study, an index of mobility into non-compe-
ting groups was developed and applied to the above classes.  It was
shown that, in all societies, middle-class origin was an aid to elite
status while working-class origin was an obstacle for upward mobility.
France, Sweden, West Germany, Puerto Rico and the United States all
provide equal opportunity for the working-class to enter middle-
class occupations.  Italy, Japan, Puerto Rico and the United States
all provide elite and middle-class people the opportunity to enter
working-class occupations; in the other countries studied, such downward

mobility is hindered. The implication here is that, in the United
States (and in Puerto Ric9), social origin is less likely to hinder
or facilitate occupational mobility than it is in other societies. (DH)

1,933.  Cahill, Imogene D.  Child-Rearing Practices in Lower Socioeconomic
Ethnic Groups.  Unpublished Ph.D. Dissertation, Columbia
University. 1966.
(Dissertation Abstracts. 27:9 (1967). p. 3139A.).

The purpose of the study was to identify what differences, if
any, exist in the child-rearing practices of lower socioeconomic
ethnic groups.  Ss were 60 mothers, representing PR, Black and
White groups equally.  The schedule used by interviewers was designed by Sears, Maccoby and Levin for their investigation of child-
rearing practices of middle-class and working-class mothers,
reported by them in Patterns of Child Rearing.  Repsonses from the
present study were broken down and rated on the Sears' schedule;
analysis of the results led to the rejection of the original hypothesis
that the child-rearing practices of PR, Black and White families of
the lower socioeconomic group differ from each other.  In fact, comparing the results of the present study to the results of the Sears'
study of middle and working-class practices, it seems that socioeconomic status has a stronger influence on the patterns of child-
rearing than ethnogeny.
Some differences exist between the present study's three
ethnic groups, however.  It was found that PR mothers were the
most permissive, and Black mothers the least.  The PR mothers
encouraged dependency and aggression much less than the Black
mothers did; White mothers fell in between the other two on both
of these measures.  (DH)

1,934.  Carter, Hugh and Bernice Doster.  "Social Characteristics of
Naturalized Americans from Mexico: Age and Marital Status."
Monthly Review, Immigration and Naturalization Service. U.S.
Department of Justice. Vol. 8 (September 1950) pp. 35-39.

1,935.  "The Challenge in Working with Puerto Rican Families." Pathways
in Child Guidance. 2:3 (April, 1960). pp. 3-6.

1,936.  Chess, Stella; and Others.  Social Class and Child-Rearing Practices.
1967 (unpublished). (Paper prepared for the American Psychological Association Divisional Meeting, November 17, 1967.)

1,937.  Commonwealth of Puerto Rico.  Department of Labor.  Migration
Division, New York City. The Jobs We Do. Migration Division.
1952.

1,938.  Commonwealth of Puerto Rico. Department of Labor, Migration
Division, New York City. Trade Unions and Puerto Rican Workers
on the Mainland.  Migration Division, 1952.

1,939.  Complaints Alleging Discriminition Because of Puerto Rican National

Origin, July 1, 1945 - September 1, 1953. New York: New York
State Commission Against Discrimination. 1958.

1, 940. Crasilneck, Harold Bernard. A Study of One Hundred Latin-American
Juvenile Delinquents in San Antonio, Texas. Unpublished Master's
thesis, University of Texas. 1948.

1,941. Cruz, Maria Angelita. Spanish-Speaking Children's Expressed Attitude
Toward Money Values. Unpublished Master's thesis, University of
Texas. 1942.

1,942. Díaz, Manual, et al. The Attitudes of Puerto Ricans in New York
City to Various Aspects of Their Environment. (Project No. 4317.
New York School of Social Work, June 1953.)

1,943. Doob, Christopher Bates. The Development of Peer Group Relationships
among Puerto Rican Boys in East Harlem. Ph.D. Dissertation,
Cornell University. 1967.
(Dissertation Abstracts. Vol. 28 (1968). p. 2788A.)

1,944. Drusine, Leon. Some Factors in Anti-Negro Prejudice among Puerto
Rican Boys in New York City. Unpublished Ph.D. Dissertation,
New York University. 1955.

1,945. Eastman, Clyde. Assessing Cultural Change in North-Central New
Mexico. New Mexico State University, Las Cruces. Agricultural
Experiment Station. Washington, D.C.: Dept. of Agriculture.
January 1972. 65pp.
(ED 063 070)

1,946. "Economic Status of Puerto Ricans: United States and New York,
New York." Manpower Report of the President, 1964. U.S.
Government Printing Office, 1964.

1,947. Elam, Sophie L. "Poverty and Acculturation in a Migrant Puerto
Rican Family." The Record (New York City). (April, 1969).
pp. 617-626.

The article is essentially a case history of a migrant Puerto
Rican family, the Mendozas, from the time of their arrival on the
mainland to the birth of their eldest child's daughter. The author's
apparent objective is to show that the full acculturation of Puerto
Rican families is thwarted because of their poverty, their different
cultural background, and American intolerance of their cultural
system. The author describes the family's problems with language,
employment and housing in some detail. It is implied that they do
not adapt to the new country until well into the first mainland born
generation's adulthood. There is some discussion of the traditional
Puerto Rican mother who, inadvertently, does not allow or encourage
her children to develop the kinds of attitudes that might help them
survive and compete better in the new cultural environment. Though
the Puerto Ricans may acquire some trappings of middle-class life in

this country, they are still effectively kept out of the mainstream
of American society because of their poverty, inferior living
conditions (barrios), language problems, and educational difficulties.
(DH)

1,948. Fantino, Eileen. "Children of Poverty." Commonweal. Vol. 62
(June 17, 1955). pp. 271-274.

1,949. Feree, William; Joseph Fitzpatrick and John Illich. Report on the
First Conference on the Spiritual Care of Puerto Rican
Migrants. Archidiocese of New York. 1955.

1,950. Fernández-Marina, R.; E.D. Maldonado-Sierra; and R.D. Trent. "Three
Basic Themes in Mexican and Puerto Rican Family Values."
Journal of Social Psychology. 48:2 (1958). pp. 167-181.

1,951. Fernández Méndez, Eugenio. La identidad y la cultura: Críticas y
valoraciones en torno a Puerto Rico. San Juan: Ediciones
el Cemi, 1959.

1,952. Fernos Isern, Antonio. "The Role of Puerto Rico and Its People in
the Americas." Journal of Educational Sociology. Vol. 35
(May, 1962). pp. 397-401.

1,953. Findling, Joav. "Bilingual Need Affiliation and Future Orientation
in Extragroup and Intragroup Relations." Modern Language
Journal. 53:4 (1969). pp. 227-231.

Reported on 2 experiments conducted using 18 male Spanish-
English bilingual teenagers of Puerto Rican descent confined to
the Spanish-speaking ghetto of Urban New York. Experiment 1 dealt
with need affiliation, hypothesizing that these subjects would exhibit greater need affiliation in English than in Spanish. Word
association scores were obtained from subjects. The test was administered in both English and Spanish. Henley's index of need
affiliation was applied, and the data subjected to analysis of
variance. Experiment II was concerned with future orientation.
Six pairs of incomplete sentences in both English and Spanish were
presented to each subject for completion. The sentences in each
pair varied with respect to future or past. An analysis of variance
was performed on this data. An analysis of variance was performed
on this data. Results indicated that both future orientation and
need affiliation were greater in English than in Spanish. It appears
that English is associated with greater social rejection than is
Spanish. (PASAR)

1,954. Fishman, Joshua A. "Attitudes and Beliefs About Spanish and English
Among Puerto Ricans." Viewpoints. Vol. 47 (March, 1971).
pp. 51-72.

356

1,955. Fitzpatrick, Joseph P. "The Adjustment of Puerto Ricans to New York City." in: Milton L. Barron, ed., Minorities in a Changing World. New York: Alfred A. Knopf, 1967. Also in: Journal of Intergroup Relations. Vol. 1 (Winter 1959-1960), pp. 43-51.

1,956. Fitzpatrick, J.P. "Attitudes of Puerto Ricans Toward Color." The American Catholic Sociological Review. 20:3 (1959). p. 219-233.

1,957. Fitzpatrick, Joseph P. "Crime and our Puerto Ricans." Catholic Mind. Vol. 43 (1960). pp. 39-50.

1,958. Fitzpatrick, J.P. Delinquency and the Puerto Ricans. New York: Migration Division, Government of Puerto Rico. 1959.

1,959. Fitzpatrick, Joseph P. "The Integration of Puerto Ricans." Thought. (Autumn, 1955).

1,960. Fitzpatrick, J.P. "Intermarriage of Puerto Ricans in New York City." The American Journal of Sociology. 71:4 (1966). pp. 395-406.

1,961. Fitzpatrick, J.P. "Mexicans and Puerto Ricans Build a Bridge." America. (December 31, 1955). pp.

1,962. Fitzpatrick, J.P. "Problems of Diverse Culture Patterns and Value Systems." Lecture, Mimeographed. 1961.

1,963. Fitzpatrick, Joseph P. Puerto Rican Americans: The Meaning of Migration to the Mainland. Ethnic Groups in American Life Series. Englewood Cliffs, New Jersey: Prentice-Hall, Inc. 1971. 215p.
(ED 061 396)

The focus of the present study is the quest of the Puerto Ricans for identity. This is the feature of their migration which they share most intimately with all other immigrant groups, and yet it is the aspect in which their experience both on the Island before they come and in New York, is unique. After they arrive in New York, they face a set of circumstances which make the quest for identity much more difficult for them than it was for earlier groups. Initial dispersal over wide areas, continued relocation, and the policy of integration in public housing make it more difficult for Puerto Ricans to establish or retain stable and strong Puerto Rican neighborhoods. The need of the great majority who are Catholics to adjust to integrated parishes, rather than having Puerto Rican parishes, largely eliminates the parish as a focus of identity. The facility of low cost travel back to Puerto Rico may make it easier to retain identity with the Island. Finally, the variety of color among Puerto Ricans also complicates the problem of identity in the presence of mainland discrimination. (RIE)

1,964. Fitzpatrick, J.P. "Puerto Ricans in Perspective: The Meaning of
       Migration to the Mainland." International Migration Review.
       Vol. 2 (1968). pp. 7-20.

       This article examines the Puerto Rican migration to New York
       City from the historical perspective of past migrations to New York.
       The author discusses the problems of assimilation and preservation of
       identity which, after years of identification with the Black
       community, are particularly difficult for the Puerto Ricans now. In
       a brief review of the outstanding literature on Puerto Rican culture
       and assimilation, Fitzpatrick presents different views of their
       present situation. Over the last ten years, there has been a shift
       in strategy from an emphasis on culture to an emphasis on power,
       largely influenced by the Black Power movement. The experiences of
       the past appear to be repeating themselves in this, the present
       migration. Fitzpatrick feels that the situation now is an optimistic
       one, that the Puerto Ricans are merely participating in the "turbulent
       social process" of becoming New Yorkers. (DH)

1,965. García, Alonso. "Discrimination Against Puerto Ricans." pp. 79-80.
       In: Governor's Advisory Commission on Civil Rights. Springfield,
       Ohio: Governor's Advisory Commission on Civil Rights, December
       1958.

1,966. Geismar, Ludwig L. and Ursula C. Gerhart. "Social Class, Ethnicity,
       and Family Functioning: Exploring Some Issues Raised by the
       Moynihan Report." Journal of Marriage and the Family. Vol. 30
       (1968). pp. 480-487.

       Investigated the relationship between the social functioning
       of urban families and their ethnic status, i.e., the influence of
       social class on the way ethnic group membership affects family
       behavior. A sample of 50 Black, 50 White, and 33 Puerto Rican
       families was used. Findings show that social status overshadows
       ethnicity in determining the nature of family functioning. (PASAR)

1,967. Glazer, Nathan and Daniel P. Moynihan. Beyond the Melting Pot: the
       Negroes, Puerto Ricans, Jews, Italians, and Irish of New York
       City. Cambridge, Massachusetts: M.I.T. and Harvard University. 1963.

1,968. Golob, Fred. "The Puerto Rican Worker in Perth Amboy, New Jersey."
       Occasional Studies: No. 2. Institute of Management and Labor
       Relations, Rutgers University, March 1956.

1,969. González, A. Problems of Adjustment of Puerto Rican Boys. Project
       4593. New York School of Social Work. 1956.

1,970. Gray, Lois. "The Labor Union and Puerto Ricans in New York City."
       Organization for Economic Cooperation and Development. December
       1963. Reprint No. 147 of the New York School of Industrial and
       Labor Relations, Cornell University, Ithaca New York.

1,971. Groty, Dorothy R. <u>Puerto Rican Families in the Navy Yard District of Brooklyn</u>. Unpublished Manuscript (1931). In Covello Papers.

1,972. Harvey, L.F. "Delinquent Mexican Boy." <u>Journal of Educational Research</u>. Vol. 42 (April 1949) pp. 573-585.

1,973. Helfgott, Roby B. "Puerto Rican Integration in the Skirt Industry in New York City." in A. Antonovsky and L. Lorwin, eds., <u>Discrimination and Low Incomes</u>. New York State Commission Against Discrimination. 1958.

1,974. <u>Helping Puerto Ricans Help Themselves</u>. New York: Commonwealth of Puerto Rico, Department of Labor, Migration Division. September 1958.

1,975. Hernández, Deluvina. "Mexican-American Challenge to a Sacred Cow." Monograph 1 (March, 1970). Los Angeles: Mexican-American Cultural Center, Los Angeles: University of California.

1,976. Hernández, Joseph William. <u>The Sociological Implications of Return Migration in Puerto Rico: An Explatory Study</u>. Ph.D. Dissertation, University of Minnesota. 1964.
(<u>Dissertation Abstracts</u>. Vol. 27 (1967). p. 4350A.).

1,977. Hillson, Maurie et al. <u>Education and the Urban Community: Schools and the Crisis of the Cities</u>. 1969. 506pp.
(ED 040 233)

Selection of 49 articles dealing with the crises and conflicts of urban education. Articles discuss the impact of urbanization, social stratification, the effects of urban poverty on Black and Puerto Rican families, and the disadvantaged school dropout. (RIE)

1,978. Howell, James D. and Others. <u>Migrant Farm Workers in Northwestern Ohio</u>. Ohio Agricultural Research and Development Center, Wooster. August 1971. 28pp.
(ED 065 228)

1,979. Illich, I. "Puerto Ricans in New York." <u>Commonweal</u>. Vol. 64 (1956). pp. 294-297.

Illich discusses the new migrants in New York City with an emphasis on the distinctness of their migration. The Puerto Rican migration has broken many of the patterns that had been followed by previous migrant groups, and this has been less than advantageous in many respects. The author demonstrates the necessity for the Puerto Rican population of New York City to gain recognition and respect for their background. He concludes, "What they need is not more help but less categorization according to previous schemes, and more understanding." (DH)

1,980. Insurralde, Adolfo. Socio-Economic Factors Affecting Families in the
        Forsyth Area. New York: Lower Eastside Neighborhoods Association.
        1964.

        Puerto Rican life in New York City.

1,981. Jackson, Anne, Ed. Ethnic Groups--Their Cultures and Contributions.
        Arkansas State Department of Education. Little Rock: September
      · 1970. 162pp.
        (ED 063 062)

1,982. Jenkins, Shirley. Intergroup Empathy: An Exploratory Study of Negro
        and Puerto Rican Groups in New York City. Unpublished Ph.D.
        Dissertation, New York University. 1957.
        (Dissertation Abstracts. Vol. 18 (1958). p. 1125.).

        The purpose of this investigation was to determine the extent
        of intergroup empathy between Black and Puerto Rican people in New
        York City. Empathy was measured by the ability of members of the
        two groups to predict the responses of each other to statements
        about intergroup relations. Ss were 250 Black and Puerto Rican
        participants in community agencies and churches in four Manhattan
        neighborhoods where there is much intergroup contact: Chelsea, the
        Lower East Side, the West Side and East Harlem. Ss completed either
        the English or Spanish version of the empathy schedule and were
        required to give a three-part response to each statement: "Do you
        agree?", "Do members of your own group agree, in general?", and "Do
        members of the other group agree, in general?" Analysis showed a
        high level of individual agreement among Black and Puerto Rican Ss
        on cooperative statements. There were significant differences in
        their responses to conflict statements, however, with individuals
        identifying closely with their own groups. Empathetic responses
        were measured by comparing intergroup predictions with both indivi-
        dual and intragroup reactions of the opposite group. Schedule
        statements with the lowest empathetic responses dealt with matters
        in which there is considerable competition between the groups:
        housing, employment, racial and ethnic status and social acceptance.
        The author concludes that the attitudes of Puerto Ricans and Blacks
        toward each other depended more on their separate problems within
        the larger community than on their intergroup associations. (DH)

1,983. Jensen, Gerald M. Investigation of Occupational Training Needs of
        Migrant Workers which May Point Toward Employment in other than
        Migrant Employment. Imperial County Schools, El Centro, Cali-
        fornia. Washington, D.C.: National Center for Educational
        Research and Development. April 28, 1972. 78pp.
        (ED 065 262)

1,984. Johnson, G.B., Jr. "Relationship Existing Between Bilingualism and
        Racial Attitude." Journal of Educational Psychology. 42:5
        (May, 1951). pp. 357-365.

Johnson measured the attitudes of bilingual male students toward
the Anglo ethnic group and found that a profound knowledge of the
Anglo culture or no knowledge of it yielded the least cultural prejudice.

1,985. Jones, Stanley E. "A Comparative Proxemics Analysis of Dyadic
Interaction in Selected Subcultures of New York City." Journal
of Social Psychology. 84:1 (June 1971). pp. 35-44.

"Two studies investigated subcultural and sex differences in
spatial orientation behavior. Two-person groups of adults in four
separate poverty subcultures (Negro, Puerto Rican, Italian, and
Chinese) were observed engaging in social interaction on the public
streets of New York City. Trained judges made estimates of the
interpersonal distance and mutual shoulder orientation of each dyad.
Regardless of subcultural group membership, women were found to be
more direct in shoulder orientation than men, an outcome which
appears to parallel the findings of previous studies of eye-contact
behavior. There was some evidence, as informants had predicted, that
Black males were less direct than males in other minority groups,
although this result did not approach statistical significance.
Finally, interaction distance was strikingly similar in all of the
subcultures studied, contrary to expectations, suggesting the in-
ference that poverty groups are rather homogeneous in the structuring
of interpersonal distance." (PASAR)

1,986. Kalarickal, Thomas V. Certain Expressed Moral Beliefs of Three
Groups of Early Adolescent Boys. St. John's, 1968.
(Dissertation Abstracts: 1968. Vol. 28 (12-A). p. 4910).

The purpose of the study was to examine whether differences in
certain expressed moral beliefs exist among Puerto Rican, Black and
White adolescent boys who live in the same socioeconomic area. The
305 Ss were all eighth grade boys from the 116 Catholic schools of
East and Central Harlem who identified themselves as Puerto Rican
(116), Black (111), or White (78), and who had lived in that area
for at least six months prior to the study. The Student Belief
Inventory was used to assess the S's expressed moral beliefs about
the following traits: friendliness, honesty, loyalty, moral courage
and responsibility. Additional data collected for the study were
the S's scores on the STA achievement series, their answers on the
Student Questionnaire, and the reports of teachers. When the samples
were compared for their expressed moral beliefs by means of the
"t" technique, without controlling any variable, significant differences were found in honesty, moral courage and responsibility. The
White group scored significantly higher when compared with the Puerto
Rican and Black groups, between whom there was no significant difference. When the samples were controlled for differences in age, social
status and academic achievement, differences in honesty and responsibility were found. Again, the White group scored higher than the
other two groups. Among the three groups there was no significant
difference in friendliness, loyalty and moral courage. There was no
significant difference between the Puerto Rican and Black samples in
any trait. (DH DC 42737 1)

361

1,987. Kantrowitz, Nathan. <u>Social Mobility of Puerto Ricans in New York,</u>
<u>1950-1960.</u> (unpublished) 1967.

1,988. Kantrowitz, Nathan. "Social Mobility of Puerto Ricans: Education,
Occupation, and Income Changes among Children of Migrants,
New York, 1950-1960. <u>International Migration Review</u>. Vol. 2
(1968). pp. 53-72.

This article tests the assumption that upward mobility of an
immigrant group is possible if the institutions of the host country
are open to social change and the immigrants' culture encourages
social mobility by analyzing the statistics of the 1950 and 1960
census concerning Puerto Ricans in the New York metropolitan area.
The conclusion is that at least the children of Puerto Rican migrants
have achieved some high school education, certain White collar jobs
and, to a lesser extent, higher income. Both Puerto Rican parents
and their children are still poor, however; but, if these data can
be used for prediction, it seems that there is a good possibility
of reaching a distribution of social class similar to that of
other groups in the city within the lifetimes of the Puerto Rican
migrants and their children. (ECK)

1,989. Kelly, Lenore Mary. <u>Community Identification among Second Genera-</u>
<u>tion Puerto Ricans; Its Relation to Occupational Success</u>. Un-
published Ph.D. Dissertation Fordham University. 1971.
(<u>Dissertation Abstracts International</u>. Vol. 32 (1971-72). p. 2223A.)

This was a study of thirty married Puerto Rican males in an
attempt to determine factors which lead to varying degrees of
occupational success. The informants had some contact with the
Puerto Rican community in Brooklyn and represented three levels of
occupational success: successful, stable and unsuccessful. The
evidence seems to indicate that those second generation Puerto
Ricans who are successful tend to retain their contact with the
Puerto Rican community, express pride in their heritage and seek to
perpetuate it in their children. The occupationally stable, as they
acquire skills necessary to mobility, also tend to follow this
pattern. The loss of community strength and ethnic identity are
more likely to be associated with failure to advance. (ECK)

1,990. Kluckhohn, Florence R. and Fred L. Strodtbeck. <u>Variations in Value</u>
<u>Orientations</u>. Evanston, Illinois: Row Peterson. 1961.

1,991. Kochman, Thomas. <u>Mainstream and Non-Mainstream Communication Norms</u>.
Cambridge, Massachusetts: Language Research Report No. 6.
January 1972. pp. 7-50.
(ED 063 814)

This document discusses significant differences between the
cultural personalities and communication patters on non-mainstream
groups in an effort to understand the nature and cause of conflict
between groups. The author seeks to identify the "combustible"
features of different communication systems to demonstrate the sys-

tematice nature of the features as they operate within their respective "natural" cultural settings by showing how they interrelate
with other aspects of the communication process, and to show the
extent to which these features can be "accounted for" in terms of
general or specific (ethnic) cultural factors. (RIE)

1,992. Lauria, Anthony. "Respeto, Relajo and Interpersonal Relations in
       Puerto Rico." Anthropological Quarterly. Vol. 37 (April,
       1964). pp. 53-67.

1,993. Leibowitz, Arnold H. "English Literacy: Legal Sanction for Discri-
       mination," Notre Dame Lawyer, 45:1 (Fall, 1969), pp. 7-67.
       (ED 040 378)

       The thesis of this article is that, in general, English
       literacy tests and other statutory sanctions applied in favor of
       English were originally formulated as indirect but effective means
       of achieving discrimination on the basis of race, color or creed.
       Many such provisions in the law are anachronistic while others
       retain their vigor and continue to operate in a discriminatory
       manner. A few contribute to the "official" character that English
       enjoys in our society or to the health and safety of the operation
       of certain institutions. Of special interest: English as the ex-
       clusive language of the American school system and the special case
       of Puerto Rico. (from document)

1,994. The Leisure Time Problems of Puerto Rican Youth in New York City:
       A Study of the Problems of Selected Group Work Programs. New
       York: Archdiocese of New York, Catholic Youth Organization,
       January 1953.

1,995. Lennon, John Joseph. A Comparative Study of the Patterns of Accul-
       turation of Selected Puerto Rican Protestants and Roman
       Catholic Families in an Urban Metropolitan Area (Chicago).
       Ph.D. Dissertation, University of Notre Dame. 1963.
       (Dissertation Abstracts. Vol. 24 (1963)p. 2613.)

       This study investigates the extent of acculturation of Puerto
       Rican Protest and Roman Catholic families in Chicago, and the role
       of the Church as an agent of acculturation for this migrant popu-
       lation. The sample consisted of 50 Protestant and 50 Roman
       Catholic couples who were interviewed (in Spanish) in their homes.
       Acculturation was measured by assigning scores to each individual on
       a weighted 16 item Index of Acculturation. Findings are as follows:
       1) the respondents have generally low acculturation scores; 2) age
       and religiousness were significantly related to acculturation;
       3) there is no significant difference between the acculturation of
       migrants from urban and rural parts of Puerto Rico, male and female
       migrants, or Protestants and Catholics; and 4) year of migration is
       not significantly related to acculturation in Chicago. Both churches
       were found to impede and assist acculturation; both migrant groups
       preferred Spanish clergymen and services. (ECK)

1,996. Levitas, Mitchel. "New York's Labor Scandal: The Puerto Rican Workers." New York Post. July 15-19 and 21, 1957.

1,997. Lewis, Oscar. "The Culture of Poverty in Puerto Rico and New York." Social Security Bulletin. (September, 1967).

1,998. Lewis, Oscar. La Vida: A Puerto Rican Family in the Culture of Poverty. San Juan and New York. New York: Random House. 1966.

1,999. Lewis, Oscar. "Mother and Son in Puerto Rican Slum, Part I, Felicita." Harper's. December, 1965. pp. 71-84.

2,000. Lewis, Oscar. "Portrait of Gabriel: A Puerto Rican Family in San Juan and New York, Part II, Gabriel." Harper's January, 1966. pp. 54-59.

2,001. Lewis, Oscar. A Study of Slum Culture: Backgrounds for La Vida. New York: Random House. 1968.

2,002. Lorain and Gary Experience with Puerto Rican Workers. (Six articles reprinted from the Gary Post Tribune). Washington: Office of the Government of Puerto Rico, 1948.

2,003. Mencher, Joan P. Child Rearing and Family Organization among Puerto Ricans in Eastville, El Barrio de Nueva York. Unpublished Ph.D. Dissertation, Columbia University. 1958. (Dissertation Abstracts. Vol. 19 (1958). pp. 931-932.).

2,004. Miller, Michael Victor. Conflict and Change in a Bifurcated Community: Anglo - Mexican-American Political Relations in a South Texas Town. Master's thesis, A and M University, College Station, Texas. December 1971. 292p. (ED 063 993)

2,005. Mintz, Sidney W. Puerto Rico: An Essay in the Definition of a National Culture. In: Status of Puerto Rico: Selected Background studies for the United States-Puerto Rican Commission on the Status of Puerto Rico. Washington, D.C.: U.S. Government Printing Office. 1966.

2,006. Mintz, Sideny. Worker in the Cane. New Haven, Connecticut: Yale University Press. 1960.

Studies the conversion of a poor sugar cane worker in Puerto Rico to a Pentecostal sect. The author discusses the idea that poor people, caught in a rapidly changing society, tend to seek security in the religious or ethnic community in which they can retain a sense of the traditional way of life. This hypothesis can be easily applied to the migrant Puerto Rican on the mainland. (DH)

2,007. Minuchin, S. et al. Families in the Slums. New York: Basic Books. 1967.

2008. Monserrat, Joseph. "Community Planning for Puerto Rican Integration in the United States." An address at the National Conference on Social Welfare, Minneapolis, Minnesota, May, 1961.

2009. Muñoz Marín, Inés María Mendoza de. "Identidad Puertoriqueña." La Prensa. (July 30, 1961).

2,010. McCauley, Margaret A. A Study of Social Class and Assimilation in Relation to Puerto Rican Family Patterns. Ph.D. Dissertation Fordham University. 1972.
(Dissertation Abstracts International. Vol. 33 (1972). p. 428A.).

Previous studies of the American family indicate that conjugal roles are conditioned to some extent by socioeconomic status. Studies of Puerto Rican families in New York City show that their husband-wife relationships are affected by both socioeconomic status (SES) and degree of assimilation (DOT). The purpose of the present study was to examine the conjugal-role relationship of Puerto Rican husbands and wives, and to attempt to determine the influence of cultural and economic factors. Data was obtained from an interview, a questionnaire and direct observation. Findings show that SES is a more important determinant for companionship and DOT is a more important determinant for division of labor and decision-making. Sex is an important variable for decision-making and division of labor only. (from abstract, abridged, DH)

2,011. McCready, Fred. "Prejudice, Language Barrier Add to Puerto Rican Problem." and Community Council Seeks Way to Ease Lot of Puerto Ricans." Allentown (Pa.) Call. May 2-3, 1958.

2,012. McKeon, John. "The Ortiz Family." Jubilee. Vol. 1 (June 1953). pp. 22-23.

2,013. Narita, Ruth. The Puerto Rican Delinquent Girl in New York City. Unpublished M.A. Thesis, Fordham University. 1954.

2,014. Newfield, Jack. "Harlem Sí, Tammy No." Commonweal. Vol. 75 (September 29, 1961). pp. 10-12.

2,015. O'Brian, Robert W. "Hawaii's Puerto Ricans: Stereotype and Reality." Social Processes in Hawaii. Vol. 23 (1959). pp. 61-64. (University of Hawaii).

2,016. O'Flannery, Ethna, "Social and Cultural Assimilation." American Catholic Sociological Review. 22-196-206 (Fall 1962).

2,017. Opler, Marvin K. "Dilemmas of Two Puerto Rican Men." In G. Seward, ed. Clinical Studies in Culture Conflict. New York: Ronald. 1958. pp. 223-244.

2,018. "Out of the Melting Pot." Economist. Vol. 211 (April 1964). p. 273.

2,019. Pakter, Jean, et al. "Out-of-Wedlock Births in New York City."
       *American Journal of Public Health.* Vol. 50 (May 1961). pp.
       683-696. Concluded in Vol. 51 (June 1961). pp. 846-865.

2,020. Pérez Justino, David. *A Suggested Human Relations Program for
       Puerto Ricans in Spanish Harlem.* Unpublished Ph.D. Dissertation,
       Columbia University. 1952.

2,021. "Pleas for the Puerto Ricans." *Social Science Review.* Vol. 26
       (September 1952). p. 26.

2,022. Poblete, R. and T.F. O'Dea. "Anomie and the Quest for Community:
       the Formation of Sects among the Puerto Ricans in New York."
       *American Catholic Sociological Review.* Vol. 21 (1960). pp. 18-36.

2,023. Preble, Edward. "The Puerto Rican American Teenager in New York
       City." in Eugene Brody (ed.) *Minority Group Adolescents in the
       United States.* Baltimore, Maryland: Williams and Wilkins. 1968.
       pp. 48-72.

       Data for this report on Puerto Rican adolescents in New York
       City has been collected over a 10-year period during which time the
       author served as a participant-observer of four predominantly Puerto
       Rican communities in the city. Preble states that he has "simply
       absorbed information through personal and social relationships" so
       that it will be understood that his conclusions have not been the
       result of a systematic research program. The report contains a brief
       description of the historical and cultural characteristics of Puerto
       Ricans, and goes on to discuss the problems the migrants encounter
       when they reach New York City. Among the issues treated in this
       report are the relationships of Puerto Ricans to non-Puerto Ricans;
       the identification of Puerto Ricans with Blacks; the physical con-
       ditions of the Puerto Rican population in New York--housing, climate;
       employment, job discrimination; return migration; the family, es-
       pecially in regard to the traditional pattern of male dominance
       which is breaking down here; and the alternatives of American-born
       children of Puerto Rican migrants. American born Puerto Ricans
       have a much greater potential for success than those who come to
       New York as adolescents because of their relative familiarity with
       English. The major factor for success for young Puerto Ricans is
       their knowledge of English. Crime and narcotics are touched upon as
       alternatives for the frustrated Puerto Rican student or worker who
       chooses to "drop out." (DH)

2,024. "The Prejudice of Having No Prejudice in Puerto Rico: Part I." *The
       Rican.* No. 2 (Winter 1972). pp. 41-54.
       (EJ 059 455).

2,025. *Project to Preserve the Integration of the Puerto Rican Migrant
       Family.* New York: Puerto Rican Family Institute. 1965.

2,026.   "The Puerto Rican Americans." in _American Diversity_. A Bibliography
         of Resources on Racial and Ethnic Minorities for Pennsylvania
         Schools. Harrisburg, Pennsylvania: Department of Education
         1969. (pp. 123-133.)

2,027.   _Puerto Rican Children:  Some Aspects of Their Needs and Related_
         _Services._ New York: City Welfare Council, 1949.

2,028.   "Puerto Rican Youth Speaks Out." _Personnel and Guidance Journal_.
         50:2 (October, 1971). pp. 91-95.

         An edited interview presents some frank, forthright responses
         relating to a great variety of concerns, from culture and stereo-
         typing to poverty and tokenism.  (CIJE)

2,029.   _Puerto Ricans Confront Problems of the Complex Urban Society:  A_
         _Design for Change._  New York City: Office of the Mayor,
         Community Conference Proceedings, 1968.

2,030.   Reiss, Paul J.  _Backgrounds of Puerto Rican Delinquency in New_
         _York City._ Unpublished M.A. thesis, Fordham University. 1954.

2,031.   Richardson, Stephen A. and Jacqueline Royce.  "Race and Physical
         Handicap in Children's Preference for Other Children." _Child_
         _Development_. 39:2 (1968). pp. 467-480.

         A rank-order preference of drawings was obtained in which skin
         color and handicap were systematically varied.  Subjects were 10-12
         years old and from lower-income Negro, White, and Puerto Rican
         families, and from upper-income White Jewish families.  Results
         suggest that, for all subjects, physical handicap is such a powerful
         cue in establishing preference that it largely masks preference
         based on skin color.  The authors suggest that attempts (in
         children's camps) to counter prejudice based on visible physical
         handicaps may be more difficult than attempts to counter prejudice
         based on race.  (PASAR and DH)

2,032.   Rivera, George, Jr.  _Theoretical Perspectives on Integration in_
         _Chicano Communities._ Paper presented at the Annual Meeting
         of the Rural Sociological Society in Baton Rouge, Louisiana.
         August 25, 1972.  14pp.
         (ED 065 248)

2,033.   Rizzo Costa, Clara; and Betty Wallace Robinett.  _La Familia Vázquez_
         _en los Estados Unidos._ San Juan: Estado Libre Asociado de
         Puerto Rico, Departamento de Instruccion Publica. 1955.

2,034.   Robinson, Sophia. _Can Delinquency be Measured?_ Columbia University
         Press. 1936. pp. 236-249.

2,035.   Rogler, L.H. and A.B. Hollingshead.  "Puerto Rican Spiritualist as a
         Psychiatrist." _American Journal of Sociology_.  67:17-21,
         July 1961. University of Chicago Press.

2,036. Ruíz, Paquita. Vocational Needs of Puerto Rican Migrants. University of Puerto Rico, Social Science Research Center, 1947.

2,037. Safa, H.I. An Analysis of Upward Mobility in Low Income Families: A Comparison of Family and Community Life among Negro₃ and Puerto Rican Poors. Syracuse, New York: Syracuse University Press. 1967.

The purpose of this report was to describe the social isolation of the poor: the problems that class and racial barriers pose for assimilation, and roles and relationships within the low-income family and how they are affected by community life.
The data used in this paper had been collected by researchers in previous studies. Safa's analysis yielded the following results: 1) that the poor are held back by a lack of opportunity, support and stimulation in the home and the community environment; 2) in Puerto Rico, the problem of upward mobility is one of class, not race, and the solution is education; 3) unity among the poor is high because of the community leaders who form a core for the community, reflecting the thoughts of the people; and 4) the family life-styles in Puerto Rico reflect the roles played by family members in the community. The author concludes with a discussion concerning the participation of government in helping the poor assimilate into the larger society. (DH)

2,038. Salazar, John J. Self-Designation Patterns of a Traditional Ethnic Minority in a Modern Society -- Conflict, Consensus, and Confusion in the Identity Crisis. Paper prepared for the Third World Congress for Rural Sociology, Baton Rouge, Louisiana, August 22-27, 1972. 26pp.
(ED 066 256)

2,039. Schaefer, Dorothy. "Prejudice in Negro and Puerto Rican Adolescents." in Robert A. Dentler et al. (eds.) The Urban R's. New York: Praeger. 1967.

2,040. Schepses, E. "Puerto Rican Delinquent Boys in New York City." Social Science Review. 23:1 (1949). pp. 51-61.

2,041. Seda-Bonilla, Edwin. The Normative Patterns of the Puerto Rican Family in Various Situational Contexts. Unpublished Dissertation, Columbia University. 1958.

2,042. Seda-Bonilla, E. "Patterns of Social Accommodation of the Migrant Puerto Rican in the American Social Structure." Revista de Ciencias Sociales. 2:2 (1958). pp. 189-201.

This article discusses the status of the Puerto Ricans in the American social system. Social status in the United States is ascribed according to the fallacious concept of "social race." Social race refers to the socially visible characteristics of a given group; these are the characteristics which will determine, to a large extent, the life chances, prestige and esteem for the individual and

the group as a whole.  The Puerto Rican has long been identified
with the Negro in dominant White society; therefore, his position
is very near the bottom in the American social structure.  Socio-
logists claim that the Puerto Rican community has not abandoned
the use of Spanish in order to preserve some sense of distinction.
The author states that Puerto Ricans have everything to gain by
rejecting their Spanish names and cultural backgrounds.  In this
way, the Puerto Rican can reject his social status and move rapidly
through American White society.  The "White middle-class group"
of Puerto Ricans in New York City has organized itself around
cultural norms and formed a tight-knit Puerto Rican community; the
Black group has assimilated into Black American society with
relative ease.  (DH)

2,043.   Seda-Bonilla, E.  "Social Structure and Race Relations." <u>Social</u>
         <u>Forces.</u> 40:2 (1961). pp. 141-148.

2,044.   Senior, Clarence.  "The Puerto Ricans in New York: A Progress Note."
         <u>International Migration Review</u>. Vol. 2 (1968). pp. 72-79.

         This article deals with specific instances of Puerto Rican in-
tegration into the larger society, in social, economic, religious
and political situations.  For example, he cites a study which compares statistics on intermarriage which concludes that Puerto Rican
migrants are assimilating as rapidly as the migrants during the
period 1908-1912.  Instances such as trade organizations, organizations to help guide and counsel youths, local organizations and labor
unions are cited as examples of Puerto Rican self-help, and the fact
that Puerto Ricans have lived in New York longer than other groups
before applying for welfare, get off the welfare rolls more quickly
or use welfare to supplement insufficient income is noted as a
reason for optimism.  The number of elected or appointed city
officials from Puerto Rican background is also noted.  In conclusion,
the author says that Puerto Rican progress "is at least equal to
and in some instances more marked than that of other immigrant
groups," and he considers that the present trend will continue. (ECK)

2,045.   Seda Bonilla, Eduardo.  <u>Two Patterns of Race Relations</u>. (1969). 52p.
         (ED 058 368)

         What North Americans term "race" is not structurally isomorphic
to and, thus, not synonymous with what Latin Americans apply the term
to.  The social identities determined by "race", and consequently the
expected behavior ascribed to these identities, are so dissimilar that
meetings between persons of both cultures produce uncertainty and
discord.  In both the United States and Latin America, the racial
phonemenon emerges from cultural assumption which attribute function as
identity credentials for the social structure, and what expectations
are ascribed to such identities.  Given the fact that what are dealt
with are cultures based on such unlike assumptions, it is difficult to
understand why the elementary principle of cultural relativism is
ignored, only to fall into rampant ethnocentrism.  Particular atten-

tion is given to Puerto Rico. Although the North American image of the Puerto Rican is of a human unaware of racism and accepting of a non-white identity, the reality is quite different. The social and political implications of racial characteristics in Puerto Rico became accentualed through the Puerto Rican's misunderstanding of what to a North American constitutes membership in a racial category other than white. (RIE)

2,046. Senior, Clarence. "Research on the Puerto Rican Family in the United States." _Marriage and Family Living_. Vol. 19 (February 1957). pp. 32-37.

2,047. Sexton, Patricia Cayo. _Spanish Harlem: Anatomy of Poverty_. New York: Harper and Row. 1965. 208pp.

2,048. Sica, Morris G. _An Analysis of the Political Orientations of Mexican-American and Anglo American Children. Final Report_. Washington, D.C.: Office of Education, Bureau of Research. February 1972. 203pp. (ED 066 481)

2,049. Siegel, Arthur L. "The Social Adjustment of Puerto Ricans in Philadelphia." _American Journal of Sociology_. (August, 1957).

2,050. Sobrino, James F. _Group Identification and Adjustment in Puerto Rican Adolescents_. Unpublished Ph.D. Dissertation, Yeshiva University. 1965.

2,051. Stuart, Irving R. "Intergroup Relations and Acceptance of Puerto Ricans and Negroes in an Immigrant Industry." _Journal of Social Psychology_. Vol. 56 (1962). pp. 89-96.

2,052. Stuart, Irving R. "Minorities vs. Minorities: Cognitive, Affective and Conative Components of Puerto Rican and Negro Acceptance and Rejection." _The Journal of Social Psychology_. Vol. 59 (February, 1963). pp. 93-99.

2,053. Stycos, J.M. "Family and Fertility in Puerto Rico." _American Sociological Review._ 17:572-580, October 1952. National Council of Family Relations

2,054. Suchman, Edward A. "Sociomedical Variations Among Ethnic Groups." _American Journal of Sociology_. Vol. 70 (November 1964). pp. 319-331.

2,055. _A Systems Analysis of Southwestern Spanish Speaking Users and Non-users of Library and Information Services Developing Criteria to Design an Optimal Model Concept. Final Report_. National Education Resources Institute, Inc. Washington, D.C. Washington, D.C.: Bureau of Libraries and Education. Technology. June 30, 1972. 463pp. (ED 066 173)

2,056.  Tendler, Diana.  <u>Social Service Needs in a Changing Community:  A Study of the Use of Voluntary Social Agencies  by Puerto Rican Clients</u>.  Ph.D. Dissertation, New York University. 1965.  (<u>Dissertation  Abstracts</u>. Vol. 27 (1966). p. 1130A.)

2,057.  Thomas, P.  <u>Down these Mean Streets</u>.  New York: Alfred A. Knopf. 1967.

2,058.  Thomas, Piri.  "Nightmare in Mi Barrio."  <u>New York Times Magazine</u>.  August 13, 1967. p. 16-17.

2,059.  Vairo, Philip D.  "Career Aspirations of Negro and Puerto Rican Youth."  <u>Negro Educational Review</u>. (April, 1964).

2,060.  Weissman, Julius.  <u>An Exploratory Study of Communication Patterns of Lower-Class Negro and Puerto Rican Mothers and Pre-School Children</u>.  Unpublished Ph.D. Dissertation,  (<u>Dissertation Abstracts</u>. 27:11 (1967). pp. 2960A-3961A.)

        The purpose of the investigation was to explore the assumption that lower-class child-rearing patterns socialize passive behavior and lack of motivation for learning in children.  Ss were mothers and pre-school age children from low-income PR and Black groups.  The nature and degree of the "assumed passivity" were studied in terms of the forms and patterns of the verbal and non-verbal communications between mother and child pairs in both home and school settings.  The findings indicate that PR mother-child pairs are much more active at home than in the school setting; the opposite was true for the Black group.  "The PR group had higher activity rates in the 'teaching' category, in the reinforcement of verbal praise, smiles, touch contacts, and related areas.  The Black group was more active in the use of verbal admonitions, 'don'ts' in critical comments, in directing and coercing verbal and non-verbal communications."  The PR mother-child pairs were more active and responsive in the interpersonal processes of communication than the Black mother-child pairs. (DH)

2,061.  Wheeler, Helen.  "The Puerto Rican Population of New York, New York."  <u>Sociology and Social Research</u>. Vol. 35 (November 1950). pp. 123-127.

2,062.  White, Trumbull.  <u>Puerto Rico and Its People</u>.  Stokes. 1937.

2,063.  Whitman, F.L.  "New York's Spanish Protestants."  <u>Christian Century</u>.  Vol. 79 (February 7, 1962).  pp. 162-164.

2,064.  <u>Workshop Conference on Puerto Ricans</u>.  New York: Brooklyn Council for Social Planning. October 1953.

2,065.  Wright, Daved E. and Others.  <u>Ambitions and Opportunities for Social Mobility and Their Consequences for Mexican Americans as Compared with Other  Youth</u>.  Washington, D.C.: Department of Agriculture.  July 1972.  41pp.  (ED 066 285)

2,066.  Yinger, J.M. and G.E. Simpson. "Integration of Americans of Mexican, Puerto Rican and Oriental Descent." <u>The Annals</u>. Vol. 304 (March 1956).  pp. 124-131.

E. The Puerto Rican Experience on the Mainland as it is Portrayed in
   Both Anglo and Puerto Rican Literature

2,067. Baglin, Roger  F.  The Mainland Experience in Selected Puerto Rican
       Literary Works. Unpublished Ph.D. Dissertation, State University
       of New York at Buffalo. 1971.
       (Dissertation Abstracts International. Vol. 32 (1971-72).
       p. 3290A.)

       This study examines the mainland experience in the Puerto Rican
       short story, novel, and theater. Themes such as liberty and identity
       appear constantly in works on this subject. The study includes an
       introduction to Puerto Rican literature dealing with these themes
       before 1940, a discussion of the radical demographic and sociological
       changes since 1940 and a detailed examination of six works on the
       mainland experience by recognized authors. (ECK)

2,068. Cordasco, F.  "Nights in the Gardens of East Harlem: Patricia Sexton's
       East Harlem." Journal of Negro Education. Vol. 34 (Fall, 1965).
       pp. 450-451.

2,069. Cordasco, F.  "Patricia Cayo Sexton's Spanish Harlem: The Anatomy of
       Poverty." Journal of Human Relations. Vol. 13 (4th Quarter,
       1965). pp. 572-574.

       Cordasco's review of Patricia Cayo Sexton's book.

2,070. Cordasco, F.  "The Puerto Rican Family and the Anthropologist:
       Oscar. Lewis, La Vida, and the Culture of Poverty." Urban
       Education. 3:1 (1967). pp. 32-38.

2,071. _____  "The Puerto Rican Family and the Anthropologist: Oscar
       Lewis, La Vida, and the Culture of Poverty." Congressional
       Record. (July 18, 1967). pp. H8914-H8915.

2,072. _____  "The Puerto Rican Family and the Anthropologist."
       Teachers College Record. Vol. 68 (May, 1967). pp. 672-675.

       Discusses Levis' concept "culture of poverty," and the many
       questions raised by that concept, mainly, the typicality of the
       Rios family: "is Professor Lewis describing exceptional people,
       leading exceptional lives, who resemble their fellow Puerto Ricans in
       limited ways?" Cordasco seems to feel that the "culture of poverty,"
       as Lewis puts it, is a gross generalization. "It will register as
       crude parodies the poetic pathos of the Puerto Rican poor and it will
       be avidly read, misinterpreted and misused." (DH)

2,073. Cordasco, F.  "Spanish Harlem: The Anatomy of Poverty." Phylon:
       The Atlanta University Review of Race and Culture. Vol. 26
       (Summer, 1965). pp. 195-196.

2,074.  Delgado, A. et al.  Los cuatro, A Poetry Anthology. Denver,
        Colorado: Barrio Publications. 1971.

2,075.  Fishman, Joshua and Heriberto Casiano.  "Puerto Ricans in Our Press."
        The Modern Language Journal. March 1969. pp. 157-162.

        The purpose of the study was to investigate the treatment of
Puerto Ricans in four New York City daily newspapers, two published
in English and two in Spanish.  Content analysis during a six-
month period showed that the English newspapers had little interest
in Puerto Ricans either before or after the major flare-up in Spanish
Harlem.  In comparison with the Spanish dailies, the English dailies
were more concerned with Puerto Rican/Anglo relations, referred
more often to the Spanish Language (generally for identification
purposes) attributed negative traits to the Puerto Ricans more
often than positive traits, frequently mentioned Blacks and Puerto
Ricans together as problem populations, discussed their needs or
problems rather than solutions or remedial measures that could be
taken to counter the problems.  In the Spanish press there was
some indication of Puerto Rican/Black tension, primarily in terms of
competition for anti-poverty funds and Puerto Rican reluctance to
being classified with Blacks in most Anglo-American references. (DH)

2,076.  Fitzpatrick, J.P.  "Oscar Lewis and the Puerto Rican Family." America.
        Vol. 115 (December 10, 1966). pp. 778-779.

2,077.  Goldberg, Gertrude S. and Edmund W. Gordon.  "La Vida:  Whose Life?"
        IRCD Bulletin.  1968.

2,078.  Moesser, Alba.  Notas sobre dos autores mejicoamericanos de California
        (Notes on Two Mexican-American Authors in California).  Speech
        presented at the annual meeting of the American Association of
        Teachers of Spanish and Portuguese, Chicago, Illinois, December
        29, 1971.  23p.
        (ED 063 829)

        This paper discusses the work of two Mexican American authors,
Jose A. Villerreal and Richard Vazquez, using "Pocho" by Villarreal
and "Chicano" by Vazquez as the focus for discussion.  Both authors
describe the world of Mexican Americans and their social conditions,
and both underscore the need for conserving their native culture
and reject the stereotype of Mexicans as seen in other literature;
differences, however, are noted in their work.  Included in this
discussion are remarks on naturalism and cultural conflict.  (RIE)

2,079.  Rivera, Thomas.  Literatura chicana: Vida en busca de forma (Chicano
        Literature:  Life in Search of Form).  Paper presented at the
        American Association of Teachers of Spanish and Portuguese annual
        convention, Chicago, Illinois, December 28-30, 1971. 12p.
        (ED 058 808)

2,080. Rivera, Tomas. Literatura chicana: Vida en busca de forma (Chicano Literature: Life in Search of Form). Paper presented at the American Association of Teachers of Spanish and Portuguese annual convention, Chicago, Illinois, December 28-30, 1971. 12p. (ED 058 808)

The Chicano culture is searching for appropriate expression in art forms and literature. The Chicano novel and essay, often written in English, seem directed toward the North American public. The short story is the most varied in viewpoint and most versatile in form. Poetry captures the Chicano sensitivity. It is almost impossible to note the variety of forms, different languages, and mixtures of language in poetry. Drama is experimental and seeks to be didactic, using sarcasm and irony. The art forms most capable of changing the stereotype are written in English. Those forms most capable of reaching Chicanos are wirtten in popular language or in Spanish. (RIE)

2,081. Romano, O. (ed.). El Espejo, A Collection of Literature by Chicano Authors. Berkely: Quinto Sol Publications. 1969.

2,082. Sexton, Patricia Cayo. Spanish Harlem: Anatomy of Poverty. New York. 1965. 208pp.

(Review of Ms. Sexton's book by Frank M. Cordasco)

Cordasco criticizes Spanish Harlem for its "strange" style, inadequate documentation and the author's gross generalizations/ oversimplifications about the residents of East Harlem ("flagrant pseudosociological nonsense"). He points to her poor treatment of the churches and schools in the ghetto and finishes by labeling the book "clinically condescending to the very people and context that is supports to study."

2,083. Simmer, Edward (ed.). The Chicano: From Caricature to Self-Portrait. New York: New American Library. 1971. 318pp.

A collection of short stories which traces the evolution of the Chicano as reflected in literature. The stories range from the sentimental stereotypes of the nineteenth century to the increasingly sympathetic and insightful portrayals by such Anglo wirters as Ray Bradbury, Jack London, William Saroyan, Paul Horgan, and John Steinbeck, to the works of such new Chicano talents as Philip D. Ortego, Nick C. Vaca, and Genarc Gonzalez. The editor's introduction provides background material. (cover abrdiged)

2,084. Slotkin, Aaron N. "The Treatment of Minorities in Textbooks: The Issues and the Outlook." Strengthening Democracy. 16:3 (May, 1964). pp. 1-2,8.

2,085. "World They Never Made: New York Puerto Ricans." Time. Vol. 55 (June 12, 1950). pp. 24-26.
A critique of C. Wright Mills, et al., The Puerto Rican Journey.

PART IV:  UNPUBLISHED MATERIALS

2,086.  (Agricultural Workers) <u>Expanded Plan of Operations Pertaining to</u>
        <u>Puerto Rico Agricultural Workers</u>. New York: Commonwealth of
        Puerto Rico. Department of Labor. Migration Division, 1953.

2,087.  (Agricultural Workers) <u>Trabajadores Agricolas de Puerto Rico:</u>
        <u>Bienvenidos a Pennsylvania, U.S.A.</u> (Puerto Rican Farm Workers:
        Welcome to Pennsylvania, U.S.A.) Harrisburg: Pennsylvania
        Bureau of Employment Security, 1957.

2,088.  "Annual Report of the Commissioner of Education." (n.d.)

2,089.  "Board of Education Statement on the Decentralization of the New
        York City School System." June 14, 1965.

2,090.  "College Readiness Program." Union Settlement. 1963.

2,091.  "Comparison of Special Programs, Classes, and Materials for Puerto
        Rican Students in Eighteen Schools." (n.d.)

2,092.  "Curriculum Development: Notes for Discussion at Principals' In-
        service Course." New York Board of Education, 1943.

2,093.  Donovan, Bernard E. and Benjamin J. Stern.  "Memorandum of Pupils
        Whose Native Language is not English." March 20, 1953.

2,094.  <u>Educating Students for Whom English is a Second Language</u>. December
        1965.

2,095.  "Education of the Non-English Speaking Child." Division of Elemen-
        tary Schools.  New York, 1962.

2,096.  "Educational Background in Puerto Rico." Welfare Council of New
        York City.  1947.

2,097.  <u>Ethnic Distribution of Pupils in the Public Schools of New York</u>
        <u>City</u>. New York City Board of Education. March 24, 1965.

2,098.  "Factors Affecting Pupil Registration: Day Schools--Migration
        Balance in the Movement of Pupil Population to and from Places
        Outside, New York City--School Years 1953-1954 to 1962-1963
        (and) Day Schools--Migration Balance in the Movement of Pupil
        Population to and from Places Outside New York City, by School
        Group and Borough--School Year 1962-1963." (Statistical)

2,099.  Finocchiaro, Mary.  "The Role of the Foreign Language Teacher in an
        Educational Program for Puerto Rican Children."  (n.d.)

2,100.  Fitzpatrick, Joseph P., Rev.,  "Delinquency and the Puerto Ricans."
        Address given to Fordham University School of Business,
        October 8, 1959.

2,101. A Five-Year Crash Program for Quality Education. October 22, 1964.

2,102. "Follow-Up Study of the Graduating Classes of Two Junior High Schools." The Puerto Rican Study. A report prepared by Maria Luisa Rodrí-guez. September 20, 1955.

2,103. "Highlights of the N-E (Non-English) Program." Division of Elementary Schools. New York, 1963.

2,104. Hillson, Henry T. and Florence Myers. The Demonstration Guidance Project, 1957-1962: Pilot Project for Higher Horizons. 1963.

2,105. Interviewing Puerto Rican Parents and Children in Spanish: A Guide for School Personnel. (n.d.)

2,106. Kouletis, Greg. "Guidance Follow-Up Study, Spring, 1964 (Compara-tive Study--JHS 13 M. and JHS 117 M)." Spring 1964. (Unpaged.)

2,107. Landers, Jacob. Higher Horizons: Progress Report. January 1963.

2,108. Letter to Dr. Leonard Covello from James R. Dumpson, Consultant. Welfare Council of New York City. May 21, 1951.

2,109. Letter to Dr. Leonard Covello from Coverly Fischer, President. Welfare Council of New York City. September 25, 1950.

2,110. Letter to Dr. Leonard Covello from Adrian P. Burke, Chairman, Committee on Puerto Ricans. Welfare Council of New York City. January 8, 1951.

2,111. "Letter to Governor Jesús T. Pinero Summarizing the Principal Findings of the Study of Puerto Rican Migrants in New York City which the Bureau has been conducting since November, 1947." Bureau of Applied Social Research of Columbia University. June 15, 1948.

2,112. "Memorandum Re: Day Care Centers." November 30, 1950.

2,113. "Migration Balance: Day Schools--Migration Balance in the Movement of Pupil Population to and from Places Outside New York City, by Borough and Geographic Area--School Year 1962-1963 (and) Day Schools--Migration Balance in the Movement of Pupil Popula-tion to and from Places Outside New York City, by Geographic Area--School Years 1953-1954 to 1962-1963." (Statistical)

2,114. "Minutes of a Conference Related to an Educational Program for Puerto Rican Children." Division of Junior High Schools. February 10, 1953. (Abstract)

2,115. ("New) AFL-CIO Racket Drive." Business Week. June 29, 1957. pp. 149-150.

2,116.  "Non-English Program, Schools Having 25 or More Students Rated as Non-English Speaking the Census of October 1958, October 1959, October 1962, October 1963." Division of High Schools.

2,117.  "Number of Candidates for Graduation--June, 1962." Division of High Schools.

2,118.  Oliveras, Candido. "What are the Educational Needs of Puerto Ricans who come to New York?" An Address given at the New York University Puerto Rican Conference, January 14, 1961.

2,119.  Pennisi, Guy V. "Some Suggestions for Helping Non-English Speaking Children. Manual for P.S. 33 Manhattan." Prepared under the direction of Principal Morris C. Finkel, P.S. 33. November 23, 1949. (Unpaged)

2,120.  Portals to the Future, Annual Report of the Superintendent of Schools, 1959-1960.

2,121.  "Practical Techniques for Teachers of Spanish Working with Puerto Rican Pupils. Questions Submitted by Members of the Class." In-Service Course, Spring Term 1963. Course C--886.

2,122.  "Proceedings of the Annual Conference for Puerto Rican Citizens of New York: 1961, 1963, 1964." New York University, School of Education. (Unpaged)

2,123.  "A Program of Education for Puerto Ricans in New York City." New York, New York: Committee of the Association of Assistant Superintendents. 1947.

2,124.  A Program of Education for Puerto Ricans in New York City. New York City Board of Education. 1947.

2,125.  "Progress Report on the Puerto Rican Migrants." Puerto Rico, Department of Labor, Employment and Migration Bureau. April 11, 1950.

2,126.  "Project for Transitional-Stage Puerto Rican Pupils in the High School, Helping the Transitional Stage Pupil in the Subject Class." The Puerto Rican Study. May 16, 1956.

2,127.  "Proposed Revision of Policy on Operation Understanding." Division of Elementary Schools. New York, 1963.

2,128.  "The Puerto Rican Bulletin: An Aid to Teachers and Supervisors of Puerto Rican Children." Division of Junior High Schools. (n.d.)

2,129.  "Puerto Rican Migration to the United States." Commonwealth of Puerto Rico, Department of Labor, Migration Division.

2,130. "Puerto Rican Population by States (according to the 1960 Census)." Commonwealth of Puerto Rico, Department of Labor, Migration Division, May 20, 1964.

2,131. "Puerto Rican Population by States and Cities." (Based on 1960 U.S. Census.) Commonwealth of Puerto Rico, Department of Labor, Migration Division.

2,132. "Puerto Ricans in New York City." Bureau of Curriculum Research. 1965.

2,133. "Questionnaire on Puerto Rican Pupils in Our Schools." New York, New York: Mayor's Committee on Puerto Rican Affairs in New York City, Sub-Committee on Education, Recreation and Parks. May 1, 1953.

2,134. "Record Sheets, Rating Sheets, and Instructional Aids for the Non-English Speaking Child." Division of Elementary Schools.

2,135. "Report of Operations, 1965 Summer Session." New York, New York: East Harlem Neighborhood Study Club.

2,136. Report of the Joint Planning Committee for More Effective Schools to the Superintendent of Schools. May 15, 1964.

2,137. "Report on Graduates--January 1962." Division of High Schools.

2,138. "A Report on School-Puerto Rican Parent Relations, 1955-1956." The Puerto Rican Study. A Report prepared by Frances Low. New York 1957.

2,139. "Report on Visits to New York City Schools Submitted to Mr. Manual Cabranes, Director, by Dr. J.J. Osuna, Educational Consultant." Puerto Rico Department of Labor, Employment and Migration Bureau. 1948.

2,140. "A Resource Unit: Understanding Our Fellow American Citizens, the Puerto Ricans. Bureau of Curriculum Research. (n.d.)

2,141. Sanguinetti, Carmen. "The Puerto Rican School Child in Puerto Rico and in New York City." An Address given at in-service course for teachers of Puerto Rican adults. New York, November 17, 1960.

2,142. Senior, Clarence. "The Newcomer Speaks Out: What Puerto Ricans Want and Need from Voluntary Agencies and the Public." A paper delivered at the National Conference on Social Welfare, Atlantic City, New Jersey, June 1960.

2,143. Shields, Osceola, et al. "Teachers College Course S 200 FA. Los Boricuas--Our Newest Neighbors." (Excerpts from a Group Report).

2,144. Sixtieth Annual Report of the Superintendent of Schools, City of New

York, Statistical Section. School Year 1957-1958. 1959, pp. 69-72.

2,145. "Some Resources Recommended for Use in the Education of Non-English Speaking Students." Division of High Schools. May 1960.

2,146. "Speech Problems of Puerto Rican Children." Department of Speech Improvement. A Report of the Committee on Individualization. November, 1948.

2,147. "Statement by the Honorable Raymond M. Hilliard, Welfare Commissioner of the City of New York upon his Arrival in Puerto Rico, August 21, 1950." New York, New York: New York City, Department of Welfare, Press and Public Relations.

2,148. "Statistics on Regular Day Schools--Pupils Newly Arrived from Places Outside New York City and Leading Sources of Immigration." 1955.

2,149. "Study on Puerto Rican Pupils in Senior and Vocational High Schools." New York, New York: Mayor's Committee on Puerto Rican Affairs in New York City, Sub-Committee on Education, Recreation and Parks. May 1, 1953.

2,150. "The Substitute Auxialiary Teacher." Division of Elementary Schools. 1958.

2,151. Teaching Children of Puerto Rican Background in New York City Schools: Suggested Plans and Procedures. 1954.

2,152. Three hundred eighty-one comulative record sheets of the Graduates of Benjamin Franklin High School, June, 1963.

2,153. Toward Greater Opportunity. A Progress Report from the Superintendent of schools to the Board of Education, Dealing with Implementations of Recommendations of the Commission on Integration, June, 1960.

2,154. Wolk, Elsie. "A Summary Report of Reading Disabilities of Children Learning English as a Second Language." New York, 1963.

2,155. Your American Pupil from Puerto Rico. School Districts 11 and 18. Benjamin E. Strumpf, Assistant Superintendent. September 1956.

INDEX TO AUTHORS' NAMES

# INDEX TO AUTHORS' NAMES

Berlant - 1535
Berle - 1917, 1918
Bernal - 906
Bernardo - 1064
Bernbaum - 907, 908
Berney - 391, 552
Beshoar - 1536
Betances - 386, 1867
Bever - 433
Beytagh - 1919
Biddick - 142
Bienstock - 1920
Bigelow - 776
Binner - 1065
Birch - 302, 361
Bird - 8
Black, ED - 915
Black, JW - 1066
Blackburn - 777
Blair, JF - 168
Blair, WC - 1538
Blancett - 679
Blanco - 916
Blatchford - 778, 1410
Blourock - 387, 680
Bodarsky - 1921
Bogardus - 1539, 1740, 1741, 1922
Boggs - 1067, 1068
Bolgar - 506
Bolger - 739
Bondarin - 681
Bone - 1540
Bonomo - 1178, 1441
Booth - 682
Bordie - 274, 779
Bordwell - 780
Boroff - 1541
Borrego - 917
Bortin - 918
Bouquet - 1923
Bourne, DD - 1542
Bourne, JR - 1542
Bowen - 600, 601, 781, 1352, 1353, 1411
Bowman - 1543
Boxhill - 1924
Boyer - 896
Bracy - 434, 782, 783, 1412-14
Braestrup - 1544, 1925
Bram - 1926
Brameld - 169, 200, 1927, 1928
Bransford - 275
Breisler - 1742

Brice - 1415
Briere - 784
Briggs - 1416
Brody - 1929
Broman - 577
Brooks, N - 435, 1069
Brooks, T - 1545
Broom - 683
Brown, BW - 1096
Brown, F - 344
Brown, FJ - 1546
Brown, MI - 1930
Brown, S - 1931
Brown, TG - 436, 1417
Brown, TH - 1335
Browning, F - 1547
Browning, HN - 578
Bruggeman - 1133
Bruner - 1871
Bryce - 1932
Bryson - 919
Bucchioni - 13, 68, 78-80, 689,
    690, 927, 1088, 1089, 1425
Budner - 1868
Bumpass - 785, 1070-72
Burbeck - 920
Burks - 1388
Burma - 1584, 1549
Burnett - 1073
Burnham, D - 1550
Burnham, S - 1550
Burt, K - 437, 1074
Burt, MK - 786

C

Cabrera - 9, 787, 1418
Cahill - 1933
Calderon - 438
Caldwell - 201, 609-611
Calitri - 1551
Callicut - 579, 612
Campbell - 1218
Cannon - 1552
Cantwell - 613
Caploritz - 1553
Capone - 388, 614
Cargas - 1168
Carleton - 1744
Carlson - 276
Carr, D - 1319
Carr, EB - 788

Lubchansky - 1877
Lucas - 234
Lumpkin - 833
Lynn - 502

## M

Ma - 561
MacCalla - 834
MacDonald - 1856
Machiran Sague - 1619
Macisco - 1797
Mackey, IS - 1230
Mackey, WF - 503, 971-74
Macnamara - 370, 504, 505, 506
Madeira - 235
Madrigal - 1231
Magana - 975
Magee - 1469
Main - 1798
Makahian - 313, 375
Maldonado, AW - 1232, 1799, 1800
Maldonado, B - 1427
Maldonado-Sierra - 1950
Malkoc - 976
Malzberg - 1878, 1879
Mangano - 640
Mangers - 155
Manrique -
Mans - 412, 715
Manuel - 314, 315, 587, 641, 1620
Marckwardt - 507, 508, 835, 836, 1233
Marden - 1621
Margolis - 105
Marland - 156
Marquardt - 509, 837, 838, 1234, 1471
Martin, J - 901
Martin, JF - 1235, 1236, 1237
Martin, JW - 601, 1353
Martinez - 157
Masnick - 1809
Massad - 376
Massimine - 1622
Materesi - 106
Matthies - 839
Matus - 1251
Maxwell - 21, 476
Mayans - 413, 714, 716
Mayerson, C - 1623
Mayerson, M - 510
Maynes - 840
Medina - 1472

Medinnos - 977
Meier - 1625
Mencher - 2003
Menton - 841
Mercer, JR - 236, 316, 642, 717, 1880
Mercer, OR - 842
Mergal - 562
Meriam - 718
Messer - 108
Meyer - 1231
Meyers, F - 2104
Meyers, GC - 1801
Meyerson, M - 719, 1627
Michel - 1473
Miller, H - 237
Miller, MV - 2004
Mills - 1629, 1630
Minigone - 238, 643
Mintz - 1802, 2005, 2006
Minuchin - 2007
Mir - 1475
Mirkin - 1631, 1632, 1633
Mishra - 317, 340, 644
Mitchell, AJ - 318
Mitchell, EG - 1261
Modiano - 979
Moesser - 2078
Modina - 1262
Monserrat - 109, 110, 1634-36, 1803, 1804, 1805, 2008
Montag - 720
Montalvo - 1047-51
Montes - 111, 721
Montez - 1637
Montilla - 63
Montross - 1806
Moore - 1592, 1638
Moquin - 1639
Moran - 586
Moreno - 1640
Morgan - 1641
Morley - 1263
Morper - 319, 645
Morris - 1876
Morrison, JC - 112, 722
Morrison, JR - 511
Morrisroe, M - 843
Morrisroe, SJ - 843
Moses - 400
Moskin - 1642, 1807
Moulton - 512, 1264

Ronch - 529
Roscoe - 1314, 1500
Rosen, CL - 47, 48, 861, 1315, 1501
1502
Rosen, P - 49, 334
Rosenthal - 395, 1890
Rosner - 1891
Ross - 1316
Rosten - 1686
Roucek - 1546
Rowan - 995
Royce - 2031
Rubinstein - 746
Ruble - 381, 599, 1004
Ruíz, A
Ruíz, P - 2036
Ruíz, R - 1688-1690
Ruíz, Ramon Eduardo - 1719
Ruíz, Ruperto E - 1687
Ruoss - 1691
Rusk - 1692
Russell - 862
Russo - 997
Rutherford - 1318
Ryan - 595

## S

Sabatino - 255, 596, 658
Sableski - 50, 530
Saer - 335
Safa - 2037
Safar - 140
Saitz - 1061, 1319
Salazar, JJ - 2038
Salazar, R - 164, 1693
Salazar, T - 747
Salinas - 165
Samora - 1587, 1694
Samuels, G - 1695, 1696, 1697
Samuels, M - 531
Sánchez, DJ - 1699
Sánchez, GI - 51, 256, 336, 337,
477, 532, 533
Sancho - 998
Sandberg - 1335
Sandis - 1841
Sanguinetti - 739, 748, 2141
Sarantos - 1336, 1337
Sardy - 564
Sauna - 1700
Saunders, J - 1503
Saunders, L - 166

Sarville - 999
Sayers - 130
Schaefer - 2039
Schmidt Mackey - 534
Schneider - 1338
Schnitzler - 1701
Schotta - 1339
Schwartz - 422, 659
Sebera - 730
Seda-Bonilla - 257, 258, 749,
2041-3, 2045
Seidl - 338
Senior - 52, 54, 132, 1703-8, 1758,
1842-48, 2044, 2046, 2142
Seplowin - 1709
Sepulveda - 167, 865
Sexton - 2047, 2082
Sharpe - 1506
Sheeler - 1341
Shepses - 2040
Shen - 360
Shields - 2143
Shiels - 565
Shotwell - 1710
Shulz - 1431
Shute - 1038, 1399
Sica - 2048
Siegel - 1849, 2049
Silen - 1711
Silverman - 566
Simmer - 2083
Simmons, RS - 1000
Simmons, WR - 1712
Simpson - 2066
Singer - 1001
Skrabanek - 597
Slager - 1342, 1507
Slaiman - 1850
Slotkin - 2084
Smalley - 966
Smart - 1851
Smith, F - 380
Smith, GW - 750
Smith, LE - 866, 1508
Smith, M - 1002
Smoker - 867
Soares, AT - 1892
Scores, LM - 1892
Sobrino - 396, 1893, 2050
Soffietti - 259
Soto - 1713
Spector - 596
Spence - 340

Walsh, JF  -  350, 351
Walsh, P  -  262
Wardaugh  -  881, 882
Wasell  -  1183
Wasserman, P  -  883
Wasserman, S  -  883
Watkins  -  54, 1848
Weales  -  1731
Webb  -  403
Weikart  -  762
Weinberg  -  57
Weissman  -  138, 569, 2060
Weitzman  -  1732
Wells  -  1862
Wenk  -  1863
Werner  -  1735, 1864
Wheeler, G  -  1382
Wheeler, H  -  2061
White, RV  -  1023
White, T  -  2062
Whitehouse  -  1383
Whitford  -  1384, 1385
Whitman  -  2063
Wiener  -  1386
Willey  -  341
Williams, F  -  588, 605, 725, 1024-6
Williams, GM  -  570, 571
Willis  -  398, 665, 763
Willoughby  -  1736
Wilson, AP  -  425, 1387
Wilson, RD  -  1027, 1288
Wineberg  -  40
Wishon  -  1388
Wissot  -  884
Withers  -  1389
Witherspoon  -  1524
Wolfram  -  549, 572, 573
Wolk  -  384, 885, 886, 2154
Woodbury  -  1737
Woods  -  604
Woolsey  -  1525
Wright, AL  -  1391
Wright, CE  -  888
Wright, DE  -  2065

## Y

Yamamoto  -  376
Yezierska  -  1738
Yinger  -  2066
Yorkey  -  1393
Yotsukura  -  550

Young, RB  -  889
Young, RW  -  551

## Z

Zimmerman  -  298
Zintz  -  890, 1394
Zirkel  -  58, 139, 263, 264, 352,
353, 390, 399, 400, 628, 666, 667,
764, 765, 1028, 1029, 1395